PENGUIN BOOKS

PENGUIN ENGLISH POETS
GENERAL EDITOR: CHRISTOPHER RICKS

John Keats
The Complete Poems

EDITED BY JOHN BARNARD

John Keats
The Complete Poems

EDITED BY JOHN BARNARD

Second Edition

PENGUIN BOOKS

Penguin Books Ltd,
Harmondsworth, Middlesex, England
Penguin Books, 625 Madison Avenue,
New York, New York 10022, U.S.A.
Penguin Books Australia Ltd,
Ringwood, Victoria, Australia
Penguin Books Canada Ltd,
41 Steelcase Road West, Markham, Ontario, Canada
Penguin Books (N.Z.) Ltd,
182–190 Wairau Road, Auckland 10, New Zealand

First published 1973
Second edition 1976
Introduction and notes copyright © John Barnard, 1973

Made and printed in Great Britain by
Richard Clay (The Chaucer Press) Ltd,
Bungay, Suffolk
Set in Monotype Ehrhardt

This book is sold subject to the condition that
it shall not, by way of trade or otherwise, be lent,
re-sold, hired out, or otherwise circulated without
the publisher's prior consent in any form of
binding or cover other than that in which it is
published and without a similar condition
including this condition being imposed on the
subsequent purchaser

Contents

Introduction *15*
Note to the Second Edition *19*
Acknowledgements *21*
Table of Dates *23*
Further Reading *29*

The Poems

Imitation of Spenser *37*
On Peace *38*
'Fill for me a brimming bowl' *38*
To Lord Byron *39*
'As from the darkening gloom a silver dove' *40*
'Can death be sleep, when life is but a dream' *40*
To Chatterton *40*
Written on the Day that Mr Leigh Hunt left Prison *41*
To Hope *41*
Ode to Apollo ('In thy western halls of gold') *43*
Lines Written on 29 May The Anniversary of the Restoration of Charles the 2nd *44*
To Some Ladies *45*
On Receiving a Curious Shell, and a Copy of Verses, from the Same Ladies *46*
To Emma *47*
Song ('Stay, ruby-breasted warbler, stay') *48*
'Woman! when I behold thee flippant, vain' *49*

'O Solitude! if I must with thee dwell' 50
To George Felton Mathew 50
To [Mary Frogley] 53
To — ('Had I a man's fair form, then might my sighs') 55
'Give me Women, Wine, and Snuff' 55
Specimen of an Induction to a Poem 56
Calidore. A Fragment 58
'To one who has been long in city pent' 62
'O! how I love, on a fair summer's eve' 63
To a Friend who Sent me some Roses 63
To my Brother George ('Many the wonders I this day have seen') 64
To my Brother George ('Full many a dreary hour have I passed') 64
To Charles Cowden Clarke 68
'How many bards gild the lapses of time!' 72
On First Looking into Chapman's Homer 72
To a Young Lady who sent me a Laurel Crown 73
On Leaving some Friends at an Early Hour 73
'Keen, fitful gusts are whispering here and there' 74
Addressed to Haydon 74
To my Brothers 75
Addressed to [Haydon] 75
'I stood tip-toe upon a little hill' 76
Sleep and Poetry 82
Written in Disgust of Vulgar Superstition 93
On the Grasshopper and Cricket 94
To Kosciusko 94
To G[eorgiana] A[ugusta] W[ylie] 95
'Happy is England! I could be content' 95
'After dark vapours have oppressed our plains' 96
To Leigh Hunt, Esq. 96

CONTENTS

Written on a Blank Space at the End of Chaucer's Tale of *The Floure and the Leafe* 97

On Receiving a Laurel Crown from Leigh Hunt 97

To the Ladies who Saw Me Crowned 98

Ode to Apollo ('God of the golden bow') 98

On Seeing the Elgin Marbles 99

To B. R. Haydon, with a Sonnet Written on Seeing the Elgin Marbles 100

On *The Story of Rimini* 100

On a Leander Gem which Miss Reynolds, my Kind Friend, Gave Me 101

On the Sea 101

Lines ('Unfelt, unheard, unseen') 102

Stanzas ('You say you love; but with a voice') 102

'Hither, hither, love —' 103

Lines Rhymed in a Letter Received (by J. H. Reynolds) From Oxford 104

'Think not of it, sweet one, so –' 105

Endymion: A Poetic Romance 106

'In drear-nighted December' 217

Nebuchadnezzar's Dream 217

Apollo to the Graces 218

To Mrs Reynolds's Cat 218

On Seeing a Lock of Milton's Hair. Ode 219

On Sitting Down to Read *King Lear* Once Again 220

'When I have fears that I may cease to be' 221

'O blush not so! O blush not so!' 221

'Hence Burgundy, Claret, and Port' 222

'God of the meridian' 222

Robin Hood 223

Lines on the Mermaid Tavern 225

To — ('Time's sea hath been five years at its slow ebb') 226

CONTENTS

To the Nile 226
'Spenser! a jealous honourer of thine' 227
'Blue! 'Tis the life of heaven, the domain' 227
'O thou whose face hath felt the Winter's wind' 228
Sonnet to A[ubrey] G[eorge] S[pencer] 229

Extracts from an Opera
i 'O! were I one of the Olympian twelve' 229
ii Daisy's Song 230
iii Folly's Song 230
iv 'O, I am frightened with most hateful thoughts' 231
v Song ('The stranger lighted from his steed') 231
vi 'Asleep! O sleep a little while, white pearl!' 232

The Human Seasons 232
'For there's Bishop's Teign' 232
'Where be ye going, you Devon maid?' 234
'Over the hill and over the dale' 235
To J. H. Reynolds, Esq. 235
To J[ames] R[ice] 238
Isabella; or, The Pot of Basil 239
To Homer 255
Ode to May. Fragment 255
Acrostic 256
'Sweet, sweet is the greeting of eyes' 256
On Visiting the Tomb of Burns 257
'Old Meg she was a gipsy' 257
A Song about Myself 258
'Ah! ken ye what I met the day' 262
To Ailsa Rock 263
'This mortal body of a thousand days' 263
'All gentle folks who owe a grudge' 264
'Of late two dainties were before me placed' 266
Lines Written in the Highlands after a Visit to Burns's Country 266
On Visiting Staffa 268

CONTENTS

'Read me a lesson, Muse, and speak it loud' *270*
'Upon my life, Sir Nevis, I am piqued' *270*
Stanzas on some Skulls in Beauly Abbey, near Inverness *272*
Translated from Ronsard *276*
''Tis "the witching time of night"' *276*
'Welcome joy, and welcome sorrow' *278*
Song ('Spirit here that reignest') *279*
'Where's the Poet? Show him, show him' *280*
Fragment of the 'Castle Builder' *280*
'And what is love? It is a doll dressed up' *282*
Hyperion. A Fragment *283*
Fancy *307*
Ode ('Bards of Passion and of Mirth') *309*
Song ('I had a dove and the sweet dove died') *310*
Song ('Hush, hush! tread softly! hush, hush my dear!') *311*
The Eve of St Agnes *312*
The Eve of St Mark *324*
'Gif ye wol stonden hardie wight' *327*
'Why did I laugh tonight?' *328*
Faery Bird's Song ('Shed no tear – O, shed no tear!') *328*
Faery Song ('Ah! woe is me! poor silver-wing!') *329*
'When they were come unto the Faery's Court' *329*
'The House of Mourning written by Mr Scott' *332*
Character of Charles Brown *333*
A Dream, after reading Dante's Episode of Paola and Francesca *334*
La Belle Dame sans Merci. A Ballad *334*
Song of Four Faeries *336*
To Sleep *339*
'If by dull rhymes our English must be chained' *340*
Ode to Psyche *340*
On Fame (I) ('Fame, like a wayward girl, will still be coy') *342*

12 CONTENTS

On Fame (II) ('How fevered is the man who cannot look') *343*
'Two or three posies' *343*
Ode on a Grecian Urn *344*
Ode to a Nightingale *346*
Ode on Melancholy *348*
Ode on Indolence *349*
Otho the Great. A Tragedy in Five Acts *352*
Lamia *414*
'Pensive they sit, and roll their languid eyes' *433*
To Autumn *434*
The Fall of Hyperion. A Dream *435*
'The day is gone, and all its sweets are gone' *449*
'What can I do to drive away' *450*
'I cry your mercy, pity, love – ay, love' *451*
'Bright star! would I were as steadfast as thou art' *452*
King Stephen. A Fragment of a Tragedy *452*
'This living hand, now warm and capable' *459*
The Cap and Bells; or, The Jealousies *459*
To Fanny *485*
'In after-time, a sage of mickle lore' *487*
Three Undated Fragments *487*

Doubtful Attributions

'See, the ship in the bay is riding' *488*
The Poet *488*
Gripus *489*

Appendix 1
Wordsworth and Hazlitt on the Origins of Greek Mythology 497

Appendix 2
The Two Prefaces to Endymion *503*

Appendix 3
The Order of Poems in Poems (*1817*) *and* Lamia, Isabella, The Eve of St Agnes, and Other Poems (*1820*)
and
The Publisher's Advertisement for 1820 *509*

Appendix 4
Keats's Notes on Milton's Paradise Lost *515*

Appendix 5
Keats on Kean's Shakespearean Acting 527

Notes *531*
Dictionary of Classical Names *697*
Index of Titles *721*
Index of First Lines *727*

Introduction

Most of Keats's poems were published in *Poems* (1817), *Endymion* (1818), and *Lamia, Isabella, The Eve of St Agnes, and other Poems* (1820), all of which Keats saw through the press, or in nineteenth-century editions of variable dependability. Four short poems were added in Galignani's *The Poetical Works of Coleridge, Shelley, and Keats* (Paris, 1829). In 1848 Richard Monckton Milnes added a substantial body of short poems to the canon in his *Life, Letters, and Literary Remains, of John Keats*, and eight years later published *The Fall of Hyperion* in *Biographical and Historical Miscellanies of the Philobiblon Society*. Since then some forty odd poems, including thirteen sonnets and a high proportion of trivia, have been found, mostly in Keats's letters.

H. W. Garrod's *The Poetical Works of John Keats* (1939, rev. edn 1958) gives the fullest available account of Keats's text, and is based on a comparison of the printed texts with the wealth of manuscript material, now mainly in American libraries. Garrod remarked that the primary concern of Keats's editors is 'not the poet's *ultima manus*, but his first fingerings and gropings' (p. xxi), a comment importantly modified by Jack Stillinger's recent work on the transmission of the texts. H. E. Rollins's edition of the letters, Robert Gittings, Alvin Whitley, Miriam Allott and Stillinger himself had earlier noted various corrections needed in Garrod's text and apparatus. Indeed, Garrod's later Oxford Standard Authors text (1956) differs in many important ways from his definitive edition, sometimes providing better readings. Apart from the 'Critical Notes' (largely concerned with textual matters) in his Oxford Standard Authors edition, Garrod gives no explanatory notes. Until the recent publication of Miriam Allott's *The Poems of John Keats* (1970), the only complete annotated text was E. De Selincourt's *Poems* (1905, 5th rev. edn 1926), which is still useful. Mrs Allott's chronologically ordered text is modernized, and based on a re-examination of the manuscripts. Her full and invaluable notes, which include a generous selection of Keats's early drafts and incorporate many of the findings of recent scholarship, make hers the most comprehensive and useful edition available to the student.

This edition is more modest. It is squarely based on the work of previous editors, and has involved no independent study of the manuscripts, though published facsimiles of some of the autograph drafts of poems have been consulted, and Dr W. H. Bond kindly checked a number of small points in the Harvard collection of Keats's manuscripts. Where possible, the text follows that of the three editions overseen by Keats (*1817*, *Endymion* and *1820*). Poems first published in R. M. Milnes's *Life, Letters, and Literary Remains, of John Keats* (1848) are sometimes based on the text which Milnes prepared with access to much of the manuscript material, though Keats's manuscripts and the transcripts made by his friends have been used wherever their readings give a more accurate record of the poet's intentions. *The Fall of Hyperion* was first published by Milnes in 1856–7, but he allowed himself greater editorial freedom than he had with *1848*, and so the text below follows Garrod's, which is based on Woodhouse's transcript. The remaining poems are based on the texts subsequently printed from various manuscript sources by such editors as H. B. Forman, C. L. Finney, Amy Lowell and H. W. Garrod, or from the versions given in H. E. Rollins's edition of the *Letters* (often the single source).

Disagreement with Garrod or Mrs Allott is usually minor. Garrod depended, perhaps too heavily, upon printed texts, while Mrs Allott places greater emphasis upon readings drawn from the manuscripts. For fuller accounts of these matters, and for a record of the 'fingerings and gropings' of Keats's creative imagination, the reader is referred to Garrod's edition and to the selection given by Mrs Allott. Like Garrod, but unlike Mrs Allott, I give '*Woman! when I behold thee flippant, vain*' as a single poem rather than as three sonnets (see p. 538), and '*God of the meridian*' is treated as a separate poem, not as the last twenty-five lines of '*Hence Burgundy, Claret, and Port*' (see p. 590). With previous editors, I have followed the earlier manuscript version of *La Belle Dame sans Merci*, since Keats's alterations for the *Indicator* coarsen the delicate texture of the poem. I have also followed the published text of *The Eve of St Agnes* like all other editors, though Jack Stillinger has argued that Keats's later alterations, which roused the puritanical objections of his publishers, should be adopted (see pp. 619–20).

In deciding which works to include in the canon, I have sought a critical neutrality. Thus, unlike Mrs Allott, but like Garrod, '*Can death be sleep, when life is but a dream*' and '*Stay, ruby-breasted warbler, stay*' are given side by side with poems undoubtedly by Keats. Although these are hardly worthy of a major poet, second-rate verse (or worse) is a feature of Keats's early work, and throughout his career he dashed off indifferent verses with no thought of publication. Badness alone is not a certain sign of Keats's innocence. Although I have placed the fragment, *Gripus*, among the Doubtful Attributions since there is no decisive external evidence one way or the other, I think it quite possibly by Keats (see headnote, p. 696).

A very detailed chronology of Keats's life is supplied by his letters, the transcripts of the poems, H. E. Rollins's *The Keats Circle: Letters and Papers 1816–1879* (1965), and by the biographical work of W. J. Bate, Robert Gittings and Aileen Ward, among others. I have arranged the poems by their date of completion, and in most cases my dating agrees with that of Mrs Allott and other scholars. The notes aim to give details of each poem's composition and early publication, to indicate characteristically Keatsian usages, to provide glosses and explanation where necessary, and to record the major critical attitudes to the poetry. Some details of draft readings are also given, though the density of annotation of textual and other matters varies according to the importance of the work – thus the *Odes* and other major poems are heavily annotated while *Otho the Great* receives little attention. Classical references, which abound, have been gathered together in a *Dictionary of Classical Names* (pp. 697–719), which draws on the reference works, particularly Lemprière, known to Keats. To have included this information in the commentary would have involved constant duplication. Allusions are noted, but the frequent echoes of other poets in Keats's work have been largely ignored in the interests of economy. De Selincourt, C. L. Finney's *The Evolution of Keats's Poetry* (1936) and Miriam Allott's notes are here especially helpful.

In modernizing the text I have interfered with punctuation and capitalization as little as possible, believing that the early texts present little difficulty of access to the modern reader. Although the punctuation, spelling, and capitalization in Keats's letters and manuscripts are notoriously irregular, it was common practice for authors at this time to leave such matters to their publishers, and Keats is on record as having asked Taylor to do so. Keats saw the proofs of the three volumes published during his lifetime, and their punctuation follows a loose, but comprehensible pattern. For instance, the early poetry's frequent catalogues usually block off the main object described with a colon, and then use semi-colons to separate each individual item. This device allows for a combination of due emphasis upon detail, while giving that sense of an excited onward rush so typical of Keats's first phase. The colon, semi-colon, dash and exclamation mark are all used to maintain a feeling of forward movement in passages which might, if punctuated by modern rules, break up into a series of phrases verging on the exclamatory (particularly in *Endymion*, where description in any case overwhelms narrative drive). These effects seem worth preserving, though I have freely re-punctuated where there is a danger of obscurity. Where Keats punctuates twice over (as ', – ') I have frequently chosen one of the alternatives offered. The use of a dash for emphasis has usually been retained, and the colon, which sometimes represents a full stop or a dash, has been replaced with alternative pointing where necessary. Keats's frequent creation of hyphenated words was not always properly marked in the early editions, and hyphens have been added throughout. Spelling is normally regularized, though in the case of Keats's inconsistent spelling of 'fairy'/'faery' I follow whichever seems the preferred spelling in an individual poem, since the latter spelling seems to have held a deliberately archaic flavour for him. The spelling 'aye' is used when the meaning is 'ever', and 'ay' when the sense is 'ah!' or 'yes'. In dealing with R. M. Milnes's *1848* text, the same conservative attitude to punctuation has been adopted: Keats's manuscripts are of little help, and Milnes went over the text carefully, pointing in basically the same style as Keats's publishers. Those texts based on Keats's manuscripts alone have been punctuated according to modern practice.

Appendixes comprise two important passages from Wordsworth and Hazlitt which affected Keats's attitude to mythology, Keats's two prefaces to *Endymion*, the publisher's advertisement for *1820*, the order of poems in *1817* and *1820*, Keats's notes on Milton's *Paradise Lost*, and Keats's account of Kean's Shakespearian acting (this item is included because, though often referred to, it is not easily available).

Note to the Second Edition

Future editorial work on Keats will be impossible without Professor Jack Stillinger's analytic account of *The Texts of Keats's Poems* (1974) and his forthcoming edition. In revising my text, many substantive corrections have been made on the basis of his study of the texts' transmission. Where possible acknowledgement is made in the Notes: for other changes, Stillinger's book should be consulted.

The canon is little affected. *To Woman (from the Greek)* has been excluded since it is not by Keats (see Garrod's edition, p. x) but there was insufficient space to add the Keats-Brown *Love and Folly* (first printed by Walter E. Peck in *Notes and Queries*, 25 February 1939). Stillinger believes that '*Can death be sleep*', *Sonnet to A[ubrey] G[eorge] S[pencer]*, and '*The House of Mourning*' *written by Mr. Scott* should be regarded as doubtful attributions. Four titles have been altered (*Lines Written on 29 May*, *The Human Seasons*, '*What can I do to drive away*', and *To Fanny*), and there are important changes in *Song* ('*Hush, hush! tread softly!*'), *Nebuchadnezzar's Dream*, *To Sleep*, *Otho the Great*, '*Bright Star!*', and *The Cap and Bells*.

20 INTRODUCTION

In some cases my decisions part company with Professor Stillinger's, most importantly over *The Eve of St. Agnes*. However, following Stillinger, I now regard '*Gif ye wol stonden hardie wight*' as a separate fragment, not as part of *The Eve of St. Mark* as Garrod and Allott believe.

March 1976

Acknowledgements

My deepest debt, and one apparent throughout the text and notes, is to the previous editors of Keats's poems, above all to H. W. Garrod's detailed record of the manuscript readings and printed texts and to Miriam Allott's careful commentary. Any editor of Keats is dependent upon the patient explorations begun by Keats's friends, Woodhouse, Clarke and Brown, and continued by several generations of critics. Among the names, those of E. De Selincourt, J. M. Murry, M. R. Ridley, Hyder Rollins, Robert Gittings, Aileen Ward, W. J. Bate, Ian Jack, John Jones and Jack Stillinger figure largely. I would also like to thank Mr O. A. Baker of Plymouth Public Library, Dr W. H. Bond of Harvard University Library, Dr David Fleeman, Geoffrey Hill, Mr D. I. Masson of the Brotherton Library in the University of Leeds, J. C. Maxwell and Dr E. T. Webb, who have generously given me their help on a number of points. Above all, I am indebted to the encouragement and detailed criticism given by Professor C. B. Ricks, the General Editor of this series.

In revising the text I have benefited very considerably from Professor Stillinger's published work and from his scholarly and personal generosity in commenting on my work in detail. I am also grateful to Father Martin Jarrett-Kerr for pointing out several misprints.

For permission to publish copyright material, I am grateful to Harvard University Press for the extracts from *The Letters of John Keats 1814–21*, ed. H. E. Rollins (1958), *The Keats Circle: Letters and Papers*, ed. H. E. Rollins (1965), and W. J. Bate, *John Keats* (1963); to the Clarendon Press for the quotations from H. W. Garrod's *The Poetical Works of John Keats* (rev. edn 1958) and from his Oxford Standard Authors text, *The Poetical Works of John Keats* (1956); and to the Longman Group for the quotations from Miriam Allott's edition, *The Poems of John Keats* (1970).

Table of Dates

1795 *31 October* Born at the Swan and Hoop Livery Stables, Finsbury.
1797 *28 February* Birth of George Keats.
1799 *18 November* Birth of Tom Keats.
1803 *3 June* Birth of Fanny (Frances Mary) Keats.
August Starts his education at the Rev. John Clarke's school at Enfield, along with George. Tom was later to attend the school.
1804 *16 April* Death of his father.
27 June His mother marries William Rawlings. The children sent to live with their grandparents, John and Alice Jennings, at Ponder's End, Enfield.
1805 *8 March* Death of his grandfather, John Jennings. With Alice Jennings the children move to Edmonton.
1810 *20 March* Burial of his mother, who died from tuberculosis, watched over by Keats.
July Alice Jennings appoints John Nowland Sandall and Richard Abbey as the children's guardians. Sandall died in 1816, leaving Abbey the only guardian.
1811 *Summer* Leaves Enfield School, and is apprenticed to Thomas Hammond, a surgeon in Edmonton.
1814 First known efforts to write verse (*Imitation of Spenser*, *To Lord Byron*, etc.)
19 December Burial of his grandmother. Fanny Keats goes to live with Richard Abbey's family.
1815 *2 February* Writes a sonnet on Leigh Hunt's release from prison.
1 October Enters Guy's Hospital as a student.
November Writes verse epistle *To George Felton Mathew*.

1816 *5 May O Solitude*, his first published poem, appears in the *Examiner*.
25 July Passes examination at Apothecaries' Hall; eligible to practise as apothecary, physician, or surgeon.
August Takes Tom to Margate, where he writes an epistle to George.
September In London, joins his brothers in their lodgings.
October Writes *On First Looking into Chapman's Homer*. Meets Leigh Hunt, Benjamin Haydon, and John Hamilton Reynolds.
November He and his brothers have moved to lodgings in Cheapside.
December Completes *Sleep and Poetry*. The Chapman's Homer sonnet is quoted by Hunt in his article on 'Young Poets' in the *Examiner*. Finishes *I stood tip-toe*.

1817 *16 February* Hunt shows some of Keats's poetry to Shelley, William Godwin, Basil Montagu, and Hazlitt at a dinner party.
1 or 2 March Sees Elgin Marbles with Haydon.
3 March His first volume, *Poems*, published by C. and J. Ollier.
25 March By this time has moved to Hampstead with his brothers.
c. 13 April Taylor and Hessey decide to publish his future books.
14 April Sets out for Isle of Wight, where he arrives the following day.
18 April Plans to begin *Endymion*. Reading Shakespeare.
c. 24 April Moves to Margate, where Tom joins him. *Endymion* has been started.
May Visits Canterbury, and meets Mrs Isabella Jones at Hastings at the end of May or beginning of June.
June Returns to Hampstead.
c. 21 August Has finished *Endymion* I–II.
c. 3 September–5 October Stays at Oxford with Bailey, where he completes *Endymion* III. Reading *Paradise Lost*.
October Blackwood's first attack on the 'Cockney School'.

TABLE OF DATES

22 November–c. 5 December Stays at Burford Bridge, is reading Shakespeare's *Poems*, and finishes *Endymion* on 28 November.
15 December Sees Kean in *Richard III* at Drury Lane.
c. 16 December Goes with Haydon to meet Wordsworth.
21 December Discusses 'intensity' in art and 'Negative Capability' in a letter to his brothers.
28 December Attends Haydon's 'immortal dinner'. Charles Lamb and William Wordsworth present, among others.
31 January Meets Wordsworth on Hampstead Heath.

1818 *January–February* Attends Hazlitt's *Lectures on the English Poets*. Corrects proof and revises *Endymion* I–III.
23 January Tom spitting blood.
March–April Stays at Teignmouth with Tom. Continues preparing *Endymion* for the press.
9–10 April Hears his Preface to *Endymion* has been rejected, and writes the second version.
27 April About this date Taylor and Hessey publish *Endymion*. Has finished *Isabella*.
3 May Writes to Reynolds on life as 'a large Mansion of Many Apartments'.
c. 28 May George Keats marries Georgiana Wylie.
24 June Begins walking tour of Scotland and the Lake District after seeing George and Georgiana Keats set out for America from Liverpool.
1 July Writes *On Visiting the Tomb of Burns*.
2 August Climbs Ben Nevis with Brown.
18 August Reaches Hampstead, having been forced to break off his tour because of a severe chill and sore throat. Finds Tom is very ill.
c. 27 September Croker's attack on *Endymion* published in the *Quarterly Review*. Has begun *Hyperion* while nursing Tom.
12 October The *Examiner* reprints Reynolds's defence of *Endymion*.
24 October Meets Mrs Isabella Jones again.

November Continues working on *Hyperion*. Before the end of this month has met Fanny Brawne.
1 December Death of Tom Keats from tuberculosis. Moves into Wentworth Place, Hampstead, with Brown.
25 December Dines with Fanny Brawne and her mother, and reaches an 'understanding' with Fanny.

1819 *January* Goes to Chichester, and visits Bedhampton with Brown. Writes *The Eve of St Agnes*.
13–17 February Writes *The Eve of St Mark*.
April–May Gives up *Hyperion*. Writes *La Belle Dame sans Merci*, experiments with the sonnet form, and composes the major odes (except for *To Autumn*).
3 April Fanny and Mrs Brawne move into the other half of Wentworth Place.
12 May Receives worrying letter from George Keats in America, and begins to consider the necessity of taking a job.
31 May Thinks of going to live near Teignmouth or becoming a ship's surgeon.
9 June Gives up both ideas.
17 June Asks Haydon and others to return loans he has made them.
28 June–10 September Stays in Shanklin, Isle of Wight, moving to Winchester with Brown on 12 August, working on *Otho the Great*, *Lamia* and *The Fall of Hyperion*.
15 September Returns to Winchester after a trip to London.
19 September Writes *To Autumn*.
21 September Has abandoned *The Fall of Hyperion*.
8 October Leaves Winchester for London, and takes lodgings in Westminster.
November Living with Brown at Wentworth Place, Hampstead, next door to Fanny Brawne. Writes *King Stephen*, starts *The Cap and Bells*, and returns to *The Fall of Hyperion*.
22 December He is 'rather unwell'. By the end of the month he is engaged to Fanny Brawne.

1820 *9–28 January* George Keats in London, having returned from America in an attempt to sort out the tangled affairs of the Keats children's inheritance. In the meantime, *Otho the Great* rejected by Covent Garden.
3 February Returns from Liverpool, having seen George off, by stage coach. At 11 p.m. has severe haemorrhage. Confined to house for the rest of the month.
c. 13 February Offers to break off his engagement with Fanny Brawne, who refuses.
12–13 March He is revising *Lamia*.
27 April Taylor and Hessey receive the manuscript of the *Lamia* volume.
May Moves to Kentish Town after Brown gives up Wentworth Place.
10 May La Belle Dame sans Merci published in Hunt's *Indicator*.
c. 11 June Reads and corrects proof of *Lamia* volume.
22 June Has an attack of blood-spitting.
23 June–mid-August Moves to Leigh Hunt's house so that he can be better looked after.
July Lamia, Isabella, The Eve of St Agnes, and Other Poems published by Taylor and Hessey.
5 July His doctor has ordered him to go to Italy.
August Is asked by Shelley to stay with him in Italy. Moves to stay with the Brawnes at Wentworth Place. Makes an informal will. Francis Jeffrey gives a belated but sympathetic review of *Endymion* and the *Lamia* volume in the *Edinburgh Review*.
23 August Abbey refuses to give him money.
13 September Severn decides to accompany him to Italy.
18 September Sails from Gravesend by night.
28 September Having been held back by bad weather and then been becalmed, he lands with Severn at Portsmouth and visits Bedhampton. Resumes voyage next day.
c. 1 October Lands at Lulworth Cove; according to Robert Gittings, writes the *Bright Star* sonnet in his copy of Shakespeare's *Poems* (but see pp. 684–5).

TABLE OF DATES

      21–31 October His ship held in quarantine at Naples for ten days.
      15 November Reaches Rome, and takes lodgings in the Piazza di Spagna.
      30 November Writes his last known letter (to Charles Brown).
      10 December Has a relapse.

1821 *23 February* Dies at 11 p.m.
      26 February Buried in Rome's Protestant Cemetery.
      17 March The news of his death reaches London.

Further Reading

Both for themselves and for the light they throw on his life and poetry, Keats's letters are indispensable further reading. The definitive edition is H. E. Rollins's *The Letters of John Keats 1814–21*, 2 vols., Harvard University Press, 1958, which contains transcripts of the single source for several of Keats's poems and corrects Garrod. Earlier editions include M. B. Forman's two-volume text, 4th edn, Oxford University Press, 1952. A useful selection, edited by Robert Gittings, is *Letters of John Keats*, Oxford University Press, 1970, which replaces F. Page's edition for the World's Classics series.

EDITIONS

John Keats, *Poems*, London, 1817.

John Keats, *Endymion*, London, 1818.

John Keats, *Lamia, Isabella, The Eve of St Agnes, and Other Poems*, London, 1820.

R. M. Milnes (ed.), *Life, Letters, and Literary Remains, of John Keats*, 2 vols., 1848.

R. M. Milnes (ed.), *Another Version of Keats's Hyperion* [i.e. *The Fall of Hyperion*], in *Miscellanies of the Philobiblion Society* III, 1856-7.

H. B. Forman (ed.), *The Poetical Works and Other Writings of John Keats*, 4 vols., 1883. Supplemented by *Poetry and Prose of John Keats*, 1890; rev. edn M. B. Forman, 8 vols., 1938-9 (Hampstead Edition).

E. De Selincourt (ed.), *The Poems of John Keats*, Methuen, 1905; 5th rev. edn, 1926.

H. W. Garrod (ed.), *The Poetical Works of John Keats*, Clarendon Press, Oxford, 1939; rev. edn, 1958. Substantial corrections are made to Garrod's edition by Jack Stillinger's important book on the text.

H. W. Garrod (ed.), *The Poetical Works of John Keats*, Oxford Standard Authors series, 1956. Text differs in minor, but significant, ways from preceding.

Douglas Bush (ed.), *Selected Poems and Letters*, Houghton Mifflin, Boston, 1959.

Miriam Allott (ed.), *The Poems of John Keats*, Longman, 1970 (2nd impression, 1972).

Robert Gittings (ed.), *The Odes of Keats and their Earliest Known Manuscripts*, Heinemann, 1970. Facsimiles, transcriptions, and useful notes. Excludes *Ode on Indolence*.

WORKS OF REFERENCE

D. L. Baldwin *et al.*, *A Concordance of the Poems of John Keats*, Carnegie Institution of Washington, 1917 (reprinted 1963).

J. R. MacGillivray, *Keats: A Bibliography and Reference Guide*, University of Toronto Press, 1949.

Keats–Shelley Journal, 1952– . Has an annual bibliography. Those for 1952–62 reprinted as *Keats, Shelley, Byron, Hunt and their Circles: A Bibliography*, 1964.

BIOGRAPHY AND CRITICISM

This is a selective list, mainly of work published in the twentieth century. For Keats's contemporary and nineteenth-century reputation, G. M. Matthews's *John Keats: The Critical Heritage*, Routledge & Kegan Paul, 1971, should be consulted: Matthews reprints the early reviews, otherwise hard to obtain, substantial extracts from later essays, and has a helpful introduction.

Matthew Arnold, 'John Keats' in *Essays in Criticism*, 1880.

W. J. Bate, *The Stylistic Development of Keats*, Modern Language Association, New York, 1945.

FURTHER READING

W. J. Bate, *John Keats*, Harvard University Press, 1963.

John Bayley, 'Keats and Reality', *Proceedings of the British Academy*, XLVIII (1962), pp. 91–126.

Harold Bloom, *The Visionary Company*, Gollancz, 1961.

Harold Bloom, 'Keats and the Embarrassments of Poetic Tradition' in *From Sensibility to Romanticism: Essays Presented to F. A. Pottle*, Yale University Press, 1965.

A. C. Bradley, 'The Letters of John Keats', *Oxford Lectures on Poetry*, Macmillan, 1909.

Robert Bridges, *John Keats, A Critical Essay*, privately printed 1895, reprinted as the introduction to G. Thorn Drury's *Poems of John Keats*, 1896.

Cleanth Brooks, 'History without Footnotes: An Account of Keats's Urn' in *The Well Wrought Urn*, Reynel and Hitchcock, New York, 1947.

Douglas Bush, *Mythology and the Romantic Tradition in English Poetry*, Harvard University Press, 1937.

Sir Sidney Colvin, *John Keats: his Life and Poetry, his Friends, Critics, and After-fame*, Macmillan, 1917.

T. S. Eliot, in *The Use of Poetry and the Use of Criticism*, Faber & Faber, 1933.

Walter H. Evert, *Aesthetic and Myth in the Poetry of Keats*, Princeton University Press, 1965.

C. L. Finney, *The Evolution of Keats's Poetry*, 2 vols., Harvard University Press, 1936. Detailed information on Keats's sources.

R. H. Fogle, *The Imagery of Keats and Shelley*, University of North Carolina Press, Chapel Hill, 1949.

G. H. Ford, *Keats and the Victorians*, Yale University Press, 1945.

N. F. Ford, *The Prefigurative Imagination of Keats*, Stanford University Press, 1951.

H. W. Garrod, *Keats*, Clarendon Press, Oxford, 1926; rev. edn, 1939.

Robert Gittings, *John Keats: The Living Year*, Heinemann, 1954.

FURTHER READING

Robert Gittings, *The Mask of Keats*, Heinemann, 1956.

Robert Gittings, *John Keats*, Heinemann, 1968.
(Gittings's work uncovers valuable new material, and corrects the work of previous scholars on many points of detail. His insistence that Keats had an affair with Mrs Isabella Jones has met with much resistance, as have other of his conclusions. There is much, however, that is challenging.)

Ian Jack, *Keats and the Mirror of Art*, Clarendon Press, Oxford, 1967.

John Jones, *John Keats's Dream of Truth*, Chatto & Windus, 1969.

G. Wilson Knight, *The Starlit Dome*, Oxford University Press, 1941.

F. R. Leavis, 'Keats' in *Revaluation*, Chatto & Windus, 1936.

Robin Mayhead, *John Keats*, Cambridge University Press, 1967.

Kenneth Muir, ed., *John Keats: A Reassessment*, Liverpool University Press, 1959.

J. Middleton Murry, *Keats and Shakespeare*, Oxford University Press, 1925.

J. Middleton Murry, *Keats*, Jonathan Cape, 1955. (A revision of two earlier works, *Studies in Keats*, 1930, and *The Mystery of Keats*, 1949.)

David Perkins, *The Quest for Permanence: The Symbolism of Wordsworth, Shelley, and Keats*, Harvard University Press, 1959.

David Perkins, 'Keats's *Odes* and Letters: Recurrent Imagery and Diction', *Keats–Shelley Journal*, II (1953), pp. 51–60.

E. C. Pettet, *On the Poetry of John Keats*, Cambridge University Press, 1957.

Christopher Ricks, *Keats and Embarrassment*, Clarendon Press, Oxford, 1974.

M. R. Ridley, *Keats's Craftsmanship: A Study in Poetic Development*, Clarendon Press, Oxford, 1933.

H. E. Rollins, ed., *The Keats Circle: Letters and Papers 1816–1879*, 2 vols., Harvard University Press, 2nd edn, 1965. Includes the supplementary material published in *More Letters and Poems of the Keats Circle*, 1955.

Bernice Slote, *Keats and the Dramatic Principle*, University of Nebraska Press, Lincoln, Nebraska, 1958.

Stuart M. Sperry, *Keats the Poet*, Princeton University Press, 1974.

Caroline Spurgeon, *Keats's Shakespeare: A Descriptive Study*, Clarendon Press, Oxford, 1928. Based on Keats's markings in his copy of Shakespeare.

Jack Stillinger, *The Hoodwinking of Madeline and other Essays on Keats's Poems*, University of Illinois Press, Urbana, 1971. Collects several important essays published separately earlier.

Jack Stillinger, *The Texts of Keats's Poems*, Harvard University Press, Cambridge, Mass., 1974. Essential corrective to Garrod and Allott on textual matters.

Clarence Thorpe, *The Mind of John Keats*, Oxford University Press, 1926.

Lionel Trilling, 'The Poet as Hero: Keats in his Letters' in *The Opposing Self*, Secker & Warburg, 1955.

Aileen Ward, *John Keats: the Making of a Poet*, Secker & Warburg, 1963.

Earl R. Wasserman, *The Finer Tone: Keats's Major Poems*, Johns Hopkins Press, 1953.

The Poems

Imitation of Spenser

    Now Morning from her orient chamber came,
    And her first footsteps touched a verdant hill;
    Crowning its lawny crest with amber flame,
    Silv'ring the untainted gushes of its rill;
    Which, pure from mossy beds, did down distill,
    And after parting beds of simple flowers,
    By many streams a little lake did fill,
    Which round its marge reflected woven bowers,
And, in its middle space, a sky that never lowers.

10   There the king-fisher saw his plumage bright
    Vying with fish of brilliant dye below;
    Whose silken fins, and golden scalès light
    Cast upward, through the waves, a ruby glow:
    There saw the swan his neck of archèd snow,
    And oared himself along with majesty;
    Sparkled his jetty eyes; his feet did show
    Beneath the waves like Afric's ebony,
And on his back a fay reclined voluptuously.

    Ah! could I tell the wonders of an isle
20   That in that fairest lake had placèd been,
    I could e'en Dido of her grief beguile;
    Or rob from aged Lear his bitter teen:
    For sure so fair a place was never seen,
    Of all that ever charmed romantic eye:
    It seemed an emerald in the silver sheen
    Of the bright waters; or as when on high,
Through clouds of fleecy white, laughs the cerulean sky.

    And all around it dipped luxuriously
    Slopings of verdure through the glossy tide,
30   Which, as it were in gentle amity,
    Rippled delighted up the flowery side;
    As if to glean the ruddy tears, it tried,
    Which fell profusely from the rose-tree stem!
    Haply it was the workings of its pride,

In strife to throw upon the shore a gem
Outvying all the buds in Flora's diadem.

On Peace

O Peace! and dost thou with thy presence bless
  The dwellings of this war-surrounded Isle;
Soothing with placid brow our late distress,
  Making the triple kingdom brightly smile?
Joyful I hail thy presence; and I hail
  The sweet companions that await on thee;
Complete my joy – let not my first wish fail,
  Let the sweet mountain nymph thy favourite be,
With England's happiness proclaim Europa's liberty.
10 O Europe! let not sceptred tyrants see
    That thou must shelter in thy former state;
  Keep thy chains burst, and boldly say thou art free;
    Give thy kings law – leave not uncurbed the great;
    So with the horrors past thou'lt win thy happier fate!

'Fill for me a brimming bowl'

*What wondrous beauty! From this moment I
efface from my mind all women.*
Terence [*Eunuch* II.3.296]

Fill for me a brimming bowl
And let me in it drown my soul:
But put therein some drug, designed
To banish Woman from my mind:
For I want not the stream inspiring
That heats the sense with lewd desiring,
But I want as deep a draught
As e'er from Lethe's waves was quaffed;
From my despairing breast to charm
10 The Image of the fairest form

That e'er my revelling eyes beheld,
That e'er my wandering fancy spelled.

'Tis vain! away I cannot chase
The melting softness of that face,
The beaminess of those bright eyes,
That breast – earth's only Paradise.

My sight will never more be blessed;
For all I see has lost its zest:
Nor with delight can I explore
20 The Classic page, the Muse's lore.

Had she but known how beat my heart,
And with one smile relieved its smart,
I should have felt a sweet relief,
I should have felt 'the joy of grief'.
Yet as a Tuscan 'mid the snow
Of Lapland thinks on sweet Arno,
Even so for ever shall she be
The Halo of my Memory.

To Lord Byron

Byron! how sweetly sad thy melody!
  Attuning still the soul to tenderness,
  As if soft Pity, with unusual stress,
Had touched her plaintive lute, and thou, being by,
Hadst caught the tones, nor suffered them to die.
  O'ershading sorrow doth not make thee less
  Delightful: thou thy griefs dost dress
With a bright halo, shining beamily,
As when a cloud a golden moon doth veil,
10 Its sides are tinged with a resplendent glow,
Through the dark robe oft amber rays prevail,
  And like fair veins in sable marble flow;
Still warble, dying swan! still tell the tale,
  The enchanting tale, the tale of pleasing woe.

'As from the darkening gloom a silver dove'

As from the darkening gloom a silver dove
   Upsoars, and darts into the Eastern light,
   On pinions that naught moves but pure delight,
So fled thy soul into the realms above,
Regions of peace and everlasting love;
   Where happy spirits, crowned with circlets bright
   Of starry beam, and gloriously bedight,
Taste the high joy none but the blest can prove.
There thou or joinest the immortal quire
   In melodies that even Heaven fair
Fill with superior bliss, or, at desire
   Of the omnipotent Father, cleavest the air
On holy message sent – What pleasures higher?
Wherefore does any grief our joy impair?

'Can death be sleep, when life is but a dream'

I

Can death be sleep, when life is but a dream,
   And scenes of bliss pass as a phantom by?
The transient pleasures as a vision seem,
   And yet we think the greatest pain's to die.

II

How strange it is that man on earth should roam,
   And lead a life of woe, but not forsake
His rugged path; nor dare he view alone
   His future doom which is but to awake.

To Chatterton

O Chatterton! how very sad thy fate!
   Dear child of sorrow – son of misery!
   How soon the film of death obscured that eye,
Whence Genius wildly flashed, and high debate.

How soon that voice, majestic and elate,
  Melted in dying murmurs! Oh! how nigh
  Was night to thy fair morning. Thou didst die
A half-blown flower which cold blasts amate.
But this is past: thou art among the stars
10 Of highest Heaven: to the rolling spheres
Thou sweetly singest: naught thy hymning mars,
  Above the ingrate world and human fears.
On earth the good man base detraction bars
  From thy fair name, and waters it with tears.

Written on the Day that Mr Leigh Hunt left Prison

What though, for showing truth to flattered state,
  Kind Hunt was shut in prison, yet has he,
  In his immortal spirit, been as free
As the sky-searching lark, and as elate.
Minion of grandeur! think you he did wait?
  Think you he naught but prison walls did see,
  Till, so unwilling, thou unturned'st the key?
Ah, no! far happier, nobler was his fate!
In Spenser's halls he strayed, and bowers fair,
10 Culling enchanted flowers; and he flew
With daring Milton through the fields of air:
  To regions of his own his genius true
Took happy flights. Who shall his fame impair
  When thou art dead, and all thy wretched crew?

To Hope

When by my solitary hearth I sit,
  And hateful thoughts enwrap my soul in gloom;
When no fair dreams before my 'mind's eye' flit,
  And the bare heath of life presents no bloom;

Sweet Hope, ethereal balm upon me shed,
And wave thy silver pinions o'er my head.

Whene'er I wander, at the fall of night,
  Where woven boughs shut out the moon's bright ray,
Should sad Despondency my musings fright,
10 And frown, to drive fair Cheerfulness away,
    Peep with the moon-beams through the leafy roof,
    And keep that fiend Despondence far aloof.

Should Disappointment, parent of Despair,
  Strive for her son to seize my careless heart;
When, like a cloud, he sits upon the air,
  Preparing on his spell-bound prey to dart:
    Chase him away, sweet Hope, with visage bright,
    And fright him as the morning frightens night!

Whene'er the fate of those I hold most dear
20 Tells to my fearful breast a tale of sorrow,
O bright-eyed Hope, my morbid fancy cheer;
  Let me awhile thy sweetest comforts borrow:
    Thy heaven-born radiance around me shed,
    And wave thy silver pinions o'er my head!

Should e'er unhappy love my bosom pain,
  From cruel parents, or relentless fair;
O let me think it is not quite in vain
  To sigh out sonnets to the midnight air!
    Sweet Hope, ethereal balm upon me shed,
30   And wave thy silver pinions o'er my head!

In the long vista of the years to roll,
  Let me not see our country's honour fade:
O let me see our land retain her soul,
  Her pride, her freedom; and not freedom's shade.
    From thy bright eyes unusual brightness shed —
    Beneath thy pinions canopy my head!

Let me not see the patriot's high bequest,
  Great Liberty! how great in plain attire!
With the base purple of a court oppressed,

40   Bowing her head, and ready to expire:
> But let me see thee stoop from heaven on wings
> That fill the skies with silver glitterings!

And as, in sparkling majesty, a star
> Gilds the bright summit of some gloomy cloud;
Brightening the half-veiled face of heaven afar:
> So, when dark thoughts my boding spirit shroud,
>> Sweet Hope, celestial influence round me shed,
>> Waving thy silver pinions o'er my head.

Ode to Apollo

In thy western halls of gold
> When thou sittest in thy state,
Bards, that erst sublimely told
> Heroic deeds, and sung of fate,
With fervour seize their adamantine lyres,
Whose chords are solid rays, and twinkle radiant fires.

There Homer with his nervous arms
> Strikes the twanging harp of war,
And even the western splendour warms,
> While the trumpets sound afar:
But, what creates the most intense surprise,
His soul looks out through renovated eyes.

Then, through thy Temple wide, melodious swells
> The sweet majestic tone of Maro's lyre:
The soul delighted on each accent dwells, –
> Enraptur'd dwells, – not daring to respire,
The while he tells of grief around a funeral pyre.

'Tis awful silence then again;
> Expectant stand the spheres;
20   Breathless the laurelled peers,
Nor move, till ends the lofty strain,
Nor move till Milton's tuneful thunders cease,
And leave once more the ravished heavens in peace.

Thou biddest Shakespeare wave his hand,
  And quickly forward spring
The Passions – a terrific band –
  And each vibrates the string
That with its tyrant temper best accords,
While from their Master's lips pour forth the inspiring words.

A silver trumpet Spenser blows,
  And, as its martial notes to silence flee,
From a virgin chorus flows
  A hymn in praise of spotless Chastity.
'Tis still! Wild warblings from the Aeolian lyre
Enchantment softly breathe, and tremblingly expire.

Next thy Tasso's ardent numbers
  Float along the pleasèd air,
Calling youth from idle slumbers,
  Rousing them from Pleasure's lair: –
Then o'er the strings his fingers gently move,
And melt the soul to pity and to love.

But when *Thou* joinest with the Nine,
And all the powers of song combine,
  We listen here on earth:
The dying tones that fill the air,
And charm the ear of evening fair,
From thee, great God of Bards, receive their heavenly birth.

Lines Written on 29 May
The Anniversary of the Restoration of Charles the 2nd

Infatuate Britons, will you still proclaim
His memory, your direst, foulest shame?
  Nor patriots revere?

Ah! when I hear each traitorous lying bell,
'Tis gallant Sidney's, Russell's, Vane's sad knell,
  That pains my wounded ear.

To Some Ladies

What though, while the wonders of nature exploring,
   I cannot your light, mazy footsteps attend;
Nor listen to accents that, almost adoring,
   Bless Cynthia's face, the enthusiast's friend:

Yet over the steep, whence the mountain stream rushes,
   With you, kindest friends, in idea I muse –
Mark the clear tumbling crystal, its passionate gushes,
   Its spray that the wild flower kindly bedews.

Why linger you so, the wild labyrinth strolling?
   Why breathless, unable your bliss to declare?
Ah! you list to the nightingale's tender condoling,
   Responsive to sylphs, in the moon-beamy air.

'Tis morn, and the flowers with dew are yet drooping,
   I see you are treading the verge of the sea:
And now! ah, I see it – you just now are stooping
   To pick up the keep-sake intended for me.

If a cherub, on pinions of silver descending,
   Had brought me a gem from the fret-work of heaven;
And, smiles with his star-cheering voice sweetly blending,
   The blessing of Tighe had melodiously given;

It had not created a warmer emotion
   Than the present, fair nymphs, I was blessed with from you,
Than the shell, from the bright golden sands of the ocean
   Which the emerald waves at your feet gladly threw.

For, indeed, 'tis a sweet and peculiar pleasure
   (And blissful is he who such happiness finds),
To possess but a span of the hour of leisure,
   In elegant, pure, and aërial minds.

On Receiving a Curious Shell, and a Copy of Verses, from the Same Ladies

Hast thou from the caves of Golconda a gem,
    Pure as the ice-drop that froze on the mountain?
Bright as the humming-bird's green diadem,
    When it flutters in sunbeams that shine through a fountain?

Hast thou a goblet for dark sparkling wine?
    That goblet right heavy, and massy, and gold?
And splendidly marked with the story divine
    Of Armida the fair, and Rinaldo the bold?

Hast thou a steed with a mane richly flowing?
    Hast thou a sword that thine enemy's smart is?
Hast thou a trumpet rich melodies blowing?
    And wear'st thou the shield of the famed Britomartis?

What is it that hangs from thy shoulder, so brave,
    Embroidered with many a spring-peering flower?
Is it a scarf that thy fair lady gave?
    And hastest thou now to that fair lady's bower?

Ah! courteous Sir Knight, with large joy thou art crowned;
    Full many the glories that brighten thy youth!
I will tell thee my blisses, which richly abound
    In magical powers to bless, and to soothe.

On this scroll thou seest written in characters fair
    A sunbeamy tale of a wreath, and a chain;
And, warrior, it nurtures the property rare
    Of charming my mind from the trammels of pain.

This canopy mark: 'tis the work of a fay;
    Beneath its rich shade did King Oberon languish,
When lovely Titania was far, far away,
    And cruelly left him to sorrow, and anguish.

There, oft would he bring from his soft-sighing lute
    Wild strains to which, spell-bound, the nightingales listened;

The wondering spirits of heaven were mute,
   And tears 'mong the dewdrops of morning oft glistened.

In this little dome, all those melodies strange,
   Soft, plaintive, and melting, for ever will sigh;
Nor e'er will the notes from their tenderness change;
   Nor e'er will the music of Oberon die.

So, when I am in a voluptuous vein,
   I pillow my head on the sweets of the rose,
And list to the tale of the wreath, and the chain,
   Till its echoes depart; then I sink to repose.

Adieu, valiant Eric! with joy thou art crowned;
   Full many the glories that brighten thy youth,
I too have my blisses, which richly abound
   In magical powers, to bless and to soothe.

To Emma

O come, dearest Emma! the rose is full blown,
And the riches of Flora are lavishly strown,
The air is all softness, and crystal the streams,
And the West is resplendently clothèd in beams.

We will hasten, my fair, to the opening glades,
The quaintly carved seats, and the freshening shades,
Where the faeries are chanting their evening hymns,
And in the last sunbeam the sylph lightly swims.

And when thou art weary I'll find thee a bed
Of mosses and flowers to pillow thy head;
There, beauteous Emma, I'll sit at thy feet,
While my story of love I enraptured repeat.

So fondly I'll breathe, and so softly I'll sigh,
Thou wilt think that some amorous Zephyr is nigh –
Ah, no! – as I breathe, I will press thy fair knee,
And then thou wilt know that the sigh comes from me.

Then why, lovely girl, should we lose all these blisses?
That mortal's a fool who such happiness misses.
So smile acquiescence, and give me thy hand,
20 With love-looking eyes, and with voice sweetly bland.

Song
Tune – *'Julia to the Wood-Robin'*

Stay, ruby-breasted warbler, stay,
  And let me see thy sparkling eye,
Oh brush not yet the pearl-strung spray
  Nor bow thy pretty head to fly.

Stay while I tell thee, fluttering thing,
  That thou of love an emblem art,
Yes! patient plume thy little wing,
  Whilst I my thoughts to thee impart.

When summer nights the dews bestow,
10 And summer suns enrich the day,
Thy notes the blossoms charm to blow,
  Each opes delighted at thy lay.

So when in youth the eye's dark glance
  Speaks pleasure from its circle bright,
The tones of love our joys enhance
  And make superior each delight.

And when bleak storms resistless rove,
  And every rural bliss destroy,
Nought comforts then the leafless grove
20 But thy soft note – its only joy –

E'en so the words of love beguile
  When Pleasure's tree no longer bears,
And draw a soft endearing smile
  Amid the gloom of grief and tears.

'Woman! when I behold thee flippant, vain'

Woman! when I behold thee flippant, vain,
   Inconstant, childish, proud, and full of fancies;
   Without that modest softening that enhances
The downcast eye, repentant of the pain
That its mild light creates to heal again:
   E'en then, elate, my spirit leaps, and prances,
   E'en then my soul with exultation dances
For that to love, so long, I've dormant lain:
But when I see thee meek, and kind, and tender,
   Heavens! how desperately do I adore
Thy winning graces; – to be thy defender
   I hotly burn – to be a Calidore –
A very Red Cross Knight – a stout Leander –
   Might I be loved by thee like these of yore.

Light feet, dark violet eyes, and parted hair,
   Soft dimpled hands, white neck, and creamy breast,
   Are things on which the dazzled senses rest
Till the fond, fixèd eyes, forget they stare.
From such fine pictures, heavens! I cannot dare
   To turn my admiration, though unpossessed
   They be of what is worthy, – though not dressed
In lovely modesty, and virtues rare.
Yet these I leave as thoughtless as a lark;
   These lures I straight forget, – e'en ere I dine,
Or thrice my palate moisten: but when I mark
   Such charms with mild intelligences shine,
My ear is open like a greedy shark,
   To catch the tunings of a voice divine.

Ah! who can e'er forget so fair a being?
   Who can forget her half-retiring sweets?
   God! she is like a milk-white lamb that bleats
For man's protection. Surely the All-seeing,
Who joys to see us with His gifts agreeing,
   Will never give him pinions, who intreats
   Such innocence to ruin, – who vilely cheats

A dove-like bosom. In truth there is no freeing
One's thoughts from such a beauty; when I hear
   A lay that once I saw her hand awake,
Her form seems floating palpable, and near;
40   Had I e'er seen her from an arbour take
A dewy flower, oft would that hand appear,
   And o'er my eyes the trembling moisture shake.

'O Solitude! if I must with thee dwell'

O Solitude! if I must with thee dwell,
   Let it not be among the jumbled heap
   Of murky buildings; climb with me the steep –
Nature's observatory – whence the dell,
Its flowery slopes, its river's crystal swell,
   May seem a span; let me thy vigils keep
   'Mongst boughs pavilioned, where the deer's swift leap
Startles the wild bee from the foxglove bell.
But though I'll gladly trace these scenes with thee,
10   Yet the sweet converse of an innocent mind,
   Whose words are images of thoughts refined,
Is my soul's pleasure; and it sure must be
   Almost the highest bliss of human-kind,
When to thy haunts two kindred spirits flee.

To George Felton Mathew

Sweet are the pleasures that to verse belong,
And doubly sweet a brotherhood in song;
Nor can remembrance, Mathew! bring to view
A fate more pleasing, a delight more true
Than that in which the brother Poets joyed,
Who with combinèd powers, their wit employed
To raise a trophy to the drama's muses.
The thought of this great partnership diffuses

TO GEORGE FELTON MATHEW

    Over the genius-loving heart, a feeling
10 Of all that's high, and great, and good, and healing.

    Too partial friend! fain would I follow thee
Past each horizon of fine poesy;
Fain would I echo back each pleasant note
As o'er Sicilian seas, clear anthems float
'Mong the light skimming gondolas far parted,
Just when the sun his farewell beam has darted –
But 'tis impossible; far different cares
Beckon me sternly from soft 'Lydian airs',
And hold my faculties so long in thrall,
20 That I am oft in doubt whether at all
I shall again see Phoebus in the morning:
Or flushed Aurora in the roseate dawning!
Or a white Naiad in a rippling stream;
Or a rapt seraph in a moonlight beam;
Or again witness what with thee I've seen,
The dew by fairy feet swept from the green,
After a night of some quaint jubilee
Which every elf and fay had come to see:
When bright processions took their airy march
30 Beneath the curvèd moon's triumphal arch.

    But might I now each passing moment give
To the coy muse, with me she would not live
In this dark city, nor would condescend
'Mid contradictions her delights to lend.
Should e'er the fine-eyed maid to me be kind,
Ah! surely it must be whene'er I find
Some flowery spot, sequestered, wild, romantic,
That often must have seen a poet frantic;
Where oaks, that erst the Druid knew, are growing,
40 And flowers, the glory of one day, are blowing;
Where the dark-leaved laburnum's drooping clusters
Reflect athwart the stream their yellow lustres,
And intertwined the cassia's arms unite,
With its own drooping buds, but very white.
Where on one side are covert branches hung,

TO GEORGE FELTON MATHEW

'Mong which the nightingales have always sung
In leafy quiet: where to pry, aloof,
Atween the pillars of the sylvan roof,
Would be to find where violet beds were nestling,
50   And where the bee with cowslip bells was wrestling.
There must be too a ruin dark, and gloomy,
To say 'joy not too much in all that's bloomy'.

Yet this is vain – O Mathew, lend thy aid
To find a place where I may greet the maid –
Where we may soft humanity put on,
And sit and rhyme, and think on Chatterton;
And that warm-hearted Shakespeare sent to meet him –
Four laurelled spirits, heaven-ward to entreat him.
With reverence would we speak of all the sages
60   Who have left streaks of light athwart their ages:
And thou shouldst moralize on Milton's blindness,
And mourn the fearful dearth of human kindness
To those who strove with the bright golden wing
Of genius, to flap away each sting
Thrown by the pitiless world. We next could tell
Of those who in the cause of freedom fell;
Of our own Alfred, of Helvetian Tell;
Of him whose name to ev'ry heart's a solace,
High-minded and unbending William Wallace.
70   While to the rugged north our musing turns
We well might drop a tear for him, and Burns.

Felton! without incitements such as these,
How vain for me the niggard Muse to tease:
For thee, she will thy every dwelling grace,
And make 'a sun-shine in a shady place':
For thou wast once a floweret blooming wild,
Close to the source, bright, pure, and undefiled,
Whence gush the streams of song: in happy hour
Came chaste Diana from her shady bower,
80   Just as the sun was from the east uprising;
And, as for him some gift she was devising,
Beheld thee, plucked thee, cast thee in the stream

To meet her glorious brother's greeting beam.
I marvel much that thou hast never told
How, from a flower, into a fish of gold
Apollo changed thee; how thou next didst seem
A black-eyed swan upon the widening stream;
And when thou first didst in that mirror trace
The placid features of a human face:
90 That thou hast never told thy travels strange,
And all the wonders of the mazy range
O'er pebbly crystal, and o'er golden sands,
Kissing thy daily food from Naiad's pearly hands.

To [Mary Frogley]

Hadst thou lived in days of old,
O what wonders had been told
Of thy lively countenance,
And thy humid eyes that dance
In the midst of their own brightness,
In the very fane of lightness.
Over which thine eyebrows, leaning,
Picture out each lovely meaning:
In a dainty bend they lie,
10 Like to streaks across the sky,
Or the feathers from a crow,
Fallen on a bed of snow.
Of thy dark hair that extends
Into many graceful bends:
As the leaves of hellebore
Turn to whence they sprung before
And behind each ample curl
Peeps the richness of a pearl.
Downward too flows many a tress
20 With a glossy waviness;
Full, and round like globes that rise
From the censer to the skies
Through sunny air. Add too, the sweetness

TO [MARY FROGLEY]

Of thy honeyed voice; the neatness
Of thine ankle lightly turned:
With those beauties, scarce discerned,
Kept with such sweet privacy,
That they seldom meet the eye
Of the little loves that fly
30 Round about with eager pry.
Saving when, with freshening lave,
Thou dipp'st them in the taintless wave;
Like twin water-lilies, born
In the coolness of the morn.
O, if thou hadst breathèd then,
Now the Muses had been ten.
Couldst thou wish for lineage higher
Than twin sister of Thalia?
At least for ever, evermore,
40 Will I call the Graces four.

Hadst thou lived when chivalry
Lifted up her lance on high,
Tell me what thou wouldst have been?
Ah! I see the silver sheen
Of thy broidered, floating vest
Covering half thine ivory breast;
Which, O heavens! I should see,
But that cruel destiny
Has placed a golden cuirass there;
50 Keeping secret what is fair.
Like sunbeams in a cloudlet nested
Thy locks in knightly casque are rested:
O'er which bend four milky plumes
Like the gentle lily's blooms
Springing from a costly vase.
See with what a stately pace
Comes thine alabaster steed;
Servant of heroic deed!
O'er his loins, his trappings glow
60 Like the northern lights on snow.

Mount his back! thy sword unsheathe!
Sign of the enchanter's death;
Bane of every wicked spell;
Silencer of dragon's yell.
Alas! thou this wilt never do –
Thou art an enchantress too,
And wilt surely never spill
Blood of those whose eyes can kill.

To —

Had I a man's fair form, then might my sighs
  Be echoed swiftly through that ivory shell
    Thine ear, and find thy gentle heart; so well
Would passion arm me for the enterprise:
But ah! I am no knight whose foeman dies;
  No cuirass glistens on my bosom's swell;
    I am no happy shepherd of the dell
Whose lips have trembled with a maiden's eyes.
Yet must I dote upon thee – call thee sweet,
10 Sweeter by far than Hybla's honeyed roses
    When steeped in dew rich to intoxication.
Ah! I will taste that dew, for me 'tis meet,
  And when the moon her pallid face discloses,
    I'll gather some by spells, and incantation.

'Give me Women, Wine, and Snuff'

Give me Women, Wine, and Snuff
Until I cry out, 'Hold, enough!'
You may do so sans objection
Till the day of resurrection;
For, bless my beard, they aye shall be
My belovèd Trinity.

Specimen of an Induction to a Poem

    Lo! I must tell a tale of chivalry;
For large white plumes are dancing in mine eye.
Not like the formal crest of latter days:
But bending in a thousand graceful ways –
So graceful, that it seems no mortal hand,
Or e'en the touch of Archimago's wand,
Could charm them into such an attitude.
We must think rather, that in playful mood,
Some mountain breeze had turned its chief delight,
10 To show this wonder of its gentle might.
Lo! I must tell a tale of chivalry;
For while I muse, the lance points slantingly
Athwart the morning air: some lady sweet,
Who cannot feel for cold her tender feet,
From the worn top of some old battlement
Hails it with tears, her stout defender sent:
And from her own pure self no joy dissembling,
Wraps round her ample robe with happy trembling.
Sometimes, when the good Knight his rest would take,
20 It is reflected, clearly, in a lake,
With the young ashen boughs, 'gainst which it rests,
And th' half-seen mossiness of linnets' nests.
Ah! shall I ever tell its cruelty,
When the fire flashes from a warrior's eye,
And his tremendous hand is grasping it,
And his dark brow for very wrath is knit?
Or when his spirit, with more calm intent,
Leaps to the honours of a tournament,
And makes the gazers round about the ring
30 Stare at the grandeur of the balancing?
No, no! this is far off: – then how shall I
Revive the dying tones of minstrelsy,
Which linger yet about lone gothic arches,
In dark green ivy, and among wild larches?
How sing the splendour of the revelries,
When butts of wine are drunk off to the lees?

SPECIMEN OF AN INDUCTION TO A POEM

And that bright lance, against the fretted wall,
Beneath the shade of stately banneral,
Is slung with shining cuirass, sword, and shield
Where ye may see a spur in bloody field?
Light-footed damsels move with gentle paces
Round the wide hall, and show their happy faces;
Or stand in courtly talk by fives and sevens,
Like those fair stars that twinkle in the heavens.
Yet must I tell a tale of chivalry –
Or wherefore comes that steed so proudly by?
Wherefore more proudly does the gentle Knight
Rein in the swelling of his ample might?

Spenser! thy brows are archèd, open, kind,
And come like a clear sun-rise to my mind;
And always does my heart with pleasure dance,
When I think on thy noble countenance:
Where never yet was aught more earthly seen
Than the pure freshness of thy laurels green.
Therefore, great bard, I not so fearfully
Call on thy gentle spirit to hover nigh
My daring steps: or if thy tender care,
Thus startled unaware,
Be jealous that the foot of other wight
Should madly follow that bright path of light
Traced by thy loved Libertas, he will speak,
And tell thee that my prayer is very meek;
That I will follow with due reverence,
And start with awe at mine own strange pretence.
Him thou wilt hear; so I will rest in hope
To see wide plains, fair trees and lawny slope,
The morn, the eve, the light, the shade, the flowers,
Clear streams, smooth lakes, and overlooking towers.

Calidore. A Fragment

Young Calidore is paddling o'er the lake,
His healthful spirit eager and awake
To feel the beauty of a silent eve,
Which seemed full loth this happy world to leave,
The light dwelt o'er the scene so lingeringly.
He bares his forehead to the cool blue sky,
And smiles at the far clearness all around,
Until his heart is well nigh over-wound,
And turns for calmness to the pleasant green
10 Of easy slopes, and shadowy trees that lean
So elegantly o'er the waters' brim
And show their blossoms trim.
Scarce can his clear and nimble eyesight follow
The freaks, and dartings of the black-winged swallow,
Delighting much, to see it half at rest,
Dip so refreshingly its wings, and breast
'Gainst the smooth surface, and to mark anon,
The widening circles into nothing gone.

And now the sharp keel of his little boat
20 Comes up with ripple, and with easy float,
And glides into a bed of water-lilies:
Broad-leaved are they and their white canopies
Are upward turned to catch the heavens' dew.
Near to a little island's point they grew;
Whence Calidore might have the goodliest view
Of this sweet spot of earth. The bowery shore
Went off in gentle windings to the hoar
And light blue mountains: but no breathing man
With a warm heart, and eye prepared to scan
30 Nature's clear beauty, could pass lightly by
Objects that looked out so invitingly
On either side. These, gentle Calidore
Greeted, as he had known them long before.
The sidelong view of swelling leafiness,
Which the glad setting sun in gold doth dress;

CALIDORE. A FRAGMENT

> Whence ever and anon the jay outsprings,
> And scales upon the beauty of its wings.
> The lonely turret, shattered, and outworn,
> Stands venerably proud – too proud to mourn
> Its long lost grandeur: fir trees grow around,
> Aye dropping their hard fruit upon the ground.
> The little chapel with the cross above
> Upholding wreaths of ivy; the white dove,
> That on the window spreads his feathers light,
> And seems from purple clouds to wing its flight.
> Green tufted islands casting their soft shades
> Across the lake; sequestered leafy glades,
> That through the dimness of their twilight show
> Large dock leaves, spiral foxgloves, or the glow
> Of the wild cat's-eyes, or the silvery stems
> Of delicate birch trees, or long grass which hems
> A little brook. The youth had long been viewing
> These pleasant things, and heaven was bedewing
> The mountain flowers, when his glad senses caught
> A trumpet's silver voice. Ah! it was fraught
> With many joys for him. The warder's ken
> Had found white coursers prancing in the glen:
> Friends very dear to him he soon will see;
> So pushes off his boat most eagerly,
> And soon upon the lake he skims along,
> Deaf to the nightingale's first undersong;
> Nor minds he the white swans that dream so sweetly:
> His spirit flies before him so completely.
>
> And now he turns a jutting point of land,
> Whence may be seen the castle gloomy, and grand:
> Nor will a bee buzz round two swelling peaches,
> Before the point of his light shallop reaches
> Those marble steps that through the water dip:
> Now over them he goes with hasty trip,
> And scarcely stays to ope the folding doors:
> Anon he leaps along the oaken floors
> Of halls and corridors.

Delicious sounds! those little bright-eyed things
That float about the air on azure wings,
Had been less heartfelt by him than the clang
Of clattering hoofs. Into the court he sprang,
Just as two noble steeds, and palfreys twain,
Were slanting out their necks with loosened rein;
While from beneath the threatening portcullis
80 They brought their happy burthens. What a kiss,
What gentle squeeze he gave each lady's hand!
How tremblingly their delicate ankles spanned!
Into how sweet a trance his soul was gone,
While whisperings of affection
Made him delay to let their tender feet
Come to the earth. With an incline so sweet
From their low palfreys o'er his neck they bent:
And whether there were tears of languishment,
Or that the evening dew had pearled their tresses,
90 He feels a moisture on his cheek, and blesses
With lips that tremble, and with glistening eye,
All the soft luxury
That nestled in his arms. A dimpled hand,
Fair as some wonder out of fairy land,
Hung from his shoulder like the drooping flowers
Of whitest cassia, fresh from summer showers:
And this he fondled with his happy cheek
As if for joy he would no further seek –
When the kind voice of good Sir Clerimond
100 Came to his ear, like something from beyond
His present being: so he gently drew
His warm arms, thrilling now with pulses new,
From their sweet thrall, and forward gently bending,
Thanked heaven that his joy was never ending,
While 'gainst his forehead he devoutly pressed
A hand heaven made to succour the distressed;
A hand that from the world's bleak promontory
Had lifted Calidore for deeds of Glory.

CALIDORE. A FRAGMENT

  Amid the pages, and the torches' glare,
There stood a knight, patting the flowing hair
Of his proud horse's mane. He was withal
A man of elegance, and stature tall,
So that the waving of his plumes would be
High as the berries of a wild ash tree,
Or as the wingèd cap of Mercury.
His armour was so dexterously wrought
In shape, that sure no living man had thought
It hard, and heavy steel, but that indeed
It was some glorious form, some splendid weed,
In which a spirit new come from the skies
Might live, and show itself to human eyes.
'Tis the far-famed, the brave Sir Gondibert,
Said the good man to Calidore alert;
While the young warrior with a step of grace
Came up – a courtly smile upon his face,
And mailèd hand held out, ready to greet
The large-eyed wonder and ambitious heat
Of the aspiring boy; who as he led
Those smiling ladies, often turned his head
To admire the visor arched so gracefully
Over a knightly brow; while they went by
The lamps that from the high-roofed hall were pendent,
And gave the steel a shining quite transcendent.

  Soon in a pleasant chamber they are seated;
The sweet-lipped ladies have already greeted
All the green leaves that round the window clamber,
To show their purple stars, and bells of amber.
Sir Gondibert had doffed his shining steel,
Gladdening in the free and airy feel
Of a light mantle; and while Clerimond
Is looking round about him with a fond
And placid eye, young Calidore is burning
To hear of knightly deeds, and gallant spurning
Of all unworthiness, and how the strong of arm
Kept off dismay, and terror, and alarm

From lovely woman: while brimful of this,
He gave each damsel's hand so warm a kiss,
And had such manly ardour in his eye,
That each at other looked half-staringly;
150 And then their features started into smiles
Sweet as blue heavens o'er enchanted isles.

Softly the breezes from the forest came,
Softly they blew aside the taper's flame;
Clear was the song from Philomel's far bower;
Grateful the incense from the lime-tree flower;
Mysterious, wild, the far heard trumpet's tone;
Lovely the moon in ether, all alone:
Sweet too the converse of these happy mortals,
As that of busy spirits when the portals
160 Are closing in the west, or that soft humming
We hear around when Hesperus is coming.
Sweet be their sleep. ...

'To one who has been long in city pent'

To one who has been long in city pent,
   'Tis very sweet to look into the fair
   And open face of heaven – to breathe a prayer
Full in the smile of the blue firmament.
Who is more happy, when, with heart's content,
   Fatigued he sinks into some pleasant lair
   Of wavy grass, and reads a debonair
And gentle tale of love and languishment?
Returning home at evening, with an ear
10   Catching the notes of Philomel – an eye
Watching the sailing cloudlet's bright career,
   He mourns that day so soon has glided by:
E'en like the passage of an angel's tear
   That falls through the clear ether silently.

'O! how I love, on a fair summer's eve'

O! how I love, on a fair summer's eve,
   When streams of light pour down the golden west,
   And on the balmy zephyrs tranquil rest
The silver clouds, far – far away to leave
All meaner thoughts, and take a sweet reprieve
   From little cares; to find, with easy quest,
   A fragrant wild, with Nature's beauty dressed,
And there into delight my soul deceive.
There warm my breast with patriotic lore,
   Musing on Milton's fate – on Sidney's bier –
     Till their stern forms before my mind arise:
Perhaps on the wing of Poesy upsoar,
   Full often dropping a delicious tear,
     When some melodious sorrow spells mine eyes.

To a Friend who Sent me some Roses

As late I rambled in the happy fields –
   What time the skylark shakes the tremulous dew
   From his lush clover covert, when anew
Adventurous knights take up their dinted shields –
I saw the sweetest flower wild nature yields,
   A fresh-blown musk-rose; 'twas the first that threw
   Its sweets upon the summer: graceful it grew
As is the wand that queen Titania wields.
And, as I feasted on its fragrancy,
   I thought the garden-rose it far excelled:
But when, O Wells! thy roses came to me
   My sense with their deliciousness was spelled:
Soft voices had they, that with tender plea
   Whispered of peace, and truth, and friendliness unquelled.

To my Brother George

Many the wonders I this day have seen:
  The sun, when first he kissed away the tears
  That filled the eyes of morn – the laurelled peers
Who from the feathery gold of evening lean –
The ocean with its vastness, its blue green,
  Its ships, its rocks, its caves, its hopes, its fears –
  Its voice mysterious, which whoso hears
Must think on what will be, and what has been.
E'en now, dear George, while this for you I write,
10   Cynthia is from her silken curtains peeping
So scantly, that it seems her bridal night,
  And she her half-discovered revels keeping.
But what, without the social thought of thee,
Would be the wonders of the sky and sea?

To my Brother George

Full many a dreary hour have I passed,
My brain bewildered, and my mind o'ercast
With heaviness; in seasons when I've thought
No sphery strains by me could e'er be caught
From the blue dome, though I to dimness gaze
On the far depth where sheeted lightning plays;
Or, on the wavy grass outstretched supinely,
Pry 'mong the stars, to strive to think divinely:
That I should never hear Apollo's song,
10 Though feathery clouds were floating all along
The purple west, and, two bright streaks between,
The golden lyre itself were dimly seen:
That the still murmur of the honey bee
Would never teach a rural song to me:
That the bright glance from beauty's eyelids slanting
Would never make a lay of mine enchanting,
Or warm my breast with ardour to unfold
Some tale of love and arms in time of old.

TO MY BROTHER GEORGE

But there are times, when those that love the bay,
Fly from all sorrowing far, far away;
A sudden glow comes on them, naught they see
In water, earth, or air, but poesy.
It has been said, dear George, and true I hold it,
(For knightly Spenser to Libertas told it,)
That when a Poet is in such a trance,
In air he sees white coursers paw, and prance,
Bestridden of gay knights, in gay apparel,
Who at each other tilt in playful quarrel,
And what we, ignorantly, sheet-lightning call,
Is the swift opening of their wide portal,
When the bright warder blows his trumpet clear,
Whose tones reach naught on earth but Poet's ear.
When these enchanted portals open wide,
And through the light the horsemen swiftly glide,
The Poet's eye can reach those golden halls,
And view the glory of their festivals:
Their ladies fair, that in the distance seem
Fit for the silvering of a seraph's dream;
Their rich brimmed goblets, that incessant run
Like the bright spots that move about the sun;
And, when upheld, the wine from each bright jar
Pours with the lustre of a falling star.
Yet further off, are dimly seen their bowers,
Of which, no mortal eye can reach the flowers –
And 'tis right just, for well Apollo knows
'Twould make the Poet quarrel with the rose.
All that's revealed from that far seat of blisses,
Is, the clear fountains' interchanging kisses,
As gracefully descending, light and thin,
Like silver streaks across a dolphin's fin,
When he upswimmeth from the coral caves,
And sports with half his tail above the waves.

These wonders strange he sees, and many more,
Whose head is pregnant with poetic lore.
Should he upon an evening ramble fare

With forehead to the soothing breezes bare,
Would he naught see but the dark, silent blue
With all its diamonds trembling through and through?
Or the coy moon, when in the waviness
Of whitest clouds she does her beauty dress,
And staidly paces higher up, and higher,
Like a sweet nun in holy-day attire?
Ah, yes! much more would start into his sight –
The revelries, and mysteries of night:
And should I ever see them, I will tell you
Such tales as needs must with amazement spell you.

These are the living pleasures of the bard:
But richer far posterity's award.
What does he murmur with his latest breath,
While his proud eye looks through the film of death?
'What though I leave this dull, and earthly mould,
Yet shall my spirit lofty converse hold
With after times. The patriot shall feel
My stern alarum, and unsheathe his steel;
Or, in the senate thunder out my numbers
To startle princes from their easy slumbers.
The sage will mingle with each moral theme
My happy thoughts sententious; he will teem
With lofty periods when my verses fire him,
And then I'll stoop from heaven to inspire him.
Lays have I left of such a dear delight
That maids will sing them on their bridal night.
Gay villagers, upon a morn of May,
When they have tired their gentle limbs with play,
And formed a snowy circle on the grass,
And placed in midst of all that lovely lass
Who chosen is their queen – with her fine head
Crownèd with flowers purple, white, and red:
For there the lily, and the musk-rose, sighing,
Are emblems true of hapless lovers dying.
Between her breasts, that never yet felt trouble,
A bunch of violets full blown, and double,

TO MY BROTHER GEORGE

  Serenely sleep: she from a casket takes
A little book and then a joy awakes
About each youthful heart, with stifled cries,
And rubbing of white hands, and sparkling eyes –
For she's to read a tale of hopes, and fears,
One that I fostered in my youthful years.
The pearls, that on each glistening circlet sleep,
100 Gush ever and anon with silent creep,
Lured by the innocent dimples. To sweet rest
Shall the dear babe, upon its mother's breast,
Be lulled with songs of mine. Fair world, adieu!
Thy dales, and hills, are fading from my view:
Swiftly I mount, upon wide spreading pinions,
Far from the narrow bounds of thy dominions.
Full joy I feel, while thus I cleave the air,
That my soft verse will charm thy daughters fair,
And warm thy sons!' Ah, my dear friend and brother,
110 Could I, at once, my mad ambition smother,
For tasting joys like these, sure I should be
Happier, and dearer to society.
At times, 'tis true, I've felt relief from pain
When some bright thought has darted through my brain:
Through all that day I've felt a greater pleasure
Than if I'd brought to light a hidden treasure.
As to my sonnets, though none else should heed them,
I feel delighted, still, that you should read them.
Of late, too, I have had much calm enjoyment,
120 Stretched on the grass at my best loved employment
Of scribbling lines for you. These things I thought
While, in my face, the freshest breeze I caught.
E'en now I'm pillowed on a bed of flowers
That crowns a lofty clift, which proudly towers
Above the ocean-waves. The stalks, and blades,
Chequer my tablet with their quivering shades.
On one side is a field of drooping oats,
Through which the poppies show their scarlet coats,
So pert and useless, that they bring to mind
130 The scarlet coats that pester human-kind.

And on the other side, outspread, is seen
Ocean's blue mantle streaked with purple, and green.
Now 'tis I see a canvassed ship, and now
Mark the bright silver curling round her prow.
I see the lark down-dropping to his nest
And the broad winged sea-gull never at rest;
For when no more he spreads his feathers free,
His breast is dancing on the restless sea.
Now I direct my eyes into the west,
140 Which at this moment is in sunbeams dressed:
Why westward turn? 'Twas but to say adieu!
'Twas but to kiss my hand, dear George, to you!

To Charles Cowden Clarke

Oft have you seen a swan superbly frowning,
And with proud breast his own white shadow crowning;
He slants his neck beneath the waters bright
So silently, it seems a beam of light
Come from the galaxy: anon he sports –
With outspread wings the Naiad Zephyr courts,
Or ruffles all the surface of the lake
In striving from its crystal face to take
Some diamond water drops, and them to treasure
10 In milky nest, and sip them off at leisure.
But not a moment can he there insure them,
Nor to such downy rest can he allure them;
For down they rush as though they would be free,
And drops like hours into eternity.

Just like that bird am I in loss of time,
Whene'er I venture on the stream of rhyme;
With shattered boat, oar snapped, and canvas rent
I slowly sail, scarce knowing my intent;
Still scooping up the water with my fingers,
20 In which a trembling diamond never lingers.

TO CHARLES COWDEN CLARKE

By this, friend Charles, you may full plainly see
Why I have never penned a line to thee:
Because my thoughts were never free, and clear,
And little fit to please a classic ear;
Because my wine was of too poor a savour
For one whose palate gladdens in the flavour
Of sparkling Helicon – small good it were
To take him to a desert rude, and bare,
Who had on Baiae's shore reclined at ease,
While Tasso's page was floating in a breeze
That gave soft music from Armida's bowers,
Mingled with fragrance from her rarest flowers:
Small good to one who had by Mulla's stream
Fondled the maidens with the breasts of cream;
Who had beheld Belphoebe in a brook,
And lovely Una in a leafy nook,
And Archimago leaning o'er his book:
Who had of all that's sweet tasted, and seen,
From silvery ripple, up to beauty's queen;
From the sequestered haunts of gay Titania,
To the blue dwelling of divine Urania:
One, who, of late, had ta'en sweet forest walks
With him who elegantly chats, and talks –
The wronged Libertas – who has told you stories
Of laurel chaplets, and Apollo's glories;
Of troops chivalrous prancing through a city,
And tearful ladies made for love, and pity:
With many else which I have never known.

Thus have I thought; and days on days have flown
Slowly, or rapidly – unwilling still
For you to try my dull, unlearned quill.
Nor should I now, but that I've known you long,
That you first taught me all the sweets of song:
The grand, the sweet, the terse, the free, the fine;
What swelled with pathos, and what right divine;
Spenserian vowels that elope with ease,
And float along like birds o'er summer seas;

Miltonian storms, and more, Miltonian tenderness;
Michael in arms, and more, meek Eve's fair slenderness.
Who read for me the sonnet swelling loudly
Up to its climax and then dying proudly?
Who found for me the grandeur of the ode,
Growing, like Atlas, stronger from its load?
Who let me taste that more than cordial dram,
The sharp, the rapier-pointed epigram?
Showed me that epic was of all the king,
Round, vast, and spanning all like Saturn's ring?
You too upheld the veil from Clio's beauty,
And pointed out the patriot's stern duty;
The might of Alfred, and the shaft of Tell;
The hand of Brutus, that so grandly fell
Upon a tyrant's head. Ah! had I never seen,
Or known your kindness, what might I have been?
What my enjoyments in my youthful years,
Bereft of all that now my life endears?
And can I e'er these benefits forget?
And can I e'er repay the friendly debt?
No, doubly no – yet should these rhymings please,
I shall roll on the grass with two-fold ease:
For I have long time been my fancy feeding
With hopes that you would one day think the reading
Of my rough verses not an hour misspent;
Should it e'er be so, what a rich content!

Some weeks have passed since last I saw the spires
In lucent Thames reflected – warm desires
To see the sun o'er-peep the eastern dimness,
And morning shadows streaking into slimness
Across the lawny fields, and pebbly water;
To mark the time as they grow broad, and shorter;
To feel the air that plays about the hills,
And sips its freshness from the little rills;
To see high, golden corn wave in the light
When Cynthia smiles upon a summer's night,
And peers among the cloudlets jet and white,

TO CHARLES COWDEN CLARKE

As though she were reclining in a bed
Of bean blossoms, in heaven freshly shed –
No sooner had I stepped into these pleasures
Than I began to think of rhymes and measures:
The air that floated by me seemed to say
100 'Write! thou wilt never have a better day.'
And so I did. When many lines I'd written,
Though with their grace I was not oversmitten,
Yet, as my hand was warm, I thought I'd better
Trust to my feelings, and write you a letter.
Such an attempt required an inspiration
Of a peculiar sort – a consummation –
Which, had I felt, these scribblings might have been
Verses from which the soul would never wean:
But many days have passed since last my heart
110 Was warmed luxuriously by divine Mozart,
By Arne delighted, or by Handel maddened,
Or by the song of Erin pierced and saddened,
What time you were before the music sitting,
And the rich notes to each sensation fitting.
Since I have walked with you through shady lanes
That freshly terminate in open plains,
And revelled in a chat that ceasèd not
When at night-fall among your books we got:
No, nor when supper came, nor after that –
120 Nor when reluctantly I took my hat;
No, nor till cordially you shook my hand
Mid-way between our homes. Your accents bland
Still sounded in my ears, when I no more
Could hear your footsteps touch the gravelly floor.
Sometimes I lost them, and then found again;
You changed the footpath for the grassy plain.
In those still moments I have wished you joys
That well you know to honour – 'Life's very toys
With him,' said I, 'will take a pleasant charm;
130 It cannot be that aught will work him harm.'
These thoughts now come o'er me with all their might –
Again I shake your hand – friend Charles, good night.

'How many bards gild the lapses of time!'

How many bards gild the lapses of time!
   A few of them have ever been the food
   Of my delighted fancy – I could brood
Over their beauties, earthly, or sublime:
And often, when I sit me down to rhyme,
   These will in throngs before my mind intrude:
   But no confusion, no disturbance rude
Do they occasion; 'tis a pleasing chime.
So the unnumbered sounds that evening store;
10   The songs of birds, the whispering of the leaves,
   The voice of waters, the great bell that heaves
With solemn sound, and thousand others more,
   That distance of recognizance bereaves,
Make pleasing music, and not wild uproar.

On First Looking into Chapman's Homer

Much have I travelled in the realms of gold,
   And many goodly states and kingdoms seen;
   Round many western islands have I been
Which bards in fealty to Apollo hold.
Oft of one wide expanse had I been told
   That deep-browed Homer ruled as his demesne;
   Yet did I never breathe its pure serene
Till I heard Chapman speak out loud and bold:
Then felt I like some watcher of the skies
10   When a new planet swims into his ken;
Or like stout Cortez when with eagle eyes
   He stared at the Pacific – and all his men
Looked at each other with a wild surmise –
   Silent, upon a peak in Darien.

To a Young Lady who sent me a Laurel Crown

Fresh morning gusts have blown away all fear
  From my glad bosom: now from gloominess
  I mount for ever – not an atom less
Than the proud laurel shall content my bier.
No! by the eternal stars! or why sit here
  In the Sun's eye, and 'gainst my temples press
  Apollo's very leaves, woven to bless
By thy white fingers and thy spirit clear.
Lo! who dares say, 'Do this'? Who dares call down
  My will from its high purpose? Who say, 'Stand',
Or 'Go'? This very moment I would frown
  On abject Caesars – not the stoutest band
Of mailèd heroes should tear off my crown:
  Yet would I kneel and kiss thy gentle hand!

On Leaving some Friends at an Early Hour

Give me a golden pen, and let me lean
  On heaped up flowers, in regions clear, and far;
  Bring me a tablet whiter than a star,
Or hand of hymning angel, when 'tis seen
The silver strings of heavenly harp atween:
  And let there glide by many a pearly car,
  Pink robes, and wavy hair, and diamond jar,
And half-discovered wings, and glances keen.
The while let music wander round my ears,
  And as it reaches each delicious ending,
    Let me write down a line of glorious tone,
And full of many wonders of the spheres:
  For what a height my spirit is contending!
  'Tis not content so soon to be alone.

'Keen, fitful gusts are whispering here and there'

Keen, fitful gusts are whispering here and there
   Among the bushes half leafless, and dry;
   The stars look very cold about the sky,
And I have many miles on foot to fare.
Yet feel I little of the cool bleak air,
   Or of the dead leaves rustling drearily,
   Or of those silver lamps that burn on high,
Or of the distance from home's pleasant lair:
For I am brimful of the friendliness
10   That in a little cottage I have found;
Of fair-haired Milton's eloquent distress,
   And all his love for gentle Lycid drowned;
Of lovely Laura in her light green dress,
   And faithful Petrarch gloriously crowned.

Addressed to Haydon

Highmindedness, a jealousy for good,
   A loving-kindness for the great man's fame,
   Dwells here and there with people of no name,
In noisome alley, and in pathless wood:
And where we think the truth least understood,
   Oft may be found a 'singleness of aim',
That ought to frighten into hooded shame
A money-mongering, pitiable brood.
How glorious this affection for the cause
10   Of steadfast genius, toiling gallantly!
What when a stout unbending champion awes
   Envy, and Malice to their native sty?
Unnumbered souls breathe out a still applause,
   Proud to behold him in his country's eye.

To my Brothers

Small, busy flames play through the fresh-laid coals,
  And their faint cracklings o'er our silence creep
  Like whispers of the household gods that keep
A gentle empire o'er fraternal souls.
And while, for rhymes, I search around the poles,
  Your eyes are fixed, as in poetic sleep,
  Upon the lore so voluble and deep,
That aye at fall of night our care condoles.
This is your birth-day Tom, and I rejoice
10   That thus it passes smoothly, quietly.
Many such eves of gently whispering noise
  May we together pass, and calmly try
What are this world's true joys — ere the great voice,
  From its fair face, shall bid our spirits fly.

Addressed to [Haydon]

Great spirits now on earth are sojourning;
  He of the cloud, the cataract, the lake,
  Who on Helvellyn's summit, wide awake,
Catches his freshness from Archangel's wing:
He of the rose, the violet, the spring,
  The social smile, the chain for Freedom's sake:
  And lo! — whose steadfastness would never take
A meaner sound than Raphael's whispering.
And other spirits there are standing apart
10   Upon the forehead of the age to come;
These, these will give the world another heart,
  And other pulses. Hear ye not the hum
Of mighty workings? —
  Listen awhile ye nations, and be dumb.

'I stood tip-toe upon a little hill'

Places of nestling green for Poets made
'The Story of Rimini'

I stood tip-toe upon a little hill,
The air was cooling, and so very still,
That the sweet buds which with a modest pride
Pull droopingly, in slanting curve aside,
Their scanty leaved, and finely tapering stems,
Had not yet lost those starry diadems
Caught from the early sobbing of the morn.
The clouds were pure and white as flocks new shorn,
And fresh from the clear brook; sweetly they slept
10 On the blue fields of heaven, and then there crept
A little noiseless noise among the leaves,
Born of the very sigh that silence heaves:
For not the faintest motion could be seen
Of all the shades that slanted o'er the green.
There was wide wandering for the greediest eye,
To peer about upon variety;
Far round the horizon's crystal air to skim,
And trace the dwindled edgings of its brim;
To picture out the quaint, and curious bending
20 Of a fresh woodland alley, never ending;
Or by the bowery clefts, and leafy shelves,
Guess where the jaunty streams refresh themselves.
I gazed awhile, and felt as light, and free
As though the fanning wings of Mercury
Had played upon my heels: I was light-hearted,
And many pleasures to my vision started;
So I straightway began to pluck a posy
Of luxuries bright, milky, soft and rosy.

A bush of May flowers with the bees about them;
30 Ah, sure no tasteful nook would be without them;
And let a lush laburnum oversweep them,
And let long grass grow round the roots to keep them
Moist, cool and green; and shade the violets,
That they may bind the moss in leafy nets.

A filbert hedge with wild briar overtwined,
And clumps of woodbine taking the soft wind
Upon their summer thrones; there too should be
The frequent chequer of a youngling tree,
That with a score of light green brethren shoots
40 From the quaint mossiness of agèd roots:
Round which is heard a spring-head of clear waters
Babbling so wildly of its lovely daughters
The spreading blue-bells – it may haply mourn
That such fair clusters should be rudely torn
From their fresh beds, and scattered thoughtlessly
By infant hands, left on the path to die.

Open afresh your round of starry folds,
Ye ardent marigolds!
Dry up the moisture from your golden lids,
50 For great Apollo bids
That in these days your praises should be sung
On many harps, which he has lately strung;
And when again your dewiness he kisses,
Tell him, I have you in my world of blisses:
So haply when I rove in some far vale,
His mighty voice may come upon the gale.

Here are sweet peas, on tip-toe for a flight:
With wings of gentle flush o'er delicate white,
And taper fingers catching at all things,
60 To bind them all about with tiny rings.

Linger awhile upon some bending planks
That lean against a streamlet's rushy banks,
And watch intently Nature's gentle doings:
They will be found softer than ring-dove's cooings.
How silent comes the water round that bend;
Not the minutest whisper does it send
To the o'erhanging sallows: blades of grass
Slowly across the chequered shadows pass –
Why, you might read two sonnets, ere they reach
70 To where the hurrying freshnesses aye preach
A natural sermon o'er their pebbly beds;

Where swarms of minnows show their little heads,
Staying their wavy bodies 'gainst the streams,
To taste the luxury of sunny beams
Tempered with coolness. How they ever wrestle
With their own sweet delight, and ever nestle
Their silver bellies on the pebbly sand.
If you but scantily hold out the hand,
That very instant not one will remain;
But turn your eye, and they are there again.
The ripples seem right glad to reach those cresses,
And cool themselves among the emerald tresses;
The while they cool themselves, they freshness give,
And moisture, that the bowery green may live:
So keeping up an interchange of favours,
Like good men in the truth of their behaviours.
Sometimes goldfinches one by one will drop
From low-hung branches; little space they stop;
But sip, and twitter, and their feathers sleek –
Then off at once, as in a wanton freak:
Or perhaps, to show their black, and golden wings,
Pausing upon their yellow flutterings.
Were I in such a place, I sure should pray
That naught less sweet, might call my thoughts away,
Than the soft rustle of a maiden's gown
Fanning away the dandelion's down;
Than the light music of her nimble toes
Patting against the sorrel as she goes.
How she would start, and blush, thus to be caught
Playing in all her innocence of thought.
O let me lead her gently o'er the brook,
Watch her half-smiling lips, and downward look;
O let me for one moment touch her wrist;
Let me one moment to her breathing list;
And as she leaves me may she often turn
Her fair eyes looking through her locks aubùrn.
What next? A tuft of evening primroses,
O'er which the mind may hover till it dozes;
O'er which it well might take a pleasant sleep,

110 But that 'tis ever startled by the leap
    Of buds into ripe flowers; or by the flitting
    Of diverse moths, that aye their rest are quitting;
    Or by the moon lifting her silver rim
    Above a cloud, and with a gradual swim
    Coming into the blue with all her light.
    O Maker of sweet poets, dear delight
    Of this fair world, and all its gentle livers;
    Spangler of clouds, halo of crystal rivers,
    Mingler with leaves, and dew and tumbling streams,
120 Closer of lovely eyes to lovely dreams,
    Lover of loneliness, and wandering,
    Of upcast eye, and tender pondering!
    Thee must I praise above all other glories
    That smile us on to tell delightful stories.
    For what has made the sage or poet write
    But the fair paradise of Nature's light?
    In the calm grandeur of a sober line,
    We see the waving of the mountain pine;
    And when a tale is beautifully staid,
130 We feel the safety of a hawthorn glade:
    When it is moving on luxurious wings,
    The soul is lost in pleasant smotherings:
    Fair dewy roses brush against our faces,
    And flowering laurels spring from diamond vases;
    O'er head we see the jasmine and sweet briar,
    And bloomy grapes laughing from green attire;
    While at our feet, the voice of crystal bubbles
    Charms us at once away from all our troubles:
    So that we feel uplifted from the world,
140 Walking upon the white clouds wreathed and curled.
    So felt he, who first told, how Psyche went
    On the smooth wind to realms of wonderment;
    What Psyche felt, and Love, when their full lips
    First touched; what amorous, and fondling nips
    They gave each other's cheeks; with all their sighs,
    And how they kissed each other's tremulous eyes;
    The silver lamp – the ravishment – the wonder –

> The darkness – loneliness – the fearful thunder;
> Their woes gone by, and both to heaven upflown,
> To bow for gratitude before Jove's throne.
> So did he feel, who pulled the boughs aside,
> That we might look into a forest wide,
> To catch a glimpse of Fauns and Dryadès
> Coming with softest rustle through the trees,
> And garlands woven of flowers wild, and sweet,
> Upheld on ivory wrists, or sporting feet:
> Telling us how fair, trembling Syrinx fled
> Arcadian Pan, with such a fearful dread.
> Poor nymph – poor Pan – how he did weep to find,
> Naught but a lovely sighing of the wind
> Along the reedy stream; a half-heard strain,
> Full of sweet desolation – balmy pain.
>
> What first inspired a bard of old to sing
> Narcissus pining o'er the untainted spring?
> In some delicious ramble, he had found
> A little space, with boughs all woven round;
> And in the midst of all, a clearer pool
> Than e'er reflected in its pleasant cool
> The blue sky here and there serenely peeping
> Through tendril wreaths fantastically creeping.
> And on the bank a lonely flower he spied,
> A meek and forlorn flower, with naught of pride,
> Drooping its beauty o'er the watery clearness,
> To woo its own sad image into nearness:
> Deaf to light Zephyrus it would not move;
> But still would seem to droop, to pine, to love.
> So while the Poet stood in this sweet spot,
> Some fainter gleamings o'er his fancy shot;
> Nor was it long ere he had told the tale
> Of young Narcissus, and sad Echo's bale.
>
> Where had he been, from whose warm head out-flew
> That sweetest of all songs, that ever new,
> That aye refreshing, pure deliciousness,
> Coming ever to bless

The wanderer by moonlight? to him bringing
Shapes from the invisible world, unearthly singing
From out the middle air, from flowery nests,
And from the pillowy silkiness that rests
Full in the speculation of the stars.
Ah! surely he had burst our mortal bars;
Into some wondrous region he had gone,
To search for thee, divine Endymion!

He was a Poet, sure a lover too,
Who stood on Latmos' top, what time there blew
Soft breezes from the myrtle vale below;
And brought in faintness solemn, sweet, and slow
A hymn from Dian's temple; while upswelling,
The incense went to her own starry dwelling.
But though her face was clear as infant's eyes,
Though she stood smiling o'er the sacrifice,
The Poet wept at her so piteous fate,
Wept that such beauty should be desolate:
So in fine wrath some golden sounds he won,
And gave meek Cynthia her Endymion.

Queen of the wide air! thou most lovely queen
Of all the brightness that mine eyes have seen!
As thou exceedest all things in thy shine,
So every tale, does this sweet tale of thine.
O for three words of honey, that I might
Tell but one wonder of thy bridal night!

Where distant ships do seem to show their keels,
Phoebus awhile delayed his mighty wheels,
And turned to smile upon thy bashful eyes,
Ere he his unseen pomp would solemnize.
The evening weather was so bright and clear,
That men of health were of unusual cheer;
Stepping like Homer at the trumpet's call,
Or young Apollo on the pedestal:
And lovely women were as fair and warm,
As Venus looking sideways in alarm.

The breezes were ethereal, and pure,
And crept through half-closed lattices to cure
The languid sick; it cooled their fevered sleep,
And soothed them into slumbers full and deep.
Soon they awoke clear-eyed: nor burnt with thirsting,
Nor with hot fingers, nor with temples bursting:
And springing up, they met the wondering sight
Of their dear friends, nigh foolish with delight;
Who feel their arms, and breasts, and kiss and stare,
And on their placid foreheads part the hair.
Young men, and maidens at each other gazed
With hands held back, and motionless, amazed
To see the brightness in each other's eyes;
And so they stood, filled with a sweet surprise,
Until their tongues were loosed in Poesy.
Therefore no lover did of anguish die:
But the soft numbers, in that moment spoken,
Made silken ties, that never may be broken.
Cynthia! I cannot tell the greater blisses,
That followed thine, and thy dear shepherd's kisses:
Was there a Poet born? – but now no more,
My wandering spirit must no further soar. –

Sleep and Poetry

As I lay in my bed slepe full unmete
Was unto me, but why that I ne might
Rest I ne wist, for there n'as earthly wight
[As I suppose] had more of hertis ese
Than I, for I n'ad sicknesse nor disese.
Chaucer

What is more gentle than a wind in summer?
What is more soothing than the pretty hummer
That stays one moment in an open flower,
And buzzes cheerily from bower to bower?
What is more tranquil than a musk-rose blowing
In a green island, far from all men's knowing?

SLEEP AND POETRY

More healthful than the leafiness of dales?
More secret than a nest of nightingales?
More serene than Cordelia's countenance?
10 More full of visions than a high romance?
What, but thee Sleep? Soft closer of our eyes!
Low murmurer of tender lullabies!
Light hoverer around our happy pillows!
Wreather of poppy buds, and weeping willows!
Silent entangler of a beauty's tresses!
Most happy listener! when the morning blesses
Thee for enlivening all the cheerful eyes
That glance so brightly at the new sun-rise.

But what is higher beyond thought than thee?
20 Fresher than berries of a mountain tree?
More strange, more beautiful, more smooth, more regal,
Than wings of swans, than doves, than dim-seen eagle?
What is it? And to what shall I compare it?
It has a glory, and naught else can share it:
The thought thereof is awful, sweet, and holy,
Chasing away all worldliness and folly;
Coming sometimes like fearful claps of thunder,
Or the low rumblings earth's regions under;
And sometimes like a gentle whispering
30 Of all the secrets of some wondrous thing
That breathes about us in the vacant air;
So that we look around with prying stare,
Perhaps to see shapes of light, aërial limning,
And catch soft floatings from a faint-heard hymning,
To see the laurel wreath, on high suspended,
That is to crown our name when life is ended.
Sometimes it gives a glory to the voice,
And from the heart up-springs, 'Rejoice! Rejoice!' –
Sounds which will reach the Framer of all things,
40 And die away in ardent mutterings.

No one who once the glorious sun has seen,
And all the clouds, and felt his bosom clean
For his great Maker's presence, but must know

What 'tis I mean, and feel his being glow:
Therefore no insult will I give his spirit,
By telling what he sees from native merit.

O Poesy! for thee I hold my pen
That am not yet a glorious denizen
Of thy wide heaven – Should I rather kneel
50 Upon some mountain-top until I feel
A glowing splendour round about me hung,
And echo back the voice of thine own tongue?
O Poesy! for thee I grasp my pen
That am not yet a glorious denizen
Of thy wide heaven; yet, to my ardent prayer,
Yield from thy sanctuary some clear air,
Smoothed for intoxication by the breath
Of flowering bays, that I may die a death
Of luxury, and my young spirit follow
60 The morning sunbeams to the great Apollo
Like a fresh sacrifice; or, if I can bear
The o'erwhelming sweets, 'twill bring to me the fair
Visions of all places: a bowery nook
Will be elysium – an eternal book
Whence I may copy many a lovely saying
About the leaves, and flowers – about the playing
Of nymphs in woods, and fountains; and the shade
Keeping a silence round a sleeping maid;
And many a verse from so strange influence
70 That we must ever wonder how, and whence
It came. Also imaginings will hover
Round my fire-side, and haply there discover
Vistas of solemn beauty, where I'd wander
In happy silence, like the clear Meander
Through its lone vales; and where I found a spot
Of awfuller shade, or an enchanted grot,
Or a green hill o'erspread with chequered dress
Of flowers, and fearful from its loveliness,
Write on my tablets all that was permitted,
80 All that was for our human senses fitted.

SLEEP AND POETRY

> Then the events of this wide world I'd seize
> Like a strong giant, and my spirit tease
> Till at its shoulders it should proudly see
> Wings to find out an immortality.
>
> Stop and consider! life is but a day;
> A fragile dew-drop on its perilous way
> From a tree's summit; a poor Indian's sleep
> While his boat hastens to the monstrous steep
> Of Montmorenci. Why so sad a moan?
> Life is the rose's hope while yet unblown;
> The reading of an ever-changing tale;
> The light uplifting of a maiden's veil;
> A pigeon tumbling in clear summer air;
> A laughing school-boy, without grief or care,
> Riding the springy branches of an elm.
>
> O for ten years, that I may overwhelm
> Myself in poesy; so I may do the deed
> That my own soul has to itself decreed.
> Then will I pass the countries that I see
> In long perspective, and continually
> Taste their pure fountains. First the realm I'll pass
> Of Flora, and old Pan: sleep in the grass,
> Feed upon apples red, and strawberries,
> And choose each pleasure that my fancy sees;
> Catch the white-handed nymphs in shady places,
> To woo sweet kisses from averted faces –
> Play with their fingers, touch their shoulders white
> Into a pretty shrinking with a bite
> As hard as lips can make it, till, agreed,
> A lovely tale of human life we'll read.
> And one will teach a tame dove how it best
> May fan the cool air gently o'er my rest;
> Another, bending o'er her nimble tread,
> Will set a green robe floating round her head,
> And still will dance with ever varied ease,
> Smiling upon the flowers and the trees:
> Another will entice me on, and on

Through almond blossoms and rich cinnamon;
Till in the bosom of a leafy world
We rest in silence, like two gems upcurled
In the recesses of a pearly shell.

And can I ever bid these joys farewell?
Yes, I must pass them for a nobler life,
Where I may find the agonies, the strife
Of human hearts – for lo! I see afar,
O'er-sailing the blue cragginess, a car
And steeds with streamy manes – the charioteer
Looks out upon the winds with glorious fear:
And now the numerous tramplings quiver lightly
Along a huge cloud's ridge; and now with sprightly
Wheel downward come they into fresher skies,
Tipped round with silver from the sun's bright eyes.
Still downward with capacious whirl they glide;
And now I see them on a green-hill's side
In breezy rest among the nodding stalks.
The charioteer with wondrous gesture talks
To the trees and mountains; and there soon appear
Shapes of delight, of mystery, and fear,
Passing along before a dusky space
Made by some mighty oaks: as they would chase
Some ever-fleeting music on they sweep.
Lo! how they murmur, laugh, and smile, and weep –
Some with upholden hand and mouth severe;
Some with their faces muffled to the ear
Between their arms; some, clear in youthful bloom,
Go glad and smilingly athwart the gloom;
Some looking back, and some with upward gaze;
Yes, thousands in a thousand different ways
Flit onward – now a lovely wreath of girls
Dancing their sleek hair into tangled curls;
And now broad wings. Most awfully intent
The driver of those steeds is forward bent,
And seems to listen: O that I might know
All that he writes with such a hurrying glow.

SLEEP AND POETRY

The visions all are fled – the car is fled
Into the light of heaven, and in their stead
A sense of real things comes doubly strong,
And, like a muddy stream, would bear along
My soul to nothingness: but I will strive
Against all doubtings, and will keep alive
The thought of that same chariot, and the strange
Journey it went.
                Is there so small a range
In the present strength of manhood, that the high
Imagination cannot freely fly
As she was wont of old? Prepare her steeds,
Paw up against the light, and do strange deeds
Upon the clouds? Has she not shown us all?
From the clear space of ether, to the small
Breath of new buds unfolding? From the meaning
Of Jove's large eye-brow, to the tender greening
Of April meadows? Here her altar shone,
E'en in this isle; and who could paragon
The fervid choir that lifted up a noise
Of harmony, to where it aye will poise
Its mighty self of convoluting sound,
Huge as a planet, and like that roll round,
Eternally around a dizzy void?
Ay, in those days the Muses were nigh cloyed
With honours; nor had any other care
Than to sing out and soothe their wavy hair.

Could all this be forgotten? Yes, a schism
Nurtured by foppery and barbarism,
Made great Apollo blush for this his land.
Men were thought wise who could not understand
His glories: with a puling infant's force
They swayed about upon a rocking horse,
And thought it Pegasus. Ah, dismal souled!
The winds of heaven blew, the ocean rolled
Its gathering waves – ye felt it not. The blue
Bared its eternal bosom, and the dew

Of summer nights collected still to make
The morning precious: beauty was awake!
Why were ye not awake? But ye were dead
To things ye knew not of – were closely wed
To musty laws lined out with wretched rule
And compass vile: so that ye taught a school
Of dolts to smooth, inlay, and clip, and fit,
Till, like the certain wands of Jacob's wit,
Their verses tallied. Easy was the task:
200 A thousand handicraftsmen wore the mask
Of Poesy. Ill-fated, impious race!
That blasphemed the bright Lyrist to his face,
And did not know it! No, they went about,
Holding a poor, decrepit standard out
Marked with most flimsy mottoes, and in large
The name of one Boileau!
                      O ye whose charge
It is to hover round our pleasant hills!
Whose congregated majesty so fills
My boundly reverence, that I cannot trace
210 Your hallowed names, in this unholy place,
So near those common folk – did not their shames
Affright you? Did our old lamenting Thames
Delight you? Did ye never cluster round
Delicious Avon, with a mournful sound,
And weep? Or did ye wholly bid adieu
To regions where no more the laurel grew?
Or did ye stay to give a welcoming
To some lone spirits who could proudly sing
Their youth away, and die? 'Twas even so.
220 But let me think away those times of woe:
Now 'tis a fairer season; ye have breathed
Rich benedictions o'er us; ye have wreathed
Fresh garlands: for sweet music has been heard
In many places – some has been upstirred
From out its crystal dwelling in a lake,
By a swan's ebon bill; from a thick brake,
Nested and quiet in a valley mild,

Bubbles a pipe – fine sounds are floating wild
About the earth: happy are ye and glad.

These things are doubtless: yet in truth we've had
Strange thunders from the potency of song;
Mingled indeed with what is sweet and strong,
From majesty: but in clear truth the themes
Are ugly clubs, the poets Polyphemes
Disturbing the grand sea. A drainless shower
Of light is Poesy; 'tis the supreme of power;
'Tis might half-slumbering on its own right arm.
The very archings of her eye-lids charm
A thousand willing agents to obey,
And still she governs with the mildest sway:
But strength alone, though of the Muses born,
Is like a fallen angel: trees uptorn,
Darkness, and worms, and shrouds, and sepulchres
Delight it; for it feeds upon the burrs,
And thorns of life; forgetting the great end
Of Poesy, that it should be a friend
To soothe the cares, and lift the thoughts of man.

Yet I rejoice: a myrtle fairer than
E'er grew in Paphos, from the bitter weeds
Lifts its sweet head into the air, and feeds
A silent space with ever sprouting green.
All tenderest birds there find a pleasant screen,
Creep through the shade with jaunty fluttering,
Nibble the little cuppèd flowers and sing.
Then let us clear away the choking thorns
From round its gentle stem; let the young fawns,
Yeaned in after times, when we are flown,
Find a fresh sward beneath it, overgrown
With simple flowers: let there nothing be
More boisterous than a lover's bended knee;
Naught more ungentle than the placid look
Of one who leans upon a closèd book;
Naught more untranquil than the grassy slopes
Between two hills. All hail delightful hopes!

As she was wont, th' imagination
Into most lovely labyrinths will be gone,
And they shall be accounted poet-kings
Who simply tell the most heart-easing things.
O may these joys be ripe before I die.

270 Will not some say that I presumptuously
Have spoken? that from hastening disgrace
'Twere better far to hide my foolish face?
That whining boyhood should with reverence bow
Ere the dread thunderbolt could reach? How!
If I do hide myself, it sure shall be
In the very fane, the light of Poesy:
If I do fall, at least I will be laid
Beneath the silence of a poplar shade;
And over me the grass shall be smooth-shaven;
280 And there shall be a kind memorial graven.
But off, Despondence! miserable bane!
They should not know thee, who, athirst to gain
A noble end, are thirsty every hour.
What though I am not wealthy in the dower
Of spanning wisdom; though I do not know
The shiftings of the mighty winds that blow
Hither and thither all the changing thoughts
Of man: though no great ministering reason sorts
Out the dark mysteries of human souls
290 To clear conceiving – yet there ever rolls
A vast idea before me, and I glean
Therefrom my liberty; thence too I've seen
The end and aim of Poesy. 'Tis clear
As anything most true; as that the year
Is made of the four seasons – manifest
As a large cross, some old cathedral's crest,
Lifted to the white clouds. Therefore should I
Be but the essence of deformity,
A coward, did my very eye-lids wink
300 At speaking out what I have dared to think.
Ah! rather let me like a madman run

SLEEP AND POETRY

    Over some precipice! let the hot sun
Melt my Dedalian wings, and drive me down
Convulsed and headlong! Say! an inward frown
Of conscience bids me be more calm awhile.
An ocean dim, sprinkled with many an isle,
Spreads awfully before me. How much toil!
How many days! what desperate turmoil!
Ere I can have explored its widenesses.
Ah, what a task! upon my bended knees,
I could unsay those – no, impossible!
Impossible!
           For sweet relief I'll dwell
On humbler thoughts, and let this strange assay
Begun in gentleness die so away.
E'en now all tumult from my bosom fades:
I turn full-hearted to the friendly aids
That smooth the path of honour; brotherhood,
And friendliness the nurse of mutual good.
The hearty grasp that sends a pleasant sonnet
Into the brain ere one can think upon it;
The silence when some rhymes are coming out;
And when they're come, the very pleasant rout:
The message certain to be done to-morrow –
'Tis perhaps as well that it should be to borrow
Some precious book from out its snug retreat,
To cluster round it when we next shall meet.
Scarce can I scribble on; for lovely airs
Are fluttering round the room like doves in pairs;
Many delights of that glad day recalling,
When first my senses caught their tender falling.
And with these airs come forms of elegance
Stooping their shoulders o'er a horse's prance,
Careless, and grand – fingers soft and round
Parting luxuriant curls – and the swift bound
Of Bacchus from his chariot, when his eye
Made Ariadne's cheek look blushingly.
Thus I remember all the pleasant flow
Of words at opening a portfolio.

Things such as these are ever harbingers
To trains of peaceful images: the stirs
Of a swan's neck unseen among the rushes;
A linnet starting all about the bushes;
A butterfly, with golden wings broad parted,
Nestling a rose, convulsed as though it smarted
With over-pleasure – many, many more,
Might I indulge at large in all my store
Of luxuries: yet I must not forget
Sleep, quiet with his poppy coronet,
For what there may be worthy in these rhymes
I partly owe to him: and thus, the chimes
Of friendly voices had just given place
To as sweet a silence, when I 'gan retrace
The pleasant day, upon a couch at ease.
It was a poet's house who keeps the keys
Of Pleasure's temple. Round about were hung
The glorious features of the bards who sung
In other ages – cold and sacred busts
Smiled at each other. Happy he who trusts
To clear Futurity his darling fame!
Then there were fauns and satyrs taking aim
At swelling apples with a frisky leap
And reaching fingers, 'mid a luscious heap
Of vine leaves. Then there rose to view a fane
Of liny marble, and thereto a train
Of nymphs approaching fairly o'er the sward:
One, loveliest, holding her white hand toward
The dazzling sun-rise: two sisters sweet
Bending their graceful figures till they meet
Over the trippings of a little child:
And some are hearing, eagerly, the wild
Thrilling liquidity of dewy piping.
See, in another picture, nymphs are wiping
Cherishingly Diana's timorous limbs –
A fold of lawny mantle dabbling swims
At the bath's edge, and keeps a gentle motion
With the subsiding crystal, as when ocean

Heaves calmly its broad swelling smoothness o'er
Its rocky marge, and balances once more
The patient weeds, that now unshent by foam
380 Feel all about their undulating home.

Sappho's meek head was there half smiling down
At nothing; just as though the earnest frown
Of over-thinking had that moment gone
From off her brow, and left her all alone.

Great Alfred's too, with anxious, pitying eyes,
As if he always listened to the sighs
Of the goaded world; and Kosciusko's worn
By horrid sufferance – mightily forlorn.

Petrarch, outstepping from the shady green,
390 Starts at the sight of Laura; nor can wean
His eyes from her sweet face. Most happy they!
For over them was seen a free display
Of out-spread wings, and from between them shone
The face of Poesy: from off her throne
She overlooked things that I scarce could tell.
The very sense of where I was might well
Keep Sleep aloof: but more than that there came
Thought after thought to nourish up the flame
Within my breast; so that the morning light
400 Surprised me even from a sleepless night;
And up I rose refreshed, and glad, and gay,
Resolving to begin that very day
These lines; and howsoever they be done,
I leave them as a father does his son.

Written in Disgust of Vulgar Superstition

The church bells toll a melancholy round,
   Calling the people to some other prayers,
   Some other gloominess, more dreadful cares,
More hearkening to the sermon's horrid sound.

Surely the mind of man is closely bound
   In some black spell; seeing that each one tears
   Himself from fireside joys, and Lydian airs,
And converse high of those with glory crowned.
Still, still they toll, and I should feel a damp –
   A chill as from a tomb – did I not know
That they are dying like an outburnt lamp;
   That 'tis their sighing, wailing ere they go
   Into oblivion – that fresh flowers will grow,
And many glories of immortal stamp.

On the Grasshopper and Cricket

The poetry of earth is never dead:
   When all the birds are faint with the hot sun,
   And hide in cooling trees, a voice will run
From hedge to hedge about the new-mown mead –
That is the Grasshopper's. He takes the lead
   In summer luxury; he has never done
   With his delights, for when tired out with fun
He rests at ease beneath some pleasant weed.
The poetry of earth is ceasing never:
   On a lone winter evening, when the frost
     Has wrought a silence, from the stove there shrills
The Cricket's song, in warmth increasing ever,
   And seems to one in drowsiness half lost,
     The Grasshopper's among some grassy hills.

To Kosciusko

Good Kosciusko, thy great name alone
   Is a full harvest whence to reap high feeling;
   It comes upon us like the glorious pealing
Of the wide spheres – an everlasting tone.
And now it tells me, that in worlds unknown,
   The names of heroes burst from clouds concealing,

And change to harmonies, for ever stealing
Through cloudless blue, and round each silver throne.
It tells me too, that on a happy day,
    When some good spirit walks upon the earth,
        Thy name with Alfred's and the great of yore
    Gently commingling, gives tremendous birth
To a loud hymn, that sounds far, far away
    To where the great God lives for evermore.

To G[eorgiana] A[ugusta] W[ylie]

Nymph of the downward smile, and sidelong glance,
    In what diviner moments of the day
    Art thou most lovely? – When gone far astray
Into the labyrinths of sweet utterance?
Or when serenely wandering in a trance
    Of sober thought? – Or when starting away,
    With careless robe, to meet the morning ray,
Thou spar'st the flowers in thy mazy dance?
Haply 'tis when thy ruby lips part sweetly,
    And so remain, because thou listenest:
But thou to please wert nurtured so completely
    That I can never tell what mood is best.
I shall as soon pronounce which Grace more neatly
    Trips it before Apollo than the rest.

'Happy is England! I could be content'

Happy is England! I could be content
    To see no other verdure than its own;
    To feel no other breezes than are blown
Through its tall woods with high romances blent:
Yet do I sometimes feel a languishment
    For skies Italian, and an inward groan
    To sit upon an Alp as on a throne,
And half forget what world or worldling meant.

Happy is England, sweet her artless daughters;
 Enough their simple loveliness for me,
  Enough their whitest arms in silence clinging:
 Yet do I often warmly burn to see
  Beauties of deeper glance, and hear their singing,
And float with them about the summer waters.

'After dark vapours have oppressed our plains'

After dark vapours have oppressed our plains
 For a long dreary season, comes a day
 Born of the gentle South, and clears away
From the sick heavens all unseemly stains.
The anxious month, relieving from its pains,
 Takes as a long-lost right the feel of May,
 The eyelids with the passing coolness play,
Like rose leaves with the drip of summer rains.
And calmest thoughts come round us – as of leaves
 Budding – fruit ripening in stillness – autumn suns
Smiling at eve upon the quiet sheaves –
Sweet Sappho's cheek – a sleeping infant's breath –
 The gradual sand that through an hour-glass runs –
A woodland rivulet – a Poet's death.

To Leigh Hunt, Esq.

Glory and loveliness have passed away;
 For if we wander out in early morn,
 No wreathèd incense do we see upborne
Into the east, to meet the smiling day:
No crowd of nymphs soft voiced and young, and gay,
 In woven baskets bringing ears of corn,
 Roses, and pinks, and violets, to adorn
The shrine of Flora in her early May.
But there are left delights as high as these,
 And I shall ever bless my destiny,

That in a time, when under pleasant trees
   Pan is no longer sought, I feel a free,
A leafy luxury, seeing I could please
   With these poor offerings, a man like thee.

Written on a Blank Space at the End of Chaucer's Tale of The Floure and the Leafe

This pleasant tale is like a little copse:
   The honeyed lines do freshly interlace
   To keep the reader in so sweet a place,
So that he here and there full-hearted stops;
And oftentimes he feels the dewy drops
   Come cool and suddenly against his face,
   And by the wandering melody may trace
Which way the tender-leggèd linnet hops.
Oh! what a power has white simplicity!
10   What mighty power has this gentle story!
   I that do ever feel athirst for glory
Could at this moment be content to lie
   Meekly upon the grass, as those whose sobbings
   Were heard of none beside the mournful robins.

On Receiving a Laurel Crown from Leigh Hunt

Minutes are flying swiftly, and as yet
   Nothing unearthly has enticed my brain
   Into a delphic labyrinth – I would fain
Catch an immortal thought to pay the debt
I owe to the kind poet who has set
   Upon my ambitious head a glorious gain.
   Two bending laurel sprigs – 'tis nearly pain
To be conscious of such a coronet.
Still time is fleeting, and no dream arises
10   Gorgeous as I would have it; only I see
A trampling down of what the world most prizes,

Turbans and crowns, and blank regality –
And then I run into most wild surmises
   Of all the many glories that may be.

To the Ladies who Saw Me Crowned

What is there in the universal Earth
   More lovely than a wreath from the bay tree?
   Haply a halo round the moon – a glee
Circling from three sweet pair of lips in mirth;
And haply you will say the dewy birth
   Of morning roses – ripplings tenderly
   Spread by the halcyon's breath upon the sea –
But these comparisons are nothing worth.
Then is there nothing in the world so fair?
10   The silvery tears of April? Youth of May?
Or June that breathes out life for butterflies?
   No – none of these can from my favourite bear
Away the palm – yet shall it ever pay
   Due reverence to your most sovereign eyes.

Ode to Apollo

God of the golden bow,
   And of the golden lyre,
And of the golden hair,
   And of the golden fire,
     Charioteer
     Round the patient year,
   Where – where slept thine ire,
When like a blank idiot I put on thy wreath,
   Thy laurel, thy glory,
10   The light of thy story,
Or was I a worm – too low-creeping, for death?
   O Delphic Apollo!

       The Thunderer grasped and grasped,
         The Thunderer frowned and frowned;
      The eagle's feathery mane
         For wrath became stiffened – the sound
           Of breeding thunder
           Went drowsily under,
      Muttering to be unbound.
20 O why didst thou pity, and beg for a worm?
         Why touch thy soft lute
         Till the thunder was mute,
    Why was I not crush'd – such a pitiful germ?
       O Delphic Apollo!

       The Pleiades were up,
         Watching the silent air;
      The seeds and roots in Earth
         Were swelling for summer fare;
         The Ocean, its neighbour,
30   Was at his old labour,
        When, who – who did dare
To tie for a moment thy plant round his brow,
         And grin and look proudly,
         And blaspheme so loudly,
And live for that honour, to stoop to thee now?
       O Delphic Apollo!

On Seeing the Elgin Marbles

My spirit is too weak – mortality
  Weighs heavily on me like unwilling sleep,
  And each imagined pinnacle and steep
Of godlike hardship, tells me I must die
Like a sick Eagle looking at the sky.
  Yet 'tis a gentle luxury to weep
  That I have not the cloudy winds to keep
Fresh for the opening of the morning's eye.
Such dim-conceivèd glories of the brain

10 Bring round the heart an undescribable feud;
So do these wonders a most dizzy pain,
   That mingles Grecian grandeur with the rude
Wasting of old Time – with a billowy main –
   A sun – a shadow of a magnitude.

To B. R. Haydon, with a Sonnet Written on Seeing the Elgin Marbles

Haydon! forgive me that I cannot speak
   Definitively on these mighty things;
   Forgive me that I have not Eagle's wings –
That what I want I know not where to seek:
And think that I would not be over-meek
   In rolling out up-followed thunderings,
   Even to the steep of Heliconian springs,
Were I of ample strength for such a freak –
Think too, that all those numbers should be thine;
10   Whose else? In this who touch thy vesture's hem?
For when men stared at what was most divine
   With browless idiotism – o'erwise phlegm –
Thou hadst beheld the Hesperian shine
   Of their star in the East, and gone to worship them.

On The Story of Rimini

Who loves to peer up at the morning sun,
   With half-shut eyes and comfortable cheek,
   Let him, with this sweet tale, full often seek
For meadows where the little rivers run;
Who loves to linger with that brightest one
   Of Heaven – Hesperus – let him lowly speak
   These numbers to the night, and starlight meek,
Or moon, if that her hunting be begun.
He who knows these delights, and too is prone
10   To moralise upon a smile or tear,

Will find at once a region of his own,
   A bower for his spirit, and will steer
To alleys, where the fir-tree drops its cone,
   Where robins hop, and fallen leaves are sear.

On a Leander Gem which Miss Reynolds, my Kind Friend, Gave Me

Come hither all sweet maidens soberly,
   Down-looking – ay, and with a chastened light
   Hid in the fringes of your eyelids white,
And meekly let your fair hands joinèd be,
Are ye so gentle that ye could not see,
   Untouched, a victim of your beauty bright –
   Sinking away to his young spirit's night,
Sinking bewildered 'mid the dreary sea:
'Tis young Leander toiling to his death.
10   Nigh swooning, he doth purse his weary lips
      For Hero's cheek, and smiles against her smile.
   O horrid dream! see how his body dips
      Dead-heavy; arms and shoulders gleam awhile:
He's gone: up bubbles all his amorous breath!

On the Sea

It keeps eternal whisperings around
   Desolate shores, and with its mighty swell
   Gluts twice ten thousand caverns, till the spell
Of Hecate leaves them their old shadowy sound.
Often 'tis in such gentle temper found,
   That scarcely will the very smallest shell
   Be moved for days from where it sometime fell,
When last the winds of Heaven were unbound.
Oh ye! who have your eye-balls vexed and tired,
10   Feast them upon the wideness of the Sea –
      Oh ye! whose ears are dinned with uproar rude,

Or fed too much with cloying melody –
    Sit ye near some old cavern's mouth and brood,
Until ye start, as if the sea-nymphs quired!

Lines

Unfelt, unheard, unseen,
  I've left my little queen,
Her languid arms in silver slumber lying:
  Ah! through their nestling touch,
  Who – who could tell how much
There is for madness – cruel, or complying?

Those faery lids how sleek!
Those lips how moist! – they speak,
In ripest quiet, shadows of sweet sounds:
  Into my fancy's ear
  Melting a burden dear,
How 'Love doth know no fullness nor no bounds.'

True! – tender monitors!
I bend unto your laws:
This sweetest day for dalliance was born!
  So, without more ado,
  I'll feel my heaven anew,
For all the blushing of the hasty morn.

Stanzas

I

You say you love; but with a voice
  Chaster than a nun's, who singeth
The soft Vespers to herself
  While the chime-bell ringeth –
    O love me truly!

II
You say you love; but with a smile
　Cold as sunrise in September,
As you were Saint Cupid's nun,
　And kept his weeks of Ember.
　　　O love me truly!

III
You say you love – but then your lips
　Coral tinted teach no blisses
More than coral in the sea –
　They never pout for kisses –
　　　O love me truly!

IV
You say you love; but then your hand
　No soft squeeze for squeeze returneth,
It is like a statue's, dead –
　While mine for passion burneth –
　　　O love me truly!

V
O breathe a word or two of fire!
　Smile, as if those words should burn me,
Squeeze as lovers should – O kiss
　And in thy heart inurn me!
　　　O love me truly!

'Hither, hither, love –'

Hither, hither, love –
　'Tis a shady mead –
Hither, hither, love,
　Let us feed and feed!

Hither, hither, sweet –
　'Tis a cowslip bed –
Hither, hither, sweet!
　'Tis with dew bespread!

Hither, hither, dear –
  By the breath of life –
Hither, hither, dear!
  Be the summer's wife!

Though one moment's pleasure
  In one moment flies,
Though the passion's treasure
  In one moment dies;

Yet it has not passed –
  Think how near, how near! –
And while it doth last,
  Think how dear, how dear!

Hither, hither, hither,
  Love this boon has sent –
If I die and wither
  I shall die content.

Lines Rhymed in a Letter Received (by J. H. Reynolds) From Oxford

The Gothic looks solemn –
  The plain Doric column
Supports an old Bishop and crosier;
  The mouldering arch,
  Shaded o'er by a larch
Stands next door to Wilson the Hosier.

Vicè – that is, by turns –
  O'er pale faces mourns
The black-tassled trencher and common hat;
  The chantry boy sings,
  The steeple bell rings,
And as for the Chancellor – *dominat*.

There are plenty of trees,
And plenty of ease,

And plenty of fat deer for parsons;
    And when it is venison,
    Short is the benison –
Then each on a leg or thigh fastens.

'Think not of it, sweet one, so – '

Think not of it, sweet one, so –
    Give it not a tear;
Sigh thou mayst, and bid it go
    Any, any where.

Do not look so sad, sweet one –
    Sad and fadingly;
Shed one drop, then it is gone,
    O 'twas born to die.

Still so pale? then, dearest, weep –
    Weep, I'll count the tears,
And each one shall be a bliss
    For thee in after years.

Brighter has it left thine eyes
    Than a sunny rill;
And thy whispering melodies
    Are tenderer still.

Yet – as all things mourn awhile
    At fleeting blisses,
E'en let us too! but be our dirge
    A dirge of kisses.

Endymion: A Poetic Romance

The stretched metre of an antique song

Inscribed to the memory of
Thomas Chatterton

BOOK I

   A thing of beauty is a joy for ever:
   Its loveliness increases; it will never
   Pass into nothingness; but still will keep
   A bower quiet for us, and a sleep
   Full of sweet dreams, and health, and quiet breathing.
   Therefore, on every morrow, are we wreathing
   A flowery band to bind us to the earth,
   Spite of despondence, of the inhuman dearth
   Of noble natures, of the gloomy days,
10 Of all the unhealthy and o'er-darkened ways
   Made for our searching: yes, in spite of all,
   Some shape of beauty moves away the pall
   From our dark spirits. Such the sun, the moon,
   Trees old, and young, sprouting a shady boon
   For simple sheep; and such are daffodils
   With the green world they live in; and clear rills
   That for themselves a cooling covert make
   'Gainst the hot season; the mid forest brake,
   Rich with a sprinkling of fair musk-rose blooms:
20 And such too is the grandeur of the dooms
   We have imagined for the mighty dead;
   All lovely tales that we have heard or read –
   An endless fountain of immortal drink,
   Pouring unto us from the heaven's brink.

   Nor do we merely feel these essences
   For one short hour; no, even as the trees
   That whisper round a temple become soon
   Dear as the temple's self, so does the moon,
   The passion poesy, glories infinite,
30 Haunt us till they become a cheering light
   Unto our souls, and bound to us so fast,
   That, whether there be shine, or gloom o'ercast,
   They alway must be with us, or we die.

   Therefore, 'tis with full happiness that I
   Will trace the story of Endymion.

The very music of the name has gone
Into my being, and each pleasant scene
Is growing fresh before me as the green
Of our own valleys: so I will begin
40 Now while I cannot hear the city's din;
Now while the early budders are just new,
And run in mazes of the youngest hue
About old forests; while the willow trails
Its delicate amber; and the dairy pails
Bring home increase of milk. And, as the year
Grows lush in juicy stalks, I'll smoothly steer
My little boat, for many quiet hours,
With streams that deepen freshly into bowers.
Many and many a verse I hope to write,
50 Before the daisies, vermeil-rimmed and white,
Hide in deep herbage; and ere yet the bees
Hum about globes of clover and sweet peas,
I must be near the middle of my story.
O may no wintry season, bare and hoary,
See it half finished; but let Autumn bold,
With universal tinge of sober gold,
Be all about me when I make an end.
And now at once, adventuresome, I send
My herald thought into a wilderness –
60 There let its trumpet blow, and quickly dress
My uncertain path with green, that I may speed
Easily onward, thorough flowers and weed.

Upon the sides of Latmos was outspread
A mighty forest; for the moist earth fed
So plenteously all weed-hidden roots
Into o'er-hanging boughs, and precious fruits.
And it had gloomy shades, sequestered deep,
Where no man went; and if from shepherd's keep
A lamb strayed far a-down those inmost glens,
70 Never again saw he the happy pens
Whither his brethren, bleating with content,
Over the hills at every nightfall went.

Among the shepherds, 'twas believèd ever,
That not one fleecy lamb which thus did sever
From the white flock, but passed unworrièd
By angry wolf, or pard with prying head,
Until it came to some unfooted plains
Where fed the herds of Pan – aye great his gains
Who thus one lamb did lose. Paths there were many,
Winding through palmy fern, and rushes fenny,
And ivy banks; all leading pleasantly
To a wide lawn, whence one could only see
Stems thronging all around between the swell
Of turf and slanting branches: who could tell
The freshness of the space of heaven above,
Edged round with dark tree tops? through which a dove
Would often beat its wings, and often too
A little cloud would move across the blue.

Full in the middle of this pleasantness
There stood a marble altar, with a tress
Of flowers budded newly; and the dew
Had taken fairy fantasies to strew
Daisies upon the sacred sward last eve,
And so the dawnèd light in pomp receive.
For 'twas the morn: Apollo's upward fire
Made every eastern cloud a silvery pyre
Of brightness so unsullied, that therein
A melancholy spirit well might win
Oblivion, and melt out his essence fine
Into the winds: rain-scented eglantine
Gave temperate sweets to that well-wooing sun,
The lark was lost in him; cold springs had run
To warm their chilliest bubbles in the grass;
Man's voice was on the mountains; and the mass
Of nature's lives and wonders pulsed tenfold,
To feel this sun-rise and its glories old.

Now while the silent workings of the dawn
Were busiest, into that self-same lawn
All suddenly, with joyful cries, there sped

110 A troop of little children garlanded;
Who gathering round the altar, seemed to pry
Earnestly round, as wishing to espy
Some folk of holiday: nor had they waited
For many moments, ere their ears were sated
With a faint breath of music, which even then
Filled out its voice, and died away again.
Within a little space again it gave
Its airy swellings, with a gentle wave,
To light-hung leaves, in smoothest echoes breaking
120 Through copse-clad valleys – ere their death, o'ertaking
The surgy murmurs of the lonely sea.

    And now, as deep into the wood as we
Might mark a lynx's eye, there glimmered light
Fair faces and a rush of garments white,
Plainer and plainer showing, till at last
Into the widest alley they all passed,
Making directly for the woodland altar.
O kindly muse! let not my weak tongue falter
In telling of this goodly company,
130 Of their old piety, and of their glee:
But let a portion of ethereal dew
Fall on my head, and presently unmew
My soul – that I may dare, in wayfaring,
To stammer where old Chaucer used to sing.

    Leading the way, young damsels danced along,
Bearing the burden of a shepherd song;
Each having a white wicker over-brimmed
With April's tender younglings; next, well trimmed,
A crowd of shepherds with as sunburnt looks
140 As may be read of in Arcadian books,
Such as sat listening round Apollo's pipe,
When the great deity, for earth too ripe,
Let his divinity o'erflowing die
In music, through the vales of Thessaly;
Some idly trailed their sheep-hooks on the ground,
And some kept up a shrilly mellow sound

111 ENDYMION: BOOK I

>With ebon-tippèd flutes; close after these,
>Now coming from beneath the forest trees,
>A venerable priest full soberly,
>Begirt with ministering looks: alway his eye
>Steadfast upon the matted turf he kept,
>And after him his sacred vestments swept.
>From his right hand there swung a vase, milk-white,
>Of mingled wine, out-sparkling generous light;
>And in his left he held a basket full
>Of all sweet herbs that searching eye could cull:
>Wild thyme, and valley-lilies whiter still
>Than Leda's love, and cresses from the rill.
>His agèd head, crownèd with beechen wreath,
>Seemed like a poll of ivy in the teeth
>Of winter hoar. Then came another crowd
>Of shepherds, lifting in due time aloud
>Their share of the ditty. After them appeared,
>Up-followed by a multitude that reared
>Their voices to the clouds, a fair-wrought car,
>Easily rolling so as scarce to mar
>The freedom of three steeds of dapple brown.
>Who stood therein did seem of great renown
>Among the throng. His youth was fully blown,
>Showing like Ganymede to manhood grown;
>And, for those simple times, his garments were
>A chieftain king's: beneath his breast, half bare,
>Was hung a silver bugle, and between
>His nervy knees there lay a boar-spear keen.
>A smile was on his countenance; he seemed,
>To common lookers-on, like one who dreamed
>Of idleness in groves Elysian:
>But there were some who feelingly could scan
>A lurking trouble in his nether lip,
>And see that oftentimes the reins would slip
>Through his forgotten hands: then would they sigh,
>And think of yellow leaves, of owlets' cry,
>Of logs piled solemnly. Ah, well-a-day.
>Why should our young Endymion pine away?

Soon the assembly, in a circle ranged,
Stood silent round the shrine: each look was changed
To sudden veneration: women meek
Beckoned their sons to silence; while each cheek
Of virgin bloom paled gently for slight fear.
Endymion too, without a forest peer,
Stood, wan, and pale, and with an awèd face,
Among his brothers of the mountain chase.
In midst of all, the venerable priest
Eyed them with joy from greatest to the least,
And, after lifting up his agèd hands,
Thus spake he: 'Men of Latmos! shepherd bands!
Whose care it is to guard a thousand flocks:
Whether descended from beneath the rocks
That overtop your mountains; whether come
From valleys where the pipe is never dumb;
Or from your swelling downs, where sweet air stirs
Blue hare-bells lightly, and where prickly furze
Buds lavish gold; or ye, whose precious charge
Nibble their fill at ocean's very marge,
Whose mellow reeds are touched with sounds forlorn
By the dim echoes of old Triton's horn;
Mothers and wives! who day by day prepare
The scrip, with needments, for the mountain air;
And all ye gentle girls who foster up
Udderless lambs, and in a little cup
Will put choice honey for a favoured youth –
Yea, every one attend! for in good truth
Our vows are wanting to our great god Pan.
Are not our lowing heifers sleeker than
Night-swollen mushrooms? Are not our wide plains
Speckled with countless fleeces? Have not rains
Greened over April's lap? No howling sad
Sickens our fearful ewes; and we have had
Great bounty from Endymion our lord.
The earth is glad: the merry lark has poured
His early song against yon breezy sky,
That spreads so clear o'er our solemnity.'

ENDYMION: BOOK I

    Thus ending, on the shrine he heaped a spire
Of teeming sweets, enkindling sacred fire;
Anon he stained the thick and spongy sod
With wine, in honour of the shepherd-god.
Now while the earth was drinking it, and while
Bay leaves were crackling in the fragrant pile,
And gummy frankincense was sparkling bright
'Neath smothering parsley, and a hazy light
Spread greyly eastward, thus a chorus sang:

    'O thou, whose mighty palace roof doth hang
From jagged trunks, and overshadoweth
Eternal whispers, glooms, the birth, life, death
Of unseen flowers in heavy peacefulness;
Who lov'st to see the hamadryads dress
Their ruffled locks where meeting hazels darken;
And through whole solemn hours dost sit, and hearken
The dreary melody of bedded reeds
In desolate places, where dank moisture breeds
The pipy hemlock to strange overgrowth;
Bethinking thee, how melancholy loth
Thou wast to lose fair Syrinx – do thou now –
By thy love's milky brow! –
By all the trembling mazes that she ran –
Hear us, great Pan!

    'O thou, for whose soul-soothing quiet, turtles
Passion their voices cooingly 'mong myrtles,
What time thou wanderest at eventide
Through sunny meadows, that outskirt the side
Of thine enmossèd realms: O thou, to whom
Broad-leavèd fig trees even now foredoom
Their ripened fruitage; yellow-girted bees
Their golden honeycombs; our village leas
Their fairest-blossomed beans and poppied corn;
The chuckling linnet its five young unborn
To sing for thee; low creeping strawberries
Their summer coolness; pent up butterflies
Their freckled wings; yea, the fresh budding year

260 All its completions – be quickly near,
By every wind that nods the mountain pine,
O forester divine!

'Thou, to whom every faun and satyr flies
For willing service; whether to surprise
The squatted hare while in half-sleeping fit;
Or upward ragged precipices flit
To save poor lambkins from the eagle's maw;
Or by mysterious enticement draw
Bewildered shepherds to their path again;
270 Or to tread breathless round the frothy main,
And gather up all fancifullest shells
For thee to tumble into Naiads' cells,
And, being hidden, laugh at their out-peeping;
Or to delight thee with fantastic leaping,
The while they pelt each other on the crown
With silvery oak apples, and fir cones brown –
By all the echoes that about thee ring,
Hear us, O satyr king!

'O Hearkener to the loud clapping shears
280 While ever and anon to his shorn peers
A ram goes bleating; Winder of the horn,
When snouted wild-boars routing tender corn
Anger our huntsmen; Breather round our farms,
To keep off mildews, and all weather harms;
Strange ministrant of undescribèd sounds,
That come a-swooning over hollow grounds,
And wither drearily on barren moors;
Dread opener of the mysterious doors
Leading to universal knowledge – see,
290 Great son of Dryope,
The many that are come to pay their vows
With leaves about their brows!

'Be still the unimaginable lodge
For solitary thinkings; such as dodge
Conception to the very bourne of heaven,

ENDYMION: BOOK I

Then leave the naked brain; be still the leaven,
That spreading in this dull and clodded earth
Gives it a touch ethereal – a new birth;
Be still a symbol of immensity;
A firmament reflected in a sea;
An element filling the space between;
An unknown – but no more! we humbly screen
With uplift hands our foreheads, lowly bending,
And giving out a shout most heaven rending,
Conjure thee to receive our humble paean,
Upon thy Mount Lycean!'

Even while they brought the burden to a close,
A shout from the whole multitude arose,
That lingered in the air like dying rolls
Of abrupt thunder, when Ionian shoals
Of dolphins bob their noses through the brine.
Meantime, on shady levels, mossy fine,
Young companies nimbly began dancing
To the swift treble pipe, and humming string.
Ay, those fair living forms swam heavenly
To tunes forgotten – out of memory;
Fair creatures! whose young children's children bred
Thermopylae its heroes – not yet dead,
But in old marbles ever beautiful.
High genitors, unconscious did they cull
Time's sweet first-fruits – they danced to weariness,
And then in quiet circles did they press
The hillock turf, and caught the latter end
Of some strange history, potent to send
A young mind from its bodily tenement.
Or they might watch the quoit-pitchers, intent
On either side; pitying the sad death
Of Hyacinthus, when the cruel breath
Of Zephyr slew him – Zephyr penitent,
Who now, ere Phoebus mounts the firmament,
Fondles the flower amid the sobbing rain.
The archers too, upon a wider plain,

Beside the feathery whizzing of the shaft
And the dull twanging bowstring, and the raft
Branch down sweeping from a tall ash top,
Called up a thousand thoughts to envelop
Those who would watch. Perhaps, the trembling knee
And frantic gape of lonely Niobe –
Poor, lonely Niobe! – when her lovely young
340 Were dead and gone, and her caressing tongue
Lay a lost thing upon her paly lip,
And very, very deadliness did nip
Her motherly cheeks. Aroused from this sad mood
By one, who at a distance loud hallooed,
Uplifting his strong bow into the air,
Many might after brighter visions stare:
After the Argonauts, in blind amaze
Tossing about on Neptune's restless ways,
Until, from the horizon's vaulted side,
350 There shot a golden splendour far and wide,
Spangling those million poutings of the brine
With quivering ore – 'twas even an awful shine
From the exaltation of Apollo's bow;
A heavenly beacon in their dreary woe.
Who thus were ripe for high contemplating,
Might turn their steps towards the sober ring
Where sat Endymion and the agèd priest
'Mong shepherds gone in eld, whose looks increased
The silvery setting of their mortal star.
360 There they discoursed upon the fragile bar
That keeps us from our homes ethereal,
And what our duties there: to nightly call
Vesper, the beauty-crest of summer weather;
To summon all the downiest clouds together
For the sun's purple couch; to emulate
In ministering the potent rule of fate
With speed of fire-tailèd exhalations:
To tint her pallid cheek with bloom, who cons
Sweet poesy by moonlight: besides these,
370 A world of other unguessed offices.

Anon they wandered, by divine converse,
Into Elysium, vying to rehearse
Each one his own anticipated bliss.
One felt heart-certain that he could not miss
His quick-gone love, among fair blossomed boughs,
Where every zephyr-sigh pouts, and endows
Her lips with music for the welcoming.
Another wished, mid that eternal spring,
To meet his rosy child, with feathery sails,
380 Sweeping, eye-earnestly, through almond vales –
Who, suddenly, should stoop through the smooth wind,
And with the balmiest leaves his temples bind;
And, ever after, through those regions be
His messenger, his little Mercury.
Some were athirst in soul to see again
Their fellow huntsmen o'er the wide champaign
In times long past; to sit with them, and talk
Of all the chances in their earthly walk;
Comparing, joyfully, their plenteous stores
390 Of happiness, to when upon the moors,
Benighted, close they huddled from the cold,
And shared their famished scrips. Thus all out-told
Their fond imaginations – saving him
Whose eyelids curtained up their jewels dim,
Endymion: yet hourly had he striven
To hide the cankering venom, that had riven
His fainting recollections. Now indeed
His senses had swooned off; he did not heed
The sudden silence, or the whispers low,
400 Or the old eyes dissolving at his woe,
Or anxious calls, or close of trembling palms,
Or maiden's sigh, that grief itself embalms:
But in the self-same fixèd trance he kept,
Like one who on the earth had never stepped.
Ay, even as dead still as a marble man,
Frozen in that old tale Arabian.

ENDYMION: BOOK I

    Who whispers him so pantingly and close?
Peona, his sweet sister – of all those,
His friends, the dearest. Hushing signs she made,
410 And breathed a sister's sorrow to persuade
A yielding up, a cradling on her care.
Her eloquence did breathe away the curse:
She led him, like some midnight spirit-nurse
Of happy changes in emphatic dreams,
Along a path between two little streams –
Guarding his forehead, with her round elbow,
From low-grown branches, and his footsteps slow
From stumbling over stumps and hillocks small –
Until they came to where these streamlets fall,
420 With mingled bubblings and a gentle rush,
Into a river, clear, brimful, and flush
With crystal mocking of the trees and sky.
A little shallop, floating there hard by,
Pointed its beak over the fringèd bank;
And soon it lightly dipped, and rose, and sank,
And dipped again, with the young couple's weight –
Peona guiding, through the water straight,
Towards a bowery island opposite,
Which gaining presently, she steerèd light
430 Into a shady, fresh, and ripply cove,
Where nested was an arbour, overwove
By many a summer's silent fingering;
To whose cool bosom she was used to bring
Her playmates, with their needle broidery,
And minstrel memories of times gone by.

    So she was gently glad to see him laid
Under her favourite bower's quiet shade,
On her own couch, new made of flower leaves,
Dried carefully on the cooler side of sheaves
440 When last the sun his autumn tresses shook,
And the tanned harvesters rich armfuls took.
Soon was he quieted to slumbrous rest:
But, ere it crept upon him, he had pressed

ENDYMION: BOOK I

Peona's busy hand against his lips,
And still, a-sleeping, held her finger-tips
In tender pressure. And as a willow keeps
A patient watch over the stream that creeps
Windingly by it, so the quiet maid
Held her in peace: so that a whispering blade
Of grass, a wailful gnat, a bee bustling
Down in the blue-bells, or a wren light rustling
Among sere leaves and twigs, might all be heard.

O magic sleep! O comfortable bird,
That broodest o'er the troubled sea of the mind
Till it is hushed and smooth! O unconfined
Restraint! imprisoned liberty! great key
To golden palaces, strange minstrelsy,
Fountains grotesque, new trees, bespangled caves,
Echoing grottoes, full of tumbling waves
And moonlight; ay, to all the mazy world
Of silvery enchantment! Who, upfurled
Beneath thy drowsy wing a triple hour,
But renovates and lives? – Thus, in the bower,
Endymion was calmed to life again.
Opening his eyelids with a healthier brain,
He said: 'I feel this thine endearing love
All through my bosom: thou art as a dove
Trembling its closèd eyes and sleekèd wings
About me; and the pearliest dew not brings
Such morning incense from the fields of May,
As do those brighter drops that twinkling stray
From those kind eyes – the very home and haunt
Of sisterly affection. Can I want
Aught else, aught nearer heaven, than such tears?
Yet dry them up, in bidding hence all fears
That, any longer, I will pass my days
Alone and sad. No, I will once more raise
My voice upon the mountain-heights; once more
Make my horn parley from their foreheads hoar;
Again my trooping hounds their tongues shall loll

Around the breathèd boar; again I'll poll
The fair-grown yew tree for a chosen bow;
And, when the pleasant sun is getting low,
Again I'll linger in a sloping mead
To hear the speckled thrushes, and see feed
Our idle sheep. So be thou cheerèd, sweet,
And, if thy lute is here, softly entreat
My soul to keep in its resolvèd course.'

Hereat Peona, in their silver source,
Shut her pure sorrow-drops with glad exclaim,
And took a lute, from which there pulsing came
A lively prelude, fashioning the way
In which her voice should wander. 'Twas a lay
More subtle cadenced, more forest wild
Than Dryope's lone lulling of her child;
And nothing since has floated in the air
So mournful strange. Surely some influence rare
Went, spiritual, through the damsel's hand;
For still, with Delphic emphasis, she spanned
The quick invisible strings, even though she saw
Endymion's spirit melt away and thaw
Before the deep intoxication.
But soon she came, with sudden burst, upon
Her self-possession – swung the lute aside,
And earnestly said: 'Brother, 'tis vain to hide
That thou dost know of things mysterious,
Immortal, starry; such alone could thus
Weigh down thy nature. Hast thou sinned in aught
Offensive to the heavenly powers? Caught
A Paphian dove upon a message sent?
Thy deathful bow against some deer-head bent
Sacred to Dian? Haply, thou hast seen
Her naked limbs among the alders green –
And that, alas! is death. No, I can trace
Something more high-perplexing in thy face!'

Endymion looked at her, and pressed her hand,
And said, 'Art thou so pale, who wast so bland

And merry in our meadows? How is this?
Tell me thine ailment – tell me all amiss!
Ah! thou hast been unhappy at the change
Wrought suddenly in me. What indeed more strange?
Or more complete to overwhelm surmise?
Ambition is no sluggard: 'tis no prize,
That toiling years would put within my grasp,
That I have sighed for; with so deadly gasp
No man e'er panted for a mortal love.
So all have set my heavier grief above
These things which happen. Rightly have they done:
I, who still saw the horizontal sun
Heave his broad shoulder o'er the edge of the world,
Out-facing Lucifer, and then had hurled
My spear aloft, as signal for the chase –
I, who, for very sport of heart, would race
With my own steed from Araby; pluck down
A vulture from his towery perching; frown
A lion into growling, loth retire –
To lose, at once, all my toil-breeding fire,
And sink thus low! but I will ease my breast
Of secret grief, here in this bowery nest.

'This river does not see the naked sky,
Till it begins to progress silverly
Around the western border of the wood,
Whence, from a certain spot, its winding flood
Seems at the distance like a crescent moon:
And in that nook, the very pride of June,
Had I been used to pass my weary eves;
The rather for the sun unwilling leaves
So dear a picture of his sovereign power,
And I could witness his most kingly hour,
When he doth tighten up the golden reins,
And paces leisurely down amber plains
His snorting four. Now when his chariot last
Its beams against the zodiac-lion cast,
There blossomed suddenly a magic bed

Of sacred ditamy, and poppies red:
At which I wondered greatly, knowing well
That but one night had wrought this flowery spell;
And, sitting down close by, began to muse
What it might mean. Perhaps, thought I, Morpheus,
560 In passing here, his owlet pinions shook;
Or, it may be, ere matron Night uptook
Her ebon urn, young Mercury, by stealth,
Had dipped his rod in it: such garland wealth
Came not by common growth. Thus on I thought,
Until my head was dizzy and distraught.
Moreover, through the dancing poppies stole
A breeze, most softly lulling to my soul,
And shaping visions all about my sight
Of colours, wings, and bursts of spangly light;
570 The which became more strange, and strange, and dim,
And then were gulfed in a tumultuous swim –
And then I fell asleep. Ah, can I tell
The enchantment that afterwards befell?
Yet it was but a dream: yet such a dream
That never tongue, although it overteem
With mellow utterance, like a cavern spring,
Could figure out and to conception bring
All I beheld and felt. Methought I lay
Watching the zenith, where the milky way
580 Among the stars in virgin splendour pours;
And travelling my eye, until the doors
Of heaven appeared to open for my flight,
I became loth and fearful to alight
From such high soaring by a downward glance:
So kept me steadfast in that airy trance,
Spreading imaginary pinions wide.
When, presently, the stars began to glide,
And faint away, before my eager view:
At which I sighed that I could not pursue,
590 And dropped my vision to the horizon's verge –
And lo! from opening clouds, I saw emerge
The loveliest moon, that ever silvered o'er

A shell for Neptune's goblet: she did soar
So passionately bright, my dazzled soul
Commingling with her argent spheres did roll
Through clear and cloudy, even when she went
At last into a dark and vapoury tent –
Whereat, methought, the lidless-eyèd train
Of planets all were in the blue again.
600 To commune with those orbs, once more I raised
My sight right upward: but it was quite dazed
By a bright something, sailing down apace,
Making me quickly veil my eyes and face:
Again I looked, and, O ye deities,
Who from Olympus watch our destinies!
Whence that completed form of all completeness?
Whence came that high perfection of all sweetness?
Speak, stubborn earth, and tell me where, O where
Hast thou a symbol of her golden hair?
610 Not oat-sheaves drooping in the western sun;
Not – thy soft hand, fair sister! let me shun
Such follying before thee – yet she had,
Indeed, locks bright enough to make me mad;
And they were simply gordianed up and braided,
Leaving, in naked comeliness, unshaded,
Her pearl-round ears, white neck, and orbèd brow;
The which were blended in, I know not how,
With such a paradise of lips and eyes,
Blush-tinted cheeks, half smiles, and faintest sighs,
620 That, when I think thereon, my spirit clings
And plays about its fancy, till the stings
Of human neighbourhood envenom all.
Unto what awful power shall I call?
To what high fane? – Ah! see her hovering feet,
More bluely veined, more soft, more whitely sweet
Than those of sea-born Venus, when she rose
From out her cradle shell. The wind out-blows
Her scarf into a fluttering pavilion;
'Tis blue, and over-spangled with a million
630 Of little eyes, as though thou wert to shed,

Over the darkest, lushest blue-bell bed,
Handfuls of daisies.' – 'Endymion, how strange!
Dream within dream!' – 'She took an airy range,
And then, towards me, like a very maid,
Came blushing, waning, willing, and afraid,
And pressed me by the hand: Ah! 'twas too much;
Methought I fainted at the charmèd touch,
Yet held my recollection, even as one
Who dives three fathoms where the waters run
640 Gurgling in beds of coral: for anon,
I felt up-mounted in that region
Where falling stars dart their artillery forth,
And eagles struggle with the buffeting north
That balances the heavy meteor-stone –
Felt too, I was not fearful, nor alone,
But lapped and lulled along the dangerous sky.
Soon, as it seemed, we left our journeying high,
And straightway into frightful eddies swooped,
Such as aye muster where grey time has scooped
650 Huge dens and caverns in a mountain's side:
There hollow sounds aroused me, and I sighed
To faint once more by looking on my bliss –
I was distracted; madly did I kiss
The wooing arms which held me, and did give
My eyes at once to death – but 'twas to live,
To take in draughts of life from the gold fount
Of kind and passionate looks; to count, and count
The moments, by some greedy help that seemed
A second self, that each might be redeemed
660 And plundered of its load of blessedness.
Ah, desperate mortal! I e'en dared to press
Her very cheek against my crownèd lip,
And, at that moment, felt my body dip
Into a warmer air – a moment more,
Our feet were soft in flowers. There was store
Of newest joys upon that alp. Sometimes
A scent of violets, and blossoming limes,
Loitered around us; then of honey cells,

ENDYMION: BOOK I

Made delicate from all white-flower bells;
And once, above the edges of our nest,
An arch face peeped – an Oread as I guessed.

'Why did I dream that sleep o'er-powered me
In midst of all this heaven? Why not see,
Far off, the shadows of his pinions dark,
And stare them from me? But no, like a spark
That needs must die, although its little beam
Reflects upon a diamond, my sweet dream
Fell into nothing – into stupid sleep.
And so it was, until a gentle creep,
A careful moving caught my waking ears,
And up I started. Ah! my sighs, my tears,
My clenchèd hands – for lo! the poppies hung
Dew-dabbled on their stalks, the ouzel sung
A heavy ditty, and the sullen day
Had chidden herald Hesperus away,
With leaden looks: the solitary breeze
Blustered, and slept, and its wild self did tease
With wayward melancholy; and I thought,
Mark me, Peona! that sometimes it brought
Faint fare-thee-wells, and sigh-shrillèd adieus! –
Away I wandered – all the pleasant hues
Of heaven and earth had faded: deepest shades
Were deepest dungeons; heaths and sunny glades
Were full of pestilent light; our taintless rills
Seemed sooty, and o'er-spread with upturned gills
Of dying fish; the vermeil rose had blown
In frightful scarlet, and its thorns out-grown
Like spiked aloe. If an innocent bird
Before my heedless footsteps stirred and stirred
In little journeys, I beheld in it
A disguisèd demon, missionèd to knit
My soul with under-darkness, to entice
My stumblings down some monstrous precipice:
Therefore I eager followed, and did curse
The disappointment. Time, that agèd nurse,

126 ENDYMION: BOOK I

  Rocked me to patience. Now, thank gentle heaven!
These things, with all their comfortings, are given
To my down-sunken hours, and with thee,
Sweet sister, help to stem the ebbing sea
710 Of weary life.'
     Thus ended he, and both
Sat silent: for the maid was very loth
To answer; feeling well that breathèd words
Would all be lost, unheard, and vain as swords
Against the enchasèd crocodile, or leaps
Of grasshoppers against the sun. She weeps,
And wonders; struggles to devise some blame;
To put on such a look as would say, *Shame
On this poor weakness!* but, for all her strife,
She could as soon have crushed away the life
720 From a sick dove. At length, to break the pause,
She said with trembling chance: 'Is this the cause?
This all? Yet it is strange, and sad, alas!
That one who through this middle earth should pass
Most like a sojourning demi-god, and leave
His name upon the harp-string, should achieve
No higher bard than simple maidenhood,
Singing alone – and fearfully – how the blood
Left his young cheek; and how he used to stray
He knew not where; and how he would say, *nay*,
730 If any said 'twas love – and yet 'twas love;
What could it be but love? How a ring-dove
Let fall a sprig of yew tree in his path;
And how he died; and then, that love doth scathe
The gentle heart, as northern blasts do roses;
And then the ballad of his sad life closes
With sighs, and an 'alas'! – Endymion!
Be rather in the trumpet's mouth – anon
Among the winds at large, that all may hearken!
Although, before the crystal heavens darken,
740 I watch and dote upon the silver lakes
Pictured in western cloudiness, that takes
The semblance of gold rocks and bright gold sands,

ENDYMION: BOOK I

  Islands, and creeks, and amber-fretted strands
With horses prancing o'er them, palaces
And towers of amethyst – would I so tease
My pleasant days, because I could not mount
Into those regions? The Morphean fount
Of that fine element that visions, dreams,
And fitful whims of sleep are made of, streams
Into its airy channels with so subtle,
So thin a breathing, not the spider's shuttle,
Circled a million times within the space
Of a swallow's nest-door, could delay a trace,
A tinting of its quality: how light
Must dreams themselves be, seeing they're more slight
Than the mere nothing that engenders them!
Then wherefore sully the entrusted gem
Of high and noble life with thoughts so sick?
Why pierce high-fronted honour to the quick
For nothing but a dream?' Hereat the youth
Looked up: a conflicting of shame and ruth
Was in his plaited brow: yet, his eyelids
Widened a little, as when Zephyr bids
A little breeze to creep between the fans
Of careless butterflies. Amid his pains
He seemed to taste a drop of manna-dew,
Full palatable; and a colour grew
Upon his cheek, while thus he lifeful spake.

  'Peona! ever have I longed to slake
My thirst for the world's praises: nothing base,
No merely slumbrous phantasm, could unlace
The stubborn canvas for my voyage prepared –
Though now 'tis tattered, leaving my bark bared
And sullenly drifting: yet my higher hope
Is of too wide, too rainbow-large a scope,
To fret at myriads of earthly wrecks.
Wherein lies happiness? In that which becks
Our ready minds to fellowship divine,
A fellowship with essence; till we shine,

ENDYMION: BOOK I

780 Full alchemized, and free of space. Behold
The clear religion of heaven! Fold
A rose leaf round thy finger's taperness,
And soothe thy lips; hist, when the airy stress
Of music's kiss impregnates the free winds,
And with a sympathetic touch unbinds
Aeolian magic from their lucid wombs;
Then old songs waken from enclouded tombs;
Old ditties sigh above their father's grave;
Ghosts of melodious prophesyings rave
790 Round every spot where trod Apollo's foot;
Bronze clarions awake, and faintly bruit,
Where long ago a giant battle was;
And, from the turf, a lullaby doth pass
In every place where infant Orpheus slept.
Feel we these things? – that moment have we stepped
Into a sort of oneness, and our state
Is like a floating spirit's. But there are
Richer entanglements, enthralments far
More self-destroying, leading, by degrees,
800 To the chief intensity: the crown of these
Is made of love and friendship, and sits high
Upon the forehead of humanity.
All its more ponderous and bulky worth
Is friendship, whence there ever issues forth
A steady splendour; but at the tip-top,
There hangs by unseen film, an orbèd drop
Of light, and that is love: its influence,
Thrown in our eyes, genders a novel sense,
At which we start and fret; till in the end,
810 Melting into its radiance, we blend,
Mingle, and so become a part of it –
Nor with aught else can our souls interknit
So wingedly. When we combine therewith,
Life's self is nourished by its proper pith,
And we are nurtured like a pelican brood.
Ay, so delicious is the unsating food,
That men, who might have towered in the van

Of all the congregated world, to fan
And winnow from the coming step of time
All chaff of custom, wipe away all slime
Left by men-slugs and human serpentry,
Have been content to let occasion die,
Whilst they did sleep in love's elysium.
And, truly, I would rather be struck dumb,
Than speak against this ardent listlessness:
For I have ever thought that it might bless
The world with benefits unknowingly,
As does the nightingale, up-perchèd high,
And cloistered among cool and bunchèd leaves –
She sings but to her love, nor e'er conceives
How tip-toe Night holds back her dark-grey hood.
Just so may love, although 'tis understood
The mere commingling of passionate breath,
Produce more than our searching witnesseth –
What I know not: but who, of men, can tell
That flowers would bloom, or that green fruit would swell
To melting pulp, that fish would have bright mail,
The earth its dower of river, wood, and vale,
The meadows runnels, runnels pebble-stones,
The seed its harvest, or the lute its tones,
Tones ravishment, or ravishment its sweet,
If human souls did never kiss and greet?

'Now, if this earthly love has power to make
Men's being mortal, immortal; to shake
Ambition from their memories, and brim
Their measure of content; what merest whim,
Seems all this poor endeavour after fame,
To one, who keeps within his steadfast aim
A love immortal, an immortal too.
Look not so wildered; for these things are true,
And never can be born of atomies
That buzz about our slumbers, like brain-flies,
Leaving us fancy-sick. No, no, I'm sure,
My restless spirit never could endure

To brood so long upon one luxury,
Unless it did, though fearfully, espy
A hope beyond the shadow of a dream.
My sayings will the less obscurèd seem,
When I have told thee how my waking sight
860 Has made me scruple whether that same night
Was passed in dreaming. Hearken, sweet Peona!
Beyond the matron-temple of Latona,
Which we should see but for these darkening boughs,
Lies a deep hollow, from whose ragged brows
Bushes and trees do lean all round athwart
And meet so nearly, that with wings outraught,
And spreaded tail, a vulture could not glide
Past them, but he must brush on every side.
Some mouldered steps lead into this cool cell,
870 Far as the slabbèd margin of a well,
Whose patient level peeps its crystal eye
Right upward, through the bushes, to the sky.
Oft have I brought thee flowers, on their stalks set
Like vestal primroses, but dark velvet
Edges them round, and they have golden pits:
'Twas there I got them, from the gaps and slits
In a mossy stone, that sometimes was my seat,
When all above was faint with midday heat.
And there in strife no burning thoughts to heed,
880 I'd bubble up the water through a reed;
So reaching back to boyhood; make me ships
Of moulted feathers, touchwood, alder chips,
With leaves stuck in them; and the Neptune be
Of their petty ocean. Oftener, heavily,
When love-lorn hours had left me less a child,
I sat contemplating the figures wild
Of o'er-head clouds melting the mirror through.
Upon a day, while thus I watched, by flew
A cloudy Cupid, with his bow and quiver,
890 So plainly charactered, no breeze would shiver
The happy chance: so happy, I was fain
To follow it upon the open plain,

And, therefore, was just going, when, behold!
A wonder, fair as any I have told –
The same bright face I tasted in my sleep,
Smiling in the clear well. My heart did leap
Through the cool depth. – It moved as if to flee –
I started up – when lo! refreshfully,
There came upon my face in plenteous showers,
Dew-drops, and dewy buds, and leaves, and flowers,
Wrapping all objects from my smothered sight,
Bathing my spirit in a new delight.
Ay, such a breathless honey-feel of bliss
Alone preserved me from the drear abyss
Of death, for the fair form had gone again.
Pleasure is oft a visitant; but pain
Clings cruelly to us, like the gnawing sloth
On the deer's tender haunches: late, and loth,
'Tis scared away by slow returning pleasure.
How sickening, how dark the dreadful leisure
Of weary days, made deeper exquisite,
By a fore-knowledge of unslumbrous night!
Like sorrow came upon me, heavier still,
Than when I wandered from the poppy hill:
And a whole age of lingering moments crept
Sluggishly by, ere more contentment swept
Away at once the deadly yellow spleen.
Yes, thrice have I this fair enchantment seen;
Once more been tortured with renewèd life.
When last the wintry gusts gave over strife
With the conquering sun of spring, and left the skies
Warm and serene, but yet with moistened eyes
In pity of the shattered infant buds –
That time thou didst adorn, with amber studs,
My hunting cap, because I laughed and smiled,
Chatted with thee, and many days exiled
All torment from my breast – 'twas even then,
Straying about, yet, cooped up in the den
Of helpless discontent, hurling my lance
From place to place, and following at chance,

ENDYMION: BOOK I

  At last, by hap, through some young trees it struck,
And, plashing among bedded pebbles, stuck
In the middle of a brook, whose silver ramble
Down twenty little falls, through reeds and bramble,
Tracing along, it brought me to a cave,
Whence it ran brightly forth, and white did lave
The nether sides of mossy stones and rock –
'Mong which it gurgled blythe adieus, to mock
Its own sweet grief at parting. Overhead,
940 Hung a lush screen of drooping weeds, and spread
Thick, as to curtain up some wood-nymph's home.
"Ah! impious mortal, whither do I roam?"
Said I, low voiced: "Ah, whither! 'Tis the grot
Of Proserpine, when Hell, obscure and hot,
Doth her resign, and where her tender hands
She dabbles, on the cool and sluicy sands;
Or 'tis the cell of Echo, where she sits,
And babbles thorough silence, till her wits
Are gone in tender madness, and anon,
950 Faints into sleep, with many a dying tone
Of sadness. O that she would take my vows,
And breathe them sighingly among the boughs,
To sue her gentle ears for whose fair head,
Daily, I pluck sweet flowerets from their bed,
And weave them dyingly – send honey-whispers
Round every leaf, that all those gentle lispers
May sigh my love unto her pitying!
O charitable Echo! hear, and sing
This ditty to her! Tell her – " So I stayed
960 My foolish tongue, and listening, half afraid,
Stood stupefied with my own empty folly,
And blushing for the freaks of melancholy.
Salt tears were coming, when I heard my name
Most fondly lipped, and then these accents came:
"Endymion! the cave is secreter
Than the isle of Delos. Echo hence shall stir
No sighs but sigh-warm kisses, or light noise
Of thy combing hand, the while it travelling cloys

ENDYMION: BOOK II

And trembles through my labyrinthine hair."
At that oppressed I hurried in. Ah! where
Are those swift moments? Whither are they fled?
I'll smile no more, Peona; nor will wed
Sorrow the way to death; but patiently
Bear up against it – so farewell, sad sigh;
And come instead demurest meditation,
To occupy me wholly, and to fashion
My pilgrimage for the world's dusky brink.
No more will I count over, link by link,
My chain of grief: no longer strive to find
A half-forgetfulness in mountain wind
Blustering about my ears. Ay, thou shalt see,
Dearest of sisters, what my life shall be;
What a calm round of hours shall make my days.
There is a paly flame of hope that plays
Where'er I look; but yet, I'll say 'tis naught –
And here I bid it die. Have not I caught,
Already, a more healthy countenance?
By this the sun is setting; we may chance
Meet some of our near-dwellers with my car.'
  This said, he rose, faint-smiling like a star
Through autumn mists, and took Peona's hand:
They stepped into the boat, and launched from land.

BOOK II

O sovereign power of love! O grief! O balm!
All records, saving thine, come cool, and calm,
And shadowy, through the mist of passèd years:
For others, good or bad, hatred and tears
Have become indolent, but touching thine,
One sigh doth echo, one poor sob doth pine,
One kiss brings honey-dew from buried days.
The woes of Troy, towers smothering o'er their blaze,
Stiff-holden shields, far-piercing spears, keen blades,
Struggling, and blood, and shrieks – all dimly fades
Into some backward corner of the brain:

Yet, in our very souls, we feel amain
The close of Troilus and Cressid sweet.
Hence, pageant history! hence, gilded cheat!
Swart planet in the universe of deeds!
Wide sea, that one continuous murmur breeds
Along the pebbled shore of memory!
Many old rotten-timbered boats there be
Upon thy vaporous bosom, magnified
To goodly vessels; many a sail of pride,
And golden keeled, is left unlaunched and dry.
But wherefore this? What care, though owl did fly
About the great Athenian admiral's mast?
What care, though striding Alexander passed
The Indus with his Macedonian numbers?
Though old Ulysses tortured from his slumbers
The glutted Cyclops, what care? – Juliet leaning
Amid her window-flowers, sighing, weaning
Tenderly her fancy from its maiden snow,
Doth more avail than these. The silver flow
Of Hero's tears, the swoon of Imogen,
Fair Pastorella in the bandit's den,
Are things to brood on with more ardency
Than the death-day of empires. Fearfully
Must such conviction come upon his head,
Who, thus far, discontent, has dared to tread,
Without one muse's smile, or kind behest,
The path of love and poesy. But rest,
In chafing restlessness, is yet more drear
Than to be crushed in striving to uprear
Love's standard on the battlements of song.
So once more days and nights aid me along,
Like legioned soldiers.

     Brain-sick shepherd prince,
What promise hast thou faithful guarded since
The day of sacrifice? Or, have new sorrows
Come with the constant dawn upon thy morrows?
Alas! 'tis his old grief. For many days,

ENDYMION: BOOK II

Has he been wandering in uncertain ways:
Through wilderness, and woods of mossèd oaks,
50 Counting his woe-worn minutes, by the strokes
Of the lone woodcutter; and listening still,
Hour after hour, to each lush-leavèd rill.
Now he is sitting by a shady spring,
And elbow-deep with feverous fingering
Stems the up-bursting cold: a wild rose tree
Pavilions him in bloom, and he doth see
A bud which snares his fancy. Lo! but now
He plucks it, dips its stalk in the water: how!
It swells, it buds, it flowers beneath his sight;
60 And, in the middle, there is softly pight
A golden butterfly, upon whose wings
There must be surely charactered strange things,
For with wide eye he wonders, and smiles oft.

Lightly this little herald flew aloft,
Followed by glad Endymion's claspèd hands:
Onward it flies. From languor's sullen bands
His limbs are loosed, and eager, on he hies
Dazzled to trace it in the sunny skies.
It seemed he flew, the way so easy was;
70 And like a new-born spirit did he pass
Through the green evening quiet in the sun,
O'er many a heath, through many a woodland dun,
Through buried paths, where sleepy twilight dreams
The summer time away. One track unseams
A wooded cleft, and, far away, the blue
Of ocean fades upon him; then, anew,
He sinks adown a solitary glen,
Where there was never sound of mortal men,
Saving, perhaps, some snow-light cadences
80 Melting to silence, when upon the breeze
Some holy bark let forth an anthem sweet,
To cheer itself to Delphi. Still his feet
Went swift beneath the merry-wingèd guide,
Until it reached a splashing fountain's side

ENDYMION: BOOK II

    That, near a cavern's mouth, for ever poured
Unto the temperate air: then high it soared,
And, downward, suddenly began to dip,
As if, athirst with so much toil, 'twould sip
The crystal spout-head: so it did, with touch
90 Most delicate, as though afraid to smutch
Even with mealy gold the waters clear.
But, at that very touch, to disappear
So fairy-quick, was strange! Bewilderèd,
Endymion sought around, and shook each bed
Of covert flowers in vain; and then he flung
Himself along the grass. What gentle tongue,
What whisperer disturbed his gloomy rest?
It was a nymph uprisen to the breast
In the fountain's pebbly margin, and she stood
100 'Mong lilies, like the youngest of the brood.
To him her dripping hand she softly kissed,
And anxiously began to plait and twist
Her ringlets round her fingers, saying: 'Youth!
Too long, alas, hast thou starved on the ruth,
The bitterness of love: too long indeed,
Seeing thou art so gentle. Could I weed
Thy soul of care, by heavens, I would offer
All the bright riches of my crystal coffer
To Amphitrite; all my clear-eyed fish,
110 Golden, or rainbow-sided, or purplish,
Vermilion-tailed, or finned with silvery gauze;
Yea, or my veinèd pebble-floor, that draws
A virgin light to the deep; my grotto-sands
Tawny and gold, oozed slowly from far lands
By my diligent springs; my level lilies, shells,
My charming rod, my potent river spells;
Yes, every thing, even to the pearly cup
Meander gave me – for I bubbled up
To fainting creatures in a desert wild.
120 But woe is me, I am but as a child
To gladden thee; and all I dare to say,
Is, that I pity thee; that on this day

I've been thy guide; that thou must wander far
In other regions, past the scanty bar
To mortal steps, before thou canst be ta'en
From every wasting sigh, from every pain,
Into the gentle bosom of thy love.
Why it is thus, one knows in heaven above:
But, a poor Naiad, I guess not. Farewell!
I have a ditty for my hollow cell.'

Hereat, she vanished from Endymion's gaze,
Who brooded o'er the water in amaze:
The dashing fount poured on, and where its pool
Lay, half asleep, in grass and rushes cool,
Quick waterflies and gnats were sporting still,
And fish were dimpling, as if good nor ill
Had fallen out that hour. The wanderer,
Holding his forehead, to keep off the burr
Of smothering fancies, patiently sat down;
And, while beneath the evening's sleepy frown
Glow-worms began to trim their starry lamps,
Thus breathed he to himself: 'Whoso encamps
To take a fancied city of delight,
O what a wretch is he! and when 'tis his,
After long toil and travailing, to miss
The kernel of his hopes, how more than vile:
Yet, for him there's refreshment even in toil;
Another city doth he set about,
Free from the smallest pebble-bead of doubt
That he will seize on trickling honey-combs –
Alas, he finds them dry; and then he foams,
And onward to another city speeds.
But this is human life: the war, the deeds,
The disappointment, the anxiety,
Imagination's struggles, far and nigh,
All human; bearing in themselves this good,
That they are still the air, the subtle food,
To make us feel existence, and to show
How quiet death is. Where soil is men grow,

ENDYMION: BOOK II

160 Whether to weeds or flowers; but for me,
There is no depth to strike in. I can see
Naught earthly worth my compassing; so stand
Upon a misty, jutting head of land –
Alone? No, no; and, by the Orphean lute,
When mad Eurydice is listening to't,
I'd rather stand upon this misty peak,
With not a thing to sigh for, or to seek,
But the soft shadow of my thrice-seen love,
Than be – I care not what. O meekest dove
170 Of heaven! O Cynthia, ten-times bright and fair!
From thy blue throne, now filling all the air,
Glance but one little beam of tempered light
Into my bosom, that the dreadful might
And tyranny of love be somewhat scared!
Yet do not so, sweet queen; one torment spared,
Would give a pang to jealous misery,
Worse than the torment's self; but rather tie
Large wings upon my shoulders, and point out
My love's far dwelling. Though the playful rout
180 Of Cupids shun thee, too divine art thou,
Too keen in beauty, for thy silver prow
Not to have dipped in love's most gentle stream.
O be propitious, nor severely deem
My madness impious; for, by all the stars
That tend thy bidding, I do think the bars
That kept my spirit in are burst – that I
Am sailing with thee through the dizzy sky!
How beautiful thou art! The world how deep!
How tremulous-dazzlingly the wheels sweep
190 Around their axle! Then these gleaming reins,
How lithe! When this thy chariot attains
Its airy goal, haply some bower veils
Those twilight eyes? Those eyes! – my spirit fails
Dear goddess, help! or the wide-gaping air
Will gulf me – help!' At this with maddened stare
And lifted hands, and trembling lips he stood;
Like old Deucalion mountained o'er the flood,

ENDYMION: BOOK II

    Or blind Orion hungry for the morn.
And, but from the deep cavern there was borne
A voice, he had been froze to senseless stone;
Nor sigh of his, nor plaint, nor passioned moan
Had more been heard. Thus swelled it forth: 'Descend,
Young mountaineer! descend where alleys bend
Into the sparry hollows of the world!
Oft hast thou seen bolts of the thunder hurled
As from thy threshold; day by day hast been
A little lower than the chilly sheen
Of icy pinnacles, and dippedst thine arms
Into the deadening ether that still charms
Their marble being: now, as deep profound
As those are high, descend! He ne'er is crowned
With immortality, who fears to follow
Where airy voices lead: so through the hollow,
The silent mysteries of earth, descend!'

    He heard but the last words, nor could contend
One moment in reflection: for he fled
Into the fearful deep, to hide his head
From the clear moon, the trees, and coming madness.

    'Twas far too strange, and wonderful for sadness;
Sharpening, by degrees, his appetite
To dive into the deepest. Dark, nor light,
The region; nor bright, nor sombre wholly,
But mingled up; a gleaming melancholy;
A dusky empire and its diadems;
One faint eternal eventide of gems.
Ay, millions sparkled on a vein of gold,
Along whose track the prince quick footsteps told,
With all its lines abrupt and angular:
Out-shooting sometimes, like a meteor-star,
Through a vast antre; then the metal woof,
Like Vulcan's rainbow, with some monstrous roof
Curves hugely: now, far in the deep abyss,
It seems an angry lightning, and doth hiss
Fancy into belief: anon it leads

Through winding passages, where sameness breeds
Vexing conceptions of some sudden change,
Whether to silver grots, or giant range
Of sapphire columns, or fantastic bridge
Athwart a flood of crystal. On a ridge
240 Now fareth he, that o'er the vast beneath
Towers like an ocean-cliff, and whence he seeth
A hundred waterfalls, whose voices come
But as the murmuring surge. Chilly and numb
His bosom grew, when first he, far away
Descried an orbèd diamond, set to fray
Old darkness from his throne. 'Twas like the sun
Uprisen o'er chaos, and with such a stun
Came the amazement, that, absorbed in it,
He saw not fiercer wonders – past the wit
250 Of any spirit to tell, but one of those
Who, when this planet's sphering time doth close,
Will be its high remembrancers. Who they?
The mighty ones who have made eternal day
For Greece and England. While astonishment
With deep-drawn sighs was quieting, he went
Into a marble gallery, passing through
A mimic temple, so complete and true
In sacred custom, that he well nigh feared
To search it inwards; whence far off appeared,
260 Through a long pillared vista, a fair shrine,
And, just beyond, on light tip-toe divine,
A quivered Dian. Stepping awfully,
The youth approached, oft turning his veiled eye
Down sidelong aisles, and into niches old.
And when, more near against the marble cold
He had touched his forehead, he began to thread
All courts and passages, where silence dead,
Roused by his whispering footsteps, murmured faint:
And long he traversed to and fro, to acquaint
270 Himself with every mystery, and awe;
Till, weary, he sat down before the maw
Of a wide outlet, fathomless and dim,

To wild uncertainty and shadows grim.
There, when new wonders ceased to float before,
And thoughts of self came on, how crude and sore
The journey homeward to habitual self!
A mad-pursuing of the fog-born elf,
Whose flitting lantern, through rude nettle-briar,
Cheats us into a swamp, into a fire,
Into the bosom of a hated thing.

What misery most drowningly doth sing
In lone Endymion's ear, now he has raught
The goal of consciousness? Ah, 'tis the thought,
The deadly feel of solitude: for lo!
He cannot see the heavens, nor the flow
Of rivers, nor hill-flowers running wild
In pink and purple chequer, nor, up-piled,
The cloudy rack slow journeying in the west,
Like herded elephants; nor felt, nor pressed
Cool grass, nor tasted the fresh slumbrous air;
But far from such companionship to wear
An unknown time, surcharged with grief, away,
Was now his lot. And must he patient stay,
Tracing fantastic figures with his spear?
'No!' exclaimed he, 'why should I tarry here?'
'No!' loudly echoed times innumerable.
At which he straightway started, and 'gan tell
His paces back into the temple's chief,
Warming and glowing strong in the belief
Of help from Dian: so that when again
He caught her airy form, thus did he plain,
Moving more near the while: 'O Haunter chaste
Of river sides, and woods, and heathy waste,
Where with thy silver bow and arrows keen
Art thou now forested! O woodland Queen,
What smoothest air thy smoother forehead woos?
Where dost thou listen to the wide halloos
Of thy disparted nymphs? Through what dark tree
Glimmers thy crescent? Wheresoe'er it be,

ENDYMION: BOOK II

310 'Tis in the breath of heaven: thou dost taste
Freedom as none can taste it, nor dost waste
Thy loveliness in dismal elements;
But, finding on our green earth sweet contents,
There livest blissfully. Ah, if to thee
It feels Elysian, how rich to me,
An exil'd mortal, sounds its pleasant name!
Within my breast there lives a choking flame –
O let me cool't the zephyr-boughs among!
A homeward fever parches up my tongue –
320 O let me slake it at the running springs!
Upon my ear a noisy nothing rings –
O let me once more hear the linnet's note!
Before mine eyes thick films and shadows float –
O let me 'noint them with the heaven's light!
Dost thou now lave thy feet and ankles white?
O think how sweet to me the freshening sluice!
Dost thou now please thy thirst with berry-juice?
O think how this dry palate would rejoice!
If in soft slumber thou dost hear my voice,
330 O think how I should love a bed of flowers! –
Young, goddess! let me see my native bowers!
Deliver me from this rapacious deep!'

Thus ending loudly, as he would o'erleap
His destiny, alert he stood: but when
Obstinate silence came heavily again,
Feeling about for its old couch of space
And airy cradle, lowly bowed his face
Desponding, o'er the marble floor's cold thrill.
But 'twas not long; for, sweeter than the rill
340 To its cold channel, or a swollen tide
To margin sallows, were the leaves he spied,
And flowers, and wreaths, and ready myrtle crowns
Up-heaping through the slab. Refreshment drowns
Itself, and strives its own delights to hide –
Nor in one spot alone; the floral pride
In a long whispering birth enchanted grew
Before his footsteps; as when heaved anew

Old ocean rolls a lengthened wave to the shore,
Down whose green back the short-lived foam, all hoar,
Bursts gradual, with a wayward indolence.

Increasing still in heart, and pleasant sense,
Upon his fairy journey on he hastes;
So anxious for the end, he scarcely wastes
One moment with his hand among the sweets:
Onward he goes – he stops – his bosom beats
As plainly in his ear, as the faint charm
Of which the throbs were born. This still alarm,
This sleepy music, forced him walk tip-toe:
For it came more softly than the east could blow
Arion's magic to the Atlantic isles;
Or than the west, made jealous by the smiles
Of thronèd Apollo, could breathe back the lyre
To seas Ionian and Tyrian.

O did he ever live, that lonely man,
Who loved – and music slew not? 'Tis the pest
Of love, that fairest joys give most unrest;
That things of delicate and tenderest worth
Are swallowed all, and made a searèd dearth,
By one consuming flame – it doth immerse
And suffocate true blessings in a curse.
Half-happy, by comparison of bliss,
Is miserable. 'Twas even so with this
Dew-dropping melody, in the Carian's ear;
First heaven, then hell, and then forgotten clear,
Vanished in elemental passion.

And down some swart abysm he had gone,
Had not a heavenly guide benignant led
To where thick myrtle branches, 'gainst his head
Brushing, awakened: then the sounds again
Went noiseless as a passing noontide rain
Over a bower, where little space he stood;
For as the sunset peeps into a wood
So saw he panting light, and towards it went

Through winding alleys – and lo, wonderment!
Upon soft verdure saw, one here, one there,
Cupids a-slumbering on their pinions fair.

After a thousand mazes overgone,
At last, with sudden step, he came upon
A chamber, myrtle walled, embowered high,
390 Full of light, incense, tender minstrelsy,
And more of beautiful and strange beside:
For on a silken couch of rosy pride,
In midst of all, there lay a sleeping youth
Of fondest beauty; fonder, in fair sooth,
Than sighs could fathom, or contentment reach:
And coverlids gold-tinted like the peach,
Or ripe October faded marigolds,
Fell sleek about him in a thousand folds –
Not hiding up an Apollonian curve
400 Of neck and shoulder, nor the tenting swerve
Of knee from knee, nor ankles pointing light;
But rather, giving them to the fillèd sight
Officiously. Sideway his face reposed
On one white arm, and tenderly unclosed,
By tenderest pressure, a faint damask mouth
To slumbery pout; just as the morning south
Disparts a dew-lipped rose. Above his head,
Four lily stalks did their white honours wed
To make a coronal; and round him grew
410 All tendrils green, of every bloom and hue,
Together intertwined and trammelled fresh:
The vine of glossy sprout; the ivy mesh,
Shading its Ethiope berries; and woodbine,
Of velvet leaves and bugle-blooms divine;
Convolvulus in streakèd vases flush;
The creeper, mellowing for an autumn blush;
And virgin's bower, trailing airily;
With others of the sisterhood. Hard by,
Stood serene Cupids watching silently.
420 One, kneeling to a lyre, touched the strings,

Muffling to death the pathos with his wings;
And, ever and anon, uprose to look
At the youth's slumber; while another took
A willow-bough, distilling odorous dew,
And shook it on his hair; another flew
In through the woven roof, and fluttering-wise
Rained violets upon his sleeping eyes.

   At these enchantments, and yet many more,
The breathless Latmian wondered o'er and o'er;
Until, impatient in embarrassment,
He forthright passed, and lightly treading went
To that same feathered lyrist, who straightway,
Smiling, thus whispered: 'Though from upper day
Thou art a wanderer, and thy presence here
Might seem unholy, be of happy cheer!
For 'tis the nicest touch of human honour,
When some ethereal and high-favouring donor
Presents immortal bowers to mortal sense –
As now 'tis done to thee, Endymion. Hence
Was I in no wise startled. So recline
Upon these living flowers. Here is wine,
Alive with sparkles – never, I aver,
Since Ariadne was a vintager,
So cool a purple: taste these juicy pears,
Sent me by sad Vertumnus, when his fears
Were high about Pomona: here is cream,
Deepening to richness from a snowy gleam;
Sweeter than that nurse Amalthea skimmed
For the boy Jupiter: and here, undimmed
By any touch, a bunch of blooming plums
Ready to melt between an infant's gums:
And here is manna picked from Syrian trees,
In starlight, by the three Hesperides.
Feast on, and meanwhile I will let thee know
Of all these things around us.' He did so,
Still brooding o'er the cadence of his lyre;
And thus: 'I need not any hearing tire

ENDYMION: BOOK II

By telling how the sea-born goddess pined
For a mortal youth, and how she strove to bind
Him all in all unto her doting self.
Who would not be so prisoned? but, fond elf,
He was content to let her amorous plea
Faint through his careless arms; content to see
An unseized heaven dying at his feet;
Content, O fool! to make a cold retreat,
When on the pleasant grass such love, lovelorn,
Lay sorrowing; when every tear was born
Of diverse passion; when her lips and eyes
Were closed in sullen moisture, and quick sighs
Came vexed and pettish through her nostrils small.
Hush! no exclaim – yet, justly mightest thou call
Curses upon his head. – I was half glad,
But my poor mistress went distract and mad,
When the boar tusked him: so away she flew
To Jove's high throne, and by her plainings drew
Immortal tear-drops down the thunderer's beard;
Whereon, it was decreed he should be reared
Each summer-time to life. Lo! this is he,
That same Adonis, safe in the privacy
Of this still region all his winter-sleep.
Ay, sleep; for when our love-sick queen did weep
Over his wanèd corse, the tremulous shower
Healed up the wound, and, with a balmy power,
Medicined death to a lengthened drowsiness:
The which she fills with visions, and doth dress
In all this quiet luxury; and hath set
Us young immortals, without any let,
To watch his slumber through. 'Tis well nigh passed,
Even to a moment's filling up, and fast
She scuds with summer breezes, to pant through
The first long kiss, warm firstling, to renew
Embowered sports in Cytherea's isle.
Look! how those wingèd listeners all this while
Stand anxious! See! behold!' – This clamant word
Broke through the careful silence; for they heard

A rustling noise of leaves, and out there fluttered
Pigeons and doves: Adonis something muttered
The while one hand, that erst upon his thigh
Lay dormant, moved convulsed and gradually
Up to his forehead. Then there was a hum
Of sudden voices, echoing, 'Come! come!
Arise! awake! Clear summer has forth walked
Unto the clover-sward, and she has talked
Full soothingly to every nested finch:
Rise, Cupids! or we'll give the blue-bell pinch
To your dimpled arms. Once more sweet life begin!'
At this, from every side they hurried in,
Rubbing their sleepy eyes with lazy wrists,
And doubling over head their little fists
In backward yawns. But all were soon alive:
For as delicious wine doth, sparkling, dive
In nectared clouds and curls through water fair,
So from the arbour roof down swelled an air
Odorous and enlivening; making all
To laugh, and play, and sing, and loudly call
For their sweet queen – when lo! the wreathèd green
Disparted, and far upward could be seen
Blue heaven, and a silver car, air-borne,
Whose silent wheels, fresh wet from clouds of morn,
Spun off a drizzling dew, which falling chill
On soft Adonis' shoulders, made him still
Nestle and turn uneasily about.
Soon were the white doves plain, with necks stretched out,
And silken traces tightened in descent;
And soon, returning from love's banishment,
Queen Venus leaning downward open-armed.
Her shadow fell upon his breast, and charmed
A tumult to his heart, and a new life
Into his eyes. Ah, miserable strife,
But for her comforting! unhappy sight,
But meeting her blue orbs! Who, who can write
Of these first minutes? The unchariest muse
To embracements warm as theirs makes coy excuse.

148 ENDYMION: BOOK II

  O it has ruffled every spirit there,
Saving Love's self, who stands superb to share
The general gladness. Awfully he stands;
A sovereign quell is in his waving hands;
No sight can bear the lightning of his bow;
His quiver is mysterious, none can know
What themselves think of it; from forth his eyes
There darts strange light of varied hues and dyes;
A scowl is sometimes on his brow, but who
Look full upon it feel anon the blue
Of his fair eyes run liquid through their souls.
Endymion feels it, and no more controls
The burning prayer within him; so, bent low,
He had begun a plaining of his woe.
But Venus, bending forward, said: 'My child,
Favour this gentle youth; his days are wild
With love – he – but alas! too well I see
Thou know'st the deepness of his misery.
Ah, smile not so, my son: I tell thee true,
That when through heavy hours I used to rue
The endless sleep of this new-born Adon',
This stranger aye I pitied. For upon
A dreary morning once I fled away
Into the breezy clouds, to weep and pray
For this my love, for vexing Mars had teased
Me even to tears. Thence, when a little eased,
Down-looking, vacant, through a hazy wood,
I saw this youth as he despairing stood:
Those same dark curls blown vagrant in the wind;
Those same full-fringèd lids a constant blind
Over his sullen eyes. I saw him throw
Himself on withered leaves, even as though
Death had come sudden; for no jot he moved,
Yet muttered wildly. I could hear he loved
Some fair immortal, and that his embrace
Had zoned her through the night. There is no trace
Of this in heaven: I have marked each cheek,
And find it is the vainest thing to seek;

And that of all things 'tis kept secretest.
Endymion! one day thou wilt be blest:
So still obey the guiding hand that fends
Thee safely through these wonders for sweet ends.
'Tis a concealment needful in extreme,
And if I guessed not so, the sunny beam
Thou shouldst mount up to with me. Now adieu!
Here must we leave thee.' – At these words up-flew
580 The impatient doves, uprose the floating car,
Up went the hum celestial. High afar
The Latmian saw them minish into naught;
And, when all were clear vanished, still he caught
A vivid lightning from that dreadful bow.
When all was darkened, with Aetnean throe
The earth closed – gave a solitary moan –
And left him once again in twilight lone.

He did not rave, he did not stare aghast,
For all those visions were o'ergone, and passed,
590 And he in loneliness: he felt assured
Of happy times, when all he had endured
Would seem a feather to the mighty prize.
So, with unusual gladness, on he hies
Through caves, and palaces of mottled ore,
Gold dome, and crystal wall, and turquoise floor,
Black polished porticoes of awful shade,
And, at the last, a diamond balustrade,
Leading afar past wild magnificence,
Spiral through ruggedest loopholes, and thence
600 Stretching across a void, then guiding o'er
Enormous chasms, where, all foam and roar,
Streams subterranean tease their granite beds;
Then heightened just above the silvery heads
Of a thousand fountains, so that he could dash
The waters with his spear – but at the splash,
Done heedlessly, those spouting columns rose
Sudden a poplar's height, and 'gan enclose
His diamond path with fretwork, streaming round

Alive, and dazzling cool, and with a sound,
Haply, like dolphin tumults, when sweet shells
Welcome the float of Thetis. Long he dwells
On this delight; for, every minute's space,
The streams with changèd magic interlace:
Sometimes like delicatest lattices,
Covered with crystal vines; then weeping trees,
Moving about as in a gentle wind,
Which, in a wink, to watery gauze refined,
Poured into shapes of curtained canopies,
Spangled, and rich with liquid broideries
Of flowers, peacocks, swans, and naiads fair.
Swifter than lightning went these wonders rare;
And then the water, into stubborn streams
Collecting, mimicked the wrought oaken beams,
Pillars, and frieze, and high fantastic roof,
Of those dusk places in times far aloof
Cathedrals called. He bade a loth farewell
To these founts Protean, passing gulf, and dell,
And torrent, and ten thousand jutting shapes,
Half seen through deepest gloom, and grisly gapes,
Blackening on every side, and overhead
A vaulted dome like Heaven's, far bespread
With starlight gems: ay, all so huge and strange,
The solitary felt a hurried change
Working within him into something dreary –
Vexed like a morning eagle, lost, and weary,
And purblind amid foggy, midnight wolds.
But he revives at once: for who beholds
New sudden things, nor casts his mental slough?
Forth from a rugged arch, in the dusk below,
Came mother Cybele! alone – alone –
In sombre chariot; dark foldings thrown
About her majesty, and front death-pale,
With turrets crowned. Four manèd lions hale
The sluggish wheels; solemn their toothèd maws,
Their surly eyes brow-hidden, heavy paws
Uplifted drowsily, and nervy tails

ENDYMION: BOOK II

  Cowering their tawny brushes. Silent sails
This shadowy queen athwart, and faints away
In another gloomy arch.
      Wherefore delay,
650 Young traveller, in such a mournful place?
Art thou wayworn, or canst not further trace
The diamond path? And does it indeed end
Abrupt in middle air? Yet earthward bend
Thy forehead, and to Jupiter cloud-borne
Call ardently! He was indeed wayworn;
Abrupt, in middle air, his way was lost;
To cloud-borne Jove he bowed, and there crossed
Towards him a large eagle, 'twixt whose wings,
Without one impious word, himself he flings,
660 Committed to the darkness and the gloom:
Down, down, uncertain to what pleasant doom,
Swift as a fathoming plummet down he fell
Through unknown things, till exhaled asphodel,
And rose, with spicy fannings interbreathed,
Came swelling forth where little caves were wreathed
So thick with leaves and mosses, that they seemed
Large honey-combs of green, and freshly teemed
With airs delicious. In the greenest nook
The eagle landed him, and farewell took.

670   It was a jasmine bower, all bestrown
With golden moss. His every sense had grown
Ethereal for pleasure; 'bove his head
Flew a delight half-graspable; his tread
Was Hesperian; to his capable ears
Silence was music from the holy spheres;
A dewy luxury was in his eyes;
The little flowers felt his pleasant sighs
And stirred them faintly. Verdant cave and cell
He wandered through, oft wondering at such swell
680 Of sudden exaltation: but, 'Alas!'
Said he, 'will all this gush of feeling pass
Away in solitude? And must they wane,

ENDYMION: BOOK II

    Like melodies upon a sandy plain,
    Without an echo? Then shall I be left
    So sad, so melancholy, so bereft!
    Yet still I feel immortal! O my love,
    My breath of life, where art thou? High above,
    Dancing before the morning gates of heaven?
    Or keeping watch among those starry seven,
690 Old Atlas' children? Art a maid of the waters,
    One of shell-winding Triton's bright-haired daughters?
    Or art – impossible – a nymph of Dian's,
    Weaving a coronal of tender scions
    For very idleness? Where'er thou art,
    Methinks it now is at my will to start
    Into thine arms; to scare Aurora's train,
    And snatch thee from the morning; o'er the main
    To scud like a wild bird, and take thee off
    From thy sea-foamy cradle; or to doff
700 Thy shepherd vest, and woo thee mid fresh leaves.
    No, no, too eagerly my soul deceives
    Its powerless self: I know this cannot be.
    O let me then by some sweet dreaming flee
    To her entrancements. Hither, Sleep, awhile!
    Hither, most gentle Sleep! and soothing foil
    For some few hours the coming solitude.'

    Thus spake he, and that moment felt endued
    With power to dream deliciously; so wound
    Through a dim passage, searching till he found
710 The smoothest mossy bed and deepest, where
    He threw himself, and just into the air
    Stretching his indolent arms, he took – O bliss! –
    A naked waist: 'Fair Cupid, whence is this?'
    A well-known voice sighed, 'Sweetest, here am I!'
    At which soft ravishment, with doting cry
    They trembled to each other. – Helicon!
    O fountained hill! Old Homer's Helicon!
    That thou wouldst spout a little streamlet o'er
    These sorry pages! Then the verse would soar

ENDYMION: BOOK II

720 And sing above this gentle pair, like lark
Over his nested young: but all is dark
Around thine agèd top, and thy clear fount
Exhales in mists to heaven. Ay, the count
Of mighty Poets is made up; the scroll
Is folded by the Muses; the bright roll
Is in Apollo's hand: our dazèd eyes
Have seen a new tinge in the western skies:
The world has done its duty. Yet, oh yet,
Although the sun of poesy is set,
730 These lovers did embrace, and we must weep
That there is no old power left to steep
A quill immortal in their joyous tears.
Long time in silence did their anxious fears
Question that thus it was; long time they lay
Fondling and kissing every doubt away;
Long time ere soft caressing sobs began
To mellow into words, and then there ran
Two bubbling springs of talk from their sweet lips.
'O known Unknown! from whom my being sips
740 Such darling essence, wherefore may I not
Be ever in these arms? in this sweet spot
Pillow my chin for ever? ever press
These toying hands and kiss their smooth excess?
Why not for ever and for ever feel
That breath about my eyes? Ah, thou wilt steal
Away from me again, indeed, indeed –
Thou wilt be gone away, and wilt not heed
My lonely madness. Speak, delicious fair!
Is – is it to be so? No! Who will dare
750 To pluck thee from me? And, of thine own will,
Full well I feel thou wouldst not leave me. Still
Let me entwine thee surer, surer – now
How can we part? Elysium! who art thou?
Who, that thou canst not be for ever here,
Or lift me with thee to some starry sphere?
Enchantress! tell me by this soft embrace,
By the most soft completion of thy face,

ENDYMION: BOOK II

    Those lips, O slippery blisses, twinkling eyes
    And by these tenderest, milky sovereignties –
760 These tenderest – and by the nectar-wine,
    The passion –' 'O doved Ida the divine!
    Endymion! dearest! Ah, unhappy me!
    His soul will 'scape us – O felicity!
    How he does love me! His poor temples beat
    To the very tune of love – how sweet, sweet, sweet.
    Revive, dear youth, or I shall faint and die;
    Revive, or these soft hours will hurry by
    In trancèd dullness; speak, and let that spell
    Affright this lethargy! I cannot quell
770 Its heavy pressure, and will press at least
    My lips to thine, that they may richly feast
    Until we taste the life of love again.
    What! dost thou move? dost kiss? O bliss! O pain!
    I love thee, youth, more than I can conceive;
    And so long absence from thee doth bereave
    My soul of any rest – yet must I hence.
    Yet, can I not to starry eminence
    Uplift thee; nor for very shame can own
    Myself to thee. Ah, dearest, do not groan
780 Or thou wilt force me from this secrecy,
    And I must blush in heaven. O that I
    Had done 't already; that the dreadful smiles
    At my lost brightness, my impassioned wiles,
    Had wanèd from Olympus' solemn height,
    And from all serious Gods; that our delight
    Was quite forgotten, save of us alone!
    And wherefore so ashamed? 'Tis but to atone
    For endless pleasure, by some coward blushes:
    Yet must I be a coward! – Horror rushes
790 Too palpable before me – the sad look
    Of Jove, Minerva's start – no bosom shook
    With awe of purity, no Cupid pinion
    In reverence vailed, my crystalline dominion
    Half lost, and all old hymns made nullity!
    But what is this to love? O I could fly

With thee into the ken of heavenly powers,
So thou wouldst thus, for many sequent hours,
Press me so sweetly. Now I swear at once
That I am wise, that Pallas is a dunce –
Perhaps her love like mine is but unknown –
O I do think that I have been alone
In chastity! Yes, Pallas has been sighing,
While every eve saw me my hair up-tying
With fingers cool as aspen leaves. Sweet love,
I was as vague as solitary dove,
Nor knew that nests were built. Now a soft kiss –
Ay, by that kiss, I vow an endless bliss,
An immortality of passion's thine.
Ere long I will exalt thee to the shine
Of heaven ambrosial: and we will shade
Ourselves whole summers by a river glade;
And I will tell thee stories of the sky,
And breathe thee whispers of its minstrelsy.
My happy love will overwing all bounds!
O let me melt into thee; let the sounds
Of our close voices marry at their birth;
Let us entwine hoveringly – O dearth
Of human words! roughness of mortal speech!
Lispings empyrean will I sometime teach
Thine honeyed tongue – lute-breathings, which I gasp
To have thee understand, now while I clasp
Thee thus, and weep for fondness – I am pained,
Endymion. Woe! woe! is grief contained
In the very deeps of pleasure, my sole life?' –
Hereat, with many sobs, her gentle strife
Melted into a languor. He returned
Entrancèd vows and tears.

                        Ye who have yearned
With too much passion, will here stay and pity
For the mere sake of truth, as 'tis a ditty
Not of these days, but long ago 'twas told
By a cavern wind unto a forest old;
And then the forest told it in a dream

To a sleeping lake, whose cool and level gleam
A poet caught as he was journeying
To Phoebus' shrine; and in it he did fling
His weary limbs, bathing an hour's space,
And after, straight in that inspirèd place
He sang the story up into the air,
Giving it universal freedom. There
840 Has it been ever sounding for those ears
Whose tips are glowing hot. The legend cheers
Yon sentinel stars; and he who listens to it
Must surely be self-doomed or he will rue it:
For quenchless burnings come upon the heart,
Made fiercer by a fear lest any part
Should be engulfèd in the eddying wind.
As much as here is penned doth always find
A resting place, thus much comes clear and plain.
Anon the strange voice is upon the wane –
850 And 'tis but echoed from departing sound,
That the fair visitant at last unwound
Her gentle limbs, and left the youth asleep. –
Thus the tradition of the gusty deep.

Now turn we to our former chroniclers. –
Endymion awoke, that grief of hers
Sweet-paining on his ear: he sickly guessed
How lone he was once more, and sadly pressed
His empty arms together, hung his head,
And most forlorn upon that widowed bed
860 Sat silently. Love's madness he had known:
Often with more than tortured lion's groan
Moanings had burst from him; but now that rage
Had passed away. No longer did he wage
A rough-voiced war against the dooming stars.
No, he had felt too much for such harsh jars.
The lyre of his soul Aeolian-tuned
Forgot all violence, and but communed
With melancholy thought. O he had swooned
Drunken from Pleasure's nipple; and his love

ENDYMION: BOOK II

870 Henceforth was dove-like. Loth was he to move
From the imprinted couch, and when he did,
'Twas with slow, languid paces, and face hid
In muffling hands. So tempered, out he strayed
Half seeing visions that might have dismayed
Alecto's serpents; ravishments more keen
Than Hermes' pipe, when anxious he did lean
Over eclipsing eyes; and at the last
It was a sounding grotto, vaulted vast,
O'er-studded with a thousand, thousand pearls,
880 And crimson-mouthèd shells with stubborn curls,
Of every shape and size, even to the bulk
In which whales arbour close, to brood and sulk
Against an endless storm. Moreover too,
Fish-semblances, of green and azure hue,
Ready to snort their streams. In this cool wonder
Endymion sat down, and 'gan to ponder
On all his life: his youth, up to the day
When 'mid acclaim, and feasts, and garlands gay,
He stepped upon his shepherd throne; the look
890 Of his white palace in wild forest nook,
And all the revels he had lorded there;
Each tender maiden whom he once thought fair,
With every friend and fellow-woodlander –
Passed like a dream before him. Then the spur
Of the old bards to mighty deeds; his plans
To nurse the golden age 'mong shepherd clans;
That wondrous night; the great Pan-festival;
His sister's sorrow; and his wanderings all,
Until into the earth's deep maw he rushed;
900 Then all its buried magic, till it flushed
High with excessive love. 'And now', thought he,
'How long must I remain in jeopardy
Of blank amazements that amaze no more?
Now I have tasted her sweet soul to the core
All other depths are shallow: essences,
Once spiritual, are like muddy lees,
Meant but to fertilize my earthly root,

And make my branches lift a golden fruit
Into the bloom of heaven. Other light,
Though it be quick and sharp enough to blight
The Olympian eagle's vision, is dark,
Dark as the parentage of chaos. Hark!
My silent thoughts are echoing from these shells;
Or they are but the ghosts, the dying swells
Of noises far away? – list!' – Hereupon
He kept an anxious ear. The humming tone
Came louder, and behold, there as he lay,
On either side out-gushed, with misty spray,
A copious spring; and both together dashed
Swift, mad, fantastic round the rocks and lashed
Among the conches and shells of the lofty grot,
Leaving a trickling dew. At last they shot
Down from the ceiling's height, pouring a noise
As of some breathless racers whose hopes poise
Upon the last few steps, and with spent force
Along the ground they took a winding course.
Endymion followed – for it seemed that one
Ever pursued, the other strove to shun –
Followed their languid mazes, till well nigh
He had left thinking of the mystery,
And was now rapt in tender hoverings
Over the vanished bliss. Ah! what is it sings
His dream away? What melodies are these?
They sound as through the whispering of trees,
Not native in such barren vaults. Give ear!

'O Arethusa, peerless nymph! why fear
Such tenderness as mine? Great Dian, why,
Why didst thou hear her prayer? O that I
Were rippling round her dainty fairness now,
Circling about her waist, and striving how
To entice her to a dive! then stealing in
Between her luscious lips and eyelids thin!
O that her shining hair was in the sun,
And I distilling from it thence to run

In amorous rillets down her shrinking form!
To linger on her lily shoulders, warm
Between her kissing breasts, and every charm
Touch raptured! – See how painfully I flow;
Fair maid, be pitiful to my great woe.
950 Stay, stay thy weary course, and let me lead,
A happy wooer, to the flowery mead
Where all that beauty snared me.' – 'Cruel god,
Desist! or my offended mistress' nod
Will stagnate all thy fountains – tease me not
With siren words – Ah, have I really got
Such power to madden thee? And is it true –
Away, away, or I shall dearly rue
My very thoughts: in mercy then away,
Kindest Alpheus, for should I obey
960 My own dear will, 'twould be a deadly bane.
O, Oread-Queen! would that thou hadst a pain
Like this of mine, then would I fearless turn
And be a criminal. Alas, I burn,
I shudder – gentle river, get thee hence.
Alpheus! thou enchanter! every sense
Of mine was once made perfect in these woods.
Fresh breezes, bowery lawns, and innocent floods,
Ripe fruits, and lonely couch, contentment gave;
But ever since I heedlessly did lave
970 In thy deceitful stream, a panting glow
Grew strong within me: wherefore serve me so,
And call it love? Alas, 'twas cruelty.
Not once more did I close my happy eye
Amid the thrushes' song. Away! Avaunt!
O 'twas a cruel thing.' – 'Now thou dost taunt
So softly, Arethusa, that I think
If thou wast playing on my shady brink,
Thou wouldst bathe once again. Innocent maid!
Stifle thine heart no more; nor be afraid
980 Of angry powers – there are deities
Will shade us with their wings. Those fitful sighs
'Tis almost death to hear. O let me pour

ENDYMION: BOOK II

    A dewy balm upon them! – fear no more,
    Sweet Arethusa! Dian's self must feel
    Sometimes these very pangs. Dear maiden, steal
    Blushing into my soul, and let us fly
    These dreary caverns for the open sky.
    I will delight thee all my winding course,
    From the green sea up to my hidden source
990 About Arcadian forests; and will show
    The channels where my coolest waters flow
    Through mossy rocks; where, 'mid exuberant green,
    I roam in pleasant darkness, more unseen
    Than Saturn in his exile; where I brim
    Round flowery islands, and take thence a skim
    Of mealy sweets, which myriads of bees
    Buzz from their honeyed wings: and thou shouldst please
    Thyself to choose the richest, where we might
    Be incense-pillowed every summer night.
1000 Doff all sad fears, thou white deliciousness,
    And let us be thus comforted; unless
    Thou couldst rejoice to see my hopeless stream
    Hurry distracted from Sol's temperate beam,
    And pour to death along some hungry sands.' –
    'What can I do, Alpheus? Dian stands
    Severe before me. Persecuting fate!
    Unhappy Arethusa! thou wast late
    A huntress free in –' At this, sudden fell
    Those two sad streams adown a fearful dell.
1010 The Latmian listened, but he heard no more,
    Save echo, faint repeating o'er and o'er
    The name of Arethusa. On the verge
    Of that dark gulf he wept, and said: 'I urge
    Thee, gentle Goddess of my pilgrimage,
    By our eternal hopes, to soothe, to assuage,
    If thou art powerful, these lovers' pains;
    And make them happy in some happy plains.'

    He turned – there was a whelming sound – he stepped –
    There was a cooler light; and so he kept

1020 Towards it by a sandy path, and lo!
More suddenly than doth a moment go,
The visions of the earth were gone and fled –
He saw the giant sea above his head.

BOOK III

There are who lord it o'er their fellow-men
With most prevailing tinsel: who unpen
Their baaing vanities, to browse away
The comfortable green and juicy hay
From human pastures; or – O torturing fact! –
Who, through an idiot blink, will see unpacked
Fire-branded foxes to sear up and singe
Our gold and ripe-eared hopes. With not one tinge
Of sanctuary splendour, not a sight
10 Able to face an owl's, they still are dight
By the blear-eyed nations in empurpled vests,
And crowns, and turbans. With unladen breasts,
Save of blown self-applause, they proudly mount
To their spirit's perch, their being's high account,
Their tip-top nothings, their dull skies, their thrones –
Amid the fierce intoxicating tones
Of trumpets, shoutings, and belaboured drums,
And sudden cannon. Ah! how all this hums,
In wakeful ears, like uproar passed and gone –
20 Like thunder clouds that spake to Babylon,
And set those old Chaldeans to their tasks. –
Are then regalities all gilded masks?
No, there are thronèd seats unscalable
But by a patient wing, a constant spell,
Or by ethereal things that, unconfined,
Can make a ladder of the eternal wind,
And poise about in cloudy thunder-tents
To watch the abysm-birth of elements.
Ay, 'bove the withering of old-lipped Fate
30 A thousand Powers keep religious state,
In water, fiery realm, and airy bourne,

And, silent as a consecrated urn,
Hold sphery sessions for a season due.
Yet few of these far majesties – ah, few! –
Have bared their operations to this globe –
Few, who with gorgeous pageantry enrobe
Our piece of heaven – whose benevolence
Shakes hand with our own Ceres, every sense
Filling with spiritual sweets to plenitude,
40　As bees gorge full their cells. And, by the feud
'Twixt Nothing and Creation, I here swear,
Eterne Apollo! that thy Sister fair
Is of all these the gentlier-mightiest.
When thy gold breath is misting in the west,
She unobservèd steals unto her throne,
And there she sits most meek and most alone;
As if she had not pomp subservient;
As if thine eye, high Poet, was not bent
Towards her with the Muses in thine heart;
50　As if the ministering stars kept not apart,
Waiting for silver-footed messages.
O Moon! the oldest shades 'mong oldest trees
Feel palpitations when thou lookest in:
O Moon! old boughs lisp forth a holier din
The while they feel thine airy fellowship
Thou dost bless everywhere, with silver lip
Kissing dead things to life. The sleeping kine,
Couched in thy brightness, dream of fields divine:
Innumerable mountains rise, and rise,
60　Ambitious for the hallowing of thine eyes;
And yet thy benediction passeth not
One obscure hiding-place, one little spot
Where pleasure may be sent. The nested wren
Has thy fair face within its tranquil ken,
And from beneath a sheltering ivy leaf
Takes glimpses of thee; thou art a relief
To the poor patient oyster, where it sleeps
Within its pearly house. The mighty deeps,
The monstrous sea is thine – the myriad sea!

ENDYMION: BOOK III

70 O Moon! far-spooming Ocean bows to thee,
And Tellus feels his forehead's cumbrous load.

   Cynthia! where art thou now? What far abode
Of green or silvery bower doth enshrine
Such utmost beauty? Alas, thou dost pine
For one as sorrowful: thy cheek is pale
For one whose cheek is pale: thou dost bewail
His tears, who weeps for thee. Where dost thou sigh?
Ah! surely that light peeps from Vesper's eye,
Or what a thing is love! 'Tis She, but lo!
80 How changed, how full of ache, how gone in woe!
She dies at the thinnest cloud; her loveliness
Is wan on Neptune's blue: yet there's a stress
Of love-spangles, just off yon cape of trees,
Dancing upon the waves, as if to please
The curly foam with amorous influence.
O, not so idle – for down-glancing thence
She fathoms eddies, and runs wild about
O'erwhelming water-courses; scaring out
The thorny sharks from hiding-holes, and frightening
90 Their savage eyes with unaccustomed lightning.
Where will the splendour be content to reach?
O love! how potent hast thou been to teach
Strange journeyings! Wherever beauty dwells,
In gulf or eyrie, mountains or deep dells,
In light, in gloom, in star or blazing sun,
Thou pointest out the way, and straight 'tis won.
Amid his toil thou gav'st Leander breath;
Thou leddest Orpheus through the gleams of death;
Thou madest Pluto bear thin element;
100 And now, O wingèd Chieftain! thou hast sent
A moon-beam to the deep, deep water-world,
To find Endymion.
                  On gold sand impearled
With lily shells, and pebbles milky-white,
Poor Cynthia greeted him, and soothed her light
Against his pallid face: he felt the charm

To breathlessness, and suddenly a warm
Of his heart's blood. 'Twas very sweet. He stayed
His wandering steps, and half-entranced laid
His head upon a tuft of straggling weeds,
To taste the gentle moon, and freshening beads,
Lashed from the crystal roof by fishes' tails.
And so he kept, until the rosy veils
Mantling the east by Aurora's peering hand
Were lifted from the water's breast, and fanned
Into sweet air and sobered morning came
Meekly through billows – when like taper-flame
Left sudden by a dallying breath of air,
He rose in silence, and once more 'gan fare
Along his fated way.
                  Far had he roamed,
With nothing save the hollow vast, that foamed,
Above, around, and at his feet – save things
More dead than Morpheus' imaginings:
Old rusted anchors, helmets, breast-plates large
Of gone sea-warriors; brazen beaks and targe;
Rudders that for a hundred years had lost
The sway of human hand; gold vase embossed
With long-forgotten story, and wherein
No reveller had ever dipped a chin
But those of Saturn's vintage; mouldering scrolls,
Writ in the tongue of heaven, by those souls
Who first were on the earth; and sculptures rude
In ponderous stone, developing the mood
Of ancient Nox; – then skeletons of man,
Of beast, behemoth, and leviathan,
And elephant, and eagle, and huge jaw
Of nameless monster. A cold leaden awe
These secrets struck into him – and unless
Dian had chased away that heaviness,
He might have died: but now, with cheerèd feel,
He onward kept, wooing these thoughts to steal
About the labyrinth in his soul of love.

'What is there in thee, Moon! that thou shouldst move
My heart so potently? When yet a child
I oft have dried my tears when thou hast smiled.
Thou seemedst my sister: hand in hand we went
From eve to morn across the firmament.
No apples would I gather from the tree,
Till thou hadst cooled their cheeks deliciously;
No tumbling water ever spake romance,
150 But when my eyes with thine thereon could dance;
No woods were green enough, no bower divine,
Until thou liftedst up thine eyelids fine;
In sowing time ne'er would I dibble take,
Or drop a seed, till thou wast wide awake;
And, in the summer-tide of blossoming,
No one but thee hath heard me blithely sing
And mesh my dewy flowers all the night.
No melody was like a passing sprite
If it went not to solemnize thy reign.
160 Yes, in my boyhood, every joy and pain
By thee were fashioned to the self-same end,
And as I grew in years, still didst thou blend
With all my ardours: thou wast the deep glen –
Thou wast the mountain-top – the sage's pen –
The poet's harp – the voice of friends – the sun.
Thou wast the river – thou wast glory won.
Thou wast my clarion's blast – thou wast my steed –
My goblet full of wine – my topmost deed.
Thou wast the charm of women, lovely Moon!
170 O what a wild and harmonizèd tune
My spirit struck from all the beautiful!
On some bright essence could I lean, and lull
Myself to immortality: I pressed
Nature's soft pillow in a wakeful rest.
But, gentle Orb! there came a nearer bliss –
My strange love came – Felicity's abyss!
She came, and thou didst fade, and fade away –
Yet not entirely. No, thy starry sway
Has been an under-passion to this hour.

180 Now I begin to feel thine orby power
Is coming fresh upon me: O be kind,
Keep back thine influence, and do not blind
My sovereign vision. – Dearest love, forgive
That I can think away from thee and live! –
Pardon me, airy planet, that I prize
One thought beyond thine argent luxuries!
How far beyond!' At this a surprised start
Frosted the springing verdure of his heart;
For as he lifted up his eyes to swear
190 How his own goddess was past all things fair,
He saw far in the concave green of the sea
An old man sitting calm and peacefully.
Upon a weeded rock this old man sat,
And his white hair was awful, and a mat
Of weeds were cold beneath his cold thin feet;
And, ample as the largest winding-sheet,
A cloak of blue wrapped up his agèd bones,
O'erwrought with symbols by the deepest groans
Of ambitious magic: every ocean-form
200 Was woven in with black distinctness; storm,
And calm, and whispering, and hideous roar,
Quicksand, and whirlpool, and deserted shore
Were emblemed in the woof; with every shape
That skims, or dives, or sleeps, 'twixt cape and cape.
The gulfing whale was like a dot in the spell.
Yet look upon it, and 'twould size and swell
To its huge self, and the minutest fish
Would pass the very hardest gazer's wish,
And show his little eye's anatomy.
210 Then there was pictured the regality
Of Neptune, and the sea nymphs round his state,
In beauteous vassalage, look up and wait.
Beside this old man lay a pearly wand,
And in his lap a book, the which he conned
So steadfastly, that the new denizen
Had time to keep him in amazèd ken,
To mark these shadowings, and stand in awe.

The old man raised his hoary head and saw
The wildered stranger – seeming not to see,
His features were so lifeless. Suddenly
He woke as from a trance; his snow-white brows
Went arching up, and like two magic ploughs
Furrowed deep wrinkles in his forehead large,
Which kept as fixedly as rocky marge,
Till round his withered lips had gone a smile.
Then up he rose, like one whose tedious toil
Had watched for years in forlorn hermitage,
Who had not from mid-life to utmost age
Eased in one accent his o'er-burdened soul,
Even to the trees. He rose: he grasped his stole,
With convulsed clenches waving it abroad,
And in a voice of solemn joy, that awed
Echo into oblivion, he said:

'Thou art the man! Now shall I lay my head
In peace upon my watery pillow: now
Sleep will come smoothly to my weary brow.
O Jove! I shall be young again, be young!
O shell-borne Neptune, I am pierced and stung
With new-born life! What shall I do? Where go,
When I have cast this serpent-skin of woe? –
I'll swim to the syrens, and one moment listen
Their melodies, and see their long hair glisten;
Anon upon that giant's arm I'll be,
That writhes about the roots of Sicily;
To northern seas I'll in a twinkling sail,
And mount upon the snortings of a whale
To some black cloud; thence down I'll madly sweep
On forkèd lightning, to the deepest deep,
Where through some sucking pool I will be hurled
With rapture to the other side of the world!
O, I am full of gladness! Sisters three,
I bow full hearted to your old decree!
Yes, every god be thanked, and power benign,
For I no more shall wither, droop, and pine.

Thou art the man!' Endymion started back
Dismayed; and, like a wretch from whom the rack
Tortures hot breath, and speech of agony,
Muttered: 'What lonely death am I to die
In this cold region? Will he let me freeze,
And float my brittle limbs o'er polar seas?
Or will he touch me with his searing hand,
And leave a black memorial on the sand?
Or tear me piece-meal with a bony saw,
And keep me as a chosen food to draw
His magian fish through hated fire and flame?
O misery of hell! resistless, tame,
Am I to be burnt up? No, I will shout,
Until the gods through heaven's blue look out! –
O Tartarus! but some few days agone
Her soft arms were entwining me, and on
Her voice I hung like fruit among green leaves:
Her lips were all my own, and – ah, ripe sheaves
Of happiness! ye on the stubble droop,
But never may be garnered. I must stoop
My head, and kiss death's foot. Love! love, farewell!
Is there no hope from thee? This horrid spell
Would melt at thy sweet breath. – By Dian's hind
Feeding from her white fingers, on the wind
I see thy streaming hair! And now, by Pan,
I care not for this old mysterious man!'

He spake, and walking to that agèd form,
Looked high defiance. Lo! his heart 'gan warm
With pity, for the grey-haired creature wept.
Had he then wronged a heart where sorrow kept?
Had he, though blindly contumelious, brought
Rheum to kind eyes, a sting to humane thought,
Convulsion to a mouth of many years?
He had in truth; and he was ripe for tears.
The penitent shower fell, as down he knelt
Before that care-worn sage, who trembling felt
About his large dark locks, and faltering spake:

ENDYMION: BOOK III

'Arise, good youth, for sacred Phoebus' sake!
I know thine inmost bosom, and I feel
A very brother's yearning for thee steal
Into mine own. For why? Thou openest
The prison gates that have so long oppressed
My weary watching. Though thou know'st it not,
Thou art commissioned to this fated spot
For great enfranchisement. O weep no more;
I am a friend to love, to loves of yore.
Ay, hadst thou never loved an unknown power,
I had been grieving at this joyous hour.
But even now most miserable old,
I saw thee, and my blood no longer cold
Gave mighty pulses: in this tottering case
Grew a new heart, which at this moment plays
As dancingly as thine. Be not afraid,
For thou shalt hear this secret all displayed,
Now as we speed towards our joyous task.'

So saying, this young soul in age's mask
Went forward with the Carian side by side:
Resuming quickly thus, while ocean's tide
Hung swollen at their backs, and jewelled sands
Took silently their foot-prints:

'My soul stands
Now past the midway from mortality,
And so I can prepare without a sigh
To tell thee briefly all my joy and pain.
I was a fisher once, upon this main,
And my boat danced in every creek and bay.
Rough billows were my home by night and day –
The sea-gulls not more constant – for I had
No housing from the storm and tempests mad,
But hollow rocks – and they were palaces
Of silent happiness, of slumbrous ease.
Long years of misery have told me so.
Ay, thus it was one thousand years ago.
One thousand years! – Is it then possible

To look so plainly through them? to dispel
A thousand years with backward glance sublime?
To breathe away as 'twere all scummy slime
From off a crystal pool, to see its deep,
And one's own image from the bottom peep?
Yes: now I am no longer wretched thrall,
My long captivity and moanings all
Are but a slime, a thin-pervading scum,
The which I breathe away, and thronging come
Like things of yesterday my youthful pleasures.

'I touched no lute, I sang not, trod no measures:
I was a lonely youth on desert shores.
My sports were lonely, 'mid continuous roars,
And craggy isles, and sea-mew's plaintive cry
Plaining discrepant between sea and sky.
Dolphins were still my playmates; shapes unseen
Would let me feel their scales of gold and green,
Nor be my desolation; and, full oft,
When a dread waterspout had reared aloft
Its hungry hugeness, seeming ready-ripe
To burst with hoarsest thunderings, and wipe
My life away like a vast sponge of fate,
Some friendly monster, pitying my sad state,
Has dived to its foundations, gulfed it down,
And left me tossing safely. But the crown
Of all my life was utmost quietude:
More did I love to lie in cavern rude,
Keeping in wait whole days for Neptune's voice,
And if it came at last, hark, and rejoice!
There blushed no summer eve but I would steer
My skiff along green shelving coasts, to hear
The shepherd's pipe come clear from aery steep,
Mingled with ceaseless bleatings of his sheep:
And never was a day of summer shine,
But I beheld its birth upon the brine,
For I would watch all night to see unfold
Heaven's gates, and Aethon snort his morning gold

ENDYMION: BOOK III

Wide o'er the swelling streams: and constantly
At brim of day-tide, on some grassy lea,
My nets would be spread out, and I at rest.
The poor folk of the sea-country I blessed
With daily boon of fish most delicate:
370 They knew not whence this bounty, and elate
Would strew sweet flowers on a sterile beach.

'Why was I not contented? Wherefore reach
At things which, but for thee, O Latmian!
Had been my dreary death? Fool! I began
To feel distempered longings: to desire
The utmost privilege that ocean's sire
Could grant in benediction – to be free
Of all his kingdom. Long in misery
I wasted, ere in one extremest fit
380 I plunged for life or death. To interknit
One's senses with so dense a breathing stuff
Might seem a work of pain; so not enough
Can I admire how crystal-smooth it felt,
And buoyant round my limbs. At first I dwelt
Whole days and days in sheer astonishment,
Forgetful utterly of self-intent,
Moving but with the mighty ebb and flow,
Then, like a new-fledged bird that first doth show
His spreaded feathers to the morrow chill,
390 I tried in fear the pinions of my will.
'Twas freedom! and at once I visited
The ceaseless wonders of this ocean-bed.
No need to tell thee of them, for I see
That thou hast been a witness – it must be –
For these I know thou canst not feel a drouth,
By the melancholy corners of that mouth.
So I will in my story straightway pass
To more immediate matter. Woe, alas!
That love should be my bane! Ah, Scylla fair!
400 Why did poor Glaucus ever, ever dare
To sue thee to his heart? Kind stranger-youth!

I loved her to the very white of truth,
And she would not conceive it. Timid thing!
She fled me swift as sea-bird on the wing,
Round every isle, and point, and promontory,
From where large Hercules wound up his story
Far as Egyptian Nile. My passion grew
The more, the more I saw her dainty hue
Gleam delicately through the azure clear,
Until 'twas too fierce agony to bear;
And in that agony, across my grief
It flashed, that Circe might find some relief –
Cruel enchantress! So above the water
I reared my head, and looked for Phoebus' daughter.
Aeaea's isle was wondering at the moon: –
It seemed to whirl around me, and a swoon
Left me dead-drifting to that fatal power.

'When I awoke, 'twas in a twilight bower;
Just when the light of morn, with hum of bees,
Stole through its verdurous matting of fresh trees.
How sweet, and sweeter! for I heard a lyre,
And over it a sighing voice expire.
It ceased – I caught light footsteps; and anon
The fairest face that morn e'er looked upon
Pushed through a screen of roses. Starry Jove!
With tears, and smiles, and honey-words she wove
A net whose thraldom was more bliss than all
The range of flowered Elysium. Thus did fall
The dew of her rich speech: "Ah! Art awake?
O let me hear thee speak, for Cupid's sake!
I am so oppressed with joy! Why, I have shed
An urn of tears, as though thou wert cold-dead.
And now I find thee living, I will pour
From these devoted eyes their silver store,
Until exhausted of the latest drop,
So it will pleasure thee, and force thee stop
Here, that I too may live: but if beyond
Such cool and sorrowful offerings, thou art fond

ENDYMION: BOOK III

Of soothing warmth, of dalliance supreme;
If thou art ripe to taste a long love-dream;
If smiles, if dimples, tongues for ardour mute,
Hang in thy vision like a tempting fruit,
O let me pluck it for thee." Thus she linked
Her charming syllables, till indistinct
Their music came to my o'er-sweetened soul;
And then she hovered over me, and stole
So near, that if no nearer it had been
This furrowed visage thou hadst never seen.

'Young man of Latmos! thus particular
Am I, that thou mayst plainly see how far
This fierce temptation went: and thou mayst not
Exclaim, "How then, was Scylla quite forgot?"

'Who could resist? Who in this universe?
She did so breathe ambrosia; so immerse
My fine existence in a golden clime.
She took me like a child of suckling time,
And cradled me in roses. Thus condemned,
The current of my former life was stemmed,
And to this arbitrary queen of sense
I bowed a trancèd vassal: nor would thence
Have moved, even though Amphion's harp had wooed
Me back to Scylla o'er the billows rude.
For as Apollo each eve doth devise
A new apparelling for western skies,
So every eve, nay, every spendthrift hour,
Shed balmy consciousness within that bower.
And I was free of haunts umbrageous;
Could wander in the mazy forest-house
Of squirrels, foxes shy, and antlered deer,
And birds from coverts innermost and drear
Warbling for very joy mellifluous sorrow –
To me new born delights!

      'Now let me borrow,
For moments few, a temperament as stern

As Pluto's sceptre, that my words not burn
These uttering lips, while I in calm speech tell
How specious heaven was changed to real hell.

'One morn she left me sleeping: half awake
I sought for her smooth arms and lips, to slake
My greedy thirst with nectarous camel-draughts;
But she was gone. Whereat the barbèd shafts
Of disappointment stuck in me so sore,
That out I ran and searched the forest o'er.
Wandering about in pine and cedar gloom
Damp awe assailed me; for there 'gan to boom
A sound of moan, an agony of sound,
Sepulchral from the distance all around.
Then came a conquering earth-thunder, and rumbled
That fierce complain to silence, while I stumbled
Down a precipitous path, as if impelled.
I came to a dark valley. – Groanings swelled
Poisonous about my ears, and louder grew,
The nearer I approached a flame's gaunt blue,
That glared before me through a thorny brake.
This fire, like the eye of gordian snake,
Bewitched me towards, and I soon was near
A sight too fearful for the feel of fear:
In thicket hid I cursed the haggard scene –
The banquet of my arms, my arbour queen,
Seated upon an up-torn forest root;
And all around her shapes, wizard and brute,
Laughing, and wailing, grovelling, serpenting,
Showing tooth, tusk, and venom-bag, and sting!
O such deformities! Old Charon's self,
Should he give up awhile his penny pelf,
And take a dream 'mong rushes Stygian,
It could not be so phantasied. Fierce, wan,
And tyrannizing was the lady's look,
As over them a gnarlèd staff she shook.
Oft-times upon the sudden she laughed out,
And from a basket emptied to the rout

ENDYMION: BOOK III

    Clusters of grapes, the which they ravened quick
And roared for more; with many a hungry lick
About their shaggy jaws. Avenging, slow,
Anon she took a branch of mistletoe,
And emptied on't a black dull-gurgling phial –
Groaned one and all, as if some piercing trial
Was sharpening for their pitiable bones.
She lifted up the charm: appealing groans
From their poor breasts went sueing to her ear
520 In vain; remorseless as an infant's bier
She whisked against their eyes the sooty oil.
Whereat was heard a noise of painful toil,
Increasing gradual to a tempest rage,
Shrieks, yells, and groans of torture-pilgrimage;
Until their grievèd bodies 'gan to bloat
And puff from the tail's end to stiflèd throat.
Then was appalling silence: then a sight
More wildering than all that hoarse affright;
For the whole herd, as by a whirlwind writhen,
530 Went through the dismal air like one huge Python
Antagonizing Boreas – and so vanished.
Yet there was not a breath of wind: she banished
These phantoms with a nod. Lo! from the dark
Came waggish fauns, and nymphs, and satyrs stark,
With dancing and loud revelry – and went
Swifter than centaurs after rapine bent.
Sighing an elephant appeared and bowed
Before the fierce witch, speaking thus aloud
In human accent: "Potent goddess! chief
540 Of pains resistless! make my being brief,
Or let me from this heavy prison fly –
Or give me to the air, or let me die!
I sue not for my happy crown again;
I sue not for my phalanx on the plain;
I sue not for my lone, my widowed wife;
I sue not for my ruddy drops of life,
My children fair, my lovely girls and boys!
I will forget them; I will pass these joys;

176 ENDYMION: BOOK III

  Ask naught so heavenward, so too, too high:
550 Only I pray, as fairest boon, to die,
  Or be delivered from this cumbrous flesh,
  From this gross, detestable, filthy mesh,
  And merely given to the cold bleak air.
  Have mercy, Goddess! Circe, feel my prayer!"

  'That cursed magician's name fell icy numb
  Upon my wild conjecturing: truth had come
  Naked and sabre-like against my heart.
  I saw a fury whetting a death-dart;
  And my slain spirit, overwrought with fright,
560 Fainted away in that dark lair of night.
  Think, my deliverer, how desolate
  My waking must have been! disgust, and hate,
  And terrors manifold divided me
  A spoil amongst them. I prepared to flee
  Into the dungeon core of that wild wood:
  I fled three days – when lo! before me stood
  Glaring the angry witch. O Dis! even now,
  A clammy dew is beading on my brow,
  At mere remembering her pale laugh, and curse.
570 "Ha! ha! Sir Dainty! there must be a nurse
  Made of rose leaves and thistledown, express,
  To cradle thee my sweet, and lull thee – yes,
  I am too flinty-hard for thy nice touch:
  My tenderest squeeze is but a giant's clutch.
  So, fairy-thing, it shall have lullabies
  Unheard of yet: and it shall still its cries
  Upon some breast more lily-feminine.
  Oh, no – it shall not pine, and pine, and pine
  More than one pretty, trifling thousand years;
580 And then 'twere pity, but fate's gentle shears
  Cut short its immortality. Sea-flirt!
  Young dove of the waters! truly I'll not hurt
  One hair of thine: see how I weep and sigh,
  That our heart-broken parting is so nigh.
  And must we part? Ah, yes, it must be so.

ENDYMION: BOOK III

    Yet ere thou leavest me in utter woe,
Let me sob over thee my last adieus,
And speak a blessing. Mark me! Thou hast thews
Immortal, for thou art of heavenly race:
But such a love is mine, that here I chase
Eternally away from thee all bloom
Of youth, and destine thee towards a tomb.
Hence shalt thou quickly to the watery vast;
And there, ere many days be overpassed,
Disabled age shall seize thee; and even then
Thou shalt not go the way of agèd men;
But live and wither, cripple and still breathe
Ten hundred years – which gone, I then bequeath
Thy fragile bones to unknown burial.
Adieu, sweet love, adieu!" – As shot stars fall,
She fled ere I could groan for mercy. Stung
And poisoned was my spirit; despair sung
A war-song of defiance 'gainst all hell.
A hand was at my shoulder to compel
My sullen steps; another 'fore my eyes
Moved on with pointed finger. In this guise
Enforcèd, at the last by ocean's foam
I found me – by my fresh, my native home.
Its tempering coolness, to my life akin,
Came salutary as I waded in;
And, with a blind voluptuous rage, I gave
Battle to the swollen billow-ridge, and drave
Large froth before me, while there yet remained
Hale strength, nor from my bones all marrow drained.

    'Young lover, I must weep – such hellish spite
With dry cheek who can tell? While thus my might
Proving upon this element, dismayed,
Upon a dead thing's face my hand I laid.
I looked – 'twas Scylla! Cursèd, cursèd Circe!
O vulture-witch, hast never heard of mercy?
Could not thy harshest vengeance be content,
But thou must nip this tender innocent

ENDYMION: BOOK III

>   Because I loved her? – Cold, O cold indeed
>   Were her fair limbs, and like a common weed
>   The sea-swell took her hair. Dead as she was
>   I clung about her waist, nor ceased to pass
>   Fleet as an arrow through unfathomed brine,
>   Until there shone a fabric crystalline,
>   Ribbed and inlaid with coral, pebble, and pearl.
> 630 Headlong I darted; at one eager swirl
>   Gained its bright portal, entered, and behold!
>   'Twas vast, and desolate, and icy-cold;
>   And all around – But wherefore this to thee
>   Who in few minutes more thyself shalt see? –
>   I left poor Scylla in a niche and fled.
>   My fevered parchings up, my scathing dread
>   Met palsy half-way: soon these limbs became
>   Gaunt, withered, sapless, feeble, cramped, and lame.
>
>   'Now let me pass a cruel, cruel space,
> 640 Without one hope, without one faintest trace
>   Of mitigation, or redeeming bubble
>   Of coloured phantasy – for I fear 'twould trouble
>   Thy brain to loss of reason – and next tell
>   How a restoring chance came down to quell
>   One half of the witch in me.
>
>   'On a day,
>   Sitting upon a rock above the spray,
>   I saw grow up from the horizon's brink
>   A gallant vessel: soon she seemed to sink
>   Away from me again, as though her course
> 650 Had been resumed in spite of hindering force –
>   So vanished; and not long, before arose
>   Dark clouds, and muttering of winds morose.
>   Old Aeolus would stifle his mad spleen,
>   But could not: therefore all the billows green
>   Tossed up the silver spume against the clouds.
>   The tempest came: I saw that vessel's shrouds
>   In perilous bustle; while upon the deck
>   Stood trembling creatures. I beheld the wreck;

The final gulfing; the poor struggling souls:
I heard their cries amid loud thunder-rolls.
O they had all been saved but crazèd eld
Annulled my vigorous cravings: and thus quelled
And curbed, think on't, O Latmian! did I sit
Writhing with pity, and a cursing fit
Against that hell-born Circe. The crew had gone,
By one and one, to pale oblivion;
And I was gazing on the surges prone,
With many a scalding tear and many a groan,
When at my feet emerged an old man's hand,
Grasping this scroll, and this same slender wand.
I knelt with pain – reached out my hand – had grasped
These treasures – touched the knuckles – they unclasped –
I caught a finger: but the downward weight
O'erpowered me – it sank. Then 'gan abate
The storm, and through chill aguish gloom outburst
The comfortable sun. I was athirst
To search the book, and in the warming air
Parted its dripping leaves with eager care.
Strange matters did it treat of, and drew on
My soul page after page, till well-nigh won
Into forgetfulness – when, stupefied,
I read these words, and read again, and tried
My eyes against the heavens, and read again.
O what a load of misery and pain
Each Atlas-line bore off! – a shine of hope
Came gold around me, cheering me to cope
Strenuous with hellish tyranny. Attend!
For thou hast brought their promise to an end.

"*In the wide sea there lives a forlorn wretch,*
Doomed with enfeeblèd carcase to outstretch
His loathed existence through ten centuries,
And then to die alone. Who can devise
A total opposition? No one. So
One million times ocean must ebb and flow,
And he oppressèd. Yet he shall not die,

*These things accomplished. If he utterly
Scans all the depths of magic, and expounds
The meanings of all motions, shapes and sounds;
If he explores all forms and substances
Straight homeward to their symbol-essences;
He shall not die. Moreover, and in chief,
He must pursue this task of joy and grief
Most piously – all lovers tempest-tossed,
And in the savage overwhelming lost,
He shall deposit side by side, until
Time's creeping shall the dreary space fulfil:
Which done, and all these labours ripened,
A youth, by heavenly power loved and led,
Shall stand before him, whom he shall direct
How to consummate all. The youth elect
Must do the thing, or both will be destroyed."'*

'Then,' cried the young Endymion, overjoyed,
'We are twin brothers in this destiny!
Say, I entreat thee, what achievement high
Is, in this restless world, for me reserved?
What! if from thee my wandering feet had swerved,
Had we both perish'd?' – 'Look!' the sage replied,
'Dost thou not mark a gleaming through the tide,
Of diverse brilliances? 'tis the edifice
I told thee of, where lovely Scylla lies;
And where I have enshrinèd piously
All lovers, whom fell storms have doomed to die
Throughout my bondage.' Thus discoursing, on
They went till unobscured the porches shone;
Which hurryingly they gained, and entered straight.
Sure never since king Neptune held his state
Was seen such wonder underneath the stars.
Turn to some level plain where haughty Mars
Has legioned all his battle; and behold
How every soldier, with firm foot, doth hold
His even breast. See, many steelèd squares,
And rigid ranks of iron – whence who dares

One step? Imagine further, line by line,
These warrior thousands on the field supine –
So in that crystal place, in silent rows,
Poor lovers lay at rest from joys and woes.
The stranger from the mountains, breathless, traced
Such thousands of shut eyes in order placed;
Such ranges of white feet, and patient lips
740 All ruddy – for here death no blossom nips.
He marked their brows and foreheads; saw their hair
Put sleekly on one side with nicest care;
And each one's gentle wrists, with reverence,
Put cross-wise to its heart.

      'Let us commence,'
Whispered the guide, stuttering with joy, 'even now.'
He spake, and, trembling like an aspen-bough,
Began to tear his scroll in pieces small,
Uttering the while some mumblings funeral.
He tore it into pieces small as snow
750 That drifts unfeathered when bleak northerns blow;
And having done it, took his dark blue cloak
And bound it round Endymion: then stroke
His wand against the empty air times nine.
'What more there is to do, young man, is thine:
But first a little patience. First undo
This tangled thread, and wind it to a clue.
Ah, gentle! 'tis as weak as spider's skein;
And shouldst thou break it – What, is it done so clean?
A power overshadows thee! O, brave!
760 The spite of hell is tumbling to its grave.
Here is a shell; 'tis pearly blank to me,
Nor marked with any sign or charactery –
Canst thou read aught? O read for pity's sake!
Olympus! we are safe! Now, Carian, break
This wand against yon lyre on the pedestal.'

 'Twas done: and straight with sudden swell and fall
Sweet music breathed her soul away, and sighed
A lullaby to silence. 'Youth! now strew

These mincèd leaves on me, and passing through
Those files of dead, scatter the same around,
And thou wilt see the issue.'

      'Mid the sound
Of flutes and viols, ravishing his heart,
Endymion from Glaucus stood apart,
And scattered in his face some fragments light.
How lightning-swift the change! a youthful wight
Smiling beneath a coral diadem,
Out-sparkling sudden like an upturned gem,
Appeared, and, stepping to a beauteous corse,
Kneeled down beside it, and with tenderest force
Pressed its cold hand, and wept – and Scylla sighed!
Endymion, with quick hand, the charm applied –
The nymph arose. He left them to their joy,
And onward went upon his high employ,
Showering those powerful fragments on the dead.
And, as he passed, each lifted up its head,
As doth a flower at Apollo's touch.
Death felt it to his inwards – 'twas too much:
Death fell a-weeping in his charnel-house.
The Latmian persevered along, and thus
All were re-animated. There arose
A noise of harmony, pulses and throes
Of gladness in the air – while many, who
Had died in mutual arms devout and true,
Sprang to each other madly; and the rest
Felt a high certainty of being blessed.
They gazed upon Endymion. Enchantment
Grew drunken, and would have its head and bent.
Delicious symphonies, like airy flowers,
Budded, and swelled, and, full-blown, shed full showers
Of light, soft, unseen leaves of sounds divine.
The two deliverers tasted a pure wine
Of happiness, from fairy-press oozed out.
Speechless they eyed each other, and about
The fair assembly wandered to and fro,

Distracted with the richest overflow
Of joy that ever poured from heaven.

      – 'Away!'
Shouted the new born god; 'Follow, and pay
Our piety to Neptunus supreme!' –
Then Scylla, blushing sweetly from her dream,
810 They led on first, bent to her meek surprise,
Through portal columns of a giant size,
Into the vaulted, boundless emerald.
Joyous all followed as the leader called,
Down marble steps, pouring as easily
As hour-glass sand – and fast, as you might see
Swallows obeying the south summer's call,
Or swans upon a gentle waterfall.

 Thus went that beautiful multitude, nor far,
Ere from among some rocks of glittering spar,
820 Just within ken, they saw descending thick
Another multitude. Whereat more quick
Moved either host. On a wide sand they met,
And of those numbers every eye was wet,
For each their old love found. A murmuring rose,
Like what was never heard in all the throes
Of wind and waters – 'tis past human wit
To tell; 'tis dizziness to think of it.

 This mighty consummation made, the host
Moved on for many a league; and gained, and lost
830 Huge sea-marks, vanward swelling in array,
And from the rear diminishing away –
Till a faint dawn surprised them. Glaucus cried,
'Behold! behold, the palace of his pride!
God Neptune's palaces!' With noise increased,
They shouldered on towards that brightening east.
At every onward step proud domes arose
In prospect – diamond gleams, and golden glows
Of amber 'gainst their faces levelling.
Joyous, and many as the leaves in spring,

840 Still onward, still the splendour gradual swelled.
Rich opal domes were seen, on high upheld
By jasper pillars, letting through their shafts
A blush of coral. Copious wonder-draughts
Each gazer drank; and deeper drank more near.
For what poor mortals fragment up as mere
As marble, was there lavish, to the vast
Of one fair palace, that far far surpassed,
Even for common bulk, those olden three,
Memphis, and Babylon, and Nineveh.

850   As large, as bright, as coloured as the bow
Of Iris, when unfading it doth show
Beyond a silvery shower, was the arch
Through which this Paphian army took its march,
Into the outer courts of Neptune's state,
Whence could be seen, direct, a golden gate,
To which the leaders sped; but not half-raught
Ere it burst open swift as fairy thought,
And made those dazzlèd thousands veil their eyes
Like callow eagles at the first sunrise.
860 Soon with an eagle nativeness their gaze
Ripe from hue-golden swoons took all the blaze,
And then, behold! large Neptune on his throne
Of emerald deep – yet not exalt alone;
At his right hand stood wingèd Love, and on
His left sat smiling Beauty's paragon.

   Far as the mariner on highest mast
Can see all round upon the calmèd vast,
So wide was Neptune's hall: and as the blue
Doth vault the waters, so the waters drew
870 Their doming curtains, high, magnificent,
Awed from the throne aloof. And when storm-rent
Disclosed the thunder-gloomings in Jove's air
(But soothed as now), flashed sudden everywhere,
Noiseless, sub-marine cloudlets, glittering
Death to a human eye: for there did spring
From natural west, and east, and south, and north,

A light as of four sunsets, blazing forth
A gold-green zenith 'bove the Sea-God's head.
Of lucid depth the floor, and far outspread
As breezeless lake, on which the slim canoe
Of feathered Indian darts about, as through
The delicatest air – air verily,
But for the portraiture of clouds and sky:
This palace floor breath-air, but for the amaze
Of deep-seen wonders motionless and blaze
Of the dome pomp, reflected in extremes,
Globing a golden sphere.

                       They stood in dreams
Till Triton blew his horn. The palace rang;
The Nereids danced; the Sirens faintly sang;
And the great Sea-King bowed his dripping head.
Then Love took wing, and from his pinions shed
On all the multitude a nectarous dew.
The ooze-born Goddess beckonèd and drew
Fair Scylla and her guides to conference;
And when they reached the thronèd eminence
She kissed the sea-nymph's cheek – who sat her down
A-toying with the doves. Then – 'Mighty crown
And sceptre of this kingdom!' Venus said,
'Thy vows were on a time to Naïs paid –
Behold!' – Two copious tear-drops instant fell
From the God's large eyes; he smiled delectable,
And over Glaucus held his blessing hands.
'Endymion! Ah! still wandering in the bands
Of love? Now this is cruel. Since the hour
I met thee in earth's bosom, all my power
Have I put forth to serve thee. What, not yet
Escaped from dull mortality's harsh net?
A little patience, youth! 'twill not be long,
Or I am skilless quite. An idle tongue,
A humid eye, and steps luxurious,
Where these are new and strange, are ominous.
Ay, I have seen these signs in one of heaven,

When others were all blind: and were I given
To utter secrets, haply I might say
Some pleasant words – but Love will have his day.
So wait awhile expectant. Prithee soon,
E'en in the passing of thine honeymoon,
Visit thou my Cythera: thou wilt find
Cupid well-natured, my Adonis kind.
And pray persuade with thee – ah, I have done,
All blisses be upon thee, my sweet son!' –
Thus the fair goddess, while Endymion
Knelt to receive those accents halcyon.

   Meantime a glorious revelry began
Before the Water-Monarch. Nectar ran
In courteous fountains to all cups outreached;
And plundered vines, teeming exhaustless, pleached
New growth about each shell and pendent lyre;
The which, in disentangling for their fire,
Pulled down fresh foliage and coverture
For dainty toying. Cupid, empire-sure,
Fluttered and laughed, and oft-times through the throng
Made a delighted way. Then dance, and song,
And garlanding grew wild; and pleasure reigned.
In harmless tendril they each other chained,
And strove who should be smothered deepest in
Fresh crush of leaves.

              O 'tis a very sin
For one so weak to venture his poor verse
In such a place as this. O do not curse,
High Muses! let him hurry to the ending.

   All suddenly were silent. A soft blending
Of dulcet instruments came charmingly;
And then a hymn.

              'King of the stormy sea!
Brother of Jove, and co-inheritor
Of elements! Eternally before
Thee the waves awful bow. Fast, stubborn rock,

At thy feared trident shrinking, doth unlock
Its deep foundations, hissing into foam.
All mountain-rivers, lost in the wide home
Of thy capacious bosom, ever flow.
Thou frownest, and old Aeolus thy foe
Skulks to his cavern, 'mid the gruff complaint
Of all his rebel tempests. Dark clouds faint
When, from thy diadem, a silver gleam
Slants over blue dominion. Thy bright team
Gulfs in the morning light, and scuds along
To bring thee nearer to that golden song
Apollo singeth, while his chariot
Waits at the doors of heaven. Thou art not
For scenes like this: an empire stern hast thou,
And it hath furrowed that large front. Yet now,
As newly come of heaven, dost thou sit
To blend and interknit
Subduèd majesty with this glad time.
O shell-borne King sublime!
We lay our hearts before thee evermore –
We sing, and we adore!

'Breathe softly, flutes;
Be tender of your strings, ye soothing lutes;
Nor be the trumpet heard! O vain, O vain –
Not flowers budding in an April rain,
Nor breath of sleeping dove, nor river's flow –
No, nor the Aeolian twang of Love's own bow,
Can mingle music fit for the soft ear
Of goddess Cytherea!
Yet deign, white Queen of Beauty, thy fair eyes
On our souls' sacrifice.

'Bright-wingèd Child!
Who has another care when thou hast smiled?
Unfortunates on earth, we see at last
All death-shadows, and glooms that overcast
Our spirits, fanned away by thy light pinions.
O sweetest essence! sweetest of all minions!

188 ENDYMION: BOOK III

    God of warm pulses, and dishevelled hair,
    And panting bosoms bare!
    Dear unseen light in darkness! eclipser
    Of light in light! delicious poisoner!
    Thy venomed goblet will we quaff until
    We fill – we fill!
990 And by thy Mother's lips – '

                    Was heard no more
    For clamour, when the golden palace door
    Opened again, and from without, in shone
    A new magnificence. On oozy throne
    Smooth-moving came Oceanus the old,
    To take a latest glimpse at his sheep-fold,
    Before he went into his quiet cave
    To muse for ever. Then a lucid wave,
    Scooped from its trembling sisters of mid-sea,
    Afloat, and pillowing up the majesty
1000 Of Doris, and the Aegean seer, her spouse –
    Next, on a dolphin, clad in laurel boughs,
    Theban Amphion leaning on his lute:
    His fingers went across it – all were mute
    To gaze on Amphitrite, queen of pearls,
    And Thetis pearly too.

                    The palace whirls
    Around giddy Endymion, seeing he
    Was there far strayèd from mortality.
    He could not bear it – shut his eyes in vain;
    Imagination gave a dizzier pain.
1010 'O I shall die! sweet Venus, be my stay!
    Where is my lovely mistress? Well-away!
    I die – I hear her voice – I feel my wing – '
    At Neptune's feet he sank. A sudden ring
    Of Nereids were about him, in kind strife
    To usher back his spirit into life:
    But still he slept. At last they interwove
    Their cradling arms, and purposed to convey
    Towards a crystal bower far away.

    Lo! while slow carried through the pitying crowd,
1020 To his inward senses these words spake aloud;
    Written in star-light on the dark above:
    'Dearest Endymion! my entire love!
    How have I dwelt in fear of fate! 'tis done –
    Immortal bliss for me too hast thou won.
    Arise then! for the hen-dove shall not hatch
    Her ready eggs, before I'll kissing snatch
    Thee into endless heaven. Awake! awake!'

    The youth at once arose: a placid lake
    Came quiet to his eyes; and forest green,
1030 Cooler than all the wonders he had seen,
    Lulled with its simple song his fluttering breast.
    How happy once again in grassy nest!

BOOK IV

    Muse of my native land! loftiest Muse!
    O first-born on the mountains! by the hues
    Of heaven on the spiritual air begot!
    Long didst thou sit alone in northern grot,
    While yet our England was a wolfish den;
    Before our forests heard the talk of men;
    Before the first of Druids was a child,
    Long didst thou sit amid our regions wild
    Rapt in a deep prophetic solitude.
10 There came an eastern voice of solemn mood –
    Yet wast thou patient. Then sang forth the Nine,
    Apollo's garland – yet didst thou divine
    Such home-bred glory, that they cried in vain,
    'Come hither, Sister of the Island!' Plain
    Spake fair Ausonia; and once more she spake
    A higher summons – still didst thou betake
    Thee to thy native hopes. O thou hast won
    A full accomplishment! The thing is done,
    Which undone, these our latter days had risen
20 On barren souls. Great Muse, thou know'st what prison,
    Of flesh and bone, curbs, and confines, and frets

Our spirit's wings. Despondency besets
Our pillows, and the fresh tomorrow morn
Seems to give forth its light in very scorn
Of our dull, uninspired, snail-pacèd lives.
Long have I said, how happy he who shrives
To thee! But then I thought on poets gone,
And could not pray – nor could I now – so on
I move to the end in lowliness of heart.

30   'Ah, woe is me! that I should fondly part
From my dear native land! Ah, foolish maid!
Glad was the hour, when, with thee, myriads bade
Adieu to Ganges and their pleasant fields!
To one so friendless the clear freshet yields
A bitter coolness; the ripe grape is sour:
Yet I would have, great gods! but one short hour
Of native air – let me but die at home.'

Endymion to heaven's airy dome
Was offering up a hecatomb of vows,
40 When these words reached him. Whereupon he bows
His head through thorny-green entanglement
Of underwood, and to the sound is bent,
Anxious as hind towards her hidden fawn.

'Is no one near to help me? No fair dawn
Of life from charitable voice? No sweet saying
To set my dull and saddened spirit playing?
No hand to toy with mine? No lips so sweet
That I may worship them? No eyelids meet
To twinkle on my bosom? No one dies
50 Before me, till from these enslaving eyes
Redemption sparkles! – I am sad and lost.'

Thou, Carian lord, hadst better have been tossed
Into a whirlpool. Vanish into air,
Warm mountaineer! for canst thou only bear
A woman's sigh alone and in distress?
See not her charms! Is Phoebe passionless?
Phoebe is fairer far – O gaze no more. –

ENDYMION: BOOK IV

  Yet if thou wilt behold all beauty's store,
  Behold her panting in the forest grass!
60 Do not those curls of glossy jet surpass
  For tenderness the arms so idly lain
  Amongst them? Feelest not a kindred pain,
  To see such lovely eyes in swimming search
  After some warm delight, that seems to perch
  Dovelike in the dim cell lying beyond
  Their upper lids? – Hist!

        'O for Hermes' wand,
  To touch this flower into human shape!
  That woodland Hyacinthus could escape
  From his green prison, and here kneeling down
70 Call me his queen, his second life's fair crown!
  Ah me, how I could love! – My soul doth melt
  For the unhappy youth – Love! I have felt
  So faint a kindness, such a meek surrender
  To what my own full thoughts had made too tender,
  That but for tears my life had fled away! –
  Ye deaf and senseless minutes of the day,
  And thou, old forest, hold ye this for true,
  There is no lightning, no authentic dew
  But in the eye of love: there's not a sound,
80 Melodious howsoever, can confound
  The heavens and earth in one to such a death
  As doth the voice of love: there's not a breath
  Will mingle kindly with the meadow air,
  Till it has panted round, and stolen a share
  Of passion from the heart!'

         Upon a bough
  He leant, wretched. He surely cannot now
  Thirst for another love. O impious,
  That he can even dream upon it thus! –
  Thought he, 'Why am I not as are the dead,
90 Since to a woe like this I have been led
  Through the dark earth, and through the wondrous sea?
  Goddess! I love thee not the less! from thee

By Juno's smile I turn not – no, no, no –
While the great waters are at ebb and flow.
I have a triple soul! O fond pretence –
For both, for both my love is so immense,
I feel my heart is cut for them in twain.'

And so he groaned, as one by beauty slain.
The lady's heart beat quick, and he could see
Her gentle bosom heave tumultuously.
He sprang from his green covert: there she lay,
Sweet as a musk-rose upon new-made hay;
With all her limbs on tremble, and her eyes
Shut softly up alive. To speak he tries.
'Fair damsel, pity me! forgive that I
Thus violate thy bower's sanctity!
O pardon me, for I am full of grief –
Grief born of thee, young angel! fairest thief!
Who stolen hast away the wings wherewith
I was to top the heavens. Dear maid, sith
Thou art my executioner, and I feel
Loving and hatred, misery and weal,
Will in a few short hours be nothing to me,
And all my story that much passion slew me,
Do smile upon the evening of my days.
And, for my tortured brain begins to craze,
Be thou my nurse; and let me understand
How dying I shall kiss that lily hand.
Dost weep for me? Then should I be content.
Scowl on, ye fates! until the firmament
Out-blackens Erebus, and the full-caverned earth
Crumbles into itself. By the cloud girth
Of Jove, those tears have given me a thirst
To meet oblivion.' – As her heart would burst
The maiden sobbed awhile, and then replied:
'Why must such desolation betide
As that thou speak'st of? Are not these green nooks
Empty of all misfortune? Do the brooks
Utter a gorgon voice? Does yonder thrush,

ENDYMION: BOOK IV

Schooling its half-fledged little ones to brush
About the dewy forest, whisper tales? –
Speak not of grief, young stranger, or cold snails
Will slime the rose tonight. Though if thou wilt,
Methinks 'twould be a guilt – a very guilt –
Not to companion thee, and sigh away
The light – the dusk – the dark – till break of day!'
'Dear lady,' said Endymion, ''tis past.
I love thee! and my days can never last.
That I may pass in patience still speak:
Let me have music dying, and I seek
No more delight – I bid adieu to all.
Didst thou not after other climates call,
And murmur about Indian streams?' – Then she,
Sitting beneath the midmost forest tree,
For pity sang this roundelay:

    'O Sorrow,
      Why dost borrow
The natural hue of health, from vermeil lips? –
      To give maiden blushes
      To the white rose bushes?
Or is't thy dewy hand the daisy tips?

    'O Sorrow
      Why dost borrow
The lustrous passion from a falcon-eye? –
      To give the glow-worm light?
      Or, on a moonless night,
To tinge, on syren shores, the salt sea-spry?

    'O Sorrow,
      Why dost borrow
The mellow ditties from a mourning tongue? –
      To give at evening pale
      Unto the nightingale,
That thou mayst listen the cold dews among?

> 'O Sorrow,
> Why dost borrow
> Heart's lightness from the merriment of May? –
>   A lover would not tread
>   A cowslip on the head,
> Though he should dance from eve till peep of day –
>   Nor any drooping flower
>   Held sacred for thy bower,
> Wherever he may sport himself and play.
>
> 'To Sorrow,
> I bade good-morrow,
> And thought to leave her far away behind.
>   But cheerly, cheerly,
>   She loves me dearly;
> She is so constant to me, and so kind:
>   I would deceive her
>   And so leave her,
> But ah! she is so constant and so kind.
>
> 'Beneath my palm trees, by the river side,
> I sat a-weeping: in the whole world wide
> There was no one to ask me why I wept –
>   And so I kept
> Brimming the water-lily cups with tears
>   Cold as my fears.
>
> 'Beneath my palm trees, by the river side,
> I sat a-weeping: what enamoured bride,
> Cheated by shadowy wooer from the clouds,
>   But hides and shrouds
> Beneath dark palm trees by a river-side?
>
> 'And as I sat, over the light blue hills
> There came a noise of revellers: the rills
> Into the wide stream came of purple hue –
>   'Twas Bacchus and his crew!
> The earnest trumpet spake, and silver thrills
> From kissing cymbals made a merry din –
>   'Twas Bacchus and his kin!

ENDYMION: BOOK IV

200 Like to a moving vintage down they came,
     Crowned with green leaves, and faces all on flame –
     All madly dancing through the pleasant valley,
         To scare thee, Melancholy!
     O then, O then, thou wast a simple name!
     And I forgot thee, as the berried holly
     By shepherds is forgotten, when, in June,
     Tall chestnuts keep away the sun and moon –
         I rushed into the folly!

     'Within his car, aloft, young Bacchus stood,
210 Trifling his ivy-dart, in dancing mood,
         With sidelong laughing;
     And little rills of crimson wine imbrued
     His plump white arms, and shoulders, enough white
         For Venus' pearly bite;
     And near him rode Silenus on his ass,
     Pelted with flowers as he on did pass
         Tipsily quaffing.

     'Whence came ye, merry Damsels! whence came ye!
     So many, and so many, and such glee?
220 Why have ye left your bowers desolate,
         Your lutes and gentler fate? –
     "We follow Bacchus! Bacchus on the wing,
         A-conquering!
     Bacchus, young Bacchus! good or ill betide,
     We dance before him thorough kingdoms wide –
     Come hither, lady fair, and joinèd be
         To our wild minstrelsy!"

     'Whence came ye, jolly Satyrs! whence came ye!
     So many, and so many, and such glee?
230 Why have ye left your forest haunts, why left
         Your nuts in oak-tree cleft? –
     "For wine, for wine we left our kernel tree;
     For wine we left our heath, and yellow brooms,
         And cold mushrooms;
     For wine we follow Bacchus through the earth –
     Great God of breathless cups and chirping mirth!

Come hither, lady fair, and joinèd be
  To our mad minstrelsy!"

'Over wide streams and mountains great we went,
And, save when Bacchus kept his ivy tent,
Onward the tiger and the leopard pants,
  With Asian elephants:
Onward these myriads – with song and dance,
With zebras striped, and sleek Arabians' prance,
Web-footed alligators, crocodiles,
Bearing upon their scaly backs, in files,
Plump infant laughers mimicking the coil
Of seamen, and stout galley-rowers' toil –
With toying oars and silken sails they glide,
      Nor care for wind and tide.

'Mounted on panthers' furs and lions' manes,
From rear to van they scour about the plains;
A three days' journey in a moment done:
And always, at the rising of the sun,
About the wilds they hunt with spear and horn,
      On spleenful unicorn.

'I saw Osirian Egypt kneel adown
    Before the vine-wreath crown!
I saw parched Abyssinia rouse and sing
    To the silver cymbals' ring!
I saw the whelming vintage hotly pierce
    Old Tartary the fierce!
The kings of Ind their jewel-sceptres vail,
And from their treasures scatter pearlèd hail.
Great Brahma from his mystic heaven groans,
    And all his priesthood moans;
Before young Bacchus' eye-wink turning pale. –
Into these regions came I following him,
Sick hearted, weary – so I took a whim
To stray away into these forests drear
    Alone, without a peer:
And I have told thee all thou mayest hear.

ENDYMION: BOOK IV

'Young stranger!
I've been a ranger
In search of pleasure throughout every clime:
Alas, 'tis not for me!
Bewitched I sure must be,
To lose in grieving all my maiden prime.

'Come then, Sorrow!
Sweetest Sorrow!
Like an own babe I nurse thee on my breast:
I thought to leave thee
And deceive thee,
But now of all the world I love thee best.

'There is not one,
No, no, not one
But thee to comfort a poor lonely maid:
Thou art her mother,
And her brother,
Her playmate, and her wooer in the shade.'

O what a sigh she gave in finishing,
And look, quite dead to every worldly thing!
Endymion could not speak, but gazed on her;
And listened to the wind that now did stir
About the crispèd oaks full drearily,
Yet with as sweet a softness as might be
Remembered from its velvet summer song.
At last he said: 'Poor lady, how thus long
Have I been able to endure that voice?
Fair Melody! kind Siren! I've no choice —
I must be thy sad servant evermore:
I cannot choose but kneel here and adore.
Alas, I must not think — by Phoebe, no!
Let me not think, soft Angel! shall it be so?
Say, beautifullest, shall I never think?
O thou couldst foster me beyond the brink
Of recollection! make my watchful care
Close up its bloodshot eyes, nor see despair!

Do gently murder half my soul, and I
Shall feel the other half so utterly! –
I'm giddy at that cheek so fair and smooth;
O let it blush so ever! let it soothe
My madness! let it mantle rosy-warm
With the tinge of love, panting in safe alarm. –
This cannot be thy hand, and yet it is;
And this is sure thine other softling – this
Thine own fair bosom, and I am so near!
Wilt fall asleep? O let me sip that tear!
And whisper one sweet word that I may know
This is this world – sweet dewy blossom!' – '*Woe!
Woe! Woe to that Endymion! Where is he?*' –
Even these words went echoing dismally
Through the wide forest – a most fearful tone,
Like one repenting in his latest moan;
And while it died away a shade passed by,
As of thunder-cloud. When arrows fly
Through the thick branches, poor ring-doves sleek forth
Their timid necks and tremble; so these both
Leant to each other trembling, and sat so
Waiting for some destruction – when lo,
Foot-feathered Mercury appeared sublime
Beyond the tall tree tops; and in less time
Than shoots the slanted hail-storm, down he dropped
Towards the ground, but rested not, nor stopped
One moment from his home: only the sward
He with his wand light touched, and heavenward
Swifter than sight was gone – even before
The teeming earth a sudden witness bore
Of his swift magic. Diving swans appear
Above the crystal circlings white and clear;
And catch the cheated eye in wide surprise,
How they can dive in sight and unseen rise –
So from the turf outsprang two steeds jet-black,
Each with large dark blue wings upon his back.
The youth of Caria placed the lovely dame
On one, and felt himself in spleen to tame

The other's fierceness. Through the air they flew,
High as the eagles. Like two drops of dew
Exhaled to Phoebus' lips, away they're gone,
Far from the earth away – unseen, alone,
Among cool clouds and winds, but that the free,
The buoyant life of song can floating be
Above their heads, and follow them untired. –
Muse of my native land, am I inspired?
This is the giddy air, and I must spread
Wide pinions to keep here; nor do I dread
Or height, or depth, or width, or any chance
Precipitous. I have beneath my glance
Those towering horses and their mournful freight.
Could I thus sail, and see, and thus await
Fearless for power of thought, without thine aid?

There is a sleepy dusk, an odorous shade
From some approaching wonder, and behold
Those wingèd steeds, with snorting nostrils bold,
Snuff at its faint extreme, and seem to tire,
Dying to embers from their native fire!

There curled a purple mist around them; soon,
It seemed as when around the pale new moon
Sad Zephyr droops the clouds like weeping willow –
'Twas Sleep slow journeying with head on pillow.
For the first time, since he came nigh dead-born
From the old womb of night, his cave forlorn
Had he left more forlorn; for the first time,
He felt aloof the day and morning's prime –
Because into his depth Cimmerian
There came a dream, showing how a young man,
Ere a lean bat could plump its wintry skin,
Would at high Jove's empyreal footstool win
An immortality, and how espouse
Jove's daughter, and be reckoned of his house.
Now was he slumbering towards heaven's gate,
That he might at the threshold one hour wait
To hear the marriage melodies, and then

Sink downward to his dusky cave again.
His litter of smooth semi-lucent mist,
Diversely tinged with rose and amethyst,
Puzzled those eyes that for the centre sought;
And scarcely for one moment could be caught
His sluggish form reposing motionless.
390 Those two on wingèd steeds, with all the stress
Of vision searched for him, as one would look
Athwart the sallows of a river nook
To catch a glance at silver-throated eels –
Or from old Skiddaw's top, when fog conceals
His rugged forehead in a mantle pale,
With an eye-guess towards some pleasant vale
Descry a favourite hamlet faint and far.

These raven horses, though they fostered are
Of earth's splenetic fire, dully drop
400 Their full-veined ears, nostrils blood wide, and stop.
Upon the spiritless mist have they outspread
Their ample feathers, are in slumber dead –
And on those pinions, level in mid-air,
Endymion sleepeth and the lady fair.
Slowly they sail, slowly as icy isle
Upon a calm sea drifting: and meanwhile
The mournful wanderer dreams. Behold! he walks
On heaven's pavement; brotherly he talks
To divine powers; from his hand full fain
410 Juno's proud birds are pecking pearly grain;
He tries the nerve of Phoebus' golden bow,
And asketh where the golden apples grow;
Upon his arm he braces Pallas' shield,
And strives in vain to unsettle and wield
A Jovian thunderbolt; arch Hebe brings
A full-brimmed goblet, dances lightly, sings
And tantalizes long; at last he drinks,
And lost in pleasure at her feet he sinks,
Touching with dazzled lips her starlight hand.
420 He blows a bugle – an ethereal band

Are visible above: the Seasons four –
Green-kirtled Spring, flush Summer, golden store
In Autumn's sickle, Winter frosty hoar –
Join dance with shadowy Hours; while still the blast,
In swells unmitigated, still doth last
To sway their floating morris. 'Whose is this?
Whose bugle?' he inquires. They smile – 'O Dis!
Why is this mortal here? Dost thou not know
Its mistress' lips? Not thou? – 'Tis Dian's: lo!
430 She rises crescented!' He looks, 'tis she,
His very goddess: good-bye earth, and sea,
And air, and pains, and care, and suffering;
Good-bye to all but love! Then doth he spring
Towards her, and awakes – and, strange, o'erhead,
Of those same fragrant exhalations bred,
Beheld awake his very dream: the gods
Stood smiling; merry Hebe laughs and nods;
And Phoebe bends towards him crescented.
O state perplexing! On the pinion bed,
440 Too well awake, he feels the panting side
Of his delicious lady. He who died
For soaring too audacious in the sun,
When that same treacherous wax began to run,
Felt not more tongue-tied than Endymion.
His heart leapt up as to its rightful throne,
To that fair shadowed passion pulsed its way –
Ah, what perplexity! Ah, welladay!
So fond, so beauteous was his bed-fellow,
He could not help but kiss her: then he grew
450 Awhile forgetful of all beauty save
Young Phoebe's, golden haired; and so 'gan crave
Forgiveness: yet he turned once more to look
At the sweet sleeper – all his soul was shook:
She pressed his hand in slumber; so once more
He could not help but kiss her and adore.
At this the shadow wept, melting away.
The Latmian started up: 'Bright goddess, stay!
Search my most hidden breast! By truth's own tongue,

ENDYMION: BOOK IV

I have no daedal heart. Why is it wrung
460 To desperation? Is there naught for me,
Upon the bourne of bliss, but misery?'

These words awoke the stranger of dark tresses:
Her dawning love-look rapt Endymion blesses
With 'haviour soft. Sleep yawned from underneath.
'Thou swan of Ganges, let us no more breathe
This murky phantasm! thou contented seemst
Pillowed in lovely idleness, nor dream'st
What horrors may discomfort thee and me.
Ah, shouldst thou die from my heart-treachery! –
470 Yet did she merely weep – her gentle soul
Hath no revenge in it. As it is whole
In tenderness, would I were whole in love!
Can I prize thee, fair maid, all price above,
Even when I feel as true as innocence?
I do, I do. – What is this soul then? Whence
Came it? It does not seem my own, and I
Have no self-passion or identity.
Some fearful end must be: where, where is it?
By Nemesis, I see my spirit flit
480 Alone about the dark. Forgive me, sweet –
Shall we away?' He roused the steeds: they beat
Their wings chivàlrous into the clear air,
Leaving old Sleep within his vapoury lair.

The good-night blush of eve was waning slow,
And Vesper, risen star, began to throe
In the dusk heavens silverly, when they
Thus sprang direct towards the Galaxy.
Nor did speed hinder converse soft and strange –
Eternal oaths and vows they interchange,
490 In such wise, in such temper, so aloof
Up in the winds, beneath a starry roof,
So witless of their doom, that verily
'Tis well nigh past man's search their hearts to see,
Whether they wept, or laughed, or grieved, or toyed –
Most like with joy gone mad, with sorrow cloyed.

Full facing their swift flight, from ebon streak,
The moon put forth a little diamond peak,
No bigger than an unobservèd star,
Or tiny point of fairy scimitar;
Bright signal that she only stooped to tie
Her silver sandals, ere deliciously
She bowed into the heavens her timid head.
Slowly she rose, as though she would have fled,
While to his lady meek the Carian turned,
To mark if her dark eyes had yet discerned
This beauty in its birth – Despair! despair!
He saw her body fading gaunt and spare
In the cold moonshine. Straight he seized her wrist;
It melted from his grasp: her hand he kissed,
And, horror! kissed his own – he was alone.
Her steed a little higher soared, and then
Dropped hawkwise to the earth.

       There lies a den,
Beyond the seeming confines of the space
Made for the soul to wander in and trace
Its own existence, of remotest glooms.
Dark regions are around it, where the tombs
Of buried griefs the spirit sees, but scarce
One hour doth linger weeping, for the pierce
Of new-born woe it feels more inly smart:
And in these regions many a venomed dart
At random flies; they are the proper home
Of every ill: the man is yet to come
Who hath not journeyed in this native hell.
But few have ever felt how calm and well
Sleep may be had in that deep den of all.
There anguish does not sting; nor pleasure pall:
Woe-hurricanes beat ever at the gate,
Yet all is still within and desolate.
Beset with plainful gusts, within ye hear
No sound so loud as when on curtained bier
The death-watch tick is stifled. Enter none

Who strive therefore: on the sudden it is won.
Just when the sufferer begins to burn,
Then it is free to him; and from an urn,
Still fed by melting ice, he takes a draught –
Young Semele such richness never quaffed
In her maternal longing! Happy gloom!
Dark Paradise! where pale becomes the bloom
Of health by due; where silence dreariest
540 Is most articulate; where hopes infest;
Where those eyes are the brightest far that keep
Their lids shut longest in a dreamless sleep.
O happy spirit-home! O wondrous soul!
Pregnant with such a den to save the whole
In thine own depth. Hail, gentle Carian!
For, never since thy griefs and woes began,
Hast thou felt so content: a grievous feud
Hath led thee to this Cave of Quietude.
Ay, his lulled soul was there, although upborne
550 With dangerous speed, and so he did not mourn
Because he knew not whither he was going.
So happy was he, not the aerial blowing
Of trumpets at clear parley from the east
Could rouse from that fine relish, that high feast.
They stung the feathered horse: with fierce alarm
He flapped towards the sound. Alas, no charm
Could lift Endymion's head, or he had viewed
A skyey masque, a pinioned multitude –
And silvery was its passing. Voices sweet
560 Warbling the while as if to lull and greet
The wanderer in his path. Thus warbled they,
While past the vision went in bright array.

'Who, who from Dian's feast would be away?
For all the golden bowers of the day
Are empty left? Who, who away would be
From Cynthia's wedding and festivity?
Not Hesperus – lo! upon his silver wings
He leans away for highest heaven and sings,

Snapping his lucid fingers merrily! –
Ah, Zephyrus! art here, and Flora too
Ye tender bibbers of the rain and dew,
Young playmates of the rose and daffodil,
Be careful, ere ye enter in, to fill
    Your baskets high
With fennel green, and balm, and golden pines,
Savory, latter-mint, and columbines,
Cool parsley, basil sweet, and sunny thyme –
Yea, every flower and leaf of every clime,
All gathered in the dewy morning. Hie
    Away! fly, fly! –
Crystalline brother of the belt of heaven,
Aquarius! to whom king Jove has given
Two liquid pulse streams 'stead of feathered wings,
Two fan-like fountains – thine illuminings
    For Dian play:
Dissolve the frozen purity of air;
Let thy white shoulders silvery and bare
Show cold through watery pinions; make more bright
The Star-Queen's crescent on her marriage night.
    Haste, haste away! –
Castor has tamed the planet Lion, see!
And of the Bear has Pollux mastery.
A third is in the race! who is the third
Speeding away swift as the eagle bird?
    The ramping Centaur!
The Lion's mane's on end – the Bear how fierce!
The Centaur's arrow ready seems to pierce
Some enemy – far forth his bow is bent
Into the blue of heaven. He'll be shent,
    Pale unrelenter,
When he shall hear the wedding lutes a-playing! –
Andromeda! sweet woman! why delaying
So timidly among the stars? Come hither!
Join this bright throng, and nimbly follow whither
    They all are going.
Danae's Son, before Jove newly bowed,

206 ENDYMION: BOOK IV

  Has wept for thee, calling to Jove aloud.
  Thee, gentle lady, did he disenthrall:
  Ye shall for ever live and love, for all
610   Thy tears are flowing. –
  By Daphne's fright, behold Apollo! – '
              More
  Endymion heard not: down his steed him bore,
  Prone to the green head of a misty hill.

   His first touch of the earth went nigh to kill.
  'Alas!' said he, 'were I but always borne
  Through dangerous winds, had but my footsteps worn
  A path in hell, for ever would I bless
  Horrors which nourish an uneasiness
  For my own sullen conquering: to him
620   Who lives beyond earth's boundary, grief is dim,
  Sorrow is but a shadow. Now I see
  The grass, I feel the solid ground – Ah, me!
  It is thy voice – divinest! Where? – who? who
  Left thee so quiet on this bed of dew?
  Behold upon this happy earth we are;
  Let us aye love each other; let us fare
  On forest-fruits, and never, never go
  Among the abodes of mortals here below,
  Or be by phantoms duped. O destiny!
630   Into a labyrinth now my soul would fly,
  But with thy beauty will I deaden it.
  Where didst thou melt to? By thee will I sit
  For ever: let our fate stop here – a kid
  I on this spot will offer. Pan will bid
  Us live in peace, in love and peace among
  His forest wildernesses. I have clung
  To nothing, loved a nothing, nothing seen
  Or felt but a great dream! O I have been
  Presumptuous against love, against the sky,
640   Against all elements, against the tie
  Of mortals each to each, against the blooms
  Of flowers, rush of rivers, and the tombs

ENDYMION: BOOK IV

    Of heroes gone! Against his proper glory
Has my own soul conspired: so my story
Will I to children utter, and repent.
There never lived a mortal man, who bent
His appetite beyond his natural sphere,
But starved and died. My sweetest Indian, here,
Here will I kneel, for thou redeemèd hast
650 My life from too thin breathing: gone and past
Are cloudy phantasms. Caverns lone, farewell!
And air of visions, and the monstrous swell
Of visionary seas! No, never more
Shall airy voices cheat me to the shore
Of tangled wonder, breathless and aghast.
Adieu, my daintiest Dream! although so vast
My love is still for thee. The hour may come
When we shall meet in pure elysium.
On earth I may not love thee; and therefore
660 Doves will I offer up, and sweetest store
All through the teeming year: so thou wilt shine
On me, and on this damsel fair of mine,
And bless our simple lives. My Indian bliss!
My river-lily bud! one human kiss!
One sigh of real breath – one gentle squeeze,
Warm as a dove's nest among summer trees,
And warm with dew at ooze from living blood!
Whither didst melt? Ah, what of that! – all good
We'll talk about – no more of dreaming. – Now,
670 Where shall our dwelling be? Under the brow
Of some steep mossy hill, where ivy dun
Would hide us up, although spring leaves were none,
And where dark yew trees, as we rustle through,
Will drop their scarlet berry cups of dew?
O thou wouldst joy to live in such a place;
Dusk for our loves, yet light enough to grace
Those gentle limbs on mossy bed reclined:
For by one step the blue sky shouldst thou find,
And by another, in deep dell below,
680 See, through the trees, a little river go

208 ENDYMION: BOOK IV

  All in its mid-day gold and glimmering.
Honey from out the gnarlèd hive I'll bring,
And apples, wan with sweetness, gather thee,
Cresses that grow where no man may them see,
And sorrel untorn by the dew-clawed stag:
Pipes will I fashion of the syrinx flag,
That thou mayst always know whither I roam,
When it shall please thee in our quiet home
To listen and think of love. Still let me speak;
690 Still let me dive into the joy I seek –
For yet the past doth prison me. The rill,
Thou haply mayst delight in, will I fill
With fairy fishes from the mountain tarn,
And thou shalt feed them from the squirrel's barn.
Its bottom will I strew with amber shells,
And pebbles blue from deep enchanted wells.
Its sides I'll plant with dew-sweet eglantine,
And honeysuckles full of clear bee-wine.
I will entice this crystal rill to trace
700 Love's silver name upon the meadow's face.
I'll kneel to Vesta, for a flame of fire;
And to god Phoebus, for a golden lyre;
To Empress Dian, for a hunting spear;
To Vesper, for a taper silver-clear,
That I may see thy beauty through the night;
To Flora, and a nightingale shall light
Tame on thy finger; to the River-gods,
And they shall bring thee taper fishing-rods
Of gold, and lines of Naiads' long bright tress.
710 Heaven shield thee for thine utter loveliness!
Thy mossy footstool shall the altar be
'Fore which I'll bend, bending, dear love, to thee:
Those lips shall be my Delphos, and shall speak
Laws to my footsteps, colour to my cheek,
Trembling or steadfastness to this same voice,
And of three sweetest pleasurings the choice:
And that affectionate light, those diamond things,
Those eyes, those passions, those supreme pearl springs,

Shall be my grief, or twinkle me to pleasure.
Say, is not bliss within our perfect seizure?
O that I could not doubt!'

              The mountaineer
Thus strove by fancies vain and crude to clear
His briared path to some tranquillity.
It gave bright gladness to his lady's eye,
And yet the tears she wept were tears of sorrow;
Answering thus, just as the golden morrow
Beamed upward from the valleys of the east:
'O that the flutter of this heart had ceased,
Or the sweet name of love had passed away.
Young feathered tyrant! by a swift decay
Wilt thou devote this body to the earth:
And I do think that at my very birth
I lisped thy blooming titles inwardly,
For at the first, first dawn and thought of thee,
With uplift hands I blest the stars of heaven.
Art thou not cruel? Ever have I striven
To think thee kind, but ah, it will not do!
When yet a child, I heard that kisses drew
Favour from thee, and so I kisses gave
To the void air, bidding them find out love:
But when I came to feel how far above
All fancy, pride, and fickle maidenhood,
All earthly pleasure, all imagined good,
Was the warm tremble of a devout kiss –
Even then, that moment, at the thought of this,
Fainting I fell into a bed of flowers,
And languished there three days. Ye milder powers,
Am I not cruelly wronged? Believe, believe
Me, dear Endymion, were I to weave
With my own fancies garlands of sweet life,
Thou shouldst be one of all. Ah, bitter strife!
I may not be thy love: I am forbidden –
Indeed I am – thwarted, affrighted, chidden,
By things I trembled at, and gorgon wrath.

Twice hast thou asked whither I went. Henceforth
Ask me no more! I may not utter it,
Nor may I be thy love. We might commit
Ourselves at once to vengeance; we might die;
We might embrace and die – voluptuous thought!
760 Enlarge not to my hunger, or I'm caught
In trammels of perverse deliciousness.
No, no, that shall not be: thee will I bless,
And bid a long adieu.'

The Carian
No word returned: both lovelorn, silent, wan,
Into the valleys green together went.
Far wandering, they were perforce content
To sit beneath a fair lone beechen tree;
Nor at each other gazed, but heavily
770 Pored on its hazel cirque of shedded leaves.

Endymion! unhappy! it nigh grieves
Me to behold thee thus in last extreme –
Enskied ere this, but truly that I deem
Truth the best music in a first-born song.
Thy lute-voiced brother will I sing ere long,
And thou shalt aid – hast thou not aided me?
Yes, moonlight Emperor! felicity
Has been thy meed for many thousand years;
Yet often have I, on the brink of tears,
Mourned as if yet thou wert a forester –
780 Forgetting the old tale.

He did not stir
His eyes from the dead leaves, or one small pulse
Of joy he might have felt. The spirit culls
Unfaded amaranth, when wild it strays
Through the old garden-ground of boyish days.
A little onward ran the very stream
By which he took his first soft poppy dream;
And on the very bark 'gainst which he leant
A crescent he had carved, and round it spent

His skill in little stars. The teeming tree
790 Had swollen and greened the pious charactery,
But not ta'en out. Why, there was not a slope
Up which he had not feared the antelope;
And not a tree, beneath whose rooty shade
He had not with his tamèd leopards played;
Nor could an arrow light, or javelin,
Fly in the air where his had never been –
And yet he knew it not.

      O treachery!
Why does his lady smile, pleasing her eye
With all his sorrowing? He sees her not.
800 But who so stares on him? His sister sure!
Peona of the woods! – Can she endure –
Impossible! how dearly they embrace!
His lady smiles, delight is in her face –
It is no treachery.

      'Dear brother mine!
Endymion, weep not so! Why shouldst thou pine
When all great Latmos so exalt will be?
Thank the great gods, and look not bitterly;
And speak not one pale word, and sigh no more.
Sure I will not believe thou hast such store
810 Of grief, to last thee to my kiss again.
Thou surely canst not bear a mind in pain,
Come hand in hand with one so beautiful.
Be happy both of you! for I will pull
The flowers of autumn for your coronals.
Pan's holy priest for young Endymion calls;
And when he is restored, thou, fairest dame,
Shalt be our queen. Now, is it not a shame
To see ye thus – not very, very sad?
Perhaps ye are too happy to be glad:
820 O feel as if it were a common day,
Free-voiced as one who never was away.
No tongue shall ask, "Whence come ye?", but ye shall
Be gods of your own rest imperial.

Not even I, for one whole month, will pry
Into the hours that have passed us by,
Since in my arbour I did sing to thee.
O Hermes! on this very night will be
A hymning up to Cynthia, queen of light;
For the soothsayers old saw yesternight
830 Good visions in the air – whence will befall,
As say these sages, health perpetual
To shepherds and their flocks; and furthermore,
In Dian's face they read the gentle lore:
Therefore for her these vesper-carols are.
Our friends will all be there from nigh and far.
Many upon thy death have ditties made;
And many, even now, their foreheads shade
With cypress, on a day of sacrifice.
New singing for our maids shalt thou devise,
840 And pluck the sorrow from our huntsmen's brows.
Tell me, my lady-queen, how to espouse
This wayward brother to his rightful joys!
His eyes are on thee bent, as thou didst poise
His fate most goddess-like. Help me, I pray,
To lure – Endymion! dear brother, say
What ails thee?' He could bear no more, and so
Bent his soul fiercely like a spiritual bow,
And twanged it inwardly, and calmly said:
'I would have thee my only friend, sweet maid!
850 My only visitor! not ignorant though,
That those deceptions which for pleasure go
'Mong men, are pleasures real as real may be:
But there are higher ones I may not see,
If impiously an earthly realm I take.
Since I saw thee, I have been wide awake
Night after night, and day by day, until
Of the empyrean I have drunk my fill.
Let it content thee, Sister, seeing me
More happy than betides mortality.
860 A hermit young, I'll live in mossy cave,
Where thou alone shalt come to me, and lave

ENDYMION: BOOK IV

Thy spirit in the wonders I shall tell.
Through me the shepherd realm shall prosper well,
For to thy tongue will I all health confide.
And, for my sake, let this young maid abide
With thee as a dear sister. Thou alone,
Peona, mayst return to me. I own
This may sound strangely: but when, dearest girl,
Thou seest it for my happiness, no pearl
Will trespass down those cheeks. Companion fair!
Wilt be content to dwell with her, to share
This sister's love with me?' Like one resigned
And bent by circumstance, and thereby blind
In self-commitment, thus that meek unknown:
'Ay, but a buzzing by my ears has flown,
Of jubilee to Dian – truth I heard?
Well then I see there is no little bird,
Tender soever, but is Jove's own care,
Long have I sought for rest, and, unaware,
Behold I find it! so exalted too!
So after my own heart! I knew, I knew
There was a place untenanted in it:
In that same void white Chastity shall sit,
And monitor me nightly to lone slumber.
With sanest lips I vow me to the number
Of Dian's sisterhood; and, kind lady,
With thy good help, this very night shall see
My future days to her fane consecrate.'

As feels a dreamer what doth most create
His own particular fright, so these three felt;
Or like one who, in after ages, knelt
To Lucifer or Baal, when he'd pine
After a little sleep; or when in mine
Far underground, a sleeper meets his friends
Who know him not. Each diligently bends
Towards common thoughts and things for very fear;
Striving their ghastly malady to cheer,
By thinking it a thing of yes and no,

ENDYMION: BOOK IV

That housewives talk of. But the spirit-blow
Was struck, and all were dreamers. At the last
Endymion said: 'Are not our fates all cast?
Why stand we here? Adieu, ye tender pair!
Adieu!' Whereat those maidens, with wild stare,
Walked dizzily away. Painèd and hot
His eyes went after them, until they got
Near to a cypress grove, whose deadly maw,
In one swift moment, would what then he saw
Engulf for ever. 'Stay!' he cried, 'ah, stay!
Turn, damsels! hist! one word I have to say.
Sweet Indian, I would see thee once again.
It is a thing I dote on: so I'd fain,
Peona, ye should hand in hand repair
Into those holy groves, that silent are
Behind great Dian's temple. I'll be yon,
At Vesper's earliest twinkle – they are gone –
But once, once, once again – ' At this he pressed
His hands against his face, and then did rest
His head upon a mossy hillock green,
And so remained as he a corpse had been
All the long day, save when he scantly lifted
His eyes abroad, to see how shadows shifted
With the slow move of time – sluggish and weary
Until the poplar tops, in journey dreary,
Had reached the river's brim. Then up he rose,
And, slowly as that very river flows,
Walked towards the temple grove with this lament:
'Why such a golden eve? The breeze is sent
Careful and soft, that not a leaf may fall
Before the serene father of them all
Bows down his summer head below the west.
Now am I of breath, speech, and speed possessed,
But at the setting I must bid adieu
To her for the last time. Night will strew
On the damp grass myriads of lingering leaves,
And with them shall I die; nor much it grieves
To die, when summer dies on the cold sward.

ENDYMION: BOOK IV

    Why, I have been a butterfly, a lord
Of flowers, garlands, love-knots, silly posies,
Groves, meadows, melodies, and arbour roses.
940 My kingdom's at its death, and just it is
That I should die with it: so in all this
We miscall grief, bale, sorrow, heartbreak, woe,
What is there to plain of? By Titan's foe
I am but rightly served.' So saying, he
Tripped lightly on, in sort of deathful glee,
Laughing at the clear stream and setting sun,
As though they jests had been: nor had he done
His laugh at nature's holy countenance,
Until that grove appeared, as if perchance,
950 And then his tongue with sober seemlihed
Gave utterance as he entered: 'Ha! I said,
"King of the butterflies", but by this gloom,
And by old Rhadamanthus' tongue of doom,
This dusk religion, pomp of solitude,
And the Promethean clay by thief endued,
By old Saturnus' forelock, by his head
Shook with eternal palsy, I did wed
Myself to things of light from infancy;
And thus to be cast out, thus lorn to die,
960 Is sure enough to make a mortal man
Grow impious.' So he inwardly began
On things for which no wording can be found,
Deeper and deeper sinking, until drowned
Beyond the reach of music: for the choir
Of Cynthia he heard not, though rough briar
Nor muffling thicket interposed to dull
The vesper hymn, far swollen, soft and full,
Through the dark pillars of those sylvan aisles.
He saw not the two maidens, nor their smiles,
970 Wan as primroses gathered at midnight
By chilly-fingered spring. 'Unhappy wight!
Endymion!' said Peona, 'we are here!
What wouldst thou ere we all are laid on bier?'
Then he embraced her, and his lady's hand

Pressed, saying: 'Sister, I would have command,
If it were heaven's will, on our sad fate.'
At which that dark-eyed stranger stood elate
And said, in a new voice, but sweet as love,
To Endymion's amaze: 'By Cupid's dove,
And so thou shalt! and by the lily truth
Of my own breast thou shalt, belovèd youth!'
And as she spake, into her face there came
Light, as reflected from a silver flame:
Her long black hair swelled ampler, in display
Full golden; in her eyes a brighter day
Dawned blue and full of love. Ay, he beheld
Phoebe, his passion! Joyous she upheld
Her lucid bow, continuing thus: 'Drear, drear
Has our delaying been; but foolish fear
Withheld me first; and then decrees of fate;
And then 'twas fit that from this mortal state
Thou shouldst, my love, by some unlooked for change
Be spiritualized. Peona, we shall range
These forests, and to thee they safe shall be
As was thy cradle; hither shalt thou flee
To meet us many a time.' Next Cynthia bright
Peona kissed, and blessed with fair good-night:
Her brother kissed her too, and knelt adown
Before his goddess, in a blissful swoon.
She gave her fair hands to him, and behold,
Before three swiftest kisses he had told,
They vanished far away! – Peona went
Home through the gloomy wood in wonderment.

'*In drear-nighted December*'

I

In drear-nighted December,
    Too happy, happy tree,
Thy branches ne'er remember
    Their green felicity:
  The north cannot undo them,
  With a sleety whistle through them,
  Nor frozen thawings glue them
    From budding at the prime.

II

In drear-nighted December,
    Too happy, happy brook,
Thy bubblings ne'er remember
    Apollo's summer look;
But with a sweet forgetting,
They stay their crystal fretting,
Never, never petting
    About the frozen time.

III

Ah! would 'twere so with many
    A gentle girl and boy!
But were there ever any
    Writhed not of passèd joy?
The feel of not to feel it,
When there is none to heal it,
Nor numbèd sense to steel it,
    Was never said in rhyme.

Nebuchadnezzar's Dream

Before he went to live with owls and bats
    Nebuchadnezzar had an ugly dream,
    Worse than a housewife's when she thinks her cream
Made a naumachia for mice and rats.

So scared, he sent for that 'Good King of Cats',
   Young Daniel, who straightway did pluck the beam
   From out his eye, and said 'I do not deem
Your sceptre worth a straw – your cushion old door-mats'.
A horrid nightmare similar somewhat
10   Of late has haunted a most valiant crew
     Of loggerheads and chapmen – we are told
That any Daniel though he be a sot
   Can make their lying lips turn pale of hue
     By drawling out, 'Ye are that head of Gold.'

Apollo to the Graces

APOLLO
   Which of the fairest three
   Today will ride with me?
My steeds are all pawing on the thresholds of Morn:
   Which of the fairest three
   Today will ride with me
Across the gold Autumn's whole kingdoms of corn?

THE GRACES *all answer*
   I will, I – I – I –
O young Apollo let me fly along with thee,
   I will, I – I – I,
10   The many, many wonders see –
   I – I – I – I –
And thy lyre shall never have a slackened string.
   I – I – I – I
Thro' the whole day will sing.

To Mrs Reynolds's Cat

Cat! who hast passed thy grand climacteric,
   How many mice and rats hast in thy days
   Destroyed? How many tit-bits stolen? Gaze

With those bright languid segments green, and prick
Those velvet ears – but prithee do not stick
   Thy latent talons in me, and up-raise
   Thy gentle mew, and tell me all thy frays
Of fish and mice, and rats and tender chick.
Nay, look not down, nor lick thy dainty wrists –
10   For all the wheezy asthma, and for all
Thy tail's tip is nicked off, and though the fists
   Of many a maid have given thee many a maul,
Still is that fur as soft as when the lists
   In youth thou enteredst on glass-bottled wall.

On Seeing a Lock of Milton's Hair. Ode

   Chief of organic numbers!
      Old scholar of the spheres!
   Thy spirit never slumbers,
      But rolls about our ears,
   For ever, and for ever!
   O what a mad endeavour
      Worketh he,
Who to thy sacred and ennoblèd hearse
Would offer a burnt sacrifice of verse
10   And melody.

   How heavenward thou soundest,
      Live temple of sweet noise,
   And discord unconfoundest,
      Give delight new joys,
   And pleasure nobler pinions!
   O, where are thy dominions?
      Lend thine ear
To a young Delian oath – ay, by thy soul,
By all that from thy mortal lips did roll,
20 And by the kernel of thy earthly love,
Beauty in things on earth and things above,
      I swear!

When every childish fashion
    Has vanished from my rhyme,
  Will I, grey-gone in passion,
    Leave to an after-time
      Hymning and harmony
Of thee, and of thy works, and of thy life;
But vain is now the burning and the strife,
30 Pangs are in vain, until I grow high-rife
      With old Philosophy,
And mad with glimpses of futurity!

For many years my offering must be hushed;
  When I do speak, I'll think upon this hour,
Because I feel my forehead hot and flushed,
  Even at the simplest vassal of thy power –
    A lock of thy bright hair.
    Sudden it came,
And I was startled, when I caught thy name
40   Coupled so unaware;
Yet, at the moment, temperate was my blood.
Methought I had beheld it from the Flood.

On Sitting Down to Read King Lear *Once Again*

O golden-tongued Romance, with serene lute!
  Fair plumèd Syren, Queen of far-away!
  Leave melodizing on this wintry day,
Shut up thine olden pages, and be mute:
Adieu! for, once again, the fierce dispute
  Betwixt damnation and impassioned clay
  Must I burn through, once more humbly assay
The bitter-sweet of this Shakespearian fruit:
Chief Poet! and ye clouds of Albion,
10   Begetters of our deep eternal theme!
When through the old oak forest I am gone,
  Let me not wander in a barren dream,
But, when I am consumèd in the fire,
Give me new Phoenix wings to fly at my desire.

'When I have fears that I may cease to be'

When I have fears that I may cease to be
  Before my pen has gleaned my teeming brain,
Before high-pilèd books, in charactery,
  Hold like rich garners the full-ripened grain;
When I behold, upon the night's starred face,
  Huge cloudy symbols of a high romance,
And think that I may never live to trace
  Their shadows, with the magic hand of chance;
And when I feel, fair creature of an hour!
10   That I shall never look upon thee more,
Never have relish in the faery power
  Of unreflecting love! – then on the shore
Of the wide world I stand alone, and think
Till love and fame to nothingness do sink.

'O blush not so! O blush not so!'

I
O blush not so! O blush not so!
  Or I shall think you knowing;
And if you smile the blushing while,
  Then maidenheads are going.

II
There's a blush for won't, and a blush for shan't,
  And a blush for having done it:
There's a blush for thought, and a blush for naught,
  And a blush for just begun it.

III
O sigh not so! O sigh not so!
10   For it sounds of Eve's sweet pippin;
By those loosened hips you have tasted the pips
  And fought in an amorous nipping.

IV

Will you play once more at nice-cut-core,
    For it only will last our youth out?
And we have the prime of the kissing time,
    We have not one sweet tooth out.

V

There's a sigh for yes, and a sigh for no,
    And a sigh for I can't bear it!
O what can be done, shall we stay or run?
    O, cut the sweet apple and share it!

'Hence Burgundy, Claret, and Port'

Hence Burgundy, Claret, and Port,
    Away with old Hock and Madeira,
Too couthly ye are for my sport;
    There's a beverage brighter and clearer.
Instead of a pitiful rummer,
My wine overbrims a whole summer;
    My bowl is the sky,
    And I drink at my eye,
    Till I feel in the brain
    A Delphian pain –
Then follow, my Caius! then follow!
    On the green of the hill
    We will drink our fill
    Of golden sunshine,
    Till our brains intertwine
With the glory and grace of Apollo!

'God of the meridian'

God of the meridian,
And of the East and West,
To thee my soul is flown,

    And my body is earthward pressed.
    It is an awful mission,
    A terrible division,
    And leaves a gulf austere
    To be filled with worldly fear.
    Ay, when the soul is fled
10 To high above our head,
    Affrighted do we gaze
    After its airy maze,
    As doth a mother wild,
    When her young infant child
    Is in an eagle's claws –
    And is not this the cause
    Of madness? – God of Song,
    Thou bearest me along
    Through sights I scarce can bear:
20 O let me, let me share
    With the hot lyre and thee,
    The staid Philosophy.
    Temper my lonely hours,
    And let me see thy bowers
    More unalarmed!

Robin Hood

TO A FRIEND

    No! those days are gone away,
    And their hours are old and grey,
    And their minutes buried all
    Under the down-trodden pall
    Of the leaves of many years;
    Many times have winter's shears,
    Frozen North, and chilling East,
    Sounded tempests to the feast
    Of the forest's whispering fleeces,
10 Since men knew nor rent nor leases.

ROBIN HOOD

No, the bugle sounds no more,
And the twanging bow no more;
Silent is the ivory shrill
Past the heath and up the hill;
There is no mid-forest laugh,
Where lone Echo gives the half
To some wight, amazed to hear
Jesting, deep in forest drear.

On the fairest time of June
You may go, with sun or moon,
Or the seven stars to light you,
Or the polar ray to right you;
But you never may behold
Little John, or Robin bold;
Never one, of all the clan,
Thrumming on an empty can
Some old hunting ditty, while
He doth his green way beguile
To fair hostess Merriment,
Down beside the pasture Trent;
For he left the merry tale
Messenger for spicy ale.

Gone, the merry morris din;
Gone, the song of Gamelyn;
Gone, the tough-belted outlaw
Idling in the 'grenè shawe';
All are gone away and past!
And if Robin should be cast
Sudden from his turfèd grave,
And if Marian should have
Once again her forest days,
She would weep, and he would craze.
He would swear, for all his oaks,
Fallen beneath the dockyard strokes,
Have rotted on the briny seas;
She would weep that her wild bees

Sang not to her – strange! that honey
　　　Can't be got without hard money!

　　　　So it is – yet let us sing,
50　　Honour to the old bow-string!
　　　Honour to the bugle-horn!
　　　Honour to the woods unshorn!
　　　Honour to the Lincoln green!
　　　Honour to the archer keen!
　　　Honour to tight little John,
　　　And the horse he rode upon!
　　　Honour to bold Robin Hood,
　　　Sleeping in the underwood!
　　　Honour to maid Marian,
60　　And to all the Sherwood-clan!
　　　Though their days have hurried by
　　　Let us two a burden try.

Lines on the Mermaid Tavern

Souls of Poets dead and gone,
What Elysium have ye known,
Happy field or mossy cavern,
Choicer than the Mermaid Tavern?
Have ye tippled drink more fine
Than mine host's Canary wine?
Or are fruits of Paradise
Sweeter than those dainty pies
Of venison? O generous food!
10 Dressed as though bold Robin Hood
Would, with his maid Marian,
Sup and bowse from horn and can.

　　I have heard that on a day
Mine host's sign-board flew away,
Nobody knew whither, till
An astrologer's old quill
To a sheepskin gave the story,

Said he saw you in your glory,
Underneath a new-old sign
20   Sipping beverage divine,
And pledging with contented smack
The Mermaid in the Zodiac.

   Souls of Poets dead and gone,
What Elysium have ye known,
Happy field or mossy cavern,
Choicer than the Mermaid Tavern?

To —*

Time's sea hath been five years at its slow ebb,
   Long hours have to and fro let creep the sand,
Since I was tangled in thy beauty's web,
   And snared by the ungloving of thy hand.
And yet I never look on midnight sky,
   But I behold thine eyes' well memoried light;
I cannot look upon the rose's dye,
   But to thy cheek my soul doth take its flight;
I cannot look on any budding flower,
10   But my fond ear, in fancy at thy lips,
And hearkening for a love-sound, doth devour
   Its sweets in the wrong sense: – Thou dost eclipse
Every delight with sweet remembering,
And grief unto my darling joys dost bring.

* A lady whom he saw for some few moments at Vauxhall.

To the Nile

Son of the old moon-mountains African!
   Chief of the pyramid and crocodile!
   We call thee fruitful, and, that very while,
A desert fills our seeing's inward span.
Nurse of swart nations since the world began,

  Art thou so fruitful? or dost thou beguile
  Such men to honour thee, who, worn with toil,
Rest for a space 'twixt Cairo and Decan?
O may dark fancies err! They surely do.
 'Tis ignorance that makes a barren waste
Of all beyond itself. Thou dost bedew
  Green rushes like our rivers, and dost taste
The pleasant sun-rise. Green isles hast thou too,
  And to the sea as happily dost haste.

'Spenser! a jealous honourer of thine'

Spenser! a jealous honourer of thine,
  A forester deep in thy midmost trees,
Did last eve ask my promise to refine
  Some English that might strive thine ear to please.
But, Elfin Poet, 'tis impossible
  For an inhabitant of wintry earth
To rise like Phoebus with a golden quell,
  Fire-winged, and make a morning in his mirth.
It is impossible to escape from toil
 O' the sudden and receive thy spiriting:
The flower must drink the nature of the soil
  Before it can put forth its blossoming.
Be with me in the summer days and I
Will for thine honour and his pleasure try.

'Blue! 'Tis the life of heaven, the domain'

ANSWER TO A SONNET ENDING THUS:
  Dark eyes are dearer far
Than orbs that mock the hyacinthine bell –
J. H. Reynolds

Blue! 'Tis the life of heaven, the domain
  Of Cynthia, the wide palace of the sun,
The tent of Hesperus, and all his train,

The bosomer of clouds, gold, grey and dun.
Blue! 'Tis the life of waters – Ocean
    And all its vassal streams, pools numberless,
May rage, and foam, and fret, but never can
    Subside, if not to dark blue nativeness.
Blue! Gentle cousin to the forest-green,
10   Married to green in all the sweetest flowers –
Forget-me-not, the blue-bell, and, that queen
    Of secrecy, the violet. What strange powers
Hast thou, as a mere shadow! But how great,
When in an eye thou art, alive with fate!

'O thou whose face hath felt the Winter's wind'

O thou whose face hath felt the Winter's wind,
    Whose eye has seen the snow-clouds hung in mist,
    And the black elm tops, 'mong the freezing stars,
    To thee the spring will be a harvest-time.
O thou, whose only book has been the light
    Of supreme darkness which thou feddest on
    Night after night when Phoebus was away,
    To thee the Spring shall be a triple morn.
O fret not after knowledge – I have none,
10   And yet my song comes native with the warmth.
O fret not after knowledge – I have none,
    And yet the Evening listens. He who saddens
At thought of idleness cannot be idle,
And he's awake who thinks himself asleep.

Sonnet

TO A[UBREY] G[EORGE] S[PENCER]
ON READING HIS ADMIRABLE VERSES IN THIS (MISS
REYNOLDS'S) ALBUM, ON EITHER SIDE OF THE FOLLOWING
ATTEMPT TO PAY SMALL TRIBUTE THERETO

Where didst thou find, young Bard, thy sounding lyre?
  Where the bland accent, and the tender tone?
A-sitting snugly by thy parlour fire?
  Or didst thou with Apollo pick a bone?
The Muse will have a crow to pick with me
  For thus assaying in thy brightening path:
Who, that with his own brace of eyes can see,
  Unthunderstruck beholds thy gentle wrath?
Who from a pot of stout e'er blew the froth
10 Into the bosom of the wandering wind,
  Light as the powder on the back of moth,
But drank thy muses with a grateful mind?
  Yea, unto thee beldams drink metheglin
  And annisies, and carraway, and gin.

Extracts from an Opera

I

O! were I one of the Olympian twelve,
Their godships should pass this into a law –
That when a man doth set himself in toil
After some beauty veilèd far away,
Each step he took should make his lady's hand
More soft, more white, and her fair cheek more fair;
And for each briar-berry he might eat,
A kiss should bud upon the tree of love,
And pulp and ripen richer every hour,
10 To melt away upon the traveller's lips.

II DAISY'S SONG

1
The sun, with his great eye,
Sees not so much as I;
And the moon, all silver-proud,
Might as well be in a cloud.

2
And O the spring – the spring!
I lead the life of a king!
Couched in the teeming grass,
I spy each pretty lass.

3
I look where no one dares,
And I stare where no one stares,
And when the night is nigh,
Lambs bleat my lullaby.

III FOLLY'S SONG

When wedding fiddles are a-playing,
    Huzza for folly O!
And when maidens go a-maying,
    Huzza, etc.
When a milk-pail is upset,
    Huzza, etc.
And the clothes left in the wet,
    Huzza, etc.
When the barrel's set abroach,
    Huzza, etc.
When Kate Eyebrow keeps a coach,
    Huzza, etc.
When the pig is over-roasted,
    Huzza, etc.
And the cheese is over-toasted,
    Huzza, etc.
When Sir Snap is with his lawyer,
    Huzza, etc.
And Miss Chip has kissed the sawyer,
    Huzza, etc.

IV

O, I am frightened with most hateful thoughts!
Perhaps her voice is not a nightingale's,
Perhaps her teeth are not the fairest pearl;
Her eye-lashes may be, for aught I know,
Not longer than the may-fly's small fan-horns;
There may not be one dimple on her hand –
And freckles many. Ah! a careless nurse,
In haste to teach the little thing to walk,
May have crumped up a pair of Dian's legs
And warped the ivory of a Juno's neck.

V SONG

1

The stranger lighted from his steed,
    And ere he spake a word,
He seized my lady's lily hand,
    And kissed it all unheard.

2

The stranger walked into the hall,
    And ere he spake a word,
He kissed my lady's cherry lips,
    And kissed 'em all unheard.

3

The stranger walked into the bower –
    But my lady first did go:
Ay, hand in hand into the bower,
    Where my lord's roses blow.

4

My lady's maid had a silken scarf,
    And a golden ring had she,
And a kiss from the stranger, as off he went
    Again on his fair palfrey.

VI

Asleep! O sleep a little while, white pearl!
And let me kneel, and let me pray to thee,
And let me call Heaven's blessing on thine eyes,
And let me breathe into the happy air,
That doth enfold and touch thee all about,
Vows of my slavery, my giving up,
My sudden adoration, my great love!

The Human Seasons

Four seasons fill the measure of the year;
　There are four seasons in the mind of man.
He has his lusty Spring, when fancy clear
　Takes in all beauty with an easy span.
He has his Summer, when luxuriously
　Spring's honeyed cud of youthful thought he loves
To ruminate, and by such dreaming nigh
　His nearest unto heaven. Quiet coves
His soul has in its Autumn, when his wings
　He furleth close; contented so to look
On mists in idleness – to let fair things
　Pass by unheeded as a threshold brook.
He has his Winter too of pale misfeature,
Or else he would forego his mortal nature.

'For there's Bishop's Teign'

I

　　For there's Bishop's Teign
　　And King's Teign
And Coomb at the clear Teign head –
　　Where close by the stream
　　You may have your cream
All spread upon barley bread.

'FOR THERE'S BISHOP'S TEIGN'

II

  There's Arch Brook
   And there's Larch Brook
Both turning many a mill;
   And cooling the drouth
    Of the salmon's mouth,
And fattening his silver gill.

III

   There is Wild Wood,
    A mild hood
To the sheep on the lea o' the down,
   Where the golden furze,
    With its green, thin spurs,
Doth catch at the maiden's gown.

IV

   There is Newton Marsh
    With its spear grass harsh –
A pleasant summer level
   Where the maidens sweet
    Of the Market Street
Do meet in the dusk to revel.

V

   There's the barton rich
    With dyke and ditch
And hedge for the thrush to live in,
   And the hollow tree
    For the buzzing bee
And a bank for the wasp to hive in.

VI

   And O, and O,
    The daisies blow
And the primroses are wakened,
   And violet white
    Sits in silver plight,
And the green bud's as long as the spike end.

VII

    Then who would go
    Into dark Soho,
And chatter with dacked-haired critics,
40   When he can stay
    For the new-mown hay,
And startle the dappled prickets?

'Where be ye going, you Devon maid'?

I

Where be ye going, you Devon maid?
    And what have ye there i' the basket?
Ye tight little fairy, just fresh from the dairy,
    Will ye give me some cream if I ask it?

II

I love your meads, and I love your flowers,
    And I love your junkets mainly,
But 'hind the door I love kissing more,
    O look not so disdainly.

III

I love your hills, and I love your dales,
10   And I love your flocks a-bleating –
But O, on the heather to lie together,
    With both our hearts a-beating!

IV

I'll put your basket all safe in a *nook*,
    And your shawl I hang up *on this willow*,
And we will sigh in the daisy's eye
    And kiss on a grass-green pillow.

'Over the hill and over the dale'

Over the hill and over the dale,
And over the bourn to Dawlish –
Where gingerbread wives have a scanty sale
And gingerbread nuts are smallish.

Rantipole Betty she ran down a hill
And kicked up her petticoats fairly.
Says I, 'I'll be Jack if you will be Jill.'
So she sat on the grass debonairly.

'Here's somebody coming, here's somebody coming!'
10 Says I,''Tis the wind at a parley.'
So without any fuss, any hawing and humming,
She lay on the grass debonairly.

'Here's somebody here, and here's somebody *there*!'
Says I, 'Hold your tongue, you young gipsy.'
So she held her tongue and lay plump and fair,
And dead as a Venus tipsy.

O who wouldn't hie to Dawlish fair,
O who wouldn't stop in a meadow?
O [who] would not rumple the daisies there,
20 And make the wild fern for a bed do?

To J. H. Reynolds, Esq.

Dear Reynolds, as last night I lay in bed,
There came before my eyes that wonted thread
Of shapes, and shadows, and remembrances,
That every other minute vex and please:
Things all disjointed come from North and South –
Two witch's eyes above a cherub's mouth,
Voltaire with casque and shield and habergeon,
And Alexander with his nightcap on,
Old Socrates a-tying his cravat,
10 And Hazlitt playing with Miss Edgeworth's cat,

And Junius Brutus, pretty well so so,
Making the best of's way towards Soho.

    Few are there who escape these visitings –
Perhaps one or two whose lives have patient wings,
And through whose curtains peeps no hellish nose,
No wild-boar tushes, and no mermaid's toes;
But flowers bursting out with lusty pride,
And young Aeolian harps personified,
Some, Titian colours touched into real life –
20 The sacrifice goes on; the pontiff knife
Gloams in the sun, the milk-white heifer lows,
The pipes go shrilly, the libation flows;
A white sail shows above the green-head cliff,
Moves round the point, and throws her anchor stiff.
The mariners join hymn with those on land.

    You know the Enchanted Castle – it doth stand
Upon a rock, on the border of a lake,
Nested in trees, which all do seem to shake
From some old magic-like Urganda's sword.
30 O Phoebus! that I had thy sacred word
To show this castle, in fair dreaming wise,
Unto my friend, while sick and ill he lies!

    You know it well enough, where it doth seem
A mossy place, a Merlin's Hall, a dream.
You know the clear lake, and the little isles,
The mountains blue, and cold near-neighbour rills,
All which elsewhere are but half animate;
Here do they look alive to love and hate,
To smiles and frowns; they seem a lifted mound
40 Above some giant, pulsing underground.

    Part of the building was a chosen see,
Built by a banished santon of Chaldee;
The other part, two thousand years from him,
Was built by Cuthbert de Saint Aldebrim;
Then there's a little wing, far from the sun,
Built by a Lapland witch turned maudlin nun;

TO J. H. REYNOLDS, ESQ.

And many other juts of agèd stone
Founded with many a mason-devil's groan.

The doors all look as if they oped themselves,
The windows as if latched by fays and elves,
And from them comes a silver flash of light,
As from the westward of a summer's night;
Or like a beauteous woman's large blue eyes
Gone mad through olden songs and poesies –

See! what is coming from the distance dim!
A golden galley all in silken trim!
Three rows of oars are lightening, moment-whiles,
Into the verdurous bosoms of those isles.
Towards the shade, under the castle wall,
It comes in silence – now 'tis hidden all.
The clarion sounds, and from a postern-grate
An echo of sweet music doth create
A fear in the poor herdsman, who doth bring
His beasts to trouble the enchanted spring.
He tells of the sweet music, and the spot,
To all his friends – and they believe him not.

O that our dreamings all, of sleep or wake,
Would all their colours from the sunset take,
From something of material sublime,
Rather than shadow our own soul's daytime
In the dark void of night. For in the world
We jostle – but my flag is not unfurled
On the admiral staff – and to philosophize
I dare not yet! O, never will the prize,
High reason, and the lore of good and ill,
Be my award! Things cannot to the will
Be settled, but they tease us out of thought.
Or is it that imagination brought
Beyond its proper bound, yet still confined,
Lost in a sort of purgatory blind,
Cannot refer to any standard law
Of either earth or heaven? It is a flaw

In happiness, to see beyond our bourne –
It forces us in summer skies to mourn;
It spoils the singing of the nightingale.

Dear Reynolds, I have a mysterious tale,
And cannot speak it. The first page I read
Upon a lampit rock of green seaweed
Among the breakers. 'Twas a quiet eve;
90 The rocks were silent, the wide sea did weave
An untumultuous fringe of silver foam
Along the flat brown sand. I was at home
And should have been most happy – but I saw
Too far into the sea, where every maw
The greater on the less feeds evermore. –
But I saw too distinct into the core
Of an eternal fierce destruction,
And so from happiness I far was gone.
Still am I sick of it; and though, today,
100 I've gathered young spring-leaves, and flowers gay
Of periwinkle and wild strawberry,
Still do I that most fierce destruction see –
The shark at savage prey, the hawk at pounce,
The gentle robin, like a pard or ounce,
Ravening a worm. – Away, ye horrid moods!
Moods of one's mind! You know I hate them well,
You know I'd sooner be a clapping bell
To some Kamchatkan missionary church,
Than with these horrid moods be left in lurch.
110 Do you get health – and Tom the same – I'll dance,
And from detested moods in new romance
Take refuge. Of bad lines a centaine dose
Is sure enough – and so 'here follows prose' . . .

To J[ames] R[ice]

O that a week could be an age, and we
    Felt parting and warm meeting every week,
Then one poor year a thousand years would be,

>   The flush of welcome ever on the cheek:
> So could we live long life in little space,
>   So time itself would be annihilate,
> So a day's journey in oblivious haze
>   To serve our joys would lengthen and dilate.
> O to arrive each Monday morn from Ind!
>   To land each Tuesday from the rich Levant!
> In little time a host of joys to bind,
>   And keep our souls in one eternal pant!
> This morn, my friend, and yester-evening taught
> Me how to harbour such a happy thought.

Isabella; or, The Pot of Basil

I

Fair Isabel, poor simple Isabel!
   Lorenzo, a young palmer in Love's eye!
They could not in the self-same mansion dwell
   Without some stir of heart, some malady;
They could not sit at meals but feel how well
   It soothed each to be the other by;
They could not, sure, beneath the same roof sleep
But to each other dream, and nightly weep.

II

With every morn their love grew tenderer,
   With every eve deeper and tenderer still;
He might not in house, field, or garden stir,
   But her full shape would all his seeing fill;
And his continual voice was pleasanter
   To her than noise of trees or hidden rill;
Her lute-string gave an echo of his name,
She spoilt her half-done broidery with the same.

III

He knew whose gentle hand was at the latch
   Before the door had given her to his eyes;
And from her chamber-window he would catch

Her beauty farther than the falcon spies;
And constant as her vespers would he watch,
  Because her face was turned to the same skies;
And with sick longing all the night outwear,
To hear her morning-step upon the stair.

IV

A whole long month of May in this sad plight
  Made their cheeks paler by the break of June:
'To-morrow will I bow to my delight,
  To-morrow will I ask my lady's boon.'
'O may I never see another night,
  Lorenzo, if thy lips breathe not love's tune.'
So spake they to their pillows; but, alas,
Honeyless days and days did he let pass –

V

Until sweet Isabella's untouched cheek
  Fell sick within the rose's just domain,
Fell thin as a young mother's, who doth seek
  By every lull to cool her infant's pain:
'How ill she is,' said he, 'I may not speak,
  And yet I will, and tell my love all plain:
If looks speak love-laws, I will drink her tears,
And at the least 'twill startle off her cares.'

VI

So said he one fair morning, and all day
  His heart beat awfully against his side;
And to his heart he inwardly did pray
  For power to speak; but still the ruddy tide
Stifled his voice, and pulsed resolve away –
  Fevered his high conceit of such a bride,
Yet brought him to the meekness of a child:
Alas! when passion is both meek and wild!

VII

So once more he had waked and anguishèd
  A dreary night of love and misery,
If Isabel's quick eye had not been wed

To every symbol on his forehead high.
She saw it waxing very pale and dead,
   And straight all flushed; so, lispèd tenderly,
'Lorenzo!' – here she ceased her timid quest,
But in her tone and look he read the rest.

VIII
'O Isabella, I can half-perceive
   That I may speak my grief into thine ear.
If thou didst ever anything believe,
   Believe how I love thee, believe how near
My soul is to its doom: I would not grieve
   Thy hand by unwelcome pressing, would not fear
Thine eyes by gazing; but I cannot live
Another night, and not my passion shrive.

IX
Love! thou art leading me from wintry cold,
   Lady! thou leadest me to summer clime,
And I must taste the blossoms that unfold
   In its ripe warmth this gracious morning time.'
So said, his erewhile timid lips grew bold,
   And poesied with hers in dewy rhyme:
Great bliss was with them, and great happiness
Grew, like a lusty flower, in June's caress.

X
Parting they seemed to tread upon the air,
   Twin roses by the zephyr blown apart
Only to meet again more close, and share
   The inward fragrance of each other's heart.
She, to her chamber gone, a ditty fair
   Sang, of delicious love and honeyed dart;
He with light steps went up a western hill,
And bade the sun farewell, and joyed his fill.

XI
All close they met again, before the dusk
   Had taken from the stars its pleasant veil,
All close they met, all eves, before the dusk

Had taken from the stars its pleasant veil,
Close in a bower of hyacinth and musk,
  Unknown of any, free from whispering tale.
Ah! better had it been for ever so,
Than idle ears should pleasure in their woe.

XII

Were they unhappy then? – It cannot be –
  Too many tears for lovers have been shed,
Too many sighs give we to them in fee,
  Too much of pity after they are dead,
Too many doleful stories do we see,
  Whose matter in bright gold were best be read;
Except in such a page where Theseus' spouse
Over the pathless waves towards him bows.

XIII

But, for the general award of love,
  The little sweet doth kill much bitterness;
Though Dido silent is in under-grove,
  And Isabella's was a great distress,
Though young Lorenzo in warm Indian clove
  Was not embalmed, this truth is not the less –
Even bees, the little almsmen of spring-bowers,
Know there is richest juice in poison-flowers.

XIV

With her two brothers this fair lady dwelt,
  Enrichèd from ancestral merchandise,
And for them many a weary hand did swelt
  In torchèd mines and noisy factories,
And many once proud-quivered loins did melt
  In blood from stinging whip – with hollow eyes
Many all day in dazzling river stood,
To take the rich-ored driftings of the flood.

XV

For them the Ceylon diver held his breath,
  And went all naked to the hungry shark;
For them his ears gushed blood; for them in death

The seal on the cold ice with piteous bark
Lay full of darts; for them alone did seethe
   A thousand men in troubles wide and dark:
Half-ignorant, they turned an easy wheel,
That set sharp racks at work to pinch and peel.

XVI

Why were they proud? Because their marble founts
   Gushed with more pride than do a wretch's tears? —
Why were they proud? Because fair orange-mounts
   Were of more soft ascent than lazar stairs? —
Why were they proud? Because red-lined accounts
   Were richer than the songs of Grecian years? —
Why were they proud? again we ask aloud,
Why in the name of Glory were they proud?

XVII

Yet were these Florentines as self-retired
   In hungry pride and gainful cowardice,
As two close Hebrews in that land inspired,
   Paled in and vineyarded from beggar-spies —
The hawks of ship-mast forests — the untired
   And panniered mules for ducats and old lies —
Quick cat's-paws on the generous stray-away —
Great wits in Spanish, Tuscan, and Malay.

XVIII

How was it these same ledger-men could spy
   Fair Isabella in her downy nest?
How could they find out in Lorenzo's eye
   A straying from his toil? Hot Egypt's pest
Into their vision covetous and sly!
   How could these money-bags see east and west? —
Yet so they did — and every dealer fair
Must see behind, as doth the hunted hare.

XIX

O eloquent and famed Boccaccio!
   Of thee we now should ask forgiving boon,
And of thy spicy myrtles as they blow,

And of thy roses amorous of the moon,
And of thy lilies, that do paler grow
150 Now they can no more hear thy gittern's tune.
For venturing syllables that ill beseem
The quiet glooms of such a piteous theme.

XX

Grant thou a pardon here, and then the tale
   Shall move on soberly, as it is meet;
There is no other crime, no mad assail
   To make old prose in modern rhyme more sweet:
But it is done – succeed the verse or fail –
   To honour thee, and thy gone spirit greet,
To stead thee as a verse in English tongue,
160 An echo of thee in the north wind sung.

XXI

These brethren having found by many signs
   What love Lorenzo for their sister had,
And how she loved him too, each unconfines
   His bitter thoughts to other, well nigh mad
That he, the servant of their trade designs,
   Should in their sister's love be blithe and glad,
When 'twas their plan to coax her by degrees
To some high noble and his olive-trees.

XXII

And many a jealous conference had they,
170 And many times they bit their lips alone,
Before they fixed upon a surest way
   To make the youngster for his crime atone;
And at the last, these men of cruel clay
   Cut Mercy with a sharp knife to the bone,
For they resolvèd in some forest dim
To kill Lorenzo, and there bury him.

XXIII

So on a pleasant morning, as he leant
   Into the sunrise, o'er the balustrade
Of the garden-terrace, towards him they bent

Their footing through the dews; and to him said,
'You seem there in the quiet of content,
   Lorenzo, and we are most loth to invade
Calm speculation; but if you are wise,
   Bestride your steed while cold is in the skies.

XXIV

'To-day we purpose, ay, this hour we mount
   To spur three leagues towards the Apennine;
Come down, we pray thee, ere the hot sun count
   His dewy rosary on the eglantine.'
Lorenzo, courteously as he was wont,
   Bowed a fair greeting to these serpents' whine;
And went in haste, to get in readiness,
With belt, and spur, and bracing huntsman's dress.

XXV

And as he to the court-yard passed along,
   Each third step did he pause, and listened oft
If he could hear his lady's matin-song,
   Or the light whisper of her footstep soft;
And as he thus over his passion hung,
   He heard a laugh full musical aloft,
When, looking up, he saw her features bright
Smile through an in-door lattice, all delight.

XXVI

'Love, Isabel!' said he, 'I was in pain
   Lest I should miss to bid thee a good morrow:
Ah! what if I should lose thee, when so fain
   I am to stifle all the heavy sorrow
Of a poor three hours' absence? but we'll gain
   Out of the amorous dark what day doth borrow.
Good bye! I'll soon be back.' 'Good bye!' said she –
And as he went she chanted merrily.

XXVII

So the two brothers and their murdered man
   Rode past fair Florence, to where Arno's stream
Gurgles through straitened banks, and still doth fan

Itself with dancing bulrush, and the bream
Keeps head against the freshets. Sick and wan
　The brothers' faces in the ford did seem,
Lorenzo's flush with love. – They passed the water
Into a forest quiet for the slaughter.

XXVIII

There was Lorenzo slain and buried in,
　There in that forest did his great love cease.
Ah! when a soul doth thus its freedom win,
　It aches in loneliness – is ill at peace
As the break-covert blood-hounds of such sin.
　They dipped their swords in the water, and did tease
Their horses homeward, with convulsèd spur,
Each richer by his being a murderer.

XXIX

They told their sister how, with sudden speed,
　Lorenzo had ta'en ship for foreign lands,
Because of some great urgency and need
　In their affairs, requiring trusty hands.
Poor girl! put on thy stifling widow's weed,
　And 'scape at once from Hope's accursèd bands;
To-day thou wilt not see him, nor to-morrow,
And the next day will be a day of sorrow.

XXX

She weeps alone for pleasures not to be;
　Sorely she wept until the night came on,
And then, instead of love, O misery!
　She brooded o'er the luxury alone:
His image in the dusk she seemed to see,
　And to the silence made a gentle moan,
Spreading her perfect arms upon the air,
And on her couch low murmuring 'Where? O where?'

XXXI

But Selfishness, Love's cousin, held not long
　Its fiery vigil in her single breast.
She fretted for the golden hour, and hung

Upon the time with feverish unrest –
Not long – for soon into her heart a throng
  Of higher occupants, a richer zest,
Came tragic – passion not to be subdued,
And sorrow for her love in travels rude.

XXXII

In the mid days of autumn, on their eves
  The breath of Winter comes from far away,
And the sick west continually bereaves
  Of some gold tinge, and plays a roundelay
Of death among the bushes and the leaves,
  To make all bare before he dares to stray
From his north cavern. So sweet Isabel
By gradual decay from beauty fell,

XXXIII

Because Lorenzo came not. Oftentimes
  She asked her brothers, with an eye all pale,
Striving to be itself, what dungeon climes
  Could keep him off so long? They spake a tale
Time after time, to quiet her. Their crimes
  Came on them, like a smoke from Hinnom's vale;
And every night in dreams they groaned aloud,
To see their sister in her snowy shroud.

XXXIV

And she had died in drowsy ignorance,
  But for a thing more deadly dark than all.
It came like a fierce potion, drunk by chance,
  Which saves a sick man from the feathered pall
For some few gasping moments; like a lance,
  Waking an Indian from his cloudy hall
With cruel pierce, and bringing him again
Sense of the gnawing fire at heart and brain.

XXXV

It was a vision. – In the drowsy gloom,
  The dull of midnight, at her couch's foot
Lorenzo stood, and wept: the forest tomb

Had marred his glossy hair which once could shoot
Lustre into the sun, and put cold doom
   Upon his lips, and taken the soft lute
From his lorn voice, and past his loamèd ears
Had made a miry channel for his tears.

XXXVI

Strange sound it was, when the pale shadow spake;
   For there was striving, in its piteous tongue,
To speak as when on earth it was awake,
   And Isabella on its music hung.
Languor there was in it, and tremulous shake,
   As in a palsied Druid's harp unstrung;
And through it moaned a ghostly under-song,
Like hoarse night-gusts sepulchral briars among.

XXXVII

Its eyes, though wild, were still all dewy bright
   With love, and kept all phantom fear aloof
From the poor girl by magic of their light,
   The while it did unthread the horrid woof
Of the late darkened time – the murderous spite
   Of pride and avarice, the dark pine roof
In the forest, and the sodden turfèd dell,
Where, without any word, from stabs he fell.

XXXVIII

Saying moreover, 'Isabel, my sweet!
   Red whortle-berries droop above my head,
And a large flint-stone weighs upon my feet;
   Around me beeches and high chestnuts shed
Their leaves and prickly nuts; a sheep-fold bleat
   Comes from beyond the river to my bed:
Go, shed one tear upon my heather-bloom,
And it shall comfort me within the tomb.

XXXIX

'I am a shadow now, alas! alas!
   Upon the skirts of human-nature dwelling
Alone. I chant alone the holy mass,

While little sounds of life are round me knelling,
  And glossy bees at noon do fieldward pass,
And many a chapel bell the hour is telling,
  Paining me through: those sounds grow strange to me,
And thou art distant in humanity.

XL

'I know what was, I feel full well what is,
  And I should rage, if spirits could go mad;
Though I forget the taste of earthly bliss,
  That paleness warms my grave, as though I had
A seraph chosen from the bright abyss
  To be my spouse: thy paleness makes me glad;
Thy beauty grows upon me, and I feel
A greater love through all my essence steal.'

XLI

The Spirit mourn'd 'Adieu!' – dissolved and left
  The atom darkness in a slow turmoil;
As when of healthful midnight sleep bereft,
  Thinking on rugged hours and fruitless toil,
We put our eyes into a pillowy cleft,
  And see the spangly gloom froth up and boil:
It made sad Isabella's eyelids ache,
And in the dawn she started up awake –

XLII

'Ha! ha!' said she, 'I knew not this hard life,
  I thought the worst was simple misery;
I thought some Fate with pleasure or with strife
  Portioned us – happy days, or else to die;
But there is crime – a brother's bloody knife!
  Sweet Spirit, thou hast schooled my infancy:
I'll visit thee for this, and kiss thine eyes,
And greet thee morn and even in the skies.'

XLIII

When the full morning came, she had devised
  How she might secret to the forest hie;
How she might find the clay, so dearly prized,

And sing to it one latest lullaby;
How her short absence might be unsurmised,
  While she the inmost of the dream would try.
Resolved, she took with her an agèd nurse,
And went into that dismal forest-hearse.

XLIV

See, as they creep along the river side,
  How she doth whisper to that agèd dame,
And, after looking round the champaign wide,
  Shows her a knife. – 'What feverous hectic flame
Burns in thee, child? – What good can thee betide,
  That thou shouldst smile again?' The evening came,
And they had found Lorenzo's earthy bed –
The flint was there, the berries at his head.

XLV

Who hath not loitered in a green church-yard,
  And let his spirit, like a demon-mole,
Work through the clayey soil and gravel hard,
  To see skull, coffined bones, and funeral stole;
Pitying each form that hungry Death hath marred
  And filling it once more with human soul?
Ah! this is holiday to what was felt
When Isabella by Lorenzo knelt.

XLVI

She gazed into the fresh-thrown mould, as though
  One glance did fully all its secrets tell;
Clearly she saw, as other eyes would know
  Pale limbs at bottom of a crystal well;
Upon the murderous spot she seemed to grow,
  Like to a native lily of the dell –
Then with her knife, all sudden, she began
To dig more fervently than misers can.

XLVII

Soon she turned up a soilèd glove, whereon
  Her silk had played in purple phantasies,
She kissed it with a lip more chill than stone,

    And put it in her bosom, where it dries
    And freezes utterly unto the bone
        Those dainties made to still an infant's cries:
    Then 'gan she work again, nor stayed her care,
    But to throw back at times her veiling hair.

XLVIII
That old nurse stood beside her wondering,
    Until her heart felt pity to the core
At sight of such a dismal labouring,
    And so she kneelèd, with her locks all hoar,
And put her lean hands to the horrid thing.
    Three hours they laboured at this travail sore –
At last they felt the kernel of the grave,
And Isabella did not stamp and rave.

XLIX
Ah! wherefore all this wormy circumstance?
    Why linger at the yawning tomb so long?
O for the gentleness of old Romance,
    The simple plaining of a minstrel's song!
Fair reader, at the old tale take a glance,
    For here, in truth, it doth not well belong
To speak – O turn thee to the very tale,
And taste the music of that vision pale.

L
With duller steel than the Persèan sword
    They cut away no formless monster's head,
But one, whose gentleness did well accord
    With death, as life. The ancient harps have said,
Love never dies, but lives, immortal Lord:
    If Love impersonate was ever dead,
Pale Isabella kissed it, and low moaned.
'Twas Love – cold, dead indeed, but not dethroned.

LI
In anxious secrecy they took it home,
    And then the prize was all for Isabel.
She calmed its wild hair with a golden comb,

And all around each eye's sepulchral cell
  Pointed each fringèd lash; the smeared loam
    With tears, as chilly as a dripping well,
She drenched away – and still she combed, and kept
Sighing all day – and still she kissed, and wept.

LII

Then in a silken scarf – sweet with the dews
  Of precious flowers plucked in Araby,
And divine liquids come with odorous ooze
  Through the cold serpent-pipe refreshfully –
She wrapped it up; and for its tomb did choose
  A garden-pot, wherein she laid it by,
And covered it with mould, and o'er it set
Sweet basil, which her tears kept ever wet.

LIII

And she forgot the stars, the moon, and sun,
  And she forgot the blue above the trees,
And she forgot the dells where waters run,
  And she forgot the chilly autumn breeze;
She had no knowledge when the day was done,
  And the new morn she saw not, but in peace
Hung over her sweet basil evermore,
And moistened it with tears unto the core.

LIV

And so she ever fed it with thin tears,
  Whence thick, and green, and beautiful it grew,
So that it smelt more balmy than its peers
  Of basil-tufts in Florence; for it drew
Nurture besides, and life, from human fears,
  From the fast mouldering head there shut from view:
So that the jewel, safely casketed,
Came forth, and in perfumèd leafits spread.

LV

O Melancholy, linger here awhile!
  O Music, Music, breathe despondingly!
  O Echo, Echo, from some sombre isle,

Unknown, Lethean, sigh to us – O sigh!
Spirits in grief, lift up your heads, and smile.
  Lift up your heads, sweet Spirits, heavily,
And make a pale light in your cypress glooms,
Tinting with silver wan your marble tombs.

LVI

Moan hither, all ye syllables of woe,
  From the deep throat of sad Melpomene!
Through bronzèd lyre in tragic order go,
  And touch the strings into a mystery;
Sound mournfully upon the winds and low;
  For simple Isabel is soon to be
Among the dead. She withers, like a palm
Cut by an Indian for its juicy balm.

LVII

O leave the palm to wither by itself;
  Let not quick Winter chill its dying hour! –
It may not be – those Baälites of pelf,
  Her brethren, noted the continual shower
From her dead eyes; and many a curious elf,
  Among her kindred, wondered that such dower
Of youth and beauty should be thrown aside
By one marked out to be a Noble's bride.

LVIII

And, furthermore, her brethren wondered much
  Why she sat drooping by the basil green,
And why it flourished, as by magic touch.
  Greatly they wondered what the thing might mean:
They could not surely give belief, that such
  A very nothing would have power to wean
Her from her own fair youth, and pleasures gay,
And even remembrance of her love's delay.

LIX

Therefore they watched a time when they might sift
  This hidden whim; and long they watched in vain:
For seldom did she go to chapel-shrift,

And seldom felt she any hunger-pain;
And when she left, she hurried back, as swift
As bird on wing to breast its eggs again;
And, patient as a hen-bird, sat her there
Beside her basil, weeping through her hair.

LX

Yet they contrived to steal the basil-pot,
    And to examine it in secret place.
The thing was vile with green and livid spot,
    And yet they knew it was Lorenzo's face:
The guerdon of their murder they had got,
    And so left Florence in a moment's space,
Never to turn again. Away they went,
With blood upon their heads, to banishment.

LXI

O Melancholy, turn thine eyes away!
    O Music, Music, breathe despondingly!
O Echo, Echo, on some other day,
    From isles Lethean, sigh to us – O sigh!
Spirits of grief, sing not your 'Well-a-way!'
    For Isabel, sweet Isabel, will die –
Will die a death too lone and incomplete,
Now they have ta'en away her basil sweet.

LXII

Piteous she looked on dead and senseless things,
    Asking for her lost basil amorously;
And with melodious chuckle in the strings
    Of her lorn voice, she oftentimes would cry
After the pilgrim in his wanderings,
    To ask him where her basil was, and why
'Twas hid from her: 'For cruel 'tis,' said she,
To steal my basil-pot away from me.'

LXIII

And so she pined, and so she died forlorn,
    Imploring for her basil to the last.
No heart was there in Florence but did mourn

500   In pity of her love, so overcast.
And a sad ditty on this story born
    From mouth to mouth through all the country passed:
Still is the burthen sung – 'O cruelty,
To steal my basil-pot away from me!'

To Homer

Standing aloof in giant ignorance,
    Of thee I hear and of the Cyclades,
As one who sits ashore and longs perchance
    To visit dolphin-coral in deep seas.
So wast thou blind! – but then the veil was rent,
    For Jove uncurtained Heaven to let thee live,
And Neptune made for thee a spumy tent,
    And Pan made sing for thee his forest-hive;
Ay, on the shores of darkness there is light,
10   And precipices show untrodden green;
There is a budding morrow in midnight;
    There is a triple sight in blindness keen;
Such seeing hadst thou, as it once befell
To Dian, Queen of Earth, and Heaven, and Hell.

Ode to May. Fragment

Mother of Hermes! and still youthful Maia!
    May I sing to thee
As thou wast hymnèd on the shores of Baiae?
    Or may I woo thee
In earlier Sicilian? or thy smiles
Seek as they once were sought, in Grecian isles,
By bards who died content in pleasant sward,
    Leaving great verse unto a little clan?
O, give me their old vigour, and unheard
10   Save of the quiet primrose, and the span
        Of Heaven and few ears,

Rounded by thee, my song should die away
    Content as theirs,
Rich in the simple worship of a day.

Acrostic

Give me your patience, sister, while I frame
Exact in capitals your golden name,
Or sue the fair Apollo, and he will
Rouse from his heavy slumber and instill
Great love in me for thee and Poesy.
Imagine not that greatest mastery
And kingdom over all the realms of verse
Nears more to Heaven in aught than when we nurse,
And surety give, to love and brotherhood.

10 Anthropophagi in Othello's mood,
Ulysses stormed, and his enchanted belt
Glow with the Muse, but they are never felt
Unbosomed so and so eternal made,
Such tender incense in their laurel shade,
To all the regent sisters of the Nine,
As this poor offering to you, sister mine.

Kind sister! ay, this third name says you are.
Enchanted has it been the Lord knows where.
And may it taste to you like good old wine,
20 Take you to real happiness and give
Sons, daughters and a home like honeyed hive.

'Sweet, sweet is the greeting of eyes'

Sweet, sweet is the greeting of eyes,
And sweet is the voice in its greeting,
When adieus have grown old and goodbyes
Fade away where old Time is retreating.

Warm the nerve of a welcoming hand,
And earnest a kiss on the brow,
When we meet over sea and o'er land
Where furrows are new to the plough.

On Visiting the Tomb of Burns

The town, the churchyard, and the setting sun,
   The clouds, the trees, the rounded hills all seem,
   Though beautiful, cold – strange – as in a dream
I dreamèd long ago. Now new begun
The short-lived, paly summer is but won
   From winter's ague, for one hour's gleam;
   Through sapphire-warm, their stars do never beam –
All is cold Beauty; pain is never done
For who has mind to relish, Minos-wise,
10   The real of Beauty, free from that dead hue
   Fickly imagination and sick pride
   Cast wan upon it! Burns! with honour due
   I have oft honoured thee. Great shadow, hide
Thy face! I sin against thy native skies.

'Old Meg she was a gipsy'

Old Meg she was a gipsy,
   And lived upon the moors,
Her bed it was the brown heath turf,
   And her house was out of doors.

Her apples were swart blackberries,
   Her currants pods o' broom,
Her wine was dew o' the wild white rose,
   Her book a churchyard tomb.

Her brothers were the craggy hills,
10   Her sisters larchen trees –
Alone with her great family
   She lived as she did please.

No breakfast had she many a morn,
   No dinner many a noon,
And 'stead of supper she would stare
   Full hard against the moon.

But every morn of woodbine fresh
   She made her garlanding,
And every night the dark glen yew
   She wove, and she would sing.

And with her fingers old and brown
   She plaited mats o' rushes,
And gave them to the cottagers
   She met among the bushes.

Old Meg was brave as Margaret Queen
   And tall as Amazon,
An old red blanket cloak she wore,
   A chip-hat had she on.
God rest her agèd bones somewhere –
   She died full long agone!

A Song about Myself

I

There was a naughty boy,
   A naughty boy was he,
He would not stop at home,
   He could not quiet be –
     He took
     In his knapsack
     A book
     Full of vowels
     And a shirt
     With some towels –
     A slight cap
     For night-cap –
     A hair brush,
     Comb ditto,

259 A SONG ABOUT MYSELF

   New stockings,
   For old ones
   Would split O!
   This knapsack
   Tight at's back
20   He rivetted close
  And followed his nose
   To the North,
   To the North,
  And followed his nose
   To the North.

II
There was a naughty boy
  And a naughty boy was he,
For nothing would he do
  But scribble poetry –
30   He took
   An inkstand
   In his hand
   And a pen
   Big as ten
   In the other
   And away
   In a pother
   He ran
   To the mountains
40   And fountains
   And ghostès
   And postès
   And witches
   And ditches,
   And wrote
   In his coat
   When the weather
   Was cool –
   Fear of gout –
50   And without

When the weather
Was warm.
Och, the charm
When we choose
To follow one's nose
To the North,
To the North,
To follow one's nose
To the North!

III

There was a naughty boy
  And a naughty boy was he,
He kept little fishes
  In washing tubs three
    In spite
    Of the might
    Of the maid,
    Nor afraid
    Of his granny-good,
    He often would
    Hurly burly
    Get up early
    And go,
    By hook or crook,
    To the brook
    And bring home
    Miller's thumb,
    Tittlebat
    Not over fat,
    Minnows small
    As the stall
    Of a glove,
    Not above
    The size
    Of a nice
    Little baby's
    Little finger –

          O he made
          ('Twas his trade)
       Of fish a pretty kettle,
90   A kettle –
          A kettle,
       Of fish a pretty kettle,
          A kettle!

    IV
    There was a naughty boy,
       And a naughty boy was he,
    He ran away to Scotland
       The people for to see –
          There he found
          That the ground
100   Was as hard,
          That a yard
          Was as long,
          That a song
          Was as merry,
          That a cherry
          Was as red,
          That lead
          Was as weighty,
          That fourscore
110   Was as eighty,
          That a door
          Was as wooden
          As in England –
       So he stood in his shoes
          And he wondered,
          He wondered,
       He stood in his
          Shoes and he wondered.

'Ah! ken ye what I met the day'

Ah! ken ye what I met the day
   Out oure the mountains,
A-coming down by craggis grey
   An mossie fountains?
Ah! goud-haired Marie yeve I pray
   Ane minute's guessing,
For that I met upon the way
   Is past expressing.
As I stood where a rocky brig
   A torrent crosses,
I spied upon a misty rig
   A troup o' horses –
And as they trotted down the glen
   I sped to meet them
To see if I might know the men
   To stop and greet them.
First Willie on his sleek mare came
   At canting gallop –
His long hair rustled like a flame
   On board a shallop.
Then came his brother Rab and then
   Young Peggy's mither
And Peggy too – adown the glen
   They went togither.
I saw her wrappit in her hood
   Fra wind and raining –
Her cheek was flush wi' timid blood
   Twixt growth and waning.
She turn'd her dazèd head full oft
   For thence her brithers
Came riding with her bridegroom soft
   An mony ithers.
Young Tam came up an' eyed me quick
   With reddened cheek.
Braw Tam was daffèd like a chick –
   He could na speak.

Ah! Marie they are all gane hame
    Through blustering weather,
An' every heart is full on flame
40   An' light as feather.
Ah! Marie they are all gone hame
    Fra happy wedding,
Whilst I – Ah! is it not a shame? –
    Sad tears am shedding.

To Ailsa Rock

Hearken, thou craggy ocean pyramid!
    Give answer by thy voice, the sea-fowls' screams!
    When were thy shoulders mantled in huge streams?
When from the sun was thy broad forehead hid?
How long is't since the mighty power bid
    Thee heave to airy sleep from fathom dreams?
    Sleep in the lap of thunder or sunbeams,
Or when grey clouds are thy cold coverlid?
Thou answer'st not; for thou art dead asleep.
10   Thy life is but two dead eternities –
The last in air, the former in the deep,
    First with the whales, last with the eagle-skies.
Drowned wast thou till an earthquake made thee steep,
    Another cannot wake thy giant size!

'This mortal body of a thousand days'

This mortal body of a thousand days
    Now fills, O Burns, a space in thine own room,
Where thou didst dream alone on budded bays,
    Happy and thoughtless of thy day of doom!
My pulse is warm with thine own barley-bree,
    My head is light with pledging a great soul,
My eyes are wandering, and I cannot see,
    Fancy is dead and drunken at its goal:

    Yet can I stamp my foot upon thy floor,
10   Yet can I ope thy window-sash to find
    The meadow thou hast trampèd o'er and o'er,
      Yet can I think of thee till thought is blind,
    Yet can I gulp a bumper to thy name –
    O smile among the shades, for this is fame!

'All gentle folks who owe a grudge'

All gentle folks who owe a grudge
    To any living thing,
Open your ears and stay your trudge
    Whilst I in dudgeon sing.

The gad-fly he hath stung me sore –
    O may he ne'er sting you!
But we have many a horrid bore
    He may sting black and blue.

Has any here an old grey mare
10   With three legs all her store?
O put it to her buttocks bare
    And straight she'll run on four.

Has any here a lawyer suit
    Of 1743?
Take lawyer's nose and put it to 't
    And you the end will see.

Is there a man in Parliament
    Dumbfoundered in his speech?
O let his neighbour make a rent
20   And put one in his breech.

O Lowther, how much better thou
    Hadst figured t'other day,
When to the folks thou mad'st a bow
    And hadst no more to say,

If lucky gad-fly had but ta'en
  His seat upon thine arse,
And put thee to a little pain
  To save thee from a worse.

Better than Southey it had been,
  Better than Mr D—,
Better than Wordsworth too, I ween,
  Better than Mr V—.

Forgive me pray, good people all,
  For deviating so.
In spirit sure I had a call –
  And now I on will go.

Has any here a daughter fair
  Too fond of reading novels,
Too apt to fall in love with care
  And charming Mister Lovels?

O put a gad-fly to that thing
  She keeps so white and pert –
I mean the finger for the ring,
  And it will breed a Wert.

Has any here a pious spouse
  Who seven times a day
Scolds as King David prayed, to chouse
  And have her holy way?

O let a gad-fly's little sting
  Persuade her sacred tongue
That noises are a common thing,
  But that her bell has rung.

And as this is the *summum bonum* of all conquering,
I leave withouten wordès mo
  The gad-fly's little sting.

'*Of late two dainties were before me placed*'

Of late two dainties were before me placed,
   Sweet, holy, pure, sacred and innocent,
   From the ninth sphere benignly sent
That Gods might know my own particular taste.
First the soft bagpipe mourned with zealous haste,
   The Stranger next, with head on bosom bent,
   Sighed; rueful again the piteous bagpipe went,
Again the Stranger sighings fresh did waste.
O Bagpipe, thou didst steal my heart away –
   O Stranger, thou my nerves from pipe didst charm –
O Bagpipe, thou didst re-assert thy sway –
   Again, thou Stranger gav'st me fresh alarm!
Alas! I could not choose. Ah! my poor heart,
Mumchance art thou with both obliged to part.

Lines Written in the Highlands after a Visit to Burns's Country

There is a joy in footing slow across a silent plain,
Where patriot battle has been fought when glory had the gain;
There is a pleasure on the heath where Druids old have been,
Where mantles grey have rustled by and swept the nettles green;
There is a joy in every spot made known by times of old,
New to the feet, although the tale a hundred times be told;
There is a deeper joy than all, more solemn in the heart,
More parching to the tongue than all, of more divine a smart,
When weary steps forget themselves upon a pleasant turf,
Upon hot sand, or flinty road, or sea-shore iron scurf,
Toward the castle or the cot, where long ago was born
One who was great through mortal days, and died of fame unshorn.

Light heather-bells may tremble then, but they are far away;
Wood-lark may sing from sandy fern, the sun may hear his lay;
Runnels may kiss the grass on shelves and shallows clear,
But their low voices are not heard, though come on travels drear;
Blood-red the sun may set behind black mountain peaks;
Blue tides may sluice and drench their time in caves and weedy creeks;
Eagles may seem to sleep wing-wide upon the air;
20 Ring-doves may fly convulsed across to some high-cedared lair;
But the forgotten eye is still fast wedded to the ground,
As palmer's that, with weariness, mid-desert shrine hath found.
At such a time the soul's a child, in childhood is the brain;
Forgotten is the worldly heart – alone, it beats in vain.
Ay, if a madman could have leave to pass a healthful day
To tell his forehead's swoon and faint when first began decay,
He might make tremble many a man whose spirit had gone forth
To find a bard's low cradle-place about the silent North!
Scanty the hour and few the steps beyond the bourn of care,
30 Beyond the sweet and bitter world – beyond it unaware;
Scanty the hour and few the steps, because a longer stay
Would bar return, and make a man forget his mortal way.
O horrible! to lose the sight of well-remembered face,
Of brother's eyes, of sister's brow, constant to every place,
Filling the air, as on we move, with portraiture intense,
More warm than those heroic tints that fill a painter's sense,
When shapes of old come striding by, and visages of old,
Locks shining black, hair scanty grey, and passions manifold.
No, no, that horror cannot be, for at the cable's length
40 Man feels the gentle anchor pull and gladdens in its strength –

One hour, half-idiot, he stands by mossy waterfall,
But in the very next he reads his soul's memorial.
He reads it on the mountain's height, where chance he may
    sit down
Upon rough marble diadem, that hill's eternal crown.
Yet be the anchor e'er so fast, room is there for a prayer.
That man may never lose his mind on mountains bleak and
    bare;
That he may stray league after league some great birth-place
    to find,
And keep his vision clear from speck, his inward sight
    unblind.

On Visiting Staffa

Not Aladdin magian
Ever such a work began;
Not the wizard of the Dee
Ever such a dream could see;
Not St John, in Patmos' Isle,
In the passion of his toil,
When he saw the churches seven,
Golden aisled, built up in heaven,
Gazed at such a rugged wonder.
10 As I stood its roofing under,
Lo! I saw one sleeping there,
On the marble cold and bare,
While the surges wash'd his feet,
And his garments white did beat
Drenched about the sombre rocks.
On his neck his well-grown locks,
Lifted dry above the main,
Were upon the curl again.
'What is this? and what art thou?'
20 Whispered I, and touched his brow.
'What art thou? and what is this?'
Whispered I, and strove to kiss

ON VISITING STAFFA

The spirit's hand, to wake his eyes.
Up he started in a trice:
'I am Lycidas,' said he,
'Famed in funeral minstrelsy!
This was architected thus
By the great Oceanus! –
Here his mighty waters play
30 Hollow organs all the day;
Here by turns his dolphins all,
Finny palmers great and small,
Come to pay devotion due –
Each a mouth of pearls must strew.
Many a mortal of these days,
Dares to pass our sacred ways,
Dares to touch audaciously
This Cathedral of the Sea!
I have been the pontiff-priest
40 Where the waters never rest,
Where a fledgy sea-bird choir
Soars for ever; holy fire
I have hid from mortal man;
Proteus is my sacristan.
But the dulled eye of mortal
Hath passed beyond the rocky portal;
So for ever will I leave
Such a taint, and soon unweave
All the magic of the place.
50 'Tis now free to stupid face,
To cutters and to fashion boats,
To cravats and to petticoats.
The great sea shall war it down,
For its fame shall not be blown
At every farthing quadrille dance.'
So saying, with a Spirit's glance
He dived!

'*Read me a lesson, Muse, and speak it loud*'

Read me a lesson, Muse, and speak it loud
    Upon the top of Nevis, blind in mist!
I look into the chasms, and a shroud
    Vapourous doth hide them; just so much I wist
Mankind do know of Hell. I look o'erhead,
    And there is sullen mist; even so much
Mankind can tell of Heaven. Mist is spread
    Before the earth, beneath me – even such,
Even so vague is man's sight of himself.
    Here are the craggy stones beneath my feet –
Thus much I know, that, a poor witless elf,
    I tread on them, that all my eye doth meet
Is mist and crag, not only on this height,
    But in the world of thought and mental might.

'*Upon my life, Sir Nevis, I am piqued*'

MRS C.
Upon my life, Sir Nevis, I am piqued
That I have so far panted tugged and reeked
To do an honour to your old bald pate
And now am sitting on you just to bate,
Without your paying me one compliment.
Alas, 'tis so with all, when our intent
Is plain, and in the eye of all mankind
We fair ones show a preference, too blind!
You gentlemen immediately turn tail –
O let me then my hapless fate bewail!
Ungrateful baldpate, have I not disdained
The pleasant valleys, have I not, mad-brained,
Deserted all my pickles and preserves,
My china closet too – with wretched nerves
To boot – say, wretched ingrate, have I not
Left my soft cushion chair and caudle pot?
'Tis true I had no corns – no! thank the fates,

'UPON MY LIFE, SIR NEVIS, I AM PIQUED'

My shoemaker was always Mr Bates.
And if not Mr Bates, why I'm not old!
Still dumb, ungrateful Nevis – still so cold!

(Here the lady took some more whiskey and was putting even more to her lips when she dashed [it] to the ground for the mountain began to grumble – which continued for a few minutes, before he thus began,)

BEN NEVIS
What whining bit of tongue and mouth thus dares
Disturb my slumber of a thousand years?
Even so long my sleep has been secure –
And to be so awaked I'll not endure.
O, pain! – for since the eagle's earliest scream
I've had a damned confounded ugly dream,
A nightmare sure. What, Madam, was it you?
It cannot be! My old eyes are not true!
Red Crag, my spectacles! Now let me see!
Good Heavens, Lady, how the gemini
Did you get here? O I shall split my sides!
I shall earthquake –

MRS C.
Sweet Nevis, do not quake, for though I love
Your honest Countenance all things above,
Truly I should not like to be conveyed
So far into your bosom – gentle maid
Loves not too rough a treatment, gentle Sir –
Pray thee be calm and do not quake nor stir,
No, not a stone, or I shall go in fits –

BEN NEVIS
I must – I shall! I meet not such tit-bits –
I meet not such sweet creatures every day!
By my old night-cap, night-cap night and day,
I must have one sweet buss – I must and shall!
Red Crag! – What, Madam, can you then repent
Of all the toil and vigour you have spent
To see Ben Nevis and to touch his nose?

Red Crag, I say! O I must have you close!
Red Crag, there lies beneath my farthest toe
A vein of sulphur – go, dear Red Crag, go –
50 And rub your flinty back against it. Budge!
Dear Madam, I must kiss you, faith I must!
I must embrace you with my dearest gust!
Blockhead, d'ye hear – Blockhead, I'll make her feel –
There lies beneath my east leg's northern heel
A cave of young earth dragons – well, my boy,
Go thither quick and so complete my joy.
Take you a bundle of the largest pines
And, where the sun on fiercest phosphor shines,
Fire them and ram them in the dragon's nest,
60 Then will the dragons fry and fizz their best,
Until ten thousand now no bigger than
Poor Alligators – poor things of one span –
Will each one swell to twice ten times the size
Of northern whale. Then for the tender prize –
The moment then – for then will Red Crag rub
His flinty back – and I shall kiss and snub
And press my dainty morsel to my breast.
Blockhead, make haste!
                O Muses weep the rest –
The lady fainted, and he thought her dead,
70 So pulled the clouds again about his head,
And went to sleep again – soon she was roused
By her affrighted servants. Next day housed
Safe on the lowly ground she blessed her fate.
That fainting fit was not delayed too late.

Stanzas on some Skulls in Beauly Abbey, near Inverness

   I shed no tears;
Deep thought, or awful vision, I had none;
By thousand petty fancies I was crossed.
Wordsworth

STANZAS ON SOME SKULLS

And mocked the dead bones that lay scattered by
Shakespeare

[Written in collaboration with Charles Brown. Keats's contributions are given in roman type.]

I

In silent barren Synod met,
Within those roofless walls *where yet*
The shafted arch and carvèd fret
   Cling to the ruin,
The brethren's skulls mourn, dewy wet,
   Their creed's undoing.

II

The mitred ones of Nice and Trent
Were not so tongue-tied – no, they went
Hot to their Councils, scarce content
   With orthodoxy;
But ye, poor tongueless things, were meant
   To speak by proxy.

III

Your chronicles no more exist,
Since Knox, the revolutionist,
Destroyed the work of every fist
   That scrawled black letter.
Well! I'm a craniologist
   And may do better.

IV

This skull-cap wore the cowl from sloth
Or discontent, perhaps from both,
And yet one day, against his oath,
   He tried escaping,
For men, though idle, may be loth
   To live on gaping.

V

A toper this! he plied his glass
More strictly than he said the Mass,
And loved to see a tempting lass
          Come to confession,
Letting her absolution pass
          O'er fresh transgression.

VI

This crawled through life in feebleness,
Boasting he never knew excess,
Cursing those crimes he sarce could guess,
          Or feel but faintly,
With prayers that Heaven would come to bless
          Men so unsaintly.

VII

Here's a true Churchman! he'd affect
Much charity, and ne'er neglect
To pray for mercy on th' elect,
          But thought no evil
In sending heathen, Turk and sect
          All to the Devil!

VIII

Poor skull, thy fingers set ablaze,
With silver Saint in golden rays,
The holy missal. Thou didst craze
          'Mid bead and spangle,
While others passed their idle days
          In coil and wrangle.

IX

Long time this sconce a helmet wore,
But sickness smites the conscience sore;
He broke his sword, and hither bore
          His gear and plunder,
Took to the cowl – then raved and swore
          At his damned blunder!

STANZAS ON SOME SKULLS

X

This lily-coloured skull, with all
The teeth complete, so white and small,
Belonged to one whose early pall
        A lover shaded;
He died ere superstition's gall
        His heart invaded.

XI

Ha! here is 'undivulgèd crime!'
Despair forbade his soul to climb
Beyond this world, this mortal time
        Of fevered sadness,
Until their monkish pantomime
        Dazzled his madness!

XII

A younger brother this! A man
Aspiring as a Tartar Khan,
But, curbed and baffled, he began
        The trade of frightening.
It smacked of power! – and here he ran
        To deal Heaven's lightning.

XIII

This idiot-skull belonged to one,
A buried miser's only son,
Who, penitent, ere he'd begun
        To taste of pleasure,
And hoping Heaven's dread wrath to shun,
        Gave Hell his treasure.

XIV

Here is the forehead of an ape,
A robber's mark – and near the nape
That bone, fie on't, bears just the shape
        Of carnal passion;
Ah! he was one for theft and rape,
        In monkish fashion!

XV

This was the Porter! – he could sing,
Or dance, or play, do anything,
And what the friars bade him bring,
        They ne'er were balked of
(Matters not worth remembering
        And seldom talked of).

XVI

Enough! why need I further pore?
This corner holds at least a score,
And yonder twice as many more
        Of Reverend Brothers;
'Tis the same story o'er and o'er –
        They're like the others!

Translated from Ronsard

Nature withheld Cassandra in the skies,
  For more adornment, a full thousand years;
She took their cream of Beauty, fairest dyes,
  And shaped and tinted her above all peers:
Meanwhile Love kept her dearly with his wings,
  And underneath their shadow filled her eyes
With such a richness that the cloudy Kings
  Of high Olympus uttered slavish sighs.
When from the Heavens I saw her first descend,
  My heart took fire, and only burning pains ...
They were my pleasures – they my Life's sad end;
  Love poured her beauty into my warm veins. ...

"'Tis "the witching time of night"'

'Tis 'the witching time of night',
Orbed is the moon and bright,
And the stars they glisten, glisten,
Seeming with bright eyes to listen –

> For what listen they?
> For a song and for a charm,
> See they glisten in alarm,
> And the moon is waxing warm
> > To hear what I shall say.
>
> 10 Moon! keep wide thy golden ears –
> Hearken, stars! and hearken, spheres!
> Hearken, thou eternal sky!
> I sing an infant's lullaby,
> > A pretty lullaby.
>
> Listen, listen, listen, listen,
> Glisten, glisten, glisten, glisten,
> > And hear my lullaby!
>
> Though the rushes that will make
> Its cradle still are in the lake;
> 20 Though the linen then that will be
> Its swathe, is on the cotton tree;
> Though the woollen that will keep
> It warm is on the silly sheep –
> Listen, stars' light, listen, listen,
> Glisten, glisten, glisten, glisten,
> > And hear my lullaby!
>
> Child, I see thee! Child, I've found thee
> Midst of the quiet all around thee!
> Child, I see thee! Child, I spy thee!
> 30 And thy mother sweet is nigh thee!
> Child, I know thee! Child no more,
> But a Poet evermore!
> See, see, the lyre, the lyre,
> In a flame of fire,
> Upon the little cradle's top
> Flaring, flaring, flaring,
> Past the eyesight's bearing.
> Awake it from its sleep,
> And see if it can keep
> 40 Its eyes upon the blaze –
> > Amaze, amaze!
>
> It stares, it stares, it stares,

It dares what no one dares!
It lifts its little hand into the flame
Unharmed, and on the strings
Paddles a little tune, and sings,
With dumb endeavour sweetly –
Bard art thou completely!
    Little child
50   O' th' western wild,
Bard art thou completely!
Sweetly with dumb endeavour,
A Poet now or never,
    Little child
    O' the western wild,
A Poet now or never!

'Welcome joy, and welcome sorrow'

Under the flag
Of each his faction, they to battle bring
Their embryon atoms.
Milton

Welcome joy, and welcome sorrow,
  Lethe's weed and Hermes' feather;
Come today, and come tomorrow,
  I do love you both together!
  I love to mark sad faces in fair weather,
And hear a merry laugh amid the thunder.
  Fair and foul I love together:
  Meadows sweet where flames burn under,
And a giggle at a wonder;
10 Visage sage at pantomime;
Funeral, and steeple-chime;
Infant playing with a skull;
Morning fair, and stormwrecked hull;
Nightshade with the woodbine kissing;
Serpents in red roses hissing;
Cleopatra regal-dressed

>   With the aspics at her breast
>   Dancing music, music sad,
>   Both together, sane and mad;
> 20 Muses bright and Muses pale;
>   Sombre Saturn, Momus hale.
>   Laugh and sigh, and laugh again –
>   O the sweetness of the pain!
>   Muses bright, and Muses pale,
>   Bare your faces of the veil!
>   Let me see! and let me write
>   Of the day and of the night –
>   Both together. Let me slake
>   All my thirst for sweet heart-ache!
> 30 Let my bower be of yew,
>   Interwreathed with myrtles new,
>   Pines and lime-trees full in bloom,
>   And my couch a low grass tomb.

Song

I

Spirit here that reignest!
Spirit here that painest!
Spirit here that burnest!
Spirit here that mournest!
    Spirit! I bow
    My forehead low,
  Enshaded with thy pinions!
    Spirit! I look
    All passion-struck
10   Into thy pale dominions!

II

Spirit here that laughest!
Spirit there that quaffest!
Spirit here that dancest!
Noble soul that prancest!

Spirit! with thee
   I join in the glee,
A-nudging the elbow of Momus!
   Spirit! I flush
   With a Bacchanal blush
20 Just fresh from the banquet of Comus.

'Where's the Poet? Show him, show him'

Where's the Poet? Show him! show him,
Muses nine, that I may know him!
'Tis the man who with a man
   Is an equal, be he king,
Or poorest of the beggar-clan,
   Or any other wondrous thing
A man may be 'twixt ape and Plato.
   'Tis the man who with a bird,
Wren or eagle, finds his way to
10   All its instincts. He hath heard
The lion's roaring, and can tell
   What his horny throat expresseth,
And to him the tiger's yell
   Comes articulate and presseth
On his ear like mother-tongue.

Fragment of the 'Castle Builder'

CASTLE BUILDER
In short, convince you that however wise
You may have grown from convent libraries,
I have, by many yards at least, been carding
A longer skein of wit in Convent Garden.

BERNARDINE
A very Eden that same place must be!
Pray what demesne? Whose lordship's legacy?

FRAGMENT OF THE 'CASTLE BUILDER'

What, have you convents in that Gothic isle?
Pray pardon me, I cannot help but smile.

CASTLE BUILDER
Sir, Convent Garden is a monstrous beast:
From morning, four o'clock, to twelve at noon,
It swallows cabbages without a spoon,
And then, from twelve till two, this Eden made is
A promenade for cooks and ancient ladies;
And then for supper, 'stead of soup and poaches,
It swallows chairmen, damns, and Hackney coaches.
In short, Sir, 'tis a very place for monks,
For it containeth twenty thousand punks,
Which any man may number for his sport,
By following fat elbows up a court ...
In such like nonsense would I pass an hour
With random friar, or rake upon his tour,
Or one of few of that imperial host
Who came unmaimèd from the Russian frost.
To-night I'll have my friar – let me think
About my room – I'll have it in the pink.
It should be rich and sombre, and the moon,
Just in its mid-life in the midst of June,
Should look through four large windows and display
Clear, but for golden fishes in the way,
Their glassy diamonding on Turkish floor.
The tapers keep aside, an hour and more,
To see what else the moon alone can show;
While the night-breeze doth softly let us know
My terrace is well bowered with oranges.
Upon the floor the dullest spirit sees
A guitar-ribband and a lady's glove
Beside a crumple-leavèd tale of love;
A tambour-frame, with Venus sleeping there,
All finished but some ringlets of her hair;
A viol, bowstrings torn, cross-wise upon
A glorious folio of Anacreon;
A skull upon a mat of roses lying,

Inked purple with a song concerning dying;
An hour-glass on the turn, amid the trails
Of passion-flower – just in time there sails
A cloud across the moon – the lights bring in!
And see what more my fantasy can win.
It is a gorgeous room, but somewhat sad;
The draperies are so, as though they had
50 Been made for Cleopatra's winding-sheet;
And opposite the steadfast eye doth meet
A spacious looking-glass, upon whose face,
In letters raven-sombre, you may trace
Old 'Mene, Mene, Tekel, Upharsin'.
Greek busts and statuary have ever been
Held, by the finest spirits, fitter far
Than vase grotesque and Siamesian jar;
Therefore 'tis sure a want of Attic taste
That I should rather love a Gothic waste
60 Of eyesight on cinque-coloured potter's clay,
Than on the marble fairness of old Greece.
My table-coverlets of Jason's fleece
And black Numidian sheep-wool should be wrought,
Gold, black, and heavy, from the Lama brought.
My ebon sofa should delicious be
With down from Leda's cygnet progeny.
My pictures all Salvator's, save a few
Of Titian's portraiture, and one, though new,
Of Haydon's in its fresh magnificence.
70 My wine – O good! 'tis here at my desire,
And I must sit to supper with my friar.

'And what is love? It is a doll dressed up'

And what is love? It is a doll dressed up
For idleness to cosset, nurse, and dandle;
A thing of soft misnomers, so divine
That silly youth doth think to make itself
Divine by loving, and so goes on

Yawning and doting a whole summer long,
   Till Miss's comb is made a pearl tiara,
   And common Wellingtons turn Romeo boots;
   Till Cleopatra lives at Number Seven,
10 And Antony resides in Brunswick Square.
   Fools! if some passions high have warmed the world,
   If queens and soldiers have played deep for hearts,
   It is no reason why such agonies
   Should be more common than the growth of weeds.
   Fools! make me whole again that weighty pearl
   The queen of Egypt melted, and I'll say
   That ye may love in spite of beaver hats.

Hyperion. A Fragment

BOOK I

   Deep in the shady sadness of a vale
   Far sunken from the healthy breath of morn,
   Far from the fiery noon, and eve's one star,
   Sat grey-haired Saturn, quiet as a stone,
   Still as the silence round about his lair;
   Forest on forest hung above his head
   Like cloud on cloud. No stir of air was there,
   Not so much life as on a summer's day
   Robs not one light seed from the feathered grass,
10 But where the dead leaf fell, there did it rest.
   A stream went voiceless by, still deadened more
   By reason of his fallen divinity
   Spreading a shade: the Naiad 'mid her reeds
   Pressed her cold finger closer to her lips.

   Along the margin-sand large foot-marks went,
   No further than to where his feet had strayed,
   And slept there since. Upon the sodden ground
   His old right hand lay nerveless, listless, dead,
   Unsceptred; and his realmless eyes were closed;
20 While his bowed head seemed listening to the Earth,
   His ancient mother, for some comfort yet.

It seemed no force could wake him from his place;
But there came one, who with a kindred hand
Touched his wide shoulders, after bending low
With reverence, though to one who knew it not.
She was a Goddess of the infant world;
By her in stature the tall Amazon
Had stood a pigmy's height: she would have ta'en
Achilles by the hair and bent his neck;
Or with a finger stayed Ixion's wheel.
Her face was large as that of Memphian sphinx,
Pedestalled haply in a palace court,
When sages looked to Egypt for their lore.
But O! how unlike marble was that face,
How beautiful, if sorrow had not made
Sorrow more beautiful than Beauty's self.
There was a listening fear in her regard,
As if calamity had but begun;
As if the vanward clouds of evil days
Had spent their malice, and the sullen rear
Was with its storèd thunder labouring up.
One hand she pressed upon that aching spot
Where beats the human heart, as if just there,
Though an immortal, she felt cruel pain;
The other upon Saturn's bended neck
She laid, and to the level of his ear
Leaning with parted lips, some words she spake
In solemn tenor and deep organ tone –
Some mourning words, which in our feeble tongue
Would come in these like accents (O how frail
To that large utterance of the early Gods!)
'Saturn, look up! – though wherefore, poor old King?
I have no comfort for thee, no, not one:
I cannot say, "O wherefore sleepest thou?"
For heaven is parted from thee, and the earth
Knows thee not, thus afflicted, for a God;
And ocean too, with all its solemn noise,
Has from thy sceptre passed; and all the air
Is emptied of thine hoary majesty.

HYPERION. A FRAGMENT

60 Thy thunder, conscious of the new command,
    Rumbles reluctant o'er our fallen house;
    And thy sharp lightning in unpractised hands
    Scorches and burns our once serene domain.
    O aching time! O moments big as years!
    All as ye pass swell out the monstrous truth,
    And press it so upon our weary griefs
    That unbelief has not a space to breathe.
    Saturn, sleep on – O thoughtless, why did I
    Thus violate thy slumbrous solitude?
70 Why should I ope thy melancholy eyes?
    Saturn, sleep on, while at thy feet I weep!'

    As when, upon a trancèd summer-night,
    Those green-robed senators of mighty woods,
    Tall oaks, branch-charmèd by the earnest stars,
    Dream, and so dream all night without a stir,
    Save from one gradual solitary gust
    Which comes upon the silence, and dies off,
    As if the ebbing air had but one wave;
    So came these words and went; the while in tears
80 She touched her fair large forehead to the ground,
    Just where her falling hair might be outspread
    A soft and silken mat for Saturn's feet.
    One moon, with alteration slow, had shed
    Her silver seasons four upon the night,
    And still these two were postured motionless,
    Like natural sculpture in cathedral cavern;
    The frozen God still couchant on the earth,
    And the sad Goddess weeping at his feet:
    Until at length old Saturn lifted up
90 His faded eyes, and saw his kingdom gone,
    And all the gloom and sorrow of the place,
    And that fair kneeling Goddess; and then spake,
    As with a palsied tongue, and while his beard
    Shook horrid with such aspen-malady:
    'O tender spouse of gold Hyperion,
    Thea, I feel thee ere I see thy face;

         Look up, and let me see our doom in it;
         Look up, and tell me if this feeble shape
         Is Saturn's; tell me, if thou hear'st the voice
100   Of Saturn; tell me, if this wrinkling brow,
         Naked and bare of its great diadem,
         Peers like the front of Saturn. Who had power
         To make me desolate? whence came the strength?
         How was it nurtured to such bursting forth,
         While Fate seemed strangled in my nervous grasp?
         But it is so; and I am smothered up,
         And buried from all godlike exercise
         Of influence benign on planets pale,
         Of admonitions to the winds and seas,
110   Of peaceful sway above man's harvesting,
         And all those acts which Deity supreme
         Doth ease its heart of love in. – I am gone
         Away from my own bosom; I have left
         My strong identity, my real self,
         Somewhere between the throne and where I sit
         Here on this spot of earth. Search, Thea, search!
         Open thine eyes eterne, and sphere them round
         Upon all space – space starred, and lorn of light;
         Space regioned with life-air; and barren void;
120   Spaces of fire, and all the yawn of hell.
         Search, Thea, search! and tell me, if thou seest
         A certain shape or shadow, making way
         With wings or chariot fierce to repossess
         A heaven he lost erewhile: it must – it must
         Be of ripe progress: Saturn must be King.
         Yes, there must be a golden victory;
         There must be Gods thrown down, and trumpets blown
         Of triumph calm, and hymns of festival
         Upon the gold clouds metropolitan,
130   Voices of soft proclaim, and silver stir
         Of strings in hollow shells; and there shall be
         Beautiful things made new, for the surprise
         Of the sky-children. I will give command:
         Thea! Thea! Thea! where is Saturn?'

HYPERION. A FRAGMENT

This passion lifted him upon his feet,
And made his hands to struggle in the air,
His Druid locks to shake and ooze with sweat,
His eyes to fever out, his voice to cease.
He stood, and heard not Thea's sobbing deep;
A little time, and then again he snatched
Utterance thus: 'But cannot I create?
Cannot I form? Cannot I fashion forth
Another world, another universe,
To overbear and crumble this to naught?
Where is another Chaos? Where?' – That word
Found way unto Olympus, and made quake
The rebel three. Thea was startled up,
And in her bearing was a sort of hope,
As thus she quick-voiced spake, yet full of awe.

'This cheers our fallen house: come to our friends,
O Saturn! come away, and give them heart.
I know the covert, for thence came I hither.'
Thus brief; then with beseeching eyes she went
With backward footing through the shade a space:
He followed, and she turned to lead the way
Through agèd boughs, that yielded like the mist
Which eagles cleave up-mounting from their nest.

Meanwhile in other realms big tears were shed,
More sorrow like to this, and such like woe,
Too huge for mortal tongue or pen of scribe.
The Titans fierce, self-hid, or prison-bound,
Groaned for the old allegiance once more,
And listened in sharp pain for Saturn's voice.
But one of the whole mammoth-brood still kept
His sovereignty, and rule, and majesty –
Blazing Hyperion on his orbèd fire
Still sat, still snuffed the incense, teeming up
From man to the sun's God – yet unsecure:
For as among us mortals omens drear
Fright and perplex, so also shuddered he –
Not at dog's howl, or gloom-bird's hated screech,

HYPERION. A FRAGMENT

    Or the familiar visiting of one
Upon the first toll of his passing-bell,
Or prophesyings of the midnight lamp;
But horrors, portioned to a giant nerve,
Oft made Hyperion ache. His palace bright
Bastioned with pyramids of glowing gold,
And touched with shade of bronzèd obelisks,
Glared a blood-red through all its thousand courts,
180 Arches, and domes, and fiery galleries;
And all its curtains of Aurorian clouds
Flushed angerly, while sometimes eagle's wings,
Unseen before by Gods or wondering men,
Darkened the place, and neighing steeds were heard,
Not heard before by Gods or wondering men.
Also, when he would taste the spicy wreaths
Of incense, breathed aloft from sacred hills,
Instead of sweets, his ample palate took
Savour of poisonous brass and metal sick:
190 And so, when harboured in the sleepy west,
After the full completion of fair day,
For rest divine upon exalted couch
And slumber in the arms of melody,
He paced away the pleasant hours of ease
With stride colossal, on from hall to hall;
While far within each aisle and deep recess,
His wingèd minions in close clusters stood,
Amazed and full of fear; like anxious men
Who on wide plains gather in panting troops,
200 When earthquakes jar their battlements and towers.
Even now, while Saturn, roused from icy trance,
Went step for step with Thea through the woods,
Hyperion, leaving twilight in the rear,
Came slope upon the threshold of the west;
Then, as was wont, his palace-door flew ope
In smoothest silence, save what solemn tubes,
Blown by the serious Zephyrs, gave of sweet
And wandering sounds, slow-breathèd melodies —
And like a rose in vermeil tint and shape,

HYPERION. A FRAGMENT

210 In fragrance soft, and coolness to the eye,
That inlet to severe magnificence
Stood full blown, for the God to enter in.

　　He entered, but he entered full of wrath;
His flaming robes streamed out beyond his heels,
And gave a roar, as if of earthly fire,
That scared away the meek ethereal Hours
And made their dove-wings tremble. On he flared,
From stately nave to nave, from vault to vault,
Through bowers of fragrant and enwreathèd light,
220 And diamond-pavèd lustrous long arcades,
Until he reached the great main cupola.
There standing fierce beneath, he stamped his foot,
And from the basement deep to the high towers
Jarred his own golden region; and before
The quavering thunder thereupon had ceased,
His voice leapt out, despite of god-like curb,
To this result: 'O dreams of day and night!
O monstrous forms! O effigies of pain!
O spectres busy in a cold, cold gloom!
230 O lank-eared Phantoms of black-weeded pools!
Why do I know ye? Why have I seen ye? Why
Is my eternal essence thus distraught
To see and to behold these horrors new?
Saturn is fallen, am I too to fall?
Am I to leave this haven of my rest,
This cradle of my glory, this soft clime,
This calm luxuriance of blissful light,
These crystalline pavilions, and pure fanes,
Of all my lucent empire? It is left
240 Deserted, void, nor any haunt of mine.
The blaze, the splendour, and the symmetry,
I cannot see – but darkness, death and darkness.
Even here, into my centre of repose,
The shady visions come to domineer,
Insult, and blind, and stifle up my pomp. –
Fall! – No, by Tellus and her briny robes!

Over the fiery frontier of my realms
I will advance a terrible right arm
Shall scare that infant thunderer, rebel Jove,
250 And bid old Saturn take his throne again.' –
He spake, and ceased, the while a heavier threat
Held struggle with his throat but came not forth;
For as in theatres of crowded men
Hubbub increases more they call out 'Hush!',
So at Hyperion's words the Phantoms pale
Bestirred themselves, thrice horrible and cold;
And from the mirrored level where he stood
A mist arose, as from a scummy marsh.
At this, through all his bulk an agony
260 Crept gradual, from the feet unto the crown,
Like a lithe serpent vast and muscular
Making slow way, with head and neck convulsed
From over-strainèd might. Released, he fled
To the eastern gates, and full six dewy hours
Before the dawn in season due should blush,
He breathed fierce breath against the sleepy portals,
Cleared them of heavy vapours, burst them wide
Suddenly on the ocean's chilly streams.
The planet orb of fire, whereon he rode
270 Each day from east to west the heavens through,
Spun round in sable curtaining of clouds;
Not therefore veilèd quite, blindfold, and hid,
But ever and anon the glancing spheres,
Circles, and arcs, and broad-belting colure,
Glowed through, and wrought upon the muffling dark
Sweet-shapèd lightnings from the nadir deep
Up to the zenith – hieroglyphics old
Which sages and keen-eyed astrologers
Then living on the earth, with labouring thought
280 Won from the gaze of many centuries –
Now lost, save what we find on remnants huge
Of stone, or marble swart, their import gone,
Their wisdom long since fled. Two wings this orb
Possessed for glory, two fair argent wings,

HYPERION. A FRAGMENT

>   Ever exalted at the God's approach:
>   And now, from forth the gloom their plumes immense
>   Rose, one by one, till all outspreaded were;
>   While still the dazzling globe maintained eclipse,
>   Awaiting for Hyperion's command.
> 290 Fain would he have commanded, fain took throne
>   And bid the day begin, if but for change.
>   He might not. – No, though a primeval God:
>   The sacred seasons might not be disturbed.
>   Therefore the operations of the dawn
>   Stayed in their birth, even as here 'tis told.
>   Those silver wings expanded sisterly,
>   Eager to sail their orb; the porches wide
>   Opened upon the dusk demesnes of night;
>   And the bright Titan, frenzied with new woes,
> 300 Unused to bend, by hard compulsion bent
>   His spirit to the sorrow of the time;
>   And all along a dismal rack of clouds,
>   Upon the boundaries of day and night,
>   He stretched himself in grief and radiance faint.
>   There as he lay, the Heaven with its stars
>   Looked down on him with pity, and the voice
>   Of Coelus, from the universal space,
>   Thus whispered low and solemn in his ear:
>   'O brightest of my children dear, earth-born
> 310 And sky-engendered, Son of Mysteries
>   All unrevealèd even to the powers
>   Which met at thy creating; at whose joys
>   And palpitations sweet, and pleasures soft,
>   I, Coelus, wonder how they came and whence;
>   And at the fruits thereof what shapes they be,
>   Distinct, and visible – symbols divine,
>   Manifestations of that beauteous life
>   Diffused unseen throughout eternal space:
>   Of these new-formed art thou, O brightest child!
> 320 Of these, thy brethren and the Goddesses!
>   There is sad feud among ye, and rebellion
>   Of son against his sire. I saw him fall,

I saw my first-born tumbled from his throne!
To me his arms were spread, to me his voice
Found way from forth the thunders round his head!
Pale wox I, and in vapours hid my face.
Art thou, too, near such doom? Vague fear there is:
For I have seen my sons most unlike Gods.
Divine ye were created, and divine
330 In sad demeanour, solemn, undisturbed,
Unrufflèd, like high Gods, ye lived and ruled:
Now I behold in you fear, hope, and wrath;
Actions of rage and passion – even as
I see them, on the mortal world beneath,
In men who die. This is the grief, O Son!
Sad sign of ruin, sudden dismay, and fall!
Yet do thou strive; as thou art capable,
As thou canst move about, an evident God;
And canst oppose to each malignant hour
340 Ethereal presence. I am but a voice;
My life is but the life of winds and tides,
No more than winds and tides can I avail. –
But thou canst. – Be thou therefore in the van
Of circumstance; yea, seize the arrow's barb
Before the tense string murmur. – To the earth!
For there thou wilt find Saturn, and his woes.
Meantime I will keep watch on thy bright sun,
And of thy seasons be a careful nurse.' –
Ere half this region-whisper had come down,
350 Hyperion arose, and on the stars
Lifted his curvèd lids, and kept them wide
Until it ceased; and still he kept them wide;
And still they were the same bright, patient stars.
Then with a slow incline of his broad breast,
Like to a diver in the pearly seas,
Forward he stooped over the airy shore,
And plunged all noiseless into the deep night.

BOOK II

Just at the self-same beat of Time's wide wings,
Hyperion slid into the rustled air
And Saturn gained with Thea that sad place
Where Cybele and the bruised Titans mourned.
It was a den where no insulting light
Could glimmer on their tears; where their own groans
They felt, but heard not, for the solid roar
Of thunderous waterfalls and torrents hoarse,
Pouring a constant bulk, uncertain where.
10 Crag jutting forth to crag, and rocks that seemed
Ever as if just rising from a sleep,
Forehead to forehead held their monstrous horns;
And thus in thousand hugest fantasies
Made a fit roofing to this nest of woe.
Instead of thrones, hard flint they sat upon,
Couches of rugged stone, and slaty ridge
Stubborned with iron. All were not assembled:
Some chained in torture, and some wandering.
Coeus, and Gyges, and Briareüs,
20 Typhon, and Dolor, and Porphyrion,
With many more, the brawniest in assault,
Were pent in regions of laborious breath;
Dungeoned in opaque element, to keep
Their clenchèd teeth still clenched, and all their limbs
Locked up like veins of metal, cramped and screwed;
Without a motion, save of their big hearts
Heaving in pain, and horribly convulsed
With sanguine feverous boiling gurge of pulse.
Mnemosyne was straying in the world;
30 Far from her moon had Phoebe wanderèd;
And many else were free to roam abroad,
But for the main, here found they covert drear.
Scarce images of life, one here, one there,
Lay vast and edgeways; like a dismal cirque
Of Druid stones, upon a forlorn moor,
When the chill rain begins at shut of eve,
In dull November, and their chancel vault,

The Heaven itself, is blinded throughout night.
Each one kept shroud, nor to his neighbour gave
40 Or word, or look, or action of despair.
Creüs was one; his ponderous iron mace
Lay by him, and a shattered rib of rock
Told of his rage, ere he thus sank and pined.
Iäpetus another; in his grasp,
A serpent's plashy neck; its barbèd tongue
Squeezed from the gorge, and all its uncurled length
Dead – and because the creature could not spit
Its poison in the eyes of conquering Jove.
Next Cottus; prone he lay, chin uppermost,
50 As though in pain, for still upon the flint
He ground severe his skull, with open mouth
And eyes at horrid working. Nearest him
Asia, born of most enormous Caf,
Who cost her mother Tellus keener pangs,
Though feminine, than any of her sons:
More thought than woe was in her dusky face,
For she was prophesying of her glory;
And in her wide imagination stood
Palm-shaded temples, and high rival fanes,
60 By Oxus or in Ganges' sacred isles.
Even as Hope upon her anchor leans,
So leant she, not so fair, upon a tusk
Shed from the broadest of her elephants.
Above her, on a crag's uneasy shelve,
Upon his elbow raised, all prostrate else,
Shadowed Enceladus – once tame and mild
As grazing ox unworried in the meads;
Now tiger-passioned, lion-thoughted, wroth,
He meditated, plotted, and even now
70 Was hurling mountains in that second war,
Not long delayed, that scared the younger Gods
To hide themselves in forms of beast and bird.
Not far hence Atlas; and beside him prone
Phorcus, the sire of Gorgons. Neighboured close
Oceanus, and Tethys, in whose lap

Sobbed Clymene among her tangled hair.
In midst of all lay Themis, at the feet
Of Ops the queen all clouded round from sight;
No shape distinguishable, more than when
Thick night confounds the pine-tops with the clouds –
And many else whose names may not be told.
For when the Muse's wings are air-ward spread,
Who shall delay her flight? And she must chant
Of Saturn, and his guide, who now had climbed
With damp and slippery footing from a depth
More horrid still. Above a sombre cliff
Their heads appeared, and up their stature grew
Till on the level height their steps found ease:
Then Thea spread abroad her trembling arms
Upon the precincts of this nest of pain,
And sidelong fixed her eye on Saturn's face.
There saw she direst strife – the supreme God
At war with all the frailty of grief,
Of rage, of fear, anxiety, revenge,
Remorse, spleen, hope, but most of all despair.
Against these plagues he strove in vain; for Fate
Had poured a mortal oil upon his head,
A disanointing poison, so that Thea,
Affrighted, kept her still, and let him pass
First onwards in, among the fallen tribe.

    As with us mortal men, the laden heart
Is persecuted more, and fevered more,
When it is nighing to the mournful house
Where other hearts are sick of the same bruise;
So Saturn, as he walked into the midst,
Felt faint, and would have sunk among the rest,
But that he met Enceladus's eye,
Whose mightiness, and awe of him, at once
Came like an inspiration; and he shouted,
'Titans, behold your God!' At which some groaned;
Some started on their feet; some also shouted;
Some wept, some wailed, all bowed with reverence;

And Ops, uplifting her black folded veil,
Showed her pale cheeks, and all her forehead wan,
Her eye-brows thin and jet, and hollow eyes.
There is a roaring in the bleak-grown pines
When Winter lifts his voice; there is a noise
Among immortals when a God gives sign,
With hushing finger, how he means to load
His tongue with the full weight of utterless thought,
With thunder, and with music, and with pomp:
Such noise is like the roar of bleak-grown pines,
Which, when it ceases in this mountained world,
No other sound succeeds; but ceasing here,
Among these fallen, Saturn's voice therefrom
Grew up like organ, that begins anew
Its strain, when other harmonies, stopped short,
Leave the dinned air vibrating silverly.
Thus grew it up: 'Not in my own sad breast,
Which is its own great judge and searcher-out,
Can I find reason why ye should be thus:
Not in the legends of the first of days,
Studied from that old spirit-leavèd book
Which starry Uranus with finger bright
Saved from the shores of darkness, when the waves
Low-ebbed still hid it up in shallow gloom –
And the which book ye know I ever kept
For my firm-basèd footstool – Ah, infirm!
Not there, nor in sign, symbol, or portent
Of element, earth, water, air, and fire –
At war, at peace, or inter-quarrelling
One against one, or two, or three, or all
Each several one against the other three,
As fire with air loud warring when rain-floods
Drown both, and press them both against earth's face,
Where, finding sulphur, a quadruple wrath
Unhinges the poor world – not in that strife,
Wherefrom I take strange lore, and read it deep,
Can I find reason why ye should be thus –
No, nowhere can unriddle, though I search,

HYPERION. A FRAGMENT

    And pore on Nature's universal scroll
Even to swooning, why ye, Divinities,
The first-born of all shaped and palpable Gods,
Should cower beneath what, in comparison,
Is untremendous might. Yet ye are here,
O'erwhelmed, and spurned, and battered, ye are here!
O Titans, shall I say, "Arise!"? – Ye groan:
Shall I say "Crouch!"? – Ye groan. What can I then?
O Heaven wide! O unseen parent dear!
What can I? Tell me, all ye brethren Gods,
How we can war, how engine our great wrath!
O speak your counsel now, for Saturn's ear
Is all a-hungered. Thou, Oceanus,
Ponderest high and deep, and in thy face
I see, astonied, that severe content
Which comes of thought and musing. Give us help!'

    So ended Saturn; and the God of the Sea,
Sophist and sage from no Athenian grove,
But cogitation in his watery shades,
Arose, with locks not oozy, and began,
In murmurs which his first-endeavouring tongue
Caught infant-like from the far-foamèd sands.
'O ye, whom wrath consumes! who, passion-stung,
Writhe at defeat, and nurse your agonies!
Shut up your senses, stifle up your ears,
My voice is not a bellows unto ire.
Yet listen, ye who will, whilst I bring proof
How ye, perforce, must be content to stoop;
And in the proof much comfort will I give,
If ye will take that comfort in its truth.
We fall by course of Nature's law, not force
Of thunder, or of Jove. Great Saturn, thou
Hast sifted well the atom-universe;
But for this reason, that thou art the King,
And only blind from sheer supremacy,
One avenue was shaded from thine eyes,
Through which I wandered to eternal truth.

And first, as thou wast not the first of powers,
So art thou not the last; it cannot be:
190 Thou art not the beginning nor the end.
From Chaos and parental Darkness came
Light, the first fruits of that intestine broil,
That sullen ferment, which for wondrous ends
Was ripening in itself. The ripe hour came,
And with it Light, and Light, engendering
Upon its own producer, forthwith touched
The whole enormous matter into life.
Upon that very hour, our parentage,
The Heavens, and the Earth, were manifest:
200 Then thou first born, and we the giant race,
Found ourselves ruling new and beauteous realms.
Now comes the pain of truth, to whom 'tis pain –
O folly! for to bear all naked truths,
And to envisage circumstance, all calm,
That is the top of sovereignty. Mark well!
As Heaven and Earth are fairer, fairer far
Than Chaos and blank Darkness, though once chiefs;
And as we show beyond that Heaven and Earth
In form and shape compact and beautiful,
210 In will, in action free, companionship,
And thousand other signs of purer life;
So on our heels a fresh perfection treads,
A power more strong in beauty, born of us
And fated to excel us, as we pass
In glory that old Darkness: nor are we
Thereby more conquered, than by us the rule
Of shapeless Chaos. Say, doth the dull soil
Quarrel with the proud forests it hath fed,
And feedeth still, more comely than itself?
220 Can it deny the chiefdom of green groves?
Or shall the tree be envious of the dove
Because it cooeth, and hath snowy wings
To wander wherewithal and find its joys?
We are such forest-trees, and our fair boughs
Have bred forth, not pale solitary doves,

HYPERION. A FRAGMENT

>   But eagles golden-feathered, who do tower
>   Above us in their beauty, and must reign
>   In right thereof. For 'tis the eternal law
>   That first in beauty should be first in might.
> 230 Yea, by that law, another race may drive
>   Our conquerors to mourn as we do now.
>   Have ye beheld the young God of the Seas,
>   My dispossessor? Have ye seen his face?
>   Have ye beheld his chariot, foamed along
>   By noble wingèd creatures he hath made?
>   I saw him on the calmèd waters scud,
>   With such a glow of beauty in his eyes,
>   That it enforced me to bid sad farewell
>   To all my empire: farewell sad I took,
> 240 And hither came, to see how dolorous fate
>   Had wrought upon ye; and how I might best
>   Give consolation in this woe extreme.
>   Receive the truth, and let it be your balm.'
>
>   Whether through posed conviction, or disdain,
>   They guarded silence, when Oceanus
>   Left murmuring, what deepest thought can tell?
>   But so it was; none answered for a space,
>   Save one whom none regarded, Clymene;
>   And yet she answered not, only complained,
> 250 With hectic lips, and eyes up-looking mild,
>   Thus wording timidly among the fierce:
>   'O Father, I am here the simplest voice,
>   And all my knowledge is that joy is gone,
>   And this thing woe crept in among our hearts,
>   There to remain for ever, as I fear.
>   I would not bode of evil, if I thought
>   So weak a creature could turn off the help
>   Which by just right should come of mighty Gods;
>   Yet let me tell my sorrow, let me tell
> 260 Of what I heard, and how it made me weep,
>   And know that we had parted from all hope.
>   I stood upon a shore, a pleasant shore,
>   Where a sweet clime was breathèd from a land

Of fragrance, quietness, and trees, and flowers.
Full of calm joy it was, as I of grief;
Too full of joy and soft delicious warmth;
So that I felt a movement in my heart
To chide, and to reproach that solitude
With songs of misery, music of our woes;
And sat me down, and took a mouthèd shell
And murmured into it, and made melody –
O melody no more! for while I sang,
And with poor skill let pass into the breeze
The dull shell's echo, from a bowery strand
Just opposite, an island of the sea,
There came enchantment with the shifting wind,
That did both drown and keep alive my ears.
I threw my shell away upon the sand,
And a wave filled it, as my sense was filled
With that new blissful golden melody.
A living death was in each gush of sounds,
Each family of rapturous hurried notes,
That fell, one after one, yet all at once,
Like pearl beads dropping sudden from their string;
And then another, then another strain,
Each like a dove leaving its olive perch,
With music winged instead of silent plumes,
To hover round my head, and make me sick
Of joy and grief at once. Grief overcame,
And I was stopping up my frantic ears,
When, past all hindrance of my trembling hands,
A voice came sweeter, sweeter than all tune,
And still it cried, "Apollo! young Apollo!
The morning-bright Apollo! young Apollo!"
I fled, it followed me, and cried "Apollo!"
O Father, and O Brethren, had ye felt
Those pains of mine – O Saturn, hadst thou felt,
Ye would not call this too indulgèd tongue
Presumptuous, in thus venturing to be heard.'

So far her voice flowed on, like timorous brook
That, lingering along a pebbled coast,

HYPERION. A FRAGMENT

    Doth fear to meet the sea: but sea it met,
    And shuddered; for the overwhelming voice
    Of huge Enceladus swallowed it in wrath:
    The ponderous syllables, like sullen waves
    In the half-glutted hollows of reef-rocks,
    Came booming thus, while still upon his arm
    He leaned – not rising, from supreme contempt:
    'Or shall we listen to the over-wise,
310 Or to the over-foolish, Giant-Gods?
    Not thunderbolt on thunderbolt, till all
    That rebel Jove's whole armoury were spent,
    Not world on world upon these shoulders piled
    Could agonize me more than baby-words
    In midst of this dethronement horrible.
    Speak! Roar! Shout! Yell! ye sleepy Titans all.
    Do ye forget the blows, the buffets vile?
    Are ye not smitten by a youngling arm?
    Dost thou forget, sham Monarch of the Waves,
320 Thy scalding in the seas? What, have I roused
    Your spleens with so few simple words as these?
    O joy! for now I see ye are not lost:
    O joy! for now I see a thousand eyes
    Wide-glaring for revenge!' – As this he said,
    He lifted up his stature vast, and stood,
    Still without intermission speaking thus:
    'Now ye are flames, I'll tell you how to burn,
    And purge the ether of our enemies;
    How to feed fierce the crooked stings of fire,
330 And singe away the swollen clouds of Jove,
    Stifling that puny essence in its tent.
    O let him feel the evil he hath done;
    For though I scorn Oceanus's lore,
    Much pain have I for more than loss of realms:
    The days of peace and slumbrous calm are fled;
    Those days, all innocent of scathing war,
    When all the fair Existences of heaven
    Came open-eyed to guess what we would speak –
    That was before our brows were taught to frown,

340 Before our lips knew else but solemn sounds;
     That was before we knew the wingèd thing,
     Victory, might be lost, or might be won.
     And be ye mindful that Hyperion,
     Our brightest brother, still is undisgraced –
     Hyperion, lo! his radiance is here!'

     All eyes were on Enceladus's face,
     And they beheld, while still Hyperion's name
     Flew from his lips up to the vaulted rocks,
     A pallid gleam across his features stern –
350 Not savage, for he saw full many a God
     Wroth as himself. He looked upon them all,
     And in each face he saw a gleam of light,
     But splendider in Saturn's, whose hoar locks
     Shone like the bubbling foam about a keel
     When the prow sweeps into a midnight cove.
     In pale and silver silence they remained,
     Till suddenly a splendour, like the morn,
     Pervaded all the beetling gloomy steeps,
     All the sad spaces of oblivion,
360 And every gulf, and every chasm old,
     And every height, and every sullen depth,
     Voiceless, or hoarse with loud tormented streams;
     And all the everlasting cataracts,
     And all the headlong torrents far and near,
     Mantled before in darkness and huge shade,
     Now saw the light and made it terrible.
     It was Hyperion: a granite peak
     His bright feet touched, and there he stayed to view
     The misery his brilliance had betrayed
370 To the most hateful seeing of itself.
     Golden his hair of short Numidian curl,
     Regal his shape majestic, a vast shade
     In midst of his own brightness, like the bulk
     Of Memnon's image at the set of sun
     To one who travels from the dusking East:
     Sighs, too, as mournful as that Memnon's harp,

HYPERION. A FRAGMENT

He uttered, while his hands contemplative
He pressed together, and in silence stood.
Despondence seized again the fallen Gods
At sight of the dejected King of Day,
And many hid their faces from the light:
But fierce Enceladus sent forth his eyes
Among the brotherhood; and, at their glare,
Uprose Iäpetus, and Creüs too,
And Phorcus, sea-born, and together strode
To where he towered on his eminence.
There those four shouted forth old Saturn's name;
Hyperion from the peak loud answered, 'Saturn!'
Saturn sat near the Mother of the Gods,
In whose face was no joy, though all the Gods
Gave from their hollow throats the name of 'Saturn!'

BOOK III

Thus in alternate uproar and sad peace,
Amazèd were those Titans utterly.
O leave them, Muse! O leave them to their woes;
For thou art weak to sing such tumults dire:
A solitary sorrow best befits
Thy lips, and antheming a lonely grief.
Leave them, O Muse! for thou anon wilt find
Many a fallen old Divinity
Wandering in vain about bewildered shores.
Meantime touch piously the Delphic harp,
And not a wind of heaven but will breathe
In aid soft warble from the Dorian flute;
For lo! 'tis for the Father of all verse.
Flush every thing that hath a vermeil hue,
Let the rose glow intense and warm the air,
And let the clouds of even and of morn
Float in voluptuous fleeces o'er the hills;
Let the red wine within the goblet boil,
Cold as a bubbling well; let faint-lipped shells,
On sands, or in great deeps, vermilion turn
Through all their labyrinths; and let the maid

HYPERION. A FRAGMENT

Blush keenly, as with some warm kiss surprised.
Chief isle of the embowered Cyclades,
Rejoice, O Delos, with thine olives green,
And poplars, and lawn-shading palms, and beech,
In which the Zephyr breathes the loudest song,
And hazels thick, dark-stemmed beneath the shade:
Apollo is once more the golden theme!
Where was he, when the Giant of the Sun
Stood bright, amid the sorrow of his peers?
Together had he left his mother fair
And his twin-sister sleeping in their bower,
And in the morning twilight wandered forth
Beside the osiers of a rivulet,
Full ankle-deep in lilies of the vale.
The nightingale had ceased, and a few stars
Were lingering in the heavens, while the thrush
Began calm-throated. Throughout all the isle
There was no covert, no retirèd cave
Unhaunted by the murmurous noise of waves,
Though scarcely heard in many a green recess.
He listened, and he wept, and his bright tears
Went trickling down the golden bow he held.
Thus with half-shut suffusèd eyes he stood,
While from beneath some cumbrous boughs hard by
With solemn step an awful Goddess came,
And there was purport in her looks for him,
Which he with eager guess began to read
Perplexed, the while melodiously he said:
'How cam'st thou over the unfooted sea?
Or hath that antique mien and robèd form
Moved in these vales invisible till now?
Sure I have heard those vestments sweeping o'er
The fallen leaves, when I have sat alone
In cool mid-forest. Surely I have traced
The rustle of those ample skirts about
These grassy solitudes, and seen the flowers
Lift up their heads, as still the whisper passed.
Goddess! I have beheld those eyes before,

HYPERION. A FRAGMENT

60 And their eternal calm, and all that face,
    Or I have dreamed.' – 'Yes,' said the supreme shape,
    Thou hast dreamed of me; and awaking up
    Didst find a lyre all golden by thy side,
    Whose strings touched by thy fingers, all the vast
    Unwearied ear of the whole universe
    Listened in pain and pleasure at the birth
    Of such new tuneful wonder. Is't not strange
    That thou shouldst weep, so gifted? Tell me, youth,
    What sorrow thou canst feel; for I am sad
70 When thou dost shed a tear. Explain thy griefs
    To one who in this lonely isle hath been
    The watcher of thy sleep and hours of life,
    From the young day when first thy infant hand
    Plucked witless the weak flowers, till thine arm
    Could bend that bow heroic to all times.
    Show thy heart's secret to an ancient Power
    Who hath forsaken old and sacred thrones
    For prophecies of thee, and for the sake
    Of loveliness new born.' – Apollo then,
80 With sudden scrutiny and gloomless eyes,
    Thus answered, while his white melodious throat
    Throbbed with the syllables: 'Mnemosyne!
    Thy name is on my tongue, I know not how;
    Why should I tell thee what thou so well seest?
    Why should I strive to show what from thy lips
    Would come no mystery? For me, dark, dark,
    And painful vile oblivion seals my eyes:
    I strive to search wherefore I am so sad,
    Until a melancholy numbs my limbs;
90 And then upon the grass I sit, and moan,
    Like one who once had wings. O why should I
    Feel cursed and thwarted, when the liegeless air
    Yields to my step aspirant? Why should I
    Spurn the green turf as hateful to my feet?
    Goddess benign, point forth some unknown thing:
    Are there not other regions than this isle?
    What are the stars? There is the sun, the sun!

And the most patient brilliance of the moon!
And stars by thousands! Point me out the way
To any one particular beauteous star,
And I will flit into it with my lyre,
And make its silvery splendour pant with bliss.
I have heard the cloudy thunder. Where is power?
Whose hand, whose essence, what Divinity
Makes this alarum in the elements,
While I here idle listen on the shores
In fearless yet in aching ignorance?
O tell me, lonely Goddess, by thy harp,
That waileth every morn and eventide,
Tell me why thus I rave, about these groves!
Mute thou remainest – mute! yet I can read
A wondrous lesson in thy silent face:
Knowledge enormous makes a God of me.
Names, deeds, grey legends, dire events, rebellions,
Majesties, sovran voices, agonies,
Creations and destroyings, all at once
Pour into the wide hollows of my brain,
And deify me, as if some blithe wine
Or bright elixir peerless I had drunk,
And so become immortal.' – Thus the God,
While his enkindlèd eyes, with level glance
Beneath his white soft temples, steadfast kept
Trembling with light upon Mnemosyne.
Soon wild commotions shook him, and made flush
All the immortal fairness of his limbs –
Most like the struggle at the gate of death;
Or liker still to one who should take leave
Of pale immortal death, and with a pang
As hot as death's is chill, with fierce convulse
Die into life: so young Apollo anguished.
His very hair, his golden tresses famed
Kept undulation round his eager neck.
During the pain Mnemosyne upheld
Her arms as one who prophesied. – At length

Apollo shrieked – and lo! from all his limbs
Celestial . . . .

Fancy

 Ever let the Fancy roam,
Pleasure never is at home:
At a touch sweet Pleasure melteth,
Like to bubbles when rain pelteth.
Then let wingèd Fancy wander
Through the thought still spread beyond her:
Open wide the mind's cage-door,
She'll dart forth, and cloudward soar.
O sweet Fancy! let her loose –
Summer's joys are spoilt by use,
And the enjoying of the Spring
Fades as does its blossoming;
Autumn's red-lipped fruitage too,
Blushing through the mist and dew,
Cloys with tasting. What do then?
Sit thee by the ingle, when
The sere faggot blazes bright,
Spirit of a winter's night;
When the soundless earth is muffled,
And the cakèd snow is shuffled
From the ploughboy's heavy shoon;
When the Night doth meet the Noon
In a dark conspiracy
To banish Even from her sky.
Sit thee there, and send abroad,
With a mind self-overawed,
Fancy, high-commissioned – send her!
She has vassals to attend her:
She will bring, in spite of frost,
Beauties that the earth hath lost;
She will bring thee, all together,
All delights of summer weather;

All the buds and bells of May,
From dewy sward or thorny spray;
All the heapèd Autumn's wealth,
With a still, mysterious stealth:
She will mix these pleasures up
Like three fit wines in a cup,
And thou shalt quaff it – thou shalt hear
Distant harvest-carols clear;
Rustle of the reapèd corn;
Sweet birds antheming the morn:
And, in the same moment – hark!
'Tis the early April lark,
Or the rooks, with busy caw,
Foraging for sticks and straw.
Thou shalt, at one glance, behold
The daisy and the marigold;
White-plumed lilies, and the first
Hedge-grown primrose that hath burst;
Shaded hyacinth, alway
Sapphire queen of the mid-May;
And every leaf, and every flower
Pearlèd with the self-same shower.
Thou shalt see the field-mouse peep
Meagre from its cellèd sleep;
And the snake all winter-thin
Cast on sunny bank its skin;
Freckled nest-eggs thou shalt see
Hatching in the hawthorn-tree,
When the hen-bird's wing doth rest
Quiet on her mossy nest;
Then the hurry and alarm
When the bee-hive casts its swarm;
Acorns ripe down-pattering,
While the autumn breezes sing.

 O, sweet Fancy! let her loose;
Every thing is spoilt by use:
Where's the cheek that doth not fade,

70 Too much gazed at? Where's the maid
Whose lip mature is ever new?
Where's the eye, however blue,
Doth not weary? Where's the face
One would meet in every place?
Where's the voice, however soft,
One would hear so very oft?
At a touch sweet Pleasure melteth
Like to bubbles when rain pelteth.
Let, then, wingèd Fancy find
80 Thee a mistress to thy mind:
Dulcet-eyed as Ceres' daughter,
Ere the God of Torment taught her
How to frown and how to chide;
With a waist and with a side
White as Hebe's, when her zone
Slipped its golden clasp, and down
Fell her kirtle to her feet,
While she held the goblet sweet,
And Jove grew languid. – Break the mesh
90 Of the Fancy's silken leash;
Quickly break her prison-string
And such joys as these she'll bring.
Let the wingèd Fancy roam,
Pleasure never is at home.

Ode

Bards of Passion and of Mirth,
Ye have left your souls on earth!
Have ye souls in heaven too,
Double-lived in regions new?
Yes, and those of heaven commune
With the spheres of sun and moon;
With the noise of fountains wondrous,
And the parle of voices thund'rous;
With the whisper of heaven's trees

10   And one another, in soft ease
     Seated on Elysian lawns
     Browsed by none but Dian's fawns;
     Underneath large blue-bells tented,
     Where the daisies are rose-scented,
     And the rose herself has got
     Perfume which on earth is not;
     Where the nightingale doth sing
     Not a senseless, trancèd thing,
     But divine melodious truth;
20   Philosophic numbers smooth;
     Tales and golden histories
     Of heaven and its mysteries.

        Thus ye live on high, and then
     On the earth ye live again;
     And the souls ye left behind you
     Teach us, here, the way to find you,
     Where your other souls are joying,
     Never slumbered, never cloying.
     Here, your earth-born souls still speak
30   To mortals, of their little week;
     Of their sorrows and delights;
     Of their passions and their spites;
     Of their glory and their shame;
     What doth strengthen and what maim.
     Thus ye teach us, every day,
     Wisdom, though fled far away.

        Bards of Passion and of Mirth,
     Ye have left your souls on earth!
     Ye have souls in heaven too,
40   Double-lived in regions new!

Song

I had a dove and the sweet dove died;
   And I have thought it died of grieving.

O, what could it grieve for? Its feet were tied,
  With a silken thread of my own hand's weaving.
Sweet little red feet! why would you die –
Why should you leave me, sweet bird! why?
You lived alone on the forest-tree,
Why, pretty thing, could you not live with me?
I kissed you oft and gave you white peas;
Why not live sweetly, as in the green trees?

Song

I

Hush, hush! tread softly! hush, hush my dear!
  All the house is asleep, but we know very well
That the jealous, the jealous old bald-pate may hear,
  Though you've padded his night-cap – O sweet Isabel!
    Though your feet are more light than a faery's feet,
    Who dances on bubbles where brooklets meet –
Hush, hush! tread softly! hush, hush my dear!
For less than a nothing the jealous can hear.

II

No leaf doth tremble, no ripple is there
  On the river – all's still, and the night's sleepy eye
Closes up, and forgets all its Lethean care,
  Charmed to death by the drone of the humming
    mayfly;
    And the moon, whether prudish or complaisant,
    Hath fled to her bower, well knowing I want
No light in the darkness, no torch in the gloom,
But my Isabel's eyes, and her lips pulped with bloom.

III

Lift the latch! ah gently! ah tenderly – sweet!
  We are dead if that latchet gives one little clink!
Well done – now those lips, and a flowery seat –
  The old man may dream, and the planets may wink;
    The shut rose may dream of our loves, and awake

Full-blown, and such warmth for the morning take,
The stock-dove shall hatch her soft brace and shall coo,
While I kiss to the melody, aching all through!

The Eve of St Agnes

I

St Agnes' Eve – Ah, bitter chill it was!
The owl, for all his feathers, was a-cold;
The hare limped trembling through the frozen grass,
And silent was the flock in woolly fold:
Numb were the Beadsman's fingers, while he told
His rosary, and while his frosted breath,
Like pious incense from a censer old,
Seemed taking flight for heaven, without a death,
Past the sweet Virgin's picture, while his prayer he saith.

II

His prayer he saith, this patient, holy man;
Then takes his lamp, and riseth from his knees,
And back returneth, meagre, barefoot, wan,
Along the chapel aisle by slow degrees:
The sculptured dead, on each side, seem to freeze,
Emprisoned in black, purgatorial rails;
Knights, ladies, praying in dumb orat'ries,
He passeth by; and his weak spirit fails
To think how they may ache in icy hoods and mails.

III

Northward he turneth through a little door,
And scarce three steps, ere Music's golden tongue
Flattered to tears this agèd man and poor;
But no – already had his deathbell rung:
The joys of all his life were said and sung:
His was harsh penance on St Agnes' Eve.
Another way he went, and soon among
Rough ashes sat he for his soul's reprieve,
And all night kept awake, for sinners' sake to grieve.

IV

That ancient Beadsman heard the prelude soft;
And so it chanced, for many a door was wide,
From hurry to and fro. Soon, up aloft,
The silver, snarling trumpets 'gan to chide:
The level chambers, ready with their pride,
Were glowing to receive a thousand guests:
The carvèd angels, ever eager-eyed,
Stared, where upon their heads the cornice rests,
With hair blown back, and wings put cross-wise on their breasts.

V

At length burst in the argent revelry,
With plume, tiara, and all rich array,
Numerous as shadows haunting faerily
The brain, new-stuffed, in youth, with triumphs gay
Of old romance. These let us wish away,
And turn, sole-thoughted, to one Lady there,
Whose heart had brooded, all that wintry day,
On love, and winged St Agnes' saintly care,
As she had heard old dames full many times declare.

VI

They told her how, upon St Agnes' Eve,
Young virgins might have visions of delight,
And soft adorings from their loves receive
Upon the honeyed middle of the night,
If ceremonies due they did aright;
As, supperless to bed they must retire,
And couch supine their beauties, lily white;
Nor look behind, nor sideways, but require
Of Heaven with upward eyes for all that they desire.

VII

Full of this whim was thoughtful Madeline:
The music, yearning like a God in pain,
She scarcely heard: her maiden eyes divine,
Fixed on the floor, saw many a sweeping train

Pass by – she heeded not at all: in vain
60 Came many a tip-toe, amorous cavalier,
And back retired – not cooled by high disdain,
But she saw not: her heart was otherwhere.
She sighed for Agnes' dreams, the sweetest of the year.

VIII

She danced along with vague, regardless eyes,
Anxious her lips, her breathing quick and short:
The hallowed hour was near at hand: she sighs
Amid the timbrels, and the thronged resort
Of whisperers in anger, or in sport;
'Mid looks of love, defiance, hate, and scorn,
70 Hoodwinked with faery fancy – all amort,
Save to St Agnes and her lambs unshorn,
And all the bliss to be before to-morrow morn.

IX

So, purposing each moment to retire,
She lingered still. Meantime, across the moors,
Had come young Porphyro, with heart on fire
For Madeline. Beside the portal doors,
Buttressed from moonlight, stands he, and implores
All saints to give him sight of Madeline
But for one moment in the tedious hours,
80 That he might gaze and worship all unseen;
Perchance speak, kneel, touch, kiss – in sooth such things have been.

X

He ventures in – let no buzzed whisper tell,
All eyes be muffled, or a hundred swords
Will storm his heart, Love's fev'rous citadel:
For him, those chambers held barbarian hordes,
Hyena foemen, and hot-blooded lords,
Whose very dogs would execrations howl
Against his lineage: not one breast affords
Him any mercy, in that mansion foul,
90 Save one old beldame, weak in body and in soul.

THE EVE OF ST AGNES

XI

Ah, happy chance! the agèd creature came,
Shuffling along with ivory-headed wand,
To where he stood, hid from the torch's flame,
Behind a broad hall-pillar, far beyond
The sound of merriment and chorus bland:
He startled her; but soon she knew his face,
And grasped his fingers in her palsied hand,
Saying, 'Mercy, Porphyro! hie thee from this place:
They are all here to-night, the whole blood-thirsty race!

XII

'Get hence! get hence! there's dwarfish Hildebrand –
He had a fever late, and in the fit
He cursèd thee and thine, both house and land:
Then there's that old Lord Maurice, not a whit
More tame for his grey hairs – Alas me! flit!
Flit like a ghost away.' 'Ah, gossip dear,
We're safe enough; here in this arm-chair sit,
And tell me how –' 'Good Saints! not here, not here;
Follow me, child, or else these stones will be thy bier.'

XIII

He followed through a lowly archèd way,
Brushing the cobwebs with his lofty plume,
And as she muttered, 'Well-a – well-a-day!'
He found him in a little moonlight room,
Pale, latticed, chill, and silent as a tomb.
'Now tell me where is Madeline,' said he,
'O tell me, Angela, by the holy loom
Which none but secret sisterhood may see,
When they St Agnes' wool are weaving piously.'

XIV

'St Agnes? Ah! it is St Agnes' Eve –
Yet men will murder upon holy days:
Thou must hold water in a witch's sieve,
And be liege-lord of all the Elves and Fays,
To venture so: it fills me with amaze

THE EVE OF ST AGNES

To see thee, Porphyro! – St Agnes' Eve!
God's help! my lady fair the conjuror plays
This very night. Good angels her deceive!
But let me laugh awhile, I've mickle time to grieve.'

XV

Feebly she laugheth in the languid moon,
While Porphyro upon her face doth look,
Like puzzled urchin on an agèd crone
Who keepeth closed a wondrous riddle-book,
As spectacled she sits in chimney nook.
But soon his eyes grew brilliant, when she told
His lady's purpose; and he scarce could brook
Tears, at the thought of those enchantments cold,
And Madeline asleep in lap of legends old.

XVI

Sudden a thought came like a full-blown rose,
Flushing his brow, and in his painèd heart
Made purple riot; then doth he propose
A stratagem, that makes the beldame start:
'A cruel man and impious thou art:
Sweet lady, let her pray, and sleep, and dream
Alone with her good angels, far apart
From wicked men like thee. Go, go! – I deem
Thou canst not surely be the same that thou didst seem.'

XVII

'I will not harm her, by all saints I swear,'
Quoth Porphyro: 'O may I ne'er find grace
When my weak voice shall whisper its last prayer,
If one of her soft ringlets I displace,
Or look with ruffian passion in her face:
Good Angela, believe me by these tears,
Or I will, even in a moment's space,
Awake, with horrid shout, my foeman's ears,
And beard them, though they be more fanged than wolves and bears.'

THE EVE OF ST AGNES

XVIII

'Ah! why wilt thou affright a feeble soul?
A poor, weak, palsy-stricken, churchyard thing,
Whose passing-bell may ere the midnight toll;
Whose prayers for thee, each morn and evening,
Were never missed.' – Thus plaining, doth she bring
A gentler speech from burning Porphyro,
So woeful, and of such deep sorrowing,
That Angela gives promise she will do
Whatever he shall wish, betide her weal or woe.

XIX

Which was, to lead him, in close secrecy,
Even to Madeline's chamber, and there hide
Him in a closet, of such privacy
That he might see her beauty unespied,
And win perhaps that night a peerless bride,
While legioned faeries paced the coverlet,
And pale enchantment held her sleepy-eyed.
Never on such a night have lovers met,
Since Merlin paid his Demon all the monstrous debt.

XX

'It shall be as thou wishest,' said the Dame:
'All cates and dainties shall be storèd there
Quickly on this feast-night; by the tambour frame
Her own lute thou wilt see. No time to spare,
For I am slow and feeble, and scarce dare
On such a catering trust my dizzy head.
Wait here, my child, with patience; kneel in prayer
The while. Ah! thou must needs the lady wed,
Or may I never leave my grave among the dead.'

XXI

So saying, she hobbled off with busy fear.
The lover's endless minutes slowly passed;
The dame returned, and whispered in his ear
To follow her; with agèd eyes aghast
From fright of dim espial. Safe at last,

Through many a dusky gallery, they gain
The maiden's chamber, silken, hushed, and chaste;
Where Porphyro took covert, pleased amain.
His poor guide hurried back with agues in her brain.

XXII

Her faltering hand upon the balustrade,
Old Angela was feeling for the stair,
When Madeline, St Agnes' charmèd maid,
Rose, like a missioned spirit, unaware:
With silver taper's light, and pious care,
She turned, and down the agèd gossip led
To a safe level matting. Now prepare,
Young Porphyro, for gazing on that bed –
She comes, she comes again, like ring-dove frayed and fled.

XXIII

Out went the taper as she hurried in;
Its little smoke, in pallid moonshine, died:
She closed the door, she panted, all akin
To spirits of the air, and visions wide –
No uttered syllable, or, woe betide!
But to her heart, her heart was voluble,
Paining with eloquence her balmy side;
As though a tongueless nightingale should swell
Her throat in vain, and die, heart-stiflèd, in her dell.

XXIV

A casement high and triple-arched there was,
All garlanded with carven imag'ries
Of fruits, and flowers, and bunches of knot-grass,
And diamonded with panes of quaint device,
Innumerable of stains and splendid dyes,
As are the tiger-moth's deep-damasked wings;
And in the midst, 'mong thousand heraldries,
And twilight saints, and dim emblazonings,
A shielded scutcheon blushed with blood of queens and kings.

THE EVE OF ST AGNES

XXV

Full on this casement shone the wintry moon,
And threw warm gules on Madeline's fair breast,
As down she knelt for heaven's grace and boon;
Rose-bloom fell on her hands, together pressed,
And on her silver cross soft amethyst,
And on her hair a glory, like a saint:
She seemed a splendid angel, newly dressed,
Save wings, for Heaven – Porphyro grew faint;
She knelt, so pure a thing, so free from mortal taint.

XXVI

Anon his heart revives; her vespers done,
Of all its wreathèd pearls her hair she frees;
Unclasps her warmèd jewels one by one;
Loosens her fragrant bodice; by degrees
Her rich attire creeps rustling to her knees:
Half-hidden, like a mermaid in sea-weed,
Pensive awhile she dreams awake, and sees,
In fancy, fair St Agnes in her bed,
But dares not look behind, or all the charm is fled.

XXVII

Soon, trembling in her soft and chilly nest,
In sort of wakeful swoon, perplexed she lay,
Until the poppied warmth of sleep oppressed
Her soothèd limbs, and soul fatigued away –
Flown, like a thought, until the morrow-day;
Blissfully havened both from joy and pain;
Clasped like a missal where swart Paynims pray;
Blinded alike from sunshine and from rain,
As though a rose should shut, and be a bud again.

XXVIII

Stolen to this paradise, and so entranced,
Porphyro gazed upon her empty dress,
And listened to her breathing, if it chanced
To wake into a slumbrous tenderness;
Which when he heard, that minute did he bless,

320 THE EVE OF ST AGNES

    And breathed himself: then from the closet crept,
250 Noiseless as fear in a wide wilderness,
    And over the hushed carpet, silent, stepped,
And 'tween the curtains peeped, where, lo! – how fast she slept.

XXIX

    Then by the bed-side, where the faded moon
Made a dim, silver twilight, soft he set
A table, and, half anguished, threw thereon
A cloth of woven crimson, gold, and jet –
O for some drowsy Morphean amulet!
The boisterous, midnight, festive clarion,
The kettle-drum, and far-heard clarinet,
260 Affray his ears, though but in dying tone;
The hall door shuts again, and all the noise is gone.

XXX

    And still she slept an azure-lidded sleep,
In blanchèd linen, smooth, and lavendered,
While he from forth the closet brought a heap
Of candied apple, quince, and plum, and gourd,
With jellies soother than the creamy curd,
And lucent syrups, tinct with cinnamon;
Manna and dates, in argosy transferred
From Fez; and spicèd dainties, every one,
270 From silken Samarkand to cedared Lebanon.

XXXI

    These delicates he heaped with glowing hand
On golden dishes and in baskets bright
Of wreathèd silver; sumptuous they stand
In the retirèd quiet of the night,
Filling the chilly room with perfume light.
'And now, my love, my seraph fair, awake!
Thou art my heaven, and I thine eremite:
Open thine eyes, for meek St Agnes' sake,
Or I shall drowse beside thee, so my soul doth ache.'

XXXII

280 Thus whispering, his warm, unnervèd arm
Sank in her pillow. Shaded was her dream
By the dusk curtains – 'twas a midnight charm
Impossible to melt as icèd stream:
The lustrous salvers in the moonlight gleam;
Broad golden fringe upon the carpet lies.
It seemed he never, never could redeem
From such a steadfast spell his lady's eyes;
So mused awhile, entoiled in woofèd fantasies.

XXXIII

Awakening up, he took her hollow lute,
290 Tumultuous, and, in chords that tenderest be,
He played an ancient ditty, long since mute,
In Provence called, 'La belle dame sans mercy',
Close to her ear touching the melody –
Wherewith disturbed, she uttered a soft moan:
He ceased – she panted quick – and suddenly
Her blue affrayèd eyes wide open shone.
Upon his knees he sank, pale as smooth-sculptured stone.

XXXIV

Her eyes were open, but she still beheld,
Now wide awake, the vision of her sleep –
300 There was a painful change, that nigh expelled
The blisses of her dream so pure and deep.
At which fair Madeline began to weep,
And moan forth witless words with many a sigh,
While still her gaze on Porphyro would keep;
Who knelt, with joinèd hands and piteous eye,
Fearing to move or speak, she looked so dreamingly.

XXXV

'Ah, Porphyro!' said she, 'but even now
Thy voice was at sweet tremble in mine ear,
Made tuneable with every sweetest vow,
310 And those sad eyes were spiritual and clear:
How changed thou art! How pallid, chill, and drear!

Give me that voice again, my Porphyro,
Those looks immortal, those complainings dear!
O leave me not in this eternal woe,
For if thou diest, my Love, I know not where to go.'

XXXVI

Beyond a mortal man impassioned far
At these voluptuous accents, he arose,
Ethereal, flushed, and like a throbbing star
Seen mid the sapphire heaven's deep repose;
Into her dream he melted, as the rose
Blendeth its odour with the violet –
Solution sweet. Meantime the frost-wind blows
Like Love's alarum pattering the sharp sleet
Against the window-panes; St Agnes' moon hath set.

XXXVII

'Tis dark: quick pattereth the flaw-blown sleet.
'This is no dream, my bride, my Madeline!'
'Tis dark: the icèd gusts still rave and beat.
'No dream, alas! alas! and woe is mine!
Porphyro will leave me here to fade and pine. –
Cruel! what traitor could thee hither bring?
I curse not, for my heart is lost in thine,
Though thou forsakest a deceivèd thing –
A dove forlorn and lost with sick unprunèd wing.'

XXXVIII

'My Madeline! sweet dreamer! lovely bride!
Say, may I be for aye thy vassal blessed?
Thy beauty's shield, heart-shaped and vermeil dyed?
Ah, silver shrine, here will I take my rest
After so many hours of toil and quest,
A famished pilgrim – saved by miracle.
Though I have found, I will not rob thy nest
Saving of thy sweet self; if thou think'st well
To trust, fair Madeline, to no rude infidel.

XXXIX

Hark! 'tis an elfin-storm from faery land,
Of haggard seeming, but a boon indeed:
Arise – arise! the morning is at hand.
The bloated wassaillers will never heed –
Let us away, my love, with happy speed –
There are no ears to hear, or eyes to see, –
Drowned all in Rhenish and the sleepy mead;
Awake! arise! my love, and fearless be,
For o'er the southern moors I have a home for thee.'

XL

She hurried at his words, beset with fears,
For there were sleeping dragons all around,
At glaring watch, perhaps, with ready spears –
Down the wide stairs a darkling way they found.
In all the house was heard no human sound.
A chain-drooped lamp was flickering by each door;
The arras, rich with horseman, hawk, and hound,
Fluttered in the besieging wind's uproar;
And the long carpets rose along the gusty floor.

XLI

They glide, like phantoms, into the wide hall;
Like phantoms, to the iron porch, they glide;
Where lay the Porter, in uneasy sprawl,
With a huge empty flaggon by his side:
The wakeful bloodhound rose, and shook his hide,
But his sagacious eye an inmate owns.
By one, and one, the bolts full easy slide –
The chains lie silent on the footworn stones –
The key turns, and the door upon its hinges groans.

XLII

And they are gone – ay, ages long ago
These lovers fled away into the storm.
That night the Baron dreamt of many a woe,
And all his warrior-guests, with shade and form
Of witch, and demon, and large coffin-worm,

Were long be-nightmared. Angela the old
Died palsy-twitched, with meagre face deform;
The Beadsman, after thousand aves told,
For aye unsought for slept among his ashes cold.

The Eve of St Mark

Upon a Sabbath-day it fell;
Twice holy was the Sabbath bell,
That called the folk to evening prayer;
The city streets were clean and fair
From wholesome drench of April rains;
And, on the western window panes,
The chilly sunset faintly told
Of unmatured green valleys cold,
Of the green thorny bloomless hedge,
10 Of rivers new with spring-tide sedge,
Of primroses by sheltered rills,
And daisies on the aguish hills.
Twice holy was the Sabbath bell:
The silent streets were crowded well
With staid and pious companies,
Warm from their fireside orat'ries,
And moving, with demurest air,
To even-song, and vesper prayer.
Each archèd porch, and entry low,
20 Was filled with patient folk and slow,
With whispers hush, and shuffling feet,
While played the organs loud and sweet.

The bells had ceased, the prayers begun,
And Bertha had not yet half done
A curious volume, patched and torn,
That all day long, from earliest morn,
Had taken captive her two eyes,
Among its golden broideries;
Perplexed her with a thousand things –

THE EVE OF ST MARK

30 The stars of Heaven, and angels' wings,
    Martyrs in a fiery blaze,
    Azure saints 'mid silver rays,
    Aaron's breastplate, and the seven
    Candlesticks John saw in Heaven,
    The wingèd Lion of Saint Mark,
    And the Covenantal Ark,
    With its many mysteries,
    Cherubim and golden mice.

    Bertha was a maiden fair,
40 Dwelling in the old Minster Square;
    From her fireside she could see,
    Sidelong, its rich antiquity,
    Far as the Bishop's garden-wall,
    Where sycamores and elm-trees tall,
    Full-leaved, the forest had outstripped,
    By no sharp north-wind ever nipped,
    So sheltered by the mighty pile.
    Bertha arose, and read awhile,
    With forehead 'gainst the window-pane.
50 Again she tried, and then again,
    Until the dusk eve left her dark
    Upon the legend of St Mark.
    From pleated lawn-frill, fine and thin,
    She lifted up her soft warm chin,
    With aching neck and swimming eyes,
    And dazed with saintly imageries.

    All was gloom, and silent all,
    Save now and then the still foot-fall
    Of one returning townwards late,
60 Past the echoing Minster gate.

    The clamorous daws, that all the day
    Above tree-tops and towers play,
    Pair by pair had gone to rest,
    Each in its ancient belfry-nest,
    Where asleep they fall betimes,
    To music of the drowsy chimes.

All was silent, all was gloom,
Abroad and in the homely room:
Down she sat, poor cheated soul!
And struck a lamp from the dismal coal,
Leaned forward, with bright drooping hair,
And slant book full against the glare.
Her shadow, in uneasy guise,
Hovered about, a giant size,
On ceiling beam and old oak chair,
The parrot's cage, and panel square;
And the warm angled winter screen,
On which were many monsters seen,
Called doves of Siam, Lima mice,
And legless birds of Paradise,
Macaw, and tender Av'davat,
And silken-furred Angora cat.
Untired she read, her shadow still
Glowered about, as it would fill
The room with wildest forms and shades,
As though some ghostly Queen of Spades
Had come to mock behind her back,
And dance, and ruffle her garments black.
Untired she read the legend page,
Of holy Mark, from youth to age,
On land, on sea, in pagan chains,
Rejoicing for his many pains.
Sometimes the learned eremite,
With golden star, or dagger bright,
Referred to pious poesies
Written in smallest crow-quill size
Beneath the text; and thus the rhyme
Was parcelled out from time to time:
'– Als writith he of swevenis
Men han beforne they wake in bliss,
Whanne that hir friendès thinke hem bound
In crimpede shroude farre under grounde;
And how a litling child mote be
A saint er its nativitie,

    Gif that the modre (God her blesse!)
    Kepen in solitarinesse,
    And kissen devoute the holy croce.
    Of Goddis love, and Sathan's force,
    He writith; and thinges many mo:
110 Of swichè thinges I may not show.
    Bot I must tellen verilie
    Somdel of Saintè Cicilie,
    And chieflie what he auctorith
    Of Saintè Markis life and death.'

    At length her constant eyelids come
    Upon the fervent martyrdom;
    Then lastly to his holy shrine,
    Exalt amid the tapers' shine
    At Venice. . . .

'Gif ye wol stonden hardie wight'

    Gif ye wol stonden hardie wight –
    Amiddès of the blackè night –
    Righte in the churchè porch, pardie,
    Ye wol behold a companie
    Approchen thee full dolourouse.
    For sooth to sain, from everich house,
    Be it in city or village,
    Wol come the phantom and image
    Of ilka gent and ilka carle,
10 Whom coldè Deathè hath in parle
    And wol some day that very year,
    Touchen with foulè venìme spear
    And sadly do them all to die:
    Hem all shalt thou see verilie.
    And everichon shall by thee pass,
    All who must die that year, alas. . . .

'Why did I laugh tonight? ...'

Why did I laugh tonight? No voice will tell:
  No God, no Demon of severe response,
Deigns to reply from Heaven or from Hell.
  Then to my human heart I turn at once –
Heart! thou and I are here sad and alone;
  Say, wherefore did I laugh! O mortal pain!
O Darkness! Darkness! ever must I moan,
  To question Heaven and Hell and Heart in vain.
Why did I laugh? I know this being's lease
  My fancy to its utmost blisses spreads;
Yet could I on this very midnight cease,
  And the world's gaudy ensigns see in shreds.
Verse, Fame, and Beauty are intense indeed,
  But Death intenser – Death is Life's high meed.

Faery Bird's Song

Shed no tear – O, shed no tear!
The flower will bloom another year.
Weep no more! O! weep no more!
Young buds sleep in the root's white core.
Dry your eyes! O! dry your eyes,
For I was taught in Paradise
To ease my breast of melodies –
        Shed no tear.

Overhead! look overhead!
'Mong the blossoms white and red –
Look up, look up. I flutter now
On this flush pomegranate bough.
See me! 'tis this silvery bill
Ever cures the good man's ill.
Shed no tear! O shed no tear!
The flower will bloom another year.
Adieu, adieu – I fly, adieu,

I vanish in the heaven's blue –
    Adieu, adieu!

Faery Song

Ah! woe is me! poor silver-wing!
  That I must chant thy lady's dirge,
And death to this fair haunt of spring,
  Of melody, and streams of flowery verge –
Poor silver-wing! ah! woe is me!
    That I must see
These blossoms snow upon thy lady's pall!
  Go, pretty page! and in her ear
  Whisper that the hour is near!
  Softly tell her not to fear
Such calm Favonian burial!
  Go, pretty page! and soothly tell –
The blossoms hang by a melting spell,
And fall they must, ere a star wink thrice
    Upon her closèd eyes,
That now in vain are weeping their last tears,
  At sweet life leaving, and these arbours green –
Rich dowry from the Spirit of the Spheres.
    Alas! poor Queen!

'When they were come unto the Faery's Court'

When they were come unto the Faery's Court
They rang – no one at home; all gone to sport
And dance and kiss and love as faeries do,
For faeries be, as humans, lovers true.
Amid the woods they were, so lone and wild,
Where even the robin feels himself exiled,
And where the very brooks as if afraid
Hurry along to some less magic shade.
'No one at home!' the fretful princess cried,

10 'And all for nothing such a dreary ride,
    And all for nothing my new diamond cross,
    No one to see my Persian feathers toss,
    No one to see my Ape, my Dwarf, my Fool,
    Or how I pace my Otahaeitan mule.
    Ape, Dwarf and Fool, why stand you gaping there?
    Burst the door open, quick – or I declare
    I'll switch you soundly and in pieces tear.'
    The Dwarf began to tremble and the Ape
    Stared at the Fool, the Fool was all agape.
20 The Princess grasped her switch, but just in time
    The Dwarf with piteous face began to rhyme.
    'O mighty Princess, did you ne'er hear tell
    What your poor servants know but too, too well?
    Know you the three 'great crimes' in faery land?
    The first – alas! poor Dwarf – I understand:
    I made a whipstock of a faery's wand.
    The next is snoring in their company.
    The next, the last, the direst of the three,
    Is making free when they are not at home.
30 I was a Prince, a baby prince – my doom
    You see – I made a whipstock of a wand.
    My top has henceforth slept in faery land.
    He was a Prince, the Fool, a grown-up Prince,
    But he has never been a King's son since
    He fell a-snoring at a faery Ball.
    Your poor Ape was a Prince, and he, poor thing,
    Picklocked a faery's boudoir – now no king,
    But ape – so pray your highness stay awhile;
    'Tis sooth indeed, we know it to our sorrow –
40 Persist and *you* may be an ape tomorrow.'
    While the Dwarf spake the Princess all for spite
    Peeled the brown hazel twig to lily white,
    Clenched her small teeth, and held her lips apart,
    Tried to look unconcerned with beating heart.
    They saw her Highness had made up her mind,
    A-quavering like three reeds before the wind –
    And they had had it, but – O happy chance! –

331 'WHEN THEY WERE COME UNTO THE FAERY'S COURT'

    The Ape for very fear began to dance
    And grinned as all his ugliness did ache –
50 She stayed her vixen fingers for his sake,
    He was so very ugly: then she took
    Her pocket mirror and began to look
    First at herself and then at him and then
    She smiled at her own beauteous face again.
    Yet for all this – for all her pretty face –
    She took it in her head to see the place.
    Women gain little from experience
    Either in lovers, husbands or expense.
    'The more the beauty, the more fortune too:
60 Beauty before the wide world never knew – '
    So each Fair reasons, though it oft miscarries.
    She thought *her* pretty face would please the faeries.
    'My darling Ape, I won't whip you today –
    Give me the picklock, sirrah, and go play.'
    They all three wept – but counsel was as vain
    As crying 'C'up, biddy' to drops of rain.
    Yet lingeringly did the sad Ape forth draw
    The picklock from the pocket in his jaw.
    The Princess took it and, dismounting straight,
70 Tripped in blue silvered slippers to the gate
    And touched the wards; the door full courteously
    Opened – she entered with her servants three.
    Again it closed, and there was nothing seen
    But the Mule grazing on the herbage green.
    End of Canto xii

    Canto the xiii
    The Mule no sooner saw himself alone
    Than he pricked up his ears – and said, 'Well done!
    At least, unhappy Prince, I may be free –
    No more a Princess shall side-saddle me.
    O King of Otahaietè – though a Mule,
80 "Ay, every inch a King", though "Fortune's fool" –
    Well done – for by what Mr Dwarfy said
    I would not give a sixpence for her head.'

Even as he spake he trotted in high glee
To the knotty side of an old pollard tree
And rubbed his sides against the mossèd bark
Till his girths burst and left him naked stark
Except his bridle – how get rid of that,
Buckled and tied with many a twist and plait?
At last it struck him to pretend to sleep
90 And then the thievish Monkeys down would creep
And filch the unpleasant trammels quite away.
No sooner thought of than adown he lay,
Shammed a good snore – the Monkey-men descended
And whom they thought to injure, they befriended.
They hung his bridle on a topmost bough,
And off he went, run, trot, or anyhow. . . .

'The House of Mourning written by Mr Scott'

The House of Mourning written by Mr Scott,
   A sermon at the Magdalen, a tear
   Dropped on a greasy novel, want of cheer
After a walk uphill to a friend's cot,
Tea with a maiden lady, a cursed lot
   Of worthy poems with the author near,
   A patron lord, a drunkenness from beer,
Haydon's great picture, a cold coffee pot
At midnight when the Muse is ripe for labour,
10   The voice of Mr Coleridge, a French bonnet
Before you in the pit, a pipe and tabour,
A damned inseparable flute and neighbour –
   All these are vile, but viler Wordsworth's sonnet
On Dover. Dover! – who *could* write upon it?

Character of Charles Brown

I

    He is to weet a melancholy carle:
Thin in the waist, with bushy head of hair,
As hath the seeded thistle when in parle
It holds the Zephyr, ere it sendeth fair
Its light balloons into the summer air;
Thereto his beard had not begun to bloom,
No brush had touched his chin or razor sheer;
No care had touched his cheek with mortal doom,
But new he was and bright as scarf from Persian loom.

II

Ne cared he for wine, or half-and-half,
Ne cared he for fish or flesh or fowl,
And sauces held he worthless as the chaff;
He 'sdained the swine-herd at the wassail-bowl,
Ne with lewd ribbalds sat he cheek by jowl,
Ne with sly Lemans in the scorner's chair,
But after water-brooks this Pilgrim's soul
Panted, and all his food was woodland air
Though he would oft-times feast on gillyflowers rare.

III

    The slang of cities in no wise he knew,
Tipping the wink to him was heathen Greek.
He sipped no olden Tom or ruin blue,
Or Nantz or cheery-brandy drank full meek
By many a damsel hoarse and rouge of cheek.
Nor did he know each agèd watchman's beat,
Nor in obscurèd purlieus would he seek
For curlèd Jewesses, with ankles neat,
Who as they walk abroad make tinkling with their feet.

A Dream, after reading Dante's Episode of Paola and Francesca

As Hermes once took to his feathers light,
    When lullèd Argus, baffled, swooned and slept,
So on a Delphic reed, my idle spright
    So played, so charmed, so conquered, so bereft
The dragon-world of all its hundred eyes;
    And, seeing it asleep, so fled away –
Not to pure Ida with its snow-cold skies,
    Nor unto Tempe where Jove grieved that day;
But to that second circle of sad hell,
    Where in the gust, the whirlwind, and the flaw
Of rain and hail-stones, lovers need not tell
    Their sorrows. Pale were the sweet lips I saw,
Pale were the lips I kissed, and fair the form
I floated with, about that melancholy storm.

La Belle Dame sans Merci. A Ballad

I

O what can ail thee, knight-at-arms,
    Alone and palely loitering?
The sedge has withered from the lake,
    And no birds sing.

II

O what can ail thee, knight-at-arms,
    So haggard and so woe-begone?
The squirrel's granary is full,
    And the harvest's done.

III

I see a lily on thy brow,
    With anguish moist and fever-dew,
And on thy cheeks a fading rose
    Fast withereth too.

IV

I met a lady in the meads,
    Full beautiful – a faery's child,
Her hair was long, her foot was light,
    And her eyes were wild.

V

I made a garland for her head,
    And bracelets too, and fragrant zone;
She looked at me as she did love,
    And made sweet moan.

VI

I set her on my pacing steed,
    And nothing else saw all day long,
For sidelong would she bend, and sing
    A faery's song.

VII

She found me roots of relish sweet,
    And honey wild, and manna-dew,
And sure in language strange she said –
    'I love thee true'.

VIII

She took me to her elfin grot,
    And there she wept and sighed full sore,
And there I shut her wild wild eyes
    With kisses four.

IX

And there she lullèd me asleep
    And there I dreamed – Ah! woe betide! –
The latest dream I ever dreamt
    On the cold hill side.

X

I saw pale kings and princes too,
    Pale warriors, death-pale were they all;
They cried – 'La Belle Dame sans Merci
    Thee hath in thrall!'

XI

I saw their starved lips in the gloam,
  With horrid warning gapèd wide,
And I awoke and found me here,
  On the cold hill's side.

XII

And this is why I sojourn here
  Alone and palely loitering,
Though the sedge is withered from the lake,
  And no birds sing.

Song of Four Faeries
Fire, Air, Earth and Water

SALAMANDER, ZEPHYR, DUSKETHA, AND BREAMA

SALAMANDER
Happy, happy glowing fire!

ZEPHYR
Fragrant air! delicious light!

DUSKETHA
Let me to my glooms retire!

BREAMA
I to green-weed rivers bright!

SALAMANDER
Happy, happy glowing fire!
Dazzling bowers of soft retire,
Ever let my nourished wing,
Like a bat's, still wandering,
Nimbly fan your fiery spaces,
Spirit sole in deadly places.
In unhaunted roar and blaze,
Open eyes that never daze,
Let me see the myriad shapes
Of men and beasts, and fish, and apes,

SONG OF FOUR FAERIES

Portrayed in many a fiery den,
And wrought by spumy bitumen
On the deep intenser roof,
Archèd every way aloof.
Let me breathe upon their skies,
And anger their live tapestries;
Free from cold, and every care,
Of chilly rain, and shivering air.

ZEPHYR
Spirit of Fire! away! away!
Or your very roundelay
Will sear my plumage newly budded
From its quillèd sheath, and studded
With the self-same dews that fell
On the May-grown asphodel.
Spirit of Fire! away! away!

BREAMA
Spirit of Fire! away! away!
Zephyr, blue-eyed, Faery, turn,
And see my cool sedge-buried urn,
Where it rests its mossy brim
'Mid water-mint and cresses dim;
And the flowers, in sweet troubles,
Lift their eyes above the bubbles,
Like our Queen, when she would please
To sleep, and Oberon *will* tease,
Love me, blue-eyed Faery true,
Soothly I am sick for you.

ZEPHYR
Gentle Breama! by the first
Violet young nature nursed,
I will bathe myself with thee,
So you sometime follow me
To my home, far, far, in west,
Beyond the nimble-wheelèd quest
Of the golden-presencèd sun;

Come with me, o'er tops of trees,
To my fragrant palaces,
Where they ever floating are
Beneath the cherish of a star
Called Vesper, who with silver veil
Ever hides his brilliance pale,
Ever gently-drowsed doth keep
Twilight for the Fays to sleep.
Fear not that your watery hair
Will thirst in drouthy ringlets there;
Clouds of storèd summer rains
Thou shalt taste, before the stains
From the mountain soil they take,
And too unlucent for thee make.
I love thee, crystal Faery, true!
Sooth I am as sick for you!

SALAMANDER
Out, ye aguish Faeries, out!
Chilly lovers, what a rout
Keep ye with your frozen breath,
Colder than the mortal death.
Adder-eyed Dusketha, speak,
Shall we leave these, and go seek
In the earth's wide entrails old
Couches warm as theirs is cold?
O for a fiery gloom and thee,
Dusketha, so enchantingly
Freckle-winged and lizard-sided!

DUSKETHA
By thee, Sprite, will I be guided!
I care not for cold or heat;
Frost or flame, or sparks, or sleet,
To my essence are the same —
But I honour more the flame.
Sprite of Fire, I follow thee
Wheresoever it may be,
To the torrid spouts and fountains,

>   Underneath earth-quakèd mountains;
> Or, at thy supreme desire,
> Touch the very pulse of fire
> With my bare unlidded eyes.
>
> SALAMANDER
> Sweet Dusketha! Paradise!
> Off, ye icy Spirits, fly!
> Frosty creatures of the sky!
>
> DUSKETHA
> 90 Breathe upon them, fiery Sprite!
>
> ZEPHYR AND BREAMA
> Away! away to our delight!
>
> SALAMANDER
> Go, feed on icicles, while we
> Bedded in tongued flames will be.
>
> DUSKETHA
> Lead me to those feverous glooms,
> Sprite of Fire!
>
> BREAMA
>   Me to the blooms,
> Blue-eyed Zephyr, of those flowers
> Far in the west where the May-cloud lowers;
> And the beams of still Vesper, when winds are all whist,
> Are shed through the rain and the milder mist,
> 100 And twilight your floating bowers.

To Sleep

> O soft embalmer of the still midnight,
>   Shutting, with careful fingers and benign,
> Our gloom-pleased eyes, embowered from the light,
>   Enshaded in forgetfulness divine:
> O soothest Sleep! if so it please thee, close
>   In midst of this thine hymn, my willing eyes,

Or wait the 'Amen', ere the poppy throws
    Around my bed its lulling charities.
Then save me, or the passèd day will shine
Upon my pillow, breeding many woes;
    Save me from curious conscience, that still hoards
Its strength for darkness, burrowing like the mole;
    Turn the key deftly in the oilèd wards,
And seal the hushèd casket of my soul.

'If by dull rhymes our English must be chained'

If by dull rhymes our English must be chained,
And, like Andromeda, the Sonnet sweet
Fettered, in spite of painèd loveliness,
Let us find out, if we must be constrained,
Sandals more interwoven and complete
To fit the naked foot of Poesy:
Let us inspect the lyre, and weigh the stress
Of every chord, and see what may be gained
By ear industrious, and attention meet;
Misers of sound and syllable, no less
Than Midas of his coinage, let us be
Jealous of dead leaves in the bay wreath crown;
So, if we may not let the Muse be free,
She will be bound with garlands of her own.

Ode to Psyche

O Goddess! hear these tuneless numbers, wrung
    By sweet enforcement and remembrance dear,
And pardon that thy secrets should be sung
    Even into thine own soft-conchèd ear:
Surely I dreamt to-day, or did I see
    The wingèd Psyche with awakened eyes?
I wandered in a forest thoughtlessly,
    And, on the sudden, fainting with surprise,

ODE TO PSYCHE

     Saw two fair creatures, couchèd side by side
10   In deepest grass, beneath the whispering roof
      Of leaves and tremblèd blossoms, where there ran
        A brooklet, scarce espied:
    'Mid hushed, cool-rooted flowers, fragrant-eyed,
      Blue, silver-white, and budded Tyrian,
    They lay calm-breathing on the bedded grass;
      Their arms embraced, and their pinions too;
      Their lips touched not, but had not bade adieu,
    As if disjoinèd by soft-handed slumber,
    And ready still past kisses to outnumber
20   At tender eye-dawn of aurorean love:
        The wingèd boy I knew;
    But who wast thou, O happy, happy dove?
        His Psyche true!

    O latest born and loveliest vision far
      Of all Olympus' faded hierarchy!
    Fairer than Phoebe's sapphire-regioned star,
      Or Vesper, amorous glow-worm of the sky;
    Fairer than these, though temple thou hast none,
      Nor altar heaped with flowers;
30 Nor virgin-choir to make delicious moan
      Upon the midnight hours;
    No voice, no lute, no pipe, no incense sweet
      From chain-swung censer teeming;
    No shrine, no grove, no oracle, no heat
      Of pale-mouthed prophet dreaming.

    O brightest! though too late for antique vows,
      Too, too late for the fond believing lyre,
    When holy were the haunted forest boughs,
      Holy the air, the water, and the fire;
40 Yet even in these days so far retired
      From happy pieties, thy lucent fans,
      Fluttering among the faint Olympians,
    I see, and sing, by my own eyes inspired.
    So let me be thy choir, and make a moan
      Upon the midnight hours;

Thy voice, thy lute, thy pipe, thy incense sweet
   From swingèd censer teeming –
Thy shrine, thy grove, thy oracle, thy heat
   Of pale-mouthed prophet dreaming.

50 Yes, I will be thy priest, and build a fane
   In some untrodden region of my mind,
Where branchèd thoughts, new grown with pleasant pain,
   Instead of pines shall murmur in the wind:
Far, far around shall those dark-clustered trees
   Fledge the wild-ridgèd mountains steep by steep;
And there by zephyrs, streams, and birds, and bees,
   The moss-lain Dryads shall be lulled to sleep;
And in the midst of this wide quietness
   A rosy sanctuary will I dress
60 With the wreathed trellis of a working brain,
   With buds, and bells, and stars without a name,
With all the gardener Fancy e'er could feign,
   Who breeding flowers, will never breed the same:
And there shall be for thee all soft delight
   That shadowy thought can win,
A bright torch, and a casement ope at night,
   To let the warm Love in!

On Fame (I)

Fame, like a wayward girl, will still be coy
   To those who woo her with too slavish knees,
But makes surrender to some thoughtless boy,
   And dotes the more upon a heart at ease;
She is gipsy, will not speak to those
   Who have not learnt to be content without her;
A jilt, whose ear was never whispered close,
   Who thinks they scandal her who talk about her –
A very gipsy is she, Nilus-born,
10   Sister-in-law to jealous Potiphar.
Ye love-sick bards! repay her scorn for scorn;

Ye artists lovelorn! madmen that ye are,
Make your best bow to her and bid adieu –
Then, if she likes it, she will follow you.

On Fame (II)
You cannot eat your cake and have it too
Proverb

How fevered is the man who cannot look
   Upon his mortal days with temperate blood,
Who vexes all the leaves of his life's book,
   And robs his fair name of its maidenhood;
It is as if the rose should pluck herself,
   Or the ripe plum finger its misty bloom,
As if a Naiad, like a meddling elf,
   Should darken her pure grot with muddy gloom:
But the rose leaves herself upon the briar,
10   For winds to kiss and grateful bees to feed,
And the ripe plum still wears its dim attire,
     The undisturbèd lake has crystal space;
      Why then should man, teasing the world for grace,
Spoil his salvation for a fierce miscreed?

'Two or three posies'

Two or three posies
With two or three simples –
Two or three noses
With two or three pimples –
Two or three wise men
And two or three ninnies –
Two or three purses
And two or three guineas –
Two or three raps
10 At two or three doors –
Two or three naps

Of two or three hours –
Two or three cats
And two or three mice –
Two or three sprats
At a very great price –
Two or three sandies
And two or three tabbies –
Two or three dandies
And two Mrs —— mum!
Two or three smiles
And two or three frowns –
Two or three miles
To two or three towns –
Two or three pegs
For two or three bonnets –
Two or three dove's eggs
To hatch into sonnets.

Ode on a Grecian Urn

I

Thou still unravished bride of quietness,
   Thou foster-child of silence and slow time,
Sylvan historian, who canst thus express
   A flowery tale more sweetly than our rhyme:
What leaf-fringed legend haunts about thy shape
    Of deities or mortals, or of both,
      In Tempe or the dales of Arcady?
    What men or gods are these? What maidens loth?
What mad pursuit? What struggle to escape?
    What pipes and timbrels? What wild ecstasy?

II

Heard melodies are sweet, but those unheard
   Are sweeter; therefore, ye soft pipes, play on;
Not to the sensual ear, but, more endeared,
   Pipe to the spirit ditties of no tone:

ODE ON A GRECIAN URN

>Fair youth, beneath the trees, thou canst not leave
>> Thy song, nor ever can those trees be bare;
>> Bold Lover, never, never canst thou kiss,
>Though winning near the goal – yet, do not grieve:
>> She cannot fade, though thou hast not thy bliss,
>>> For ever wilt thou love, and she be fair!

III

>Ah, happy, happy boughs! that cannot shed
>> Your leaves, nor ever bid the Spring adieu;
>And, happy melodist, unwearièd,
>> For ever piping songs for ever new;
>More happy love! more happy, happy love!
>> For ever warm and still to be enjoyed,
>>> For ever panting, and for ever young –
>All breathing human passion far above,
>> That leaves a heart high-sorrowful and cloyed,
>>> A burning forehead, and a parching tongue.

IV

>Who are these coming to the sacrifice?
>> To what green altar, O mysterious priest,
>Lead'st thou that heifer lowing at the skies,
>> And all her silken flanks with garlands dressed?
>What little town by river or sea shore,
>> Or mountain-built with peaceful citadel,
>>> Is emptied of this folk, this pious morn?
>And, little town, thy streets for evermore
>> Will silent be; and not a soul to tell
>>> Why thou art desolate, can e'er return.

V

>O Attic shape! Fair attitude! with brede
>> Of marble men and maidens overwrought,
>With forest branches and the trodden weed;
>> Thou, silent form, dost tease us out of thought
>As doth eternity: Cold Pastoral!
>> When old age shall this generation waste,
>>> Thou shalt remain, in midst of other woe

Than ours, a friend to man, to whom thou say'st,
  'Beauty is truth, truth beauty, – that is all
    Ye know on earth, and all ye need to know.'

Ode to a Nightingale

I

My heart aches, and a drowsy numbness pains
  My sense, as though of hemlock I had drunk,
Or emptied some dull opiate to the drains
  One minute past, and Lethe-wards had sunk:
'Tis not through envy of thy happy lot,
  But being too happy in thine happiness –
    That thou, light-wingèd Dryad of the trees,
      In some melodious plot
Of beechen green, and shadows numberless,
  Singest of summer in full-throated ease.

II

O, for a draught of vintage! that hath been
  Cooled a long age in the deep-delvèd earth,
Tasting of Flora and the country green,
  Dance, and Provençal song, and sunburnt mirth!
O for a beaker full of the warm South,
  Full of the true, the blushful Hippocrene,
    With beaded bubbles winking at the brim,
      And purple-stainèd mouth,
That I might drink, and leave the world unseen,
  And with thee fade away into the forest dim –

III

Fade far away, dissolve, and quite forget
  What thou among the leaves hast never known,
The weariness, the fever, and the fret
  Here, where men sit and hear each other groan;
Where palsy shakes a few, sad, last grey hairs,
  Where youth grows pale, and spectre-thin, and dies;
    Where but to think is to be full of sorrow

    And leaden-eyed despairs;
  Where Beauty cannot keep her lustrous eyes,
    Or new Love pine at them beyond to-morrow.

IV

Away! away! for I will fly to thee,
  Not charioted by Bacchus and his pards,
But on the viewless wings of Poesy,
  Though the dull brain perplexes and retards.
Already with thee! tender is the night,
  And haply the Queen-Moon is on her throne,
    Clustered around by all her starry Fays;
    But here there is no light,
  Save what from heaven is with the breezes blown
    Through verdurous glooms and winding mossy ways.

V

I cannot see what flowers are at my feet,
  Nor what soft incense hangs upon the boughs,
But, in embalmèd darkness, guess each sweet
  Wherewith the seasonable month endows
The grass, the thicket, and the fruit-tree wild –
  White hawthorn, and the pastoral eglantine;
    Fast fading violets covered up in leaves;
    And mid-May's eldest child,
  The coming musk-rose, full of dewy wine,
    The murmurous haunt of flies on summer eves.

VI

Darkling I listen; and, for many a time
  I have been half in love with easeful Death,
Called him soft names in many a musèd rhyme,
  To take into the air my quiet breath;
Now more than ever seems it rich to die,
  To cease upon the midnight with no pain,
    While thou art pouring forth thy soul abroad
    In such an ecstasy!
  Still wouldst thou sing, and I have ears in vain –
    To thy high requiem become a sod.

VII

Thou wast not born for death, immortal Bird!
  No hungry generations tread thee down;
The voice I hear this passing night was heard
  In ancient days by emperor and clown:
Perhaps the self-same song that found a path
  Through the sad heart of Ruth, when, sick for home,
    She stood in tears amid the alien corn;
      The same that oft-times hath
  Charmed magic casements, opening on the foam
    Of perilous seas, in faery lands forlorn.

VIII

Forlorn! the very word is like a bell
  To toll me back from thee to my sole self!
Adieu! the fancy cannot cheat so well
  As she is famed to do, deceiving elf.
Adieu! adieu! thy plaintive anthem fades
  Past the near meadows, over the still stream,
    Up the hill-side; and now 'tis buried deep
      In the next valley-glades:
  Was it a vision, or a waking dream?
    Fled is that music – Do I wake or sleep?

Ode on Melancholy

I

No, no, go not to Lethe, neither twist
  Wolf's-bane, tight-rooted, for its poisonous wine:
Nor suffer thy pale forehead to be kissed
  By nightshade, ruby grape of Proserpine;
Make not your rosary of yew-berries,
  Nor let the beetle, nor the death-moth be
    Your mournful Psyche, nor the downy owl
A partner in your sorrow's mysteries;
  For shade to shade will come too drowsily,
    And drown the wakeful anguish of the soul.

II
But when the melancholy fit shall fall
   Sudden from heaven like a weeping cloud,
That fosters the droop-headed flowers all,
   And hides the green hill in an April shroud;
Then glut thy sorrow on a morning rose,
   Or on the rainbow of the salt sand-wave,
     Or on the wealth of globèd peonies;
Or if thy mistress some rich anger shows,
   Emprison her soft hand, and let her rave,
20   And feed deep, deep upon her peerless eyes.

III
She dwells with Beauty – Beauty that must die;
   And Joy, whose hand is ever at his lips
Bidding adieu; and aching Pleasure nigh,
   Turning to poison while the bee-mouth sips:
Ay, in the very temple of Delight
   Veiled Melancholy has her sovran shrine,
     Though seen of none save him whose strenuous tongue
Can burst Joy's grape against his palate fine;
   His soul shall taste the sadness of her might,
30   And be among her cloudy trophies hung.

Ode on Indolence
They toil not, neither do they spin

I
One morn before me were three figures seen,
   With bowèd necks, and joinèd hands, side-faced;
And one behind the other stepped serene,
   In placid sandals, and in white robes graced;
They passed, like figures on a marble urn,
   When shifted round to see the other side;
     They came again; as when the urn once more
Is shifted round, the first seen shades return;
   And they were strange to me, as may betide
10   With vases, to one deep in Phidian lore.

II

How is it, Shadows! that I knew ye not?
    How came ye muffled in so hush a masque?
Was it a silent deep-disguisèd plot
    To steal away, and leave without a task
My idle days? Ripe was the drowsy hour;
    The blissful cloud of summer-indolence
        Benumbed my eyes; my pulse grew less and less;
Pain had no sting, and pleasure's wreath no flower:
    O, why did ye not melt, and leave my sense
        Unhaunted quite of all but – nothingness?

III

A third time passed they by, and, passing, turned
    Each one the face a moment whiles to me;
Then faded, and to follow them I burned
    And ached for wings because I knew the three;
The first was a fair Maid, and Love her name;
    The second was Ambition, pale of cheek,
        And ever watchful with fatiguèd eye;
The last, whom I love more, the more of blame
    Is heaped upon her, maiden most unmeek –
        I knew to be my demon Poesy.

IV

They faded, and, forsooth! I wanted wings.
    O folly! What is love! and where is it?
And, for that poor Ambition – it springs
    From a man's little heart's short fever-fit.
For Poesy! – no, she has not a joy –
    At least for me – so sweet as drowsy noons,
        And evenings steeped in honeyed indolence.
O, for an age so sheltered from annoy,
    That I may never know how change the moons,
        Or hear the voice of busy common-sense!

V

A third time came they by – alas! wherefore?
    My sleep had been embroidered with dim dreams;

ODE ON INDOLENCE

My soul had been a lawn besprinkled o'er
   With flowers, and stirring shades, and baffled beams:
The morn was clouded, but no shower fell,
    Though in her lids hung the sweet tears of May;
      The open casement pressed a new-leaved vine,
   Let in the budding warmth and throstle's lay;
O Shadows! 'twas a time to bid farewell!
    Upon your skirts had fallen no tears of mine.

VI

So, ye three Ghosts, adieu! Ye cannot raise
   My head cool-bedded in the flowery grass;
For I would not be dieted with praise,
   A pet-lamb in a sentimental farce!
Fade softly from my eyes, and be once more
   In masque-like figures on the dreamy urn.
     Farewell! I yet have visions for the night,
And for the day faint visions there is store.
     Vanish, ye Phantoms! from my idle sprite,
   Into the clouds, and never more return!

Otho the Great. A Tragedy in Five Acts

Dramatis Personae

OTHO THE GREAT Emperor of Germany
LUDOLPH his son
CONRAD Duke of Franconia
ALBERT a Knight, favoured by Otho
SIGIFRED an Officer friend of Ludolph
THEODORE } Officers
GONFRED }
ETHELBERT an Abbot
GERSA Prince of Hungary
An Hungarian Captain
Physician
Page
Nobles, Knights, Attendants, and Soldiers

ERMINIA Niece of Otho
AURANTHE Conrad's Sister
Ladies and Attendants

Scene: the Castle of Friedburg, its vicinity, and the Hungarian Camp

Time: one day

OTHO THE GREAT: I.1

ACT I

Scene 1 *An Apartment in the Castle. Enter* CONRAD.

CONRAD So, I am safe emergèd from these broils!
Amid the wreck of thousands I am whole;
For every crime I have a laurel-wreath,
For every lie a lordship. Nor yet has
My ship of fortune furled her silken sails –
Let her glide on! This dangered neck is saved,
By dexterous policy, from the rebel's axe;
And of my ducal palace not one stone
Is bruised by the Hungarian petards.
Toil hard, ye slaves, and from the miser-earth
Bring forth once more my bullion, treasured deep,
With all my jewelled salvers, silver and gold,
And precious goblets that make rich the wine.
But why do I stand babbling to myself?
Where is Auranthe? I have news for her
Shall –

[*Enter* AURANTHE]

AURANTHE Conrad! what tidings? Good, if I may guess
From your alert eyes and high-lifted brows.
What tidings of the battle? Albert? Ludolph? Otho?
CONRAD You guess aright. And, sister, slurring o'er
Our by-gone quarrels, I confess my heart
Is beating with a child's anxiety,
To make our golden fortune known to you.
AURANTHE So serious?
CONRAD Yes, so serious, that before
I utter even the shadow of a hint
Concerning what will make that sin-worn cheek
Blush joyous blood through every lineament,
You must make here a solemn vow to me.
AURANTHE I prithee, Conrad, do not overact
The hypocrite. What vow would you impose?
CONRAD Trust me for once. That you may be assured
'Tis not confiding in a broken reed,

A poor court-bankrupt, outwitted and lost,
Revolve these facts in your acutest mood,
In such a mood as now you listen to me.
A few days since, I was an open rebel –
Against the Emperor, had suborned his son –
Drawn off his nobles to revolt, and shown
Contented fools causes for discontent,
Fresh hatched in my ambition's eagle nest.
40 So thrived I as a rebel, and, behold –
Now I am Otho's favourite, his dear friend,
His right hand, his brave Conrad!

AURANTHE   I confess
You have intrigued with these unsteady times
To admiration. But to be a favourite –

CONRAD I saw my moment. The Hungarians,
Collected silently in holes and corners,
Appeared, a sudden host, in the open day.
I should have perished in our empire's wreck,
But, calling interest loyalty, swore faith
50 To most believing Otho; and so helped
His blood-stained ensigns to the victory
In yesterday's hard fight, that it has turned
The edge of his sharp wrath to eager kindness.

AURANTHE So far yourself. But what is this to me
More than that I am glad? I gratulate you.

CONRAD Yes, sister, but it does regard you greatly,
Nearly, momentously – ay, painfully!
Make me this vow –

AURANTHE   Concerning whom or what?

CONRAD Albert!

AURANTHE   I would inquire somewhat of him:
60 You had a letter from me touching him?
No treason 'gainst his head in deed or word!
Surely you spared him at my earnest prayer?
Give me the letter – it should not exist!

CONRAD At one pernicious charge of the enemy,
I, for a moment-whiles, was prisoner ta'en
And rifled – stuff! the horses' hoofs have minced it!

AURANTHE He is alive?
CONRAD   He is! but here make oath
  To alienate him from your scheming brain,
  Divorce him from your solitary thoughts,
70 And cloud him in such utter banishment,
  That when his person meets again your eye,
  Your vision shall quite lose its memory,
  And wander past him as through vacancy.
AURANTHE I'll not be perjured.
CONRAD   No, nor great, nor mighty;
  You would not wear a crown, or rule a kingdom.
  To you it is indifferent.
AURANTHE   What means this?
CONRAD You'll not be perjured! Go to Albert then,
  That camp-mushroom – dishonour of our house.
  Go, page his dusty heels upon a march,
80 Furbish his jingling baldric while he sleeps,
  And share his mouldy ratioo in a siege.
  Yet stay – perhaps a charm may call you back,
  And make the widening circlets of your eyes
  Sparkle with healthy fevers. The Emperor
  Hath given consent that you should marry Ludolph!
AURANTHE Can it be, brother? For a golden crown
  With a queen's awful lips I doubly thank you!
  This is to wake in Paradise! Farewell
  Thou clod of yesterday – 'twas not myself!
90 Not till this moment did I ever feel
  My spirit's faculties! I'll flatter you
  For this, and be you ever proud of it;
  Thou, Jove-like, struck'd'st thy forehead,
  And from the teeming marrow of thy brain
  I spring complete Minerva! But the prince –
  His highness Ludolph – where is he?
CONRAD   I know not:
  When, lackeying my counsel at a beck,
  The rebel lords, on bended knees, received
  The Emperor's pardon, Ludolph kept aloof,
100 Sole, in a stiff, fool-hardy, sulky pride;

        Yet, for all this, I never saw a father
        In such a sickly longing for his son.
        We shall soon see him, for the Emperor
        He will be here this morning.
AURANTHE   That I heard
        Among the midnight rumours from the camp.
CONRAD You give up Albert to me?
AURANTHE   Harm him not!
        E'en for his highness Ludolph's sceptry hand,
        I would not Albert suffer any wrong.
CONRAD Have I not laboured, plotted – ?
AURANTHE   See you spare him:
110   Nor be pathetic, my kind benefactor,
        On all the many bounties of your hand –
        'Twas for yourself you laboured – not for me!
        Do you not count, when I am queen, to take
        Advantage of your chance discoveries
        Of my poor secrets, and so hold a rod
        Over my life?
CONRAD   Let not this slave – this villain –
        Be cause of feud between us. See! he comes!
        Look, woman, look, your Albert is quite safe!
        In haste it seems. Now shall I be in the way,
120   And wish'd with silent curses in my grave,
        Or side by side with 'whelmèd mariners.

        [*Enter* ALBERT]

ALBERT Fair on your graces fall this early morrow!
        So it is like to do, without my prayers,
        For your right noble names, like favourite tunes,
        Have fall'n full frequent from our Emperor's lips,
        High commented with smiles.
AURANTHE   Noble Albert!
CONRAD [*aside*]   Noble!
AURANTHE Such salutation argues a glad heart
        In our prosperity. We thank you, sir.
ALBERT Lady! O, would to Heaven your poor servant
130   Could do you better service than mere words!

But I have other greeting than mine own,
From no less man than Otho, who has sent
This ring as pledge of dearest amity;
'Tis chosen I hear from Hymen's jewel'ry,
And you will prize it, lady, I doubt not,
Beyond all pleasures past, and all to come.
To you great duke –
CONRAD   To me! What of me, ha?
ALBERT What pleased your grace to say?
CONRAD   Your message, sir!
ALBERT You mean not this to me?
CONRAD   Sister, this way;
For there shall be no 'gentle Alberts' now,
No 'sweet Auranthes!' [*aside*]

[*Exeunt* CONRAD *and* AURANTHE]

ALBERT (*solus*) The duke is out of temper; if he knows
More than a brother of a sister ought,
I should not quarrel with his peevishness.
Auranthe – Heaven preserve her always fair! –
Is in the heady, proud, ambitious vein;
I bicker not with her – bid her farewell!
She has taken flight from me, then let her soar –
He is a fool who stands at pining gaze!
But for poor Ludolph, he is food for sorrow:
No levelling bluster of my licensed thoughts,
No military swagger of my mind,
Can smother from myself the wrong I've done him –
Without design, indeed – yet it is so –
And opiate for the conscience have I none! [*Exit*]

Scene 2 *The Court-yard of the Castle.*
[*Martial Music. Enter, from the outer gate,* OTHO, *Nobles, Knights, and Attendants. The Soldiers halt at the gate, with banners in sight*]

OTHO Where is my noble herald?

[*Enter* CONRAD, *from the Castle, attended by two Knights and Servants, Albert following*]

      Well, hast told
Auranthe our intent imperial?
Lest our rent banners, too o' the sudden shown,
Should fright her silken casements, and dismay
Her household to our lack of entertainment.
A victory!
CONRAD God save illustrious Otho!
OTHO Ay, Conrad, it will pluck out all grey hairs;
 It is the best physician for the spleen;
 The courtliest inviter to a feast;
10 The subtlest excuser of small faults;
 And a nice judge in the age and smack of wine.

[*Enter, from the Castle,* AURANTHE, *followed by Pages holding up her robes, and a train of Women. She kneels*]

Hail my sweet hostess! I do thank the stars,
Or my good soldiers, or their ladies' eyes,
That, after such a merry battle fought,
I can, all safe in body and in soul,
Kiss your fair hand and Lady Fortune's too.
My ring! now, on my life, it doth rejoice
These lips to feel't on this soft ivory!
Keep it, my brightest daughter; it may prove
20 The little prologue to a line of kings.
I strove against thee and my hot-blood son,
Dull blockhead that I was to be so blind,
But now my sight is clear; forgive me, lady.
AURANTHE My lord, I was a vassal to your frown,
 And now your favour makes me but more humble;
 In wintry winds the simple snow is safe,
 But fadeth at the greeting of the sun:
 Unto thine anger I might well have spoken,
 Taking on me a woman's privilege,
30 But this so sudden kindness makes me dumb.
 OTHO What need of this? Enough, if you will be

OTHO THE GREAT: I . 2

  A potent tutoress to my wayward boy,
  And teach him, what it seems his nurse could not,
  To say, for once, I thank you. Sigifred!
ALBERT He has not yet returned, my gracious liege.
OTHO What then! No tidings of my friendly Arab?
CONRAD None, mighty Otho.

[To one of his Knights, who goes out]

     Send forth instantly
  An hundred horsemen from my honoured gates,
  To scour the plains and search the cottages.
40   Cry a reward, to him who shall first bring
  News of that vanishèd Arabian,
  A full-heaped helmet of the purest gold.
OTHO More thanks, good Conrad; for, except my son's,
  There is no face I rather would behold
  Than that same quick-eyed pagan's. By the saints,
  This coming night of banquets must not light
  Her dazzling torches; nor the music breathe
  Smooth, without clashing cymbal, tones of peace
  And in-door melodies; nor the ruddy wine
50   Ebb spouting to the lees; if I pledge not,
  In my first cup, that Arab!
ALBERT   Mighty Monarch,
  I wonder not this stranger's victor-deeds
  So hang upon your spirit. Twice in the fight
  It was my chance to meet his olive brow,
  Triumphant in the enemy's shattered rhomb;
  And, to say truth, in any Christian arm
  I never saw such prowess.
OTHO   Did you ever?
  O, 'tis a noble boy! – tut! – what do I say?
  I mean a triple Saladin, whose eyes,
60   When in the glorious scuffle they met mine,
  Seemed to say – 'Sleep, old man, in safety sleep;
  I am the victory!'
CONRAD   Pity he's not here.
OTHO And my son too, pity he is not here.

Lady Auranthe, I would not make you blush,
But can you give a guess where Ludolph is?
Know you not of him?
AURANTHE   Indeed, my liege, no secret –
OTHO Nay, nay, without more words, dost know of him?
AURANTHE I would I were so over-fortunate,
  Both for his sake and mine, and to make glad
70 A father's ears with tidings of his son.
OTHO I see 'tis like to be a tedious day.
  Were Theodore and Gonfred and the rest
  Sent forth with my commands?
ALBERT   Ay, my lord.
OTHO And no news! No news! 'Faith! 'tis very strange
  He thus avoids us. Lady, is't not strange?
  Will he be truant to you too? It is a shame.
CONRAD Will't please your highness enter, and accept
  The unworthy welcome of your servant's house?
  Leaving your cares to one whose diligence
80 May in few hours make pleasures of them all.
OTHO Not so tedious, Conrad. No, no, no, no –
  I must see Ludolph or the – What's that shout!
VOICES WITHOUT Huzza! huzza! Long live the Emperor!
OTHER VOICES Fall back! Away there!
OTHO   Say, what noise is that?

[ALBERT *advancing from the back of the stage, whither he had hastened on hearing the cheers of the soldiery*]

ALBERT It is young Gersa, the Hungarian prince,
  Picked like a red stag from the fallow herd
  Of prisoners. Poor prince, forlorn he steps,
  Slow, and demure, and proud in his despair.
  If I may judge by his so tragic bearing.
90 His eye not downcast, and his folded arm,
  He doth this moment wish himself asleep
  Among his fallen captains on yon plains.

[*Enter* GERSA, *in chains, and guarded*]

OTHO Well said, Sir Albert.
GERSA   Not a word of greeting,
  No welcome to a princely visitor,
  Most mighty Otho? Will not my great host
  Vouchsafe a syllable, before he bids
  His gentlemen conduct me with all care
  To some securest lodging? – cold perhaps!
OTHO What mood is this? Hath fortune touched thy brain?
GERSA O kings and princes of this feverous world,
  What abject things, what mockeries must ye be,
  What nerveless minions of safe palaces!
  When here, a monarch, whose proud foot is used
  To fallen princes' necks, as to his stirrup,
  Must needs exclaim that I am mad forsooth,
  Because I cannot flatter with bent knees
  My conqueror!
OTHO   Gersa, I think you wrong me:
  I think I have a better fame abroad.
GERSA I prithee mock me not with gentle speech,
  But, as a favour, bid me from thy presence;
  Let me no longer be the wondering food
  Of all these eyes; prithee command me hence!
OTHO Do not mistake me, Gersa. That you may not,
  Come, fair Auranthe, try if your soft hands
  Can manage those hard rivets to set free
  So brave a prince and soldier.
AURANTHE [*sets him free*]   Welcome task!
GERSA I am wound up in deep astonishment!
  Thank you, fair lady. Otho! emperor!
  You rob me of myself; my dignity
  Is now your infant; I am a weak child.
OTHO Give me your hand, and let this kindly grasp
  Live in our memories.
GERSA   In mine it will.
  I blush to think of my unchastened tongue;
  But I was haunted by the monstrous ghost
  Of all our slain battalions. Sire, reflect,

And pardon you will grant, that, at this hour,
The bruisèd remnants of our stricken camp
Are huddling undistinguished my dear friends,
With common thousands, into shallow graves.
OTHO Enough, most noble Gersa. You are free
To cheer the brave remainder of your host
By your own healing presence, and that too,
Not as their leader merely, but their king;
For, as I hear, the wily enemy,
Who eased the crownet from your infant brows,
Bloody Taraxa, is among the dead.
GERSA Then I retire, so generous Otho please,
Bearing with me a weight of benefits
Too heavy to be borne.
OTHO   It is not so;
Still understand me, King of Hungary,
Nor judge my open purposes awry.
Though I did hold you high in my esteem
For your self's sake, I do not personate
The stage-play emperor to entrap applause,
To set the silly sort o' the world agape,
And make the politic smile; no, I have heard
How in the Council you condemned this war,
Urging the perfidy of broken faith –
For that I am your friend.
GERSA   If ever, sire,
You are my enemy, I dare here swear
'Twill not be Gersa's fault. Otho, farewell!
OTHO Will you return, Prince, to our banqueting?
GERSA As to my father's board I will return.
OTHO Conrad, with all due ceremony, give
The prince a regal escort to his camp;
Albert, go thou and bear him company.
Gersa, farewell!
GERSA   All happiness attend you!
OTHO Return with what good speed you may; for soon
We must consult upon our terms of peace.

[*Exeunt* GERSA *and* ALBERT *with others*]

OTHO THE GREAT: I . 2

160 And thus a marble column do I build
To prop my empire's dome. Conrad, in thee
I have another steadfast one, to uphold
The portals of my state; and, for my own
Pre-eminence and safety, I will strive
To keep thy strength upon its pedestal.
For, without thee, this day I might have been
A show-monster about the streets of Prague,
In chains, as just now stood that noble prince:
And then to me no mercy had been shown,
170 For when the conquered lion is once dungeoned,
Who lets him forth again? or dares to give
An old lion sugar-cates of mild reprieve?
Not to thine ear alone I make confession,
But to all here, as, by experience,
I know how the great basement of all power
Is frankness, and a true tongue to the world;
And how intriguing secrecy is proof
Of fear and weakness, and a hollow state.
Conrad, I owe thee much.

CONRAD   To kiss that hand,
180 My emperor, is ample recompense,
For a mere act of duty.

OTHO   Thou art wrong;
For what can any man on earth do more?
We will make trial of your house's welcome,
My bright Auranthe!

CONRAD   How is Friedburg honoured!

[*Enter* ETHELBERT *and six Monks*]

ETHELBERT The benison of heaven on your head,
Imperial Otho!

OTHO   Who stays me? Speak! Quick!

ETHELBERT Pause but one moment, mighty conqueror,
Upon the threshold of this house of joy.

OTHO Pray, do not prose, good Ethelbert, but speak
190 What is your purpose.

ETHELBERT   The restoration of some captive **maids**,
Devoted to Heaven's pious ministries,
Who, driven forth from their religious cells,
And kept in thraldom by our enemy,
When late this province was a lawless spoil,
Still weep amid the wild Hungarian camp,
Though hemmed around by thy victorious arms.
OTHO Demand the holy sisterhood in our name
From Gersa's tents. Farewell, old Ethelbert.
ETHELBERT The saints will bless you for this pious care.
200 OTHO Daughter, your hand; Ludolph's would fit it best.
CONRAD Ho! let the music sound!

[*Music.* ETHELBERT *raises his hands, as in benediction of* OTHO.
Exeunt severally. The scene closes on them]

Scene 3 *The Country, with the Castle in the distance.*

[*Enter* LUDOLPH *and* SIGIFRED]

LUDOLPH You have my secret; let it not be breath'd.
SIGIFRED Still give me leave to wonder that the Prince
Ludolph and the swift Arab are the same;
Still to rejoice that 'twas a German arm
Death doing in a turbaned masquerade.
LUDOLPH The Emperor must not know it, Sigifred.
SIGIFRED I prithee, why? What happier hour of time
Could thy pleased star point down upon from heaven
With silver index, bidding thee make peace?
10 LUDOLPH Still it must not be known, good Sigifred;
The star may point oblique.
SIGIFRED   If Otho knew
His son to be that unknown Mussulman
After whose spurring heels he sent me forth,
With one of his well-pleased Olympian oaths,
The charters of man's greatness, at this hour
He would be watching round the castle walls,
And, like an anxious warder, strain his sight

> For the first glimpse of such a son returned –
> Ludolph, that blast of the Hungarians,
> That Saracenic meteor of the fight,
> That silent fury, whose fell scimitar
> Kept danger all aloof from Otho's head,
> And left him space for wonder.
>
> LUDOLPH   Say no more.
> Not as a swordsman would I pardon claim,
> But as a son. The bronzed centurion,
> Long toiled in foreign wars, and whose high deeds
> Are shaded in a forest of tall spears,
> Known only to his troop, hath greater plea
> Of favour with my sire than I can have.
>
> SIGIFRED My lord, forgive me that I cannot see
> How this proud temper with clear reason squares.
> What made you then, with such an anxious love,
> Hover around that life, whose bitter days
> You vexed with bad revolt? Was't opium,
> Or the mad-fumèd wine? Nay, do not frown,
> I rather would grieve with you than upbraid.
>
> LUDOLPH I do believe you. No, 'twas not to make
> A father his son's debtor, or to heal
> His deep heart-sickness for a rebel child.
> 'Twas done in memory of my boyish days,
> Poor cancel for his kindness to my youth,
> For all his calming of my childish griefs,
> And all his smiles upon my merriment.
> No, not a thousand foughten fields could sponge
> Those days paternal from my memory,
> Though now upon my head he heaps disgrace.
>
> SIGIFRED My Prince, you think too harshly –
> LUDOLPH   Can I so?
> Hath he not galled my spirit to the quick?
> And with a sullen rigour obstinate
> Poured out a phial of wrath upon my faults?
> Hunted me as a Tartar does the boar,
> Driven me to the very edge o' the world,
> And almost put a price upon my head?

SIGIFRED Remember how he spared the rebel lords.
LUDOLPH Yes, yes, I know he hath a noble nature
   That cannot trample on the fallen. But his
   Is not the only proud heart in his realm.
   He hath wronged me, and I have done him wrong;
   He hath loved me, and I have shown him kindness;
   We should be almost equal.
SIGIFRED   Yet, for all this,
   I would you had appeared among those lords,
   And taken his favour.
LUDOLPH   Ha! till now I thought
   My friend had held poor Ludolph's honour dear.
   What! would you have me sue before his throne
   And kiss the courtier's missal, its silk steps?
   Or hug the golden housings of his steed,
   Amid a camp, whose steelèd swarms I dared
   But yesterday? And, at the trumpet sound,
   Bow like some unknown mercenary's flag,
   And lick the soilèd grass? No, no, my friend,
   I would not, I, be pardoned in the heap,
   And bless indemnity with all that scum –
   Those men I mean, who on my shoulders propped
   Their weak rebellion, winning me with lies,
   And pitying forsooth my many wrongs;
   Poor self-deceivèd wretches, who must think
   Each one himself a king in embryo,
   Because some dozen vassals cried – 'My Lord!'
   Cowards, who never knew their little hearts,
   Till flurried danger held the mirror up,
   And then they owned themselves without a blush,
   Curling, like spaniels, round my father's feet.
   Such things deserted me and are forgiven,
   While I, least guilty, am an outcast still,
   And will be, for I love such fair disgrace.
SIGIFRED I know the clear truth; so would Otho see,
   For he is just and noble. Fain would I
   Be pleader for you –
LUDOLPH   He'll hear none of it;

You know his temper, hot, proud, obstinate;
Endanger not yourself so uselessly.
I will encounter his thwart spleen myself,
To-day, at the Duke Conrad's, where he keeps
His crowded state after the victory,
There will I be, a most unwelcome guest,
And parley with him, as a son should do,
Who doubly loathes a father's tyranny;
Tell him how feeble is that tyranny;
How the relationship of father and son
Is no more valid than a silken leash
Where lions tug adverse, if love grow not
From interchangèd love through many years.
Ay, and those turreted Franconian walls,
Like to a jealous casket, hold my pearl –
My fair Auranthe! Yes, I will be there.

SIGIFRED Be not so rash; wait till his wrath shall pass,
Until his royal spirit softly ebbs
Self-influenced; then, in his morning dreams
He will forgive thee, and awake in grief
To have not thy good morrow.

LUDOLPH   Yes, today
I must be there, while her young pulses beat
Among the new-plumed minions of the war.
Have you seen her of late? No? Auranthe,
Franconia's fair sister, 'tis I mean.
She should be paler for my troublous days –
And there it is – my father's iron lips
Have sworn divorcement 'twixt me and my right.

SIGIFRED [*aside*] Auranthe! I had hoped this whim had passed.

LUDOLPH And, Sigifred, with all his love of justice,
When will he take that grandchild in his arms,
That, by my love I swear, shall soon be his?
This reconcilement is impossible,
For see – but who are these?

SIGIFRED   They are messengers
From our great emperor; to you, I doubt not,

For couriers are abroad to seek you out.

[*Enter* THEODORE *and* GONFRED]

THEODORE Seeing so many vigilant eyes explore
The province to invite your highness back
To your high dignities, we are too happy.
GONFRED We have no eloquence to colour justly
The emperor's anxious wishes.
LUDOLPH   Go. I follow you.

[*Exeunt* THEODORE *and* GONFRED]

130 I play the prude: it is but venturing –
Why should he be so earnest? Come, my friend,
Let us to Friedburg castle.

ACT II

Scene 1 *An Antechamber in the Castle.*

[*Enter* LUDOLPH *and* SIGIFRED]

LUDOLPH No more advices, no more cautioning:
I leave it all to fate – to any thing!
I cannot square my conduct to time, place,
Or circumstance; to me 'tis all a mist!
SIGIFRED I say no more.
LUDOLPH   It seems I am to wait
Here in the anteroom – that may be a trifle.
You see now how I dance attendance here,
Without that tyrant temper, you so blame,
Snapping the rein. You have medicined me
10 With good advices; and I here remain,
In this most honourable anteroom,
Your patient scholar.
SIGIFRED   Do not wrong me, Prince.
By Heavens, I'd rather kiss Duke Conrad's slipper,
When in the morning he doth yawn with pride,
Than see you humbled but a half-degree!
Truth is, the Emperor would fain dismiss
The nobles ere he sees you.

[Enter GONFRED, from the Council-room]

LUDOLPH   Well, sir! what?
GONFRED   Great honour to the Prince! The Emperor,
Hearing that his brave son had re-appeared,
Instant dismissed the Council from his sight,
As Jove fans off the clouds. Even now they pass.

[Enter the Nobles from the Council-room. They cross the stage, bowing with respect to LUDOLPH, he frowning on them. CONRAD follows. Exeunt Nobles]

LUDOLPH   Not the discoloured poisons of a fen,
Which he who breathes feels warning of his death,
Could taste so nauseous to the bodily sense
As these prodigious sycophants disgust
The soul's fine palate.
CONRAD   Princely Ludolph, hail!
Welcome, thou younger sceptre to the realm!
Strength to thy virgin crownet's golden buds,
That they, against the winter of thy sire,
May burst, and swell, and flourish round thy brows,
Maturing to a weighty diadem!
Yet be that hour far off; and may he live,
Who waits for thee, as the chapped earth for rain.
Set my life's star! I have lived long enough,
Since under my glad roof, propitiously,
Father and son each other re-possess.
LUDOLPH   Fine wording, Duke! but words could never yet
Forestall the fates; have you not learnt that yet?
Let me look well – your features are the same;
Your gait the same; your hair of the same shade;
As one I knew some passèd weeks ago,
Who sung far different notes into mine ears.
I have mine own particular comments on't;
You have your own, perhaps.
CONRAD   My gracious Prince,
All men may err. In truth I was deceived
In your great father's nature, as you were.

Had I known that of him I have since known,
And what you soon will learn, I would have turned
My sword to my own throat, rather than held
Its threatening edge against a good King's quiet:
Or with one word fevered you, gentle Prince,
Who seemed to me, as rugged times then went,
Indeed too much oppressed. May I be bold
To tell the Emperor you will haste to him?
LUDOLPH Your Dukedom's privilege will grant so much.

[*Exit* CONRAD]

He's very close to Otho, a tight leech!
Your hand – I go. Ha! here the thunder comes
Sullen against the wind! If in two angry brows
My safety lies, then Sigifred, I'm safe.

[*Enter* OTHO *and* CONRAD]

OTHO Will you make Titan play the lackey-page
To chattering pigmies? I would have you know
That such neglect of our high Majesty
Annuls all feel of kindred. What is son –
Or friend, or brother, or all ties of blood –
When the whole kingdom, centred in ourself,
Is rudely slighted? Who am I to wait?
By Peter's chair! I have upon my tongue
A word to fright the proudest spirit here! –
Death! – and slow tortures to the hardy fool,
Who dares take such large charter from our smiles!
Conrad, we would be private. Sigifred!
Off! And none pass this way on pain of death!

[*Exeunt* CONRAD *and* SIGIFRED]

LUDOLPH This was but half expected, my good sire,
Yet I am grieved at it, to the full height,
As though my hopes of favour had been whole.
OTHO How you indulge yourself! What can you hope for?
LUDOLPH Nothing, my liege; I have to hope for nothing.

> I come to greet you as a loving son,
> And then depart, if I may be so free,
> Seeing that blood of yours in my warm veins
> Has not yet mitigated into milk.
>
> OTHO What would you, sir?
>
> LUDOLPH A lenient banishment;
> So please you let me unmolested pass
> This Conrad's gates, to the wide air again.
> I want no more. A rebel wants no more.
>
> OTHO And shall I let a rebel loose again
> To muster kites and eagles 'gainst my head?
> No, obstinate boy, you shall be kept caged up,
> Served with harsh food, with scum for Sunday-drink.
>
> LUDOLPH Indeed!
>
> OTHO And chains too heavy for your life:
> I'll choose a gaoler, whose swart monstrous face
> Shall be a hell to look upon, and she –
>
> LUDOLPH Ha!
>
> OTHO Shall be your fair Auranthe.
>
> LUDOLPH Amaze! Amaze!
>
> OTHO Today you marry her.
>
> LUDOLPH This is a sharp jest!
>
> OTHO No. None at all. When have I said a lie?
>
> LUDOLPH If I sleep not, I am a waking wretch.
>
> OTHO Not a word more. Let me embrace my child.
>
> LUDOLPH I dare not. 'Twould pollute so good a father!
> O heavy crime! that your son's blinded eyes
> Could not see all his parent's love aright,
> As now I see it. Be not kind to me –
> Punish me not with favour.
>
> OTHO Are you sure,
> Ludolph, you have no saving plea in store?
>
> LUDOLPH My father, none!
>
> OTHO Then you astonish me.
>
> LUDOLPH No, I have no plea. Disobedience,
> Rebellion, obstinacy, blasphemy,
> Are all my counsellors. If they can make
> My crooked deeds show good and plausible,

Then grant me loving pardon, but not else,
Good Gods! not else, in any way, my liege!
OTHO You are a most perplexing, noble boy.
LUDOLPH You not less a perplexing noble father.
OTHO Well, you shall have free passport through the gates.
Farewell!
LUDOLPH Farewell! and by these tears believe,
And still remember, I repent in pain
All my misdeeds!
OTHO   Ludolph, I will! I will!
But, Ludolph, ere you go, I would inquire
If you, in all your wandering, ever met
A certain Arab haunting in these parts.
LUDOLPH No, my good lord, I cannot say I did.
OTHO Make not your father blind before his time;
Nor let these arms paternal hunger more
For an embrace, to dull the appetite
Of my great love for thee, my supreme child!
Come close, and let me breathe into thine ear.
I knew you through disguise. You are the Arab!
You can't deny it. [*Embracing him*]
LUDOLPH   Happiest of days!
OTHO We'll make it so.
LUDOLPH   'Stead of one fatted calf
Ten hecatombs shall bellow out their last,
Smote 'twixt the horns by the death-stunning mace
Of Mars, and all the soldiery shall feast
Nobly as Nimrod's masons, when the towers
Of Nineveh new kissed the parted clouds!
OTHO Large as a God speak out, where all is thine.
LUDOLPH Ay, father, but the fire in my sad breast
Is quenched with inward tears! I must rejoice
For you, whose wings so shadow over me
In tender victory, but for myself
I still must mourn. The fair Auranthe mine!
Too great a boon! I prithee let me ask
What more than I know of could so have changed
Your purpose touching her?

OTHO   At a word, this:
      In no deed did you give me more offence
      Than your rejection of Erminia.
      To my appalling, I saw too good proof
      Of your keen-eyed suspicion – she is naught!
LUDOLPH You are convinced?
OTHO   Ay, spite of her sweet looks.
      O, that my brother's daughter should so fall!
      Her fame has passed into the grosser lips
150   Of soldiers in their cups.
LUDOLPH   'Tis very sad.
OTHO No more of her, Auranthe – Ludolph, come!
      This marriage be the bond of endless peace! [*Exeunt*]

Scene 2 *The Entrance of* GERSA's *Tent in the Hungarian
    Camp.*
    [*Enter* ERMINIA]

ERMINIA Where! where! where shall I find a messenger?
      A trusty soul? a good man in the camp?
      Shall I go myself? Monstrous wickedness!
      O cursed Conrad! devilish Auranthe!
      Here is proof palpable as the bright sun!
      O for a voice to reach the Emperor's ears!

    [*Shouts in the Camp*]

    [*Enter an Hungarian Captain*]

CAPTAIN Fair prisoner, you hear those joyous shouts?
      The king – ay, now our king – but still your slave,
      Young Gersa, from a short captivity
10   Has just returned. He bids me say, bright Dame,
      That even the homage of his rangèd chiefs
      Cures not his keen impatience to behold
      Such beauty once again. What ails you, lady?
ERMINIA Say, is not that a German, yonder? There!
CAPTAIN Methinks by his stout bearing he should be –
      Yes – it is Albert; a brave German knight,
      And much in the Emperor's favour.

ERMINIA   I would fain
   Inquire of friends and kinsfolk, how they fared
   In these rough times. Brave soldier, as you pass
20 To royal Gersa with my humble thanks,
   Will you send yonder knight to me?
CAPTAIN   I will. [*Exit*]
ERMINIA Yes, he was ever known to be a man
   Frank, open, generous; Albert I may trust.
   O proof! proof! proof! Albert's an honest man;
   Not Ethelbert the monk, if he were here,
   Would I hold more trustworthy. Now!

   [*Enter* ALBERT]

ALBERT   Good Gods!
   Lady Erminia! are you prisoner
   In this beleaguered camp? Or are you here
   Of your own will? You pleased to send for me.
30 By Venus, 'tis a pity I knew not
   Your plight before and, by her son, I swear
   To do you every service you can ask.
   What would the fairest –?
ERMINIA   Albert, will you swear?
ALBERT I have. Well?
ERMINIA   Albert, you have fame to lose.
   If men, in court and camp, lie not outright,
   You should be, from a thousand, chosen forth
   To do an honest deed. Shall I confide –?
ALBERT Ay, anything to me, fair creature. Do;
   Dictate my task. Sweet woman –
ERMINIA   Truce with that.
40 You understand me not; and, in your speech,
   I see how far the slander is abroad.
   Without proof could you think me innocent?
ALBERT Lady, I should rejoice to know you so.
ERMINIA If you have any pity for a maid,
   Suffering a daily death from evil tongues;
   Any compassion for that Emperor's niece,
   Who, for your bright sword and clear honesty,

OTHO THE GREAT: II . 2

      Lifted you from the crowd of common men
      Into the lap of honour – save me, knight!
ALBERT How? Make it clear; if it be possible,
    I, by the banner of Saint Maurice, swear
    To right you.
ERMINIA   Possible! – Easy. O my heart!
    This letter's not so soiled but you may read it –
    Possible! There – that letter! Read – read it.

    [*Gives him a letter*]

ALBERT [*reads it*] 'To the Duke Conrad. – Forget the
    threat you made at parting, and I will forget to send
    the Emperor letters and papers of yours I have become
    possessed of. His life is no trifle to me; his death you
    shall find none to yourself.' [*Speaks to himself*] 'Tis me
    – my life that's pleaded for! [*Reads*] 'He, for his own
    sake, will be dumb as the grave. Erminia has my shame
    fixed upon her, sure as a wen. We are safe. *Auranthe.*'
    A she-devil! A dragon! I her imp!
    Fire of Hell! Auranthe – lewd demon!
    Where got you this? Where? When?
ERMINIA I found it in the tent, among some spoils
    Which, being noble, fell to Gersa's lot.
    Come in, and see.   [*They go in and return*]
ALBERT   Villainy! Villainy!
    Conrad's sword, his corselet, and his helm,
    And his letter. Caitiff, he shall feel –
ERMINIA I see you are thunderstruck. Haste, haste away!
ALBERT O I am tortured by this villainy.
ERMINIA You needs must be. Carry it swift to Otho;
    Tell him, moreover, I am prisoner
    Here in this camp, where all the sisterhood,
    Forced from their quiet cells, are parcelled out
    For slaves among these Huns. Away! Away!
ALBERT I am gone.
ERMINIA   Swift be your steed! Within this hour
    The Emperor will see it.

ALBERT   Ere I sleep:
That I can swear. [*Hurries out*]
GERSA [*without*]   Brave captains! thanks. Enough
Of loyal homage now!

[*Enter* GERSA]

ERMINIA   Hail, royal Hun!
GERSA What means this, fair one? Why in such alarm?
Who was it hurried by me so distract?
It seemed you were in deep discourse together;
Your doctrine has not been so harsh to him
As to my poor deserts. Come, come, be plain.
I am no jealous fool to kill you both,
Or, for such trifles, rob the adornèd world
Of such a beauteous vestal.
ERMINIA   I grieve, my Lord,
To hear you condescend to ribald phrase.
GERSA This is too much! Hearken, my lady pure!
ERMINIA Silence! and hear the magic of a name –
Erminia! I am she – the Emperor's niece!
Praised be the Heavens, I now dare own myself!
GERSA Erminia! Indeed! I've heard of her.
Prithee, fair lady, what chance brought you here?
ERMINIA Ask your own soldiers.
GERSA   And you dare own your name.
For loveliness you may – and for the rest
My vein is not censorious.
ERMINIA   Alas! poor me!
'Tis false indeed.
GERSA   Indeed you are too fair:
The swan, soft leaning on her fledgy breast,
When to the stream she launches, looks not back
With such a tender grace; nor are her wings
So white as your soul is, if that but be
Twin-picture to your face. Erminia!
Today, for the first day, I am a king,
Yet would I give my unworn crown away
To know you spotless.

ERMINIA   Trust me one day more,
Generously, without more certain guarantee,
Than this poor face you deign to praise so much;
After that, say and do whate'er your please.
If I have any knowledge of you, sir,
I think, nay I am sure, you will grieve much
To hear my story. O be gentle to me,
For I am sick and faint with many wrongs,
Tired out, and weary-worn with contumelies.
GERSA Poor lady!

[*Enter* ETHELBERT]

ERMINIA   Gentle Prince, 'tis false indeed.
Good morrow, holy father! I have had
Your prayers, though I looked for you in vain.
ETHELBERT Blessings upon you, daughter! Sure you look
Too cheerful for these foul pernicious days.
Young man, you heard this virgin say 'twas false –
'Tis false, I say. What! can you not employ
Your temper elsewhere, 'mong these burly tents,
But you must taunt this dove, for she hath lost
The Eagle Otho to beat off assault?
Fie! fie! But I will be her guard myself;
In the Emperor's name, I here demand of you
Herself, and all her sisterhood. She false!
GERSA Peace! peace, old man! I cannot think she is.
ETHELBERT Whom I have known from her first infancy,
Baptized her in the bosom of the Church,
Watched her, as anxious husbandmen the grain,
From the first shoot till the unripe mid-May,
Then to the tender ear of her June days,
Which, lifting sweet abroad its timid green,
Is blighted by the touch of calumny;
You cannot credit such a monstrous tale.
GERSA I cannot. Take her. Fair Erminia,
I follow you to Friedburg – is't not so?
ERMINIA Ay, so we purpose.

ETHELBERT   Daughter, do you so?
    How's this? I marvel! Yet you look not mad.
ERMINIA I have good news to tell you, Ethelbert.
GERSA Ho! ho, there! Guards!
    Your blessing, father! Sweet Erminia,
    Believe me, I am well nigh sure –
ERMINIA   Farewell!
    Short time will show.

    [*Enter Chiefs*]

                  Yes, father Ethelbert,
    I have news precious as we pass along.
ETHELBERT Dear daughter, you shall guide me.
ERMINIA   To no ill.
150 GERSA Command an escort to the Friedburg lines.

    [*Exeunt Chiefs*]

    Pray let me lead. Fair lady, forget not
    Gersa, how he believed you innocent.
    I follow you to Friedburg with all speed.   [*Exeunt*]

ACT III

Scene 1 *The Country*.
    [*Enter* ALBERT]

ALBERT O that the earth were empty, as when Cain
    Had no perplexity to hide his head!
    Or that the sword of some brave enemy
    Had put a sudden stop to my hot breath,
    And hurled me down the illimitable gulf
    Of times past, unremembered! Better so
    Than thus fast-limèd in a cursèd snare,
    The limbo of a wanton. This the end
    Of an aspiring life! My boyhood passed
10 In feud with wolves and bears, when no eye saw
    The solitary warfare, fought for love
    Of honour 'mid the growling wilderness.
    My sturdier youth, maturing to the sword,

OTHO THE GREAT: III . I

    Won by the siren-trumpets, and the ring
    Of shields upon the pavement, when bright-mailed
    Henry the Fowler passed the streets of Prague.
    Was't to this end I louted and became
    The menial of Mars, and held a spear
    Swayed by command, as corn is by the wind?
20   Is it for this, I now am lifted up
    By Europe's thronèd Emperor, to see
    My honour be my executioner –
    My love of fame, my prided honesty
    Put to the torture for confessional?
    Then the damned crime of blurting to the world
    A woman's secret! – though a fiend she be,
    Too tender of my ignominious life –
    But then to wrong the generous Emperor
    In such a searching point, were to give up
30   My soul for football at Hell's holiday!
    I must confess – and cut my throat – today?
    Tomorrow? Ho! some wine!

    [*Enter* SIGIFRED]

SIGIFRED   A fine humour –
ALBERT Who goes there? Count Sigifred? Ha! Ha! Ha!
SIGIFRED What, man, do you mistake the hollow sky
    For a thronged tavern – and these stubbèd trees
    For old serge hangings – me, your humble friend,
    For a poor waiter? Why, man, how you stare!
    What gipsies have you been carousing with?
    No, no more wine; methinks you've had enough.
40 ALBERT You well may laugh and banter. What a fool
    An injury may make of a staid man!
    You shall know all anon.
SIGIFRED   Some tavern brawl?
ALBERT 'Twas with some people out of common reach;
    Revenge is difficult.
SIGIFRED   I am your friend;
    We meet again today, and can confer
    Upon it. For the present I'm in haste.

ALBERT Whither?

SIGIFRED   To fetch King Gersa to the feast.
  The Emperor on this marriage is so hot,
  Pray Heaven it end not in apoplexy!
50 The very porters, as I passed the doors,
  Heard his loud laugh, and answered in full choir.
  I marvel, Albert, you delay so long
  From these bright revelries; go, show yourself,
  You may be made a duke.

ALBERT   Ay, very like:
  Pray, what day has his Highness fixed upon?

SIGIFRED For what?

ALBERT   The marriage. What else can I mean?

SIGIFRED Today! O, I forgot, you could not know;
  The news is scarce a minute old with me.

ALBERT Married today! Today! You did not say so?

60 SIGIFRED Now, while I speak to you, their comely heads
  Are bowed before the mitre.

ALBERT   O! monstrous!

SIGIFRED What is this?

ALBERT   Nothing, Sigifred. Farewell!
  We'll meet upon our subject. Farewell, count! [*Exit*]

SIGIFRED Is this clear-headed Albert? He brain-turned!
  'Tis as portentous as a meteor. [*Exit*]

Scene 2 *An Apartment in the Castle.*
  [*Enter, as from the Marriage,* OTHO, LUDOLPH,
  AURANTHE, CONRAD, *Nobles, Knights, Ladies, etc.
  Music*]

OTHO Now, Ludolph! Now, Auranthe! Daughter fair!
  What can I find to grace your nuptial day
  More than my love, and these wide realms in fee?

LUDOLPH I have too much.

AURANTHE   And I, my liege, by far.

LUDOLPH Auranthe! I have! O, my bride, my love!
  Not all the gaze upon us can restrain
  My eyes, too long poor exiles from thy face,

From adoration, and my foolish tongue
From uttering soft responses to the love
I see in thy mute beauty beaming forth!
Fair creature, bless me with a single word!
All mine!

AURANTHE Spare, spare me, my Lord; I swoon else.
LUDOLPH Soft beauty! by tomorrow I should die,
Wert thou not mine. [*They talk apart*]
FIRST LADY   How deep she has bewitched him!
FIRST KNIGHT Ask you for her receipt for love philtres.
SECOND LADY They hold the Emperor in admiration.
OTHO If ever king was happy, that am I!
What are the cities 'yond the Alps to me,
The provinces about the Danube's mouth,
The promise of fair sail beyond the Rhone;
Or routing out of Hyperborean hordes,
To these fair children, stars of a new age?
Unless perchance I might rejoice to win
This little ball of earth, and chuck it them
To play with!

AURANTHE   Nay, my Lord, I do not know.
LUDOLPH Let me not famish.
OTHO [*to Conrad*]   Good Franconia,
You heard what oath I sware, as the sun rose,
That unless Heaven would send me back my son,
My Arab, no soft music should enrich
The cool wine, kissed off with a soldier's smack;
Now all my empire, bartered for one feast,
Seems poverty.

CONRAD   Upon the neighbour-plain
The heralds have prepared a royal lists;
Your knights, found war-proof in the bloody field,
Speed to the game.

OTHO   Well, Ludolph, what say you?
LUDOLPH My lord!
OTHO   A tourney?
CONRAD   Or, if't please you best –
LUDOLPH I want no more!

FIRST LADY   He soars!
SECOND LADY   Past all reason.
LUDOLPH Though heaven's choir
  Should in a vast circumference descend
40 And sing for my delight, I'd stop my ears!
  Though bright Apollo's car stood burning here,
  And he put out an arm to bid me mount,
  His touch an immortality, not I!
  This earth, this palace, this room, Auranthe!
OTHO This is a little painful; just too much.
  Conrad, if he flames longer in this wise,
  I shall believe in wizard-woven loves
  And old romances; but I'll break the spell.
  Ludolph!
CONRAD He'll be calm, anon.
LUDOLPH   You called?
50 Yes, yes, yes, I offend. You must forgive me;
  Not being quite recovered from the stun
  Of your large bounties. A tourney, is it not?

[*A sennet heard faintly*]

CONRAD The trumpets reach us.
ETHELBERT [*without*]   On your peril, sirs,
  Detain us!
FIRST VOICE [*without*] Let not the Abbot pass.
SECOND VOICE [*without*]   No,
  On your lives!
FIRST VOICE [*without*] Holy father, you must not.
ETHELBERT [*without*] Otho!
OTHO   Who calls on Otho?
ETHELBERT [*without*]   Ethelbert!
OTHO Let him come in.

[*Enter* ETHELBERT *leading in* ERMINIA]

            Thou cursèd Abbot, why
  Hast brought pollution to our holy rites?
  Hast thou no fear of hangmen, or the faggot?
60 LUDOLPH What portent – what strange prodigy is this?

CONRAD Away!
ETHELBERT   You, Duke?
ERMINIA   Albert has surely failed me!
  Looked at the Emperor's brow upon me bent!
ETHELBERT A sad delay!
CONRAD   Away, thou guilty thing!
ETHELBERT You again, Duke? Justice, most noble
    Otho!
  You – go to your sister there and plot again,
  A quick plot, swift as thought to save your heads;
  For lo! the toils are spread around your den,
  The world is all agape to see dragged forth
  Two ugly monsters.
LUDOLPH   What means he, my lord?
70 CONRAD I cannot guess.
ETHELBERT   Best ask your lady sister,
  Whether the riddle puzzles her beyond
  The power of utterance.
CONRAD   Foul barbarian, cease:
  The Princess faints!
LUDOLPH   Stab him! O, sweetest wife!

  [*Attendants bear off* AURANTHE]

ERMINIA Alas!
ETHELBERT   Your wife?
LUDOLPH   Ay, Satan! does that yerk ye?
ETHELBERT Wife! so soon!
LUDOLPH   Ay, wife! O, impudence!
  Thou bitter mischief! Venomous bad priest!
  How darest thou lift those beetle brows at me?
  Me – the prince Ludolph, in this presence here,
  Upon my marriage-day, and scandalize
80 My joys with such opprobrious surprise?
  Wife! Why dost linger on that syllable,
  As if it were some demon's name pronounced
  To summon harmful lightning, and make yawn
  The sleepy thunder? Hast no sense of fear?
  No ounce of man in thy mortality?

Tremble! for, at my nod, the sharpened axe
Will make thy bold tongue quiver to the roots,
Those grey lids wink, and thou not know it, monk!
ETHELBERT O, poor deceivèd Prince! I pity thee!
Great Otho! I claim justice –
LUDOLPH   Thou shalt have 't!
Thine arms from forth a pulpit of hot fire
Shall sprawl distracted! O that that dull cowl
Were some most sensitive portion of thy life,
That I might give it to my hounds to tear!
Thy girdle some fine zealous-painèd nerve
To girth my saddle! And those devil's beads
Each one a life, that I might, every day,
Crush one with Vulcan's hammer!
OTHO   Peace, my son;
You far outstrip my spleen in this affair.
Let us be calm, and hear the abbot's plea
For this intrusion.
LUDOLPH   I am silent, sire.
OTHO Conrad, see all depart not wanted here.

[Exeunt Knights, Ladies, etc.]

Ludolph, be calm. Ethelbert, peace awhile.
This mystery demands an audience
Of a just judge, and that will Otho be.
LUDOLPH Why has he time to breathe another word?
OTHO Ludolph, old Ethelbert, be sure, comes not
To beard us for no cause; he's not the man
To cry himself up an ambassador
Without credentials.
LUDOLPH   I'll chain up myself.
OTHO Old Abbot, stand here forth. Lady Erminia,
Sit. And now, Abbot! what have you to say?
Our ear is open. First we here denounce
Hard penalties against thee, if 't be found
The cause for which you have disturbed us here,
Making our bright hours muddy, be a thing
Of little moment.

ETHELBERT   See this innocent!
   Otho! thou father of the people called,
   Is her life nothing? Her fair honour nothing?
120 Her tears from matins until even-song
   Nothing? Her burst heart nothing? Emperor!
   Is this your gentle niece – the simplest flower
   Of the world's herbal – this fair lily blanched
   Still with the dews of piety, this meek lady
   Here sitting like an angel newly-shent,
   Who veils its snowy wings and grows all pale –
   Is she nothing?
OTHO   What more to the purpose, Abbot?
LUDOLPH Whither is he winding?
CONRAD   No clue yet!
ETHELBERT You have heard, my liege, and so, no doubt, all here,
130 Foul, poisonous, malignant whisperings;
   Nay open speech, rude mockery grown common,
   Against the spotless nature and clear fame
   Of the princess Erminia, your niece.
   I have intruded here thus suddenly,
   Because I hold those base weeds, with tight hand,
   Which now disfigure her fair growing stem,
   Waiting but for your sign to pull them up
   By the dark roots, and leave her palpable,
   To all men's sight, a lady, innocent.
140 The ignominy of that whispered tale
   About a midnight gallant, seen to climb
   A window to her chamber neighboured near,
   I will from her turn off, and put the load
   On the right shoulders; on that wretch's head,
   Who, by close stratagems, did save herself,
   Chiefly by shifting to this lady's room
   A rope-ladder for false witness.
LUDOLPH   Most atrocious!
OTHO Ethelbert, proceed.
ETHELBERT   With sad lips I shall:
   For, in the healing of one wound, I fear

150 To make a greater. His young highness here
Today was married.
LUDOLPH   Good.
ETHELBERT   Would it were good!
Yet why do I delay to spread abroad
The names of those two vipers, from whose jaws
A deadly breath went forth to taint and blast
This guileless lady?
OTHO   Abbot, speak their names.
ETHELBERT A minute first. It cannot be – but may
I ask, great judge, if you today have put
A letter by unread?
OTHO   Does 't end in this?
CONRAD Out with their names!
ETHELBERT   Bold sinner, say you so?
160 LUDOLPH Out, tedious monk!
OTHO   Confess, or by the wheel –
ETHELBERT My evidence cannot be far away;
And, though it never come, be on my head
The crime of passing an attaint upon
The slanderers of this virgin.
LUDOLPH   Speak aloud!
ETHELBERT Auranthe, and her brother there.
CONRAD   Amaze!
LUDOLPH Throw them from the windows!
OTHO Do what you will!
LUDOLPH   What shall I do with them?
Something of quick dispatch, for should she hear,
My soft Auranthe, her sweet mercy would
170 Prevail against my fury. Damnèd priest!
What swift death wilt thou die? As to the lady
I touch her not.
ETHELBERT   Illustrious Otho, stay!
An ample store of misery thou hast,
Choke not the granary of thy noble mind
With more bad bitter grain, too difficult
A cud for the repentance of a man
Grey-growing. To thee only I appeal,

OTHO THE GREAT: III . 2

>   Not to thy noble son, whose yeasting youth
>   Will clear itself, and crystal turn again.
> 180 A young man's heart, by Heaven's blessing, is
>   A wide world, where a thousand new-born hopes
>   Empurple fresh the melancholy blood:
>   But an old man's is narrow, tenantless
>   Of hopes, and stuffed with many memories,
>   Which, being pleasant, ease the heavy pulse –
>   Painful, clog up and stagnate. Weight this matter
>   Even as a miser balances his coin;
>   And, in the name of mercy, give command
>   That your knight Albert be brought here before you.
> 190 He will expound this riddle; he will show
>   A noon-day proof of bad Auranthe's guilt.
> OTHO Let Albert straight be summoned.

[Exit one of the Nobles]

> LUDOLPH   Impossible!
>   I cannot doubt – I will not – no – to doubt
>   Is to be ashes! – withered up to death!
> OTHO My gentle Ludolph, harbour not a fear;
>   You do yourself much wrong.
> LUDOLPH   O, wretched dolt!
>   Now, when my foot is almost on thy neck,
>   Wilt thou infuriate me? Proof! Thou fool!
>   Why wilt thou tease impossibility
> 200 With such a thick-skulled persevering suit?
>   Fanatic obstinacy! Prodigy!
>   Monster of folly! Ghost of a turned brain!
>   You puzzle me – you haunt me – when I dream
>   Of you my brain will split! Bald sorcerer!
>   Juggler! May I come near you? On my soul
>   I know not whether to pity, curse, or laugh.

[Enter ALBERT, and the Nobleman]

>   Here, Albert, this old phantom wants a proof!
>   Give him his proof! A camel's load of proofs!
> OTHO Albert, I speak to you as to a man

210   Whose words once uttered pass like current gold;
    And therefore fit to calmly put a close
    To this brief tempest. Do you stand possessed
    Of any proof against the honourableness
    Of Lady Auranthe, our new-spoused daughter?
ALBERT You chill me with astonishment. How's this?
    My Liege, what proof should I have 'gainst a fame
    Impossible of slur? [OTHO *rises*]
ERMINIA   O wickedness!
ETHELBERT Deluded monarch, 'tis a cruel lie.
OTHO Peace, rebel-priest!
CONRAD   Insult beyond credence!
220 ERMINIA Almost a dream!
LUDOLPH   We have awaked from
    A foolish dream that from my brow hath wrung
    A wrathful dew. O folly! why did I
    So act the lion with this silly gnat?
    Let them depart. Lady Erminia!
    I ever grieved for you, as who did not?
    But now you have, with such a brazen front,
    So most maliciously, so madly striven
    To dazzle the soft moon, when tenderest clouds
    Should be unlooped around to curtain her;
230   I leave you to the desert of the world
    Almost with pleasure. Let them be set free
    For me! I take no personal revenge
    More than against a nightmare, which a man
    Forgets in the new dawn. [*Exit Ludolph*]
OTHO Still in extremes! No, they must not be loose.
ETHELBERT Albert, I must suspect thee of a crime
    So fiendish –
OTHO   Fear'st thou not my fury, monk?
    Conrad, be they in your safe custody
    Till we determine some fit punishment.
240   It is so mad a deed, I must reflect
    And question them in private; for perhaps,
    By patient scrutiny, we may discover

Whether they merit death, or should be placed
In care of the physicians.

[*Exeunt* OTHO *and Nobles,* ALBERT *following*]

CONRAD My guards, ho!
ERMINIA   Albert, wilt thou follow there?
Wilt thou creep dastardly behind his back,
And shrink away from a weak woman's eye?
Turn, thou court-Janus! thou forget'st thyself;
Here is the Duke, waiting with open arms,

[*Enter Guards*]

250 To thank thee; here congratulate each other;
Wring hands; embrace; and swear how lucky 'twas
That I, by happy chance, hit the right man
Of all the world to trust in.
ALBERT   Trust! to me!
CONRAD [*aside*] He is the sole one in this mystery.
ERMINIA Well, I give up, and save my prayers for
    Heaven!
You, who could do this deed, would ne'er relent,
Though, at my words, the hollow prison-vaults
Would groan for pity.
CONRAD   Manacle them both!
ETHELBERT I know it – it must be – I see it all!
260 Albert, thou art the minion!
ERMINIA   Ah! too plain –
CONRAD Silence! Gag up their mouths! I cannot bear
More of this brawling. That the Emperor
Had placed you in some other custody!
Bring them away. [*Exeunt all but* ALBERT]
ALBERT Though my name perish from the book of
    honour,
Almost before the recent ink is dry,
And be no more remembered after death,
Than any drummer's in the muster-roll;
Yet shall I season high my sudden fall
270 With triumph o'er that evil-witted duke!

He shall feel what it is to have the hand
Of a man drowning, on his hateful throat.

[*Enter* GERSA *and* SIGIFRED]

GERSA What discord is at ferment in this house?
SIGIFRED We are without conjecture; not a soul
We met could answer any certainty.
GERSA Young Ludolph, like a fiery arrow, shot
By us.
SIGIFRED The Emperor, with crossed arms, in thought.
GERSA In one room music, in another sadness,
Perplexity everywhere!
ALBERT   A trifle mere!
Follow; your presences will much avail
To tune our jarrèd spirits. I'll explain.   [*Exeunt*]

ACT IV
Scene 1   AURANTHE'S *Apartment*.
   [AURANTHE *and* CONRAD *discovered*]

CONRAD Well, well, I know what ugly jeopardy
We are caged in; you need not pester that
Into my ears. Prithee, let me be spared
A foolish tongue, that I may bethink me
Of remedies with some deliberation.
You cannot doubt but 'tis in Albert's power
To crush or save us?
AURANTHE   No, I cannot doubt.
He has, assure yourself, by some strange means,
My secret; which I ever hid from him,
Knowing his mawkish honesty.
CONRAD   Cursed slave!
AURANTHE Ay, I could almost curse him now myself.
Wretched impediment! Evil genius!
A glue upon my wings, that cannot spread,
When they should span the provinces! A snake,
A scorpion, sprawling on the first gold step,
Conducting to the throne, high canopied.

CONRAD You would not hear my counsel, when his life
  Might have been trodden out, all sure and hushed;
  Now the dull animal forsooth must be
20 Entreated, managed! When can you contrive
  The interview he demands?
AURANTHE   As speedily
  It must be done as my bribed woman can
  Unseen conduct him to me; but I fear
  'Twill be impossible, while the broad day
  Comes through the panes with persecuting glare.
  Methinks, if 't now were night I could intrigue
  With darkness, bring the stars to second me,
  And settle all this trouble.
CONRAD   Nonsense! Child!
  See him immediately; why not now?
30 AURANTHE Do you forget that even the senseless doorposts
  Are on the watch and gape through all the house?
  How many whisperers there are about,
  Hungry for evidence to ruin me;
  Men I have spurned, and women I have taunted?
  Besides, the foolish prince sends, minute whiles,
  His pages – so they tell me – to inquire
  After my health, entreating, if I please,
  To see me.
CONRAD   Well, suppose this Albert here;
  What is your power with him?
AURANTHE   He should be
40 My echo, my taught parrot! but I fear
  He will be cur enough to bark at me;
  Have his own say; read me some silly creed
  'Bout shame and pity.
CONRAD   What will you do then?
AURANTHE What I shall do, I know not: what I would
  Cannot be done; for see, this chamber-floor
  Will not yield to the pick-axe and the spade –
  Here is no quiet depth of hollow ground.
CONRAD Sister, you have grown sensible and wise,

Seconding, ere I speak it, what is now,
I hope, resolved between us.
AURANTHE   Say, what is 't?
CONRAD You need not be his sexton too: a man
  May carry that with him shall make him die
  Elsewhere – give that to him; pretend the while
  You will tomorrow succumb to his wishes,
  Be what they may, and send him from the Castle
  On some fool's errand; let his latest groan
  Frighten the wolves!
AURANTHE   Alas! he must not die!
CONRAD Would you were both hearsed up in stifling lead!
  Detested –
AURANTHE Conrad, hold! I would not bear
  The little thunder of your fretful tongue,
  Though I alone were taken in these toils,
  And you could free me; but remember, sir,
  You live alone in my security:
  So keep your wits at work, for your own sake,
  Not mine, and be more mannerly.
CONRAD   Thou wasp!
  If my domains were emptied of these folk,
  And I had thee to starve –
AURANTHE   O, marvellous!
  But Conrad, now be gone; the host is looked for;
  Cringe to the Emperor, entertain the lords.
  And, do ye mind, above all things, proclaim
  My sickness, with a brother's saddened eye,
  Condoling with Prince Ludolph. In fit time
  Return to me.
CONRAD   I leave you to your thoughts. [*Exit*]
AURANTHE [*sola*] Down, down, proud temper! down,
    Auranthe's pride!
  Why do I anger him when I should kneel?
  Conrad! Albert! help! help! What can I do?
  O wretched woman! Lost, wrecked, swallowed up,
  Accursèd, blasted! O, thou golden Crown,
  Orbing along the serene firmament

OTHO THE GREAT: IV . I

80 Of a wide empire, like a glowing moon;
And thou, bright sceptre! lustrous in my eyes –
There – as the fabled fair Hesperian tree,
Bearing a fruit more precious! Graceful thing,
Delicate, godlike, magic! must I leave
Thee to melt in the visionary air,
Ere, by one grasp this common hand is made
Imperial? I do not know the time
When I have wept for sorrow; but methinks
I could now sit upon the ground, and shed
90 Tears, tears of misery. O, the heavy day!
How shall I bear my life till Albert comes?
Ludolph! Erminia! Proofs! O heavy day!
Bring me some mourning weeds, that I may 'tire
Myself, as fits one wailing her own death:
Cut off these curls, and brand this lily hand,
And throw these jewels from my loathing sight –
Fetch me a missal, and a string of beads –
A cup of bittered water, and a crust –
I will confess, O holy Abbot! – How!
100 What is this? Auranthe! thou fool, dolt,
Whimpering idiot! Up! Up! and quell!
I am safe! Coward! why am I in fear?
Albert! he cannot stickle, chew the cud
In such a fine extreme – impossible!
Who knocks?

[*Goes to the door, listens, and opens it*]

[*Enter* ALBERT]

Albert, I have been waiting for you here
With such an aching heart, such swooning throbs
On my poor brain, such cruel – cruel sorrow,
That I should claim your pity! Art not well?
110 ALBERT Yes, lady, well.
AURANTHE You look not so, alas!
But pale, as if you brought some heavy news.
ALBERT You know full well what makes me look so **pale.**
AURANTHE No! Do I? Surely I am still to learn

>   Some horror; all I know, this present, is
>   I am near hustled to a dangerous gulf,
>   Which you can save me from – and therefore safe,
>   So trusting in thy love; that should not make
>   Thee pale, my Albert.
> ALBERT   It doth make me freeze.
> AURANTHE Why should it, love?
> ALBERT   You should not ask me that,
> But make your own heart monitor, and save
> Me the great pain of telling. You must know.
> AURANTHE Something has vexed you, Albert. There are times
>   When simplest things put on a sombre cast;
>   A melancholy mood will haunt a man,
>   Until most easy matters take the shape
>   Of unachievable tasks; small rivulets
>   Then seem impassable.
> ALBERT   Do not cheat yourself
>   With hope that gloss of words, or suppliant action,
>   Or tears, or ravings, or self-threatened death,
>   Can alter my resolve.
> AURANTHE   You make me tremble;
>   Not so much at your threats, as at your voice,
>   Untuned, and harsh, and barren of all love.
> ALBERT You suffocate me! Stop this devil's parley,
>   And listen to me; know me once for all.
> AURANTHE I thought I did. Alas! I am deceived.
> ALBERT No, you are not deceived. You took me for
>   A man detesting all inhuman crime;
>   And therefore kept from me your demon's plot
>   Against Erminia. Silence? Be so still –
>   For ever! Speak no more; but hear my words,
>   Thy fate. Your safety I have bought today
>   By blazoning a lie, which in the dawn
>   I'll expiate with truth.
> AURANTHE   O cruel traitor!
> ALBERT For I would not set eyes upon thy shame;
>   I would not see thee dragged to death by the hair,

Penanced, and taunted on a scaffolding!
Tonight, upon the skirts of the blind wood
That blackens northward of these horrid towers,
I wait for you with horses. Choose your fate.
150 Farewell.
AURANTHE Albert, you jest; I'm sure you must.
You, an ambitious soldier! I, a Queen,
One who could say, – Here, rule these provinces!
Take tribute from those cities for thyself!
Empty these armouries, these treasuries,
Muster thy warlike thousands at a nod!
Go! conquer Italy!
ALBERT   Auranthe, you have made
The whole world chaff to me. Your doom is fixed.
AURANTHE Out, villain! dastard!
ALBERT   Look there to the door!
Who is it?
AURANTHE Conrad, traitor!
ALBERT   Let him in.

[*Enter* CONRAD]

160 Do not affect amazement, hypocrite,
At seeing me in this chamber.
CONRAD   Auranthe?
ALBERT Talk not with eyes, but speak your curses out
Against me, who would sooner crush and grind
A brace of toads, than league with them t'oppress
An innocent lady, gull an Emperor,
More generous to me than autumn sun
To ripening harvests.
AURANTHE   No more insult, sir!
ALBERT Ay, clutch your scabbard; but, for prudence' sake,
Draw not the sword; 'twould make an uproar, Duke,
170 You would not hear the end of. At nightfall
Your lady sister, if I guess aright,
Will leave this busy castle. You had best
Take farewell too of worldly vanities.

CONRAD Vassal!
ALBERT   Tomorrow, when the Emperor sends
For loving Conrad, see you fawn on him.
Good even!
AURANTHE You'll be seen!
ALBERT   See the coast clear then.
AURANTHE [*as he goes*] Remorseless Albert! Cruel, cruel,
wretch!

[*She lets him out*]

CONRAD So, we must lick the dust?
AURANTHE   I follow him.
CONRAD How? Where? The plan of your escape?
AURANTHE   He waits
For me with horses by the forest-side,
Northward.
CONRAD   Good, good! he dies. You go, say you?
AURANTHE Perforce.
CONRAD   Be speedy, darkness! Till that comes,
Fiends keep you company! [*Exit*]
AURANTHE   And you! And you!
And all men! Vanish! Oh! Oh! Oh!

[*Retires to an inner apartment*]

Scene 2 *An Apartment in the Castle.*
[*Enter* LUDOLPH *and Page*]

PAGE Still very sick, my Lord; but now I went
[Knowing my duty to so good a Prince;]
And there her women in a mournful throng
Stood in the passage whispering: if any
Moved 'twas with careful steps and hushed as death;
They bade me stop.
LUDOLPH   Good fellow, once again
Make soft enquiry; prithee be not stayed
By any hindrance, but with gentlest force
Break through her weeping servants, till thou com'st

OTHO THE GREAT: IV . 2

10   E'en to her chamber door, and there, fair boy –
       If with thy mother's milk thou hast sucked in
       Any diviner eloquence – woo her ears
       With plaints for me, more tender than the voice
       Of dying Echo, echoed.

PAGE   Kindest master!
       To know thee sad thus, will unloose my tongue
       In mournful syllables. Let but my words reach
       Her ears and she shall take them coupled with
       Moans from my heart and sighs not counterfeit.
       May I speed better! [*Exit Page*]

LUDOLPH   Auranthe! My Life!
20   Long have I loved thee, yet till now not loved:
       Remembering, as I do, hard-hearted times
       When I had heard even of thy death perhaps,
       And thoughtless! suffered thee to pass alone
       Into Elysium! Now I follow thee
       A substance or a shadow, wheresoe'er
       Thou leadest me – whether thy white feet press,
       With pleasant weight, the amorous-aching earth
       Or through the air thou pioneerest me,
       A shade! Yet sadly I predestinate!
30   O unbenignest Love, why wilt thou let
       Darkness steal out upon the sleepy world
       So wearily, as if night's chariot wheels
       Were clogged in some thick cloud. O, changeful Love,
       Let not her steeds with drowsy-footed pace
       Pass the high stars, before sweet embassage
       Comes from the pillowed beauty of that fair
       Completion of all delicate nature's wit.
       Pout her faint lips anew with rubious health,
       And with thine infant fingers lift the fringe
40   Of her sick eyelids; that those eyes may glow
       With wooing light upon me, ere the morn
       Peers with disrelish, grey, barren, and cold.

       [*Enter* GERSA *and Courtiers*]

       Otho calls me his Lion – should I blush

To be so tamed? so —
GERSA   Do me the courtesy
  Gentlemen to pass on.
COURTIER   We are your servants.

[*Exeunt Courtiers*]

LUDOLPH It seems then, Sir, you have found out the man
  You would confer with – me?
GERSA   If I break not
  Too much upon your thoughtful mood, I will
  Claim a brief while your patience.
LUDOLPH   For what cause
50 Soe'er I shall be honoured.
GERSA   I not less.
LUDOLPH What may it be? No trifle can take place
  Of such deliberate prologue, serious 'haviour.
  But be it what it may I cannot fail
  To listen with no common interest –
  For though so new your presence is to me,
  I have a soldier's friendship for your fame –
  Please you explain.
GERSA   As thus – for, pardon me,
  I cannot in plain terms grossly assault
  A noble nature; and would faintly sketch
60 What your quick apprehension will fill up,
  So finely I esteem you.
LUDOLPH   I attend.
GERSA Your generous father, most illustrious Otho,
  Sits in the banquet-room among his chiefs:
  His wine is bitter, for you are not there,
  His eyes are fixed still on the open doors,
  And every passer in he frowns upon,
  Seeing no Ludolph comes.
LUDOLPH   I do neglect —
GERSA And for your absence, may I guess the cause?
LUDOLPH Stay there! No! Guess? More princely you must be
70 Than to make guesses at me. 'Tis enough.
  I'm sorry I can hear no more.

GERSA   And I
As grieved to force it on you so abrupt;
Yet, one day, you must know a grief whose sting
Will sharpen more the longer 'tis concealed.
LUDOLPH Say it at once, sir! Dead – dead – is she dead?
GERSA Mine is a cruel task: she is not dead –
And would, for your sake, she were innocent.
LUDOLPH Hungarian! thou amazest me beyond
All scope of thought; convulsest my heart's blood
To deadly churning! – Gersa, you are young
As I am; let me observe you face to face:
Not grey-browed like the poisonous Ethelbert,
No rheumèd eyes, no furrowing of age,
No wrinkles where all vices nestle in
Like crannied vermin – no! but fresh and young
And hopeful featured. Ha! by Heaven you weep
Tears, human tears! Do you repent you then
Of a cursed torturer's office! Why shouldst join –
Tell me – the league of Devils? Confess – confess
The lie!
GERSA Lie! – but begone all ceremonious points
Of honour battailous! I could not turn
My wrath against thee for the orbèd world.
LUDOLPH Your wrath, weak boy? Tremble at mine unless
Retraction follow close upon the heels
Of that late stounding insult. Why has my sword
Not done already a sheer judgement on thee?
Despair, or eat thy words! Why, thou wast nigh
Whimpering away my reason! Harkee, Sir,
It is no secret that Erminia,
Erminia, Sir, was hidden in your tent –
O blessed asylum! Comfortable home!
Begone! I pity thee; thou art a gull –
Erminia's fresh puppet –
GERSA   Furious fire!
Thou mak'st me boil as hot as thou canst flame!
And in thy teeth I give thee back the lie!
Thou liest! Thou, Auranthe's fool! A wittol!

LUDOLPH Look! look at this bright sword;
There is no part of it to the very hilt
But shall indulge itself about thine heart!
Draw! but remember thou must cower thy plumes,
As yesterday the Arab made thee stoop.
GERSA Patience! Not here, I would not spill thy blood
Here underneath this roof where Otho breathes,
Thy father – almost mine –
LUDOLPH   O faltering coward!

[*Re-enter Page*]

Stay, stay; here is one I have half a word with –
Well? What ails thee, child?
PAGE   My lord...
LUDOLPH   What wouldst say?
PAGE They are fled!
LUDOLPH   They! Who?
PAGE   When anxiously
I hastened back, your grieving messenger,
I found the stairs all dark, the lamps extinct,
And not a foot or whisper to be heard.
I thought her dead, and on the lowest step
Sat listening; when presently came by
Two muffled up – one sighing heavily,
The other cursing low, whose voice I knew
For the Duke Conrad's. Close I followed them
Through the dark ways they chose to the open air;
And, as I followed, heard my lady speak.
LUDOLPH Thy life answer the truth!
PAGE   The chamber's empty!
LUDOLPH As I will be of mercy! So, at last,
This nail is in my temples!
GERSA   Be calm in this.
LUDOLPH I am.
GERSA   And Albert too has disappeared;
Ere I met you, I sought him everywhere;
You would not hearken.
LUDOLPH   Which way went they, boy?

GERSA I'll hunt with you.
LUDOLPH   No, no, no. My senses are
Still whole. I have survived. My arm is strong,
My appetite sharp – for revenge! I'll no sharer
In my feast; my injury is all my own,
And so is my revenge, my lawful chattels!
Terrier, ferret them out! Burn – burn the witch!
Trace me their footsteps! Away! [*Exeunt*]

ACT V

Scene 1 *A Part of the Forest.*
   [*Enter* CONRAD *and* AURANTHE]

AURANTHE Go no further; not a step more. Thou art
A master-plague in the midst of miseries.
Go – I fear thee! I tremble every limb,
Who never shook before. There's moody death
In thy resolvèd looks! Yes, I could kneel
To pray thee far away. Conrad, go! go! –
There! yonder underneath the boughs I see
Our horses!
CONRAD   Aye, and the man.
AURANTHE   Yes, he is there!
Go, go – no blood! no blood! Go, gentle Conrad!
CONRAD Farewell!
AURANTHE   Farewell, for this Heaven pardon you.

   [*Exit* AURANTHE]

CONRAD If he survive one hour, then may I die
In unimagined tortures – or breathe through
A long life in the foulest sink o' the world!
He dies. 'Tis well she do not advertize
The caitiff of the cold steel at his back. [*Exit* CONRAD]

   [*Enter* LUDOLPH *and* Page]

LUDOLPH Missed the way, boy? Say not that on your peril!

PAGE Indeed, indeed I cannot trace them further.
LUDOLPH Must I stop here? Here solitary die?
  Stifled beneath the thick oppressive shade
  Of these dull boughs – this oven of dark thickets –
  Silent – without revenge? Pshaw! – bitter end –
  A bitter death – a suffocating death –
  A gnawing – silent – deadly, quiet death!
  Escaped? – Fled? – Vanished? Melted into air?
  She's gone! I cannot clutch her! No revenge!
  A muffled death, ensnared in horrid silence!
  Sucked to my grave amid a dreary calm!
  O, where is that illustrious noise of war,
  To smother up this sound of labouring breath,
  This rustle of the trees!

   [AURANTHE *shrieks at a distance*]

PAGE   My Lord, a noise!
  This way – hark!
LUDOLPH   Yes, yes! A hope! A music!
  A glorious clamour! Now I live again!   [*Exeunt*]

Scene 2 *Another Part of the Forest.*
   [*Enter* ALBERT (*wounded*)]

ALBERT O for enough life to support me on
  To Otho's feet!

   [*Enter* LUDOLPH]

LUDOLPH   Thrice villainous, stay there!
  Tell me where that detested woman is,
  Or this is through thee!
ALBERT   My good Prince, with me
  The sword has done its worst; not without worst
  Done to another – Conrad has it home!
  I see you know it all!
LUDOLPH   Where is his sister?

   [AURANTHE *rushes in*]

AURANTHE   Albert!

LUDOLPH Ha! There! there! – He is the paramour! –
There – hug him – dying! O, thou innocence,
Shrive him and comfort him at his last gasp,
Kiss down his eyelids! Was he not thy love?
Wilt thou forsake him at his latest hour?
Keep fearful and aloof from his last gaze,
His most uneasy moments, when cold death
Stands with the door ajar to let him in?
ALBERT O, that that door with hollow slam would close
Upon me sudden, for I cannot meet,
In all the unknown chambers of the dead,
Such horrors!
LUDOLPH   Auranthe! what can he mean?
What horrors? Is it not a joyous time?
Am I not married to a paragon
'Of personal beauty and untainted soul?'
A blushing fair-eyed purity! A sylph,
Whose snowy timid hand has never sinned
Beyond a flower plucked, white as itself?
Albert, you do insult my bride – your mistress –
To talk of horrors on our wedding night.
ALBERT Alas! poor Prince, I would you knew my heart!
'Tis not so guilty –
LUDOLPH   Hear, he pleads not guilty!
You are not? or, if so, what matters it?
You have escaped me, free as the dusk air,
Hid in the forest – safe from my revenge.
I cannot catch you! You should laugh at me,
Poor cheated Ludolph! Make the forest hiss
With jeers at me! You tremble – faint at once,
You will come to again. O cockatrice,
I have you! Whither wander those fair eyes
To entice the Devil to your help, that he
May change you to a spider, so to crawl
Into some cranny to escape my wrath?
ALBERT Sometimes the counsel of a dying man
Doth operate quietly when his breath is gone:
Disjoin those hands – part – part, do not destroy

Each other – forget her! Our miseries
Are equal shared, and mercy is –
LUDOLPH   A boon
When one can compass it. Auranthe, try
Your oratory; your breath is not so hitched –
Ay, stare for help –

[ALBERT *dies*]

There goes a spotted soul
Howling in vain along the hollow night!
Hear him! He calls you – sweet Auranthe, come!
AURANTHE Kill me!
LUDOLPH   No! What? Upon our marriage-night?
The earth would shudder at so foul a deed –
A fair bride! A sweet bride! An innocent bride!
No, we must revel it, as 'tis in use
In times of delicate brilliant ceremony:
Come, let me lead you to our halls again!
Nay, linger not – make no resistance, sweet –
Will you? – Ah wretch, thou canst not, for I have
The strength of twenty lions 'gainst a lamb!
Now – one adieu for Albert! – Come away!   [*Exeunt*]

Scene 3 *An inner Court of the Castle.*
[*Enter* SIGIFRED, GONFRED, *and* THEODORE *meeting*]

THEODORE Was ever such a night?
SIGIFRED   What horrors more?
Things unbelieved one hour, so strange they are,
The next hour stamps with credit.
THEODORE   Your last news?
GONFRED After the page's story of the death
Of Albert and Duke Conrad?
SIGIFRED   And the return
Of Ludolph with the Princess.
GONFRED   No more, save
Prince Gersa's freeing Abbot Ethelbert,

And the sweet lady, fair Erminia,
From prison.
THEODORE   Where are they now? Hast yet heard?
GONFRED With the sad Emperor they are closeted;
I saw the three pass slowly up the stairs,
The lady weeping, the old Abbot cowled.
SIGIFRED What next?
THEODORE   I ache to think on't.
GONFRED   'Tis with fate.
THEORORE One while these proud towers are hushed as death.
GONFRED The next our poor Prince fills the archèd rooms
With gastly ravings.
SIGIFRED   I do fear his brain.
GONFRED I will see more. Bear you so stout a heart?

[*Exeunt into the Castle.*]

Scene 4 *A Cabinet, opening towards a Terrace.*
[OTHO, ERMINIA, ETHELBERT, *and a Physician, discovered*]

OTHO O, my poor boy! My son! My son! My Ludolph!
Have ye no comfort for me, ye physicians
Of the weak body and soul?
ETHELBERT   'Tis not in medicine
Either of heaven or earth can cure, unless
Fit time be chosen to administer.
OTHO A kind forbearance, holy Abbot – come
Erminia; here, sit by me, gentle girl;
Give me thy hand – hast thou forgiven me?
ERMINIA Would I were with the saints to pray for you!
OTHO Why will ye keep me from my darling child?
PHYSICIAN Forgive me, but he must not see thy face.
OTHO Is then a father's countenance a Gorgon?
Hath it not comfort in it? Would it not
Console my poor boy, cheer him, heal his spirits?
Let me embrace him, let me speak to him;
I will! Who hinders me? Who's Emperor?

PHYSICIAN You may not, Sire; 'twould overwhelm him quite,
   He is so full of grief and passionate wrath;
   Too heavy a sigh would kill him, or do worse.
20 He must be saved by fine contrivances,
   And most especially we must keep clear
   Out of his sight a father whom he loves;
   His heart is full, it can contain no more,
   And do its ruddy office.
ETHELBERT   Sage advice;
   We must endeavour how to ease and slacken
   The tight-wound energies of his despair,
   Not make them tenser.
OTHO   Enough! I hear, I hear.
   Yet you were about to advise more – I listen.
ETHELBERT This learned doctor will agree with me,
30 That not in the smallest point should he be thwarted,
   Or gainsaid by one word; his very motions,
   Nods, becks and hints, should be obeyed with care,
   Even on the moment: so his troubled mind
   May cure itself.
PHYSICIAN   There are no other means.
OTHO Open the door: let's hear if all is quiet.
PHYSICIAN Beseech you, Sire, forbear.
ERMINIA   Do, do.
OTHO   I command!
   Open it straight – hush! – quiet! – my lost boy!
   My miserable child!
LUDOLPH [*indistinctly without*] Fill full
   My goblet – here's a health!
ERMINIA   O, close the door!
40 OTHO Let, let me hear his voice; this cannot last –
   And fain would I catch up his dying words
   Though my own knell they be – this cannot last –
   O let me catch his voice – for lo! I hear
   A whisper in this silence that he's dead!
   It is so! Gersa?

[*Enter* GERSA]

PHYSICIAN   Say, how fares the prince?
GERSA More calm – his features are less wild and flushed;
Once he complained of weariness.
PHYSICIAN   Indeed!
'Tis good – 'tis good; let him but fall asleep,
That saves him.
OTHO   Gersa, watch him like a child;
50 Ward him from harm – and bring me better news!
PHYSICIAN Humour him to the height. I fear to go;
For should he catch a glimpse of my dull garb,
It might affright him, fill him with suspicion
That we believe him sick, which must not be.
GERSA I will invent what soothing means I can.

[*Exit* GERSA]

PHYSICIAN This should cheer up your Highness; the weariness
Is a good symptom, and most favourable;
It gives me pleasant hopes. Please you, walk forth
Upon the terrace; the refreshing air
60 Will blow one half of your sad doubts away.   [*Exeunt*]

Scene 5 *A Banqueting Hall, brilliantly illuminated, and set forth with all costly magnificence, with supper-tables, laden with services of gold and silver. A door in the back scene, guarded by two Soldiers. Lords, Ladies, Knights, Gentlemen, etc., whispering sadly, and ranging themselves; part entering and part discovered.*

FIRST KNIGHT Grievously are we tantalized, one and all;
Swayed here and there, commanded to and fro
As though we were the shadows of a sleep,
And linked to a dreaming fancy. What do we here?
GONFRED I am no seer; you know we must obey
The prince from A to Z, though it should be
To set the place in flames. I pray hast heard
Where the most wicked Princess is?

FIRST KNIGHT   There, sir,
   In the next room. Have you remarked those two
10 Stout soldiers posted at the door?
GONFRED   For what? [*They whisper*]
FIRST LADY How ghast a train!
SECOND LADY Sure this should be some splendid burial.
FIRST LADY What fearful whispering! See, see – Gersa
   there!

[*Enter* GERSA]

GERSA Put on your brightest looks; smile if you can;
   Behave as all were happy; keep your eyes
   From the least watch upon him; if he speaks
   To any one, answer collectedly,
   Without surprise, his questions, howe'er strange.
   Do this to the utmost – though, alas! with me
20 The remedy grows hopeless! Here he comes –
   Observe what I have said – show no surprise.

[*Enter* LUDOLPH, *followed by* SIGIFRED *and Page*]

LUDOLPH A splendid company! rare beauties here!
   I should have Orphean lips, and Plato's fancy,
   Amphion's utterance, tonèd with his lyre,
   Or the deep key of Jove's sonorous mouth,
   To give fit salutation. Methought I heard,
   As I came in, some whispers – what of that?
   'Tis natural men should whisper; at the kiss
   Of Psyche given by Love, there was a buzz
30 Among the gods! – and silence is as natural.
   These draperies are fine, and, being a mortal,
   I should desire no better; yet, in truth,
   There must be some superior costliness,
   Some wider-domèd high magnificence!
   I would have, as a mortal I may not,
   Hangings of heaven's clouds, purple and gold,
   Slung from the spheres; gauzes of silver mist,
   Looped up with cords of twisted wreathèd light,
   And tasselled round with weeping meteors!

These pendent lamps and chandeliers are bright
　　As earthly fires from dull dross can be cleansed;
　　Yet could my eyes drink up intenser beams
　　Undazzled – this is darkness. When I close
　　These lids, I see far fiercer brilliances –
　　Skies full of splendid moons, and shooting stars,
　　And spouting exhalations, diamond fires,
　　And panting fountains quivering with deep glows!
　　Yes – this is dark – is it not dark?
SIGIFRED　　　　　　　　　　　　My Lord,
　　'Tis late; the lights of festival are ever
　　Quenched in the morn.
LUDOLPH　　　　　　　　'Tis not tomorrow then?
SIGIFRED 'Tis early dawn.
GERSA　　　　　　　　Indeed full time we slept;
　　Say you so, Prince?
LUDOLPH　　　　　　I say I quarrelled with you;
　　We did not tilt each other – that's a blessing,
　　Good gods! No innocent blood upon my head!
SIGIFRED Retire, Gersa!
LUDOLPH　　　　　　　There should be three more here:
　　For two of them, they stay away perhaps,
　　Being gloomy-minded, haters of fair revels –
　　They know their own thoughts best.
　　　　　　　　　　　　　　　As for the third,
　　Deep blue eyes, semi-shaded in white lids,
　　Finished with lashes fine for more soft shade,
　　Completed by her twin-arched ebon brows;
　　White temples of exactest elegance,
　　Of even mould felicitous and smooth;
　　Cheeks fashioned tenderly on either side,
　　So perfect, so divine that our poor eyes
　　Are dazzled with the sweet proportioning,
　　And wonder that 'tis so – the magic chance!
　　Her nostrils, small, fragrant, faery-delicate;
　　Her lips – I swear no human bones e'er wore
　　So taking a disguise – you shall behold her!
　　We'll have her presently; ay, you shall see her,

And wonder at her, friends, she is so fair –
She is the world's chief jewel, and by heaven
She's mine by right of marriage! – she is mine!
Patience, good people, in fit time I send
A summoner. She will obey my call,
Being a wife most mild and dutiful.
First I would hear what music is prepared
To herald and receive her – let me hear!

SIGIFRED Bid the musicians soothe him tenderly.

[*A soft strain of music*]

LUDOLPH Ye have none better? No – I am content;
'Tis a rich sobbing melody, with reliefs
Full and majestic; it is well enough,
And will be sweeter, when ye see her pace
Sweeping into this presence, glistened o'er
With emptied caskets, and her train upheld
By ladies, habited in robes of lawn,
Sprinkled with golden crescents, others bright
In silks, with spangles showered, and bow'd to
By Duchesses and pearlèd Margravines!
Sad, that the fairest creature of the earth –
I pray you mind me not – 'tis sad, I say,
That the extremest beauty of the world
Should so entrench herself away from me,
Behind a barrier of engendered guilt!

SECOND LADY Ah! what a moan!

FIRST KNIGHT   Most piteous indeed!

LUDOLPH She shall be brought before this company,
And then – then –

FIRST LADY   He muses.

GERSA   O, Fortune, where will this end?

SIGIFRED I guess his purpose! Indeed he must not have
That pestilence brought in – that cannot be,
There we must stop him.

GERSA   I am lost! Hush, hush!
He is about to rave again.

LUDOLPH A barrier of guilt! I was the fool,
She was the cheater! Who's the cheater now,
And who the fool? The entrapped, the cagèd fool,
The bird-limed raven? She shall croak to death
Secure! Methinks I have her in my fist,
To crush her with my heel! Wait, wait! I marvel
My father keeps away. Good friend – ah! Sigifred!
Do bring him to me – and Erminia
I fain would see before I sleep – and Ethelbert,
That he may bless me, as I know he will
Though I have cursed him.
SIGIFRED   Rather suffer me
To lead you to them.
LUDOLPH   No, excuse me, no!
The day is not quite done. Go bring them hither.

[*Exit* SIGIFRED]

Certes, a father's smile should, like sunlight,
Slant on my sheavèd harvest of ripe bliss.
Besides, I thirst to pledge my lovely bride
In a deep goblet: let me see – what wine?
The strong Iberian juice, or mellow Greek?
Or pale Calabrian? Or the Tuscan grape?
Or of old Aetna's pulpy wine presses,
Black stained with the fat vintage, as it were
The purple slaughter-house, where Bacchus' self
Pricked his own swollen veins? Where is my Page?
PAGE   Here, here!
LUDOLPH Be ready to obey me; anon thou shalt
Bear a soft message for me; for the hour
Draws near when I must make a winding up
Of bridal mysteries – a fine-spun vengeance!
Carve it on my tomb, that when I rest beneath,
Men shall confess – This Prince was gulled and cheated,
But from the ashes of disgrace he rose
More than a fiery dragon, and did burn
His ignominy up in purging fires!

Did I not send, sir, but a moment past,
For my father?
GERSA   You did.
LUDOLPH   Perhaps 'twould be
Much better he came not.
GERSA   He enters now!

[*Enter* OTHO, ERMINIA, ETHELBERT, SIGIFRED, *and Physician*]

LUDOLPH O thou good man, against whose sacred head
I was a mad conspirator, chiefly too
For the sake of my fair newly wedded wife,
Now to be punished – do not look so sad!
Those charitable eyes will thaw my heart,
Those tears will wash away a just resolve,
A verdict ten times sworn! Awake – awake –
Put on a judge's brow, and use a tongue
Made iron-stern by habit! Thou shalt see
A deed to be applauded, 'scribed in gold!
Join a loud voice to mine, and so denounce
What I alone will execute!
OTHO   Dear son,
What is it? By your father's love, I sue
That it be nothing merciless!
LUDOLPH   To that demon?
Not so! No! She is in temple-stall
Being garnished for the sacrifice, and I,
The Priest of Justice, will immolate her
Upon the altar of wrath! She stings me through! –
Even as the worm doth feed upon the nut,
So she, a scorpion, preys upon my brain!
I feel her gnawing here! Let her but vanish,
Then, father, I will lead your legions forth,
Compact in steelèd squares, and spearèd files
And bid our trumpets speak a fell rebuke
To nations drowsed in peace!
OTHO   Tomorrow, son,
Be your word law; forget today –

LUDOLPH   I will
   When I have finished it! Now, now I'm pight,
   Tight-footed for the deed!
ERMINIA   Alas! Alas!
LUDOLPH What angel's voice is that? Erminia!
   Ah! gentlest creature, whose sweet innocence
   Was almost murdered; I am penitent,
   Wilt thou forgive me? And thou, holy man,
170 Good Ethelbert, shall I die in peace with you?
ERMINIA Die, my lord!
LUDOLPH   I feel it possible.
OTHO   Physician?
PHYSICIAN I fear me he is past my skill.
OTHO   Not so!
LUDOLPH I see it – I see it – I have been wandering!
   Half-mad – not right here – I forget my purpose.
   Bestir – bestir – Auranthe! Ha! ha! ha!
   Youngster! Page! go bid them drag her to me!
   Obey! This shall finish it! [*Draws a dagger*]
OTHO   O my son! my son!
SIGIFRED This must not be – stop there!
LUDOLPH   Am I obeyed?
   A little talk with her – no harm – haste! haste!

   [*Exit Page*]

180 Set her before me – never fear I can strike.
SEVERAL VOICES My Lord! My Lord!
GERSA   Good Prince!
LUDOLPH Why do ye trouble me? Out – out away!
   There she is! take that! and that! no, no –
   That's not well done. Where is she?

   [*The doors open. Enter Page. Several women are
   seen grouped about* AURANTHE *in the inner room*]

PAGE Alas! My Lord, my Lord! they cannot move her!
   Her arms are stiff – her fingers clenched and cold!
LUDOLPH She's dead! [*Staggers and falls into their arms*]

ETHELBERT   Take away the dagger.
GERSA   Softly; so!
OTHO Thank God for that!
SIGIFRED   It could not harm him now.
GERSA No! – brief be his anguish!
LUDOLPH She's gone – I am content – Nobles, good
    night!
  Where is your hand? Father, what sultry air!
  We are all weary – faint – set ope the doors –
  I will to bed! – Tomorrow – [*Dies*]
      [*The curtain falls*]

Lamia

PART I

Upon a time, before the faery broods
Drove Nymph and Satyr from the prosperous woods,
Before King Oberon's bright diadem,
Sceptre, and mantle, clasped with dewy gem,
Frighted away the Dryads and the Fauns
From rushes green, and brakes, and cowslipped lawns,
The ever-smitten Hermes empty left
His golden throne, bent warm on amorous theft:
From high Olympus had he stolen light,
On this side of Jove's clouds, to escape the sight
Of his great summoner, and made retreat
Into a forest on the shores of Crete.
For somewhere in that sacred island dwelt
A nymph, to whom all hoofèd Satyrs knelt,
At whose white feet the languid Tritons poured
Pearls, while on land they withered and adored.
Fast by the springs where she to bathe was wont,
And in those meads where sometime she might haunt,
Were strewn rich gifts, unknown to any Muse,
Though Fancy's casket were unlocked to choose.
Ah, what a world of love was at her feet!

LAMIA

    So Hermes thought, and a celestial heat
Burnt from his wingèd heels to either ear,
That from a whiteness, as the lily clear,
Blushed into roses 'mid his golden hair,
Fallen in jealous curls about his shoulders bare.
From vale to vale, from wood to wood, he flew,
Breathing upon the flowers his passion new,
And wound with many a river to its head
30 To find where this sweet nymph prepared her secret bed.
In vain; the sweet nymph might nowhere be found,
And so he rested, on the lonely ground,
Pensive, and full of painful jealousies
Of the Wood-Gods, and even the very trees.
There as he stood, he heard a mournful voice,
Such as, once heard, in gentle heart destroys
All pain but pity; thus the lone voice spake:
'When from this wreathèd tomb shall I awake!
When move in a sweet body fit for life,
40 And love, and pleasure, and the ruddy strife
Of hearts and lips! Ah, miserable me!'
The God, dove-footed, glided silently
Round bush and tree, soft-brushing, in his speed,
The taller grasses and full-flowering weed,
Until he found a palpitating snake,
Bright, and cirque-couchant in a dusky brake.

    She was a gordian shape of dazzling hue,
Vermilion-spotted, golden, green, and blue;
Striped like a zebra, freckled like a pard,
50 Eyed like a peacock, and all crimson barred;
And full of silver moons, that, as she breathed,
Dissolved, or brighter shone, or interwreathed
Their lustres with the gloomier tapestries –
So rainbow-sided, touched with miseries,
She seemed, at once, some penanced lady elf,
Some demon's mistress, or the demon's self.
Upon her crest she wore a wannish fire
Sprinkled with stars, like Ariadne's tiar;

416 LAMIA

Her head was serpent, but ah, bitter-sweet!
60 She had a woman's mouth with all its pearls complete;
And for her eyes – what could such eyes do there
But weep, and weep, that they were born so fair,
As Proserpine still weeps for her Sicilian air.
Her throat was serpent, but the words she spake
Came, as through bubbling honey, for Love's sake,
And thus – while Hermes on his pinions lay,
Like a stooped falcon ere he takes his prey –

'Fair Hermes, crowned with feathers, fluttering light,
I had a splendid dream of thee last night:
70 I saw thee sitting, on a throne of gold,
Among the Gods, upon Olympus old,
The only sad one; for thou didst not hear
The soft, lute-fingered Muses chanting clear,
Nor even Apollo when he sang alone,
Deaf to his throbbing throat's long, long melodious moan.
I dreamt I saw thee, robed in purple flakes,
Break amorous through the clouds, as morning breaks,
And, swiftly as a bright Phoebean dart,
Strike for the Cretan isle; and here thou art!
80 Too gentle Hermes, hast thou found the maid?'
Whereat the star of Lethe not delayed
His rosy eloquence, and thus inquired:
'Thou smooth-lipped serpent, surely high inspired!
Thou beauteous wreath, with melancholy eyes,
Possess whatever bliss thou canst devise,
Telling me only where my nymph is fled –
Where she doth breathe!' 'Bright planet, thou hast said,'
Returned the snake, 'but seal with oaths, fair God!'
'I swear,' said Hermes, 'by my serpent rod,
90 And by thine eyes, and by thy starry crown!'
Light flew his earnest words, among the blossoms blown.
Then thus again the brilliance feminine:
'Too frail of heart! for this lost nymph of thine,
Free as the air, invisibly, she strays
About these thornless wilds; her pleasant days

LAMIA

>   She tastes unseen; unseen her nimble feet
>   Leave traces in the grass and flowers sweet;
>   From weary tendrils, and bowed branches green,
>   She plucks the fruit unseen, she bathes unseen;
>   And by my power is her beauty veiled
>   To keep it unaffronted, unassailed
>   By the love-glances of unlovely eyes
>   Of Satyrs, Fauns, and bleared Silenus' sighs.
>   Pale grew her immortality, for woe
>   Of all these lovers, and she grievèd so
>   I took compassion on her, bade her steep
>   Her hair in weïrd syrops, that would keep
>   Her loveliness invisible, yet free
>   To wander as she loves, in liberty.
>   Thou shalt behold her, Hermes, thou alone,
>   If thou wilt, as thou swearest, grant my boon!'
> Then, once again, the charmèd God began
> An oath, and through the serpent's ears it ran
> Warm, tremulous, devout, psalterian.
> Ravished, she lifted her Circean head,
> Blushed a live damask, and swift-lisping said,
>   'I was a woman, let me have once more
>   A woman's shape, and charming as before.
>   I love a youth of Corinth – O the bliss!
>   Give me my woman's form, and place me where he is.
>   Stoop, Hermes, let me breathe upon thy brow,
>   And thou shalt see thy sweet nymph even now.'
> The God on half-shut feathers sank serene,
> She breathed upon his eyes, and swift was seen
> Of both the guarded nymph near-smiling on the green.
> It was no dream; or say a dream it was,
> Real are the dreams of Gods, and smoothly pass
> Their pleasures in a long immortal dream.
> One warm, flushed moment, hovering, it might seem
> Dashed by the wood-nymph's beauty, so he burned;
> Then, lighting on the printless verdure, turned
> To the swooned serpent, and with languid arm,
> Delicate, put to proof the lithe Caducean charm.

LAMIA

So done, upon the nymph his eyes he bent
Full of adoring tears and blandishment,
And towards her stepped: she, like a moon in wane,
Faded before him, cowered, nor could restrain
Her fearful sobs, self-folding like a flower
That faints into itself at evening hour:
But the God fostering her chillèd hand,
She felt the warmth, her eyelids opened bland,
And, like new flowers at morning song of bees,
Bloomed, and gave up her honey to the lees.
Into the green-recessèd woods they flew;
Nor grew they pale, as mortal lovers do.

Left to herself, the serpent now began
To change; her elfin blood in madness ran,
Her mouth foamed, and the grass, therewith besprent,
Withered at dew so sweet and virulent;
Her eyes in torture fixed, and anguish drear,
Hot, glazed, and wide, with lid-lashes all sear,
Flashed phosphor and sharp sparks, without one cooling tear.
The colours all inflamed throughout her train,
She writhed about, convulsed with scarlet pain:
A deep volcanian yellow took the place
Of all her milder-moonèd body's grace;
And, as the lava ravishes the mead,
Spoilt all her silver mail, and golden brede;
Made gloom of all her frecklings, streaks and bars,
Eclipsed her crescents, and licked up her stars.
So that, in moments few, she was undressed
Of all her sapphires, greens, and amethyst,
And rubious-argent; of all these bereft,
Nothing but pain and ugliness were left.
Still shone her crown; that vanished, also she
Melted and disappeared as suddenly;
And in the air, her new voice luting soft,
Cried, 'Lycius! gentle Lycius!' – Borne aloft
With the bright mists about the mountains hoar
These words dissolved: Crete's forests heard no more.

LAMIA

    Whither fled Lamia, now a lady bright,
A full-born beauty new and exquisite?
She fled into that valley they pass o'er
Who go to Corinth from Cenchreas' shore;
And rested at the foot of those wild hills,
The rugged founts of the Peraean rills,
And of that other ridge whose barren back
Stretches, with all its mist and cloudy rack,
South-westward to Cleone. There she stood
180 About a young bird's flutter from a wood,
Fair, on a sloping green of mossy tread,
By a clear pool, wherein she passionèd
To see herself escaped from so sore ills,
While her robes flaunted with the daffodils.

    Ah, happy Lycius! – for she was a maid
More beautiful than ever twisted braid,
Or sighed, or blushed, or on spring-flowered lea
Spread a green kirtle to the minstrelsy:
A virgin purest lipped, yet in the lore
190 Of love deep learnèd to the red heart's core;
Not one hour old, yet of sciential brain
To unperplex bliss from its neighbour pain,
Define their pettish limits, and estrange
Their points of contact, and swift counterchange;
Intrigue with the specious chaos, and dispart
Its most ambiguous atoms with sure art;
As though in Cupid's college she had spent
Sweet days a lovely graduate, still unshent,
And kept his rosy terms in idle languishment.

200   Why this fair creature chose so faerily
By the wayside to linger, we shall see;
But first 'tis fit to tell how she could muse
And dream, when in the serpent prison-house,
Of all she list, strange or magnificent:
How, ever, where she willed, her spirit went;
Whether to faint Elysium, or where
Down through tress-lifting waves the Nereids fair

420 LAMIA

  Wind into Thetis' bower by many a pearly stair;
  Or where God Bacchus drains his cups divine,
210 Stretched out, at ease, beneath a glutinous pine;
  Or where in Pluto's gardens palatine
  Mulciber's columns gleam in far piazzian line.
  And sometimes into cities she would send
  Her dream, with feast and rioting to blend;
  And once, while among mortals dreaming thus,
  She saw the young Corinthian Lycius
  Charioting foremost in the envious race,
  Like a young Jove with calm uneager face,
  And fell into a swooning love of him.
220 Now on the moth-time of that evening dim
  He would return that way, as well she knew,
  To Corinth from the shore; for freshly blew
  The eastern soft wind, and his galley now
  Grated the quaystones with her brazen prow
  In port Cenchreas, from Egina isle
  Fresh anchored; whither he had been awhile
  To sacrifice to Jove, whose temple there
  Waits with high marble doors for blood and incense rare.
  Jove heard his vows, and bettered his desire;
230 For by some freakful chance he made retire
  From his companions, and set forth to walk,
  Perhaps grown wearied of their Corinth talk:
  Over the solitary hills he fared,
  Thoughtless at first, but ere eve's star appeared
  His fantasy was lost, where reason fades,
  In the calmed twilight of Platonic shades.
  Lamia beheld him coming, near, more near –
  Close to her passing, in indifference drear,
  His silent sandals swept the mossy green;
240 So neighboured to him, and yet so unseen
  She stood: he passed, shut up in mysteries,
  His mind wrapped like his mantle, while her eyes
  Followed his steps, and her neck regal white
  Turned – syllabling thus, 'Ah, Lycius bright,
  And will you leave me on the hills alone?

421 LAMIA

>   Lycius, look back! and be some pity shown.'
> He did – not with cold wonder fearingly,
> But Orpheus-like at an Eurydice –
> For so delicious were the words she sung,
> It seemed he had loved them a whole summer long.
> And soon his eyes had drunk her beauty up,
> Leaving no drop in the bewildering cup,
> And still the cup was full – while he, afraid
> Lest she should vanish ere his lip had paid
> Due adoration, thus began to adore
> (Her soft look growing coy, she saw his chain so sure):
> 'Leave thee alone! Look back! Ah, Goddess, see
> Whether my eyes can ever turn from thee!
> For pity do not this sad heart belie –
> Even as thou vanished so I shall die.
> Stay! though a Naiad of the rivers, stay!
> To thy far wishes will thy streams obey.
> Stay! though the greenest woods be thy domain,
> Alone they can drink up the morning rain:
> Though a descended Pleiad, will not one
> Of thine harmonious sisters keep in tune
> Thy spheres, and as thy silver proxy shine?
> So sweetly to these ravished ears of mine
> Came thy sweet greeting, that if thou shouldst fade
> Thy memory will waste me to a shade –
> For pity do not melt!' – 'If I should stay,'
> Said Lamia, 'here, upon this floor of clay,
> And pain my steps upon these flowers too rough,
> What canst thou say or do of charm enough
> To dull the nice remembrance of my home?
> Thou canst not ask me with thee here to roam
> Over these hills and vales, where no joy is –
> Empty of immortality and bliss!
> Thou art a scholar, Lycius, and must know
> That finer spirits cannot breathe below
> In human climes, and live. Alas! poor youth,
> What taste of purer air hast thou to soothe
> My essence? What serener palaces,

Where I may all my many senses please,
And by mysterious sleights a hundred thirsts appease?
It cannot be – Adieu!' So said, she rose
Tip-toe with white arms spread. He, sick to lose
The amorous promise of her lone complain,
Swooned, murmuring of love, and pale with pain.
290 The cruel lady, without any show
Of sorrow for her tender favourite's woe,
But rather, if her eyes could brighter be,
With brighter eyes and slow amenity,
Put her new lips to his, and gave afresh
The life she had so tangled in her mesh;
And as he from one trance was wakening
Into another, she began to sing,
Happy in beauty, life, and love, and every thing,
A song of love, too sweet for earthly lyres,
300 While, like held breath, the stars drew in their panting fires.
And then she whispered in such trembling tone,
As those who, safe together met alone
For the first time through many anguished days,
Use other speech than looks; bidding him raise
His drooping head, and clear his soul of doubt,
For that she was a woman, and without
Any more subtle fluid in her veins
Than throbbing blood, and that the self-same pains
Inhabited her frail-strung heart as his.
310 And next she wondered how his eyes could miss
Her face so long in Corinth, where, she said,
She dwelt but half retired, and there had led
Days happy as the gold coin could invent
Without the aid of love; yet in content
Till she saw him, as once she passed him by,
Where 'gainst a column he leant thoughtfully
At Venus' temple porch, 'mid baskets heaped
Of amorous herbs and flowers, newly reaped
Late on that eve, as 'twas the night before
320 The Adonian feast; whereof she saw no more,

LAMIA

>   But wept alone those days, for why should she adore?
> Lycius from death awoke into amaze,
> To see her still, and singing so sweet lays;
> Then from amaze into delight he fell
> To hear her whisper woman's lore so well;
> And every word she spake enticed him on
> To unperplexed delight and pleasure known.
> Let the mad poets say whate'er they please
> Of the sweets of Faeries, Peris, Goddesses,
> There is not such a treat among them all,
> Haunters of cavern, lake, and waterfall,
> As a real woman, lineal indeed
> From Pyrrha's pebbles or old Adam's seed.
> Thus gentle Lamia judged, and judged aright,
> That Lycius could not love in half a fright,
> So threw the goddess off, and won his heart
> More pleasantly by playing woman's part,
> With no more awe than what her beauty gave,
> That, while it smote, still guaranteed to save.
> Lycius to all made eloquent reply,
> Marrying to every word a twinborn sigh;
> And last, pointing to Corinth, asked her sweet,
> If 'twas too far that night for her soft feet.
> The way was short, for Lamia's eagerness
> Made, by a spell, the triple league decrease
> To a few paces; not at all surmised
> By blinded Lycius, so in her comprised.
> They passed the city gates, he knew not how,
> So noiseless, and he never thought to know.
>
>   As men talk in a dream, so Corinth all,
> Throughout her palaces imperial,
> And all her populous streets and temples lewd,
> Muttered, like tempest in the distance brewed,
> To the wide-spreaded night above her towers.
> Men, women, rich and poor, in the cool hours,
> Shuffled their sandals o'er the pavement white,
> Companioned or alone; while many a light

Flared, here and there, from wealthy festivals,
And threw their moving shadows on the walls,
360 Or found them clustered in the corniced shade
Of some arched temple door, or dusky colonnade.

    Muffling his face, of greeting friends in fear,
Her fingers he pressed hard, as one came near
With curled grey beard, sharp eyes, and smooth bald crown,
Slow-stepped, and robed in philosophic gown:
Lycius shrank closer, as they met and passed,
Into his mantle, adding wings to haste,
While hurried Lamia trembled: 'Ah,' said he,
'Why do you shudder, love, so ruefully?
370 Why does your tender palm dissolve in dew?' –
'I'm wearied,' said fair Lamia, 'tell me who
Is that old man? I cannot bring to mind
His features – Lycius! wherefore did you blind
Yourself from his quick eyes?' Lycius replied,
''Tis Apollonius sage, my trusty guide
And good instructor; but tonight he seems
The ghost of folly haunting my sweet dreams.'

    While yet he spake they had arrived before
A pillared porch, with lofty portal door,
380 Where hung a silver lamp, whose phosphor glow
Reflected in the slabbèd steps below,
Mild as a star in water; for so new,
And so unsullied was the marble hue,
So through the crystal polish, liquid fine,
Ran the dark veins, that none but feet divine
Could e'er have touched there. Sounds Aeolian
Breathed from the hinges, as the ample span
Of the wide doors disclosed a place unknown
Some time to any, but those two alone,
390 And a few Persian mutes, who that same year
Were seen about the markets: none knew where
They could inhabit; the most curious
Were foiled, who watched to trace them to their house.

And but the flitter-wingèd verse must tell,
For truth's sake, what woe afterwards befell,
'Twould humour many a heart to leave them thus,
Shut from the busy world, of more incredulous.

PART II

Love in a hut, with water and a crust,
Is – Love, forgive us! – cinder, ashes, dust;
Love in a palace is perhaps at last
More grievous torment than a hermit's fast.
That is a doubtful tale from faery land,
Hard for the non-elect to understand.
Had Lycius lived to hand his story down,
He might have given the moral a fresh frown,
Or clenched it quite: but too short was their bliss
10 To breed distrust and hate, that make the soft voice hiss.
Besides, there, nightly, with terrific glare,
Love, jealous grown of so complete a pair,
Hovered and buzzed his wings, with fearful roar,
Above the lintel of their chamber door,
And down the passage cast a glow upon the floor.

    For all this came a ruin: side by side
They were enthronèd, in the eventide,
Upon a couch, near to a curtaining
Whose airy texture, from a golden string,
20 Floated into the room, and let appear
Unveiled the summer heaven, blue and clear,
Betwixt two marble shafts. There they reposed,
Where use had made it sweet, with eyelids closed,
Saving a tithe which love still open kept,
That they might see each other while they almost slept;
When from the slope side of a suburb hill,
Deafening the swallow's twitter, came a thrill
Of trumpets – Lycius started – the sounds fled,
But left a thought a-buzzing in his head.
30 For the first time, since first he harboured in
That purple-linèd palace of sweet sin,

His spirit passed beyond its golden bourne
Into the noisy world almost forsworn.
The lady, ever watchful, penetrant,
Saw this with pain, so arguing a want
Of something more, more than her empery
Of joys; and she began to moan and sigh
Because he mused beyond her, knowing well
That but a moment's thought is passion's passing-bell.
'Why do you sigh, fair creature?' whispered he:
'Why do you think?' returned she tenderly,
'You have deserted me – where am I now?
Not in your heart while care weighs on your brow:
No, no, you have dismissed me; and I go
From your breast houseless – ay, it must be so.'
He answered, bending to her open eyes,
Where he was mirrored small in paradise,
'My silver planet, both of eve and morn!
Why will you plead yourself so sad forlorn,
While I am striving how to fill my heart
With deeper crimson, and a double smart?
How to entangle, trammel up and snare
Your soul in mine, and labyrinth you there
Like the hid scent in an unbudded rose?
Ay, a sweet kiss – you see your mighty woes.
My thoughts! shall I unveil them? Listen then!
What mortal hath a prize, that other men
May be confounded and abashed withal,
But lets it sometimes pace abroad majestical,
And triumph, as in thee I should rejoice
Amid the hoarse alarm of Corinth's voice.
Let my foes choke, and my friends shout afar,
While through the thronged streets your bridal car
Wheels round its dazzling spokes.' – The lady's cheek
Trembled; she nothing said, but, pale and meek,
Arose and knelt before him, wept a rain
Of sorrows at his words; at last with pain
Beseeching him, the while his hand she wrung,
To change his purpose. He thereat was stung,

LAMIA

70 Perverse, with stronger fancy to reclaim
    Her wild and timid nature to his aim:
    Besides, for all his love, in self-despite,
    Against his better self, he took delight
    Luxurious in her sorrows, soft and new.
    His passion, cruel grown, took on a hue
    Fierce and sanguineous as 'twas possible
    In one whose brow had no dark veins to swell.
    Fine was the mitigated fury, like
    Apollo's presence when in act to strike
80 The serpent – Ha, the serpent! Certes, she
    Was none. She burnt, she loved the tyranny,
    And, all subdued, consented to the hour
    When to the bridal he should lead his paramour.
    Whispering in midnight silence, said the youth,
    'Sure some sweet name thou hast, though, by my truth,
    I have not asked it, ever thinking thee
    Not mortal, but of heavenly progeny,
    As still I do. Hast any mortal name,
    Fit appellation for this dazzling frame?
90 Or friends or kinsfolk on the citied earth,
    To share our marriage feast and nuptial mirth?'
    'I have no friends,' said Lamia, 'no, not one;
    My presence in wide Corinth hardly known:
    My parents' bones are in their dusty urns
    Sepulchred, where no kindled incense burns,
    Seeing all their luckless race are dead, save me,
    And I neglect the holy rite for thee.
    Even as you list invite your many guests;
    But if, as now it seems, your vision rests
100 With any pleasure on me, do not bid
    Old Apollonius – from him keep me hid.'
    Lycius, perplexed at words so blind and blank,
    Made close inquiry; from whose touch she shrank,
    Feigning a sleep; and he to the dull shade
    Of deep sleep in a moment was betrayed.

    It was the custom then to bring away
    The bride from home at blushing shut of day,

428 LAMIA

    Veiled, in a chariot, heralded along
By strewn flowers, torches, and a marriage song,
With other pageants: but this fair unknown
Had not a friend. So being left alone,
(Lycius was gone to summon all his kin)
And knowing surely she could never win
His foolish heart from its mad pompousness,
She set herself, high-thoughted, how to dress
The misery in fit magnificence.
She did so, but 'tis doubtful how and whence
Came, and who were her subtle servitors.
About the halls, and to and from the doors,
There was a noise of wings, till in short space
The glowing banquet-room shone with wide-archèd grace.
A haunting music, sole perhaps and lone
Supportress of the faery-roof, made moan
Throughout, as fearful the whole charm might fade.
Fresh carvèd cedar, mimicking a glade
Of palm and plantain, met from either side,
High in the midst, in honour of the bride;
Two palms and then two plaintains, and so on,
From either side their stems branched one to one
All down the aislèd place; and beneath all
There ran a stream of lamps straight on from wall to wall.
So canopied, lay an untasted feast
Teeming with odours. Lamia, regal dressed,
Silently paced about, and as she went,
In pale contented sort of discontent,
Missioned her viewless servants to enrich
The fretted splendour of each nook and niche.
Between the tree-stems, marbled plain at first,
Came jasper panels; then anon, there burst
Forth creeping imagery of slighter trees,
And with the larger wove in small intricacies.
Approving all, she faded at self-will,
And shut the chamber up, close, hushed and still,
Complete and ready for the revels rude,
When dreadful guests would come to spoil her solitude.

The day appeared, and all the gossip rout.
O senseless Lycius! Madman! wherefore flout
The silent-blessing fate, warm cloistered hours,
And show to common eyes these secret bowers?
150 The herd approached; each guest, with busy brain,
Arriving at the portal, gazed amain,
And entered marvelling – for they knew the street,
Remembered it from childhood all complete
Without a gap, yet ne'er before had seen
That royal porch, that high-built fair demesne.
So in they hurried all, mazed, curious and keen –
Save one, who looked thereon with eye severe,
And with calm-planted steps walked in austere.
'Twas Apollonius: something too he laughed,
160 As though some knotty problem, that had daffed
His patient thought, had now begun to thaw,
And solve and melt – 'twas just as he foresaw.

He met within the murmurous vestibule
His young disciple. ''Tis no common rule,
Lycius,' said he, 'for uninvited guest
To force himself upon you, and infest
With an unbidden presence the bright throng
Of younger friends; yet must I do this wrong,
And you forgive me.' Lycius blushed, and led
170 The old man through the inner doors broad-spread;
With reconciling words and courteous mien
Turning into sweet milk the sophist's spleen.

Of wealthy lustre was the banquet-room,
Filled with pervading brilliance and perfume:
Before each lucid panel fuming stood
A censer fed with myrrh and spicèd wood,
Each by a sacred tripod held aloft,
Whose slender feet wide-swerved upon the soft
Wool-woofèd carpets; fifty wreaths of smoke
180 From fifty censers their light voyage took
To the high roof, still mimicked as they rose
Along the mirrored walls by twin-clouds odorous.

Twelve spherèd tables, by silk seats ensphered,
High as the level of a man's breast reared
On libbard's paws, upheld the heavy gold
Of cups and goblets, and the store thrice told
Of Ceres' horn, and, in huge vessels, wine
Come from the gloomy tun with merry shine.
Thus loaded with a feast the tables stood,
Each shrining in the midst the image of a God.

When in an antechamber every guest
Had felt the cold full sponge to pleasure pressed,
By ministering slaves, upon his hands and feet,
And fragrant oils with ceremony meet
Poured on his hair, they all moved to the feast
In white robes, and themselves in order placed
Around the silken couches, wondering
Whence all this mighty cost and blaze of wealth could
      spring.

Soft went the music the soft air along,
While fluent Greek a vowelled undersong
Kept up among the guests, discoursing low
At first, for scarcely was the wine at flow;
But when the happy vintage touched their brains,
Louder they talk, and louder come the strains
Of powerful instruments. The gorgeous dyes,
The space, the splendour of the draperies,
The roof of awful richness, nectarous cheer,
Beautiful slaves, and Lamia's self, appear,
Now, when the wine has done its rosy deed,
And every soul from human trammels freed,
No more so strange; for merry wine, sweet wine,
Will make Elysian shades not too fair, too divine.
Soon was God Bacchus at meridian height;
Flushed were their cheeks, and bright eyes double bright:
Garlands of every green, and every scent
From vales deflowered, or forest-trees branch-rent,
In baskets of bright osiered gold were brought
High as the handles heaped, to suit the thought

LAMIA

    Of every guest – that each, as he did please,
220 Might fancy-fit his brows, silk-pillowed at his ease.

    What wreath for Lamia? What for Lycius?
What for the sage, old Apollonius?
Upon her aching forehead be there hung
The leaves of willow and of adder's tongue;
And for the youth, quick, let us strip for him
The thyrsus, that his watching eyes may swim
Into forgetfulness; and, for the sage,
Let spear-grass and the spiteful thistle wage
War on his temples. Do not all charms fly
230 At the mere touch of cold philosophy?
There was an awful rainbow once in heaven:
We know her woof, her texture; she is given
In the dull catalogue of common things.
Philosophy will clip an Angel's wings,
Conquer all mysteries by rule and line,
Empty the haunted air, and gnomèd mine –
Unweave a rainbow, as it erewhile made
The tender-personed Lamia melt into a shade.

    By her glad Lycius sitting, in chief place,
240 Scarce saw in all the room another face,
Till, checking his love trance, a cup he took
Full brimmed, and opposite sent forth a look
'Cross the broad table, to beseech a glance
From his old teacher's wrinkled countenance,
And pledge him. The bald-head philosopher
Had fixed his eye, without a twinkle or stir
Full on the alarmèd beauty of the bride,
Brow-beating her fair form, and troubling her sweet pride.
Lycius then pressed her hand, with devout touch,
250 As pale it lay upon the rosy couch:
'Twas icy, and the cold ran through his veins;
Then sudden it grew hot, and all the pains
Of an unnatural heat shot to his heart.
'Lamia, what means this? Wherefore dost thou start?
Know'st thou that man?' Poor Lamia answered not.

He gazed into her eyes, and not a jot
Owned they the lovelorn piteous appeal;
More, more he gazed; his human senses reel;
Some hungry spell that loveliness absorbs;
There was no recognition in those orbs.
'Lamia!' he cried – and no soft-toned reply.
The many heard, and the loud revelry
Grew hush; the stately music no more breathes;
The myrtle sickened in a thousand wreaths.
By faint degrees, voice, lute, and pleasure ceased;
A deadly silence step by step increased,
Until it seemed a horrid presence there,
And not a man but felt the terror in his hair.
'Lamia!' he shrieked; and nothing but the shriek
With its sad echo did the silence break.
'Begone, foul dream!' he cried, gazing again
In the bride's face, where now no azure vein
Wandered on fair-spaced temples; no soft bloom
Misted the cheek; no passion to illume
The deep-recessèd vision. All was blight;
Lamia, no longer fair, there sat a deadly white.
'Shut, shut those juggling eyes, thou ruthless man!
Turn them aside, wretch! or the righteous ban
Of all the Gods, whose dreadful images
Here represent their shadowy presences,
May pierce them on the sudden with the thorn
Of painful blindness; leaving thee forlorn,
In trembling dotage to the feeblest fright
Of conscience, for their long offended might,
For all thine impious proud-heart sophistries,
Unlawful magic, and enticing lies.
Corinthians! look upon that grey-beard wretch!
Mark how, possessed, his lashless eyelids stretch
Around his demon eyes! Corinthians, see!
My sweet bride withers at their potency.'
'Fool!' said the sophist, in an undertone
Gruff with contempt; which a death-nighing moan
From Lycius answered, as heart-struck and lost,

>   He sank supine beside the aching ghost.
>   'Fool! Fool!' repeated he, while his eyes still
>   Relented not, nor moved: 'From every ill
>   Of life have I preserved thee to this day,
>   And shall I see thee made a serpent's prey?'
>   Then Lamia breathed death-breath; the sophist's eye,
> 300 Like a sharp spear, went through her utterly,
>   Keen, cruel, perceant, stinging: she, as well
>   As her weak hand could any meaning tell,
>   Motioned him to be silent; vainly so,
>   He looked and looked again a level – *No!*
>   'A Serpent!' echoed he; no sooner said,
>   Than with a frightful scream she vanishèd:
>   And Lycius' arms were empty of delight,
>   As were his limbs of life, from that same night.
>   On the high couch he lay! – his friends came round –
> 310 Supported him – no pulse, or breath they found,
>   And, in its marriage robe, the heavy body wound.

'Pensive they sit, and roll their languid eyes'

>   Pensive they sit, and roll their languid eyes,
>   Nibble their toasts and cool their tea with sighs;
>   Or else forget the purpose of the night,
>   Forget their tea, forget their appetite.
>   See, with crossed arms they sit – Ah! hapless crew,
>   The fire is going out and no one rings
>   For coals, and therefore no coals Betty brings.
>   A fly is in the milk-pot – must he die
>   Circled by a Humane Society?
> 10 No, no; there, Mr Werter takes his spoon,
>   Inverts it, dips the handle, and lo! soon
>   The little struggler, saved from perils dark,
>   Across the teaboard draws a long wet mark.
>   Romeo! Arise! take snuffers by the handle,
>   There's a large cauliflower in each candle.
>   A winding-sheet – ah, me! I must away

To No. 7, just beyond the Circus gay.
'Alas, my friend, your coat sits very well;
Where may your tailor live?' 'I may not tell.
20 O pardon me – I'm absent now and then.
Where *might* my tailor live? I say again
I cannot tell. Let me no more be teased –
He lives in Wapping, *might* live where he pleased.'

To Autumn

I

Season of mists and mellow fruitfulness,
  Close bosom-friend of the maturing sun,
Conspiring with him how to load and bless
  With fruit the vines that round the thatch-eves run;
To bend with apples the mossed cottage-trees,
  And fill all fruit with ripeness to the core;
    To swell the gourd, and plump the hazel shells
  With a sweet kernel; to set budding more,
And still more, later flowers for the bees,
10 Until they think warm days will never cease,
    For Summer has o'er-brimmed their clammy cells.

II

Who hath not seen thee oft amid thy store?
  Sometimes whoever seeks abroad may find
Thee sitting careless on a granary floor,
  Thy hair soft-lifted by the winnowing wind;
Or on a half-reaped furrow sound asleep,
  Drowsed with the fume of poppies, while thy hook
    Spares the next swath and all its twinèd flowers;
And sometimes like a gleaner thou dost keep
20 Steady thy laden head across a brook;
  Or by a cider-press, with patient look,
    Thou watchest the last oozings hours by hours.

III

Where are the songs of Spring? Ay, where are they?

Think not of them, thou hast thy music too –
While barrèd clouds bloom the soft-dying day,
  And touch the stubble-plains with rosy hue:
Then in a wailful choir the small gnats mourn
  Among the river sallows, borne aloft
    Or sinking as the light wind lives or dies;
And full-grown lambs loud bleat from hilly bourn;
  Hedge-crickets sing; and now with treble soft
  The red-breast whistles from a garden-croft;
    And gathering swallows twitter in the skies.

The Fall of Hyperion. A Dream

CANTO I

Fanatics have their dreams, wherewith they weave
A paradise for a sect, the savage too
From forth the loftiest fashion of his sleep
Guesses at Heaven; pity these have not
Traced upon vellum or wild Indian leaf
The shadows of melodious utterance.
But bare of laurel they live, dream, and die;
For Poesy alone can tell her dreams,
With the fine spell of words alone can save
Imagination from the sable charm
And dumb enchantment. Who alive can say,
'Thou art no Poet – mayst not tell thy dreams'?
Since every man whose soul is not a clod
Hath visions, and would speak, if he had loved,
And been well nurtured in his mother tongue.
Whether the dream now purposed to rehearse
Be Poet's or Fanatic's will be known
When this warm scribe my hand is in the grave.

Methought I stood where trees of every clime,
Palm, myrtle, oak, and sycamore, and beech,
With plantain, and spice-blossoms, made a screen –
In neighbourhood of fountains, by the noise
Soft-showering in mine ears, and, by the touch

Of scent, not far from roses. Turning round,
I saw an arbour with a drooping roof
Of trellis vines, and bells, and larger blooms,
Like floral censers, swinging light in air;
Before its wreathèd doorway, on a mound
Of moss, was spread a feast of summer fruits,
Which, nearer seen, seemed refuse of a meal
By angel tasted, or our Mother Eve;
For empty shells were scattered on the grass,
And grape-stalks but half bare, and remnants more,
Sweet-smelling, whose pure kinds I could not know.
Still was more plenty than the fabled horn
Thrice emptied could pour forth at banqueting
For Proserpine returned to her own fields,
Where the white heifers low. And appetite
More yearning than on earth I ever felt
Growing within, I ate deliciously;
And, after not long, thirsted, for thereby
Stood a cool vessel of transparent juice,
Sipped by the wandered bee, the which I took,
And, pledging all the mortals of the world,
And all the dead whose names are in our lips,
Drank. That full draught is parent of my theme.
No Asian poppy, nor elixir fine
Of the soon-fading jealous Caliphat;
No poison gendered in close monkish cell,
To thin the scarlet conclave of old men,
Could so have rapt unwilling life away.
Among the fragrant husks and berries crushed,
Upon the grass I struggled hard against
The domineering potion; but in vain –
The cloudy swoon came on, and down I sunk,
Like a Silenus on an antique vase.
How long I slumbered 'tis a chance to guess.
When sense of life returned, I started up
As if with wings; but the fair trees were gone,
The mossy mound and arbour were no more.
I looked around upon the carvèd sides

THE FALL OF HYPERION. A DREAM

    Of an old sanctuary with roof august,
Builded so high, it seemed that filmèd clouds
Might spread beneath, as o'er the stars of heaven.
So old the place was, I remembered none
The like upon the earth: what I had seen
Of grey cathedrals, buttressed walls, rent towers,
The superannuations of sunk realms,
Or Nature's rocks toiled hard in waves and winds,
70 Seemed but the faulture of decrepit things
To that eternal domèd monument.
Upon the marble at my feet there lay
Store of strange vessels and large draperies,
Which needs had been of dyed asbestos wove,
Or in that place the moth could not corrupt,
So white the linen; so, in some, distinct
Ran imageries from a sombre loom.
All in a mingled heap confused there lay
Robes, golden tongs, censer and chafing-dish,
80 Girdles, and chains, and holy jewelleries –

    Turning from these with awe, once more I raised
My eyes to fathom the space every way –
The embossèd roof, the silent massy range
Of columns north and south, ending in mist
Of nothing, then to eastward, where black gates
Were shut against the sunrise evermore.
Then to the west I looked, and saw far off
An Image, huge of feature as a cloud,
At level of whose feet an altar slept,
90 To be approached on either side by steps,
And marble balustrade, and patient travail
To count with toil the innumerable degrees.
Towards the altar sober-paced I went,
Repressing haste, as too unholy there;
And, coming nearer, saw beside the shrine
One ministering; and there arose a flame.
When in mid-May the sickening East wind
Shifts sudden to the south, the small warm rain

THE FALL OF HYPERION. A DREAM

    Melts out the frozen incense from all flowers,
100 And fills the air with so much pleasant health
    That even the dying man forgets his shroud –
    Even so that lofty sacrificial fire,
    Sending forth Maian incense, spread around
    Forgetfulness of everything but bliss,
    And clouded all the altar with soft smoke,
    From whose white fragrant curtains thus I heard
    Language pronounced: 'If thou canst not ascend
    These steps, die on that marble where thou art.
    Thy flesh, near cousin to the common dust,
110 Will parch for lack of nutriment – thy bones
    Will wither in few years, and vanish so
    That not the quickest eye could find a grain
    Of what thou now art on that pavement cold.
    The sands of thy short life are spent this hour,
    And no hand in the universe can turn
    Thy hourglass, if these gummèd leaves be burnt
    Ere thou canst mount up these immortal steps.'
    I heard, I looked: two senses both at once,
    So fine, so subtle, felt the tyranny
120 Of that fierce threat, and the hard task proposed.
    Prodigious seemed the toil; the leaves were yet
    Burning – when suddenly a palsied chill
    Struck from the pavèd level up my limbs,
    And was ascending quick to put cold grasp
    Upon those streams that pulse beside the throat.
    I shrieked; and the sharp anguish of my shriek
    Stung my own ears – I strove hard to escape
    The numbness, strove to gain the lowest step.
    Slow, heavy, deadly was my pace: the cold
130 Grew stifling, suffocating, at the heart;
    And when I clasped my hands I felt them not.
    One minute before death, my iced foot touched
    The lowest stair; and as it touched, life seemed
    To pour in at the toes: I mounted up,
    As once fair Angels on a ladder flew
    From the green turf to Heaven. 'Holy Power,'

THE FALL OF HYPERION. A DREAM

  Cried I, approaching near the hornèd shrine,
'What am I that should so be saved from death?
What am I that another death come not
To choke my utterance sacrilegious, here?'
Then said the veilèd shadow: 'Thou hast felt
What 'tis to die and live again before
Thy fated hour. That thou hadst power to do so
Is thy own safety; thou hast dated on
Thy doom.' 'High Prophetess,' said I, 'purge off,
Benign, if so it please thee, my mind's film.'
'None can usurp this height,' returned that shade,
'But those to whom the miseries of the world
Are misery, and will not let them rest.
All else who find a haven in the world,
Where they may thoughtless sleep away their days,
If by a chance into this fane they come,
Rot on the pavement where thou rotted'st half.'
'Are there not thousands in the world,' said I,
Encouraged by the sooth voice of the shade,
'Who love their fellows even to the death;
Who feel the giant agony of the world;
And more, like slaves to poor humanity,
Labour for mortal good? I sure should see
Other men here: but I am here alone.'
'They whom thou spak'st of are no visionaries,'
Rejoined that voice – 'They are no dreamers weak,
They seek no wonder but the human face;
No music but a happy-noted voice –
They come not here, they have no thought to come –
And thou art here, for thou art less than they –
What benefit canst thou do, or all thy tribe,
To the great world? Thou art a dreaming thing,
A fever of thyself. Think of the Earth;
What bliss even in hope is there for thee?
What haven? Every creature hath its home;
Every sole man hath days of joy and pain,
Whether his labours be sublime or low –
The pain alone; the joy alone; distinct:

THE FALL OF HYPERION. A DREAM

    Only the dreamer venoms all his days,
    Bearing more woe than all his sins deserve.
    Therefore, that happiness be somewhat shared,
    Such things as thou art are admitted oft
    Into like gardens thou didst pass erewhile,
180 And suffered in these Temples; for that cause
    Thou standest safe beneath this statue's knees.'
    'That I am favoured for unworthiness,
    By such propitious parley medicined
    In sickness not ignoble, I rejoice –
    Ay, and could weep for love of such award.'
    So answered I, continuing, 'If it please,
    Majestic shadow, tell me: sure not all
    Those melodies sung into the world's ear
    Are useless: sure a poet is a sage,
190 A humanist, physician to all men.
    That I am none I feel, as vultures feel
    They are no birds when eagles are abroad.
    What am I then? Thou spakest of my tribe:
    What tribe?' – The tall shade veiled in drooping white
    Then spake, so much more earnest, that the breath
    Moved the thin linen folds that drooping hung
    About a golden censer from the hand
    Pendant. – 'Art thou not of the dreamer tribe?
    The poet and the dreamer are distinct,
200 Diverse, sheer opposite, antipodes.
    The one pours out a balm upon the world,
    The other vexes it.' Then shouted I,
    Spite of myself, and with a Pythia's spleen,
    'Apollo! faded, far-flown Apollo!
    Where is thy misty pestilence to creep
    Into the dwellings, through the door crannies,
    Of all mock lyrists, large self-worshippers
    And careless hectorers in proud bad verse.
    Though I breathe death with them it will be life
210 To see them sprawl before me into graves.
    Majestic shadow, tell me where I am,
    Whose altar this; for whom this incense curls;

THE FALL OF HYPERION. A DREAM

What Image this, whose face I cannot see,
For the broad marble knees; and who thou art,
Of accent feminine so courteous?'

Then the tall shade, in drooping linens veiled,
Spake out, so much more earnest, that her breath
Stirred the thin folds of gauze that drooping hung
About a golden censer from her hand
Pendant; and by her voice I knew she shed
Long-treasured tears. 'This temple, sad and lone,
Is all spared from the thunder of a war
Foughten long since by giant hierarchy
Against rebellion; this old Image here,
Whose carvèd features wrinkled as he fell,
Is Saturn's; I Moneta, left supreme
Sole Priestess of his desolation.'
I had no words to answer, for my tongue,
Useless, could find about its roofèd home
No syllable of a fit majesty
To make rejoinder to Moneta's mourn.
There was a silence, while the altar's blaze
Was fainting for sweet food: I looked thereon,
And on the pavèd floor, where nigh were piled
Faggots of cinnamon, and many heaps
Of other crispèd spice-wood – then again
I looked upon the altar, and its horns
Whitened with ashes, and its languorous flame,
And then upon the offerings again;
And so by turns – till sad Moneta cried:
'The sacrifice is done, but not the less
Will I be kind to thee for thy goodwill.
My power, which to me is still a curse,
Shall be to thee a wonder; for the scenes
Still swooning vivid through my globèd brain,
With an electral changing misery,
Thou shalt with those dull mortal eyes behold,
Free from all pain, if wonder pain thee not.'
As near as an immortal's spherèd words

THE FALL OF HYPERION. A DREAM

250 Could to a mother's soften, were these last:
But yet I had a terror of her robes,
And chiefly of the veils, that from her brow
Hung pale, and curtained her in mysteries
That made my heart too small to hold its blood.
This saw that Goddess, and with sacred hand
Parted the veils. Then saw I a wan face,
Not pined by human sorrows, but bright-blanched
By an immortal sickness which kills not;
It works a constant change, which happy death
260 Can put no end to; deathwards progressing
To no death was that visage; it had passed
The lily and the snow; and beyond these
I must not think now, though I saw that face –
But for her eyes I should have fled away.
They held me back, with a benignant light,
Soft-mitigated by divinest lids
Half-closed, and visionless entire they seemed
Of all external things – they saw me not,
But in blank splendour beamed like the mild moon,
270 Who comforts those she sees not, who knows not
What eyes are upward cast. As I had found
A grain of gold upon a mountain's side,
And twinged with avarice strained out my eyes
To search its sullen entrails rich with ore,
So at the view of sad Moneta's brow
I ached to see what things the hollow brain
Behind enwombèd; what high tragedy
In the dark secret chambers of her skull
Was acting, that could give so dread a stress
280 To her cold lips, and fill with such a light
Her planetary eyes; and touch her voice
With such a sorrow – 'Shade of Memory!'
Cried I, with act adorant at her feet,
'By all the gloom hung round thy fallen house,
By this last Temple, by the golden age,
By great Apollo, thy dear foster child,
And by thyself, forlorn Divinity,

THE FALL OF HYPERION. A DREAM

The pale Omega of a withered race,
Let me behold, according as thou said'st,
What in thy brain so ferments to and fro.'
No sooner had this conjuration passed
My devout lips, than side by side we stood
(Like a stunt bramble by a solemn pine)
Deep in the shady sadness of a vale,
Far sunken from the healthy breath of morn,
Far from the fiery noon and eve's one star.
Onward I looked beneath the gloomy boughs,
And saw, what first I thought an Image huge,
Like to the Image pedestalled so high
In Saturn's Temple. Then Moneta's voice
Came brief upon mine ear: 'So Saturn sat
When he had lost his realms.' Whereon there grew
A power within me of enormous ken
To see as a God sees, and take the depth
Of things as nimbly as the outward eye
Can size and shape pervade. The lofty theme
At those few words hung vast before my mind,
With half-unravelled web. I set myself
Upon an eagle's watch, that I might see,
And seeing ne'er forget. No stir of life
Was in this shrouded vale, not so much air
As in zoning of a summer's day
Robs not one light seed from the feathered grass,
But where the dead leaf fell there did it rest.
A stream went voiceless by, still deadened more
By reason of the fallen Divinity
Spreading more shade; the Naiad 'mid her reeds
Pressed her cold finger closer to her lips.
Along the margin-sand large footmarks went
No farther than to where old Saturn's feet
Had rested, and there slept – how long a sleep!
Degraded, cold, upon the sodden ground
His old right hand lay nerveless, listless, dead,
Unsceptred; and his realmless eyes were closed,
While his bowed head seemed listening to the Earth,

444 THE FALL OF HYPERION. A DREAM

    His ancient mother, for some comfort yet.

      It seemed no force could wake him from his place;
    But there came one who, with a kindred hand
    Touched his wide shoulders, after bending low
330 With reverence, though to one who knew it not.
    Then came the grieved voice of Mnemosyne,
    And grieved I hearkened. 'That Divinity
    Whom thou saw'st step from yon forlornest wood,
    And with slow pace approach our fallen King,
    Is Thea, softest-natured of our brood.'
    I marked the Goddess in fair statuary
    Surpassing wan Moneta by the head,
    And in her sorrow nearer woman's tears.
    There was a listening fear in her regard,
340 As if calamity had but begun;
    As if the vanward clouds of evil days
    Had spent their malice, and the sullen rear
    Was with its storèd thunder labouring up.
    One hand she pressed upon that aching spot
    Where beats the human heart, as if just there,
    Though an immortal, she felt cruel pain;
    The other upon Saturn's bended neck
    She laid, and to the level of his hollow ear
    Leaning with parted lips, some words she spake
350 In solemn tenor and deep organ tune,
    Some mourning words, which in our feeble tongue
    Would come in this-like accenting – how frail
    To that large utterance of the early Gods! –
    'Saturn! look up – and for what, poor lost King?
    I have no comfort for thee, no – not one;
    I cannot cry, *Wherefore thus sleepest thou?*
    For Heaven is parted from thee, and the Earth
    Knows thee not, so afflicted, for a God;
    And Ocean too, with all its solemn noise,
360 Has from thy sceptre passed, and all the air
    Is emptied of thine hoary Majesty.
    Thy thunder, captious at the new command,

THE FALL OF HYPERION. A DREAM

Rumbles reluctant o'er our fallen house;
And thy sharp lightning, in unpractised hands,
Scorches and burns our once serene domain.
With such remorseless speed still come new woes
That unbelief has not a space to breathe.
Saturn! sleep on. Me thoughtless, why should I
Thus violate thy slumbrous solitude?
Why should I ope thy melancholy eyes?
Saturn, sleep on, while at thy feet I weep.'

As when, upon a trancèd summer-night,
Forests, branch-charmèd by the earnest stars,
Dream, and so dream all night without a noise,
Save from one gradual solitary gust,
Swelling upon the silence; dying off;
As if the ebbing air had but one wave –
So came these words, and went; the while in tears
She pressed her fair large forehead to the earth,
Just where her fallen hair might spread in curls,
A soft and silken mat for Saturn's feet.
Long, long those two were postured motionless,
Like sculpture builded-up upon the grave
Of their own power. A long awful time
I looked upon them: still they were the same;
The frozen God still bending to the earth,
And the sad Goddess weeping at his feet.
Moneta silent. Without stay or prop,
But my own weak mortality, I bore
The load of this eternal quietude,
The unchanging gloom, and the three fixèd shapes
Ponderous upon my senses a whole moon.
For by my burning brain I measured sure
Her silver seasons shedded on the night,
And every day by day methought I grew
More gaunt and ghostly. Oftentimes I prayed
Intense, that Death would take me from the vale
And all its burthens. Gasping with despair
Of change, hour after hour I cursed myself –

THE FALL OF HYPERION. A DREAM

400 Until old Saturn raised his faded eyes,
     And looked around and saw his kingdom gone,
     And all the gloom and sorrow of the place,
     And that fair kneeling Goddess at his feet.
     As the moist scent of flowers, and grass, and leaves,
     Fills forest dells with a pervading air
     Known to the woodland nostril, so the words
     Of Saturn filled the mossy glooms around,
     Even to the hollows of time-eaten oaks,
     And to the windings in the foxes' hole,
410 With sad low tones, while thus he spake, and sent
     Strange musings to the solitary Pan:
     'Moan, brethren, moan; for we are swallowed up
     And buried from all godlike exercise
     Of influence benign on planets pale,
     And peaceful sway above man's harvesting,
     And all those acts which Deity supreme
     Doth ease its heart of love in. Moan and wail.
     Moan, brethren, moan; for lo! the rebel spheres
     Spin round, the stars their ancient courses keep,
420 Clouds still with shadowy moisture haunt the earth,
     Still suck their fill of light from sun and moon,
     Still buds the tree, and still the sea-shores murmur.
     There is no death in all the universe,
     No smell of death – there shall be death – moan, moan,
     Moan, Cybele, moan; for thy pernicious babes
     Have changed a God into a shaking palsy.
     Moan, brethren, moan, for I have no strength left,
     Weak as the reed – weak – feeble as my voice –
     O, O, the pain, the pain of feebleness.
430 Moan, moan, for still I thaw – or give me help:
     Throw down those imps, and give me victory.
     Let me hear other groans, and trumpets blown
     Of triumph calm, and hymns of festival,
     From the gold peaks of heaven's high-pilèd clouds –
     Voices of soft proclaim, and silver stir
     Of strings in hollow shells; and let there be
     Beautiful things made new for the surprise

Of the sky-children – ' So he feebly ceased,
With such a poor and sickly sounding pause,
Methought I heard some old man of the earth
Bewailing earthly loss; nor could my eyes
And ears act with that pleasant unison of sense
Which marries sweet sound with the grace of form,
And dolorous accent from a tragic harp
With large-limbed visions. More I scrutinized:
Still fixed he sat beneath the sable trees,
Whose arms spread straggling in wild serpent forms,
With leaves all hushed; his awful presence there
(Now all was silent) gave a deadly lie
To what I erewhile heard – only his lips
Trembled amid the white curls of his beard.
They told the truth, though, round, the snowy locks
Hung nobly, as upon the face of heaven
A midday fleece of clouds. Thea arose,
And stretched her white arm through the hollow dark,
Pointing some whither; whereat he too rose
Like a vast giant, seen by men at sea
To grow pale from the waves at dull midnight.
They melted from my sight into the woods;
Ere I could turn, Moneta cried: 'These twain
Are speeding to the families of grief,
Where roofed in by black rocks they waste, in pain
And darkness, for no hope.' – And she spake on,
As ye may read who can unwearied pass
Onward from the antechamber of this dream,
Where even at the open doors awhile
I must delay, and glean my memory
Of her high phrase – perhaps no further dare.

CANTO II
'Mortal, that thou mayst understand aright,
I humanize my sayings to thine ear,
Making comparisons of earthly things;
Or thou mightst better listen to the wind,
Whose language is to thee a barren noise,

Though it blows legend-laden through the trees –
In melancholy realms big tears are shed,
More sorrow like to this, and such-like woe,
Too huge for mortal tongue, or pen of scribe.
The Titans fierce, self-hid or prison-bound,
Groan for the old allegiance once more,
Listening in their doom for Saturn's voice.
But one of our whole eagle-brood still keeps
His Sovereignty, and Rule, and Majesty;
Blazing Hyperion on his orbèd fire
Still sits, still snuffs the incense teeming up
From man to the sun's God – yet unsecure.
For as upon the earth dire prodigies
Fright and perplex, so also shudders he:
Nor at dog's howl or gloom-bird's even screech,
Or the familiar visitings of one
Upon the first toll of his passing-bell:
But horrors, portioned to a giant nerve,
Make great Hyperion ache. His palace bright,
Bastioned with pyramids of glowing gold,
And touched with shade of bronzèd obelisks,
Glares a blood-red through all the thousand courts,
Arches, and domes, and fiery galleries;
And all its curtains of Aurorian clouds
Flush angerly: when he would taste the wreaths
Of incense breathed aloft from sacred hills,
Instead of sweets, his ample palate takes
Savour of poisonous brass and metals sick.
Wherefore, when harboured in the sleepy West,
After the full completion of fair day,
For rest divine upon exalted couch
And slumber in the arms of melody,
He paces through the pleasant hours of ease
With strides colossal, on from hall to hall;
While far within each aisle and deep recess
His wingèd minions in close clusters stand
Amazed, and full of fear; like anxious men,
Who on a wide plain gather in sad troops,

When earthquakes jar their battlements and towers.
Even now, while Saturn, roused from icy trance,
Goes, step for step, with Thea from yon woods,
Hyperion, leaving twilight in the rear,
Is sloping to the threshold of the West –
Thither we tend.' – Now in clear light I stood,
50 Relieved from the dusk vale. Mnemosyne
Was sitting on a square-edged polished stone,
That in its lucid depth reflected pure
Her priestess-garments. My quick eyes ran on
From stately nave to nave, from vault to vault,
Through bowers of fragrant and enwreathèd light
And diamond-pavèd lustrous long arcades.
Anon rushed by the bright Hyperion;
His flaming robes streamed out beyond his heels,
And gave a roar, as if of earthly fire,
60 That scared away the meek ethereal Hours,
And made their dove-wings tremble. On he flared . . .

'The day is gone, and all its sweets are gone!'

The day is gone, and all its sweets are gone!
   Sweet voice, sweet lips, soft hand, and softer breast,
Warm breath, light whisper, tender semi-tone,
   Bright eyes, accomplished shape, and languorous waist!
Faded the flower and all its budded charms,
   Faded the sight of beauty from my eyes,
Faded the shape of beauty from my arms,
   Faded the voice, warmth, whiteness, paradise –
Vanished unseasonably at shut of eve,
10   When the dusk holiday – or holinight –
Of fragrant-curtained love begins to weave
   The woof of darkness thick, for hid delight;
But, as I've read love's missal through today,
He'll let me sleep, seeing I fast and pray.

What can I do to drive away

What can I do to drive away
Remembrance from my eyes? for they have seen,
Ay, an hour ago, my brilliant Queen!
Touch has a memory. O say, love, say,
What can I do to kill it and be free
In my old liberty?
When every fair one that I saw was fair,
Enough to catch me in but half a snare,
Not keep me there;
10 When, howe'er poor or parti-coloured things,
My muse had wings,
And ever ready was to take her course
Whither I bent her force,
Unintellectual, yet divine to me –
Divine, I say! What sea-bird o'er the sea
Is a philosopher the while he goes
Winging along where the great water throes?

    How shall I do
    To get anew
20 Those moulted feathers, and so mount once more
    Above, above
    The reach of fluttering Love,
And make him cower lowly while I soar?
Shall I gulp wine? No, that is vulgarism,
A heresy and schism,
    Foisted into the canon law of love;
No – wine is only sweet to happy men;
    More dismal cares
    Seize on me unawares –
30 Where shall I learn to get my peace again?
To banish thoughts of that most hateful land,
Dungeoner of my friends, that wicked strand
Where they were wrecked and live a wreckèd life;
That monstrous region, whose dull rivers pour,
Ever from their sordid urns into the shore,

Unowned of any weedy-hairèd gods;
Whose winds, all zephyrless, hold scourging rods,
Iced in the great lakes, to afflict mankind;
Whose rank-grown forests, frosted, black, and blind,
40 Would fright a Dryad; whose harsh-herbaged meads
Make lean and lank the starved ox while he feeds;
There flowers have no scent, birds no sweet song,
And great unerring Nature once seems wrong.

O, for some sunny spell
To dissipate the shadows of this hell!
Say they are gone – with the new dawning light
Steps forth my lady bright!
O, let me once more rest
My soul upon that dazzling breast!
50 Let once again these aching arms be placed,
The tender gaolers of thy waist!
And let me feel that warm breath here and there
To spread a rapture in my very hair –
O, the sweetness of the pain!
Give me those lips again!
Enough! Enough! It is enough for me
To dream of thee!

'I cry your mercy, pity, love – ay, love!'

I cry your mercy, pity, love – ay, love!
   Merciful love that tantalizes not,
One-thoughted, never-wandering, guileless love,
   Unmasked, and being seen – without a blot!
O! let me have thee whole, – all, all, be mine!
   That shape, that fairness, that sweet minor zest
Of love, your kiss – those hands, those eyes divine,
   That warm, white, lucent, million-pleasured breast –
Yourself – your soul – in pity give me all,
10   Withhold no atom's atom or I die;
Or living on perhaps, your wretched thrall,

Forget, in the mist of idle misery,
Life's purposes – the palate of my mind
Losing its gust, and my ambition blind!

'Bright star! would I were steadfast as thou art'

Bright star! would I were steadfast as thou art –
   Not in lone splendour hung aloft the night
And watching, with eternal lids apart,
   Like nature's patient, sleepless Eremite,
The moving waters at their priestlike task
   Of pure ablution round earth's human shores,
Or gazing on the new soft-fallen mask
   Of snow upon the mountains and the moors –
No – yet still steadfast, still unchangeable,
   Pillowed upon my fair love's ripening breast,
To feel for ever its soft swell and fall,
   Awake for ever in a sweet unrest,
Still, still to hear her tender-taken breath,
And so live ever – or else swoon to death.

King Stephen. A Fragment of a Tragedy

ACT I

Scene 1 *Field of Battle.*
[*Alarm. Enter* KING STEPHEN, *Knights, and Soldiers*]

STEPHEN If shame can on a soldier's vein-swollen front
   Spread deeper crimson than the battle's toil,
   Blush in your casing helmets! for see, see!
   Yonder my chivalry, my pride of war,
   Wrenched with an iron hand from firm array,
   Are routed loose about the plashy meads,
   Of honour forfeit. O, that my known voice
   Could reach your dastard ears, and fright you more!
   Fly, cowards, fly! Gloucester is at your backs!

KING STEPHEN: I . I

10 Throw your slack bridles o'er the flurried manes,
    Ply well the rowel with faint trembling heels,
    Scampering to death at last!
FIRST KNIGHT   The enemy
    Bears his flaunt standard close upon their rear.
SECOND KNIGHT Sure of a bloody prey, seeing the fens
    Will swamp them girth-deep.
STEPHEN   Over head and ears,
    No matter! 'Tis a gallant enemy;
    How like a comet he goes streaming on.
    But we must plague him in the flank – hey, friends.
    We are well breathèd – follow!

[*Enter* EARL BALDWIN *and Soldiers, as defeated*]

STEPHEN   De Redvers!
20 What is the monstrous bugbear that can fright
    Baldwin?
BALDWIN   No scarecrow, but the fortunate star
    Of boisterous Chester, whose fell truncheon now
    Points level to the goal of victory.
    This way he comes, and if you would maintain
    Your person unaffronted by vile odds,
    Take horse, my Lord.
STEPHEN   And which way spur for life?
    Now I thank Heaven I am in the toils,
    That soldiers may bear witness how my arm
    Can burst the meshes. Not the eagle more
30 Loves to beat up against a tyrannous blast,
    Than I to meet the torrent of my foes.
    This is a brag – be't so – but if I fall,
    Carve it upon my 'scutcheon'd sepulchre.
    On, fellow soldiers! Earl of Redvers, back!
    Not twenty Earls of Chester shall browbeat
    The diadem. [*Exeunt. Alarum*]

Scene 2 *Another Part of the Field.*

[Trumpets sounding a victory. Enter GLOUCESTER, *Knights, and Forces]*

GLOUCESTER Now may we lift our bruisèd vizors up,
And take the flattering freshness of the air,
While the wide din of battle dies away
Into times past, yet to be echoed sure
In the silent pages of our chroniclers.
FIRST KNIGHT Will Stephen's death be marked there, my good Lord,
Or that we gave him lodging in yon towers?
GLOUCESTER Fain would I know the great usurper's fate.

[Enter two Captains severally]

FIRST CAPTAIN My Lord!
SECOND CAPTAIN   Most noble Earl!
FIRST CAPTAIN   The King –
SECOND CAPTAIN The Empress greets –
GLOUCESTER What of the King?
FIRST CAPTAIN   He sole and lone maintains
A hopeless bustle mid our swarming arms,
And with a nimble savageness attacks,
Escapes, makes fiercer onset, then anew
Eludes death, giving death to most that dare
Trespass within the circuit of his sword!
He must by this have fallen. Baldwin is taken;
And for the Duke of Bretagne, like a stag
He flies, for the Welsh beagles to hunt down.
God save the Empress!
GLOUCESTER   Now our dreaded Queen:
What message from her Highness?
SECOND CAPTAIN   Royal Maud
From the thronged towers of Lincoln hath looked down,
Like Pallas from the walls of Ilion,
And seen her enemies havocked at her feet.
She greets most noble Gloucester from her heart,
Entreating him, his captains, and brave knights,

To grace a banquet. The high city gates
Are envious which shall see your triumph pass;
The streets are full of music.

[*Enter* SECOND KNIGHT]

GLOUCESTER   Whence come you?
SECOND KNIGHT From Stephen, my good Prince –
   Stephen! Stephen!
GLOUCESTER Why do you make such echoing of his name?
SECOND KNIGHT Because I think, my lord, he is no man,
   But a fierce demon, 'nointed safe from wounds,
   And misbaptizèd with a Christian name.
GLOUCESTER A mighty soldier! – Does he still hold out?
SECOND KNIGHT He shames our victory. His valour still
   Keeps elbow-room amid our eager swords,
   And holds our bladed falchions all aloof –
   His gleaming battle-axe being slaughter-sick,
   Smote on the morion of a Flemish knight,
   Broke short in his hand; upon the which he flung
   The heft away with such a vengeful force,
   It paunched the Earl of Chester's horse, who then
   Spleen-hearted came in full career at him.
GLOUCESTER Did no one take him at a vantage then?
SECOND KNIGHT Three then with tiger leap upon him flew,
   Whom, with his sword swift-drawn and nimbly held,
   He stung away again, and stood to breathe,
   Smiling. Anon upon him rushed once more
   A throng of foes, and in this renewed strife,
   My sword met his and snapped off at the hilts.
GLOUCESTER Come, lead me to this Mars – and let us move
   In silence, not insulting his sad doom
   With clamorous trumpets. To the Empress bear
   My salutation as befits the time.

[*Exeunt* GLOUCESTER *and Forces*]

Scene 3 [*The Field of Battle. Enter* STEPHEN *unarmed*]

STEPHEN Another sword! And what if I could seize
One from Bellona's gleaming armoury,
Or choose the fairest of her sheavèd spears!
Where are my enemies? Here, close at hand,
Here comes the testy brood. O, for a sword!
I'm faint – a biting sword! A noble sword!
A hedge-stake – or a ponderous stone to hurl
With brawny vengeance, like the labourer Cain.
Come on! Farewell my kingdom, and all hail
10 Thou superb, plumed, and helmeted renown,
All hail! I would not truck this brilliant day
To rule in Pylos with a Nestor's beard –
Come on!

[*Enter* DE KAIMS *and Knights, etc.*]

DE KAIMS Is't madness, or a hunger after death,
That makes thee thus unarmed throw taunts at us?
Yield, Stephen, or my sword's point dips in
The gloomy current of a traitor's heart.
STEPHEN Do it, De Kaims, I will not budge an inch.
DE KAIMS Yes, of thy madness thou shalt take the meed.
STEPHEN Darest thou?
DE KAIMS   How dare, against a man disarmed?
20 STEPHEN What weapon has the lion but himself?
Come not near me, De Kaims, for by the price
Of all the glory I have won this day,
Being a king, I will not yield alive
To any but the second man of the realm,
Robert of Gloucester.
DE KAIMS   Thou shalt vail to me.
STEPHEN Shall I, when I have sworn against it, sir?
Thou think'st it brave to take a breathing king,
That, on a court-day bowed to haughty Maud,
The awèd presence-chamber may be bold
30 To whisper, there's the man who took alive

KING STEPHEN: I . 4

Stephen – me – prisoner. Certes, De Kaims,
The ambition is a noble one.
DE KAIMS   'Tis true,
And, Stephen, I must compass it.
STEPHEN   No, no,
Do not tempt me to throttle you on the gorge,
Or with my gauntlet crush your hollow breast,
Just when your knighthood is grown ripe and full
For lordship.
A SOLDIER   Is an honest yeoman's spear
Of no use at a need? Take that.
STEPHEN   Ah, dastard!
DE KAIMS What, you are vulnerable! my prisoner!
40 STEPHEN No, not yet. I disclaim it, and demand
Death as a sovereign right unto a king
Who 'sdains to yield to any but his peer,
If not in title, yet in noble deeds,
The Earl of Gloucester. Stab to the hilts, De Kaims,
For I will never by mean hands be led
From this so famous field. Do ye hear! Be quick!

[*Trumpets. Enter the* EARL OF CHESTER *and Knights*]

Scene 4 *A Presence Chamber*.
[QUEEN MAUD *in a Chair of State, the* EARLS OF
GLOUCESTER *and* CHESTER, *Lords, Attendants*]

MAUD Gloucester, no more: I will behold that Boulogne:
Set him before me. Not for the poor sake
Of regal pomp and a vainglorious hour,
As thou with wary speech, yet near enough,
Hast hinted.
GLOUCESTER Faithful counsel have I given;
If wary, for your Highness' benefit.
MAUD The Heavens forbid that I should not think so,
For by thy valour have I won this realm,
Which by thy wisdom I will ever keep.
10 To sage advisers let me ever bend
A meek attentive ear, so that they treat
Of the wide kingdom's rule and government,

>   Not trenching on our actions personal.
>   Advised, not schooled, I would be; and henceforth
>   Spoken to in clear, plain, and open terms,
>   Not sideways sermoned at.
> GLOUCESTER   Then, in plain terms,
>   Once more for the fallen king –
> MAUD   Your pardon, brother,
>   I would no more of that; for, as I said,
>   'Tis not for worldly pomp I wish to see
>   The rebel, but as dooming judge to give
>   A sentence something worthy of his guilt.
> GLOUCESTER If 't must be so, I'll bring him to your
>   presence. [*Exit* GLOUCESTER]
> MAUD A meaner summoner might do as well –
>   My Lord of Chester, is't true what I hear
>   Of Stephen of Boulogne, our prisoner,
>   That he, as a fit penance for his crimes,
>   Eats wholesome, sweet, and palatable food
>   Off Gloucester's golden dishes – drinks pure wine,
>   Lodges soft?
> CHESTER   More than that, my gracious Queen,
>   Has angered me. The noble Earl, methinks,
>   Full soldier as he is, and without peer
>   In counsel, dreams too much among his books.
>   It may read well, but sure 'tis out of date
>   To play the Alexander with Darius.
> MAUD Truth! I think so. By Heavens it shall not last!
> CHESTER It would amaze your Highness now to mark
>   How Gloucester overstrains his courtesy
>   To that crime-loving rebel, that Boulogne –
> MAUD That ingrate!
> CHESTER   For whose vast ingratitude
>   To our late sovereign lord, your noble sire,
>   The generous Earl condoles in his mishaps,
>   And with a sort of lackeying friendliness,
>   Talks off the mighty frowning from his brow,
>   Woos him to hold a duet in a smile,
>   Or, if it please him, play an hour at chess –

MAUD A perjured slave!
CHESTER   And for his perjury,
  Gloucester has fit rewards – nay, I believe,
  He sets his bustling household's wits at work
  For flatteries to ease this Stephen's hours,
50 And make a heaven of his purgatory;
  Adorning bondage with the pleasant gloss
  Of feasts and music, and all idle shows
  Of indoor pageantry; while siren whispers,
  Predestined for his ear, 'scape as half-checked
  From lips the courtliest and the rubiest
  Of all the realm, admiring of his deeds.
MAUD A frost upon his summer!
CHESTER   A queen's nod
  Can make his June December. Here he comes. . . .

'This living hand, now warm and capable'

This living hand, now warm and capable
Of earnest grasping, would, if it were cold
And in the icy silence of the tomb,
So haunt thy days and chill thy dreaming nights
That thou would wish thine own heart dry of blood
So in my veins red life might stream again,
And thou be conscience-calmed – see here it is –
I hold it towards you.

The Cap and Bells; or, The Jealousies
A FAERY TALE – UNFINISHED

I

  In midmost Ind, beside Hydaspes cool,
  There stood, or hovered, tremulous in the air,
  A faery city, 'neath the potent rule
  Of Emperor Elfinan – famed everywhere
  For love of mortal women, maidens fair,

Whose lips were solid, whose soft hands were made
Of a fit mould and beauty, ripe and rare,
To pamper his slight wooing, warm yet staid:
He loved girls smooth as shades, but hated a mere shade.

II

This was a crime forbidden by the law;
And all the priesthood of his city wept,
For ruin and dismay they well foresaw,
If impious prince no bound or limit kept,
And faery Zendervester overstepped.
They wept, he sinned, and still he would sin on,
They dreamt of sin, and he sinned while they slept;
In vain the pulpit thundered at the throne,
Caricature was vain, and vain the tart lampoon.

III

Which seeing, his high court of parliament
Laid a remonstrance at his Highness' feet,
Praying his royal senses to content
Themselves with what in faery land was sweet,
Befitting best that shade with shade should meet:
Whereat, to calm their fears, he promised soon
From mortal tempters all to make retreat –
Ay, even on the first of the new moon,
An immaterial wife to espouse as heaven's boon.

IV

Meantime he sent a fluttering embassy
To Pigmio, of Imaus sovereign,
To half beg, and half demand, respectfully,
The hand of his fair daughter Bellanaine.
An audience had, and speeching done, they gain
Their point, and bring the weeping bride away;
Whom, with but one attendant, safely lain
Upon their wings, they bore in bright array,
While little harps were touched by many a lyric fay.

V

As in old pictures tender cherubim
A child's soul through the sapphired canvas bear,
So, through a real heaven, on they swim
With the sweet princess on her plumaged lair,
Speed giving to the winds her lustrous hair;
And so she journeyed, sleeping or awake,
Save when, for healthful exercise and air,
She chose to *promener à l'aile*, or take
A pigeon's somerset, for sport or change's sake.

VI

'Dear Princess, do not whisper me so loud,'
Quoth Corallina, nurse and confidant,
'Do not you see there, lurking in a cloud,
Close at your back, that sly old Crafticant?
He hears a whisper plainer than a rant.
Dry up your tears, and do not look so blue;
He's Elfinan's great state-spy militant,
His running, lying, flying footman too –
Dear mistress, let him have no handle against you!

VII

'Show him a mouse's tail, and he will guess,
With metaphysic swiftness, at the mouse;
Show him a garden, and with speed no less,
He'll surmise sagely of a dwelling house,
And plot, in the same minute, how to chouse
The owner out of it; show him a – ' 'Peace!
Peace! nor contrive thy mistress' ire to rouse!'
Returned the Princess, 'my tongue shall not cease
Till from this hated match I get a free release.

VIII

'Ah, beauteous mortal!' 'Hush!' quoth Coralline,
'Really you must not talk of him, indeed.'
'*You* hush!' replied the mistress, with a shine
Of anger in her eyes, enough to breed
In stouter hearts than nurse's fear and dread:

'Twas not the glance itself made Nursey flinch,
But of its threat she took the utmost heed,
Not liking in her heart an hour-long pinch,
Or a sharp needle run into her back an inch.

IX

So she was silenced, and fair Bellanaine,
Writhing her little body with ennui,
Continued to lament and to complain,
That Fate, cross-purposing, should let her be
Ravished away far from her dear countree;
That all her feelings should be set at naught,
In trumping up this match so hastily,
With lowland blood; and lowland blood she thought
Poison, as every staunch true-born Imaian ought.

X

Sorely she grieved, and wetted three or four
White Provence rose-leaves with her faery tears,
But not for this cause – alas! she had more
Bad reasons for her sorrow, as appears
In the famed memoirs of a thousand years,
Written by Crafticant, and publishèd
By Parpaglion and Co. (those sly compeers
Who raked up every fact against the dead)
In Scarab Street, Panthea, at the Jubal's Head.

XI

Where, after a long hypercritic howl
Against the vicious manners of the age,
He goes on to expose, with heart and soul,
What vice in this or that year was the rage,
Backbiting all the world in every page;
With special strictures on the horrid crime
(Sectioned and subsectioned with learning sage),
Of faeries stooping on their wings sublime
To kiss a mortal's lips, when such were in their prime.

XII

100 Turn to the copious index, you will find
Somewhere in the column, headed letter B,
The name of Bellanaine, if you're not blind;
Then pray refer to the text, and you will see
An article made up of calumny
Against this highland princess, rating her
For giving way, so over-fashionably,
To this new-fangled vice, which seems a burr
Stuck in his moral throat, no coughing e'er could stir.

XIII

There he says plainly that she loved a man!
110 That she around him fluttered, flirted, toyed,
Before her marriage with great Elfinan;
That after marriage too, she never joyed
In husband's company, but still employed
Her wits to 'scape away to Angle-land;
Where lived the youth, who worried and annoyed
Her tender heart, and its warm ardours fanned
To such a dreadful blaze, her side would scorch her hand.

XIV

But let us leave this idle tittle-tattle
To waiting-maids, and bedroom coteries,
120 Nor till fit time against her fame wage battle.
Poor Elfinan is very ill at ease –
Let us resume his subject if you please:
For it may comfort and console him much
To rhyme and syllable his miseries;
Poor Elfinan! whose cruel fate was such,
He sat and cursed a bride he knew he could not touch.

XV

Soon as (according to his promises)
The bridal embassy had taken wing,
And vanished, bird-like, o'er the suburb trees,
130 The Emperor, empierced with the sharp sting
Of love, retirèd, vexed and murmuring

Like any drone shut from the fair bee-queen,
Into his cabinet, and there did fling
His limbs upon a sofa, full of spleen,
And damned his House of Commons, in complete chagrin.

XVI

'I'll trounce some of the members,' cried the Prince,
'I'll put a mark against some rebel names,
I'll make the Opposition benches wince,
I'll show them very soon, to all their shames,
What 'tis to smother up a Prince's flames;
That ministers should join in it, I own,
Surprises me! – they too at these high games!
Am I an Emperor? Do I wear a crown?
Imperial Elfinan, go hang thyself or drown!

XVII

'I'll trounce 'em! – there's the square-cut chancellor,
His son shall never touch that bishopric;
And for the nephew of old Palfior,
I'll show him that his speeches made me sick,
And give the colonelcy to Phalaric;
The tip-toe marquis, moral and gallant,
Shall lodge in shabby taverns upon tick;
And for the Speaker's second cousin's aunt,
She shan't be maid of honour – by heaven that she shan't!

XVIII

'I'll shirk the Duke of A.; I'll cut his brother;
I'll give no garter to his eldest son;
I won't speak to his sister or his mother!
The Viscount B. shall live at cut-and-run;
But how in the world can I contrive to stun
That fellow's voice, which plagues me worse than any,
That stubborn fool, that impudent state-dun,
Who sets down every sovereign as a zany –
That vulgar commoner, Esquire Biancopany?

XIX

'Monstrous affair! Pshaw! pah! what ugly minx
Will they fetch from Imaus for my bride?
Alas! my wearied heart within me sinks,
To think that I must be so near allied
To a cold dullard fay– ah, woe betide!
Ah, fairest of all human loveliness!
Sweet Bertha! what crime can it be to glide
About the fragrant pleatings of thy dress,
Or kiss thine eyes, or count thy locks, tress after tress?'

XX

So said, one minute's while his eyes remained
Half lidded, piteous, languid, innocent;
But, in a wink, their splendour they regained,
Sparkling revenge with amorous fury blent.
Love thwarted in bad temper oft has vent:
He rose, he stamped his foot, he rang the bell,
And ordered some death-warrants to be sent
For signature – somewhere the tempest fell,
As many a poor felon does not live to tell.

XXI

'At the same time Eban' (this was his page,
A fay of colour, slave from top to toe,
Sent as a present, while yet under age,
From the Viceroy of Zanguebar – wise, slow,
His speech, his only words were 'yes' and 'no',
But swift of look, and foot, and wing was he),
'At the same time, Eban, this instant go
To Hum the soothsayer, whose name I see
Among the fresh arrivals in our empery.

XXII

'Bring Hum to me! But stay – here, take my ring,
The pledge of favour, that he not suspect
Any foul play, or awkward murdering,
Though I have bowstrung many of his sect;
Throw in a hint, that if he should neglect

One hour, the next shall see him in my grasp,
And the next after that shall see him necked,
Or swallowed by my hunger-starvèd asp –
And mention ('tis as well) the torture of the wasp.'

XXIII

These orders given, the Prince, in half a pet,
Let o'er the silk his propping elbow slide,
Caught up his little legs, and, in a fret,
Fell on the sofa on his royal side.
The slave retreated backwards, humble-eyed,
And with a slave-like silence closed the door,
And to old Hum through street and alley hied;
He 'knew the city', as we say, of yore,
For shortest cuts and turns, was nobody knew more.

XXIV

It was the time when wholesale houses close
Their shutters with a moody sense of wealth,
But retail dealers, diligent, let loose
The gas (objected to on score of health),
Conveyed in little soldered pipes by stealth,
And make it flare in many a brilliant form,
That all the powers of darkness it repell'th,
Which to the oil-trade doth great scathe and harm,
And supersedeth quite the use of the glow-worm.

XXV

Eban, untempted by the pastry-cooks
(Of pastry he got store within the palace),
With hasty steps, wrapped cloak, and solemn looks,
Incognito upon his errand sallies,
His smelling-bottle ready for the alleys.
He passed the hurdy-gurdies with disdain,
Vowing he'd have them sent on board the galleys;
Just as he made his vow, it 'gan to rain,
Therefore he called a coach, and bade it drive amain.

XXVI

'I'll pull the string,' said he, and further said,
'Polluted Jarvey! Ah, thou filthy hack!
Whose springs of life are all dried up and dead,
Whose linsey-woolsey lining hangs all slack,
Whose rug is straw, whose wholeness is a crack;
And evermore thy steps go clatter-clitter;
Whose glass once up can never be got back,
Who prov'st, with jolting arguments and bitter,
That 'tis of modern use to travel in a litter.

XXVII

'Thou inconvenience! thou hungry crop
For all corn! thou snail-creeper to and fro,
Who while thou goest ever seem'st to stop,
And fiddle-faddle standest while you go;
I' the morning, freighted with a weight of woe,
Unto some lazar-house thou journeyest,
And in the evening tak'st a double row
Of dowdies, for some dance or party dressed,
Besides the goods meanwhile thou movest east and west.

XXVIII

'By thy ungallant bearing and sad mien,
An inch appears the utmost thou couldst budge;
Yet at the slightest nod, or hint, or sign,
Round to the curb-stone patient dost thou trudge,
Schooled in a beckon, learned in a nudge,
A dull-eyed Argus watching for a fare;
Quiet and plodding, thou dost bear no grudge
To whisking tilburies, or phaetons rare,
Curricles, or mail-coaches, swift beyond compare.'

XXIX

Philosophizing thus, he pulled the check,
And bade the Coachman wheel to such a street,
Who, turning much his body, more his neck,
Louted full low, and hoarsely did him greet:
'Certes, Monsieur were best take to his feet,

… Seeing his servant can no further drive
For press of coaches, that tonight here meet
Many as bees about a straw-capped hive,
When first for April honey into faint flowers they dive.'

XXX

Eban then paid his fare, and tip-toe went
To Hum's hotel; and, as he on did pass
With head inclined, each dusky lineament
Showed in the pearl-paved street, as in a glass;
His purple vest, that ever peeping was
Rich from the fluttering crimson of his cloak,
His silvery trousers, and his silken sash
Tied in a burnished knot, their semblance took
Upon the mirrored walls, wherever he might look.

XXXI

He smiled at self, and, smiling, showed his teeth,
And seeing his white teeth, he smiled the more;
Lifted his eye-brows, spurned the path beneath,
Showed teeth again, and smiled as heretofore,
Until he knocked at the magician's door;
Where, till the porter answered, might be seen,
In the clear panel, more he could adore –
His turban wreathed of gold, and white, and green,
Mustachios, ear-ring, nose-ring, and his sabre keen.

XXXII

'Does not your master give a rout tonight?'
Quoth the dark page. 'Oh, no!' returned the Swiss,
'Next door but one to us, upon the right,
The *Magazin des Modes* now open is
Against the Emperor's wedding – and, sir, this
My master finds a monstrous horrid bore,
As he retired, an hour ago I wis,
With his best beard and brimstone, to explore
And cast a quiet figure in his second floor.

XXXIII

'Gad! he's obliged to stick to business!
For chalk, I hear, stands at a pretty price;
And as for aqua-vitae – there's a mess!
The *dentes sapientiae* of mice,
Our barber tells me too, are on the rise –
Tinder's a lighter article – nitre pure
Goes off like lightning – grains of Paradise
At an enormous figure! Stars not sure! –
Zodiac will not move without a sly douceur!

XXXIV

'Venus won't stir a peg without a fee,
And master is too partial, *entre nous*,
To –' 'Hush – hush!' cried Eban, 'sure that is he
Coming down stairs. By St Bartholomew!
As backwards as he can – is't something new?
Or is't his custom, in the name of fun?'
'He always comes down backward, with one shoe',
Returned the porter, 'off, and one shoe on,
Like, saving shoe for sock or stocking, my man John!'

XXXV

It was indeed the great Magician,
Feeling, with careful toe, for every stair,
And retrograding careful as he can,
Backwards and downwards from his own two pair:
'Salpietro!' exclaimed Hum, 'is the dog there?
He's always in my way upon the mat!'
'He's in the kitchen, or the Lord knows where,'
Replied the Swiss, 'the nasty, yelping brat!'
'Don't beat him!' returned Hum, and on the floor came pat.

XXXVI

Then facing right about, he saw the Page,
And said: 'Don't tell me what you want, Eban;
The Emperor is now in a huge rage –
'Tis nine to one he'll give you the rattan!

470 THE CAP AND BELLS; OR, THE JEALOUSIES

320   Let us away!' Away together ran
    The plain-dressed sage and spangled blackamoor,
    Nor rested till they stood to cool, and fan,
    And breathe themselves at the Emperor's chamber door,
When Eban thought he heard a soft imperial snore.

XXXVII

    'I thought you guessed, foretold, or prophesied,
    That's Majesty was in a raving fit?'
    'He dreams,' said Hum, 'or I have ever lied,
    That he is tearing you, sir, bit by bit.'
    'He's not asleep, and you have little wit,'
330   Replied the page, 'that little buzzing noise,
    Whate'er your palmistry may make of it,
    Comes from a play-thing of the Emperor's choice,
From a Man-Tiger-Organ, prettiest of his toys.'

XXXVIII

    Eban then ushered in the learned seer:
    Elfinan's back was turned, but, ne'ertheless,
    Both, prostrate on the carpet, ear by ear,
    Crept silently, and waited in distress,
    Knowing the Emperor's moody bitterness;
    Eban especially, who on the floor 'gan
340   Tremble and quake to death – he feared less
    A dose of senna-tea or nightmare Gorgon
Than the Emperor when he played on his Man-Tiger-
        Organ.

XXXIX

    They kissed nine times the carpet's velvet face
    Of glossy silk, soft, smooth, and meadow-green,
    Where the close eye in deep rich fur might trace
    A silver tissue, scantly to be seen,
    As daisies lurked in June-grass, buds in treen.
    Sudden the music ceased, sudden the hand
    Of majesty, by dint of passion keen,
350   Doubled into a common fist, went grand,
And knocked down three cut glasses, and his best inkstand.

XL

 Then turning round, he saw those trembling two.
'Eban,' said he, 'as slaves should taste the fruits
Of diligence, I shall remember you
Tomorrow, or the next day, as time suits,
In a finger conversation with my mutes –
Begone! – for you, Chaldean! here remain!
Fear not, quake not, and as good wine recruits
A conjurer's spirits, what cup will you drain?
Sherry in silver, hock in gold, or glassed champagne?'

XLI

 'Commander of the Faithful!' answered Hum,
'In preference to these, I'll merely taste
A thimble-full of old Jamaica rum.'
'A simple boon!' said Elfinan, 'thou mayst
Have Nantz, with which my morning-coffee's laced.'
'I'll have a glass of Nantz, then,' said the Seer,
'Made racy (sure my boldness is misplaced!)
With the third part (yet that is drinking dear!)
Of the least drop of *crème de citron*, crystal clear.'

XLII

 'I pledge you, Hum! and pledge my dearest love,
My Bertha!' 'Bertha! Bertha!' cried the sage,
'I know a many Berthas!' 'Mine's above
All Berthas!' sighed the Emperor. 'I engage,'
Said Hum, 'in duty, and in vassalage,
To mention all the Berthas in the Earth –
There's Bertha Watson, and Miss Bertha Page,
This famed for languid eyes, and that for mirth –
There's Bertha Blount of York – and Bertha Knox of Perth.'

XLIII

 'You seem to know – ' 'I do know,' answered Hum,
'Your Majesty's in love with some fine girl
Named Bertha, but her surname will not come,
Without a little conjuring.' ''Tis Pearl,

'Tis Bertha Pearl what makes my brains so whirl;
  And she is softer, fairer than her name!'
'Where does she live?' asked Hum. 'Her fair locks curl
  So brightly, they put all our fays to shame! –
Live? – O! at Canterbury, with her old grand-dame.'

XLIV

'Good! good!' cried Hum, 'I've known her from a child!
  She is a changeling of my management.
She was born at midnight in an Indian wild;
  Her mother's screams with the striped tiger's blent,
  While the torch-bearing slaves a halloo sent
Into the jungles; and her palanquin,
  Rested amid the desert's dreariment,
  Shook with her agony, till fair were seen
The little Bertha's eyes ope on the stars serene.'

XLV

'I can't say,' said the monarch, 'that may be
  Just as it happened, true or else a bam!
Drink up your brandy, and sit down by me,
  Feel, feel my pulse, how much in love I am;
  And if your science is not all a sham,
Tell me some means to get the lady here.'
  'Upon my honour!' said the son of Cham,
  'She is my dainty changeling, near and dear,'
Although her story sounds at first a little queer.'

XLVI

'Convey her to me, Hum, or by my crown,
  My sceptre, and my cross-surmounted globe,
I'll knock you' – 'Does your majesty mean – *down*?
  No, no, you never could my feelings probe
  To such a depth!' The Emperor took his robe,
And wept upon its purple palatine,
  While Hum continued, shamming half a sob,
  'In Canterbury doth your lady shine?
But let me cool your brandy with a little wine.'

XLVII

Whereat a narrow Flemish glass he took,
That once belonged to Admiral de Witt,
Admired it with a connoisseuring look,
And with the ripest claret crownèd it,
And, ere one lively bead could burst and flit,
He turned it quickly, nimbly upside down,
His mouth being held conveniently fit
To save 'the creature'. 'Best in all the town!'
He said, smacked his moist lips, and gave a pleasant frown.

XLVIII

'Ah! good my Prince, weep not!' And then again
He filled a bumper. 'Great Sire, do not weep!
Your pulse is shocking, but I'll ease your pain.'
'Fetch me that Ottoman, and prithee keep
Your voice low,' said the Emperor, 'and steep
Some lady's-fingers nice in Candy wine;
And prithee, Hum, behind the screen do peep
For the rose-water vase, magician mine!
And sponge my forehead – so my love doth make me pine.

XLIX

'Ah, cursèd Bellanaine!' 'Don't think of her,'
Rejoined the Mago, 'but on Bertha muse;
For, by my choicest best barometer,
You shall not throttled be in marriage noose.
I've said it, Sire; you only have to choose
Bertha or Bellanaine.' So saying, he drew
From the left pocket of his threadbare hose,
A sampler hoarded slyly, good as new,
Holding it by his thumb and finger full in view.

L

'Sire, this is Bertha Pearl's neat handy-work,
Her *name*, see here, *Midsummer, ninety-one*.'
Elfinan snatched it with a sudden jerk,
And wept as if he never would have done,
Honouring with royal tears the poor homespun,

Whereon were broidered tigers with black eyes,
And long-tailed pheasants, and a rising sun,
Plenty of posies, great stags, butterflies
Bigger than stags, a moon – with other mysteries.

LI

The monarch handled o'er and o'er again
These day-school hieroglyphics with a sigh;
Somewhat in sadness, but pleased in the main,
Till this oracular couplet met his eye
Astounded: *Cupid I – do thee defy!*
It was too much. He shrunk back in his chair,
Grew pale as death, and fainted – very nigh!
'Pho! nonsense!' exclaimed Hum, 'now don't despair;
She does not mean it really. Cheer up, hearty – there!

LII

'And listen to my words. You say you won't,
On any terms, marry Miss Bellanaine;
It goes against your conscience – good! Well, don't.
You say you love a mortal. I would fain
Persuade your honour's Highness to refrain
From peccadilloes. But, Sire, as I say,
What good would that do? And, to be more plain,
You would do me a mischief some odd day,
Cut off my ears and hands, or head too, by my fay!

LIII

'Besides, manners forbid that I should pass any
Vile strictures on the conduct of a prince
Who should indulge his genius, if he has any,
Not, like a subject, foolish matters mince.
Now I think on't, perhaps I could convince
Your Majesty there is no crime at all
In loving pretty little Bertha, since
She's very delicate – not over tall –
A faery's hand, and in the waist, why – very small.'

LIV

'Ring the repeater, gentle Hum!' ''Tis five,'
Said gentle Hum, 'the nights draw in apace;
The little birds I hear are all alive;
I see the dawning touched upon your face;
Shall I put out the candles, please your Grace?'
'Do put them out, and, without more ado,
Tell me how I may that sweet girl embrace –
How you can bring her to me.' 'That's for you,
Great Emperor! to adventure, like a lover true.'

LV

'I fetch her!' – 'Yes, an't like your Majesty;
And as she would be frightened wide awake
To travel such a distance through the sky,
Use of some soft manoeuvre you must make,
For your convenience, and her dear nerves' sake.
Nice way would be to bring her in a swoon,
Anon, I'll tell what course were best to take;
You must away this morning.' 'Hum! so soon?'
'Sire, you must be in Kent by twelve o'clock at noon.'

LVI

At this great Caesar started on his feet,
Lifted his wings, and stood attentive-wise.
'Those wings to Canterbury you must beat,
If you hold Bertha as a worthy prize.
Look in the Almanack – *Moore* never lies –
April the twenty-fourth, this coming day,
Now breathing its new bloom upon the skies,
Will end in St Mark's Eve – you must away,
For on that eve alone can you the maid convey.'

LVII

Then the magician solemnly 'gan frown,
So that his frost-white eyebrows, beetling low,
Shaded his deep-green eyes, and wrinkles brown
Plaited upon his furnace-scorchèd brow:
Forth from the hood that hung his neck below,

476 THE CAP AND BELLS; OR, THE JEALOUSIES

510 He lifted a bright casket of pure gold,
  Touched a spring-lock, and there in wool, or snow
  Charmed into ever-freezing, lay an old
And legend-leavèd book, mysterious to behold.

LVIII
 'Take this same book, – it will not bite you, Sire –
  There, put it underneath your royal arm;
  Though it's a pretty weight it will not tire,
  But rather on your journey keep you warm.
  This is the magic, this the potent charm,
  That shall drive Bertha to a fainting fit!
520 When the time comes, don't feel the least alarm,
  Uplift her from the ground, and swiftly flit
Back to your palace, where I wait for guerdon fit.'

LIX
 'What shall I do with that same book?' 'Why merely
  Lay it on Bertha's table, close beside
  Her work-box, and 'twill help your purpose dearly.
  I say no more.' 'Or good or ill betide,
  Through the wide air to Kent this morn I glide!'
  Exclaimed the Emperor. 'When I return,
  Ask what you will – I'll give you my new bride!
530 And take some more wine, Hum – O Heavens! I burn
To be upon the wing! Now, now, that minx I spurn!'

LX
 'Leave her to me,' rejoined the magian,
  'But how shall I account, illustrous fay!
  For thine imperial absence? Pho! I can
  Say you are very sick, and bar the way
  To your so loving courtiers for one day;
  If either of their two Archbishops' graces
  Should talk of extreme unction, I shall say
  You do not like cold pig with Latin phrases,
540 Which never should be used but in alarming cases.'

LXI

'Open the window, Hum; I'm ready now!'
'Zooks!' exclaimed Hum, as up the sash he drew,
'Behold, your Majesty, upon the brow
Of yonder hill, what crowds of people!' 'Whew!
The monster's always after something new,'
Returned his Highness, 'they are piping hot
To see my pigsney Bellanaine. Hum! do
Tighten my belt a little – so, so – not
Too tight. The book! – my wand! – so, nothing is forgot.'

LXII

550 'Wounds! how they shout!' said Hum, 'and there, – see, see!
The Ambassador's returned from Pigmio!
The morning's very fine – uncommonly!
See, past the skirts of yon white cloud they go,
Tinging it with soft crimsons! Now below
The sable-pointed heads of firs and pines
They dip, move on, and with them moves a glow
Along the forest side! Now amber lines
Reach the hill top, and now throughout the valley shines.'

LXIII

'Why, Hum, you're getting quite poetical!
560 Those *nows* you managed in a special style.'
'If ever you have leisure, Sire, you shall
See scraps of mine will make it worth your while,
Tit-bits for Phoebus! – yes, you well may smile.
Hark! Hark! the bells!' 'A little further yet,
Good Hum, and let me view this mighty coil.'
Then the great Emperor full graceful set
His elbow for a prop, and snuffed his mignonette.

LXIV

The morn is full of holiday: loud bells
With rival clamours ring from every spire;
570 Cunningly-stationed music dies and swells
In echoing places; when the winds respire,

Light flags stream out like gauzy tongues of fire;
A metropolitan murmur, lifeful, warm,
Comes from the northern suburbs; rich attire
Freckles with red and gold the moving swarm;
While here and there clear trumpets blow a keen alarm.

LXV

And now the faery escort was seen clear,
Like the old pageant of Aurora's train,
Above a pearl-built minster, hovering near:
First wily Crafticant, the chamberlain,
Balanced upon his grey-grown pinions twain,
His slender wand officially revealed;
Then black gnomes scattering sixpences like rain;
Then pages three and three; and next, slave-held,
The Imaian 'scutcheon bright – one mouse in argent field.

LXVI

Gentlemen pensioners next; and after them,
A troop of wingèd Janizaries flew;
Then slaves, as presents bearing many a gem;
Then twelve physicians fluttering two and two;
And next a chaplain in a cassock new;
Then Lords in waiting; then (what head not reels
For pleasure?) the fair Princess in full view,
Borne upon wings – and very pleased she feels
To have such splendour dance attendance at her heels.

LXVII

For there was more magnificence behind.
She waved her handkerchief. 'Ah, very grand!'
Cried Elfinan, and closed the window-blind.
'And, Hum, we must not shilly-shally stand –
Adieu! adieu! I'm off for Angle-land!
I say, old Hocus, have you such a thing
About you – feel your pockets, I command –
I want, this instant, an invisible ring –
Thank you, old mummy! Now securely I take wing.'

LXVIII

Then Elfinan swift vaulted from the floor,
And lighted graceful on the window-sill;
Under one arm the magic book he bore,
The other he could wave about at will;
Pale was his face, he still looked very ill.
He bowed at Bellanaine, and said, 'Poor Bell!
Farewell! farewell! and if for ever! still
For ever fare thee well!' – and then he fell
A-laughing! – snapped his fingers! shame it is to tell!

LXIX

'By'r Lady! he is gone!' cries Hum, 'and I
(I own it) have made too free with his wine;
Old Crafticant will smoke me by the bye!
This room is full of jewels as a mine –
Dear valuable creatures, how ye shine!
Sometime today I must contrive a minute,
If Mercury propitiously incline,
To examine his scrutoire, and see what's in it,
For of superfluous diamonds I as well may thin it.

LXX

'The Emperor's horrid bad – yes, that's my cue!'
Some histories say that this was Hum's last speech;
That, being fuddled, he went reeling through
The corridor, and scarce upright could reach
The stair-head; that being glutted as a leech,
And used, as we ourselves have just now said,
To manage stairs reversely, like a peach
Too ripe, he fell, being puzzled in his head
With liquor and the staircase: verdict – *found stone dead*.

LXXI

This as a falsehood Crafticanto treats;
And as his style is of strange elegance,
Gentle and tender, full of soft conceits
(Much like our Boswell's) we will take a glance
At his sweet prose, and, if we can, make dance

His woven periods into careless rhyme.
O, little faery Pegasus! rear – prance –
Trot round the quarto – ordinary time!
March, little Pegasus, with pawing hoof sublime!

LXXII

Well, let us see – *tenth book and chapter nine* –
Thus Crafticant pursues his diary:
''Twas twelve o'clock at night, the weather fine,
Latitude thirty-six; our scouts descry
A flight of starlings making rapidly
Toward Tibet. Mem. – birds fly in the night;
From twelve to half-past – wings not fit to fly
For a thick fog – the Princess sulky quite
Called for an extra shawl, and gave her nurse a bite.

LXXIII

'Five minutes before one – brought down a moth
With my new double-barrel – stewed the thighs
And made a very tolerable broth –
Princess turned dainty; to our great surprise,
Altered her mind, and thought it very nice.
Seeing her pleasant, tried her with a pun,
She frowned. A monstrous owl across us flies
About this time – a sad old figure of fun;
Bad omen – this new match can't be a happy one.

LXXIV

'From two to half-past, dusky way we made,
Above the plains of Gobi – desert, bleak;
Beheld afar off, in the hooded shade
Of darkness, a great mountain (strange to speak)
Spitting, from forth its sulphur-baken peak,
A fan-shaped burst of blood-red, arrowy fire,
Turbaned with smoke, which still away did reek,
Solid and black from that eternal pyre,
Upon the laden winds that scantly could respire.

LXXV

'Just upon three o'clock a falling star
Created an alarm among our troop,
Killed a man-cook, a page, and broke a jar,
A tureen, and three dishes, at one swoop,
Then passing by the Princess, singed her hoop.
Could not conceive what Coralline was at –
She clapped her hands three times and cried out
  "Whoop!"
Some strange Imaian custom. A large bat
Came sudden 'fore my face, and brushed against my hat.

LXXVI

'Five minutes thirteen seconds after three,
Far in the west a mighty fire broke out.
Conjectured, on the instant, it might be
The city of Balk – 'twas Balk beyond all doubt.
A griffin, wheeling here and there about,
Kept reconnoitring us – doubled our guard –
Lighted our torches, and kept up a shout,
Till he sheered off – the Princess very scared –
And many on their marrowbones for death prepared.

LXXVII

'At half-past three arose the cheerful moon –
Bivouacked for four minutes on a cloud –
Where from the earth we heard a lively tune
Of tambourines and pipes, serene and loud,
While on a flowery lawn a brilliant crowd
Cinque-parted danced, some half-asleep reposed
Beneath the green-faned cedars, some did shroud
In silken tents, and 'mid light fragrance dozed,
Or on the open turf their soothèd eyelids closed.

LXXVIII

'Dropped my gold watch, and killed a kettledrum –
It went for apoplexy – foolish folks! –
Left it to pay the piper – a good sum
(I've got a conscience, maugre people's jokes).

>   To scrape a little favour 'gan to coax
>   Her Highness' pug-dog – got a sharp rebuff.
> 700 She wished a game at whist – made three revokes –
>   Turned from myself, her partner, in a huff.
> His Majesty will know her temper time enough.

LXXIX

>   'She cried for chess – I played a game with her.
>   Castled her king with such a vixen look,
>   It bodes ill to his Majesty (refer
>   To the second chapter of my fortieth book,
>   And see what hoity-toity airs she took).
>   At half-past four the morn essayed to beam –
>   Saluted, as we passed, an early rook –
> 710 The Princess fell asleep, and, in her dream,
> Talked of one Master Hubert, deep in her esteem.

LXXX

>   'About this time, making delightful way,
>   Shed a quill-feather from my larboard wing –
>   Wished, trusted, hoped 'twas no sign of decay –
>   Thank heaven, I'm hearty yet! – 'twas no such thing.
>   At five the golden light began to spring,
>   With fiery shudder through the bloomèd east.
>   At six we heard Panthea's churches ring –
>   The city all her unhived swarms had cast,
> 720 To watch our grand approach, and hail us as we passed.

LXXXI

>   'As flowers turn their faces to the sun,
>   So on our flight with hungry eyes they gaze,
>   And, as we shaped our course, this, that way run,
>   With mad-cap pleasure, or hand-clasped amaze.
>   Sweet in the air a mild-toned music plays,
>   And progresses through its own labyrinth.
>   Buds gathered from the green spring's middle-days,
>   They scattered – daisy, primrose, hyacinth –
> Or round white columns wreathed from capital to plinth.

LXXXII

730 'Onward we floated o'er the panting streets,
That seemed throughout with upheld faces paved.
Look where we will, our bird's-eye vision meets
Legions of holiday; bright standards waved,
And fluttering ensigns emulously craved
Our minute's glance; a busy thunderous roar,
From square to square, among the buildings raved,
As when the sea, at flow, gluts up once more
The craggy hollowness of a wild reefèd shore.

LXXXIII

'And "Bellanaine for ever!" shouted they,
740 While that fair Princess, from her wingèd chair,
Bowed low with high demeanour, and, to pay
Their new-blown loyalty with guerdon fair,
Still emptied, at meet distance, here and there,
A plenty horn of jewels. And here I
(Who wish to give the devil her due) declare
Against that ugly piece of calumny,
Which calls them Highland pebble-stones not worth a fly.

LXXXIV

'Still "Bellanaine!" they shouted, while we glide
'Slant to a light Ionic portico,
750 The city's delicacy, and the pride
Of our Imperial Basilic. A row
Of lords and ladies, on each hand, make show
Submissive of knee-bent obeisance,
All down the steps; and, as we entered, lo!
The strangest sight – the most unlooked-for chance –
All things turned topsy-turvy in a devil's dance.

LXXXV

''Stead of his anxious Majesty and court
At the open doors, with wide saluting eyes,
Congées and scapegraces of every sort,
760 And all the smooth routine of gallantries,
Was seen, to our immoderate surprise,

A motley crowd thick gathered in the hall,
Lords, scullions, deputy-scullions, with wild cries
Stunning the vestibule from wall to wall,
Where the Chief Justice on his knees and hands doth crawl.

LXXXVI

'Counts of the palace, and the state purveyor
Of moth's-down, to make soft the royal beds,
The Common Council and my fool Lord Mayor
Marching a-row, each other slipshod treads;
Powdered bag-wigs and ruffy-tuffy heads
Of cinder wenches meet and soil each other;
Toe crushed with heel ill-natured fighting breeds,
Frill-rumpling elbows brew up many a bother,
And fists in the short ribs keep up the yell and pother.

LXXXVII

'A Poet, mounted on the Court-Clown's back,
Rode to the Princess swift with spurring heels,
And close into her face, with rhyming clack,
Began a Prothalamion – she reels,
She falls, she faints! while laughter peals
Over her woman's weakness. "Where!" cried I,
"Where is his Majesty?" No person feels
Inclined to answer; wherefore instantly
I plunged into the crowd to find him or to die.

LXXXVIII

'Jostling my way I gained the stairs, and ran
To the first landing, where, incredible!
I met, far gone in liquor, that old man,
That vile impostor Hum –'
                          So far so well,
For we have proved the Mago never fell
Down stairs on Crafticanto's evidence;
And therefore duly shall proceed to tell,
Plain in our own original mood and tense,
The sequel of this day, though labour 'tis immense!

LXXXIX

>Now Hum, new fledged with high authority,
>Came forth to quell the hubbub in the hall. . . .

To Fanny

I

Physician Nature! let my spirit blood!
    O ease my heart of verse and let me rest;
Throw me upon thy tripod till the flood
    Of stifling numbers ebbs from my full breast.
A theme! a theme! Great Nature! give a theme;
    Let me begin my dream.
I come – I see thee, as thou standest there,
Beckon me out into the wintry air.

II

Ah! dearest love, sweet home of all my fears,
    And hopes, and joys, and panting miseries,
Tonight, if I may guess, thy beauty wears
        A smile of such delight,
        As brilliant and as bright,
    As when with ravished, aching, vassal eyes,
        Lost in a soft amaze,
        I gaze, I gaze!

III

Who now, with greedy looks, eats up my feast?
    What stare outfaces now my silver moon!
Ah! keep that hand unravished at the least;
        Let, let, the amorous burn –
        But, prithee, do not turn
    The current of your heart from me so soon.
        O save, in charity,
        The quickest pulse for me!

IV

Save it for me, sweet love! though music breathe
    Voluptuous visions into the warm air,

Though swimming through the dance's dangerous wreath,
    Be like an April day,
    Smiling and cold and gay,
30 A temperate lily, temperate as fair;
    Then, Heaven! there will be
    A warmer June for me.

V

Why, this – you'll say, my Fanny! – is not true:
  Put your soft hand upon your snowy side,
Where the heart beats; confess – 'tis nothing new –
    Must not a woman be
    A feather on the sea,
  Swayed to and fro by every wind and tide?
    Of as uncertain speed
40   As blow-ball from the mead?

VI

I know it – and to know it is despair
  To one who loves you as I love, sweet Fanny!
Whose heart goes fluttering for you everywhere,
    Nor, when away you roam,
    Dare keep its wretched home.
  Love, Love alone, has pains severe and many:
    Then, loveliest! keep me free
    From torturing jealousy.

VII

Ah! if you prize my subdued soul above
50   The poor, the fading, brief, pride of an hour,
Let none profane my Holy See of Love,
    Or with a rude hand break
    The sacramental cake;
  Let none else touch the just new-budded flower;
    If not – may my eyes close,
    Love! on their last repose.

'In after-time, a sage of mickle lore'

In after-time, a sage of mickle lore
Y-cleped Typographus, the Giant took,
And did refit his limbs as heretofore,
And made him read in many a learned book,
And into many a lively legend look;
Thereby in goodly themes so training him,
That all his brutishness he quite forsook,
When, meeting Artegall and Talus grim,
The one he struck stone-blind, the other's eyes wox dim.

Three Undated Fragments

I
I am as brisk
As a bottle of Wisk –
Ey and as nimble
As a Milliner's thimble.

II
O grant that like to Peter I
May like to Peter B,
And tell me, lovely Jesus, Y
This Peter went to C.

O grant that like to Peter I
May like to Peter B,
And tell me, lovely Jesus, Y
Old Jonah went to C.

III
They weren fully glad of their gude hap
And tasten all the pleasaunces of joy.

Doubtful Attributions

'See, the ship in the bay is riding'

See, the ship in the bay is riding,
Dearest Ellen, I go from thee –
Boldly go, in thy love confiding,
Over the deep and trackless sea:
When thy dear form no longer is near me,
This soothing thought shall at midnight cheer me:
'My love is breathing a prayer for me'.

When the thunder of war is roaring,
When the bullets around me fly,
When the rage of the tempest pouring,
Blends the billowy sea and sky,
Yet shall my heart, to fear a stranger,
Cherish its fondest hopes for thee –
This dear reflection disarming danger,
'My love is breathing a prayer for me'.

The Poet

At morn, at noon, at eve, and middle night,
   He passes forth into the charmèd air,
   With talisman to call up spirits rare
From plant, cave, rock, and fountain. To his sight
The husk of natural objects opens quite
   To the core, and every secret essence there
   Reveals the elements of good and fair,
Making him see, where Learning hath no light.

Sometimes above the gross and palpable things
    Of this diurnal sphere, his spirit flies
    On awful wing; and with its destined skies
Holds premature and mystic communings;
    Till such unearthly intercourses shed
    A visible halo round his mortal head.

Gripus

GRIPUS And gold and silver are but filthy dross.
    Then seek not gold and silver which are dross,
    But rather lay thy treasure up in heaven! –
SLIM Hem!
GRIPUS And thou has meat and drink and lodging too
    And clothing too, what more can man require?
    And thou art single –
    But I must lay up money for my children,
    My children's children and my great-grandchildren;
    For, Slim! thy master will be shortly married –
SLIM Married!
GRIPUS   Yea! married. Wherefore dost thou stare,
    As though my words had spoke of aught impossible?
SLIM My lord, I stare not but my ears played false.
    Methought you had said married.
GRIPUS   Married, fool!
    Is't aught unlikely? I'm not very old,
    And my intended has a noble fortune.
SLIM My lord 'tis likely.
GRIPUS   Haste, then, to the butchers,
    And ere thou go, tell Bridget she is wanted –
SLIM I go – Gods! what a subject for an ode.
    With Hymen, Cupids, Venus, Loves and Graces!

    [*Exit*]

GRIPUS [*solus*] This matrimony is no light affair;
    'Tis downright venture and mere speculation.
    Less risk there is in what the merchant trusts

To winds and waves and the uncertain elements –
For he can have assurance for his goods
And put himself beyond the reach of losses –
But who can e'er ensure to me a wife
Industrious and managing and frugal,
Who will not spend far more than she has brought,
But be almost a saving to her husband? –
But none can tell – the broker cannot tell
He is not cheated in the wares he buys,
And to judge well of women or the seas
Would oft surpass the wisest merchant's prudence;
For both are deep alike – capricious too –
And the worst things that money can be sunk in.
But Bridget comes –

BRIDGET   Your pleasure, Sir, with me?
GRIPUS Bridget, I wish to have a little converse
Upon a matter that concerns us both
Of like importance both to thee and me.
BRIDGET Of like importance and concerning both!
What can your Honour have to say to me?
[*aside*] O lord! I would give all that I am worth
To know what 'tis –
GRIPUS   Then prithee rein thy tongue
That ever battles with thine own impatience.
But to the point. Thou knowst, for twenty years
Together we have lived as man and wife,
But never hath the sanction of the Church
Stamped its legality upon our union.
BRIDGET Well, what of that?
GRIPUS   Why, when in wiser years
Men look upon the follies of their youth,
They oft repent, and wish to make amends,
And seek for happier in more virtuous days.
In such a case, and such is mine I own,
'Tis marriage offers us the readiest way
To make atonement for our former deeds.
And thus have I determined in my heart
To make amends – in other words to marry.

BRIDGET O Lord! how overjoyed I am to hear it!
  I vow that I have often thought myself,
  What wickedness it was to live as we did!
  But do you joke?
GRIPUS   Not so upon my oath.
  I am resolved to marry and beget
  A little heir to leave my little wealth to.
  I am not old, my hair is hardly grey,
  My health is good – what hast thou to object?
BRIDGET O dear! how close your honour puts the question!
  I've said as much already as was fit
  And incompatible with female modesty –
  But would your honour please to name a day?
GRIPUS To name a day! But hark! I hear a knock –
  'Tis perhaps young Prodigal, I did expect him.
BRIDGET But Sir – a day?
GRIPUS   Zounds! dost thou hear the bell?
  Wilt thou not run? He was to bring me money!

  [*Exit* BRIDGET *and returns*]

BRIDGET 'Tis he, I've shown him to the little study.
GRIPUS Then stay thee here, and when I've settled him
  I will return and hold more converse with thee.

  [*Exit*]

BRIDGET [*sola*] My head runs round! O, what a happy change!
  Now I shall be another woman quite.
  Dame Bridget, then, adieu! and don't forget
  Your Lady Gripus now that is to be;
  Great Lady Gripus – O Lord! –
  The Lady of the old and rich Sir Gripus!
  O how will people whisper, as I pass,
  'There goes my Lady' – 'What a handsome gownd,
  All scarlet silk embroiderèd with gold!'
  Or green and gold will perhaps become me better –

492 GRIPUS

  How vastly fine, how handsome I shall be
  In green and gold! Besides, a lady too!
  I'll have a footman too, to walk behind me.
90 Slim is too slender to set off a livery,
  I must have one more lustier than him,
  A proper man to walk behind his lady.
  O how genteel! methinks I see myself
  In green and gold and carrying my fan –
  Or perhaps I'd have a redicule *about me!*
  The lusty footman all so spruce behind me
  Walking on tip-toes in a bran new livery;
  And he shall have a favour in his hat
  As sure as ever I am Lady Gripus!

 [*Enter* SLIM]

100 SLIM Why how now, Bridget, you're turned actress sure!
 BRIDGET An actor, fellow, no! To something better,
  To something grander and more ladylike,
  Know I am turned!
 SLIM   A lunatic, 'tis plain.
  But, lovee, leave this jesting for a while,
  And hear thy servant, who thus pleads for favour.
 BRIDGET For favour Sirrah! But I must be kind,
  I will forget your insolence this once,
  And condescend to keep you in my service.
  But no! I want a much more lustier man,
110 You are too slender to become my livery
  I must excard you, you must suit yourself!
 SLIM Why, how now, Bridget –
 BRIDGET   You forget me, sure!
 SLIM Forget thee, Bridget? Never from my heart
  Shall thy dear image part.
    Ah! no,
     I love you so
   No language can impart!
  Alas! 'tis love that makes me thin,
  I have a fiery flame within,
120   That burns and shrivels up my skin –

                     'Tis Cupid's little dart,
                     And by this kiss I swear –

[*Attempts to kiss her*]

BRIDGET Ruffin, begone, or I will tell my lord.
  Do you not care for difference of rank,
  Nor make distinction between dirt and dignity?
SLIM Why, Bridget, once you did not treat me thus.
BRIDGET No, times are altered, Fortune's wheel is turned,
  You still are Slim, but, though I once was Bridget,
  I'm Lady Gripus now that is to be.
  Did not his Honour tell you he should marry?
SLIM Yea, to a lady of an ample fortune.
BRIDGET Why, that, you fool, he said in allegolly.
  A virtuous woman, is she not a crown,
  A crown of gold and glory to her husband?
SLIM Heavens is it possible? I pray forgive me
  That I could doubt a moment of that fortune
  Which is but due to your assembled merits.
BRIDGET Well, Slim, I do not wish to harbour malice,
  But while you show a proper due respect
  You may be certain of my condescension.
  But hark! I hear his lordship on the stairs,
  And we must have some privacy together. [*Exit* SLIM]
  O lord, how overjoyed I am your honour –
GRIPUS Bridget, I thank thee for thy friendly zeal,
  That seems to glory in thy master's bliss;
  And much it grieves me that I can't requite it
  Except by mere reciprocal good-wishes.
  For as a change in my domestic government
  Will make thy place in future but a sinecure,
  It grieves me much that I must warn you thus
  To seek and get a situation elsewhere.
BRIDGET O dear! O lord! O what a shock! O lord!

  [*Faints*]

GRIPUS Ho! Slim – the devil's in the fool, to faint.

494 GRIPUS

  Halloo! – What shall I do? Halloo! Halloo!
  Ho! Slim, I say – run, Sirrah, for the brandy!
SLIM The brandy, Sir? there is none in the house!
GRIPUS No brandy! None! What, none at all, thou
  knave?
What, none at all? Thou rascal thou hast drunk it.
Why Bridget, Bridget – what, no brandy, knave?
160 Zounds! what a fit! Where is my brandy, wretch!
Thou toping villain, say, or I will slay thee!

[*Lets* BRIDGET *fall and collars* SLIM]

SLIM O lord! Forgive me, Bridget had the wind,
And drank the brandy up to warm her stomach.
GRIPUS A tipsy Bacchanal! Then let her lie!
I'll not be drunken out of house and home.
Zounds! brandy for the wind – a cure indeed!
A little water had done just as well.
This is the way, then, when I want a drop;
I always find my cellar is stark naked.
170 But both shall go, yes, I discard ye. Thieves!
Begone, ye thieves!

[BRIDGET *jumps up*]

BRIDGET   No, not without my wages!
I'll have a month's full wages or my warning!
I'll not be left at nonplush for a place.
GRIPUS A month's full warning! What, another month,
To sack, to ransack, and to strip the house,
And then depart in triumph with your booty!
Begone, I say!
BRIDGET   No, not without my wages!
And I'll have damages, you cruel man!
I will convict you of a breach of marriage!
180 GRIPUS Begone, I say! Deceitful thing! begone –
Who ever dared to promise such a match
But thy own fancy, and thy lying tongue?
What, marry one as poor as a church mouse,
And equally devoid of rank and beauty!

GRIPUS

Reason would sleep and prudence would be blind,
And Gripus then would be no longer Gripus,
But only fitting for more sober men
To lodge in Bedlam and to call a lunatic.

APPENDIX I

*Wordsworth and Hazlitt on the
Origins of Greek Mythology*

William Wordsworth
The Excursion (1814), IV, 687–756, 840–81

These lines had a deep influence on Keats. Wordsworth's claim that the Classical deities originated in man's animistic response to natural forces lies behind several important passages in Keats's poetry: see '*I stood tip-toe . . .*' 124–205, *Endymion* I, 232–306, II, 830–39, and *Ode to Psyche* 38–45. Hazlitt described Wordsworth's lines as 'a succession of splendid passages equally enriched with philosophy and poetry, tracing the fictions of Eastern mythology to the immediate intercourse of the imagination with nature, and to the habitual propensity of the human mind to endow the outward forms of being with life and conscious motion', *Works*, ed. P. P. Howe (1930–34), IV, pp. 114–15. For Wordsworth's dismissive attitude to Keats's 'Paganism', see *Endymion* I, 232–306 *n*, p. 563.

Chaldean Shepherds, ranging trackless fields,
Beneath the concave of unclouded skies
Spread like a sea, in boundless solitude,
Looked on the Polar Star, as on a Guide
And Guardian of their course, that never closed
His steadfast eye. The Planetary Five
With a submissive reverence they beheld;
Watched, from the centre of their sleeping flocks,
Those radiant Mercuries, that seemed to move
Carrying through Ether, in perpetual round,
Decrees and resolutions of the Gods;
And, by their aspects, signifying works
Of dim futurity, to Man revealed.
– The Imaginative Faculty was Lord
Of observations natural; and, thus
Led on, those Shepherds made report of Stars
In set rotation passing to and fro.
Between the orbs of our apparent sphere
And its invisible counterpart, adorned
With answering Constellations, under earth
Removed from all approach of living sight,

But present to the Dead; who, so they deemed,
Like those celestial Messengers, beheld
All accidents, and Judges were of all.

    The lively Grecian, in a land of hills,
Rivers, and fertile plains, and sounding shores,
Under a cope of variegated sky,
Could find commodious place for every God,
Promptly received, as prodigally brought,
From the surrounding Countries – at the choice
Of all Adventurers. With unrivalled skill,
As nicest observation furnished hints
For studious fancy, did his hand bestow
On fluent Operations a fixed Shape;
Metal or Stone, idolatrously served.
And yet – triumphant o'er this pompous show
Of Art, this palpable array of Sense,
On every side encountered; in despite
Of the gross fictions, chaunted in the streets
By wandering Rhapsodists; and in contempt
Of doubt and bold denial hourly urged
Amid the wrangling Schools – a SPIRIT hung,
Beautiful Region! o'er thy Towns and Farms,
Statues and Temples, and Memorial Tombs;
And emanations were perceived; and acts
Of immortality, in Nature's course,
Exemplified by mysteries, that were felt
As bonds, on grave Philosopher imposed
And armed Warrior; and in every grove
A gay or pensive tenderness prevailed
When piety more awful had relaxed. . . .
And, doubtless, sometimes . . .
. . . a thought arose
Of Life continuous, Being unimpaired;
That hath been, is, and where it was and is
There shall be, – seen, and heard, and felt, and known,
And recognized, – existence unexposed
To the blind walk of mortal accident;
From diminution safe and weakening age;

While Man grows old, and dwindles, and decays;
And countless generations of Mankind
Depart; and leave no vestige where they trod.
(ll. 687–756)

Once more to distant Ages of the world
Let us revert, and place before our thoughts
The face which rural Solitude might wear
To the unenlightened Swains of pagan Greece.
– In that fair Clime, the lonely Herdsman, stretched
On the soft grass through half a summer's day,
With music lulled his indolent repose:
And, in some fit of weariness, if he,
When his own breath was silent, chanced to hear
A distant strain, far sweeter than the sounds
Which his poor skill could make, his Fancy fetched,
Even from the blazing Chariot of the Sun,
A beardless Youth, who touched a golden lute,
And filled the illumined groves with ravishment.
The nightly Hunter, lifting up his eyes
Towards the crescent Moon, with grateful heart
Called on the lovely wanderer who bestowed
That timely light, to share his joyous sport:
And hence, a beaming Goddess with her Nymphs,
Across the lawn and through the darksome grove
(Not unaccompanied with tuneful notes
By echo multiplied from rock or cave)
Swept in the storm of chase, as Moon and Stars
Glance rapidly along the clouded heavens,
When winds are blowing strong. The Traveller slaked
His thirst from Rill or gushing Fount, and thanked
The Naiad. – Sunbeams, upon distant Hills
Gliding apace, with Shadows in their train,
Might, with small help from fancy, be transformed
Into fleet Oreads sporting visibly.
The Zephyrs, fanning as they passed, their wings,
Lacked not, for love, fair Objects, whom they wooed
With gentle whisper. Withered Boughs grotesque,

Stripped of their leaves and twigs by hoary age,
From depth of shaggy covert peeping forth
In the low vale, or on steep mountain side;
And, sometimes, intermixed with stirring horns,
Of the live Deer, or Goat's depending beard;
These were the lurking Satyrs, a wild brood
Of gamesome Deities! or Pan himself,
The simple Shepherd's awe-inspiring God.
(ll. 840–81)

William Hazlitt

from Lecture 4, *Lectures on the English Poets* (1818)

Keats had met Hazlitt in the winter of 1816–17, and admired his 'depth of Taste'. Hazlitt's eight lectures were first given at the Surrey Institution. Keats was a frequent member of the audience, and attended this lecture, given on 10 February 1818 (*L* I, p. 227). The extract is taken from *Works*, ed. P. P. Howe (1930–34), V, p. 102:

If we have once enjoyed the cool shade of a tree, and been lulled into a deep repose by the sound of a brook running at its foot, we are sure that wherever we can find a shady stream, we can enjoy the same pleasure again; so that when we imagine these objects, we can easily form a mystic personification of the friendly power that inhabits them, Dryad or Naiad, offering its cool fountain or its tempting shade. Hence the origin of the Grecian mythology.

Hazlitt was sharply aware that Wordsworth did not share his own (or, indeed, Keats's) enthusiasm for classical mythology. In Lecture 8 he remarked that the Lake Poets, in their search for the 'natural and new', had discarded 'the whole heathen mythology', and that they considered a classical allusion 'as a piece of antiquated foppery' (*Works*, edn cit., V, p. 162).

APPENDIX 2
The Two Prefaces to Endymion

(1) *Published Version*

Appeared with *Endymion* when it was published in May 1818.

Knowing within myself the manner in which this Poem has been produced, it is not without a feeling of regret that I make it public.

What manner I mean, will be quite clear to the reader, who must soon perceive great inexperience, immaturity, and every error denoting a feverish attempt, rather than a deed accomplished. The two first books, and indeed the two last, I feel sensible are not of such completion as to warrant their passing the press; nor should they if I thought a year's castigation would do them any good; – it will not: the foundations are too sandy. It is just that this youngster should die away: a sad thought for me, if I had not some hope that while it is dwindling I may be plotting, and fitting myself for verses fit to live.

This may be speaking too presumptuously, and may deserve a punishment: but no feeling man will be forward to inflict it: he will leave me alone, with the conviction that there is not a fiercer hell than the failure in a great object. This is not written with the least atom of purpose to forestall criticisms of course, but from the desire I have to conciliate men who are competent to look, and who do look with a zealous eye, to the honour of English literature.

The imagination of a boy is healthy, and mature imagination of a man is healthy; but there is a space of life between, in which the soul is in a ferment, the character undecided, the way of life uncertain, the ambition thick-sighted: thence proceeds mawkishness, and all the thousand bitters which those men I speak of must necessarily taste in going over the following pages.

I hope I have not in too late a day touched the beautiful mythology of Greece, and dulled its brightness: for I wish to try once more, before I bid it farewell.

Teignmouth, 10 April 1818

(2) *Rejected Dedication and Preface*

Keats's original preface and dedication met with strong objections from J. H. Reynolds, and his publishers, Taylor and Hessey. The Dedication originally read: 'INSCRIBED,/ WITH EVERY FEELING OF PRIDE AND REGRET/ AND WITH 'A BOWED MIND',/ TO THE MEMORY OF/ THE MOST ENGLISH OF POETS EXCEPT SHAKESPEARE,/ THOMAS CHATTERTON.' The preface, written 19 March 1818, and sent to the publishers on 21 March, originally read:

In a great nation, the work of an individual is of so little importance; his pleadings and excuses are so uninteresting; his 'way of life' such a nothing, that a preface seems a sort of impertinent bow to strangers who care nothing about it.

A preface, however, should be down in so many words; and such a one that by an eye-glance over the type the Reader may catch an idea of an Author's modesty, and non-opinion of himself – which I sincerely hope may be seen in the few lines I have to write, notwithstanding many proverbs of many ages' old which men find a great pleasure in receiving for gospel.

About a twelve month since, I published a little book of verses; it was read by some dozen of my friends who lik'd it; and some dozen whom I was unacquainted with, who did not. Now, when a dozen human beings are at words with another dozen, it becomes a matter of anxiety to side with one's friends: – more especially when excited thereto by a great love of Poetry.

I fought under disadvantages. Before I began I had no inward feel of being able to finish; and as I proceeded my steps were all uncertain. So this Poem must rather be considered as an endeavour than a thing accomplish'd; a poor prologue to what, if I live, I humbly hope to do. In duty to the Public I should have kept it back for a year or two, knowing it to be so faulty: but I really cannot do so: – by repetition my favorite Passages sound vapid in my ears, and I would rather redeem myself with a new Poem – should this one be found of any interest.

I have to apologise to the lovers of simplicity for touching the spell of loveliness that hung about *Endymion*: if any of my lines plead for me with such people I shall be proud.

It has been too much the fashion of late to consider men bigotted and addicted to every word that may chance to escape their lips: now I here declare that I have not any particular affection for any particular phrase, word, or letter in the whole affair. I have written to please myself and in hopes to please others, and for a love of fame; if I neither please myself, nor others, nor get fame, of what consequence is Phraseology?

I would fain escape the bickerings that all works not exactly in chime, bring upon their begetters, – but this is not fair to expect, there must be conversation of some sort and to object shows a man's consequence. In case of a London drizzle or a Scotch Mist, the following quotation from Marston may perhaps 'stead me as an umbrella for an hour or so: ' let it be the Curtesy of my peruser rather to pity my self hindering labours than to malice me.'

One word more: – for we cannot help seeing our own affairs in every point of view – Should any one call my dedication to Chatterton affected I answer as followeth: 'Were I dead, sir, I should like a Book dedicated to me' –

Teignmouth March 19th 1818

Keats explained why his preface had taken such a self-dismissive tone, and gives an account of the reasons for changing it, in his letter to Reynolds, 9 April 1818 (*L* I, pp. 266–7):

Since you all agree that the thing is bad, it must be so – though I am not aware there is anything like Hunt in it, (and if there is, it is my natural way, and I have something in common with Hunt) look it over again and examine into the motives, the seeds from which any one sentence sprung – I have not the slightest feel of humility towards the Public – or to any thing in existence, – but the eternal Being, the Principle of Beauty, – and the Memory of great Men – When I am writing for myself for mere the Moment's enjoyment, perhaps nature has its course with me – but a Preface is written to the Public; a thing I cannot help looking upon as an Enemy, and which I cannot address without feelings of Hostility – If I write a Preface in a supple or subdued style, it will not be in character with me as a publis speaker – I wo[ul]d be subdued before my friends, and thank them for subduing me – but among Multitudes of Men – I have no feel of stooping, I hate the idea of humility to them –

I never wrote one single Line of Poetry with the least Shadow of public thought.

Forgive me for vexing you and making such a Trojan Horse of such a Trifle, both with respect to the matter in Question, and myself – but it eases me to tell you – I could not live without the love of my friends. – I would jump down Aetna for any great Public good – but I hate a Mawkish Popularity. – I cannot be subdued before them. My glory would be to daunt and dazzle the thousand jabberers about Pictures and Books – I see swarms of Porcupines with their Quills erect 'like limetwigs set to catch my Winged Book' and I would fright 'em away with a torch. You will say my preface is not much of a Torch. It would have been too insulting 'to begin from Jove' and I could not [set] a golden head upon a thing of clay – if there is any fault in the preface it is not affectation: but an undersong of disrespect to the Public. If I write another preface, it must be done without a thought of those people – I will think about it. If it should not reach you in four- or five -days – tell Taylor to publish it without a preface, and let the Dedication simply stand 'inscribed to the memory of Thomas Chatterton'.

APPENDIX 3

The Order of Poems in Poems (*1817*) *and* Lamia, Isabella, The Eve of St Agnes, and Other Poems (*1820*)
and
The Publisher's Advertisement for 1820

The Order of Poems

For a discussion of the possible reasoning behind the order adopted by Keats in these two volumes, see *Stillinger*, pp. 1-13, 116-17.

Poems (1817)

[The title page has the epigraph, 'What more felicity can fall to creature,/ Than to enjoy liberty with delight', Spenser, *Muiopotomos: or The Fate of the Butterflie* 209-10, with a vignette head of Spenser below. On p. vi, following the dedicatory Sonnet to Hunt, is a Note stating that 'The Short Pieces in the middle of the Book, as well as some of the Sonnets, were written at an earlier period than the rest of the Poems.']

POEMS
Dedication. To Leigh Hunt, Esq. ('Glory and loveliness have passed away')
'I stood tip-toe upon a little hill'
Specimen of an Induction to a Poem
Calidore. A Fragment
To Some Ladies
On Receiving a Curious Shell, and a Copy of Verses, from the Same Ladies
To [Mary Frogley]
To Hope
Imitation of Spenser
'Woman! when I behold thee flippant, vain'

EPISTLES

[Preceded by a motto, 'Among the rest a shepheard (though but young/ Yet hartned to his pipe) with all the skill / His few yeeres could, began to fit his quill', from William Browne's *Britannia's Pastorals* II (1616), Song 3, 748–50.]

To George Felton Mathew

To my Brother George ('Full many a dreary hour have I passed')

To Charles Cowden Clarke

SONNETS

To my Brother George ('Many the wonders I this day have seen')

To . . . ('Had I a man's fair form, then might my sighs')

Written on the Day that Mr Leigh Hunt left Prison

'How many bards gild the lapses of time'

To a Friend who Sent me some Roses

To G[eorgiana] A[ugusta] W[ylie]

'O Solitude! if I must with thee dwell'

To my Brothers

'Keen, fitful gusts are whispering here and there'

'To one who has been long in city pent'

On First Looking into Chapman's Homer

On Leaving some Friends at an Early Hour

Addressed to Haydon ('Highmindedness, a jealousy for good')

Addressed to the Same ('Great spirits now on earth are sojourning')

On the Grasshopper and Cricket

To Kosciusko

'Happy is England! I could be content'

Sleep and Poetry

THE ORDER OF POEMS

Lamia, Isabella, The Eve of St Agnes, and Other Poems (1820)

Lamia
Isabella
The Eve of St Agnes
Ode to a Nightingale
Ode on a Grecian Urn
Ode to Psyche
Fancy
Ode ('Bards of passion and of mirth')
Lines on the Mermaid Tavern
Robin Hood
To Autumn
Ode on Melancholy
Hyperion. A Fragment

The Publisher's Advertisement for 1820

Advertisement

If any apology be thought necessary for the appearance of the unfinished poem of *Hyperion*, the publishers beg to state that they alone are responsible, as it was printed at their particular request, and contrary to the wish of the author. The poem was intended to have been of equal length with *Endymion*, but the reception given to that work discouraged the author from proceeding.

Fleet Street, 26 June 1820

According to Rollins, this Advertisement was written by John Taylor. Keats commented on it, 'This is none of my doing – I was ill at the time. This is a lie' (see *Lowell* II, p. 424). 'This is a lie' refers only to the final sentence, the rest to the whole Advertisement. *G* and *KC* II, pp. 115–16, give Woodhouse's draft of the Advertisement which has several important variants from the version finally printed.

APPENDIX 4
Keats's Notes on Milton's Paradise Lost

Keats's annotated copy of *Paradise Lost* is now in the Hampstead Museum. His marginalia are reproduced in *Forman* (1938–9) V, pp. 292–305, which is the basis of the text here. Keats's underlinings are marked by italics.

1 ON THE POET AND THE POEM

The Genius of Milton, more particularly in respect to its span in immensity, calculated him, by a sort of birthright, for such an 'argument' as the paradise lost: he had an exquisite passion for what is properly, in the sense of ease and pleasure, poetical Luxury; and with that it appears to me he would fain have been content, if he could, so doing, have preserved his self-respect and feel of duty performed; but there was working in him as it were that same sort of thing as operates in the great world to the end of a Prophecy's being accomplished: therefore he devoted himself rather to the Ardours than the pleasures of Song, solacing himself at intervals with cups of old wine; and those are with some exceptions the finest parts of the Poem. With some exceptions – for the spirit of mounting and adventure can never be unfruitful or unrewarded: had he not broken through the clouds which envellope so deliciously the Elysian fields of Verse, and committed himself to the Extreme, we never should have seen Satan as described –

> But his face
> Deep Scars of thunder had entrench'd, etc.

2 ON 'THE ARGUMENT'

There is a greatness which the *Paradise Lost* possesses over every other Poem – *the Magnitude of Contrast*, and that is softened by the contrast being ungrotesque to a degree. Heaven moves on like music throughout. Hell is also peopled with angels; it also move[s] on like music, not grating and harsh, but like a grand accompaniment in the Base to Heaven.

3 ON THE OPENING

There is always a great charm in the openings of great Poems, more particularly where the action begins – that of Dante's Hell. Of Hamlet, the first step must be heroic and full of power; and nothing can be more impressive and shaded than the commencement of the action here – 'Round he throws his baleful eyes –'

518 APPENDIX 4

4 BOOK I, 53-75

>   But his doom
> Reserv'd him to more wrath; for now the thought
> Both of lost happiness and lasting pain
> Torments him: *round he throws his baleful eyes,*
> *That witness'd huge affliction and dismay*
> *Mix'd with obdurate pride and stedfast hate:*
> *At once, as far as Angel's ken, he views*
> *The dismal situation waste and wild;*
> A dungeon horrible on all sides round
> As one great furnace flamed, yet from those flames
> No light, but rather darkness visible
> Serv'd only to discover *sights of woe,*
> *Regions of sorrow, doleful shades, where peace*
> *And rest can never dwell; hope never comes*
> *That comes to all;* but torture without end
> Still urges, and a fiery deluge, fed
> With ever-burning sulphur unconsumed.
> Such place eternal Justice had prepared
> For those rebellious, here their prison ordain'd
> In utter darkness, and their portion set
> As far removed from God and light of Heaven,
> As from the centre thrice to the utmost pole.
> Oh how unlike the place from whence they fell!

One of the most mysterious of semi-speculations is, one would suppose, that of one Mind's imagining into another. Things may be described by a Man's self in parts so as to make a grand whole which that Man himself would scarcely inform to its excess. A Poet can seldom have justice done to his imagination – for men are as distinct in their conceptions of material shadowings as they are in matters of spiritual understanding: it can scarcely be conceived how Milton's Blindness might here ade [for 'aid'] the magnitude of his conceptions as a bat in a large gothic vault.

5 BOOK I, 318-21

>   or have ye chosen this place
> After the toil of battle to repose
> Your wearied virtue, for the ease you find

APPENDIX 4

To slumber here, as in the vales of Heaven?

There is a cool pleasure in the very sound of vale. The english word is of the happiest chance. Milton has put vales in heaven and hell with the very utter affection and yearning of a great Poet. It is a sort of delphic Abstraction – a beautiful thing made more beautiful by being reflected and put in a Mist. The next mention of Vale is one of the most pathetic in the whole range of Poetry.

> Others, more mild,
> Retreated in a silent Valley etc.

[II, 546–7]

How much of the charm is in the Valley! –

6 BOOK I, 527–67

> but he, his wonted pride
> Soon recollecting, with high words, that bore
> Semblance of worth not substance, gently raised
> Their fainting courage, and dispell'd their fears.
> Then straight commands that at the warlike sound
> Of trumpets loud and clarions be uprear'd
> His mighty standard: that proud honour claim'd
> Azazel as his right, a Cherub tall;
> Who forthwith from *the glittering staff unfurl'd*
> *The imperial ensign, which full high advanced*
> *Shone like a meteor streaming to the wind,*
> *With gems and golden lustre rich emblazed,*
> *Seraphic arms and trophies; all the while*
> *Sonorous metal blowing martial sounds:*
> *At which the universal host up-sent*
> *A shout, that tore Hell's concave, and beyond*
> *Frighted the reign of Chaos and old Night.*
> *All in a moment through the gloom were seen*
> *Ten thousand banners rise into the air*
> *With orient colours waving: with them rose*
> *A forest huge of spears, and thronging helms*
> *Appear'd, and serried shields in thick array*
> *Of depth immeasurable: anon they move*
> *In perfect phalanx to the Dorian mood*

520 APPENDIX 4

Of flutes and soft recorders; such as raised
To height of noblest temper heroes old
Arming to battle, and instead of rage
Deliberate valour breath'd, firm and unmoved
With dread of death to flight or foul retreat;
Nor wanting power to mitigate and swage
With solemn touches, troubled thoughts, and chase
Anguish, and doubt, and fear, and sorrow, and pain,
From mortal or immortal minds. Thus they
Breathing united force with fixed thought
Moved on in silence to soft pipes, that charm'd
Their painful steps o'er the burnt soil; and now
Advanced in view they stand, a horrid front
Of dreadful length and dazzling arms, in guise
Of warriors old with order'd spear and shield,
Awaiting what command their mighty chief
Had to impose.

The light and shade – the sort of black brightness – the ebon diamonding – the ethiop Immortality – the sorrow, the pain, the sad-sweet Melody – the P[h]alanges of Spirits so depressed as to be 'uplifted beyond hope' – the short mitigation of Misery – the thousand Melancholies and Magnificences of this Page – leaves no room for anything to be said thereon but '*so it is*'.

7 BOOK I, 591–9
           his form had not yet lost
All her original brightness, nor appear'd
Less than Arch-Angel ruin'd, and the excess
Of glory obscured; as when the sun new risen
Looks through the horizontal misty air
Shorn of his beams; or from behind the moon
In dim eclipse disastrous twilight sheds
On half the nations, and with fear of change
Perplexes monarchs.

How noble and collected an indignation against Kings, '*and for fear of change perplexes Monarchs*' etc. His very wishing should have had power to pull that feeble animal Charles from his bloody throne. 'The evil days' had come to him; he hit the new System of things a mighty mental blow; the exertion must have had or is yet to have some sequences.

8 BOOK I, 710-30

Anon out of the earth a fabric huge
Rose like an exhalation, with the sound
Of dulcet symphonies and voices sweet,
Built like a temple, where pilasters round
Were set, and Doric pillars overlaid
With golden architrave; nor did there want
Cornice or frieze, with bossy sculptures graven;
The roof was fretted gold. Not Babylon,
Nor great Alcairo such magnificence
Equall'd in all their glories, to inshrine
Belus or Serapis their Gods, or seat
Their kings, when Egypt with Assyria strove
In wealth and luxury. The ascending pile
Stood fix'd her stately height; and straight the doors
Opening their brazen folds, discover, wide
Within, her ample spaces, o'er the smooth
And level pavement: from the arched roof
Pendent by subtle magic many a row
Of starry lamps and blazing cressets, fed
With Naphtha and Asphaltus, yielded light
As from a sky.

What creates the intense pleasure of not knowing? A sense of independence, of power, from the fancy's creating a world of its own by the sense of probabilities. We have read the Arabian Nights and hear there are thousands of those sort of Romances lost – we imagine after them – but not their realities if we had them nor our fancies in their strength can go further than this Pandemonium –

'Straight the doors opening' etc.
'rose like an exhalation' –

9 BOOK II, 546–61

>   *Others, more mild,*
> *Retreated in a silent valley, sing*
> *With notes angelical to many a harp*
> *Their own heroic deeds and hapless fall*
> *By doom of battle; and complain that Fate*
> *Free Virtue should inthrall to force or chance.*
> *Their song was partial, but the harmony*
> *(What could it less when Spirits immortal sing?)*
> *Suspended Hell,* and took with ravishment
> The thronging audience. *In discourse more sweet*
> *(For eloquence the soul, song charms the sense)*
> *Others apart sat on a hill retired,*
> In thoughts more elevate, and reason'd high
> Of providence, foreknowledge, will, and fate,
> Fixed fate, free will, foreknowledge absolute,
> And found no end, in wandering mazes lost.

Milton is godlike in the sublime pathetic. In Demons, fallen Angels, and Monsters the delicacies of passion, living in and from their immortality, is of the most softening and dissolving nature. It is carried to the utmost here – 'Others more mild' – nothing can express the sensation one feels at '*Their song was partial*' etc. Examples of this nature are divine to the utmost in other poets – in Caliban '*Sometimes a thousand twangling instruments*' etc. In Theocritus, Polyphemus – and Homer's Hymn to Pan where Mercury is represented as taking his '*homely fac'd*' to heaven. There are numerous other instances in Milton – where Satan's progeny is called his '*daughter dear*', and where this same Sin, a female, and with a feminine instinct for the showy and martial is in pain lest death should sully his bright arms, '*nor vainly hope to be invulnerable in those bright arms.*' Another instance is '*pensive I sat* alone.' We need not mention '*Tears such as Angels weep.*'

523 APPENDIX 4

10 BOOK III, 1, 51-9
Hail, holy Light, offspring of Heaven first-born!

*   *   *

So much the rather thou, celestial Light,
Shine inward, and the mind through all her powers
Irradiate; there plant eyes, all mist from thence
Purge and disperse, that I may see and tell
Of things invisible to mortal sight.
  Now had the Almighty Father from above,
From the pure empyrean where he sits
High throned above all height, bent down his eye,
His own works and their works at once to view.

The management of this Poem is Apollonian. Satan first '*throws round his baleful eyes,*' the[n] awakes his legions, he consults, he sets forward on his voyage – and just as he is getting to the end of it we see the Great God and our first parent, and that same satan all brought in one's vision – we have the invocation to light before we mount to heaven – we breathe more freely – we feel the great Author's consolations coming thick upon him at a time when he complains most – we are getting ripe for diversity – the immediate topic of the Poem opens with a grand Perspective of all concerned.

11 BOOK III, 135-7
Thus while God spake, ambrosial fragrance fill'd
All Heaven, and in the blessed Spirits elect
Sense of new joy ineffable diffused.

Hell is finer than this.

12 BOOK III, 487-9
A violent cross wind from either coast
Blows them transverse, ten thousand leagues awry
Into the devious air.

This part in its sound is unaccountably expressive of the description.

13 BOOK III, 606-17

What wonder then if fields and regions here
Breathe forth Elixir pure, and rivers run
Potable gold, *when with one virtuous touch
The arch-chemic Sun*, so far from us remote,
Produces with terrestrial humour mix'd,
Here in the dark so many precious things
Of colour glorious and effect so rare?
Here matter new to gaze the Devil met
Undazzled, far and wide his eye commands,
For sight no obstacle found here, nor shade,
But all sunshine, *as when his beams at noon
Culminate from the Equator*, ...

A Spirit's eye.

14 BOOK IV, 1-5

*O for that warning voice, which he who saw
The Apocalypse heard cry in Heaven aloud,
Then when the Dragon, put to second rout,
Came furious down to be revenged on men,
'Woe to the inhabitants on earth!'*

A friend of mine [probably Benjamin Bailey] says this Book has the finest opening of any – the point of time is gigantically critical – the wax is melted, the seal is about to be applied – and Milton breaks out, '*O for that warning voice,*' etc. There is moreover an op[p]ortunity for a Grandeur of Tenderness – the opportunity is not lost. Nothing can be higher – Nothing so more than delphic.

15 BOOK IV, 268-72

*Not that fair field
Of Enna, where Proserpin gathering flowers,
Herself a fairer flower, by gloomy Dis
Was gather'd, which cost Ceres all that pain
To seek her through the world;*

There are two specimens of a very extraordinary beauty in the *Paradise Lost*; they are of a nature as far as I have read, unexampled elsewhere – they are entirely distinct from the brief

525 APPENDIX 4

pathos of Dante — and they are not to be found even in Shakespeare — these are according to the great prerogative of poetry better described in themselves than by a volume. The one is in the fol[lowing] — '*which cost Ceres all that pain*' — the other is that ending '*Nor could the Muse defend her son*'* — they appear exclusively Miltonic without the shadow of another mind ancient or modern.

16 BOOK VI, 58–9
    reluctant flames, the sign
Of wrath awaked; ...

'Reluctant' with its original and modern meaning combined and woven together, with all its shades of signification has a powerful effect.

17 BOOK VII, 420–23
    but feather'd soon and fledge
They summ'd their pens, and, soaring the air sublime
With clang despised the ground, under a cloud
In prospect.

Milton in every instance pursues his imagination to the utmost — he is 'sagacious of his Quarry,' he sees Beauty on the wing, pounces upon it and gorges it to the producing his essential verse. 'So from the root the springs lighter the green stalk,' etc.† But in no instance is this sort of perseverance more exemplified than in what may be called his *stationing or statu[a]ry*. He is not content with simple description, he must station, — thus here, we not only see how the Birds '*with clang despised the ground,*' but we see them '*under a cloud in prospect.*' So we see Adam '*Fair indeed and tall — under a plantane*' — and so we see Satan '*disfigured — on the Assyrian Mount.*' This last with all its accompaniments, and keeping in mind the Theory of Spirits' eyes and the simile of Gallilio [sic], has a dramatic vastness and solemnity fit and worthy to hold one amazed in the midst of this *Paradise Lost* —

 * V, 32–8 (underlined in Keat's copy).
 † V, 479–80 (slightly misquoted).

18 BOOK IX, 41-7

>   Me, of these
> Nor skill'd nor studious, higher argument
> Remains, sufficient of itself to raise
> That name, unless an age too late, or cold
> Climate, or years, damp my intended wing
> Depress'd; and much they may, if all be mine,
> Not hers who brings it nightly to my ear.

Had not Shakespeare liv'd?

19 BOOK IX, 179-91

> *So saying, through each thicket, dank or dry,*
> *Like a black mist low creeping, he held on*
> *His midnight search,* where soonest he might find
> The serpent: *him fast sleeping soon he found*
> *In labyrinth of many a round self-roll'd,*
> *His head the midst, well stored with subtle wiles.*
> *Not yet in horrid shade or dismal den,*
> *Nor nocent yet; but, on the grassy herb*
> *Fearless, unfear'd, he slept: in at his mouth*
> *The Devil enter'd, and his brutal sense,*
> *In heart or head, possessing, soon inspired*
> *With act intelligential; but his sleep*
> *Disturb'd not, waiting close the approach of morn.*

Satan having entered the Serpent, and inform'd his brutal sense – might seem sufficient – but Milton goes on '*but his sleep disturb'd not.*' Whose spirit does not ache at the smothering and confinement – the unwilling stillness – the '*waiting close*'? Whose head is not dizzy at the prosaible* speculations of satan in the serpent prison – no passage of poetry ever can give a greater pain of suffocation.

* Forman emends to 'possible', suggesting that Keats at first intended to write 'probable', and then changed his mind. 'Prosaible' may be an invented word.

APPENDIX 5

Keats on Kean's Shakespearean Acting

Keats was asked by his friend, John Reynolds, the dramatic critic of the *Champion*, to review Edmund Kean's return to the stage. Kean had been ill at the end of November 1817, and did not resume his role as Richard III until Monday, 15 December. Keats's review appeared in the *Champion*, 21 December 1817 (reprinted *Forman* [1938–9] V, pp. 227–32). A second Shakespearean piece, published in the *Champion*, 28 December 1817, is commonly attributed to Keats, but Leonidas M. Jones (*KSJ*, III [1954], pp. 55–65) has argued persuasively for Reynolds's authorship. It is reprinted by *Forman* (1938–9) V, pp. 233–46. Two further reviews by Keats for the *Champion*, one on *Harlequin's Vision*, a pantomime, and the other on the tragedy, *Retribution*, appeared on 4 January 1818 (reprinted *Forman* [1938–9] V, pp. 247–56).

Champion, 21 December 1817

Mr Kean

'In our unimaginative days' – *Habeas Corpus'd* as we are, out of all wonder, uncertainty and fear; – in these fireside, delicate, gilded days, – these days of sickly safety and comfort, we feel very grateful to Mr Kean for giving us some excitement by his old passion in one of the old plays. He is a relict of romance; – a Posthumous ray of chivalry, and always seems just arrived from the camp of Charlemagne. In Richard he is his sword's dear cousin; in Hamlet his footing is germain to the platform. In Macbeth his eye laughs siege to scorn; in Othello he is welcome to Cyprus. In Timon he is of the palace – of Athens – of the woods, and is worthy to sleep in a grave 'which once a day with its embossed froth, the turbulent surge doth cover.' For all these was he greeted with enthusiasm on his reappearance in Richard; for all these, his sickness will ever be a public misfortune. His return was full of power. He is not the man to 'bate a jot'. On Thursday evening, he acted *Luke* in *Riches* [Sir James Bland Burges's version of Massinger's *City Madam*], as far as the stage will permit, to perfection. In the hypocritical self-possession, in the caution, and afterwards the pride, cruelty, and avarice, Luke appears to us a man incapable of imagining to the extreme heinousness of crimes. To him, they are mere magic-lantern horrors. He is at no trouble to deaden his conscience.

Mr Kean's two characters of this week, comprising as they do, the utmost of quiet and turbulence, invite us to say a few words on his acting in general. We have done this before, but we do it again without remorse. Amid his numerous excellencies, the one which at this moment most weighs upon us, is the elegance, gracefulness, and music of elocution. A melodious passage in poetry is full of pleasures both sensual and spiritual. The spiritual is felt when the very letters and prints of charactered language show like the hieroglyphics of beauty; – the mysterious signs of an immortal freemasonry! 'A thing to dream of, not to tell!' The sensual life of verse springs warm from the lips of Kean, and to one learned in Shakespearian hieroglyphics, – learned in the spiritual portion of those lines to which Kean adds a sensual grandeur: his tongue must seem to have robbed 'the Hybla bees, and left them honeyless' [*Julius Caesar* V. 1. 34–5]. There is an indescribable gusto in his voice, by which we feel that the utterer is thinking of the past and the future, while speaking of the instant. When he says in Othello 'put up your bright swords, for the dew will rust them,' we feel that his throat had commanded where swords were as thick as reeds. From eternal risk, he speaks as though his body were unassailable. Again, his exclamation of 'blood, blood, blood!' is direful and slaughterous to the deepest degree, the very words appear stained and gory. His nature hangs over them, making a prophetic repast. His voice is loosed on them, like the wild dogs on the savage relics of an eastern conflict; and we can distinctly hear it 'gorging, and growling o'er carcase and limb.' In Richard, 'Be stirring with the lark to-morrow, gentle

Norfolk!' [*Richard III* V. 3. 56] comes from him, as through the morning atmosphere, towards which he yearns. We could cite a volume of such immortal scraps, and dote upon them with our remarks; but as an end must come, we will content ourselves with a single syllable. It is in those lines of impatience to the night who, 'like a foul and ugly witch, doth limp so tediously away' [*Henry V* IV, Chorus 21–2]. Surely this intense power of anatomizing the passion of every syllable – of taking to himself the wings of verse, is the mean[s] by which he becomes a storm with such fiery decision; and by which, with a still deeper charm, he 'does his spiriting gently' [*The Tempest* I. 2. 298]. Other actors are continually thinking of their sum-total effect throughout a play. Kean delivers himself up to the instant feeling, without a shadow of a thought about any thing else. He feels his being as deeply as Wordsworth, or any other of our intellectual monopolists. From all his comrades he stands alone, reminding us of him, whom Dante has so finely described in his Hell:

And sole apart retir'd, the Soldan fierce.

[*Inferno* IV, 126; Henry Carey's translation (1814)]

Although so many times he has lost the battle of Bosworth Field, we can easily conceive him really expectant of victory, and a different termination of the piece. Yet we are as moths about a candle in speaking of this great man. 'Great, let us call him, for he has conquered us!' [Edward Young, *The Revenge*]. We will say no more. Kean! Kean! have a carefulness of thy health, an in-nursed respect for thy own genius, a pity for us in these cold and enfeebling times! Cheer us a little in the failure of our days! for romance lives but in books. The goblin is driven from the heath, and the rainbow is robbed of its mystery![1]

[1] Compare *Lamia* II, 229–37 and *n* (p. 673).

Notes

The notes are both explanatory and textual. They give the first appearance of each poem, an indication of the textual source if it is not in the editions published in Keats's lifetime or R. M. Milnes's *Life, Letters, and Literary Remains* (1848), and some indication of its place in Keats's life and development. Textual variants are given where a manuscript reading has been adopted, where the alternative readings are of unusual importance, and, in the case of the more important poems, when they throw light on the poem's genesis. Unless otherwise stated, *Garrod (OSA)* agrees with G. Mythological names from classical literature are placed in the *Dictionary of Classical Names*, which follows the notes (pp. 697–719).

Several substantial quotations from Keats's important statements on the nature of poetry made in the letters are given in the Notes:

22 November 1817, to Benjamin Bailey ('the holiness of the Heart's affections and the truth of the Imagination', 'Adam's dream', 'O for a Life of Sensations'), p. 582.

21–7 December 1817, to George and Tom Keats ('Negative Capability'), p. 587.

13 March 1818, to Benjamin Bailey ('Things real – things semireal – and no things'), pp. 593–4.

3 May 1818, to J. H. Reynolds ('the Chamber of Maiden-Thought'), pp. 677–8.

27 October 1818, to Richard Woodhouse ('the poetical Character . . . has no self', 'gusto', 'the chameleon Poet'), pp. 607–608.

14 February–3 May 1819, to George and Georgiana Keats ('the Vale of soul-making'), p. 644.

22 September 1819, to Richard Woodhouse (on *Isabella* being 'smokeable'), p. 666.

The following abbreviations have been used:

KEATS'S WORKS

1817   *Poems* (1817).
Endymion   *Endymion: A Poetical Romance* (1818).
1820   *Lamia, Isabella, The Eve of St Agnes, and Other Poems* (1820).

532 NOTES

Galignani	*The Poetical Works of Coleridge, Shelley, and Keats*, Paris, 1829.
1848	*Life, Letters, and Literary Remains, of John Keats*, ed. R. M. Milnes, 2 vols., 1848.
1876	*The Poetical Works of John Keats*, Aldine edition, ed. R. M. Milnes, 1876.
Forman (1883)	*The Poetical Works and Other Writings of John Keats*, ed. H. B. Forman, 4 vols., 1883.
Forman (1938–9)	*The Poetical Works and Other Writings of John Keats*, ed. H. B. Forman, rev. M. B. Forman, 8 vols., 1938–9.
Colvin (1915)	*The Poems of John Keats*, ed. S. Colvin, 1915.
De Selincourt	*The Poems of John Keats*, ed. E. de Selincourt, 1905, rev. edn 1926.
G	*The Poetical Works of John Keats*, ed. H. W. Garrod, 1939, rev. edn 1958.
Garrod (OSA)	*The Poetical Works of John Keats*, ed. H. W. Garrod, Oxford Standard Authors, 1956.
L	*The Letters of John Keats 1814–1821*, ed. H. E. Rollins, 2 vols., 1958.
KC	*The Keats Circle: Letters and Papers 1816–1879*, ed. H. E. Rollins, 2 vols., 1965. Combines the original edn of 1948 with supplementary material published in *More Letters and Poems of the Keats Circle* (1955).
Allott	*The Poems of John Keats*, ed. M. Allott, 1970.
Gittings (1970)	*The Odes of Keats and Their Earliest Known Manuscripts* (1970).

OTHER WORKS FREQUENTLY REFERRED TO

Baldwin	'Edward Baldwin' [William Godwin], *The Pantheon: or Ancient History of the Gods of Greece and Rome*, 1806, 2nd edn 1809.
Bate (1945)	W. J. Bate, *The Stylistic Development of John Keats*, 1945.
Bate (1963)	W. J. Bate, *John Keats*, 1963.
Colvin (1917)	S. Colvin, *John Keats: his Life and Poetry, his Friends, Critics, and After-fame*, 1917.
Cowden Clarke	Charles and Mary Cowden Clarke, *Recollections of Writers*, 1878.
Critical Heritage	*Keats: The Critical Heritage*, ed. G. M. Matthews, 1971.
Finney	C. L. Finney, *The Evolution of Keats's Poetry*, 2 vols., 1936.
Gittings (1954)	R. Gittings, *John Keats: The Living Year*, 1954.
Gittings (1956)	R. Gittings, *The Mask of Keats*, 1956.
Gittings (1968)	R. Gittings, *John Keats*, 1968.
Jack	Ian Jack, *Keats and the Mirror of Art*, 1967.
Jones	John Jones, *John Keats's Dream of Truth*, 1967.

KSJ	Keats–Shelley Journal
Lemprière	Bibliotheca Classica; or, A Classical Dictionary ... (2nd edn 1792).
Lowell	A. Lowell, John Keats, 2 vols., 1925.
Morgan Library	Pierpont Morgan Library, New York.
Murry (1925)	J. M. Murry, Keats and Shakespeare, 1925.
Murry (1930)	J. M. Murry, Studies in Keats, 1930.
N & Q	Notes and Queries.
OED	Oxford English Dictionary
Pettet	E. C. Pettet, On the Poetry of John Keats, 1957.
PMLA	Publications of the Modern Language Association of America
PQ	Philological Quarterly.
RES	The Review of English Studies
Ridley	M. R. Ridley, Keats's Craftsmanship, 1933.
Spence's Polymetis	J. Spence, Polymetis; or an Enquiry concerning the Agreement between the works of the Roman Poets and the Remains of the antient Artists ..., 1747.
Stillinger	Jack Stillinger, The Hoodwinking of Madeline and other Essays on Keats's Poetry, 1970.
Texts	Jack Stillinger, The Texts of Keats's Poems, 1974.
TLS	Times Literary Supplement.
Ward (1963)	A. Ward, John Keats: The Making of a Poet, 1963.
Woodhouse (1817)	Stuart M. Sperry, 'Richard Woodhouse's Interleaved and Annotated Copy of Keats's Poems (1817)', Literary Monographs 1, ed. E. Rothstein and T. K. Dunseath, 1967.
W1–3	Woodhouse's transcripts of Keats's poems. W1–2 are in Harvard Library. W3 is now in the Morgan Library. For details, see G, pp. lx–iv, lxviii–lxxv, passim.

IMITATION OF SPENSER

Written early in 1814. Published 1817. Keats was introduced to Spenser by Cowden Clarke. Charles Brown reported, 'It was the "Faery Queen" that awakened his genius. In Spenser's fairy land he was enchanted ... till, enamoured of the stanza, he attempted to imitate it, and succeeded' (*KC* II p. 55). However, the poem owes more to eighteenth-century Spenserians like Thomson, Beattie, and Mary Tighe, than to Spenser himself. On the versification, see *Bate* (1945), pp. 189–91.

22 *teen* grief (Spenser).
27 *cerulean* azure.

ON PEACE

Written in spring 1814 to celebrate the Peace of Paris. Published *N&Q*, 4 February 1905. This irregular Shakespearian sonnet echoes the tone of the editorials written for the *Examiner* by Leigh Hunt, who hoped that the Peace might bring constitutional monarchy to Europe. On Hunt, see *Written on the Day that Mr Leigh Hunt left Prison* and headnote (p. 535).

9 *With England's happiness proclaim Europa's liberty* compare with the inscription on the peace decorations on Somerset House, '*Europa Instaurata, Aupice Britanniae / Tyrannide Subversa, Vindice Libertatis*' ('Europe restored, tyranny overthrown under the leadership of Britain, by the defender of liberty').

14 *horrors*] *Forman* (1883); honors *MSS*, *G*. *Allott* silently rejects the emendation, but none of the MSS is in Keats's hand, while 'horrors' makes more obvious sense, and fits in with imagery of imprisonment in l. 12. Although Keats does use 'honours' in this sense ('Leaps to the honours of a tournament', *Specimen of an Induction* 28), 'horrors' is more common in his work, the most famous example being, 'But horrors, portioned to a giant nerve' (*Hyperion* I, 175); see also *Endymion* IV, 468, 618, *Hyperion* I, 233, and *Otho the Great* V.2. 19, etc.

'FILL FOR ME A BRIMMING BOWL'

Written August 1814 after 'obtaining a casual sight' of a lady at Vauxhall, on whom Keats later wrote '*When I have fears . . .*' and *To —* ('Time's sea . . .'). Published *N & Q*, 4 February 1905. The text is based on the autograph MS in the Morgan Library, which marks the stanza divisions, unlike *W*3, *Garrod* (*OSA*), or *Allott*. M. A. E. Steele reproduces the MS in *KSJ*, I (1952), pp. 57–63, and thinks the poem was written at the same time as *To Emma* and '*O Solitude! if I must with thee dwell*'. *Texts*, pp. 95–8, argues for Mary Frogley's text.

6] That fills the mind with fond desiring *W*2–3, *G*. As *Allott* suggests, probably a watered down version to suit the tastes of Mary Frogley (see p. 539).
9 *breast*] heart *W*2–3, *G*.
13 *'Tis*] In *W*2–3, *G*.
25 *a*] the *G*, *Allott*.

TO LORD BYRON

Published *1848*. Written December 1814; sometimes said to have been written after his grandmother's death, but ll. 6–7 refer not to Keats's 'griefs', but Byron's.

9 *a golden*] *W*2, *Allott*; the golden, *1848*, *G*.

'AS FROM THE DARKENING GLOOM A SILVER DOVE'

Written December 1814. Published *1876*. According to Woodhouse 'he said he had written it on the death of his grandmother, about five days after; but he had never told anyone, not even his brother, the occasion on which it was written; he said he was tenderly attached to her' (*W*3). Keats's grandmother was buried 19 December.

7 *bedight* adorned (Spenser).
9 *quire* archaic spelling of 'choir' (though still a possible spelling in Keats's time).

13 *pleasures*] *W*1, *W*3, Allott; pleasure's *W*2, *1876*, G.

'CAN DEATH BE SLEEP, WHEN LIFE IS BUT A DREAM'

Written 1814. Published *Forman* (1883). *G* and *Allott* reject this poem. It occurs in the Keats–Wylie Scrap-Book, and is unsigned, though copied out by George Keats. The verses may represent Keats's attempt to reconcile himself to the death of his grandmother in December 1814. The weakness of the lines is not conclusive evidence against Keats's authorship: he was still ill-formed as a poet at this stage. See *Bate* (1963), pp. 39–40n. *Texts* (pp. 271–2) also rejects.

TO CHATTERTON

Written early spring 1815. Published *1848*. Thomas Chatterton (1752–70), who came of humble origins, fabricated a number of poems purporting to be the work of an imaginary fifteenth-century poet, Thomas Rowley. The fraud was exposed in 1777 and 1778 by Thomas Tyrwhitt, but the poems are nevertheless the product of a remarkably gifted writer. Chatterton moved to London in 1770, but despite the success of his burlesque opera, *The Revenge*, he was reduced to despair by poverty, and poisoned himself with arsenic at the age of seventeen. For the Romantics he became a symbol of society's neglect of the artist. Keats dedicated *Endymion* to him, and mentions him in *To George Felton Mathew* 56. In September 1819 he wrote, 'The purest english ... is Chatterton's – The Language had existed long enough to be entirely uncorrupted of Chaucer's gallicisms and still the old words are used – Chatterton's language is entirely northern – I prefer the native music of it to Milton's cut by feet' (*L* II, 212). For his influence on Keats, see *Gittings* (1956), pp. 88–97.

4 *wildly*] *W*2–3, *G*, Allott; mildly *1848*, Garrod (*OSA*).
6 *murmurs*] *W*2–3, Allott; numbers *1848*, *G*.
8 *flower*] *W*2–3; flower'ts *1848*, *G*, Allott.
8 *amate* daunt, subdue (archaic). Like 'elate' (l. 5), 'ingrate' (l. 12) and 'floweret', this echoes Chatterton's usage, who took it from Spenser. Keats's fondness for '-ate' endings persisted.

WRITTEN ON THE DAY THAT MR LEIGH HUNT LEFT PRISON

Written 2 February 1815. Published *1817*. Hunt had just finished a two-year sentence for libelling the Prince Regent in the *Examiner*. Keats did not meet Hunt until October 1816, but his influence is apparent on the poetry until 1817. Cowden Clarke lent Keats copies of the *Examiner*.

TO HOPE

Written February 1815. Published *1817*. Composed when Keats was living in as an apprentice with the surgeon, Thomas Hammond, in Edmonton (l. 1). The family was dispersed after the death of Keats's grandmother. Fanny and George were living with their guardian, Richard Abbey. Tom may have been with them or at Enfield School. As the eldest, Keats felt his responsibility (ll. 19–20).

3 'mind's eye' quoted from *Hamlet* I. 2. 185.

536 NOTES FOR PP. 43-5

ODE TO APOLLO

Written February 1815. Published *1848*. An announcement of Keats's early pre-occupation with the grandeur of poetry, and of the attraction held for him by Apollo (see *Jack*, pp. 176–90, and W. Evert, *Aesthetic and Myth in the Poetry of Keats*, 1965, pp. 23–87). The 'Ode' is influenced by earlier ones, particularly Gray's *Progress of Poesy* (1757).

5 *adamantine* diamond. Keats characteristically fuses the connotations of hardness and brilliance.
7 *nervous* sinewy, muscular.
14 *Maro* Virgil's name for Publius Virgilius Maro.
33 See Spenser, *The Faerie Queene* III.
34 *Aeolian lyre* a wind-harp, a stringed instrument hung so that it vibrated with the movement of the air: a favourite symbol of inspiration among Romantic poets.
42 *Nine* the Nine Muses.

LINES WRITTEN ON 29 MAY, THE ANNIVERSARY OF THE RESTORATION OF CHARLES THE 2ND

Written 29 May 1815. Published *Lowell*. Written during the Hundred Days following Napoleon's escape from Elba. Louis XVIII sought asylum in England, and was met by huge crowds. On 29 May bells were rung all over England to commemorate Charles II's restoration. Keats approved of neither reaction, taking a liberal stance: legitimacy alone was not sufficient. For Hazlitt, Waterloo was 'the sacred triumph of kings over mankind'. Text from *W*3 (*Texts*, pp. 93–4).

1 *will*] *G* (*from W*3), *Allott*; while *Lowell*.
4 *when*] *Texts* (p. 94); while *Lowell*, *G*, *Allott*.
5 Algernon Sidney (1622–83), Lord William Russell (1639–83), and Sir Henry Vane (1613–62) were all executed for treason against Charles II. They were regarded as heroes by the Whigs.

TO SOME LADIES

Probably written summer 1815. Published *1817*. Sent to Misses Anne and Caroline Mathew, when they were staying at Hastings with their cousin, George Felton Mathew. Mathew attempted to write poetry himself, and occupied an important place as a friend and admirer of Keats in 1815. The taste of Mathew and his cousins for sentiment and the jingling quatrains of Thomas Moore had a short-lived influence on Keats's work (see the next six poems and *To George Felton Mathew*).

6 *muse*] *G* (*from MS*), *Allott*; rove *1817*.
8 *Its*] *1817*; In *MS*.
20 *Tighe* Mary Tighe (1772–1810), popular Irish poetess, whose *Psyche* (1805), a six-canto poem in Spenserian stanzas, was admired by Moore. For a somewhat too eager account of her influence on Keats, see E. V. Weller, *Keats and Mary Tighe* (1928).

NOTES FOR PP. 46-8

28 *aërial* thin as air, ethereal.

ON RECEIVING A CURIOUS SHELL AND A COPY OF VERSES, FROM THE SAME LADIES

Written summer 1815. Published *1817*. Addressed to G. F. Mathew, who had written some verses to accompany his cousin's gifts of a 'Dome shaped' sea shell and a copy of Moore's *The Wreath and the Chain* (1801).

1 *Golconda* Indian city, west of Hyderabad, famous for its diamonds. In fact, Golconda had no mines, but diamonds were cut and polished there.
8 *Armida ... Rinaldo* heroine and hero of Tasso's *Gerusalemme Liberata*.
12 *Britomartis* heroine of *The Faerie Queene* III, representing chastity and purity.
17 *Sir Knight* i.e., G. F. Mathew.
21 Refers to Moore's poem (see headnote).
24 *trammels* shackles.
25 *This canopy* that is, its shell, which is later called 'this little dome' (l. 33).
25-30 *A Midsummer Night's Dream* is the obvious source, but Mathew introduced Keats to W. Sotheby's translation (1798) of Wieland's *Oberon* (1780), and the influence of its romantic pathos is evident here – see W. Beyer, *Keats and the Demon King* (1947). The idea of fairies held a strong interest for Keats: in 1815-16 he is reported as saying, 'the other day ... during the lecture [at St Thomas's Hospital], there came a sunbeam into the room, and with it a whole troop of creatures floating in the ray, and I was off with them to Oberon – and fairyland' (*Cowden Clarke*, pp. 131-2).
41 *Eric* a playful nickname for Mathew.

TO EMMA

Probably written in summer 1815. Published *Forman* (1883). It is likely that the poem was addressed to one of two Mathew sisters, though neither was called 'Emma'. *De Selincourt*, p. 563, suggests that Keats borrows the name from Wordsworth, who had used it when addressing his sister Dorothy. George Keats later used the poem, with the name appropriately changed, during his courtship (see headnote *To G[eorgiana] A[ugusta] W[ylie]*, p. 554).

Text from autograph MS in Morgan Library, reproduced by M. A. E. Steele, *KSJ*, I (1952), pp. 57-63, who argues that the poem was written at the same time as *Fill for me a brimming bowl*' and '*O Solitude! if I must with thee dwell*'. Title from *W*2.

1 *dearest*] my dear *W*2, *G*.
5] O Come! let us haste to the freshening shades *W*2, *G*.
6 *freshening shades*] opening glades *W*2, *G*.
17 *Then*] Ah! *W*2, *G*, *Allott*.
17 *lovely*] dearest *W*2, *G*.

SONG ('Stay, ruby-breasted warbler, stay')

Dated 'About 1815/6' (*W*3); *Bate* (1963), p. 40*n*, thinks it was written before

538 NOTES FOR PP. 48-50

autumn 1815. Published *1876*. 'This song was written at the request of some young ladies who were tired of singing the words printed with the air and desired fresh words to the same tune' (*W*3). The 'young ladies' are identified as the Misses Mathew. Forman rejected this poem. *Allott*, p. 744, thinks the attribution doubtful, and considers it may be by his brother, George. Woodhouse, however, transcribed the poem, which argues in favour of Keats's authorship. See also *Texts*, pp. 94-5.

22 *longer*] Keats-Wylie Scrapbook (*Texts*, ibid.); flower *G*, *Allott*.

'WOMAN! WHEN I BEHOLD THEE FLIPPANT, VAIN'

Probably written March to December 1815. 'From Mathew's later enthusiastic endorsement ... we can conclude that the [poem was] written while he and Keats were seeing one another most frequently (March to December, 1815)', *Bate* (1963), p. 40*n*. *Allott* dates *c*. March 1816, but the earlier date is preferable since the poem seems to belong with the preceding group of poems to the Misses Mathew. Published *1817*. Like other editors, *G* and *Allott* print the three stanzas as separate sonnets, but in *1817* the three sonnets are given as stanzas in a single poem, and *Garrod* (*OSA*) adopts this arrangement. Further, see *Stillinger*, p. 8*n*. The structure of this poem should be connected with Keats's later experiments with the 'sonnet stanza' which led to the stanzaic structure of the major odes (see headnote to *Ode to Psyche*, p. 645).

12-13 *Calidore ... Red Cross Knight ... Leander* three examples of devoted lovers; the two first are from *The Faerie Queene*. Leander swam the Hellespont to reach Hero.

14 *of yore* of old (archaic).

31-2 'When Keats had written these lines he burst into tears overpowered by the tenderness of his own imagination (conceptions)', *Woodhouse* (1817), p. 145.

'O SOLITUDE! IF I MUST WITH THEE DWELL'

Written *c*. October 1815, shortly after Keats entered Guy's Hospital after leaving Edmonton. On the date, see *Murry* (1930), pp. 2-5. This, Keats's first published poem, appeared in the *Examiner*, 5 May 1816, where it is entitled *To Solitude*: it has no title in *1817*. The 'kindred spirit' of l. 14 is probably George Keats, but the style of the poem suggests G. F. Mathew's influence. M. A. E. Steele believes the sonnet was written at the same time as '*Fill for me a brimming bowl*' and *To Emma*.

TO GEORGE FELTON MATHEW

Written November 1815, as a verse letter to George Felton Mathew (*L* I, pp. 100-103). Published *1817*. Mathew was an important friend and influence on Keats in 1815. For a while Keats thought his sentimental poeticizing endowed him with a power it did not possess. They read and explored poetry together, as this letter suggests. Keats's poem is probably a reply to Mathew's verses *To a poetical Friend*, published in the *European Magazine*, LXX (1816), p. 365; further, see *Murry* (1930), pp. 1-6, and for Mathew's comments on Keats's

NOTES FOR PP. 50-53

epistle, see *KC* II, p. 181, pp. 186-8. Several other of Keats's early poems are connected with the Mathew family circle: see *To Some Ladies, On Receiving a Curious Shell*, '*Stay, ruby-breasted warbler, stay*' and '*Woman! when I behold thee flippant, vain*'.

5 *brother Poets* a reference to Beaumont and Fletcher according to Woodhouse (1817), p. 145.

17 *far different cares* Keats's medical studies at Guy's Hospital.

18 '*Lydian airs*' quoted from Milton, *L'Allegro* 135-6.

24 *rapt seraph* see Pope, *An Essay on Man* (1733) I, 78: 'As the rapt Seraph that adores and burns'.

25-8 probably a reply to Mathew's poem, where he had urged Keats not to let his medical studies turn him from the poetry, especially Wieland's 'strange tales of the elf and fay', which they had appreciated together. For Keats's interest in fairies and Wieland's *Oberon*, see *On Receiving a Curious Shell* 25-30*n* (p. 537).

39 *Druid* for the pre-Romantics a symbol of the poet-priest.

40 *blowing* blooming (poeticism).

43 *cassia* not the 'casia' (cassia) of Virgil, Ovid, the Psalms and Milton, whose flowers were yellow or greenish-yellow (and whose bark provided a gentle laxative). Here Keats's 'cassia' intertwines with itself and its flowers are white (as in *Calidore* 96). The woodbine or 'Morning Glory' is probably intended.

45 *covert branches* here contains the meaning 'hidden branches' as well as the idea of the branches making a 'covert', i.e. hiding-place – 'Like a deer ... to the covert doth himself betake' (Drayton).

47 *aloof* the observer's height makes him 'aloof' from the 'violet beds' nestling on the ground.

56 *Chatterton* see *To Chatterton* headnote (p. 535).

62-5 *And mourn ... world* compare Keats's letter of 9 June 1819, 'One of the great reasons that the english have produced the finest writers in the world; is, that the English world has ill-treated them during their lives and foster'd them after their deaths' (*L* II, p. 115).

67-9 *Alfred ... Tell ... Wallace* the liberal spirit, and the admiration for these national heroes, was encouraged by Cowden Clarke and by the *Examiner*: compare *To Charles Cowden Clarke* 70-71.

75 '*a sun-shine in a shady place*' quoted from *The Faerie Queene* I. iii. 4.

77-8 *Close ... song* that is, close to the Pierian spring, the inspiration of the Muses.

85-9 the metamorphoses here are inspired by Ovid.

TO [MARY FROGLEY]

Written 14 February 1816 as a valentine for George Keats to send to Mary Frogley, who was a cousin of Richard Woodhouse. Published, in an altered form, *1817* (for the changes, see *G*). According to Woodhouse, Keats wrote two other valentines on the same occasion. One may have been the sonnet, *To —*

540 NOTES FOR PP. 53–5

('Had I a man's fair form'), possibly addressed to Mary Frogley or one of the Mathew sisters.

6 *fane* temple (poeticism), as in 'Old Iona's holy fane' (Scott).

15 *hellebore* botanical name for a species of garden plant, here probably referring to the Christmas rose.

21 *globes* 'i.e. of smoke', *Woodhouse* (1817), p. 144.

29 *little loves* putti, or winged cherubs, common in Renaissance paintings. Echoes Spenser, *Epithalamion*, where the phrase 'little winged loves' is used (l. 357), and ll. 231–3, where angels '... forget their service and about her fly, / Oft peeping in her face that seems more fayre, / The more they on it stare.' *Cowden Clarke*, p. 125, remarks, 'How often, in after-times, have I heard him quote these lines.'

31 *lave* normally a verb meaning 'bathe' (poeticism). Here used as a noun. The *OED* gives only one example, and that after Keats, of this form.

33 compare Spenser, *Epithalamion* 176, 'Her paps lyke lyllies budded'.

39–40 compare Spenser, *The Shepheardes Calendar*, April 112–13, 'Wants not a fourth grace, to make the daunce even? / Let that rowme to my Lady be yeuen...'

48–58 Mary Frogley is pictured as Spenser's chaste Britomartis, *The Faerie Queene* III. Compare *On Receiving a Curious Shell* 12.

55 *vase* Keats uses the eighteenth-century and early nineteenth-century pronunciation which rhymed with 'face'. Compare Byron, *Don Juan* VI, 97.

57 *alabaster* white (figurative).

60 *northern lights* the Aurora Borealis.

TO — ('Had I a man's fair form, then might my sighs')

Probably written *c*. 14 February 1816 as a valentine. See note to preceding poem. Published *1817*. Woodhouse wrote that Keats was here playing on the 'idea that the diminutiveness of his size makes him contemptible and that no woman can like a man of small stature' (*Woodhouse* (1817), p. 148). J. Burke Severs is probably right in thinking the speaker is a fairy, *KSJ*, VI (1957), pp. 109–13. Keats was sensitive about his height: he was only five foot and three quarters of an inch.

'GIVE ME WOMEN, WINE, AND SNUFF'

Written between autumn 1815 and July 1816 while Keats was studying medicine. Tentatively placed in March. Henry Stephens, a fellow student, recorded, 'In my Syllabus of Chemical Lectures [Keats] scribbled many lines on the paper cover, This cover has long been torn off, except one small piece on which is the following fragment of Doggrel rhyme' (*KC* II, p. 210). Published H. B. Forman's *Poetical Works of John Keats* (1884).

541 NOTES FOR PP. 56-8

SPECIMEN OF AN INDUCTION TO A POEM

Probably written late spring 1816; *Allott* dates *c.* February–March 1816. Colvin characterized this as an attempt 'to embody the spirit of Spenser in the metre of *Rimini*'. Keats had yet to meet Hunt, but *The Story of Rimini* had appeared in February 1816. Published *1817*.

Title the 'Poem' is *Calidore*.

2 compare *To [Mary Frogley]* 52–3.
6 *Archimago* the magician in *The Faerie Queene* I and II.
7 *attitude* see *Ode on a Grecian Urn* 41n (p. 651).
18 *trembling* for Keats's use of participal nouns, see *Calidore* 5n.
33 *lone*] long *Galignani, Allott*.
38 *banneral* a standard, pennon (not recorded in *OED*). See *The Faerie Queene* VI. vii 26, 'knightly banneral'.
40 *a spur in bloody field* describes the heraldic device on the knight's shield.
51 *And always does my heart with pleasure dance* compare Wordsworth, '*I wandered lonely as a cloud*' 23–4, 'And then my heart with pleasure fills, / And dances with the daffodils.'
61 *Libertas* Leigh Hunt, on whose imprisonment for the liberal views expressed in the *Examiner* see headnote to *Written on the Day that Mr Leigh Hunt left Prison* (p. 535). The name is also used in *To my Brother George* 24 and *To Charles Cowden Clarke* 44–5.

CALIDORE. A FRAGMENT

Precise date unknown, but probably written in late spring 1816, immediately after the preceding poem. Published *1817*. Sir Calidore, the Knight of Courtesy in *The Faerie Queene* VI, was a particular favourite with Keats. As in the *Specimen of an Induction*, Leigh Hunt's *The Story of Rimini* is a strong influence on the diction and conception of the poem.

5 *lingeringly* Keats's liking for adverbs made from participles was encouraged by Hunt's example. Other examples occur in ll. 16, 31, 82, 149. Examples of this word are recorded by the *OED* from 1589 onwards.
7 *clearness* Keats's liking for '-ness' endings was also supported by Hunt's practice. Other examples occur in ll. 9, 34, 48, 144.
10 *shadowy* the use of adjectives ending in '-y' derived from verbs or nouns was encouraged by Hunt's example. Other instances occur in ll. 26, 50, 139.
11 *So elegantly* again drawn from Hunt. *Allott*, p. 37n, quotes W. T. Arnold: 'Both [Keats and Hunt] have a curious way of using "so" . . . a sort of appeal to the reader, a tacit question whether he has not noted the same thing, and felt the same pleasure from it'. For other examples, see ll. 16, 130.
12 The six-syllable line here and at ll. 72, 84, 92 probably derives from Spenser's *Epithalamion*, a poem much admired by Keats (see *To [Mary Frogley]* 29–33, 39–40 nn).
14 *freaks* tricks.
20 *float* the use of verbs as nouns was supported by Hunt. Further, see ll. 69, 86, 139.

542 NOTES FOR PP. 58–62

30–45 *1817* prints as quatrains.
41 *Aye dropping their hard fruit upon the ground* Hunt praised the 'Greek simplicity' of this line when he reviewed *1817* in the *Examiner*, reprinted in *Critical Heritage*, p. 60.
44 *window*] Tom Keats's *MS, G, Allott*; *windows 1817*.
49 *spiral* 'Rising like a spire; tall and tapering or pointed', used of rocks, buildings, trees, etc. (*OED*). Steuart's *Planter's Garden* (1828), p. 338, has, 'It is indispensably necessary ... that the standard or grove Trees should be kept spiral. ...'
50 *cat's-eyes* the speedwell or forget-me-not, or various other small bright flowers. The *OED* gives this as the earliest example.
56 *ken* range of vision.
61 *undersong* a subordinate song or strain, especially one serving as an accompaniment or burden to another: 'Who the Roundelay should singe / And who againe the vndersong should beare' (Drayton).
67 *shallop* dinghy.
73 *bright-eyed things* fairies.
82 *their delicate ankles spanned* helped the ladies dismount by placing his hand under the foot, so 'spanning' the ankle.
84 *affection* Allott reads this as four syllables.
87 *palfrey* 'a saddle-horse for ordinary riding as distinguished from a war-horse; esp. a small saddle-horse for ladies' (*OED*). By the late eighteenth century the word had become a poeticism.
96 *cassia* probably woodbine ('Morning Glory') which is white, rather than honeysuckle. See *To George Felton Mathew* 43n (p. 539).
119 *weed* dress (Spenser).
146 *brimful* a typical word in Keats's early style.
155 *incense* the scent of flowers, a poetic usage Keats could have found in Milton, Pope, or Gray, and was to use again, most notably in *Ode to a Nightingale* 42, 'soft incense hangs upon the boughs'. See also *Endymion* I, 470, *Hyperion* I, 167, *The Fall of Hyperion* I, 99, 103, and 'incense-pillowed', *Endymion* II, 999. Compare Shelley, *Ginevra* (1821), 126, 'The matin winds from the expanded flowers / Scatter their hoarded incense.'

'TO ONE WHO HAS BEEN LONG IN CITY PENT'

'Written in the Fields. June 1816' (Keats-Wylie Scrap-Book). Published *1817*. Like *O Solitude! if I must with thee dwell*, a reaction against being bound down in London by his medical studies, though as *Bate* (1963), pp. 63–4, suggests, it is also an attempt to write another version of his first published poem. The sonnet starts from an adaptation of Milton's 'As one who long in populous City pent' (*Paradise Lost* IX, 445). Also echoes Coleridge, 'How many bards in city garret pent' (*To the Nightingale* [1796], 2).

7 *debonair* gentle, gracious (Spenser).
7–8 probably another reference to Hunt's *The Story of Rimini*.

'O! HOW I LOVE, ON A FAIR SUMMER'S EVE'

Written summer 1816, probably June–July. Published *1848*.

10 *Sidney* a reference probably to Algernon Sidney (for whom see *Written on 29 May 5n*, p. 536), though possibly to Sir Philip Sidney. Keats refers to 'the two Sidneys' in his journal-letter to George and Georgiana Keats, October 1818 (*L* I, p. 397). A little earlier, he remarks, 'We have no Milton, no Algernon Sidney'.
12 *the wing*] *W* 1–3, *G*; wing *1848*, *Garrod (OSA)*. Compare this line with *Ode to a Nightingale* 33, 'on the viewless wings of Poesy'.
14 *spells* bewitches, binds as with a spell.

TO A FRIEND WHO SENT ME SOME ROSES

Written 29 June 1816. *G* records that it is so dated in Tom Keats's transcript, and has the title, *To Charles Wells on receiving a bunch of roses*. The roses settled a disagreement between Wells and Keats. Wells (1800–79) was a minor writer and friend of Tom. Published *1817*.

3 *lush* see '*I stood tip-toe . . .*' 31*n* (p. 549).
6 *musk-rose* a favourite flower in Keats's poetry. It is a rambling rose, with fragrant white flowers. But there are also literary sources – Shakespeare, *A Midsummer Night's Dream* II. 1. 252, 'With sweet musk roses, and with eglantine', and Milton, *Lycidas* 146, 'The Musk-rose, and the well-attir'd Woodbine'. Keats's most notable reference is in *Ode to a Nightingale* 49, 'The coming musk-rose, full of dewy wine . . .'
8 *Titania* the fairy queen in *A Midsummer Night's Dream*.
12 *spelled* bewitched, bound as with a spell.

TO MY BROTHER GEORGE ('Many the wonders I this day have seen')

Written Margate, August 1816. Published *1817*. This sonnet, like the following poem, was written to George from Margate, where Keats had gone for a holiday after taking his examinations at the Apothecaries Hall on 25 July. The holiday was an attempt to give himself to writing for a while: Keats could not practise as a surgeon or apothecary until he came of age on 31 October.

3 *laurelled peers* repeated from *Ode to Apollo* 20.

TO MY BROTHER GEORGE ('Full many a dreary hour have I passed')

Written Margate, August 1816. Published *1817*. For the occasion, see note to preceding sonnet. This is the second of Keats's three verse epistles, the first being *To George Felton Mathew*, and the third *To Charles Cowden Clarke*. Bate (1963), pp. 70–72, regards this poem as important in Keats's early development, and shows him facing his central problem, that of the function and status of poetry. Clarke's notions on the 'visions' of poetry and Hunt's example still dominate however.

544 NOTES FOR PP. 64-8

12 *golden lyre* Apollo's lyre, symbol of poetic achievement. For other references, see *Ode to Apollo* 2, *Endymion* IV, 702, *Hyperion* III, 63.

19 *bay* the poet's (and Apollo's) laurel wreath.

24 *Libertas* Leigh Hunt (see *Specimen of an Induction* 61n, p. 541).

38 *seraph* angel of the highest of the nine orders, but Keats's source is probably literary rather than biblical (see *To George Felton Mathew* 24n, p. 539).

54 *poetic lore* compare *To my Brothers* 6-7.

66 *spell* bewitch, bind as with a spell.

74 *alarum* tri-syllabic.

121 *you* Woodhouse noted that *To [Mary Frogley]*, *To Georgiana Augusta Wylie*, and 'perhaps' '*O Solitude! if I must with thee dwell*', 'were written for his brother', and that this poem and the two sonnets, *To my Brother George* and *To my Brothers*, were written to him: see *Woodhouse* (1817), pp. 146-7.

123-42 Isabella Towers's copy of *1817* notes, 'Written on the cliff at Margate' (G).

124 *clift* a by-form of 'cliff' due to a confusion with 'cleft' (fissure). 'Exceedingly common in 16-18th centuries, and used by some writers in the 19th century', including Shelley (*OED*). The text in *L* has 'cliff'.

126 *tablet* 'a small smooth inflexible or stiff sheet or leaf for writing upon' (*OED*).

130 *scarlet coats* soldiers.

TO CHARLES COWDEN CLARKE

Written September 1816 as a verse epistle. Published *1817*. An autograph MS is now in the Huntington Library. This is the last of the three poems Keats wrote during his two month stay at Margate. Clarke (1787-1877), the son of Keats's headmaster at Enfield, had early encouraged Keats's interests in poetry, music and liberal politics. Clarke had just moved to London to take up publishing as his father was about to retire.

6 *With outspread wings the Naiad Zephyr courts* Allott considers 'the naiad' a 'slip, as the swan here is masculine'. But the 'Naiad Zephyr' is a composite figure invented by Keats, not a synonym for the swan. Keats imagines the swan half-flying ('With outspread wings'), half-treading across the water in the act of courting the 'Naiad Zephyr'. A Naiad was an inferior deity, presiding over springs, rivers, etc., usually pictured as a beautiful virgin. Zephyrs were wind deities, normally masculine, and usually so for Keats. However, he elsewhere relates them to women and streams – Woodhouse's transcript of the draft of *Endymion* has 'Upon some breast more zephyr-feminine' (III, 577), while the text in *L* of the *Ode to Psyche* 56 has 'Zephyrs' streams'; see also *Endymion* I, 376-7. The fusion of the two figures creates a suitable mistress for the swan, who also belongs to both air and water.

15-20 Keats's stay at Margate was marked by despondency: inspiration failed to come.

NOTES FOR PP. 68–72

17 *shattered boat* compare *Endymion* I, 46–7, 'I'll smoothly steer / My little boat'.

29–30 Clarke had introduced Keats to Tasso. 'Baiae' refers to the Bay of Naples, Tasso's home.

31 *Armida* heroine of *Gerusalemme Liberata*: see *On Receiving a Curious Shell* 8n (p. 537).

33–7 all Spenserian references. 'Mulla' is the stream near Spenser's last home, Kilcolman, Ireland. Line 34 can be compared to *Epithalamion* 175, 'Her brest like to a bowle of creame uncrudded'. Archimago is the magician in *The Faerie Queene* I and II; Una and Belphoebe are the heroines in the same books.

40 *Titania* the fairy queen in *A Midsummer Night's Dream* and Wieland's *Oberon*.

41 *Urania* the Muse of astronomy as well as Venus. Compare with the astronomical image in l. 67.

44 *wronged Libertas* Leigh Hunt, wronged because imprisoned. See *Specimen of an Induction* 61 and preceding poem, l. 24.

46–7 Refers to Hunt's *The Story of Rimini* I, 147ff.

49] *autograph MS* marks a paragraph, as do *G*, Allott; *1817* and Garrod *(OSA)* runs straight on.

52–3 Keats met Clarke first in 1803 at Enfield school, which was run by his father.

57 refers to the halcyon: see *To the Ladies who Saw Me Crowned* 7n (p. 556).

59 refers to *Paradise Lost* IV–VI, and VIII.

67 *Saturn's ring* Keats won Bonnycastle's *Introduction to Astronomy* (1807 edn) as a school prize.

70–71 *Alfred ... Tell ... Brutus* compare *To George Felton Mathew* 67–9.

94 *cloudlets*] *autograph MS*, Garrod *(OSA)*, Allott; cloudlet's *1817*, *G*.

100 Compare this use of quotation with the urn's statement at the end of *Ode on a Grecian Urn*.

110 *Mozart* Keats reacted strongly to Mozart. On 14 October 1818 he wrote, '... she kept me awake one Night as a tune of Mozart's might do' (*LI*, p. 395). Clarke was a good pianist, and first excited Keats's love of music.

111 *Arne* Thomas Arne (1710–88), a prolific composer, responsible, among other things, for the tune of 'Rule Britannia'.

112 *Erin* Ireland. Probably the 'song of Erin' refers to Thomas Moore's *Irish Melodies*.

'HOW MANY BARDS GILD THE LAPSES OF TIME!'

Probably written *c*. October 1816. Often dated March 1816, but see *Woodhouse* (1817), pp. 110–11, and Allott. One of the 'two or three' poems Keats showed to Leigh Hunt when he finally met him in Hampstead in October 1816, *Cowden Clarke*, pp. 132–3. Published *1817*.

1 compare '*To one who has been long in city pent*' 1. Leigh Hunt, reviewing *1817* in the *Examiner*, commented, 'by no contrivance of any sort can we prevent this from jumping out of the heroic measure into mere rhythmicality' (*Critical Heritage*, p. 59).

546 NOTES FOR P. 72

13 *That distance of recognizance bereaves* 'which distance prevents from being distinctly recognized' *Woodhouse* (1817), p. 148.

ON FIRST LOOKING INTO CHAPMAN'S HOMER

Written early one morning in October 1816 after Keats returned to his lodgings in Dean Street, having stayed late at Clarke's lodgings in Clerkenwell. First published in the *Examiner*, 1 December 1816, where it is quoted in an article by Leigh Hunt, whom Keats first met some time after 9 October.

Later critics have agreed with Hunt that this sonnet 'completely announced the new poet taking possession', *Lord Byron and Some of his Contemporaries* (1828), p. 248. Chapman offered Keats a masculine poetry opposed to the indulgent softness of Hunt's work. *Cowden Clarke*, p. 130, recalled introducing Keats to Chapman – 'One scene I could not fail to introduce to him – the shipwreck of Ulysses, in the fifth book of the *Odysseis*, and I had the reward of one of his delighted stares upon reading the following lines: "Then forth he came, his both knees falt'ring, both / His strong hands hanging down, and all with froth / His cheeks and nostrils flowing, voice and breath / Spent to all use, and down he sank to death. / *The sea had soak'd his heart through*...."' Clarke says that Keats departed 'at day-spring, yet he contrived that I should receive the poem from a distance of, may be, two miles by ten o'clock'. For discussion of the poem's sources and structure see *Murry* (1930), pp. 15–33, and B. Ifor Evans, 'Keats's Approach to the Chapman Sonnet', *Essays and Studies of the English Association*, XVI (1931).

The final text in *1817* differs from that in the *Examiner* or Keats's draft and fair copy (both in Harvard Library, though *G* and *Allott* report the draft as being in the Morgan Library).

1 *realms of gold* a reference to El Dorado, though probably also to the gold leaf embossing on the covers and spines of books.

4 *in fealty* poets are bound to Apollo by the feudal obligation of fidelity.

5 *Oft*] But *Examiner*.

6 *deep-browed*] deep *written over* low *in Fair copy*.

6 *demesne* 'a district, region, territory' (*OED*, which cites this example). But here may include overtones of the feudal sense of possession as by right (see l. 4*n* above).

7] Yet could I never judge what Men could mean *Draft, Fair copy, Examiner*. *Cowden Clarke*, p. 130, reports that Keats first wrote, 'Yet could I never tell what men could mean', but altered the line because this was 'bald and too simply wondering'.

7 *pure serene* 'serene' is derived from the Latin, *serenum*, which means a clear, bright or serene sky. Compare Coleridge, *Hymn before Sunrise, in the Vale of Chamouni* (1802), 72, 'glittering through the pure serene'.

9–10 an echo of the vivid description of Herschel's discovery of the planet Uranus in John Bonnycastle's *Introduction to Astronomy* given to Keats as a school prize in 1811.

NOTES FOR PP. 72-4

11-12 the sources of these lines are varied. *De Selincourt* gives a passage from William Gilbert's *The Hurricane* (1796) which is quoted by Wordsworth, *The Excursion* (1814) III, 931*n*: '... the Man of Mind ... would certainly be swallowed up by the first Pizarro that crossed him. But when he ... contemplates, from a sudden promontory, the distant, vast Pacific – and feels himself a freeman in this vast theatre ... his exaltation is not less than imperial.' Also influenced by Robertson's description of Balboa first sighting the Pacific in his *History of America* (1777) I, pp. 289–90. Tennyson pointed out to Palgrave that 'History requires here *Balbóa*' and not Cortez (*The Golden Treasury* [1861], p. 320).

11 *eagle*] wond'ring *Fair copy*. Leigh Hunt called Cortez's 'eagle eyes', '... a piece of historical painting, as the reader may see by Titian's portrait of him', *Lord Byron and Some of his Contemporaries* (1828), p. 249. *Allott* points out that no such painting by Titian is known. *Jack*, pp. 141–2, p. 265, says that in the sestet Keats designs his own 'historical painting', 'stationing' Cortez so as to dominate the scene.

13 *surmise*] look *Draft*.

14 *Darien* a reference to the wild region south and east of the Panama canal between Darien, a town in the middle of the isthmus, and Colombia.

TO A YOUNG LADY WHO SENT ME A LAUREL CROWN

Date of composition unknown. *Gittings* (1968), p. 93, points out a parallel between ll. 11–12 ('I would frown / On abject Caesars') and a sonnet by Horace Smith *Addressed by the Statue of Jupiter, lately arrived from Rome, to his Royal Highness the Prince Regent*, 'Caesars, whene'er I frowned, stood petrified'. Smith's poem appeared in the *Examiner*, 27 October 1816. October–November 1816 therefore seems a likely period for Keats to have written his poem. *Allott* argues for March 1817. Published *1848*.

ON LEAVING SOME FRIENDS AT AN EARLY HOUR

Probably written October–November 1816 in response to Keats's entry into the circle surrounding Hunt in Hampstead. Keats met Hunt for the first time somewhere between 9 and 27 October. Published *1817*.

3 *tablet* see *To my Brother George* 126*n* (p. 544).
6 *car* chariot (poeticism).

'KEEN, FITFUL GUSTS ARE WHISPERING HERE AND THERE'

Written October or early November 1816 after a visit to Leigh Hunt's cottage in the Vale of Health, Hampstead. Published *1817*. Composed 'on the day after one of our visits' according to *Cowden Clarke*, p. 134. Keats would have had to walk over five miles to get back to his lodgings in London.

13-14 *lovely Laura ... faithful Petrarch* Petrarch (1304–74) epxressed his spiritualized passion for Laura in his *Canzoniere*. In his cottage Hunt had a portrait of the famous lovers, which is mentioned again in *Sleep and Poetry* 389–91.

548 NOTES FOR PP. 74-6

ADDRESSED TO HAYDON ('Highmindedness, a jealousy for good')

Date uncertain, but possibly written after Keats's first visit to Haydon's studio, 3 November 1816. However, it could have been written before the two men had met. Gittings thinks a date in March more likely. Published *1817*. Benjamin Robert Haydon (1786–1846) was a successful historical painter at this point, and a friend of Wordsworth, Reynolds and Hunt, through whom Keats met him. From 1812 Haydon had carried out a vigorous war with the Academy in the pages of the *Examiner*, continued later in *Annals of the Fine Arts*. A man of energy, convinced of his own genius, Haydon was an important influence on Keats, and tried to turn him away from Hunt's manner. Haydon's devotion to art, his 'gusto', his admiration for Shakespeare, and his love of the Elgin Marbles came at a crucial point in Keats's development (see *On Seeing the Elgin Marbles*). Further see Bate (1963), pp. 97–101, and *Jack*, pp. 23–57.

6 *'singleness of aim'* quoted from Wordsworth's *Character of the Happy Warrior* (1807), 40.
11-12 Haydon played an active part in the campaign to persuade the Government to purchase the marble reliefs brought back from the Parthenon by Lord Elgin in 1803, and offered for sale to the nation in 1811. The Government gave way early in 1816.

TO MY BROTHERS

Written 18 November 1816 to mark Tom Keats's seventeenth birthday. Published *1817*. It probably celebrates the brothers' coming together in their new lodgings at 76 Cheapside.

ADDRESSED TO [HAYDON] ('Great spirits now on earth are sojourning')

Sent to Haydon in a letter, 20 November 1816 (*L* I, p. 117). Probably composed on the evening of 19 November, after dining with Haydon, or the following morning. Published *1817*. The poem is the second of three addressed to Haydon: see *Addressed to Haydon* and *To B. R. Haydon*. The three 'spirits' celebrated are Wordsworth (2–4), Hunt (5–6) and Haydon (7–8).

3 *Helvellyn* mountain five miles from Grasmere, frequently referred to by Wordsworth.
6 *the chain for Freedom's sake* another reference to Hunt's imprisonment (see headnote to *Written on the Day that Mr Leigh Hunt left Prison*, p. 535).
13 *Of mighty workings?* —] Of mighty Workings in a distant Mart? *L* and *MS*. Keats altered the line at Haydon's suggestion, and wrote to him on 21 November 1816, 'My feelings entirely fall in with yours in regard to the Elipsis and I glory in it' (*L* I, p. 118).

'I STOOD TIP-TOE UPON A LITTLE HILL'

Completed in December 1816. On 17 December Keats wrote to Cowden Clarke, 'I have done little to Endymion [this poem's original title] lately – I

549 NOTES FOR PP. 76–7

hope to finish it in one more attack' (*L* I, p. 121). Haydon reported to Wordsworth on 31 December, Keats 'is now writing a longer sort of poem of "Diana and Endymion" to publish with his smaller production' (*Correspondence and Table Talk*, ed. F. W. Haydon [1876] II, p. 30). Probably begun in spring–summer of 1816. Published as the first poem in *1817*. Hunt said the poem was suggested 'by a delightful summer-day, as he stood beside the gate that leads from the Battery on Hampstead Heath into a field by Caen Wood' (*Lord Byron and Some of his Contemporaries* [1828], p. 249). *Ward* (1963), pp. 420–21, attempts to date the progress of the poem's composition. Lines 1–114 may have been drafted during Keats's stay in Margate, lines 115–92 may belong to October or November, and lines 193–end were written in 'attacks' in December, when the whole poem was revised. It is placed here before *Sleep and Poetry* in the chronological, sequence: although finished later, '*I stood tip-toe* . . .' was begun earlier, and is an attempt to explore the issues more fully realized in *Sleep and Poetry*. For a discussion, see *Jones*, p. 123–6. The manuscripts are widely distributed and their relationship complicated (see *G*, pp. lxxxiv–viii). A recently discovered fragment shows Keats eliminating 'Huntisms' such as 'gently', 'nestling', 'embower', 'dainties', 'delicious', etc., from what is nevertheless his most Huntian poem: see N. Rogers and M. Steele, '*I stood tip-toe*: A Hitherto Uncollated Fragment', *KSJ*, X (1962), pp. 12–13.

Motto Leigh Hunt, *The Story of Rimini* III, 430.

6 *starry diadems* 'the dew Drops', *Woodhouse* (1817), p. 141.

20 *alley* a walk in a park, etc., lined with trees: 'every alley green . . . of this wilde Wood' (Milton, *Comus* 310–11).

22 *where*] *G*, *Allott*; *were 1817*. 'Jaunty' is glossed as 'wandering' by *Woodhouse* (1817), p. 141.

31 *lush* cited by *OED*, along with *Endymion* I, 940 ('a lush screen of drooping weeds'), as an example of the meaning, used of plants (esp. grass), 'succulent and luxuriant in growth'. *OED* points out that the literary currency of this sense stemmed from Theobald's emendation of 'luscious woodbine' in *A Midsummer Night's Dream* II.1.251 to 'lush woodbine', a reading adopted by Johnson. Woodhouse, however, glossed the meaning as 'deep coloured', and his note on *To a Friend who Sent me some Roses* 3 ('From his lush clover covert') reads, 'full-coloured – in opposition to faint-coloured' (*Woodhouse* [1817], pp. 141, 149). This sense, which is recorded in Johnson's *Dictionary*, stemmed from Hanmer's explanation of 'lush' in *The Tempest* II.1.52 as 'of a dark deep Colour, opposite to pale, faint' (*Shakespeare's Works* [1774] VI). It is probable that Woodhouse is right about this instance: compare the 'lush laburnum' here with 'the dark-leaved laburnum's drooping clusters' (*To George Felton Mathew* 41). Something of both meanings is usually present in Keats's use of the word; see *Endymion* I, 46, 631, 940, II, 52.

51–2 for other examples of Keats's enthusiasm for his contemporaries at this point, see *Addressed to [Haydon]* and *Sleep and Poetry* 220–30.

59 *taper fingers* the sweet peas's tendrils. The adjectival use of 'taper' lasted through the nineteenth century.

550 NOTES FOR PP. 77-82

61-106 a 'recollection of having frequently loitered over the rail of a foot-bridge that spanned ... a little brook in the last field upon entering Edmonton' according to *Cowden Clarke*, pp. 138-9. These lines do not occur in the draft, and *Ward* (1963), pp. 420-21, suggests that they were written in Margate in August-September 1816.

67 *sallows* willows. For other occurrences see *Endymion* II, 341, IV, 392, and *To Autumn* 28.

70-71 compare Shakespeare, *As You Like It* II.i.15-17, 'And this our life ... / Finds tongues in trees, books in the running brooks, / Sermons in stones and good in everything.'

113-15 *moon ... light* anticipates *Endymion* in celebrating the moon's influence over the poetic imagination. Cowden Clarke said that 'one of the earliest things J. K. wrote was a sonnet to the moon' (*W*3). It is, of course, a common Romantic theme.

114 *swim* see *Endymion* I, 571*n* (p. 566).

125-204 Keats engages here with the central problem of the function and nature of poetry. The source of the ideas lies in his reading of Wordsworth's *The Excursion* (1814), IV, 687-765, 840-81, which suggests that the Classical deities originated in man's animistic response to the forces of nature. These views on the origins of myth had a profound influence on Keats. See Appendix 1, p. 497.

134 *vases* rhymes with 'faces'. Compare *To [Mary Frogley]* 55*n*.

141-50 compare this handling of the Psyche story with that in *Ode to Psyche* (see headnote, p. 642). Keats's sources are Lemprière, Spence's *Polymetis*, and paintings of Arcadian scenes such as Poussin's. The cluster of figures here – Psyche and Cupid, Pan and Syrinx (ll. 157-62), Echo and Narcissus (ll. 163-80), and Endymion and Cynthia (ll. 181-204) – were associated in Keats's mind: all of them could be used to describe the origin of poetry, and they had all provided subjects for painters; see *Jack*, pp. 144 ff.

151-2 *Woodhouse* (1817), p. 141, identifies the figure here with Ovid.

163-80 this passage is probably indebted to memories of Poussin's *Landscape with Narcissus and Echo* as well as to the more obvious source in Ovid, *Metamorphoses* III.

180 *bale* torment, woe (poeticism), also mental suffering, misery (Spenser).

189 *speculation* the act of observing (archaic by Keats's time). Keats 'almost always used the word ... with the meaning ... of "contemplation" or "simple vision" or with a meaning in which the contemplative element predominates', *Murry* (1930), p. 93.

194 *Latmos* the mountain where Endymion pastured his sheep and was visited by Diana: see *Endymion* I, 63-88 for another handling of this incident.

218 *young Apollo on the pedestal* a reference to the Apollo Belvedere. *Allott* points out that Keats knew the illustration in *Spence* (Plate XI).

221-30 Probably, as *Ward* (1963), p. 59, suggests, a memory of Keats's experiences as a student in the wards of Guy's Hospital.

220 *Venus* the Venus de Medici.

233 *other's*] *G, Allott*; others' *1817*; others *MSS*.

551 NOTES FOR PP. 82-6

SLEEP AND POETRY

Completed December 1816, written largely in Leigh Hunt's Hampstead cottage, and therefore started sometime after 9 October. 'It was in the library at Hunt's cottage, where an extemporary bed had been made up for him on the sofa, that [Keats] composed the frame-work and many lines of the poem... the last sixty or seventy being an inventory of the art garniture of the room', *Cowden Clarke*, pp. 133-4. It is closely related to '*I stood tip-toe...*' (see note to preceding poem), and was published as the final poem in *1817*.

Sleep and Poetry takes up the themes raised by his verse letters, and the loose framework allows Keats to make the first serious effort to outline his major concerns. Discussed by *Bate* (1963), pp. 124-30, *Jack*, pp. 130-40, and *Jones*, pp. 40-48, *passim*.

Motto *The Floure and the Leafe* 17-21. The poem is no longer attributed to Chaucer. See also *Written on a Blank Space at the End of Chaucer's Tale of 'The Floure and the Leafe'*.

5 *blowing* blooming (poeticism). For 'musk-rose', see *To a Friend who Sent Me some Roses* 6n (p. 543).

28 *rumblings* Woodhouse altered to 'rumbleings' with the note, '3 syllables', *Woodhouse* (1817), p. 153.

33 *shapes of light, aërial limning* delicately outlined spirits made of light: the participle also suggests that the spirits are 'limning' themselves in light.

48 *denizen* citizen, inhabitant, often used in a poetic sense by this time. The word may here have something of its legal meaning, for which *OED* cites Blackstone, *Commentaries* (1765) I, p. 374, 'A Denizen is an alien born, but who has obtained ... letters patent to make him an English subject.'

56 *clear air* 'i.e. of poetic inspiration', *Woodhouse* (1817), p. 153.

69-71 compare Wordsworth, *To the Daisy* (1807), 70-72, 'A happy, genial influence, / Coming one knows not how, nor whence, / Nor whither going'.

71-2 *imaginings will hover / Round my fireside* see *To My Brothers*.

74 *Meander*] G, *Allott*; meander *1817*. In classical geography, a river in Asia Minor celebrated for its windings.

79 *tablets* writing pad, though dignified perhaps by an echo of the Mosaic 'tablets'.

88-9 *steep / Of Montmorenci* a river in Quebec with a waterfall.

96-154 Keats gives an account of the development of the artist. It resembles *Tintern Abbey*, and anticipates his later discussion of life as 'a large Mansion of Many Apartments' (3 May 1818, *L* I, pp. 280-81, quoted in part in headnote to *The Fall of Hyperion*, p. 677-8).

101-21 *the realm.../ Of Flora, and old Pan* the carefree world of pastoral. Flora was the Roman goddess of flowers. Pan ('God of all') was the god of pastoral mythology, represented as a satyr. The ultimate source for Keats's 'realm of Flora' is Ovid, but Ovid mediated through Sandys, eighteenth-century poets, and through the work of painters. Spence called the garden of Flora 'the paradise of the Roman mythology'. Poussin's *Bacchanalian Revel before a Term of Pan* probably contributes details to this passage, while his

552 NOTES FOR PP. 86-8

Realm of Flora provides a more basic inspiration: see *Jack*, pp. 135-40. Further, see *Dictionary of Classical Names* (pp. 706, 713).

126-33 the image of the charioteer 'O'ersailing the blue cragginess' above the world of Flora and Pan is taken from Poussin's painting *The Realm of Flora*, *Jack*, pp. 136-8. The charioteer is therefore to be identified with Apollo, god of the sun (and poetry). Woodhouse commented on ll. 127-8, 'Personification of the Epic poet, when the enthusiasm of inspiration is upon him', *Woodhouse* (1817), p. 154.

134 *a green*] the green *Garrod (O S A)*, *Allott*.

135 *stalks* '"poetical expression for "trees"' *Woodhouse* (1817), p. 154.

162-229 Keats gives a brief history of the development of English poetry. In his account the greatness of the Elizabethans and seventeenth-century writers (ll. 171-80) was betrayed by the formalism of neo-classicism (ll. 181-206). He ends by turning to the resurgence of poetry in his own time (ll. 221-9).

180 *soothe*] *Allott*; sooth *1817, G*. John Jones suggests emending to 'smooth', *Jones*, p. 58n; *G* notes it as a possible reading. Keats, however, regularly spelt 'soothe' as 'sooth', and its occurrence here should be compared with *Endymion* I, 783, 'soothe thy lips', and *Isabella* 403, 'calmed its wild hair'. See also the otherwise unexampled superlative, 'O soothest Sleep', in *To Sleep* 5. *Jones*, p. 61, comments, 'Did he spell ["sooth"] that way in order to bring it visually – and thus magically-truly – closer to "smooth"? Or perhaps its private rationale is to be found in the private Keatsian adjective "sooth" which exists in his poetry alongside the public "sooth" (meaning of course "true") and appears to conflate "smooth" and "soothing" – at any rate in *St Agnes Eve*'s "jellies soother than the creamy curd".'

186 *rocking horse* the Augustan heroic couplet. Hazlitt said in the *Examiner* 20 August 1815, 'Dr Johnson and Pope would have converted his vaulting Pegasus [Milton's versification] into a rocking horse', *Works*, ed. P. P. Howe (1930-34), IV, p. 40.

198 *the certain wands of Jacob's wit* Jacob's payment for looking after Laban's flock was the right to all speckled cattle, goats and sheep. Genesis xxx 37-42 gives the story of how Jacob used rods of poplar, hazel and chestnut in a magical variety of selective breeding.

202 *Lyrist* Apollo.

206 *Boileau* Boileau (1636-1711), French poet and critic, whose *Art poétique* formulated neo-classical critical attitudes. Like most of his generation, Keats thought of Augustanism as an interregnum in English poetry, dominated by French taste.

206 *O ye whose charge* 'Oh ye elder & better poets, who sang in your day of our pleasant hills, & of natural scenes, & whose spirits may be imagined now to haunt those places', *Woodhouse* (1817), p. 155.

209 *boundly* either bounden or boundless (coinage).

218 *lone spirits* 'alluding to H[enry] Kirke White [1785-1806] – Chatterton – & other poets of great promise, neglected by the age, who died young', *Woodhouse* (1817), p. 155.

NOTES FOR PP. 88-92

226 *swan's ebon bill* refers to Wordsworth according to *Woodhouse* (1817), p. 155.

226-8 *from a thick brake .../Bubbles a pipe* 'Leigh Hunt's poetry is here alluded to, in terms too favorable', *Woodhouse* (1817), p. 155. A 'brake' is a thicket, or clump of bushes. 'Pipe' refers to the bird's song.

231 *Strange thunders from the potency of song* 'Allusion to Lord Byron, & his terrific stile of poetry – to Christabel by Coleridge &c.', *Woodhouse* (1817), p. 155.

233-5 *the themes | Are ugly clubs, the poets Polyphemes | Disturbing the grand sea* 'The poets, says Keats, are giants like Polyphemus and his brethren, of superhuman strength, but like the eyeless Polyphemus without ability to direct their energies fitly, so that their clubs (the themes they write on ...) only succeed in disturbing the grand sea (of poetry? or life?)', *De Selincourt* (who further suggests that Keats was probably thinking of Byron). Hunt took the lines as an attack on the Lake School. *Woodhouse* (1817) suggests 'cubs' for 'clubs'.

237 *'Tis might half-slumbering on its own right arm* echoed by Coleridge in the lines added to *The Eolian Harp* in 1817, 'Is Music slumbering on its instrument' (l. 33). *De Selincourt* comments on Keats's characteristic power 'of presenting in his poetry the effects of sculpture', and *Woodhouse* (1817), p. 155 refers to the Elgin Marbles. *Jack*, p. 135, notes that the Dionysus on the East pediment is the only figure bearing any resemblance to the line, and suggests Michelangelo's Adam in the Sistine Chapel as a possible source.

241-2 'Alluding still to Lord Byron', *Woodhouse* (1817), p. 155.

248 *a myrtle fairer* 'Allusion to the coming age of poetry under the type of a myrtle. The author appears to think (perhaps justly) very favourably of the approaching generation of poets ...', *Woodhouse* (1817), p. 156.

257 *Yeaned* brought forth, born (used of sheep, goats, and occasionally other beasts).

276 *fane* temple (poeticism).

303 *Dedalian wings* see under 'Dedalus', *Dictionary of Classical Names* (p. 703).

322 *pleasant rout* 'rout' usually means uproar, clamour, but here means 'A fashionable gathering or assembly, a large evening party or reception, much in vogue in the 18th and early 19th centuries' (*OED*).

324 *perhaps* pronounced as one syllable.

344-6 *the swift bound | Of Bacchus from his chariot, when his eye | Made Ariadne's cheek look blushingly* Ariadne, daughter of King Minos, was abandoned on Naxos by Theseus, where she was found by Bacchus. The latter's 'swift bound' is drawn from Titian's *Bacchus and Ariadne*, exhibited in London in 1816 and which Keats much admired (see *Jack*, pp. 130-31). See also *Endymion* IV, 193-272 and *n* (p. 583).

338 *portfolio* portfolios of engravings of paintings were the best way to gain acquaintance with art in the early nineteenth-century. Keats was given the run of Hunt's collection.

354 *a poet's house* Hunt's cottage (see headnote). Keats goes on to describe its library in the following lines (354–91). For a discussion of the paintings by Poussin, Claude, and Titian which probably influenced these lines see *Jack*, pp. 132–3.

377 *smoothness*] G, Allott; smoothiness *1817*.
379 *unshent* unsullied, unspoiled (now archaic).
381 *Sappho's meek head* a bust of the Greek poetess.
385 *Great Alfred* a patriotic hero of Keats; see *To George Felton Mathew* 67–9n (p. 539).
387 *Kosciusko* see headnote, *To Kosciusko*, below.
389–90 *Petrarch ... Laura* for an earlier reference see *Keen, fitful gusts* 13–14n (p. 547).

WRITTEN IN DISGUST OF VULGAR SUPERSTITION

Written on Sunday evening, 22 December 1816. Keats's autograph (Harvard) has a note, which may be in Tom Keats's hand, 'J. Keats Written in 15 Minutes'. Published *1876*. An important poem for the light it throws on Keats's religious attitudes; see *Bate* (1963), pp. 133–6.

7 *Lydian airs* compare *To George Felton Mathew* 18. Echoes Milton's *L'Allegro* 136.

ON THE GRASSHOPPER AND CRICKET

Written 30 December 1816. Published *1817*. 'The author & Leigh Hunt challenged each other to write a sonnet in a Quarter of an hour. – 'The Grasshopper & Cricket' was the subject. – Both performed the task within the time allotted', *Woodhouse* (1817), p. 151. 'Keats won as to time', *Cowden Clarke*, p. 135. *On Receiving a Laurel Crown*, *On Seeing a Lock of Milton's Hair*, and *To the Nile* were also written in competitions with Hunt.

TO KOSCIUSKO

Written December 1816. So dated when it appeared in the *Examiner*, 16 February 1817. Reprinted in *1817*. Tadeusz Kosciusko (1746–1817) was a Polish patriot who fought against Russia. At Dubjenka in 1792 he held off 16,000 Russians with only 4,000 troops. He had also fought for the United States in the War of Independence. He died a hero of English liberals. Hunt had a bust of him in his cottage, see *Sleep and Poetry* 387–8.

7 *And change*] Garrod (*OSA*), Allott; And changed *1817*; Are changed *Examiner*, G. Emendation follows *Woodhouse* (1817), p. 152.
8 *and round*] around *Examiner*.

TO G[EORGIANA] A[UGUSTA] W[YLIE]

Written December 1816. Published *1817*. Georgiana Wylie (c. 1797–1879) became the wife of Keats's brother, George, in May 1818, and they emigrated to America in June of the same year. Probably written on behalf of his brother like *To [Mary Frogley]* (see headnote, p. 539). Keats had a strong affection for his future sister-in-law.

'HAPPY IS ENGLAND! I COULD BE CONTENT'

Probably written December 1816 (see *Bate* [1963], p. 120). Published *1817*.
7 *Alp* used in the singular by Milton, *Paradise Lost* II, 620, 'many a Fierie Alp'. See also *Endymion* I, 666.

'AFTER DARK VAPOURS HAVE OPPRESSED OUR PLAINS'

Dated 31 January 1817 (*W*1–2). Published in *Examiner*, 23 February 1817, and in *1848*. Keats had *1817* ready for the press on 1 January: this is the only poem he wrote that month.

5 *month, relieving from*] *W*1–2, *G*; month, relieving of *Examiner*; mouth, relieved from *1848*; month, relievèd of *Garrod* (*OSA*), *Allott*. 'Mouth' is a possible reading in view of the images of sickness (ll. 1, 4) and the reference to 'eyelids' (l. 7). 'Month', however, fits in with the seasonal imagery, and also fits the period in which Keats wrote the poem. 'Relieving from' is a rare intransitive use: *OED* records the sense, 'to lift or raise up again' (1533).
6 *the feel of* compare *In drear-nighted December* 21n.
10 *fruit ... suns* anticipates *To Autumn* 1–2.
14 *a Poet's death* Chatterton, perhaps. 'I always somehow associate Chatterton with autumn' (*L* II, p. 167).

TO LEIGH HUNT, ESQ.

Probably written *c.* February 1817, and published as the Dedication to *1817*. Although Hunt's answering sonnet is dated 'Dec. 1, 1816' by Keats's publisher, Charles Ollier, Clarke reports that when the last batch of proofs reached Keats one evening, he 'drew to a side-table, and in the buzz of a mixed conversation ... he composed ... the Dedication sonnet to Leigh Hunt' (*Cowden Clarke*, p. 138).

3 *wreathèd incense* 'smoke of sacrifice', *Woodhouse* (1817), p. 140.
5–8 *Jack*, p. 117, compares with Poussin's *The Triumph of Flora*. Compare also *Sleep and Poetry* 101–21.

WRITTEN ON A BLANK SPACE AT THE END OF CHAUCER'S TALE OF 'THE FLOURE AND THE LEAFE'

Probably written on 27 February 1817. Published *Examiner*, 16 March 1817, reprinted *1848*. According to *Cowden Clarke*, p. 139, 'the sonnet ... was an extempore effusion'. It was written in Clarke's copy of *The Poetical Works of Geoffrey Chaucer* (1782), now in the British Museum. *The Floure and the Leafe* is no longer attributed to Chaucer: Keats had used a quotation from the poem as the motto to *Sleep and Poetry*. Text based on the *Examiner*.

2 *do*] so *1848*.
9 *has*] hath autograph *MS*, *G*, *Allott*.
9 *white simplicity* *The Floure and the Leafe* praises chastity.

11 *do*] *Examiner, 1848*; for autograph *MS*, *G*, *Allott*.
13-14 an allusion to the Babes in the Wood. The robins covered the sleeping children with leaves.

ON RECEIVING A LAUREL CROWN FROM LEIGH HUNT

Date uncertain. Assigned to 1 March 1817 or before, as Hunt's two sonnets on being given an *ivy* crown by Keats are so dated, and the two crownings are supposed to belong to the same occasion. Further, see Bate (1963), pp. 138-9. The sonnet is another by-product of Hunt's poetry contests: see also *On the Grasshopper and Cricket* and *To the Nile*. Woodhouse records, 'As Keats and Leigh Hunt were taking their wine together after dinner at the house of the latter, the whim seized them to crown themselves with laurel after the fashion of the elder Bards' (*W*2). Giving laurel crowns seems to have been one of Hunt's pastimes judging by *To Charles Cowden Clarke* 44-5, 'Libertas – who has told you stories / Of laurel chaplets, and Apollo's glories...'. Garrod thinks that Keats and Hunt may have been given crowns by the woman celebrated in *To a Young Lady who Sent me a Laurel Crown* (*G*, p. 529). However, the date of that poem is uncertain (see p. 547). First published *The Times*, 18 May 1914.

3 *delphic labyrinth* Apollo's oracle was at Delphi. The meaning is 'the labyrinth of poetic inspiration'.

4 *immortal*] *Allott*; unmortal *G*. Keats's MS is unclear, but see H. E. Rollins, *Harvard Library Bulletin*, VI (1954), p. 164.

13 *wild surmises* compare *On First Looking into Chapman's Homer* 13, 'with a wild surmise'.

TO THE LADIES WHO SAW ME CROWNED

Date uncertain, and dependent on preceding poem. Tentatively, 1 March 1817 or before. Published *The Times*, 18 May 1914. Woodhouse's reconstruction of the events indicates that Hunt and Keats were still wearing their wreaths when visitors called: '... Hunt removed the wreath from his own brows... Keats however in his mad enthusiastic way, vowed that he would not take off his crown for any human being: and ... wore it ... as long as the visit lasted' (*W*2). The visitors were probably the Reynolds sisters: for other poems addressed to them see headnote to *On a Leander Gem* (p. 558). On the whole episode, see Bate (1963), pp. 137-40.

7 *halcyon* 'A bird of which the ancients fabled that it bred about the time of the winter solstice in a nest floating on the sea, and that it charmed the wind and the waves so that the sea was specially calm' (*OED*). Further references occur in *To Charles Cowden Clarke* 57 and *Endymion* I, 453-5.

ODE TO APOLLO

Written immediately after the two preceding poems, spring 1817. Keats regretted the 'folly of his conduct' and 'was determined to record it by an apologetic ode to Apollo' (*W*2). Published *Western Messenger* (Louisville), 1

557   NOTES FOR PP. 98-100

June 1836; reprinted *1848*. The text is based on the autograph MS in the Morgan Library. Keats's draft is in Harvard Library.
Title] W2-3, *Western Messenger*, *G*; *no title in MSS*; Hymn to Apollo *1848*; To Apollo *Allott*. W1 has 'A Fragment of an Ode ...'

6   *Round*] Of *Draft, Western Messenger, 1848, G, Allott*.
11   *-creeping*] Crawling W2-3, *Western Messenger, 1848, G, Allott*.
13   *grasped*   grasped his thunderbolt.
15   *eagle*   one of Jupiter's emblems.
23   *germ*   seed (Latin *germen*), both literally and figuratively (from 1823), or, more loosely (as here), a shoot, 'the rudiment of a new organ', used of plants and animals (*OED*). Compare Cowper, *The Task* (1784) III, 521, 'Then rise the tender germes, upstarting quick / And spreading wide their spongy lobes.'
25   *Pleiades*   a constellation of seven stars. *Lemprière* notes that it was also the name given to seven poets 'near the age of Philadelphus Ptolemy, king of Egypt'.
32   *for a moment*] like a madman *Draft, Western Messenger, 1848, Garrod* (*OSA*).

ON SEEING THE ELGIN MARBLES

Written before 3 March 1817, after visiting the British Museum with Haydon to see the Marbles, which had been bought recently for the nation (see *Addressed to Haydon* 11-12n, p. 548). Published in the *Examiner* and the *Champion*, 9 March 1817; reprinted *Annals of the Fine Arts*, April 1818, *1848*. On 3 March Haydon wrote, 'Many thanks My dear fellow for your two noble sonnets' (*L* I, p. 122): for the second sonnet, see next poem. For the influence of the Marbles on Keats's poetry, see S. A. Larrabee, *English Bards and Grecian Marbles* (1943), pp. 209-32, and *Jack*, pp. 31-6 passim.
14   *shadow of a magnitude*   'the conception of something so great that it can only be dimly apprehended' (*Allott*). Possibly the scientific sense of 'magnitude' (a system of classification applied to the stars, ranging them in order of brilliancy), current from the Renaissance onwards, is relevant. So used by Milton, *Paradise Lost* VII, 356-7, 'then formd the Moon / Globose, and everie magnitude of Starrs'.

TO B. R. HAYDON,
WITH A SONNET WRITTEN ON SEEING THE ELGIN MARBLES

Written before 3 March 1817. See headnote to preceding poem, with which Keats was unsatisfied. This is a second attempt at the theme. Published in the *Examiner* and the *Champion*, 9 March 1817; reprinted *Annals of the Fine Arts*, April 1818, *1848*. Text based on the *Champion*.

2   *on*] of *1848*.
8   *freak*   several meanings of the word are present: 1. a monstrosity in nature, 2. a product of irregular fancy (1784 onwards), 3. a prank, or caper (eighteenth and nineteenth centuries). Keats is stressing the gap between his youthful powers and the immensity of his subject.

12 *browless idiotism* 'without shame, unabashed' (*OED*), a seventeenth-century usage. Idiotism means ignorance, vulgarity. For 'browless' *1848* has 'brainless'.

12 *o'erwise*] o'erweening *Keats's MS* (*Harvard*); and o'erwise *1848*.

ON 'THE STORY OF RIMINI'

Written before 25 March 1817 (see *L* I, p. 127). Published *1848*. Hunt was revising *The Story of Rimini*, which was reprinted in 1817, and Keats was living a few minutes away in Well Walk.

8 *moon, if that her hunting be begun* the moon is seen in its role as Diana, the huntress.

ON A LEANDER GEM WHICH MISS REYNOLDS, MY KIND FRIEND, GAVE ME

Probably written March 1817, though dated March 1816 in the autograph MS. Published *Gem* (1829); reprinted *Galignani*. Keats met the Reynolds family late in 1816, and his relationship with the sisters was to continue until Fanny Brawne appeared. Jane Reynolds married Thomas Hood in 1825. The other sisters were Marianne, Eliza, and Charlotte, who was only fourteen. Keats wrote several poems to the sisters (see '*Spenser! a jealous honourer of thine*', *To Mrs Reynolds's Cat*, '*Hush, hush! tread softly . . .*', and possibly '*I had a dove*' and *To the Ladies who Saw Me Crowned*). *On a Leander Gem* acknowledged Jane Reynolds's gift of one of James Tassie's reproductions of ancient gems: for an illustration of a 'Leander Gem' see *Jack* (Plate IXb).
Title] *G* (a conflation of *MSS* titles).

2 —*ay,*] *G*; —aye autograph (*Harvard*); aye, *Gem, Galignani*; ay, *Allott*.
5 *Are ye*] autograph (*Harvard*), *Allott*; As if *Gem, G*. The MS may be meant to read 'So gentle are ye' (*Texts*, pp. 135–6).
13 *Dead-heavy* compare with the passage quoted from *Cowden Clarke* in headnote, *On First Looking into Chapman's Homer* (p. 546).

ON THE SEA

Written 16 or 17 April 1817 on the Isle of Wight. Published *Champion*, 17 August 1817; reprinted *1848*. Keats took lodgings in Carisbrooke. In the letter to John Hamilton Reynolds, in which he sent a copy of the poem on 17–18 April, Keats said he had been 'haunted' by 'the passage in *Lear* – "Do you not hear the sea?"' (*L* I, pp. 132–3). See *Lear* IV.6.4.

3 *Gluts* under 'glut' *OED* (4) gives 'To fill (a receptacle, channel, pipe, etc.) to excess, to choke up . . .'. Compare *Hyperion* II, 306, and *The Cap and Bells* 737–8. See also the Keatsian use of 'glut' in *Ode on Melancholy* 15 and *n* (p. 659).
3–4 *spell | Of Hecate* refers to the moon's control of the tides.
7 *where*] *Champion, 1848, G, Allott*. On MS evidence *Texts* (p. 139) prefers 'whence'.

NOTES FOR PP. 102-104

LINES ('Unfelt, unheard, unseen')

Date uncertain, but written before 17 August 1817, when J. H. Reynolds quoted l.9 in the *Champion*. Published *1848*. Keats's fair copy is now in the Morgan Library. This poem is often grouped with 'You say you love . . .', '*Hither, hither love* –', and '*Think not of it* . . .'. Ward (1963), pp. 124, 424 sees them moving from excited anticipation, to tender farewell, to dissuasion from remorse, and finally to reproaches for coldness, dating them all before mid-August. However, '*Think not of it* . . .' probably belongs to a later date (see p. 560). Any biographical order is highly speculative: these three poems may or may not belong together. There is a possibility that '*You say you love* . . .' is connected with Isabella Jones (see headnote, below), or that at least two, and possibly more, of the poems are connected with the Misses Reynolds.

12 *nor*] autograph *MS, G, Allott*; and *1848*.
17 *feel my heaven anew* an example of Keats's use of sexual slang, noted by Gittings (1968), p. 453.

STANZAS ('You say you love; but with a voice')

Date unknown. Usually grouped with the preceding poem. According to Allott, *W3* has 'From Miss Reynolds and Mrs Jones'. Keats met Mrs Jones in Hastings, May–June 1817, and was to meet her again in October 1818 (see p. 608). Published *TLS*, 16 April 1914. Text from Charlotte Reynolds's transcript (see *Texts*, pp. 141–2).

6 *with a*] then you *Allott*.
9 *Ember* 'The English name of the four periods of fasting and prayer . . . in the four periods of the year' (*OED*).
19 *for*] to *TLS, G, Allott*.

'HITHER, HITHER LOVE–'

Date unknown. Usually grouped with the two preceding poems (see headnote to *Lines*, above). Published *Ladies Home Companion* (New York 1837); reprinted Lowell (1925). Text from holograph (Yale).

4 *us*] me *Garrod* (*OSA*).
22 *has*] *MS* (*Texts*, pp. 140–1); hath *G, Allott*.

LINES RHYMED IN A LETTER RECEIVED
(BY J. H. REYNOLDS) FROM OXFORD

Written September 1817, while Keats was visiting Benjamin Bailey at Magdalen Hall, Oxford, *c.* 3 September–*c.* 5 October. Keats was working on *Endymion* III. Published Forman (1883). Text from Forman (from a lost Brown transcript, see Texts, pp. 143–4), which differs substantially from the earlier version in *L*. The *Lines* are a loose parody of Wordsworth: 'Wordsworth sometimes, though in a fine way, gives us sentences in the Style of School exercises – for Instance / "The lake doth glitter / Small birds twitter &c." [*Written in March, while Resting on the Bridge at the Foot of Brother's Water* (1807), 3–4].'

560 NOTES FOR PP. 104–106

8 *faces*] visages *W 1–2, G, Allott*.
9 *black-tasslled trencher and common hat* 'trencher-cap' is an eighteenth-century name for mortar-board, 'in shape thought to resemble an inverted trencher with a basin on it' (*OED*). Black tassels were worn by commoners, but gold by noblemen. 'Common hat', i.e. 'commoner's cap'.
10 *chantry boy* Magdalen College Chapel supports a boy's choir.
12 *dominat* he rules.
13–18 Magdalen College still keeps deer in its park, and has a notoriously good high-table.
17 *benison* blessing, grace.

'THINK NOT OF IT, SWEET ONE, SO–'

Written *c*. 11 November 1817 according to *W2–3*. Probably a song for the Reynolds sisters. *Ward* (1963) argues for an earlier date (see headnote to *Lines*, p. 559). Published *1848*. Keats's autograph *MS* is in the Morgan Library, and provides the text.

7 *then it is gone*] and only one *1848*.
11] For each I will invent a bliss *1848*.
16 *tenderer*] More tender *1848*.
19 *E'en let*] Let *1848*.

ENDYMION: A POETIC ROMANCE

Started *c*. 18 April 1817 at Carisbrooke on the Isle of Wight. Finished by 28 November 1817 at Burford Bridge, Surrey. A certain amount of revision took place before its publication as a volume in May 1818. Text based on *Endymion*, with some variants noted from Keats's draft (recorded by Woodhouse in his copy of the poem, and printed in *G* from H. B. Forman's collation) and from the author's fair copy (now in the Morgan Library).

Keats saw the poem as a 'test, a trial of my Powers of Imagination and chiefly of my invention ... by which I must make 4000 Lines of one bare circumstance and fill them with Poetry ... Besides a long Poem is a test of Invention which I take to be the Polar Star of Poetry, as Fancy is the Sails, and Imagination the Rudder. Did our great Poets ever write short Pieces?' (*L* I, pp. 169–70). He had discovered the legend of Endymion (for which see *Dictionary of Classical Names*, p. 705) at school, where his 'recurrent sources of attraction were Tooke's *Pantheon*, Lemprière's *Classical Dictionary* which he seemed to *learn*, and Spence's *Polymetis*. This was the store whence he acquired his intimacy with the Greek mythology' (*Cowden Clarke*, p. 124). An earlier attempt to handle the story appears in '*I stood tip-toe* ...' 181–93. Keats drew on his reading of the Elizabethans (see *De Selincourt*, pp. 414–17), taking ideas from Drayton's *Man in the Moone* (1606), and Ovid's *Metamorphoses*, both in the original and in Sandys's translation. Lyly's *Endimion* may have provided some suggestions, as may Mary Tighe's *Psyche* (1805), Wieland's *Oberon*, Southey's *Curse of Kehama* (1810), and other contemporary narrative poems. Shelley's *Alastor* (1816) offered a challenge, and may have been a 'sort of "anti-model"' as *Bate* (1963), p. 177, suggests. When he begun the poem in May, Keats was excited by Shakespeare (see *On the Sea* headnote, p. 558): he wrote to Haydon, '. . . you had notions of a good Genius presiding over you – I have of late had the same thought. . . . Is it too daring to Fancy Shakspeare this Presider?' (*L* I, pp. 141–2).

Keats was uneasy about *Endymion*, which he thought an 'endeavour' rather than 'a thing accomplished': further see his Preface and the rejected version Appendix 2 (pp. 506–508). The early reception was mixed: see *Critical Heritage*, pp. 75–148. Lockhart's attack in Blackwood's *Edinburgh Magazine* in August 1818 and Croker's assault in the *Quarterly Magazine* in September created the myth that Keats was 'killed off by one critique', but see *Critical Heritage*, pp. 16–17.

Some critics read the poem as a coherent and continued allegory, with a neoplatonic colouring – 'a parable of the poetic soul in man seeking communion with the spirit of essential Beauty in the world' (Colvin). De Selincourt, C. Thorpe (1926), C. L. Finney, *The Evolution of Keats's Poetry* (1936) and J. M. Murry's various books take a generally similar position. Objections to a sustained allegorical reading are:

1. allegory is foreign to Keats's early work
2. Platonism is alien to Keats's pragmatism
3. the loose suggestiveness of the poem spawns too many allegorical readings to allow for coherence
4. nineteenth-century readers took the poem as a narrative.

Further, see *Pettet*, pp. 123–45, N. F. Ford, *The Prefigurative Imagination of John Keats* (1951), pp. 13–19, pp. 46–8, and *Bate* (1963), pp. 168–92. John Jones illuminates, among other things, Keats's difficulty in handling sexuality in the poem (*Jones*, pp. 127–49). See also J. Bayley, 'Keats and Reality', *Proceedings of the British Academy*, LXVIII (1962), pp. 91–125. *Jack*, pp. 143–60, discusses the influence of painting and sculpture.

Motto from Shakespeare, Sonnet xvii 12.

BOOK I

Begun *c.* April 1817 but it is not known when Keats finished it. Book II was finished *c.* 28 August 1817 in Hampstead. Between 16 April and early September Keats stayed at Carisbrooke, Margate, Canterbury, Hastings and London. The 'Hymn to Pan' (I, 232–306) may have been begun at Margate on 26 April 1817.

I, 1 Henry Stephens, for whom see '*Give me Wine, Women, and Snuff*' headnote (p. 540), told Sir Benjamin Richardson that he and Keats were sitting together one evening, 'Stephens at his medical studies, Keats at his dreaming. Keats breaks out to Stephens that he has composed a new line: – "A thing of beauty is a constant joy." "What think you of that, Stephens?" "It has the true ring, but is wanting in some way," replies the latter, as he dips once more into his medical studies. An interval of silence, and again the poet: – "A thing of beauty is a joy for ever." "What think of that, Stephens?" "That it will live for ever"' (*Aesculapiad* [April 1884], pp. 148–9). There is probably an

562 NOTES FOR PP. 107–111

element of fantasy in this account, and it is significant that Stephens did not send the story to Monckton Milnes with his reminiscences. See further, F. W. Bateson, *English Poetry: A Critical Introduction* (1951), pp. 47–8.

I, 8–9 But compare *Addressed [to Haydon]* ('Great spirits . . .').

I, 19 *musk-rose* a rambling rose with fragrant white flowers. See *To a Friend who Sent me some Roses* 6n (p. 543).

I, 25 *essences* see I, 777–81n (p. 567).

I, 39–57 Keats announces a remarkably demanding timetable for his poem, which he more or less fulfilled.

I, 46 *lush* see '*I stood tip-toe . . .*' 31n (p. 549).

I, 50 *vermeil* bright scarlet, vermilion (Spenser): see *The Faerie Queene* III. i. 46 'a vermeill Rose'. Used again I, 696, IV, 148 below, etc.

I, 63 *Latmos* the mountain in Caria, Asia Minor, where Endymion pastured his sheep.

I, 76 *pard* leopard.

I, 78 *aye* the sense is probably 'always', but *Allott* puts a comma after 'aye', giving the meaning 'ah!'.

I, 80 *palmy* on Keats's liking for adjectives ending in '-y' see *Calidore* 10n (p. 541).

I, 86 *Edged round with dark tree tops* compare *Ode to Psyche* 54–5.

I, 89–392 Keats's description of the festival of Pan draws on his reading in Elizabethan pastoral poetry, particularly Drayton's *The Man in the Moone*. *Cowden Clarke*, p. 131, says that the *Hymn to Pan* was 'his favourite among Chapman's "Hymns of Homer"'. On Pan see *Dictionary of Classical Names* (p. 713).

I, 95 *Apollo's upward fire* the sun's rays at dawn.

I, 100 *eglantine* the sweetbriar rather than the honeysuckle. See IV, 697n (p. 586).

I, 107–13 Keats's description draws upon Titian's *The Worship of Venus* and Rubens's *Sacrifice to Venus* or *The Feast of Venus* (*Jack*, p. 149).

I, 121 *The surgy murmurs of the lonely sea* Keats was staying on the Isle of Wight, and the sea made a strong impression on him: see *On the Sea* and notes (p. 558).

I, 132 *unmew* a neologism for 'set free'. A 'mew' is a cage, especially one for hawks.

I, 134 Keats left for Canterbury on 16 May 1817.

I, 135–74 'we are once again in the country of Poussin and Claude' (*Jack*, pp. 150–51) in this description of pagan festivals.

I, 138 *younglings* young plants, rather than lambs.

I, 140–44 Apollo spent a period of exile in Thessaly as a shepherd: 'here he taught to the shepherds of Admetus the use of the pipe and other instruments of music; and those pastoral people, who had before had a savage life, became so happy, that the Gods, fearful lest mortals should become happier than themselves, suddenly recalled Apollo to Heaven' (*Baldwin*, p. 314).

I, 150 *Begirt* surrounded.

563 NOTES FOR PP. 111-15

I, 154 *mingled wine* different kinds of wine mixed together for sacrificial rites.

I, 160 *poll* 'the part of the head on which the hair grows' (*OED*).

I, 172 *chieftain king* Endymion appears in classical mythology both as a prince and as a shepherd.

I, 174 *nervy* sinewy, muscular.

I, 199 *overtop* probably a coinage meaning 'crown', though the obsolescent sense, 'To render top-heavy', is possibly intended (*OED* gives only a single example from 1643).

I, 208 *scrip, with needments* 'scrip' is an archaic word for a small bag, especially one carried by a shepherd or pilgrim. Croker thought 'needments' one of the 'new words . . . in imitation of Mr Leigh Hunt' which Keats had unnecessarily added to the language (*Critical Heritage*, p. 114). However, Spenser, *The Faerie Queene* I. i. 6 has 'bag / Of needments at his backe', and *OED* cites an occurrence in Thomson's *The Castle of Indolence* (1748) II. vi.

I, 210 *Udderless* without their mother's milk.

I, 228-9 *Baldwin*, p. 21, gives a description of Greek sacrifices — '. . . the whole temple was pervaded with the smell of fragrant woods, myrtle, cedar and sandal-wood, together with incense, burning on the altar'.

I, 232-306 this stanzaic hymn to Pan, which owes something to Chapman's Homeric hymns (see I, 89-392n), is an important step towards the major odes. Shelley recognized its 'promise of ultimate excellence', but Wordsworth thought it no more than 'a Very pretty piece of Paganism' (*KC* II, p. 144). This is particularly ironic in view of the importance to Keats of Wordsworth's passage on the origin of the Classical deities in *The Excursion* (see Appendix 1, p. 499). Keats's account of Pan's activities is largely drawn from the Elizabethan poets (*Finney* I, pp. 260-68). Douglas Bush notes, 'The goat-god, the tutelary divinity of shepherds, had long been allegorized on various levels, from Christ to "Universall Nature" (Sandys); here he becomes the symbol of the romantic imagination, of supra-mortal knowledge' (*Selected Poems and Letters* [1959], p. 317).

I, 241 *pipy hemlock* the poisonous variety has hollow stems.

I, 247 *turtles* turtle-doves.

I, 248 *Passion* to affect or imbue with passion. Spenser, *The Faerie Queene* II. ix. 41 has 'Great wonder had the knight, to see the mayd / So straungely passioned'. See also II, 201 below. For the intransitive use of the verb, see *Lamia* I, 182n (p. 669).

I, 253 *yellow-girted* 'girted' is a false formation. It should be 'girt'.

I, 256 *chuckling* clucking, an eighteenth-century usage.

I, 261 *pine* one of Pan's emblems.

I, 285-7 'All the strange, mysterious and unaccountable sounds which were heard in solitary places, were attributed to Pan' (*Baldwin*, p. 84).

I, 295 *bourne* boundary.

I, 298 *ethereal* a favourite word, which should here be connected with 'essence' (I, 25, 779). Compare the use of 'ethereal' here with Keats's letter to Bailey, 13 March 1818, quoted headnote '*Four seasons fill the measure of the*

564 NOTES FOR PP. 115–18

year' (p. 593). R. T. Davies notes, 'Keats uses ethereal in a variety of senses. When applied to physical things and actions it can mean "having the insubstantiality and rarity of *ether*, delicate, refined, volatile". It seems to be derived from Keats's medical studies in which he would have found ether contrasted with heavy spirits ... Sometimes it means spirit-like, aerial, heavenly' (*John Keats: A Reassessment*, ed. K. Muir (1959), p. 136).

I, 305 *paean* hymn or chant of thanksgiving, originally addressed to Apollo or Artemis.

I, 311 *bob* Woodhouse records, 'The words *raise, push* were suggested to the author: but he insisted on retaining *bob*' (*W*2).

I, 318 *Thermopylae* a pass, leading from Thessaly to Locris, which three hundred Spartans, led by Leonidas, defended bravely but hopelessly against the whole might of Xerxes' army.

I, 319 Possibly suggested by the Elgin Marbles.

I, 320 *genitors* parents (in the singular, male parent, father). *OED* notes, 'now rare', and draws the bulk of its examples from the sixteenth and seventeenth centuries.

I, 334 *raft* torn off (an archaic form of 'reft'). *OED* gives only this example of the participial form. Spenser uses the verb – 'He raft her hatefull head ...', *The Faerie Queene* I. i. 24.

I, 337–43 *Niobe* see *Dictionary of Classical Names* (p. 712). For the sculptural and pictorial representations probably known to Keats, see *Jack*, pp. 152–3.

I, 341 *paly* pale or somewhat pale. An Elizabethan poeticism revived in the eighteenth and nineteenth centuries (see Gray's *Propertius* [1748], II, 20, for example). Used again I, 984 below and *On Visiting the Tomb of Burns* 5.

I, 347–54 Keats would not have found this incident in *Lemprière*, and may be indebted to Shelley or to Fawkes's translation of Apollonius Rhodius' *Argonautica*: further, see *Dictionary of Classical Names*, p. 700.

I, 358 *eld* old age (poeticism).

I, 363 *Vesper* the evening star. See *Dictionary of Classical Names* under 'Hesperus', p. 707.

I, 367 *fire-tailèd exhalations* comets.

I, 376 *zephyr-sigh* Keats may be thinking of the zephyrs as feminine; see *To Charles Cowden Clarke* 6n (p. 544).

I, 379 *feathery sails* wings.

I, 386 *champaign* an expanse of level, open country. 'Fair champain with less rivers interveined', Milton, *Paradise Regained* III, 257.

I, 392 *famished scrips* the food in their bags is depleted (see I, 208n, for 'scrips').

I, 405–6 a reference to 'The History of the Young King of the Black Isles' in *The Arabian Nights*. Like other Romantic writers, Keats took great pleasure in these exotic tales.

I, 408 *Peona* the idea of giving Endymion a sister as confidante may have come from Chapman's continuation of *Hero and Leander* where Leander is given 'a most kind sister' who 'all his secrets knew'. Peona's healing powers

565 NOTES FOR PP. 118–20

are probably drawn from Paeon, 'A celebrated physician who cured the wounds which the gods received during the Trojan war. From him physicians are sometimes called *Poeonii*, and herbs serviceable in medicinal processes *Poeniae herbae*' (Lemprière). Paeon also appears in Ovid, *Metamorphoses* XV, and Spenser's Poeana in *The Faerie Queene* IV. ix. 3–16 may have suggested some features.

I, 413 *midnight spirit-nurse*] *Fair copy* (in text), *Allott*; midnight-spirit Nurse *Fair copy* (in margin); midnight spirit nurse *Endymion*, G.

I, 423 *shallop* dinghy.

I, 432 *fingering* possibly refers to musical 'fingering' in addition to the obvious sense.

I, 440–41] When last the Harvesters rich armfuls took. / She tied a little bucket to a Crook, / Ran some swift paces to a dark wells side, / And in a sighing-time return'd, supplied / With spar cold water; in which she did squeeze / A snowy napkin, and upon her knees / Began to cherish her poor Brother's face; / Damping refreshfully his forehead's space, / His eyes, his Lips: then in a cupped shell / She brought him ruby wine; then let him smell, / Time after time, a precious amulet, / Which seldom took she from its cabinet. *Fair copy* (cancelled). On the opposite page in the *Fair copy* Keats wrote, 'When last the Sun his autumn tresses shook / And the tan[n]'d Harvesters rich armfuls took.'

I, 450 *wailful gnat* compare *To Autumn* 27, 'Then in a wailful choir the small gnats mourn'.

I, 453–5 *O comfortable bird ... smooth!* a reference to the halcyon: see *To the Ladies who Saw Me Crowned* 7n (p. 556) 'Comfortable' has the obsolete sense of strengthening, inspiriting, or consoling.

I, 466–7] He said: 'Dear Maid, may I this moment die, / If I feel not this thine endearing Love' *Fair copy (cancelled)*. Keats commented in his journal-letter of 23–4 January 1818, 'Hunt ... says the conversation is unnatural & too high-flown for the Brother & Sister. Says it should be simple forgetting ... that they are both overshadowed by a Supernatural Power, & of force could not speak like Franchesca [in Hunt's *The Story of Rimini*]. He must first prove that Caliban's poetry is unnatural, – This with me completely overturns his objections' (*L* I, pp. 213–14).

I, 470 *incense* the scent of flowers, compare *Calidore* 155n (p. 542).

I, 481 *poll* 'cut off the top (of a tree or plant) ... to lop the branches of' (*OED*).

I, 494–5] More forest-wild, more subtle-cadenced / Than can be told by mortal: even wed / The fainting tenors of a thousand Shells, / To a million whisperings of Lilly bells; / And, mingle too, the Nightingale's complain / Caught in its hundredth echo; 'twould be vain: *Fair copy (cancelled)*.

I, 499 *Delphic* divinely inspired.

I, 510 *Paphian dove* a dove from Venus' temple in Paphos.

I, 511 *deer-head*] *Fair copy*, *Allott*; deer-herd *Endymion*, *Garrod* (*OSA*); dear-head G.

I, 512–14 Actaeon saw Diana bathing naked. In punishment he was changed into a stag and torn to pieces by his own hounds (Ovid, *Metamorphoses* III, 138–252).

NOTES FOR PP. 120–24

I, 516–20] And I do pray thee by thy utmost aim / To tell me all. No little fault or blame / Canst thou lay on me for a teasing Girl; / Ever as an unfathomable pearl / Has been thy secrecy to me: but now / I needs must hunger after it, and vow / To be its jealous Guardian for aye. / Uttering these words she got nigh and more nigh, / And put at last her arms about his neck; / Nor was there any tart, ungentle check, / Nor any frown or stir dissatisfied, / But smooth compliance and tender slide / Of arm in arm, and what is written next. / 'Doubtless, Peona, thou hast been perplex'd, / And pained oft, in thinking of the change *Fair copy* (*cancelled*).

I, 517 *bland* mild.

I, 545] And in that spot the most endowing boon / Of balmy Air, sweet blooms, and coverts fresh / Has been outshed; yes, all that could enmesh / Our human senses – make us fealty sware / To gadding Flora. In this grateful lair *Fair copy* (*cancelled*).

I, 553 *the zodiac-lion* Leo, one of the constellations of the Zodiac.

I, 555 *ditamy ... poppies* both plants sacred to Diana. Ditamy (or dittany), a plant from Dittany in Crete, was famous for its medicinal properties (including the ability to expel weapons from wounds). Both White and Bastard Dittany are to be found in Britain.

I, 563 *rod* Mercury's caduceus.

I, 571 *gulfed in a tumultuous swim* 'gulfed' means 'swallowed like a gulf, or as in a gulf, engulfed' (*OED*). The verb was coined in the Romantic period, and is used several times in *Endymion* (see II, 195, III, 205, 351, 659, 956), but not elsewhere. The use of 'swim' as a noun here, along with that in '*I stood tip-toe ...*' 114, is given by *OED* as an example of 'A swimming motion; *colloqu.* or *dial.*, a swimming or dizzy sensation'.

I, 595 *argent spheres* 'argent' means silvery white (esp. in heraldry). The spheres were, in pre-Renaissance astronomy, supposed to be the concentric, transparent globes round each planet.

I, 614–16 possibly suggested by the simplicity of Phoebe's (i.e. Diana's) appearance in Spence's *Polymetis*, reproduced *Jack* Plate XV. 'Gordianed' is a Keatsian verb derived from the Gordian knot.

I, 622 *human neighbourhood* being in the company of mankind.

I, 624–32 this description of Diana echoes that in eighteenth-century works of classical reference (*Jack*, p. 154); see I, 614–16*n*. Any resemblance to Botticelli's *Birth of Venus* is accidental as the painting was unknown in England at the time.

I, 631 *lushest* see '*I stood tip-toe ...*' 31*n* (p. 549).

I, 638 *recollection* memory. 'The scene of the preceding night ran in his recollection' (Scott, cited by *OED*).

I, 641 *region* pronounced here with three syllables.

I, 643–4 *buffeting north ... meteor-stone* 'Northern gales so strong that they can balance a heavy meteor in the air' (*Allott*).

I, 646] Sleepy with deep foretasting, that did bless / My Soul from Madness, twas such certainty *Fair copy* (*cancelled*). For 'along the dangerous sky' Keats first tried 'in safe deliriousness'.

I, 665-6 *There was ... alp*] Hurry o'er / O sacrilegeous tongue the – best be dumb; / For should one little accent from thee come / On such a daring theme, all other sounds / Would sicken at it, as would beaten hounds / Scare the elysian Nightingales *Fair copy* (cancelled). 'Alp' here means mountain pastures.

I, 679 *a gentle creep* one of the many Huntisms.

I, 683 *ouzel* the blackbird or merle.

I, 696 *vermeil* bright scarlet. See I, 50*n*.

I, 714 *enchasèd crocodile* the crocodile's protective covering is patterned (i.e. 'enchased') like armour. *OED* cites J. Lane, *The Squire's Tale* (1651), 'Camballo ... came armed in bright enchased steele'. It is perhaps possible that 'enchased' is, as Allott suggests, a poeticism meaning 'hunted'.

I, 722 *Yet it is strange, and sad, alas!*] Yet it is wonderful – exceeding – / And yet a shallow dream, for ever breeding / Tempestuous Weather in that very Soul / That should be twice content, twice smooth, twice whole, / As is a double Peach. 'Tis sad Alas! *Fair copy* (cancelled).

I, 759 *high-fronted* of noble bearing.

I, 762 *plaited*] pleated *Fair copy, Allott*.

I, 765 *careless* carefree.

I, 766 *manna-dew* this compound is used again in *La Belle Dame sans Merci* 26. 'Manna' is the mysterious food which God gave the Israelites in the desert. Exodus xvi 21 says they gathered manna each morning, 'and when the sun waxed hot it melted'. Keats thought of it as an actual fruit – *Endymion* II, 452 has 'And here is manna picked from Syrian trees', and *The Eve of St Agnes* 268-9 has 'Manna and dates, in argosy transferred from Fez'. Keats's medical studies would have introduced him to the pharmaceutical meaning, 'a sweet pale yellow or whitish concrete juice obtained from ... the Manna ash' or from Mediterranean trees, known variously as Persian, Hebrew Manna, etc. (*OED*), though its use as a laxative would hardly have suited the poetic context here. The source of Keats's idea is probably Nathan Bailey's *Universal Etymological English Dictionary*, which he owned, where manna is described as '... also a Sort of fat Dew in a Morning from the Leaves of Mulberry-trees, &c. in *Calabria*, and other hot Countries, used as a gentle Purge'. (It may also be relevant that until 1753 'manna' could refer to frankincense in granular form.)

I, 772-4 Compare *To J. H. Reynolds, Esq.* 72-3 and *To Charles Cowden Clarke* 17.

I, 777-81] Wherein lies happiness? In that which becks / Our ready minds to blending pleasureable: / And that delight is the most treasureable / That makes the richest Alchymy. Behold / Where in lies happiness Peona / The clear Religion of Heaven ! *Fair copy*. These lines, and the following passage (ll. 782-842), are the most disputed in the poem. Keats made his revision some two months after completing the poem. On 30 January 1818 he wrote to Taylor, sending the new lines, 'You must indulge me by putting this in for setting aside the badness of the other, such a preface is necessary to the Subject. The whole thing must I think have appeared to you, who are a consequitive

568 NOTES FOR PP. 127-9

Man, as a thing almost of mere words – but I assure you than when I wrote it, it was a regular stepping of the Imagination towards a Truth. My having written that Argument will perhaps be of the greatest Service to me of any thing I ever did – It set before me at once the gradations of Happiness even like a kind of Pleasure Thermometer – and is my first Step towards the chief Attempt in the Drama – the playing of different Natures with Joy and Sorrow' (*L* I, pp. 218-19).

The revised passage and Keats's comments raise two main problems:

1. What is the meaning of 'fellowship with essence' (779)? Colvin, De Selincourt, Middleton Murry, and Finney take it in a transcendental sense, regarding Keats's 'Pleasure Thermometer' as an idealizing or neoplatonic hierarchy. For a summary of the argument, see N. F. Ford, 'The Meaning of "Fellowship with Essence" in *Endymion*', *PMLA*, LXII (1947), pp. 1061-76 and his *The Prefigurative Imagination of John Keats* (1951), pp. 13-19, 46-8. Ford argues that the word 'essence' is used as a synonym for 'a thing of beauty' or 'shape of beauty' (I, 12, and I, 1 and 12). 'Essence' is later apostrophized as the God of warm pulses, and dishevelled hair,/ And panting bosoms bare ...' (III, 983-5).

2. Does Keats's 'Pleasure Thermometer' refer to the new lines (777-81) or does it refer to the whole passage (777-842)? *Bate* (1963), pp. 182-3, argues for the former, but Keats's letter suggests that the new lines will make clearer what Taylor had read *before* ('the *whole thing* must have appeared ... to you'). The 'Thermometer', then, is described in ll. 780-802 or ll. 780-842, probably the latter. The scale, according to the 'clear religion of heaven' (I, 781), runs from physical enjoyment of the natural world (I, 782) to the pleasures of music (and poetry) (I, 783-97), to friendship (I, 800-805), and culminates in the passionate love of men and women (I, 805-842), which makes 'Men's being mortal, immortal' (I, 844) – further, see I, 833-42n and IV, 146-81n.

I, 781 *religion* four syllables.

I, 786 *Aeolian magic* on the Aeolian lyre see *Ode to Apollo* 34n (p. 536).

I, 791 *bruit* rumour, report.

I, 792 *giant battle* refers to the war between the Titans and the gods of Olympus, the subject of *Hyperion*.

I, 799 *self-destroying* subduing the sense of self. Compare II, 275-6 and *Ode to a Nightingale* 72, 'To toll me back from thee to my sole self'.

I, 808 *genders* engenders, generates.

I, 815 *pelican brood* the pelican was reputed to nourish its young with its own blood.

I, 825 *ardent listlessness* describes Keats's notion of the poetic trance. Compare *Sleep and Poetry*, and *passim*.

I, 833 *commingling* intermingling.

I, 833-42 Bailey commented on *Endymion's* 'inclination... to that abominable principle of *Shelley's* – that *Sensual Love* is the principle of *things*. Of this I believe him to be unconscious, & can see how by a process of imagination he might arrive at so false, delusive, & dangerous conclusion' (*KC* I, pp. 34-5).

Keats's argument, however, is quite clear, though it should be noted that in the letter to Taylor quoted above he says the passage was 'a regular stepping of the Imagination towards *a* Truth' (*L* I, p. 218), not *the* truth.

I, 850 *wildered* bewildered.

I, 851 *atomies* diminutive or tiny beings, mites, pigmies. Compare *Romeo and Juliet* I. 4. 58–9. 'Drawn with a team of little atomies / Athwart men's noses as they lie asleep . . .'

I, 890 *charactered* plainly visible, or clearly written or inscribed. Compare Shakespeare, *Sonnet* cviii, 'What's in the brain that ink may character'.

I, 896–7 *Smiling . . . depth*] In the green opening smiling. Gods that keep, / Mercifully, a little strength of heart / Unkill'd in us by raving, pang and smart; / And do preserve it, like a lilly root, / That, in another spring, it may outshoot / From its wintry prison; let this hour go / Drawling along its heavy weight of woe / And leave me living! 'Tis not more than need – / Your veriest help. Ah! how long did I feed / On that crystailine life of Portraiture! / How long I hover'd breathless at the tender lure! / How many times dimpled the watery glass / With kisses maddest kisses; and, till they did pass / And leave the liquid smooth again, how mad! / O 'twas as if the absolute sisters had / My life into the compass of a Nut; / Or all my breathing minished and shut / To a scanty straw. To look above I fear'd / Lest my hot eyeballs might be burnt and sear'd / By a blank naught *Fair copy (cancelled)*.

I, 907 *gnawing sloth* Keats is thinking not of the sloth, but of the 'slothbear', an Indian species of bear. At this time the word could also mean koala bear. Keats's natural history belongs to the world of imagination: bears are herbivores.

I, 924 *amber studs* compare with Marlowe's *The Passionate Shepherd to his Love* 18, 'With Corall clasps and Amber studs.'

I, 940 *screen*] *Fair copy*, G, Allott; scene *Endymion*. For 'lush', see '*I stood tip-toe* . . .' 31*n* (p. 549).

I, 962 *freaks* tricks; see also *To B. R. Haydon* 8*n* (p. 557).

I, 968 *cloys* a favourite Keatsian word, here used to suggest the slowly sensual movement of the hand through the hair. Possibly echoes the rare verb used in *Cymbeline* V. 4. 118–19, 'His royal bird / Prunes the immortal wing, and cloys his beak'.

I, 989 *car* chariot.

BOOK II

Finished Hampstead *c.* 28 August 1817. *Gittings* (1968), p. 140, suggests that the beginning (II, 1–130) was written on Keats's return to London in early June, and was influenced by his meeting with Mrs Isabella Jones at Hastings shortly before.

II, 1–43 Keats's defence of love as 'the chiefest intensity' (see I, 777–81*n* and 833–42*n*, pp. 567–9).

II, 4–5 *others . . . indolent* 'Records other than those of love have become too shadowy to cause either hatred or grief' (*Allott*).

570 NOTES FOR PP. 133–7

II, 8 *towers smothering o'er their blaze* the towers are either smothered by the smoke from the blaze, or they smother the blaze when they collapse into it.

II, 12 *amain* with full force, violently (Elizabethan).

II, 13 *The close of Troilus and Cressid* 'close' (embrace) is drawn from Shakespeare. See *Twelfth Night* V.1.152, 'Attested by the holy close of lips', and *Two Gentlemen of Verona* V.4.117, 'Let me be blest to make this happy close'. Used as a verb in *Troilus and Cressida* III.2.51.

II, 15 *Swart* dark in colour, black.

II, 22–3 in Plutarch's account, Themistocles was debating with his officers over the advisability of attacking, when an owl appeared as a good omen. Keats's source was probably J. Potter's *Antiquities of Greece* (1697; 1827 edn I, p. 379).

II, 24–5 Alexander crossed the Indus in 326 B.C.

II, 26–7 Odysseus blinded the sleeping Cyclops so that he and his band could escape (*Odyssey* IX).

II, 27–30 *Juliet ... flow*] Juliet leans / Amid her window flowers, sighs, – and as she weans / Her maiden thoughts from their young firstling snow, / What sorrows from the melting whiteness grow *Draft* (*cancelled*). The Draft also has another cancelled variant for l. 29, 'Tenderly from their first young snow her maiden breast'.

II, 31–2 *Hero ... Imogen ... Pastorella* the heroines of Marlowe's *Hero and Leander*, Shakespeare's *Cymbeline*, and *The Faerie Queene* VI. xi.

II, 52 *lush* see '*I stood tip-toe ...*' 31*n* (p. 549).

II, 60 *pight* archaic form of 'pitched', a favourite Spenserian word, but also found in Shakespeare and Chatterton. Here extended to mean settled. *Allott* compares with *Troilus and Cressida* V. 10. 23–4, 'tents / Thus proudly pight upon our Phrygian plains ...' See also *Otho the Great* V.5.164*n* (p. 665).

II, 62 *charactered* engraved, written.

II, 81–2 *holy bark ... Delphi* a ship filled with pilgrims on their way to Delphi, near Mount Parnassus, which had an important temple dedicated to Apollo.

II, 90 *smutch* smudge.

II, 91 *mealy gold* dust from the butterfly's wings. 'Mealy' is derived from 'meal' (powder) produced by grinding grain. Compare *Troilus and Cressida* III.3.78–9, '... men, like butterflies, / Show not their mealy wings but to the summer ...'.

II, 95 *covert* hidden, sheltered.

II, 96–7] His sullen limbs upon the grass – what tongue, / What airy whisperer spoilt his angry rest? *Draft*.

II, 112–13 *draws ... deep* 'The limpid reflections of light in a pebbled bed of clear water' (*Allott*).

II, 116 *charming* magical.

II, 118 *Meander* see *Sleep and Poetry* 74*n* (p. 551).

II, 136 *dimpling* refers to the circles made in water by the fishes breaking the surface.

II, 138 *burr* 'A circle of light round the moon (or a star)' (*OED*), which cites, 'A burre about the moone is ... a presage of a tempest' (1631), and an example from Herschel (1802). Here it describes the wanderer's blurred mind.

II, 143 unrhymed line.

II, 145 *travailing*] Draft, *Allott*; travelling, *Endymion*, G. 'Travailing' means 'toiling' or 'working hard'.

II, 149 *pebble-bead*] L, G, *Allott*; pebble head *Endymion*. The *Draft* is hard to decipher.

II, 153–6 Compare *Sleep and Poetry* 122–54.

II, 155 *Imagination's struggles*] Imaginings and searchings *Draft*.

II, 168–70 Endymion does not realize his 'thrice-seen love' is Diana.

II, 179–80 *Though ... shun thee* Cynthia's (i.e. Diana's) reputation for chastity causes her to conceal her love: see II, 778–94, IV, 751–4.

II, 187–95 Endymion rides in Diana's chariot in Drayton's *The Man in the Moone* 430–35.

II, 189 *tremulous-dazzingly*] *Draft* has the following attempts: 'silently and tremulous', 'bright and tremulous', 'tremulous and dazzling'.

II, 195 *gulf* see I, 571n.

II, 198 *blind Orion* Keats's account of Orion watching for the dawn probably combines memories of Ovid (*Metamorphoses* I, 316–29) and Poussin's *Landscape with Orion*, which includes Diana watching from above (*Jack*, p. 156). See further, *Dictionary of Classical Names* (p. 712). Hazlitt used the line for a motto to his essay 'On a Landscape of Nicolas Poussin' (1821).

II, 201 *passioned* see I, 248n.

II, 203 *alleys* see 'I stood tip-toe ...' 20n (p. 549).

II, 204 *sparry* rich in spar, i.e. 'crystalline minerals more or less lustrous in appearance and admitting or easy cleavage' (*OED*).

II, 207 *sheen* brilliance.

II, 221–39 this underworld is indebted to Keats's reading of *The Arabian Nights* and William Beckford's *Vathek* (1786).

II, 230 *vast antre* 'antre' is a poeticism meaning cave (Latin, *antrum*). Echoes *Othello* I.3.140, 'antres vast and desarts idle', the only earlier example cited by *OED*.

II, 230–31 *metal woof* / *Like Vulcan's rainbow* 'woof' is a woven fabric. Vulcan was the blacksmith of the gods, and made Jupiter's thunderbolts. His forges were supposed to be under Mount Aetna.

II, 240 *vast* used as a noun. Compare with *The Tempest* I.2.327, 'that vast of night', which Keats quoted in a letter of April 1817 (*L* I, p. 133).

II, 245 *fray* frighten, or scare away. *OED* cites, 'A Puritan is a Protestant frayed out of his wits' (1604). See *The Eve of St Agnes* 198n (p. 624).

II, 247 *stun* the act of stunning (rare eighteenth-century noun). Used again *Otho the Great* III. 2. 51.

II, 248 *amazement* mental stupefaction, as in Milton, *Paradise Regained* IV, 561, 'Satan, smitten with amazement fell'.

NOTES FOR PP. 140-44

II, 251 *sphering time* The world circles the sun, and so will exist in its 'sphering time' until the dissolution of the universe.

II, 262 *quivered Dian* Diana in her role as huntress.

II, 275-6 *self* compare the use of 'self-destroying' at I, 799.

II, 277 *fog-born elf* Will-o'-the-wisp. Keats's image of the *ignis fatuus* (ll. 277-80) may echo *King Lear* III.4.50-53, '... the foul fiend hath led through fire and through flame, through ford and whirlpool, o'er bog and quagmire....' A few lines earlier Edgar mentions the 'sharp hawthorn'. Here 'elf' means a dwarfish malignant spirit. For Keats's use of the word, see II, 461*n*, and *Ode to a Nightingale* 73-4*n* (p. 657).

II, 279-80 *into ... thing*] cuttings and shreds / Of old Vexations plaited to a rope/ Wherewith to drag us from the sight of hope, / And fix us to our earthly bating-ring *Fair copy (cancelled), Draft (with variants)*.

II, 282 *raught*] *Fair copy, G, Allott*; caught *Endymion*. 'Raught' means 'reached' (Spenser).

II, 288 *rack* 'Clouds, or a mass of cloud, driven before the wind in the upper air' (*OED*).

II, 292 *surcharged* overloaded, weighed down.

II, 298 *chief* upper end (Spenserian archaism).

II, 301 *plain* complain.

II, 308 *disparted* separated (Spenser).

II, 309 *crescent* one of Diana's emblems was the crescent moon.

II, 313 *on*] *Fair copy*; in *Endymion, G, Allott*.

II, 318 *the zephyr-boughs among*] *Draft* (recorded by Woodhouse), *G, Allott*; among the zephyr-boughs *Endymion*.

II, 340 *cold*] *G*; old *Endymion, Allott*.

II, 341 *sallows* willows.

II, 362 unrhymed line owing to revisions.

II, 363-72] To seas Ionian and Tyrian. Dire / Was the love torn despair to which it wrought / Endymion – for dire is the bare thought / That among lovers things of tenderest worth / Are swallow'd all, and made a blank – a dearth / By one devouring flame; and far far worse / Blessing to them become a heavy curse / Half happy till comparisons of bliss / To misery lead them. 'Twas even so with this *Draft*. H. B. Forman conjecturally emended 'Tyrian' to 'seas of Tyre'.

II, 364-5 *O ... music slew not?* for Keats's feeling for music see *To Charles Cowden Clarke* 110-11 and *n* (p. 545).

II, 373 *the Carian* Endymion.

II, 376 *swart* black.

II, 389-427 details for Keats's bower of Adonis are taken from Spenser's Garden of Adonis in *The Faerie Queene* III. vi.

II, 392-411 possibly a recollection of Poussin's *Echo and Narcissus* (see *Jack* Plate XVII).

II, 396 *coverlids* variant spelling of 'coverlet'.

573 NOTES FOR PP. 144-6

II, 400 *tenting swerve* 'Like the top of a tent' (Woodhouse).

II, 405 *damask* 'A rich silk fabric' (*OED*), originally made in Damascus. The 'rose' at l. 407 suggests that the 'damask-plum' (damson) may also have been in Keats's mind.

II, 407 *Disparts* separates (Spenser).

II, 409-18 various climbing plants twine themselves into a bower. Compare *The Faerie Queene* III. vi. 44, 'Which knitting their rancke braunches part to part, / With wanton yvie twyne entrayld athwart, / And Eglantine, and Caprifole emong . . .'.

II, 411 *trammelled* entangled, fastened up (Elizabethan). From 'trammel', a fishing- or fowling-net.

II, 414 *bugle-blooms* the woodbine's flowers.

II, 415 *streakèd vases flush* the flowers of the convolvulus in full bloom.

II, 416 *autumn blush* probably referring to the Virginia creeper which turns to red in the autumn.

II, 417 'The British climbing shrub *Clematis Vitalba*, traveller's joy' (*OED*).

II, 419] Stood Cupids holding o'er an upward gaze / Each a slim wand tipt with a silver blaze / Each one a silver torch *Draft*.

II, 441-4 *Here is wine ... purple* anticipates *Ode to a Nightingale* 16-18. See also '*Hence Burgundy, Claret and Port*' 1-2n (p. 590).

II, 452 *manna* see I, 766n (p. 567).

II, 457-80 this account of Venus and Adonis is mainly drawn from Shakespeare's *Venus and Adonis*, *The Faerie Queene* III. i. 34-8 and vi. 46-9, and Ovid's *Metamorphoses* X, 519-52.

II, 458 *sea-born goddess* Venus, who rose from the sea near Cythera.

II, 461 *elf* a favourite word in Keats, here based on Spenser's constant use of it to refer to his knights in their 'faerie land'. For other examples of this sense, see *Isabella* 453, 'Read me a lesson . . .' 11, and '*How fevered is the man* . . .' 7, where, as here, it is used as a rhyme-word. Keats also used 'elf' in other senses. See II, 227n (p. 572) and *Ode to a Nightingale* 73-4n (p. 657).

II, 473-4 *But my poor mistress ... tusked him* compare *Venus and Adonis* 1027-62 and Ovid, *Metamorphoses* X, 708-23.

II, 474-8 *so away ... to life* Venus does not plead with Jupiter in the literary sources. 'Venus was inconsolable for his loss, and at length obtained from Jupiter that he should return to life for six months in every year; so that Adonis revives and dies in incessant succession' (*Baldwin*, p. 207).

II, 474 *tusked*] tushed *Fair copy*. Compare *To J. H. Reynolds Esq.* 16n (p. 595).

II, 475 *plainings* complainings.

II, 475-6 *drew ... beard* echoes Milton's *Il Penseroso* 107, 'Drew Iron tears down Pluto's cheek . . .'.

II, 490 *scuds* compare Shakespeare on Adonis's horse, 'Sometimes he scuds far off', *Venus and Adonis* 301. Used again II, 698, III, 956, and *Hyperion* II, 236.

NOTES FOR PP. 146-51

II, 494 *clamant* literally, crying out, clamorous, noisy, first used in the seventeenth century. According to *OED*, Keats first used it of sound, but see Thomson, *Autumn* (1730), 350, 'a train / Of clamant children dear'.

II, 497 *Pigeons and doves* emblems of Venus.

II, 505] Cupids awake! or black and blue we'll pinch *Draft (cancelled)*.

II, 517 *Disparted* separated (Spenser).

II, 518 *car* chariot.

II, 524 *tightened*] *Draft*, *Fair copy*, *G*; lightened *Endymion*, *Allott*.

II, 526–34] Queen Venus bending downward, so o'ertaken, / So suffering sweet, so blushing mad, so shaken / That the wild warmth prob'd the young sleeper's heart / Enchantingly; and with a sudden start / His trembling arms were out in instant time / To catch his fainting love. – O foolish rhyme / What mighty power in thee that so often / Thou strivest rugged syllables to soften / Even to the telling of a sweet like this. / Away! let them embrace alone! that kiss / Was far too rich for thee to talk upon. / Poor wretch! mind not these sobs and sighs! begone! / Speak not one atom of thy paltry stuff, / That they are met is poetry enough. / O this has ruffled every spirit there *Draft (cancelled)*.

II, 532 *unchariest* least coy.

II, 535 *Love's self* Cupid.

II, 535 *superb* 'Grand, stately, majestic, 1784' (*OED*).

II, 537 *quell* power or means to quell, a rare archaism. Compare '*Spenser! a jealous honourer ...*' 7.

II, 569 *zoned* embraced. A Keatsian verb from the noun meaning, 'A girdle or belt, as part of dress' (poeticism), 'hence, any encircling band' (*OED*).

II, 578–81 *Now adieu ... celestial* Cowden Clarke recorded, 'I have often thought of that Sunday afternoon, when [Keats] ... read to Mr Severn and myself the description of the "Bower of Adonis"; and the conscious pleasure with which he looked up when he came to the passage that tells the ascent of the car of Venus' (*KC* II, p. 151).

II, 601–4 compare Coleridge, *Kubla Khan* (1816), 17–19, and Shelley's *Alastor* (1816), 377–81, both known to Keats.

II, 607 *'gan enclose*] *Fair copy*; 'gan to enclose *Endymion*, *G*, *Allott*.

II, 613–27 *Allott* points out that this depiction of the 'founts Protean' may owe something to contemporary stage effects as well as to Drayton's *Man in the Moone* 145–220.

II, 625 *aloof* at a distance, usually referring to space, but here meaning far in the future.

II, 629 *grisly gapes* probably referring to crevices or rents in the rocks.

II, 636 *purblind ... wolds* 'purblind' means of impaired or defective vision. 'Wolds' are hilly uplands.

II, 646 *nervy* sinewy, muscular.

II, 658 *eagle* emblem of Jupiter.

II, 663 *asphodel* a genus of liliaceous plants, in Greek mythology supposed

NOTES FOR PP. 151–9

to cover the Elysian fields. From the Greek; earlier written 'affodil' in English, whence 'daffodil'.

II, 668–71 *In the ... moss*] Long he hung about / Before his nice enjoyment could pick out / The resting place: but at the last he swung / Into the greenest cell of all – among / Dark leaved jasmine: star flower'd and bestrown / With golden moss *Draft*.

II, 672 *Ethereal* here, purged of dross, 'pertaining to the upper atmosphere' (*OED*). On Keats's use of the word, see *Endymion* I, 298n (p. 563).

II, 686–94 *O my love ... idleness* Endymion fails to recognize his love as the goddess she is. He thinks she may be one of the Horae (l. 688), one of the Pleiades (ll. 689–90), a sea nymph (ll. 690–91), or an attendant of Diana (ll. 692–4).

II, 693 *scions* twigs, shoots (archaic).

II, 700 *vest* garment (poeticism).

II, 726 *dazèd*] mortal *Draft*.

II, 727–8 *a new tinge ... duty* 'The sun is setting: the world has completed its poetic task' (*Allott*).

II, 740 *essence* see I, 777–81n (p. 567).

II, 748 *delicious*] *L, Draft, G, Allott*; kindest *Fair copy, Endymion*.

II, 773 *O bliss! O pain!* for this typically Keatsian conjunction of pain and pleasure see also II, 823–4 and, most notably, *Ode to a Nightingale* 1–6.

II, 789 *Horror*] *Fair copy, G, Allott*; The thing or idea *Draft*; Honour *Endymion*.

II, 793 *vailed*] *Fair copy, G, Allot*; veiled *Endymion*. 'Vailed' is an Elizabethan word meaning lowered in sign of submission or respect.

II, 819 *empyrean* 'Of or pertaining to the sphere of fire or highest heaven' (*OED*).

II, 823–4 *is ... pleasure* compare *Ode on Melancholy* 25–6.

II, 833ff. Shelley praised this passage, and III, 113–20, 193ff., as having the 'promise of ultimate excellence' in a letter to the *Quarterly Review* in 1820 (*Critical Heritage*, p. 124).

II, 830–39 *long ago. ... freedom* see Appendix I (pp. 499–502) for some important sources of Keats's ideas on the source of myths.

II, 853 *gusty deep* refers back to 'cavern wind' (l. 831).

II, 854 *former chroniclers* earlier tellers of the tale.

II, 866 *Aeolian-tuned* tuned like the strings of the Aeolian harp (see *Ode to Apollo* 34n, p. 536).

II, 885 *snort their streams* a reference to the 'blowing' of whales.

II, 896 *golden age* see *Dictionary of Classical Names* (pp. 715–16).

II, 899 *maw* here, entrails, bowels.

II, 905 *essences* see I, 777–81n (p. 567).

II, 906 *lees* dregs.

II, 912 *Dark as the parentage of chaos* compare *Hyperion* II, 190–91.

II, 945 *rillets* rivulet, brooklet (Elizabethan).

II, 948–9] Kiss, raptur'd, even to her milky toes. / O foolish maid be gentle to my woes. *Draft*.

576 NOTES FOR PP. 160-63

II, 993-4 *more unseen ... exile* a reference to Saturn's overthrow by the Olympians. See *Hyperion* I, 1-14.

II, 996 *mealy*] powdery *Draft*. For 'mealy' see II, 91n.

II, 1008-9 *At this ... fearful dell* 'The fountain Arethusa is in Ortygia, a small island near Syracuse; and the ancients affirm, that the river Alpheus passes under the sea from Peleponnesus, rises again in Ortygia, and joins the stream of Arethusa' (*Lemprière*).

II, 1023 possibly based on Dante's practice of finishing a canto with a single line. See *Gittings* (1968), p. 146.

BOOK III

Written September 1817, mainly at Oxford where Keats stayed with Benjamin Bailey at Magdalen Hall. Keats wrote about fifty lines a day (*KC* II, 270). He was reading *Paradise Lost* during this period, which is occasionally reflected in the phrasing and syntax of the poem.

III, 1-21 an attack on the Tory government and other reactionary regimes, which echoes Hunt's articles in the *Examiner*, August 1817.

III, 7-8 *Fire-branded ... hopes* refers to Judges xv 4-5, 'And Samson went and caught three hundred foxes, and took firebrands, and turned tail to tail, and put a firebrand in the midst between two tails. And when he had set the brands on fire, he let them go into the standing corn of the Philistines, and burnt up both the shocks, and also the standing corn, with the vineyards and olives.'

III, 10 *dight* dress, array (Spenser, Milton, Chatterton).

III, 11 *empurpled vests* Hunt, as *Allott* points out, ridiculed the French clergy for wearing 'the Roman purple', adding, 'The Roman purple ... the garb of the Antonines, – and of the Neros!' (*Examiner*, 31 August 1817).

III, 17-18 *trumpets ... cannon* there were noisy peace celebrations following Napoleon's abdication on 6 April 1814.

III, 25 *ethereal* see I, 298n.

III, 31 *bourne* here domain; but properly, a boundary.

III, 31-2] In the several vastnesses of air and fire; / And silent, as a corpse upon a pyre *Draft* (*cancelled*).

III, 38-9] Salutes our native Ceres – every sense / With spiritual honey fills to plenitude *Draft*.

III, 42 *thy Sister* Diana, the moon.

III, 56-7 *Thou ... life*] Thou dost bless all things – even dead things sip / A midnight life from thee *Draft*.

III, 57 *kine* cattle.

III, 69 *monstrous* inhabited by monsters.

III, 70-71 the moon causes tides, whose waves break on the forehead of Tellus (the earth). 'Spooming' means foaming.

III, 80 anticipates *The Eve of St. Agnes* 311, 'How changed thou art! how pallid, chill, and drear ...'.

III, 82-3 *stress | Of love-spangles* the spread of moonbeams reflected in the water.

III, 97-9 *Leander .. Orpheus ... Pluto* classical figures who braved the sea, the underworld, and the upper air for the sake of love.

III, 100 *wingèd Chieftain* Cupid.

III, 106-7 *a warm | Of his heart's blood* compare Keats's letter to Reynolds, 22 September 1818, 'This morning Poetry has conquered ... There is an awful warmth about my heart like a load of Immortality' (*L* I, p. 370).

III, 119-29 *Far ... vintage* echoes *Richard III* I.4.22-8, 'What dreadful noise of waters in my ears! / What sights of ugly death within my eyes! / Methought I saw a thousand fearful wrecks; / Ten thousand men that fishes gnaw'd upon; / Wedges of gold, great anchors, heaps of pearl, / Inestimable stones, unvalued jewels, / All scattered in the bottom of the sea. ...' Also Virgil, *Aeneid* VII, 183-6.

III, 120 *vast* the sea. See II, 240n.

III, 124 *brazen beaks and targe* the bronze figureheads and shields of the wrecked ships.

III, 129 *of Saturn's vintage* from earliest times. Saturn was one of the first gods.

III, 134 *behemoth ... leviathan* the first is a Biblical word for one of the largest and most powerful of animals (see Job xl 15), the second a word meaning sea-monster which occurs frequently in Hebrew poetry. Both words echo Keats's recent reading of *Paradise Lost* VII, 471-2, 412-16.

III, 150 *eyes*] soul Draft.

III, 153 *dibble* 'An instrument used to make holes in the ground for seeds, bulbs, or young plants' (*OED*).

III, 157 *mesh* weave (figurative).

III, 172 *essence* see I, 777-81n (p. 567)

III, 173-4 *I pressed ... wakeful rest* compare '*Bright star! would I were steadfast as thou art*' 10-12.

III, 175-6 the moon and Endymion's 'strange love' are of course identical, both being Diana.

III, 176 *Felicity's abyss* 'Pleasure so profound that it is unfathomable' (*Allott*).

III, 179 *under-passion* compare Steele, *Spectator*, no. 208, 1711, 'The Under-Passion (as I may so call it) of a noble Spirit, Pity.'

III, 192 *old man* Glaucus. The following lines may owe a debt to Salvator Rosa's *Glaucus and Scylla* according to *Jack* (see his Plate XVIII).

III, 202] Draft, G, Allott; not in Fair copy or Endymion.

III, 203 *woof* woven fabric.

III, 205 *gulfing* see I, 571n, though 'gulf' here may have its Elizabethan meaning, 'To rush along like a gulf or whirlpool; to eddy, swirl' (*OED*).

III, 222-5 *and like ... smile* Bailey later reported Keats reading 'the fine & affecting story of the old man, Glaucus ... '. These lines struck him 'as peculiarly fine ... I remember his upward look when he read of the "magic ploughs"' (*KC* II, p. 271). The lines echo Keats's reading of Shakespeare's

NOTES FOR PP. 167-73

sonnets: 'When forty winters shall besiege thy brow, / And dig deep trenches ...', 'But when in thee time's furrows I behold', 'And delves the parallels in beauty's brow' (*Sonnets* ii, 1-2, xxii, 3, lx, 10).

III, 230 *stole* a long robe, frequently used in translations from Greek and Latin, referring to classical antiquity.

III, 234 (and 255) *Thou art the man* 2 Samuel xii 7, 'And Nathan said to David, Thou art the man.'

III, 243 *that giant* Typhon.

III, 251 *Sisters three* the Fates. *Allott* suggests that Keats may be remembering the witches in *Macbeth* as well.

III, 254 *wither, droop, and pine* compare *Macbeth* I.3.22-3, 'Weary se'nnights nine times nine / Shall he dwindle, peak and pine ...'

III, 261-2 Endymion fears Glaucus may burn him to a cinder.

III, 265 *magian* magical. See *On Visiting Staffa* (p. 605).

III, 285 *contumelious* superciliously arrogant (Elizabethan).

III, 286 *humane*] Fair copy, *G*, *Allott*; human *Endymion*.

III, 315 *the midway from mortality* the half way point between life and death.

III. 318-638 the story of Glaucus and Scylla is a free adaptation from Ovid, *Metamorphoses* XIII, 898-968, XIV, 1-74.

III, 342 *discrepant* apart or separate in space (rare). *OED* cites only two earlier examples. 'Plaining' means complaining.

III, 351 *gulfed* see I, 571*n*.

III, 366 *brim of day-tide* noon. 'Lea' means meadow.

III, 372-92 in Ovid, *Metamorphoses* XIII, 940-8, Glaucus is changed into a sea-deity by eating a magic herb.

III, 375 *distempered* disordered, deranged.

III, 380-84 *To interknit ... limbs* as *Allott* notes, this illustrates Keats's theory of 'fellowship with essence'. See I, 795-7, '... that moment have we stepped / Into a sort of oneness, and our state / Is like a floating spirit's', and I, 777-81*n* (p. 567).

III, 386 *self-intent* refers to the loss of self necessary for 'fellowship with essence'. See I, 799 and 777-81*n* (p. 567).

III, 402 *the very white of truth* the 'white' is the bull's eyes at the centre of an archery target. Hence the meaning is 'absolutely true'.

III, 406 Hercules burnt himself on a pyre on Mount Oetna.

III, 414 *Phoebus' daughter* i.e. Circe.

III, 446-7] And then I felt a hovering influence / A breathing on my foreheat *Draft*.

III, 449-72 in Ovid, *Metamorphoses* XIV, 37-74, Glaucus resists Circe, who in revenge changes Scylla into a monster.

III, 454 *ambrosia* the food of the gods. 'It was sweeter than honey, and of a most odoriferous smell. ... The gods used generally to perfume their hair with ambrosia, as Juno when she adorned herself to captivate Jupiter, and Venus when she appeared to Aeneas' (*Lemprière*).

III, 459 *arbitrary* unrestrained in the exercise of will, hence despotic. *OED* cites, 'Acts of Will and Tyranny, which make up an Arbitrary Government' (1642).

III, 459–60 *And ... vassal* as Allott notes, probably suggested by Sandy's 'The Mind of the Frontispiece, and argument of this Work' 11–15, prefixed to his translation of Ovid: '... who forsake that faire *Intelligence*, / To follow *Passion* and voluptuous *Sence*; / That shun the Path and Toyles of HERCULES, / Such charmèd by CIRCE's luxurie and ease, / Themselves deforme. ...'.

III, 466 *balmy consciousness*] nectareous Influence *Draft*.

III, 485 *moan* A Spenserian usage. See *La Belle Dame sans Merci* 20n (p. 639).

III, 488 *complain* complaint.

III, 494 *gordian* intertwined.

III, 496 *the feel of fear* compare 'the feel of not to feel it' in '*In drear-nighted December*' 21 and n (p. 587).

III, 500–531 Circe metamorphosed her lovers into beasts (Homer, *Odyssey* X, 210–43, Ovid, *Metamorphoses* XIV, 276–87). See also Milton's treatment of the 'monstrous rout' led by Circe's son, Comus, in *Comus* 19–38.

III, 504 *penny pelf* refers to the obolus, Charon's fee for ferrying the dead over the Styx and Acheron.

III, 511 *ravened* devoured greedily (Elizabethan).

III, 529 *writhen* made to writhe.

III, 534 *stark* either harsh or powerful.

III, 588 *thews* the bodily powers or forces of a man (Shakespeare).

III, 590–99 Allott compares with Lyly's *Endimion* (1591), II. 3. 29–36, 'Thou that liest downe with golden lockes shalt not awake untill they bee turned to silver haires; and that chin, on which scarcely appeareth soft downe, shall be filled with brissels as hard as broome, thou shalt sleep out thy youth and flowring time, and become dry hay before thou knowest thy selfe greene grass, and ready by age to step into the grave when thou wakest, that was youthfull in the Court when thou laidst thee downe to sleepe. The malice of *Tellus* hath brought thee to this passe. ...'

III, 621–35 an alteration from the original in which Scylla is transformed into a monster.

III, 654–60 *all the billows ... thunder-rolls* echoes *The Tempest* I. 2. 3–9, 'The sky, it seems, would pour down stinking pitch, / But that the sea, mounting to th'welkin's cheek, / Dashes the fire out. O! I have suffered / With those I saw suffer: a brave vessel, / Who had, no doubt, some noble creature in her, / Dashed all to pieces. O! the cry did knock / Against my very heart. Poor souls, they perished. ...'

III, 659 *gulfing* see I, 571n).

III, 661 *eld* old age (archaism).

III, 675 *aguish* compare *The Eve of St Mark* 12, 'the aguish hills'.

III, 685 *Atlas-line* lines as strong as Atlas.

III, 695–6 *he oppressèd. ... These things accomplished* inversions reflecting Keats's reading of *Paradise Lost* at this time.

III, 700 *symbol-essences* compare the lines on 'fellowship with essence', I, 777–81 and *n* (p. 567).

II, 728–44 this description of the dead lovers echoes Milton's account of Satan's host in *Paradise Lost* I, 344–5, 544–71. The magical aura is reminiscent of *The Arabian Nights* and Beckford's *Vathek*.

III, 752 *stroke*] Fair copy, G; struck *Endymion, Garrod (OSA), Allott*. 'Stroke' is a Spenserian archaism.

III, 756 *clue* a ball of thread or yarn.

III, 762 *charactery* printed or written symbols. Compare '*When I have fears* . . .' 3, 'high-pilèd books, in charactery'.

III, 766–806 possibly written 20 September 1817 (see *KC* I, p. 7).

III, 786 *Apollo's touch* the sun's rays.

III, 796 *Enchantment*] Ravishment *Draft (cancelled)*.

III, 816 *Swallows obeying the south summer's call* compare *To Autumn* 33, '. . . gathering swallows twitter in the skies'.

III, 819 *spar* see II, 204*n* (p. 571).

III, 820 *ken* sight.

III, 845–6 *poor mortals fragment up as mere | As marble, was there lavish* this makes difficult sense. 'Mere' (*OED* 5) now means 'Having no greater extent, range, value, power or importance than the designation implies; that is, barely or only what it is said to be'. However, it earlier meant 'pure', as in 'mere Chalk', or 'absolute, entire, sheer, perfect' (*OED* 1c, 4). *Endymion*, and all other texts, place the comma after 'up'. The repunctuated lines mean, 'whatever mankind treasures up in fragments which are as pure as marble, was lavishly used there'.

III, 849 *Memphis . . . Babylon . . . Nineveh* ancient cities notable for their magnificence.

III, 856 *raught* reached (Spenser).

III, 859 *callow* unfledged.

III, 862–5 possibly influenced by Poussin's *The Triumph of Venus and Amphitrite* as well as Tooke's *Pantheon* and Spence's *Polymetis* (*Jack*, p. 159). These images inspired the Hymn to Neptune (III, 943–90).

III, 867 *vast* sea.

III, 879–87 *Of lucid depth . . . sphere* the floor of Neptune's hall is transparent and looks down into the sea. Its shining expanse resembles a lake in which Red Indians dart about in canoes. The lake could be thought to be air, were it not for the reflection of the clouds and sky. So too the palace floor might be taken for air, but for the wonders which can be seen beneath it, and the reflection of its own blazing dome. The dome and its reflection together create the illusion of an encircling 'golden sphere'.

III, 893 *ooze-born Goddess* Venus.

III, 897 *doves* those in attendance upon Venus.

III, 909–15 Venus has realized that Diana loves Endymion.

III, 918 *Visit thou my Cythera*] Hunt's copy of *Endymion* (Keats Museum), *G, Allott*; Visit my Cytherea *Endymion*. Keats refers to the island, not to Venus (Cytherea) herself.

581 NOTES FOR PP. 186–91

III, 923 *halcyon* see *To the Ladies who Saw Me Crowned* 7n (p. 556)

III, 927 *pleached* intertwined. Compare *Much Ado About Nothing* III. 1. 7–9, '... the pleached bower / Where honey suckles, ripened by the sun, / Forbid the sun to enter ...'

III, 930 *coverture* shelter. Compare ibid., III. i. 30, 'couched in the woodbine coverture'.

III, 934–5 *and pleasure ... chained*] and wildness reigns. / They bound each other up in tendril chains. *Draft*.

III, 943–90 For the pictorial influences on this passage, see III, 862–5n above.

III, 956 *Gulfs in* engulfs, but also gulps up. See also I, 571n.

III, 973 *Aeolian twang* the sound of an Aeolian harp. See *Ode to Apollo* 34n (p. 536).

III, 975 *Cytherea* Venus.

III, 983 *essence* see I, 777–81n (p. 567).

III, 997 *lucid* shining, resplendent.

III, 1009 *dizzier pain* compare *On Seeing the Elgin Marbles* 11, 'a most dizzy pain'.

III, 1016–18] They gave him nectar – shed bright drops, and strove / Long time in vain. At last they interwove / Their cradling arms, and carefully conveyed / His body towards a quiet bowery shade *Draft*.

BOOK IV

Written between *c.* 5 October and 28 November 1817 at Hampstead and Burford Bridge, Surrey. By 30 October Keats had written only 300 lines.

IV, 1–29 This Miltonic invocation echoes Keats's recent reading of *Paradise Lost*.

IV, 10 *an eastern voice of solemn mood* the sublime Hebrew style of the Bible.

IV, 14–16 *Plain ... summons* Ausonia is the classical name for Italy, and her two voices here are those of Dante and Virgil.

IV, 26 *shrives* confesses. An archaism. Strictly speaking, 'shrive' means absolution.

IV, 34 *freshet* small stream of clear water.

IV, 39 *hecatomb* literally, a great public sacrifice, extended to mean a large number.

IV, 49–54 *No one ... mountaineer!*] false! 'twas false / They said how beautiful I was! who calls / Me now divine? Who now kneels down and dies / Before me till from these enslaving eyes / Redemption sparkles. Ah me how sad I am! / Of all the poisons sent to make us mad / Of all death's overwhelmings' – Stay Beware / Young Mountaineer! *Draft*.

IV, 56 *Phoebe* Diana. An indication perhaps that Keats had recently read Drayton's *Endimion and Phoebe* (1595).

IV, 66 *Hermes' wand* i.e., Mercury's caduceus.

IV, 82 *As doth the voice of love*] As will a lover's voice *Draft*.

582 NOTES FOR PP. 192–3

IV, 94–5 *While ... soul*] While the fair moon gives light, or rivers flow / My adoration of thee is yet pure / As infants prattling. How is this – why sure / I have a tripple soul *Draft*.

IV, 97 *for them in twain*] Hunt's copy of *Endymion* (Keats Museum), G, Allott; in twain for them *Endymion*.

IV, 101 *covert* hiding-place.

IV, 104–5 *To speak he tries. / 'Fair damsel, pity me!'*] Ye harmonies / Ye tranced visions – ye flights ideal / Nothing are ye to life so dainty real / O Lady pity me! *Draft*.

IV, 110 *sith* since.

IV, 111 *Thou art my executioner* echoes *As You Like It* III. 5. 8, 'I would not be thy executioner ...'.

IV, 118 *that lily hand* a detail which gives some evidence to support the suggestion that *The Lay of Aristotle*, printed in G. L. Way's translation of Le Grand's *Fabliaux* (1800), provided the source for Keats's Indian Maid. See Colvin (1917), p. 33, pp. 551–3, and Finney, p. 276.

IV, 126 *desolation* here given five syllables.

IV, 129 *gorgon* petrifying, terrible.

IV, 136–7]*Draft continues Diana's speech*, Canst thou do so? Is there no balm, no cure / Could not a beckoning Hebe soon allure / Thee into Paradise? What sorrowing / So weighs thee down what utmost woe could bring / This madness – Sit thee down by me, and ease / Thine heart in whispers – haply by degrees / I may find out some soothing medicine,' – / 'Dear Lady,' said Endymion, 'I pine / I die – the tender accents thou hast spoken / Have finish'd all – my heart is lost and broken *Draft*.

IV, 139 *patience* three syllables.

IV, 146–81 Keats comments on his 'Ode to Sorrow' in a letter to Bailey on 22 November 1817. 'I am certain of nothing but of the holiness of the Heart's affections and the truth of Imagination – What the imagination seizes as Beauty must be truth – whether it existed before or not – or I have the same Idea of all our Passions as of Love they are all in their sublime, creative of essential Beauty – In a Word, you may know my favorite Speculation by my first Book [i.e. *Endymion* I, 777ff.] and the little song I sent in my last [i.e. the 'Ode to Sorrow'] – which is a representation from the fancy of the probable mode of operating in these Matters – The Imagination may be compared to Adam's dream – he awoke and found it truth. I am the more zealous in this affair, because I have never yet been able to perceive how any thing can be known for truth by consequitive reasoning – and yet it must be – Can it be that even the greatest Philosopher ever arrived at his goal without putting aside numerous objections – However it may be, O for a Life of Sensations rather than of Thoughts!' (*L* I, pp. 184–5). See N. Ford, *The Prefigurative Imagination of John Keats* (1951), pp. 20–38, on the relationship between this letter and *Endymion*.

IV, 148 *vermeil* bright scarlet. See I, 50*n* (p. 562).

IV, 157 *spry* variant spelling of 'spray'.

NOTES FOR PP. 194-200

IV, 186 *Brimming the water-lily cups with tears* echoes Milton, *Lycidas* 150, 'And Daffadillies fill their cups with tears ...'

IV, 193-272 Keats includes details from several sources in this portrayal of Bacchus' triumphal progress, for which see Finney, pp. 276-91. Jack, pp. 159-60, discusses the influence of Poussin and Titian's *Bacchus and Ariadne*. For Lemprière's description of the rout, see *Dictionary of Classical Names* (p. 701).

IV, 203 *To scare thee, Melancholy!* Bacchus was also the deliverer from care. See *Dictionary of Classical Names* (p. 697).

IV, 210 *ivy-dart* his thyrsus (spear), bound about with ivy.

IV, 212 *imbrued* stained or dyed (with blood).

IV, 232 *kernel tree* possibly refers to the pine tree with its cones.

IV, 241 *leopard* a detail from Titian's *Bacchus and Ariadne*.

IV, 247 *coil* noisy disturbance, bustle (sixteenth and seventeenth centuries).

IV, 251 *panthers' furs* the panther was sacred to Bacchus.

IV, 256 *spleenful unicorn* unicorns are not traditionally associated with Bacchus' rout. Keats is not thinking of the fabulous medieval beast, the guardian of chastity, but of the rhinoceros (see *OED* Ib and II. 7), here made to perform as a saddle animal. Finney, p. 289, suggests an echo of Chapman's *Hymnus ad Cynthiam* 284-5, '... in eager chase drew neare, / Mounted on Lyons, Unicorns, and Bores ...'.

IV, 257 *Osirian Egypt* Osiris was 'a great deity of the Egyptians, son of Jupiter and Niobe'. During his life he was King of Egypt, and after civilizing his own subjects, he 'resolved to spread civilization in the other parts of the earth', taking a great army through most of Asia and Europe (*Lemprière*). He thus provides a parallel with Bacchus, who has now superseded him.

IV, 265 *Brahma* the divine reality in Hinduism.

IV, 266 *And all his priesthood moans* Bacchus' victory over Osiris and Brahma echoes the passing of the pagan gods in Milton's *Nativity Ode* 189-91, 'In consecrated Earth, / And on the holy Hearth / The *Lars* and *Lemures* moan with midnight plaint ...'. Compare *Ode to Psyche* 37-45.

IV, 311-14] That – oh how beautiful – how giddy smooth! / Blush so for ever! let those glances soothe / My madness for did I no mercy spy / Dear lady I should shudder and then die *Draft*.

IV, 336 *wand* caduceus.

IV, 341 *wide*] *Draft, Fair copy, G, Allott*; wild *Endymion*.

IV, 349 *Exhaled to Phoebus' lips* drawn up (through a kind of evaporation) to the sun's lips.

IV, 349 *they're*] *Fair copy;* they are *all other texts.*

IV, 377 *plump* compare *To Autumn* 7, 'plump the hazel shells'.

IV, 380 *Jove's daughter* i.e., Diana (Phoebe), daughter of Latona by Jupiter.

IV, 392 *sallows* willows.

IV, 394 *Skiddaw* Keats did not visit the Lake District until summer 1818, but knew of Skiddaw through his reading of Wordsworth.

584 NOTES FOR PP. 200-205

IV, 399 *splenetic* compare with the usage 'in spleen' (IV, 346), where it means 'with strong determination, resolution'.

IV, 400 *blood wide* 'wide open and suffused with blood' (*Allott*).

IV, 407 *The mournful wanderer* Endymion.

IV, 409 *fain* content.

IV, 410 *proud birds* peacocks, which were associated with Juno.

IV, 413 *Pallas' shield* Pallas Athene (Minerva) was goddess of war, wisdom, and the liberal arts. 'In one hand she held a spear, in the other a shield, with the dying head of Medusa upon it' (*Lemprière*).

IV, 422 *-kirtled* dressed in a garment which reached to the knees.

IV, 426 *floating morris* airy dance.

IV, 429-31 *'Tis Dian's ... goddess* Endymion's unknown goddess and Diana are identical.

IV, 436 *Beheld awake his very dream* compare Keats's remark in his letter to Bailey, 'The Imagination may be compared to Adam's dream – he awoke and found it truth' (*LI*, p. 185). See IV, 146-81*n*.

IV, 438 *Phoebe ... crescented* the crescent moon was a symbol of Diana (Phoebe).

IV, 441-4 a reference to Icarus.

IV, 453 *shook* an archaism for 'shaken'.

IV, 459 *daedal* cunning, a word derived from Daedalus, the master artificer. Spenser uses it to mean 'skilful' in *The Faerie Queene* III, Prologue 13, 'His daedale hand would faile', and Shelley used it frequently – *Prometheus Unbound* (1820) IV, 416, 'Daedal harmony'.

IV, 461 *bourne* boundary, limit.

IV, 476-7 For this loss of 'self-passion or identity' in 'fellowship with essence', see I, 777-81*n*, and 799*n* (pp. 567-8).

IV, 486 *silverly*] *Draft, Fair copy, G, Allott*; silvery *Endymion*.

IV, 512-48 Keats's 'Cave of Quietude' explores his ideas about the connection between suffering and creativity. On this passage, see J. M. Murry, *The Mystery of Keats* (1949), pp. 118-50, who interprets the Cave as a state of profound content, beyond sorrow and joy. But misery and apathy are dwelt upon more than renewal.

IV, 531 *The death-watch tick is stifled* the tick of the death-watch beetle portends death. It is 'stifled' because death has taken place.

IV, 552 A hypermetrical line.

IV, 558 *masque*] *G* (*from Hunt's copy of Endymion in Keats Museum*), *Allott*; mask *Draft, Fair copy, Endymion*.

IV, 569 *lucid* shining.

IV, 575 *balm, and golden pines* 'Balm' is a fragrant garden herb, esp. balm-gentle, balm-mint. 'Golden pine' is a pineapple.

IV, 576 *Savory, latter-mint, and columbines* 'savory' is a garden herb, 'latter-mint' a neologism for late-growing mint, and 'columbine', not strictly a herb, is the English name for plants of the ranunculus ('crowfoot') family.

IV, 581 *belt of heaven* the zodiac, which is in astronomy 'a belt of the celestial sphere extending eight or nine degrees on each side of the ecliptic, within which the apparent motions of the sun, and principal planets takes place'.

IV, 582 *Aquarius* a sign of the zodiac, the water-carrier, frequently, as here, identified with Ganymede, Jupiter's cup-bearer. *Allott* cites Sandys's *Ovid*, '*Ganymed* . . . is . . . faigned to have been converted into the winter signe of *Aquarius*, and because abundance of raine is powred upon the Earth from the clouds when the sunne is in that signe, he is said to be Jupiter's cup-bearer' (1640 edn, p. 196).

IV, 589 *Star-Queen* Diana.

IV, 591–611 Aquarius having been called upon to brighten Diana's wedding night, Keats has Castor and Pollux (Gemini) defeat inappropriate constellations, the 'Lion' (Leo) and the 'Bear' (Ursa Major, the Big Dipper), while the 'Centaur' (Sagittarius) speeds away in pursuit of Scorpio. The constellations of Andromeda and Perseus (ll. 602–609), whose story is analogous to that of Endymion and Diana, are then called upon to attend the festivities in their role as lovers.

IV, 597–9 *The Centaur's arrow . . . heaven* Spence's commentary on the Farnese Globe is relevant: 'Arcitens . . . was represented under the figure of a satyr. . . . He holds his bow as just ready to shoot it off; and the arrow in it seems to aim at the tail of Scorpius. The artists, in process of time, substituted the form of a Centaur, instead of that of a Satyr, for this sign of the Zodiac' (*Polymetis*, p. 171).

IV, 599 *shent* reproached, reviled (Elizabethan).

IV, 606 *Danae's Son* Perseus, lover of Andromeda (l. 602). The two lovers were transformed into closely related constellations. For their story, see *Dictionary of Classical Names* (p. 698).

IV, 622 *The grass*] The real grass *Draft, Fair copy*.

IV, 623 *It is thy voice – divinest! Where?* Diana has reassumed her disguise as the Indian Maid.

IV, 646–55 this should perhaps be taken as a rebuttal of Shelley's visionary idealism in *Alastor* (1816).

IV, 663 *simple*] silver *Garrod (OSA)*, Allott. 'Silver' would mean lives lived out under the influence of the moon.

IV, 670–721 this 'invitation to love' belongs to the pastoral tradition, and may be indebted to Polyphemus' wooing of Galatea, Ovid, *Metamorphoses* XIII, 810–37, as well as to Marlowe's *The Passionate Shepherd to his Love* (1599).

IV, 685 *dew-clawed stag* the 'claws' may be the stag's hooves (*OED* 6 cites examples of this sense up to 1661). It is also possible that Keats is referring figuratively to the stag's antlers.

IV, 686 an echo of the myth of Pan and Syrinx.

NOTES FOR PP. 208–15

IV, 697 *eglantine* the sweet-briar, a fragrant white rose. The word can also mean 'honeysuckle', which, however, appears in the next line. *Ode to a Nightingale* 46, 'White hawthorn, and the pastoral eglantine', also suggests a thorny plant.

IV, 699 *trace* write out in letters.

IV, 700] *followed in Fair copy by* And by it shalt thou sit and sing, hey nonny! / While doves coo to thee for a little honey.

IV, 716] And the most velvet peaches to my choice *Draft*.

IV, 721 *mountaineer* Endymion.

IV, 730 *Young feathered tyrant* Cupid.

IV, 750–51 *With ... all*] My own imaginations to sweet life / Thou would'st o'ertop them all *Draft*.

IV, 759 compare *Ode to a Nightingale* 55, 'Now more than ever seems it rich to die'.

IV, 761 *trammels* see II, 411*n* (p. 573).

IV, 769 *cirque* circle (poetic spelling).

IV, 774 *Thy lute-voiced brother* Apollo.

IV, 783 *amaranth* an imaginary flower that never fades.

IV, 784 *the old garden-ground of boyish days* the garden of Eden of childhood.

IV, 790 *charactery* letters incised in the tree's bark.

IV, 792 *feared* frightened.

IV, 801 *Can she endure –* can she endure to see Endymion's misery?

IV, 808 *and sigh no more* compare Balthazar's song in *Much Ado About Nothing* II. 3. 58, 'Sigh no more, ladies, sigh no more ...'

IV, 811–13] Were this sweet damsel like a long neck'd crane / Or an old rocking barn owl half asleep / Some reason would there be for thee to keep / So dull-eyed – but thou knowst she's beautiful / Yes, Yes! and thou dost love her well – I'll pull *Draft*.

IV, 814 *coronals* coronets, wreaths.

IV, 834 *vesper-carols* evening songs.

IV, 877–8 see Matthew x 29–31, 'Are not two sparrows sold for a farthing? and one of them shall not fall on the ground without your Father. But the very hairs of your head are all numbered. Fear ye not therefore, ye are of more value than many sparrows.'

IV, 884 *monitor* guide (a Keatsian coinage from the noun).

IV, 892 *Lucifer or Baal* 'Lucifer' is here a name for Satan. 'Baal' is a general name for the Syrian gods. In the Bible used of the god of the Canaanites, and hence means a false god.

IV, 906 *maw* throat, mouth.

IV, 929 *serene father* Apollo as the sun.

IV, 942 *bale* misery (poeticism).

IV, 943 *Titan's foe* Jupiter.

IV, 949–50] Until he saw that grove, as if perchance, / And then his soul was changed *Draft*.

IV, 950 *seemlihed* a becoming appearance. A Spenserian archaism: see *The Faerie Queen*, IV. viii. 14, 'by his persons secret seemlyhed'.

IV, 956–7 *By ... palsy* anticipates *Hyperion* I, 89–90, 92–4.
IV, 967 *vesper* evening.
IV, 984–6 *in display ... love*] while it turned / Golden – and her eyes of jet dawned forth a brighter day / Blue – blue – and full of love *Draft*.
IV, 988 *lucid* resplendent, shining.
IV, 1002–3 compare with '*I stood tip-toe ...*' 141–2, '... how Psyche went / On the smooth wind to realms of wonderment'.

'IN DREAR-NIGHTED DECEMBER'

Dated 1817 in 'Miss Reynolds' Album' (*W*2). Published *Literary Gazette*, 19 September 1829. Text, like that of *Garrod (OSA)* and *Allott*, based on Keats's manuscript in Bristol University Library, which is reproduced and its relationship with early MSS and printed versions discussed, by A. Whitley in *Harvard Library Bulletin*, V (1951), pp. 116–22.

The poem reflects Keats's ideas on 'Negative Capability' and 'intensity', which he outlined in his important letter to George and Tom Keats on 21–7 December 1817. '*Death on the Pale horse ... is a wonderful picture, when West's age is considered; But there is nothing to be intense upon; no women one feels mad to kiss; no face swelling into reality. The excellence of every Art is its intensity, capable of making all disagreeables evaporate, from their being in close relationship with Beauty & Truth – Examine King Lear & you will find this examplified throughout; but in this picture we have unpleasantness without any momentous depth of speculation excited, in which to bury its repulsiveness – .... I had not a dispute but a disquisition with Dilke, on various subjects; several things dovetailed in my mind, & at once it struck me, what quality went to form a Man of Achievement especially in Literature & which Shakespeare posessed so enormously – I mean Negative Capability, that is when man is capable of being in uncertainties, Mysteries, doubts, without any irritable reaching after fact & reason – Coleridge, for instance, would let go by a fine isolated verisimilitude caught from the Penetralium of mystery, from being incapable of remaining content with half knowledge. This pursued through Volumes would perhaps take us no further than this, that with a great poet the sense of Beauty overcomes every other consideration, or rather obliterates all consideration*' (I, pp. 192–4).

1, 9 *In*] In a *Literary Gazette, G*.
15 *petting* sulking, taking offence.
20 *joy?*] *G, Allott; MS* unpunctuated.
21 *The feel of not to feel it*] To know the change and feel it *Literary Gazette, G*. The variant line, often accepted as the final reading, comes from Woodhouse's objections to the Keatsian 'feel of not to feel it' (see *KC* I, p. 64). The MS reading is undoubtedly correct, though the syntax of ll. 20–24 is difficult since the MS is unpunctuated. Thus, l. 21 could stand in apposition to l. 20, but that makes the rest of the poem hard to construe. As Whitley says, l. 21 'wrenches itself loose from the poem and grows greater in intensity and suggestion'. Further, see *G*, pp. lvi–vii, *Murry* (1930), pp. 62–70, and *Jones*, pp. 36–8, which also analyses the Keatsian use of 'of' in l. 20.

23 *steel*] *Literary Gazette, G, Allott*; steal *MS*. 'Steal' is a possible reading, but is probably an error. See, however, the exchange between J. F. Muirhead and Sir S. Colvin in *TLS*, 9, 16, and 23 July 1925.

NEBUCHADNEZZAR'S DREAM

Date uncertain, but probably December 1817. Published *Literary Anecdotes of the Nineteenth Century* (1896). Text here is based on Charles Brown's transcript rather than the holograph in the Huntingdon Library. In *Philological Quarterly*, XXXIV (1955), pp. 177–88, A. Ward has shown that this hitherto obscure poem is a political satire upon the repressive measures taken by the Tory government to silence its critics in 1817. 'Daniel' probably stands for William Hone (1780–1842), who had attacked the government in parodies of the Catechism, the Creed, and the Litany. He was tried for blasphemous and seditious writings on 18–20 December 1817, but defended himself brilliantly, pointing out that the employment of biblical parallels in political satire was nothing new, and citing several examples which had used the story of Daniel. Keats followed the trial with interest (*L* I, p. 191), as did Hunt in the *Examiner*, and Hone's acquittal was a liberal triumph. The poem is based on Daniel ii–iv, in which Nebuchadnezzar erects an image of gold, and suffers from nightmares. Daniel fearlessly interprets these dreams, which foretell the overthrow of Nebuchadnezzar's kingdom, for he is the 'head of gold' (ii 38). In Keats's sonnet Nebuchadnezzar probably represents George III, while the 'valiant crew' of 'loggerheads and chapmen' (ll. 10–11) stands for the Tory ministry, who were terrified that the regime, maintained by force, might be overthrown by popular revolt. They have 'lying lips' (l. 13) because they subvert the Constitutional liberties they are supposed to defend, but will be defeated by the truth voiced by Daniel (i.e. Hone). Keats also uses the image of the downfall of Babylon to prophesy the end of Tory tyranny in *Endymion* III, 18–21. *G* and *Allott* mix readings from Brown's transcript and the draft (*Texts*, pp. 142–3).

4 *naumachia* a 'Serpentine Naumachia' or 'sham naval fight' was an item in the Peace celebrations of 1814 (see *Endymion* III, 17–18).

5 *'Good King of Cats'* quoted from *Romeo and Juliet* III. i. 76, and used to refer to Daniel in the lion's den.

6–7 *beam ... eye* see Luke vi 42.

11 *loggerheads and chapmen* blockheads and pedlars (i.e. the ministry).

14 *'Ye are that head of Gold'* see headnote above.

APOLLO TO THE GRACES

Written as a song for the Reynolds sisters, probably in January 1818. Published *TLS*, 16 April 1914. Woodhouse records, 'Written to the tune of an air in Don Giovanni' (*W2*), i.e. a tune in the Christmas entertainment, *Harlequin's Vision*, put on at Drury Lane Theatre in 1817, and reviewed by Keats in the *Champion*, 4 January 1818. Text based on *G*, which follows the autograph MS at Harvard.

TO MRS REYNOLDS'S CAT

Dated 16 January 1818 in Keats's autograph (Buffalo and Erie County Library). Published *The Comic Annual* (1830). Text based on autograph.

1 *grand climacteric* the sixty-third year of life.

ON SEEING A LOCK OF MILTON'S HAIR. ODE

Written 21 January 1818. Published *Plymouth and Devon Weekly Journal*, 15 November 1838, reprinted *1848*. Keats told Bailey on 23 January, 'I was at Hunt's the other day, and he surprised me with a real authenticated Lock of Milton's Hair' (*L*, I, p. 210). Text based on Brown's transcript.

1 *organic numbers* poetry which is 'organ-like' (*OED* cites examples from Donne and Leigh Hunt).
18 *Delian oath* the oath of a young poet. Delos was Apollo's birthplace.
22 *I swear*] Brown's transcript, *1848*, G, Allott; not in L or W1, though added in pencil in W2.
37–8] some *MSS* give as a single line, but Woodhouse noted the need for a rhyme with 'unaware' (*W2*).

ON SITTING DOWN TO READ *KING LEAR* ONCE AGAIN

Written 22 January 1818. Published *Plymouth and Devonport Weekly*, 8 November 1838, reprinted *1848*. The fair copy of the sonnet is in the folio Shakespeare in the Keats Museum (Hampstead). Keats was preparing *Endymion* for the press, which forced upon him the contrast between Shakespearian poetry and 'golden-tongued Romance'. For Keats's early reading of *King Lear* see headnote to *On the Sea* (p. 558).

2 *Fair plumèd Syren* Romance is imagined as a Spenserian heroine. Compare *Specimen of an Induction* 1–2 and *To [Mary Frogley]* 52–3.
6 *damnation*] Fair copy, G, Allott; Hell torment L, *1848*.
7 *assay* test, make trial of (esp. when analysing metals).

'WHEN I HAVE FEARS THAT I MAY CEASE TO BE'

Written between 22 and 31 January 1818. Published *1848*. This sonnet marks the beginning of Keats's preference for the Shakespearian sonnet form over the Petrarchan pattern. For an analysis, see M. A. Goldberg, *Modern Language Quarterly*, XVIII, (1957), pp. 125–31.

3 *charactery* written or printed words (Shakespearean).
5–6 compare with Keats's remark of 19 February 1818, '... man should ... weave a tapestry empyrean – full of Symbols for his spiritual eye' (*L* I, p. 232).
7–8 Woodhouse noted 'These lines give some insight into Keats's mode of writing Poetry. He has repeatedly said ... that he never sits down to write, unless he is full of ideas – and then thoughts come about him in troops ... one of his Maxims is that if P[oetry] does not come naturally, it had better not come at all' (*KC* I, p. 128).

590 NOTES FOR PP. 221-2

9 *fair creature of an hour* Woodhouse claimed that Keats was thinking of the same woman he had seen in the summer of 1814 at Vauxhall Gardens: see '*Fill for me a brimming bowl*' and *To —* ('Time's sea . . .') for two other poems inspired by her.

'O BLUSH NOT SO! O BLUSH NOT SO!'

Written 31 January 1818. Published *Forman* (1883). Text from the transcript made by Brown. The poem, whose sexual puns led Swinburne to think it unfit for publication, attempts to catch the tone of seventeenth-century rondeaus.

9 *O sigh not so! O sigh not so!* echoes Balthazar's song in *Much Ado About Nothing*. See '*Think not of it, sweet one, so*' 3 (p. 105) and *Endymion* IV, 808n (p. 586).
10-13 Keats's letter of February–May 1819 glosses this: 'On going he leaves her three pips of eve's apple – and some how – she, having liv'd a virgin all her life, begins to repent of it' (*L* II, p. 61).
11 *hips*] lips *W*3, *G*.
20 *cut the sweet apple* an injunction to abandon virginity (see ll. 10–13n).

'HENCE BURGUNDY, CLARET, AND PORT'

Written 31 January 1818 in Keats's letter to Reynolds (*L* I, p. 220). Published *1848*. Text based on *L*. This poem and '*God of the meridian*' occur in the letter one after the other. As in *G*, they are treated as two poems here. *Allott* and other editors treat them as a single poem. *1848* does not make it clear whether they are two poems or two stanzas of a single poem.

1-2 Keats reports the pleasures of a convivial evening spent with Wells and Severn in his letter to his brothers of 5 January 1818 (*L* I, pp. 196-7). His enjoyment of wine is celebrated in '*Fill for me a brimming bowl*'. The most famous example of Keats's abjuring the pleasures of wine for those of poetic inspiration occurs in *Ode to a Nightingale* 11–34.
3 *couthly*] *L*, *Allott*; courtly *W*2; earthly Brown's transcript, 1848, *G. Texts*, pp. 164–5, argues for 'earthly'. 'Couthly' is an archaism for 'well-known' or 'familiar'.
5 *rummer* 'a large drinking-glass' (*OED*).
10 *Delphian* poetic.
11 *Caius* i.e. Reynolds, who used this pseudonym in the *Yellow Dwarf*.

'GOD OF THE MERIDIAN'

Written 31 January 1818. Published *1848*. See headnote to preceding poem, of which this is regarded as the second stanza by some editors.

1 *meridian* noon. The god invoked is Apollo, 'God of Song' (l. 17).

ROBIN HOOD

Written *c.* 3 February 1818, and sent to Reynolds on that date (*L* I, p. 225). Published *1820*. The poem answers Reynolds's 'Robin Hood' sonnets which were to appear in the *Yellow Dwarf*, 21 February 1818. In his letter Keats attacks modern poetry which has a 'palpable design' on the reader as contrasted to the 'great & unobtrusive' poetry of the Elizabethans – 'Let us have the old Poets, & robin Hood ...' (*L* I, pp. 224–5).

10 Keats is here attacking Reynolds's decision to abandon poetry for law.
13 *ivory* probably, hunting horn.
21–22 *seven stars ... polar ray* Pleiades and the North Star.
26 *can* metal drinking cup.
30 *pasture* a neologism, probably meaning, as *Allott* suggests, pastoral.
33 *morris* morris dance.
34 *Gamelyn* *The Tale of Gamelyn* is a medieval metrical romance, once attributed to Chaucer. Gamelyn, an oppressed younger brother, takes to the forest, where he becomes king of the outlaws.
36 *'grenè shawe'* quotation from Chaucer, *The Friar's Tale* 88.
55 *tight* compact, trim, applied ironically to Little John, so named for his unusual height.

LINES ON THE MERMAID TAVERN

Written *c.* 3 February 1818, and sent with preceding poem to Reynolds (*L* I, p. 225). Published *1820*. Like the preceding poem this expresses Keats's liking for the 'unobtrusiveness' of Elizabethan poetry as opposed to the 'grandeur' of modern poets. A lost letter of Keats recorded that he wrote the poem after visiting the Mermaid Tavern, Cheapside, the famous meeting-place of Elizabethan wits and writers, including Shakespeare, Ben Jonson, Beaumont, and Fletcher (see *L* I, p. 225*n*).

12 *Sup and bowse* both words mean drink, esp. liquor.

TO— ('Time's sea hath been five years at its slow ebb')

Written 4 February 1818. Published *Hood's Magazine*, September 1844, *1848*. Addressed to the same woman Keats had seen in the summer of 1814 in Vauxhall Gardens and celebrated in '*Fill for me a brimming bowl*'. She also appears in '*When I have fears ...*' 9–10. The sonnet shows Shakespeare's influence, and Bridges thought 'it might have been written by Shakespeare'. For an illuminating discussion of the interplay between Keats's poem and his reading of Shakespeare, see *Jones*, pp. 197–8.

TO THE NILE

Written 4 February 1818. Published *Plymouth and Devonport Weekly Journal*, 19 July 1838, *1848*. Text follows Brown's transcript, which includes Keats's final alterations, as recorded in *G*. This sonnet was composed in a fifteen-

592 NOTES FOR PP. 226-8

minute contest between Keats, Shelley, and Hunt. Keats and Shelley finished on time, but Hunt ran over and produced one of his best sonnets (*It flows through old hushed Egypt*). For other poems written by Keats in similar competitions, see headnote to *On the Grasshopper and Cricket* (p. 554).

1 *moon-mountains African* the mountains in which the Nile rose were known as the 'Mountains of the Moon'.
2 *Chief*] *Brown's transcript, Garrod (OSA), Allott;* Stream *1848, G.*
3-4 the upper Nile flows through a desert even while its flood is making Egypt fruitful.
5 *swart* black.
7 *Such*] *Brown's transcript, Garrod (OSA), Allott;* Those *1848.*
8 *for*] *Brown's transcript, Garrod (OSA), Allott;* them *1848, G.*

'SPENSER! A JEALOUS HONOURER OF THINE'

Written 5 February 1818. Published *1848*. The poem is addressed to Reynolds, though the first draft was presented to his sister, Eliza. On the early drafts and the occasion, see E. B. Clark, *Harvard Library Bulletin*, I (1947), pp. 90-100.

1 *jealous honourer* i.e. Reynolds.
2 *forester* an allusion to Reynolds's 'Robin Hood' sonnets. See headnote to *Robin Hood* (p. 591).
5 *Elfin Poet* by analogy with Spenser's 'Elfin knight', which occurs frequently in *The Faerie Queene*. For Keats's use of 'elf', see *Endymion* II, 461n (p. 573).
7 *quell*] *MSS, G, Allott;* quill *1848*. 'Quell' means the power to subdue. Compare *Endymion* II, 537, 'A sovereign quell is in his waving hands ...'.
9 *toil* Keats was still preparing Endymion for the press.

'BLUE! 'TIS THE LIFE OF HEAVEN, THE DOMAIN'

Written 8 February 1818 in reply to Reynolds's sonnet, '*Sweet poets of the gentle antique line*' (published in his *Garden of Florence* [1821]). Published *1848*. Text from *W2* (see *Texts*, pp. 175-6).

'O THOU WHOSE FACE HATH FELT THE WINTER'S WIND'

Written 19 February 1818. Published *1848*. Keats sent the sonnet to Reynolds on the same day, remarking that he had been 'led into these thoughts ... by the beauty of the morning operating on a sense of Idleness – I have not read any Books – the Morning said I was right – I had no Idea but of the Morning and the Thrush said I was right – seeming to say ...' (*L* I, pp. 232-3). An unrhymed sonnet.

SONNET TO A[UBREY] G[EORGE] S[PENCER] ...

Date of composition unknown, but probably between 22 January and end of February 1818 (*Ward*, 1963, pp. 158–9). Published *TLS*, 27 November 1937, where Garrod argues for Keats's authorship. Stillinger considers this a doubtful attribution (*Texts*, pp. 273–4). The sonnet's tone resembles that of *To Mrs Reynolds's Cat*. Text from *G*.

Title] *G* (from *W*3). Aubrey George Spencer (1795–1872) was a contemporary of Benjamin Bailey at Magdalen Hall, Oxford. The 'admirable verses' are two sonnets transcribed in *W*3.

5 *a crow to pick* 'to have something disagreeable or awkward to settle ... to have some fault to find' (*OED*).

13 *metheglin* spiced mead.

14 *annisies* either an odd spelling of 'anise' in the plural (*OED* records several variants), or a word hovering between 'anise' and 'aniseed'. The aniseed and caraway are either liqueurs, or added spice to the beldams' gin.

EXTRACTS FROM AN OPERA

Dated 1818 by Woodhouse. Probably written in February of that year. Keats told his brothers on 14(?) February that he was 'writing at intervals many songs & Sonnets' (*L* I, p. 228). *Finney*, p. 370, suggests that Keats may have attempted an opera with the encouragement of Charles Brown. Published *1848*.

I, 1 *the Olympian twelve* the twelve gods who ruled on Olympus.

I, 9 *pulp* compare '*Hush, hush! tread softly* ...' 16, 'her lips pulped with bloom'.

II Similar in style to '*For there's Bishop's Teign*' and '*Where be ye going* ...?'

IV, 2–7 Ironical version of Shakespeare's *Sonnet* cxxx, 'My mistress' eyes are nothing like the sun. ...'

IV, 9 *crumped* bent into a curve, or crook (current in Keats's day).

V Keats's first attempt at a ballad, followed by '*Old Meg she was a gipsy*', and culminating in *La Belle Dame sans Merci*.

THE HUMAN SEASONS

Written between 7 and 13 March 1818. Published Leigh Hunt's *Literary Pocket Book* (1819), reprinted *Galignani*. Keats sent the poem to Bailey on 13 March with the following remarks: 'I am sometimes so very sceptical as to think Poetry itself a mere Jack a lanthern ... probably every mental pursuit takes its reality and worth from the ardour of the pursuer – being in itself a nothing – Ethereal thing[s] may at least be thus real, divided under three heads – Things real – things semireal – and no things – Things real – such as existences of Sun Moon & Stars and passages of Shakespeare – Things semireal such as Love, the Clouds &c which require a greeting of the Spirit to make them wholly exist – and Nothings which are made great and Dignified by an ardent pursuit ... I have written a Sonnet here [i.e. at Teignmouth] of a somewhat collateral nature' (*L* I, pp. 242–3). *Texts* (pp. 178–9) would adopt the very different version in *L*. Text based on *Pocket Book*.

1 *Title*] *Pocket Book*; untitled in *MSS*, *G*, *Allott*.
7–8 nigh / His] *Pocket Book*, *G*, *Allott*; high / Is *1876*, *Garrod* (*OSA*). Garrod's second thoughts in his OSA text make obvious sense, but the weight of early readings is against the emendation. The sense of ll. 7–8 is 'and by such dreaming the youth comes almost as close to heaven as is possible'.
12 *threshold brook* presumably a brook running just outside a house.
13 *misfeature* distorted feature. *OED* gives this as the word's first occurrence, citing later examples from Carlyle and Bridges.
14 forget] *MSS*; forge *Pocket Book*; forego *Galignani*, *G*, *Allott*.

'FOR THERE'S BISHOP'S TEIGN'

Written *c.* 21 March 1818, the latter being the postmarked date on the letter to Haydon in which Keats sent him the poem. Published T. Taylor's *Autobiography of Haydon* (1853) and *Forman* (1883). Text based on *L* I, pp. 249–50. Keats remarked, 'I have enjoyed the most delightful Walks these three fine days beautiful enough to make me content here all the summer could I stay' (*L* I, p. 249). This light-hearted poem belongs with the two following, and was written while Keats was completing *Endymion* for publication, and also working on *Isabella*.

1–3 *Bishop's Teign ... King's Teign ... Coomb* Bishopsteignton and Kingsteignton are on the north side of the Teign estuary, while Combeinteignhead is to the south.
7–8 *Arch Brook* on the south side of the Teign estuary, about a mile from Teignmouth. It runs through Mill Bottom. Larch Brook does not appear on the six-inch Ordnance Survey Map.
13 *Wild Wood* Wildwoods Point and Copse are on the south side of the Teign, half a mile from Newton Abbot.
19 *Newton Marsh* probably refers to the Teign's estuarial marshes at Newton Abbot, now largely reclaimed and occupied by the racecourse.
25 *barton* strictly 'a demesne farm ... of a manor, not let out to tenants but retained for the lord's own use' (*OED*), but also a common name for 'farm' in Devon and Cornwall.
35 *plight* attire, array (Spenser).
36 *spike* an ear of grain (chiefly poetic).
39 *dacked-haired* possibly meant for 'docked hair', i.e., short-haired, but the word is probably, as Garrod suggests, related to 'dag', one of the locks of wool clotted with dirt, in the neighbourhood of a sheep's tail (hence, 'dag-tailed'). H. E. Rollins thinks there might be an oblique reference to Hazlitt, though this seems unlikely.
42 *prickets* 'a buck in its second year, having straight unbranched horns' (*OED*).

'WHERE BE YE GOING, YOU DEVON MAID?'

Sent to Haydon with preceding poem (see headnote). Published *1848* (without the second stanza); Forman (1883) printed the first accurate version. Text from *L* I, p. 251.

3 *tight* trim, compact.

'OVER THE HILL AND OVER THE DALE'

Written *c.* 23 March 1818 in a letter to James Rice (*L* I, pp. 256–7), after visiting Dawlish Fair on Easter Monday, 23 March. Published T. Taylor, *Life of Benjamin Robert Haydon* (1853). Text based on *L*.

2 *bourn* small stream, brook. Dawlish is about three miles from Teignmouth.
5 *Rantipole* 'wild, disorderly, rakish' (*OED*).
16 *Venus* a prostitute (colloquial).

TO J. H. REYNOLDS, ESQ.

A verse letter written 24 March 1818 from Devon. Published *1848* (without the last four lines). Text based on *L*. Reynolds was ill at the time. Keats wrote, 'In hopes of cheering you through a Minute or two I was determined nill he will he to send you some lines so you will excuse this unconnected subject and careless verse' (*L* I, p. 263). Although the poem was written casually over a hundred lines in an evening, after a light-hearted opening Keats turns in ll. 67–105 to the perplexing problem of suffering and the place of the imagination, anticipating the concerns which dominate his mature verse. For discussions of the poem, see *Murry* (1925), pp. 65–7, *Bate* (1963), pp. 307–9, Douglas Bush, *John Keats* (1966), pp. 73–5, and M. Visick, '"Tease us out of Thought": Keats's *Epistle to Reynolds* and the Odes', *KSJ*, XV (1966), pp. 87–98.

10 Maria Edgeworth liked cats: Hazlitt disliked Miss Edgeworth.
11 *Junius Brutus* the Shakespearean actor, Junius Brutus Booth.
14 *patient*] *Allott*; patent *L, 1848, G*. For the emendation, see S. R. Swaminathan, *N&Q*, August 1967, p. 307. 'Perhaps' should be pronounced as a single syllable, 'p'raps'.
16 *tushes* variant spelling of 'tusks'.
18 *Aeolian harps* wind harps, see *Ode to Apollo* 34n (p. 536).
19–20 The punctuation of these lines, based on *L*, is difficult. The sense is that 'some' of the nocturnal images of 'flowers' and 'Aeolian harps' resemble Titian's paintings.
20 *pontiff* here, a high priest rather than the Pope.
20–22 the details are suggestive of Claude's *Landscape with the Father of Psyche*. See *Jack*, pp. 129–30 and Plate XXV.
21 *Gloams*] *L*; Gleams *1848, G, Allott*. The silent emendation in *1848* and subsequent texts corrects what might seem an obvious slip (Keats's letter, transcribed by Woodhouse, who wrote '[so]' against 'Gloams', is the single

596 NOTES FOR PP. 236–8

source). However, *OED* records the rare Scots verb, 'to gloam' ('to darken, become dusk'), in 1819, and the noun, 'gloaming', is to be found in Hogg, Byron (1807), and Tennyson (1830). Keats has, 'I saw their starved lips in the gloam', *La Belle Dame sans Merci* 41. The idea is that the knife is dusky as compared to the sun, and the word's connotations add an element of threat to the scene. Further, the 'o' sound echoes throughout ll. 20–22.

26–66 the description of the 'Enchanted Castle' draws on Claude's painting of that name in the National Gallery. Further, see *Jack*, pp. 67–8, 127–30.

29 *Urganda's sword* Urganda the Unknown is the enchantress in the medieval romance, *Amadis of Gaul*.

41 *see* dwelling-place.

42 *santon* 'A European designation for a kind of monk or hermit among the Mohammedans' (*OED*). Used in oriental tales written in the Romantic period.

46 *Lapland witch* echoes Milton, *Paradise Lost* II, 664–5, 'Lur'd with the smell of infant blood, to dance / With Lapland Witches . . .'.

57 *lightening* emitting flashes of light.

61 -grate] L, Allott; gate *1848*, G.

68–9 echoes Wordsworth, *Tintern Abbey* (1798), 95–7, '. . . a sense sublime / Of something far more deeply interfused, / Whose dwelling is the light of setting suns . . .'

72–3 *my flag . . . admiral staff* Keats has not yet achieved his maturity. The image, as *Allott* notes, was suggested by North's translation of Plutarch's *Lives* (1676), p. 178, 'Alcibiades setting up a Flag on the top of his Admiral Galley, to show what he was'.

75 lore] L, G, Allott; Love *1848*, Garrod (*OSA*).

77 *tease us out of thought* Keats uses the words again in *Ode on a Grecian Urn* 44–5.

88 *lampit* variant spelling of 'limpet'.

94 *maw* jaw or throat.

108 *Kamchatkan missionary church* Keats had read of the mission established in this bleak peninsula in Russia from Robertson's *History of America* (1777) and other sources, for which see A. D. Atkinson, *N&Q*, August, 1951, pp. 343–5.

109 in] L, G, Allott; i'the *1848*.

111 *new romance* refers to *Isabella*, which Keats was writing.

112 *centaine* a hundred (a rare and obsolete word; *OED* records one occurrence only, in 1560).

TO J[AMES] R[ICE]

Written 18–20 April 1818, when Rice visited Keats at Teignmouth. Published *1848*, with the inaccurate title 'To J. H. Reynolds'. Reynolds introduced Keats to Rice in 1817, and in 1819 Keats said 'He is the most sensible, and even wise Man I know' (*L* II, p. 187).

ISABELLA; OR, THE POT OF BASIL

Probably begun in March 1818, completed by 27 April. Published *1820*. Some variants given from Keats's fair copy (British Museum, Egerton MS 2780), his draft (fragments of which are now scattered in several libraries: see *G*), and the readings in *W*1–3. The narrative follows Keats's source, the fifth novel of the fourth day in Boccaccio's *Decameron*, fairly closely (for a convenient comparison, see *Allott's* notes). *Isabella* was written for a proposed joint volume by Reynolds and Keats based on Boccaccio, the idea of translating him probably being suggested by Hazlitt's lecture 'On Dryden and Pope', given 3 February 1818. Keats's use of *ottava rima*, which is Italian in origin, was influenced by Fairfax's translation of Tasso's *Gerusalemme Liberata* (1600). The verse texture moves away from Hunt's influence – 'Feminine endings, so abundant in the 1817 volume (about 25 per cent), have now been cut to about 3 per cent; Hunt's limp use of feminine caesuras late in the line ... has drastically waned. The soft polysyllabic diction of Hunt and the early Keats is beginning to give way to shorter words of stronger consonantal body; adjectives generally decrease, and the proportion of verbs rises' (*Bate*, 1963, p. 313).

Keats was uneasy about the poem. He wrote to Woodhouse on 22 September 1819, 'I shall persist in not publishing The Pot of Basil – It is too smokeable ... There is too much inexperience of life, and simplicity of knowledge in it – which might do very well after one's death – but not while one is alive. There are very few would look to the reality. I intend to use more finesse with the Public. It is possible to write fine things which cannot be laugh'd at in any way. Isabella is what I should call were I a reviewer "A weak-sided Poem" with an amusing sober-sadness about it ... If I may say so, in my dramatic capacity I enter fully into the feeling: but in Propria Persona I should be apt to quiz it myself – There is no objection of this kind to Lamia – a good deal to St Agnes' Eve – only not so glaring' (*L* II, p. 174). Keats's difficulties are apparent in the revealing alterations made in the drafts of the poem. Contemporary reaction was mixed: see *Critical Heritage*, pp. 149–50, 162, 170–72, 193–201, 213–14, 217–18. Lamb (*ibid.* 157–8) thought it the 'finest thing' in *1820*. For recent discussions, see *Ridley*, pp. 18–56, *Bate* (1945), pp. 32–42, H. Wright's *Boccaccio in England* (1957), pp. 397–407, and Miriam Allott in *John Keats: A Reassessment*, ed. K. Muir (1958), pp. 50–54, and *Jones*, pp. 13–31.

2 *palmer* pilgrim. The religious imagery is maintained throughout the poem.
4 *some malady* lovesickness.
21 *vespers* evening prayers.
26 *break* beginning.
28 *boon* gift.
34 *the rose's just domain* that part of the cheek which should be rosy.
46 *conceit* conception, idea, thought, though the meaning 'fancy, fanciful notion' may also be present.

NOTES FOR PP. 241-3

52 *every symbol on his forehead high* 'every mark of emotion on his forehead'.

55-6] *Fair copy* has two attempts at a longer version:
1. 'Lorenzo, I would clip my ringlet hair / To make thee laugh again and debonair // "Then should I be," said he, "full deified; / And yet I would not have it, clip it not; / For Lady I do love it where 'tis tied / About the Neck I dote on; and that spot / That anxious dimple it doth take a pride / To play about. – Aye Lady I have got / Its shadow in my heart and ev'ry sweet / Its Mistress owns there summed all complete"' 2. 'Lorenzo in the twilight Morn was wont / To rouse the clamorous Kennel to the hunt; // And then his cheek inherited the Ray / Of the outpouring Sun; and ere the Horn / Could call the Hunter to the Chase away / His Voice more softly woke the sun: Many a Morn / From sweetest Dreams it drew me to a Day / More sweet; but now Lorenzo holds in scorn / His Hunting [Health?] and all those by-gone Joys are Dreams / To me – to him, somehow – so chang'd he seems –' (the last eight lines of 2 were first printed by *Allott*). For the readings in *W*1-2, see *G*.

62 *fear* make afraid.

64 *shrive* confess. See *Endymion* IV, 26n (p. 581).

78 *dart* Cupid's arrow.

80 *joyed* rejoiced.

83 *all eves* every evening.

91 *in fee* because legally obliged to.

95 *Theseus' spouse* Ariadne.

99 *Though Dido silent is in under-grove* refers to Virgil's *Aeneid* VI, 442-51, *hic, quos durus amor crudeli tabe peredit, / secreti celant calles et myrtea circum / silva tegit; curae non ipsa in morte relinquunt. . . . / inter quas Phoenissa recens a volnere Dido / errabat silva in magna . . .* ('Here those whom stern Love has consumed with cruel wasting are hidden in walks withdrawn, embowered in a myrtle grove; even in death the pangs leave them not. . . . Among them, with wound still fresh, Phoenician Dido was wandering in the great forest' [Loeb edn]).

101 *warm Indian clove* the warmth refers to the taste of the cloves.

103 *almsmen* the buzzing of the bees sounds like the murmured prayers of almsmen.

105-44 Keats supplies Isabella with two brothers, not three, as in Boccaccio, and emphasizes their greedy capitalism, an element not present in Boccaccio's story.

107 *swelt* given by *OED* as the most recent example of the sense, 'to suffer oppressive heat, to swelter'. It is possible that 'hand' means workman, and that 'swelt' here bears the archaic sense of 'swoon, faint'.

116 *Allott* cites Buffon's *Natural History* (English translation 1792) IX, p. 68, 'The voice of the seal may be compared to the barking of an angry dog.'

123 *orange-mounts* probably, a hillside terraced with orange trees.

124 *lazar stairs* stairs in a lazar-house, which housed the poor, especially lepers.

NOTES FOR PP. 243–7

131 *that land inspired* Palestine.

132–6 the syntax is difficult, and not made easier by the punctuation. The idea is that the brothers live a retired life, and avoid the sight or knowledge of how their wealth is attained. *Allott* introduces a full stop after 'beggar-spies', which leaves ll. 133–6 without a verb.

135 *hirelings* ('cat's-paws'), who take advantage of free-spending young men ('generous stray-aways').

136] *Fair copy* and *W*3 give an extra stanza: 'Two young Orlandos far away they seem'd, / But on a near inspect their vapid Miens – / Very alike, – at once themselves redeem'd / From all suspicion of Romantic spleens – /No fault of theirs, for their good Mother dream'd / In the longing time of Units in their teens / Of proudly bas'd addition and of net – / And both their backs were mark'd with tare and tret.'

140 *Hot Egypt's pest* the plague of darkness visited upon the Egyptians (Exodus x 21–3).

150 *gittern's* a cithern is a form of guitar.

159 *stead* render service.

165–8 Boccaccio does not supply these motives for the brothers' violence. 'Olive-trees' here means estates.

188 *eglantine* sweet-briar. See *Endymion* IV, 697n (p. 586).

199–200 *bright ... delight* fair ... debonair *W*1 (*cancelled*). In *W*1 Keats wrote the following note on 'debonair', 'As I have used this word before in the poem you may use your judgement between your lines and mine. I think my last alteration [the *1820* reading] will do.' On the preceding leaf is the following couplet in Taylor's [?] hand, 'When Io an indoor lattice met his view, / And her fair features smiling playful through.'

200 *in-door lattice* the hyphen in *1820* suggests that Keats is describing a door with a lattice window set in it, rather than a lattice window within the house. *Allott* alters to 'indoor'.

209 *their murdered man* this prolepsis was first praised by Lamb: see *Critical Heritage*, p. 158.

213 *freshets* 'a stream or rush of fresh water flowing into the sea'.

221 *break-covert blood-hounds* the image is of blood-hounds breaking from cover in pursuit of their victim.

236 *luxury* meant to suggest the intensity of her sensitivity, rather than self-indulgence.

237] What might have been too plainly did she see *Draft*.

248] Exalting her to patient Fortitude *Draft* (*cancelled*).

251 *sick west* the West wind.

262 *Hinnom's vale* a valley into which the Jews cast refuse and the bodies of animals and criminals, keeping fires going to prevent infection.

269–72 Keats echoes William Robertson's account of American Indians' methods of torture and their tests of endurance. 'Some burn their limbs with red-hot irons, some mangle their bodies with knives ... they often prolong this ... anguish for several days ...' and (on the trial of a warrior), 'A fire of

NOTES FOR PP. 248-55

stinking herbs is kindled underneath so as he may feel its heat, and be involved in smoke. Though scorched and almost suffocated, he must continue to endure with ... patient insensibility' (*History of America* [1777], I, p. 364).

278] Upon his [soiled] lips and took the mellow lute *Draft* (*cancelled*).
286 *Druid* see *To George Felton Mathew* 39n (p. 539).
292 *woof* woven fabric.
303 *my heather-bloom* heather is growing on Lorenzo's grave.
315 *the taste of earthly bliss*] what Pleasure was a kiss *Draft*; the heaven of a kiss *Fair copy*.
316 *That paleness* i.e., Isabella's.
317 *bright abyss* heaven.
320 *essence* being. See *Endymion* I, 99, 'his essence fine', I, 777–81n (p. 567) and *Hyperion* I, 232.
347 *champaign* see *Endymion* I, 386n (p. 564).
356 *stole* a long robe (poeticism).
370 Isabella had embroidered the glove for Lorenzo.
373-4 *unto the bone ... cries*] Love's sighful throne *W*1 (*in Keats's hand*).
374 *Those dainties made to still an infant's cries* a periphrasis for 'breasts'.
385-92 Keats admits the distance between the laconic objectivity of ballads when dealing with gruesome events, and his own sensuous and romantic style.
393 *Persèan sword* the sword with which Perseus cut off the Gorgon's head.
393-4] With duller sliver than the persean sword/They cut away no foul Medusa's head *Fair copy*.
398] If ever any piece of love were dead *Fair copy*, *W*1-3. *W*1 has the additional attempts: 'With fond caress as if it were not dead' and 'The ghastly features of her lover dead'.
409 *dews* scents.
412 *cold serpent-pipe* the coiled pipes used in distilling the perfume.
416 *basil* an aromatic herb.
432 *leafits* small leaves, a variant of 'leaflet' in the late eighteenth and early nineteenth centuries.
436 *Lethean* from a forgotten past life.
450 *quick Winter chill*] th ['h]ot lightning sear *Draft*.
451 *Baälites of pelf* worshippers of the false god, money.
453 *elf* see *Endymion* II, 461n (p. 573).
477 *guerdon* reward (poeticism).
482 *breathe despondingly*] slumber silently *Draft*.
484 *Lethean*] hesperrian *Draft*.
491-2 *melodious chuckle in the strings / Of her lorn voice* now that Isabella is demented, her still beautiful, but uncontrolled, voice makes grotesque laughter.
492] Of her dissolving account would she cry *Draft*.
503 *burthen* refrain.

601 NOTES FOR PP. 255-7

TO HOMER

Probably written April 1818. Published *1848*. Text from Brown's transcript.

1 *giant ignorance* Keats knew no Greek, but knew Homer through Chapman. See *On First Looking into Chapman's Homer*.
5 *the veil was rent* quoted from Matthew xxvii 51.
5-8 Homer is seen as a poet of natural rather than bookish inspiration.
7 *spumy*] Brown's transcript, *G*, *Allott*; spermy *1848*.
12 *triple* looks back to the heaven, sea and earth of Jupiter, Neptune and Pan (ll. 6-8) and forward to Diana (l. 14), the tri-form goddess.

ODE TO MAY. FRAGMENT

Written 1 May 1818 and sent to Reynolds on 3 May (*L* I, p. 278). Published *1848*.

5 *earlier Sicilian* the manner of Theocritus.

ACROSTIC

Written 27 June 1818 at the 'Foot of Helvellyn', and included in Keats's journal-letter of 27-8 June; copied out with some revisions in his journal-letter of 17-27 September 1819 (*L* II, p. 195), which provides the basis for the text. Published *New York World*, 25 June 1877, *Forman* (1883). The acrostic spells out the name 'Georgiana Augusta Keats'. For Keats's affection for his sister-in-law see *To G[eorgiana] A[ugusta] W[ylie]*. This, like the fourteen poems which follow, was written during Keats's walking tour of the Lake District and Scotland with Charles Brown, 24 June-8 August 1818.

10 alludes to *Othello* I. 3. 142-3, '... the cannibals that each other eat, / The anthropophagi ...'.
11-12 sense is difficult to make out. Ulysses is threatened by storms, but is saved by a magic veil given him by Leucothea in *Odyssey* V, 346-7.
12 *Glow*] Glowed *G*.
15 *sisters of the Nine* the nine Muses.

'SWEET, SWEET IS THE GREETING OF EYES'

Written 28 June 1818 for George and Georgiana Keats (*L* I, p. 304). Published *Lowell*.

7 *When we meet* Keats at one point planned to spend a year with George in America, where the newly married couple had settled.

ON VISITING THE TOMB OF BURNS

Written at Dumfries on 1 July 1818. Published *1848*. Keats recorded his feelings, 'This Sonnet I have written in a strange mood, half asleep. I know not how it is, the Clouds, the sky, the Houses, all seem anti-Grecian and anti-Charlemagnish – I will endeavour to get rid of my prejudices, & tell you fairly about the Scotch ...' (*L* I, p. 309). The punctuation and meaning of the poem

602 NOTES FOR PP. 257-8

are uncertain: see *Murry* (1930), pp. 62-4, J. C. Maxwell, *KSJ*, IV (1955), pp. 77-80, G. Yost, *JECP*, LVII (1958), pp. 220-29 and *Allott*. The only MS is the imperfect transcript in the hand of John Jeffrey given in *L*. This is the basis of the text given here which differs from both *G* and *Allott*.

Lines 8-12 should probably be regarded as meaning, 'Pain is never done for him who has a mind to relish the full reality of beauty, and to discount (as can Minos, the judge of the dead in the underworld) the pallor which the deceiving imagination and human arrogance cast upon it!' Keats, as he says in his letter, was in a 'strange mood'. The landscape and cold weather of Scotland oppressed him, and seemed to deny the vitality of Grecian art or medieval romance. His consequent awareness of human suffering made him feel that humanity could not, in this unpropitious country, perceive beauty without distortion. The final couplet takes the form of an apology to Burns, who had after all written true poetry in Scotland. Keats asks Burns's shade to ignore his own temporary betrayal of the high idea of poetry.

4   *ago. Now new begun*] *Allott*; ago, now new begun *L*; ago now new begun. *1848*, *G*. The emendation made in *1848* is unnecessary. It is the Scottish summer which starts late, and is there 'new begun'.

7   *Through*] *L*, *Allott*; Though *1848*, *G*. Again, an unnecessary emendation. Compare *Ode to Psyche* 26 and *n* (p. 646), 'Phoebe's sapphire-regioned star'.

7   *beam—*] beam, *L*; beam: *1848*, *G*; beam; *Allott*. The real difficulty in this line is the plural 'their stars', which could refer either to the summer's stars, or to the features pictured by Keats in the opening lines. Garrod suggested (but did not adopt) the attractive emendation, 'those stars'.

8   *done*] *L* (Rollins incorrectly prints a full stop, *Texts*, p. 189), *Allott*; done: *1848*, *G*. *Allott* comments, 'The colon [or full-stop] converts the following clause ... into a question – Garrod substitutes "?" for the "!" of the transcript – and Keats from one who is trying to face reality into one who seeks illusion.'

9   *Minos-wise*   on Minos's wisdom, see *Dictionary of Classical Names* (p. 710).

11   *Fickly*] *L*; Sickly *1848*, *G*, *Allott*. The emendation seems obvious, but the *OED* gives 'Fickly, *adv.* (now rare), in a fickle manner ... deceitfully'. See J. C. Maxwell, *KSJ*, IV (1955), pp. 77-80.

12   *Cast*] conjectural reading in *1848*. *L* has a blank.

12   *it!*] *L*, *1848*, Garrod (*OSA*), *Allott*; it? *G* (*following Murry's emendation*).

13   *have oft*] *L*, *Allott*; oft have *1848*, *G*.

'OLD MEG SHE WAS A GIPSY'

Written on 3 July 1818. Published *Plymouth and Devonport Weekly Journal*, 22 November 1838, *1848*. As Brown and Keats walked to Kirkcudbright through Auchencairn, Brown told the story of Meg Merrilies in Scott's novel, *Guy Mannering* (1814), which Keats had not read. The result was this poem.

28   *chip-hat*   hat made from thin strips of wood or woody fibre.

NOTES FOR PP. 258-64

A SONG ABOUT MYSELF

Written 3 July 1818 for Fanny when Keats and Brown stopped for the night in Kirkcudbright. Published *Forman* (1883). Text based on *L* I, p. 312.

76 *Miller's thumb* small freshwater fish, otherwise called a bullhead.
77 *Tittlebat* variant of stickleback, usually used by children.

'AH! KEN YE WHAT I MET THE DAY'

Written 9 or 10 July at Ballantrae. Published *Forman* (1883). Sent to Tom in Keats's journal-letter of 10–14 July, which provides the basis of the text, and where Keats records, 'The reason for my writing these lines was that Brown wanted to impose a galloway song upon [Charles] Dilke – but it won't do – The subject I got from a wedding just as we came down into this place' (*L* I, p. 328).

2 *oure* o'er.
5 *yeve* give (an English archaism).
35 *daffèd* daunt (northern dialect).

TO AILSA ROCK

Written 10 July 1818 in an inn at Girvan. Published Leigh Hunt's *Literary Pocket Book* (1819). Text based on journal-letter to Tom Keats, 10–14 July, where Keats says, '... we had a gradual descent and got among the tops of the Mountains whence in a little time I descried in the Sea Ailsa Rock 940 feet high – it was 15 Miles distant and seemed close upon us – The effect of Ailsa with the peculiar perspective of the Sea ... and the misty rain then falling gave me a complete Idea of a deluge – Ailsa struck me very suddenly – really I was a little alarmed ...' (*L* I, pp. 329–30).

2 *by*] *L*; *from G, Allott*.

'THIS MORTAL BODY OF A THOUSAND DAYS'

Written 11 July 1818 in Robert Burns's Ayrshire cottage. Published *1848*. Keats told Reynolds, 'We went to the Cottage and took some Whiskey – I wrote a sonnet for the mere sake of writing some lines under the roof – they are so bad I cannot transcribe them – The Man at the Cottage was a great Bore with his Anecdotes ... O the flummery of a birth place! Cant! Cant! Cant!' (*L* I, p. 324).

3 *budded bays* the poet's laurel wreath.
5 *own*] *1876, Garrod (OSA), Allott*; *old 1848, G*.
5 *barley-bree* malt liquor, whiskey.
13 *bumper* a cup or glass filled to the brim, especially for a toast.

'ALL GENTLE FOLKS WHO OWE A GRUDGE'

Written 17 July 1818. Published *Forman* (1883). Text based on *L* I, pp. 334–6. Keats had been bathing in Lock Fyne which was 'quite pat and fresh but for the cursed Gad flies'.

21 *Lowther* William Lowther (1787–1872), later second Earl of Lonsdale, a Tory who had been supported by Wordsworth in 1818 against the Whig candidate, Henry Brougham (1778–1868), later Baron, to Keats's disgust (*L* I, p. 299).

29 *Southey* Southey had abandoned his early liberal ideals, and was regarded by Keats, and by Byron, as a turncoat.

30, 32 *Mr D— ... Mr V—* M. Buxton Forman suggests the references are to Robert Dundas, second Viscount Melville (1771–1851), referred to in Wordsworth's *Two Addresses to the Freeholders of Westmoreland* (1818), and Nicholas Vansittart, Baron Bexley (1766–1851), then Chancellor of the Exchequer. *Allott* suggests that 'Mr D' may be Burridge Davenport, the irritating neighbour of the Keats brothers (*L* II, pp. 76–7), and that 'Mr V' may be the 'Vincent' referred to casually by Keats in October 1818 (*L* I, p. 376n).

40 *Mister Lovels* the hero of Scott's *The Antiquary* (1816).

47 *chouse* dupe, trick, deceive (colloquial).

55 *withouten wordès mo* a Chaucerian tag.

'OF LATE TWO DAINTIES WERE BEFORE ME PLACED'

Written 17 or 18 July 1818. Published *Athenaeum*, 7 June 1873, *Forman* (1883). Text from *L* I, p. 337. Keats had gone, without Brown, to watch a performance of Kotzebue's *The Stranger* in Inverary. It was badly acted, and the bag-piper entertained the audience during the *entr'acte*.

14 *Mumchance* silent, tongue-tied (archaic).

LINES WRITTEN IN THE HIGHLANDS AFTER A VISIT TO BURNS'S COUNTRY

Written 18 July 1818, and copied out for Bailey in Keats's letter of 18–22 July (*L* I, pp. 344–5). Published *New Monthly Magazine* (1822) in part; *Examiner*, 14 July 1822, *1848* (in full). Text based on *L*. The poem is an attempt to make up for the 'wretched' sonnet, '*This mortal body of a thousand days*', which Keats felt had to do justice to Burns. It re-creates his excitement when approaching Burns's cottage on 11 July.

1 *joy*] charm *1848, G.*

2 *when*] where *Garrod (OSA), Allott.*

10 *scurf* 'any incrustation upon the surface of a body; rust, a scab; a saline or sulphurous deposit, mould, or the like' (*OED*).

29 *bourn* boundary, limit.

36 *fill*] *L, Allott;* pain *G.*

ON VISITING STAFFA

Written 26 July 1818 in Isle of Mull. Published *Plymouth and Devonport Weekly Journal*, 20 September 1838, *1848*. Keats's first version was sent to Tom in the journal-letter of 23–26 July (*L* I, pp. 349–51), and copied out again in September 1819 (*L* II, pp. 199–200), omitting ll. 7–8 and 45–57. Text from the earlier letter (*L*1) with some variants from the September letter (*L*2) noted. The poem was inspired by Keats's visit to Fingal's Cave on the Isle of Staffa (see *L* I, pp. 348–9).

Title] *G* (based on *W*1–2).

1 *magian* probably a noun, 'One of the Magi; a follower or believer in the Magi; a magician, wizard' (*OED*). Examples occur in the sixteenth century, but Byron, *Manfred* (1817) II, 4, has 'A Magian of great power, and fearful skill'. However, the adjective may be intended, as in *Endymion* III, 265, 'His magian fish', which the *OED* gives as the only example of this rare poetic usage.

3 *wizard of the Dee* Merlin.

5–8 St John is reputed to have written the Apocalypse on Patmos, Revelation i 9–12.

7–8] *not in L*2; the same reference occurs in *The Eve of St Mark* 33–4.

9 *at*] on *L*2.

19 *what art*] who art *L*2.

24 *trice*] *G*, Allott; thrice *L* 1–2.

25–6 alludes to Milton's *Lycidas*.

37 *touch*] see *L*2.

39 *pontiff-priest* high priest.

45–57] *not in L*2.

45 *dulled*] Brown's transcript, *1848*; stupid *L*1, *G*, Allott. The alteration avoids the repetition of 'stupid' in l. 50.

57 *breaking off* in *L*1, Keats comments, 'I am sorry I am so indolent as to write such stuff as this.'

'READ ME A LESSON, MUSE, AND SPEAK IT LOUD'

Written 2 August 1818 on the top of Ben Nevis. Published *Plymouth and Devonport Weekly Journal*, 6 September 1838. Brown recalled, '[Keats] sat on the stones a few feet from the edge of that fearful precipice, fifteen hundred perpendicular from the valley below, and wrote this sonnet' (*KC* II, p. 63). The sonnet's mood is related to that of *On Visiting the Tomb of Burns* (see headnote, p. 601).

3 *chasms* Keats told Tom, 'Talking of chasms they are the finest wonder of the whole – the[y] appear great rents in the very heart of the mountain . . .' (*L* I, p. 353).

11 *elf* a Spenserian word (see *Endymion* II, 461n, p. 573), here used to stress the smallness of man.

'UPON MY LIFE, SIR NEVIS, I AM PIQUED'

Written 3 August 1818 in a letter to Tom Keats. Published *Forman* (1883). Keats's letter records that a fifty-year-old woman, Mrs Cameron, had climbed Ben Nevis only a few years before. His poem invents 'a little conversation ... between the mountain and the Lady – After taking a glass of Wiskey as she was tolerably seated at her ease she thus begun —' (*L* I, p. 354). Text based on *L*.

2 Keats describes the difficulties of climbing the mountain in his letter (*L* I, p. 354).
4 *bate* variant spelling of 'bait', 'to make a brief stay or sojourn' (used of travellers' stops to feed the horses and refresh themselves) (*OED*).
9 *gentlemen*] *Allott*; gentleman *L, G*; Gentle man *Garrod* (*OSA*).
16 *caudle* a warm spiced drink, or thin gruel.
29 *Red Crag* Keats adds the note, 'A domestic of Ben's'.
52 *gust* means both 'blast' and 'taste' here.
53 *Blockhead* Keats adds a note, 'another domestic of Ben's'.
66 *snub* a colloquial word, not in *OED*. Probably means 'pet'.

STANZAS ON SOME SKULLS IN BEAULY ABBEY, NEAR INVERNESS

Written *c.* 6–8 August 1818, in collaboration with Brown. Published *New Monthly Magazine* 1822. Only the lines in roman type are Keats's. The poem is indebted to the grave-digging scene in *Hamlet* V.1. 77–210. Keats had caught a violent cold in Mull, and his illness put a stop to his tour shortly after this date. For the text, see *Texts*, pp. 201–2.
Mottoes The first is quoted from Wordsworth's '*Beloved vale!*' *I said* (1807), 7–9, later revised to '... from mine eyes escaped no tears; / Deep thought, or dread remembrance, had I none. / By doubts and thousand petty fancies crossed ...'. The second is from *Richard III* I. 4. 33.

6 *Their creed's undoing* the Reformation.
7 *Nice and Trent* the Councils of Nice (A.D. 325, 787) and of Trent (1545).
14 *Knox* John Knox (1505–72), Scottish religious reformer.
17 *craniologist* phrenologist.
43–6 the monks' illuminated missals.
48 *coil* fuss, bother.

TRANSLATED FROM RONSARD

Written *c.* mid-September 1818. Published *1848*. Text from *W*3. Woodhouse lent Keats a copy of Ronsard while he was nursing Tom through his last illness. Ronsard's '*Nature ornant Cassandre* ...' is the second sonnet in *Le Premier Livre des Amours* (*Amours de Cassandre*) (1552). Keats read the 1584 text, taken here from *Oeuvres de P. de Ronsard*, ed. C. Marty-Laveaux, vol. 1, 1887, p. 4:

Nature ornant Cassandre qui devoit
  De sa douceur forcer les plus rebelles,
  La composa de cent beautez nouvelles
  Que dés mille ans en espargne elle audit!
De tous les biens qu'Amour-oiseau couvoit
  Au plus beau Ciel cherement sous ses ailes,
  Elle enrichit les graces immortelles
  De son bel oeil, qui les Dieux esmouvoit.
Du Ciel à peine elle estoit descendue
  Quand ie la vey, quand mon ame esperdue
  En devint folle, et d'un si poignant trait
Amour coula ses beautez en mes veines,
  Qu'autres plaisirs ie ne sens que mes peines,
  Ny autre bien qu'adorer son pourtrait.

3 *Beauty*,] Beauty—*MSS* (see *Texts*, pp. 202–3); Beauty's *1848*, *G*, *Allott*.
9–10 Keats sent the poem to Reynolds *c.* 22 September. In the same letter he wrote, 'I never was in love – Yet the voice and the shape of a woman has haunted me these two days' (*L* I, pl 370). The woman should probably be identified with Jane Cox, Reynolds's cousin.
12] *1848* supplies a concluding couplet, 'So that her image in my soul upgrew, / The only thing adorable and true.' Keats probably did not finish the translation: 'I had not the original by me when I wrote it, and did not recollect the purport of the last lines' (*L* I, p. 371).

'"TIS "THE WITCHING TIME OF NIGHT"'

Written 14 October 1818. Published *1848*. Composed as a lullaby for George and Georgiana Keats's first child, born in February 1819. The poem is given in the journal-letter of 14–31 October 1818, where Keats comments, 'If I had a prayer to make for any great good, next to Tom's recovery, it should be that one of your Children should be the first American Poet. I have a great mind to make a prophecy and they say prophecies work out their own fulfilment' (*L* I, p. 398). Text follows that in *L*.

1 *time*] hour *1848*, *G*. The line quotes *Hamlet*, III. 2. 378.
20–21 in fact linen is made from flax, not cotton.
20 *then*] *not in 1848*, *G*.
24 *stars' light*] *Allott*; stars light *L*; starlight *1848*, *G*.
41 *Amaze* amazement (poeticism).
46 *Paddles* 'to paddle' means 'to finger idly, playfully, fondly' (*OED*). A seventeenth-century usage.

'WELCOME JOY, AND WELCOME SORROW'

Dated 1818 in transcripts: *Allott* argues convincingly for October 1818. Published *1848*. Keats's letter to Woodhouse of 27 October 1818 expresses, in more serious vein, the poem's theme: 'As to the poetical Character . . . it has no self – it is every thing and nothing – It has no character – it enjoys light and

shade; it lives in gusto, be it foul or fair, high or low, rich or poor, mean or elevated – It has as much delight in conceiving an Iago as an Imogen. What shocks the virtuous philosopher, delights the chameleon Poet. It does no harm from its relish of the dark side of things any more than from its taste for the bright one; because they both end in speculation' (*L* I, pp. 386–7).
Motto adapted from *Paradise Lost* II, 898–903.

1 the idea here, as well as the 'Muses bright and Muses pale' of ll. 20 and 24, was probably suggested by Milton's *L'Allegro* and *Il Penseroso*.

SONG ('Spirit here that reignest!')

Allott dates *c.* October 1818, pointing out its close connection with the preceding poem. Published *1848* (but not in *Plymouth and Devonport Weekly Journal*, 25 October 1838, as *G* reports).

17 *A-nudging*] *G*, *Allott*; While nudging *1848*.
19–20 compare Milton's *Comus* 102–4, '... welcome Joy and Feast,/Midnight shout and revelry, / Tipsie dance and Jollity ...'.

'WHERE'S THE POET? SHOW HIM, SHOW HIM'

Dated 1818 in transcripts: *Allott* links with '*Welcome joy, and welcome sorrow*', which is concerned with the same ideas. Published *1848*.
8–15 compare with Keats's remarks to Bailey on 22 November 1817, '... if a Sparrow come before my Window I take part in its existence and pick about the Gravel' (*L* I, p. 186).

FRAGMENT OF THE 'CASTLE BUILDER'

Dated 1818 by Woodhouse: *Allott* argues convincingly for late October 1818. Published *1848* (ll. 24–71) and *TLS*, 16 April 1914 (ll. 1–23). Text based on *W*2. Various earlier dates in 1818 are suggested by *Finney*, pp. 351–2, *Ward*, p. 151, and *Bate* (1963), p. 302n, but *Allott* show that ll. 61 ff., and other details, are linked with Keats's description of Mrs Isabella Jones's rooms, which he described on 24 October (*L* I, p. 403). *Allott* thinks the poem 'part of an unfinished satire on fashionable Romantic taste'.

4 *Convent Garden* i.e. Covent Garden.
6 *demesne* the territory of a sovereign or state.
14 *poaches* poached food (*OED* does not record the noun).
16–17 compare with the satire in *Stanzas on some Skulls in Beauly Abbey, near Inverness*.
22–3 survivors from Napoleon's disastrous retreat from Moscow (1812).
29 *golden fishes*] *W*2 (see *Texts*, p. 203); gold-fish vases *1848*, *Garrod* (*OSA*); golden vases *G*, *Allott*.
30 *glassy diamonding* the light thrown on the floor by the 'four windows' of l. 28. 'Turkish' means covered with Turkish carpets.
40 *A viol, bowstrings torn*] *W*2, *1848*, *G*; A viol-bow, strings torn *Forman* (1883), *Allott* (though her footnote gives the *W*2 reading).
41 *Anacreon* sixth-century Greek lyric poet.

54 *Mene, Mene, Tekel, Upharsin* Daniel v 25-8. The meaning is 'God hath numbered thy kingdom, and finished it ... Thou art weighed in the balances, and art found wanting ... Thy kingdom is divided, and given to the Medes and Persians'.

58 *Attic* Grecian.

60 *cinque-coloured* decorated with five colours.

63 *Numidian* African.

67 *Salvator* Salvator Rosa (1615-73), popular Italian landscape painter.

68 *Titian* see *To J. H. Reynolds, Esq.* 19 and *Sleep and Poetry* 334-6n (p. 553), 354-91.

68-9 *one ... Of Haydon's* Haydon's unfinished *Christ's Triumphal Entry into Jerusalem*, first exhibited March 1820.

'AND WHAT IS LOVE? IT IS A DOLL DRESSED UP'

Dated 1818 (*W*2). Published *1848*, with the unauthorized title *Modern Love*. Allott suggests that it belongs in October with the preceding poem. Text, *W*2.

8 *Wellingtons* 'a high boot covering the knee in front and cut away behind.' Named after the Duke of Wellington *c*. 1817 (*OED*).

12 *deep*] *1848, G*; high *W*2, Allott.

15-16 Cleopatra is reputed to have dissolved and drunk a pearl.

HYPERION. A FRAGMENT

Mainly written between late September 1818, and the death of Tom Keats on 1 December 1818. Finally abandoned April 1819. Placed here because the fragment was substantially finished (Books I-II) by December, and its genesis clearly precedes that of the following poem. Published *1820*. Some variants are given from Keats's autograph draft (British Museum, Add. MSS 37000).

Keats's interest in the subject of *Hyperion* was well-established (see *Endymion* III, 993-7). On 23 January 1818 he had written to Haydon, '... in Endymion I think you may have many bits of the deep and sentimental cast – the nature of *Hyperion* will lead me to treat it in a more naked and grecian Manner – and the march of passion and endeavour will be undeviating – and one great contrast between them will be – that the Hero of [*Endymion*], – being mortal, is led on, like Buonaparte, by circumstance; whereas the Apollo in Hyperion being a fore-seeing God will shape his actions like one' (*L* I, p. 207). Keats's narrative describes the displacement of the obscurely-known pre-Hellenic gods, the Titans, by their offspring, who, led by Jupiter, established the rule of the Olympian gods. The poem opens with Saturn and his fellow Titans already defeated. Hyperion, the sun-god, is the sole exception, and he succeeds in rousing their almost broken spirits (Books I-II). In Book III Apollo is introduced in the process of being transformed into the god of the sun, music, healing, and prophecy, by the Titan goddess, Mnemosyne (who has changed her allegiance). Woodhouse noted, 'The poem, if completed, would have treated of the dethronement of Hyperion, the former God of the Sun, by Apollo – and incidentally, of those of Oceanus by Neptune, of Saturn

610 NOTES FOR P. 283

by Jupiter, etc. – and of the war of the Giants [i.e. Titans] for Saturn's reestablishment, with other events, of which we have but very dark hints in the mythological poets of Greece and Rome. In fact, the incidents would have been pure creations of the poet's brain' (written in Woodhouse's copy of *Endymion*).

Keats's theme of the 'march of passion and endeavour' – that is, of human progress in which Apollo's disinterested suffering makes him into a symbolic representative of the dreamer-poet, a new and higher force born out of the pain of the 'vale of soul-making', in which Hyperion and the Titans suffer – is his own interpretation of the ancient myth. The mythological sources are much the same as those for *Endymion*, though to the Elizabethan poets, Lemprière and Tooke's *Pantheon* should be added Hesoid's *Theogony* and Hyginus's *Fabulae* (further see *Dictionary of Classical Names*, especially under 'Hyperion' and 'Titans', pp. 708, 717). The poem's style and imagery reflect his recent reading of Dante (see *Gittings* [1956], pp. 5–44), Shakespeare, and, most importantly, Milton's *Paradise Lost*. Keats's MSS show his struggle with his material: see further *G*, *Allott*, and E. De Selincourt, *Hyperion* (1905). For the publishers' Advertisement, which Keats disowned, see Appendix 3 (p. 514).

For the immediate reception of the poem by Hunt, Byron, Shelley and others, see *Critical Heritage*, pp. 131–2, 174–6, 124–7, etc. For recent discussions, see K. Muir, 'The Meaning of *Hyperion*' in *John Keats: A Reassessment*, ed. K. Muir (1958), J. Bayley, 'Keats and Reality', *Proceedings of the British Academy*, XLVIII (1962), pp. 91–125. *Bate* (1963), pp. 388–417, Douglas Bush, *John Keats* (1966), pp. 95–108, and *Jones*, pp. 74–91. The sources in the visual arts are discussed by *Jack*, pp. 161–75.

I, 1–14   Keats commented in a marginal note to *Paradise Lost* I, 318–21, 'There is a cool pleasure in the very sound of vale. The english word is of the happiest chance. Milton has put vales in heaven and hell with the very utter affection and yearning of a great Poet. It is a sort of delphic Abstraction – a beautiful thing made more beautiful by being reflected and put in a Mist' (see Appendix 4, p. 516). On Keats's 'stationing' of his God, see *Jack*, pp. 162–3. Bailey, Keats's Oxford friend, gives ll. 1–7 as an instance of Keats's 'theory' of melody in verse, 'particularly in the management of open & close vowels' which should 'not clash with one another so as to mar the melody, – & yet ... should be interchanged, like differing notes of music to prevent monotony' (*KC* II, p. 277). Further, see *Bate* (1945), pp. 51–6 and *Bate* (1963), pp. 413–17.

I, 6   *above*] *MS*, *G*; *about 1820*, *Allott*, *Garrod* (*OSA*).

I, 8–9   ] *MS at first had* Not so much Life as what an eagle's [a young vulture's *written above*] wing / Would spread upon a field of green ear'd corn; *this is cancelled and an alternative given marginally*: Not so much life as on a summer's day / Robs not at all the dandelion's fleece.

611 NOTES FOR PP. 283-6

I, 16   *strayed*] stayed *MS*, *W*1. 'Strayed' may be a misprint. *The Fall of Hyperion* I, 321 has 'rested', and compare the use of 'stayed' in *Endymion* III, 107-8. Cary's translation of Dante's *Inferno* XIV, 13 has 'Our steps we stay'd'.

I, 21   ] *followed in MS by* Thus the old Eagle drowsy with his great grief / Sat moulting his weak Plumage never more / To be restored or soar against the Sun, / While his three Sons upon Olympus stood –

I, 31-3   these lines reflect Keats's interest in Egyptian antiquities. Napoleon's Egyptian campaign of 1798 created considerable interest in the subject. Further, see *Jack*, pp. 166-70 and B. Garlitz, 'Egypt and *Hyperion*', *PQ*, XXXIV (1955), pp. 189-96.

I, 31   *Memphian*   Memphis was ancient Egypt's second city.

I, 34-6   compare *The Fall of Hyperion* I, 256-63.

I, 39-41   *vanward clouds ... storèd thunder*   clouds of skirmishers followed up by the slower-moving artillery.

I, 46   *ear*] hollow ear *MS* (and *The Fall of Hyperion* I, 348).

I, 60-62   *Thy thunder ... thy sharp lightning*   the weapons of Saturn have now passed into Jupiter's hands.

I, 61   *Rumbles reluctant*   a Miltonic inversion. See Keats's comment on Milton's use of 'reluctant' (Appendix 4, p. 525).

I, 62   *unpractised*] impetuous *MS* (*cancelled*).

I, 63   *once serene domain*   a reference to the idyllic order of the Saturnian Golden Age.

I, 81   *falling*] 1820, Allott, Garrod (*OSA*); fallen *MS*, G.

I, 85-8   another example of Miltonic 'stationing': see I, 1-14n.

I, 87   *couchant*   a heraldic word meaning 'lying down'. This seems to conflict with Saturn's posture at I, 17-19. See N. F. Ford, 'Keats's Saturn: Person or Statue?', *Modern Language Quarterly*, XIV (1953), pp. 253-7 and *Jack*, p. 164.

I, 94   *horrid ... aspen-malady*   'horrid' is used in its Latin sense, 'bristling', as in Milton. Aspen leaves shiver in the slightest breeze.

I, 98-103   the portrait of Saturn reflects Keats's reading of *King Lear*. See especially I. 4. 226-30.

I, 102   *front*   forehead.

I, 105   *nervous*   sinewy, muscular.

I, 107-8   Jupiter has taken over the control of the heavenly bodies.

I, 111   *acts*] 1820; Allott misreports as 'arts'.

I, 112   *Doth ease its heart of love in.*] Must do to ease itself, lest two [*sic*] hot grown *MS* (*cancelled*). *After* 'in.', *MS* had just as tears / Leave a calm pleasure in the human breast. – / O Thea I must burn – my Spirit gasps ... (*cancelled*).

I, 113-16   The Titans depend upon their power and personal identity. They are the antithesis of the qualities represented by Apollo, who embodies Keats's notions of the 'poetical character' which has 'no self', 'no identity' (*L* I, 386-7).

I, 129   *gold clouds metropolitan*   the clouds are the Gods' metropolis. 'Metropolis' here may have the meaning of parent-state of a colony (Saturn was born of Coelus [the heavens] as well as Tellus [the earth]).

I, 137 *Druid locks* the phrasing probably recalls Gray's *The Bard* 17-20. See also the 'cirque / Of Druid stone', II, 33-8n. Keats owned a copy of Edward Davies's *Celtic Researches* (1804) which tried to link the Titans and the Celts.

I, 145 *Chaos* Saturn is depicted as the creator of the ordered universe. 'Chaos' is spelt without a capital here and at II, 191 in *1820*. Both have been altered to conform with the usage elsewhere in the poem.

I, 147 *The rebel three* Saturn's sons, Jupiter, Neptune, and Pluto, who divided their father's kingdom among themselves.

I, 152 *covert* hiding-place.

I, 166 *orbèd fire* the sun (Hyperion is the sun god).

I, 167 *snuffed the incense* echoes *Paradise Lost* X, 272-3, '... with delight he snuffed the smell / Of mortal change on earth...'.

I, 171 *gloom-bird* the owl, whose hoot was an ill-omen.

I, 172 *familiar visiting* Allott suggests that Keats means the 'relatives and friends attending a death-bed', pointing out that 'familiar' could mean 'familial' in the eighteenth century. Douglas Bush thinks Keats may be recalling the custom of sending the bellman or town crier to a criminal before execution, or to the tolling of a church-bell for a dying man. See *Macbeth* II. 2. 3-4, 'the fatal bellman / Which gives the stern'st goodnight'. The reference is possibly to a 'familiar spirit' ('a demon supposed to attend at call', *OED*).

I, 174 occult prophecies obtained through witchcraft.

I, 175 *portioned* proportioned.

I, 176-82 Hyperion's palace is part Greek, part Byzantine, and part Egyptian (see *Jack*, pp. 170-71). Milton's description of the palace in Hell (*Paradise Lost* I, 710-30) may have served as a general inspiration, but Keats also had the example of the palaces which appear in Wordsworth, *The Excursion* (1814) II, 834-69, Southey's *Thalaba* (1801) I, xii-xiii, xxix-xxxiv, and Beckford's *Vathek*.

I, 182-3 the description is possibly indebted to John Martin's painting, *The Fall of Babylon*. See *Jack*, p. 172.

I, 196-200 echoes Milton's description of the fallen angels in Pandemonium, *Paradise Lost* I, 767-71.

I, 203] He of the Sun just Lighted from the Air *MS* (cancelled).

I, 204 *slope* sloping downward.

I, 205] *followed in MS by* Most like a Rosebud to a fairie's Lute (cancelled).

I, 206 *tubes* the pipes of a musical instrument, such as an organ.

I, 209 *vermeil* bright scarlet (poeticism).

I, 216 *Hours* the attendant nymphs of the sun (i.e. 'Horae').

I, 217 *flared*] went *MS* (cancelled).

I, 232 *essence* being. Used again at II, 331, III, 104. See *Endymion* I, 777-81n (p. 567).

I, 239 *lucent* shining (Milton).

I, 258-63 partly inspired in all probability by Milton's description of Satan entering Eden in *Paradise Lost* IX, 180-90, but also by the sculpture of Laocoon (see *Jack*, pp. 173-4).

613 NOTES FOR PP. 290-93

I, 271-83] Spun at his round in darkest curtaining of clouds / Not therefore hidden up and muffled quite / But ever and anon the glancing spheres / Glow'd through and still about the sable shroud / Made sweet-shap'd light: Wings this Orb *MS* (*cancelled*).

I, 274 *colure* an astronomical term meaning 'Each of two great circles which intersect each other at right angles at the poles, and divide the equinoctial and the ecliptic into four equal parts' (*OED*).

I, 277 *hieroglyphics old* the Signs of the Zodiac.

I, 282 *swart* black.

I, 299 *bright*] enraged *MS* (*cancelled*).

I, 302 *rack* 'clouds, or a mass of cloud, driven before the wind in the upper air' (*OED*). Compare *Endymion* II, 288.

I, 305-8 Keats plays down the traditionally hostile relationship between Coelus and his sons.

I, 311 *the powers* i.e. Coelus and Terra.

I, 316-18 *symbols divine ... eternal space* compare with Baldwin's account of the festival of Ceres: 'to this were appropriated the Mysteries ... it has been conjectured that the doctrine revealed by the high-priest was the fallacy of vulgar polytheism, and the unity of the great principle of the universe; thus the religion of the common people was left undisturbed; and the enlightened were satisfied ... secretly to worship one God under the emblems of the various manners and forms in which he operates' (pp. 19-20). See also Appendix 1.

I, 317 *beauteous life*].Life and Beauty *MS* (*cancelled*).

I, 322 *son against his sire* Jupiter's rebellion against Saturn.

I, 326 *wox* waxed (Spenser).

I, 331 *Unrufflèd*] Passionless *MS* (*cancelled*).

I, 334] In widest speculation I do see *MS* (*cancelled*).

I, 349 *region-whisper* Coelus (heaven) is a place and so cannot be made to speak like a person.

BOOK II

II, 1-2] Upon the very point of winged time / That saw Hyperion / Hyperion slid *cancelled start in MS*.

II, 4 *the bruised Titans*] her bruised Children *MS* (*cancelled*). The alteration corrects the confusion of Cybele with Tellus, her daughter, and mother of the Titans. However, the two figures are often run into one another in classical mythology.

II, 5-17 another passage echoing John Martin's painting, according to *Jack*, p. 173.

II, 7-12 recollects the waterfalls and mountains which had impressed Keats on his tour through the Lake District and Scotland in the summer of 1818. See '*Read me a lesson, Muse, and speak it loud*'.

II, 19-81 some of the Titans are called by traditional names, others are less usually thought of as Titans, while Dolor qualifies, if at all, with difficulty. Further see *Dictionary of Classical Names* (p. 704).

614 NOTES FOR PP. 293-7

II, 22-8 the eruption of Mount Etna was supposed to be caused by the struggles of Typhon, whom Jupiter had imprisoned under the island of Sicily.

II, 28 *boiling gurge of pulse* 'gurge' is a rare Miltonic word meaning 'whirlpool' (from the Latin '*gurges*'): see *Paradise Lost* XII, 41. 'Pulse' refers to the pulsing of blood in the heart (compare *Isabella* 45).

II, 33-8 Keats describes the prehistoric circle of stones at Castlerigg near Keswick as a 'Druid temple' when writing to Tom on 29 June 1818 (*L* I, p. 306). *De Selincourt* points out that the parallel between the Greek Titans and the Druids' heroes can be found in Davies' *Celtic Researches* (1804), a book owned by Keats.

II, 34 *cirque* circle.

II, 36 *at shut of eve* the phrase is used again in '*The day is gone, and all its sweets are gone*' 9.

II, 39 *shroud* shrouded.

II, 53 *most enormous Caf* an invented parent for Asia, drawn from Keats's reading of Oriental romances, in which Kaf or Caf appears as an enormous mountain. See Beckford's *Vathek* (1816), pp. 248-9.

II, 56-63 Asia appears as the goddess of a future oriental cult. 'This part of the globe [Asia] has given birth to many of the greatest monarchies of the universe, and to the ancient inhabitants of Asia we are indebted for most of the arts and sciences' (*Lemprière*).

II, 61 *Hope ... anchor* a traditional emblem of hope.

II, 69-72 it was probably Keats's intention to deal with this 'second war' between the Titans and the Olympians in a later book.

II, 83 *chant*] trill *M S (cancelled)*.

II, 98 *disanointing poison* the oil of mortality ('mortal oil') of the preceding line deprives Saturn of his godhead.

II, 120 *utterless* unutterable, but also thoughts which cannot be uttered because they are those of a god.

II, 128] Leaving and leave the air vibrations silver in the roof *M S (cancelled). This variant occurs in the Morgan Library M S according to G.*

II, 161 *engine our great wrath* 'transform our wrath into an instrument of war' (*Allott*).

II, 165 *astonied* (archaic variant, probably drawn from Spenser).

II, 168 *no Athenian grove* Oceanus has not gained his wisdom from a Greek academy. 'Sophist' is used here in a favourable sense.

II, 170 *not oozy* Oceanus's locks are dry because he is out of his watery element.

II, 181-243 Oceanus's speech reflects Keats's belief that both personal experience and the history of mankind obey a law of progress. See his views on the ordered extension of individual knowledge in *Sleep and Poetry* 101-21, 122-54, and his letter to Reynolds of May 1818 (quoted in headnote to *The Fall of Hyperion*, pp. 677-8). In September 1819 he wrote to George and Georgiana Keats, 'All civil[iz]ed countries become gradually more enlighten'd, and there should be a continual change for the better ...', going on to give a survey of English history and contemporary politics, in order to substantiate his belief (*L* II, pp. 193-4).

II, 190   compare *Genesis* 1–4.

II, 191   *Chaos and parental Darkness*] chaos and darkness *1820*. See I, 145*n*.

II, 195   *Light, and Light*] light, and light *1820*. See I, 145*n*.

II, 196   *its own producer*   the darkness of Chaos.

II, 208   *show beyond*   are manifestly superior to.

II, 232   *the young God of the Seas*   Neptune, who was (ll. 234–6) traditionally depicted as travelling over the sea in a chariot.

II, 244   *posed*   either 'nonplussed' or 'pretended', though it may be a verb invented from 'composed'.

II, 250   *hectic*   feverish.

II, 280   *golden melody*   Joseph Severn claimed that 'a beautiful air of Glucks ... furnishd the groundwork of the coming of Apollo in Hyperion' (*KC* II, p. 133).

II, 289   *joy and grief at once*   as *Allott* points out, joy at the music, and grief that her own has been surpassed.

II, 306   *half-glutted*   see *On the Sea* 3*n* (p. 558).

II, 310   *Giant-Gods*] *MS*, *G*, *Allott*; giant, gods *1820*.

II, 329   *crooked stings of fire*   flashes of lightning.

II, 330   *singe ... swollen clouds*] lick ... cloudy tent *MS* (*cancelled*).

II, 341–2   *the wingèd thing, | Victory*   'the goddess of Victory ... was represented with wings' (*Lemprière*).

II, 357–71   ] Till suddenly a full-blown Splendour fill'd / Those native spaces of oblivion / And every glulph [*sic*] *was seen* and every chasm old / And every height and *every* sullen depth / Voiceless or filled with hoarse tormented Streams; / And all the everlasting Cataracts / And all the *headlong* Torrents far and near, / And all the Caverns soft with moss and weed / Or blazon'd with bright *clear spar* and barren gems; / And all the Gods. It was Hyperion: / He stood upon a granite peak aloof / With golden hair of short numidian curl, / Rich as the colchian fleece, *MS* (*cancelled*). *The italicized words are given above the line.*

II, 371   *Numidian curl*   Keats is probably thinking of the tight curls of Hyperion's hair, which are like those of an African negro (so contrasting with Apollo's 'golden tresses' at III, 131). *Allott* suggests, 'Like the mane of an African lion'.

II, 372   *Regal his shape majestic*   an example of Miltonic inversion.

II, 373   *bulk*] shade *MS* (*cancelled*).

II, 374–6   *Memnon's image ... Memnon's harp*   Keats probably had the statue of Rameses II in the British Museum in mind. *Baldwin*, p. 269, records that 'an exquisite statue' was erected to Memnon, 'near the Egyptian Thebes; and, as he was the son of Aurora, this statue had the peculiar property of uttering a melodious sound every morning when touched by the first beams of the day as if to salute his mother; and every night at sunset, it gave another sound, low and mournful, as lamenting the departure of the day'. Hyperion, god of the sun, gives way to Apollo, god of sun and music. Further, see *Jack*, pp. 168–70.

II, 376   *mournful*] melodious *MS* (*cancelled*).

BOOK III

III, 2 *Amazèd* both 'overcome with a sense of wonder', and 'astounded' (Milton). Possibly the seventeenth-century sense of 'filled with panic' (*OED*) is present. Keats first wrote 'Perplexed'.

III, 8 *fallen*] *MS has two cancelled readings,* lonely *and* 'mateless'.

III, 12 *Dorian flute* the flute of classical Greece, which replaces the more primitive instruments heard earlier – strings in hollow shells (I, 131) and Clymene's shell (II, 270). The 'Dorian flute' and 'Delphic harp' (l. 10) usher in Apollo's new rule. See also Keats's note on *Paradise Lost* I, 527–67 (Appendix 4, p. 519).

III, 14] Let a warm rosy hue distain ... *MS (cancelled).*

III, 14 *vermeil* bright scarlet, vermilion.

III, 14–28 this gentle dawn scene contrasts with the angry sunrise at I, 176–82.

III, 16] And the corn haunting poppy *MS (cancelled).*

III, 29 *Giant of the Sun* Hyperion.

III, 31–2 *mother ... twin-sister* Latona and Diana (Artemis).

III, 39 *covert* hiding-place.

III, 46 *awful Goddess* Mnemosyne. Compare the later treatment of Mnemosyne as Moneta in *The Fall of Hyperion* I, 107–41, 141–81.

III, 76 *Show*] Develop *MS (cancelled).*

III, 77 Mnemosyne has abandoned her fellow Titans and gone over to Apollo's side.

III, 82–120 Keats told Woodhouse that Apollo's speech 'seemed to come by chance or magic – to be as it were something given to him' (*KC* I, p. 129).

III, 87 *oblivion* ignorance.

III, 88–end Leigh Hunt commented on the deification of Apollo, 'It strikes us that there is something too effeminate and human in the way which Apollo receives the exaltation which his wisdom is giving him. He weeps and wonders somewhat too fondly; but his powers gather nobly on him as he proceeds' (*Critical Heritage*, pp. 174–5).

III, 92 *liegeless* under no-one's rule.

III, 104 *essence* see I, 232n, and *Endymion* I, 777–81n (p. 567).

III, 113–20 Apollo attains godhead through knowledge of suffering, and the relationship between poetic power and this knowledge is central to the meaning of *Hyperion*. On 3 May 1818 Keats had written, 'Until we are sick, we understand not; – in fine, as Byron says, "Knowledge is Sorrow"; and I go on to say that "Sorrow is Wisdom"' (*L* I, p. 279).

III, 115 *sovran* a Miltonic spelling of 'sovereign'.

III, 125] *Keat's first attempt at this line was* And while through all his frame ... *MS (cancelled); his second attempt reads* and a wild commotion throughout ... *MS (cancelled).*

III, 125] *in MS followed by the cancelled line* Roseate and pained as a ravish'd nymph *which is then expanded to* Into a hue more roseate than sweet pain / Gives to a ravish'd Nymph when her warm tears / Gush luscious with no sob. Or more severe, –

III, 129 *convulse* convulsion.

III, 131–2 *golden tresses ... Kept undulation round his eager neck* contrasts with Hyperion's 'Numidian curl' (II, 371).

III, 135–6 *from ... Celestial*] he was the God! / And godlike *MS (cancelled)*.

FANCY

Probably written in December 1818. Published *1820*. Keats copied the poem out, with its companion-piece (next poem), on 2 January 1819, and commented, 'These are specimens of a sort of rondeau which I think I shall become partial to – because you have one idea amplified with greater ease and more delight and freedom than in the sonnet' (*L* II, p. 26). Keats had used four-stressed lines earlier in *Lines on the Mermaid Tavern* and *Robin Hood* (which are grouped with the present poems in *1820*). His search for a more discursive form was not resolved until he began the great *Odes* some four months later. *Fancy* is an uncertain move towards them, and argues that the Fancy can improve on reality because it brings together pleasures that cannot actually be enjoyed simultaneously. Possible echoes of Herrick are noted by J. H. Wagenblass, 'Keats's Roaming Fancy', *Harvard Studies and Notes in Philology and Literature*, XX (1938), and N. T. Ting, *KSJ*, V (1956).

21 *shoon* shoes (poeticism).

27 *high-commissioned* the mind has over-ruled itself, and commissioned Fancy to search for the pleasures of the seasons.

28 *vassals* as the Fancy is in control, other faculties (especially memory) are now its servants.

33 *buds and bells* the phrase is used again in *Ode to Psyche* 61.

37–8 Fancy mixes the pleasures of spring, summer and autumn, just as wine is blended.

52 *mid-May* compare *Ode to a Nightingale* 48–9, 'mid-May's eldest child, / The coming musk-rose'.

56 the field-mouse is 'meagre' because it has been hibernating all winter.

81 *Ceres' daughter* Proserpine.

82 *God of Torment* Pluto.

89–92 for the image of a bird held by a silken leash, see '*I had a dove ...*' 3–4, written at about the same time as this poem.

ODE ('Bards of Passion and of Mirth')

Probably written in December 1818 (see preceding poem). Published *1820*. The poem takes up the idea Keats had expressed to Bailey on 22 November 1817, '... O for a Life of Sensations rather than of Thoughts! It is "a Vision in the form of Youth" a Shadow of reality to come – and this consideration has further conv[i]nced me for it has come as auxiliary to another favourite Speculation of mine, that we shall enjoy ourselves here after by having what we call happiness on Earth repeated in a finer tone. ...' (*L* I, p. 185). Keats said the poem was 'on the double immortality of Poets' (*L* II, 25).

8 *parle* conversation, speech (a recently revived archaism).

17-20 in eternity, beauty and truth are undivided, so the nightingale's song is not 'tranced' or deceptive. Compare *Ode to a Nightingale*, where Keats cannot allow himself so easy an answer. Keats's union of 'philosophy' and music probably draws on *Comus* 475-7, 'How charming is divine Philosophy!/ Not harsh, and crabbed as dull fools suppose, / But musical as is *Apollo*'s lute ...'

24 the bards are immortalized by their poetry.

30 *little week* brief lives.

SONG ('I had a dove and the sweet dove died')

Probably written in December 1818. Published *1848*. When he copied it into his journal-letter of December 1818-January 1819, Keats called the poem 'a little thing I wrote off to some Music as it was playing' (*L* II, p. 27). Charlotte Reynolds is usually supposed to have provided the occasion (see headnote to following poem). *Allott* bases her text on *L*, but *1848* follows Woodhouse's later transcript. *G*'s text is eclectic. Text from *W2* (*Texts*, p. 210).

4 compare *Fancy* 90-93.

SONG ('Hush, hush! tread softly! hush, hush my dear!')

Probably written in December 1818. Published *Hood's Magazine*, April 1845, *1848*. Both *W2* and *1848* date the poem '1818'; Fanny Brawne's copy gives 21 January 1819, but the date probably refers to the date of transcription. The biographical background to this poem is in dispute. *Forman* (1883) reported, 'Miss Charlotte Reynolds tells me that ... [Keats] was passionately fond of music, and would sit for hours while she played the piano for him. It was to a Spanish air that the song ... was composed.' In the *Athenaeum*, 15 October 1859, the following note is given: 'Steibelt [1765-1823] ... was a melodist, besides a fancier of finger-wonders, as the tune to which Keats wrote the song "Hush! hush! tread softly ..." may remind those who care to seek no further.' Despite this strong connection with the Reynolds sisters (and Fanny Brawne) there is internal evidence to suggest that the poem might refer to Keats's relations with Mrs Isabella Jones. See *Gittings* (1954), pp. 57-60, 83-5, and (1956), pp. 45-53. The 'jealous old baldpate' (l. 3) could then refer to Donat O'Callaghan, a man of seventy who had formed an association with Mrs Jones. Keats had first met (and flirted with) Mrs Jones in 1817, and she is reputed to have suggested the idea of *The Eve of St Agnes*. The playfulness of the poem (and of Steibelt's music) support the suggestion, made by *Bate* (1963), p. 382n, that Keats wrote the poem in a puckish mood for the Reynolds sisters (who were, presumably, ignorant of the reference to Mrs Jones). Text from Fanny Brawne's transcript (*Texts*, pp. 210-12). *Allott*'s text is based on the earlier authorial MS; *G* follows *1848*.

23 *soft brace and shall coo*] Fanny Brawne's transcript, *G*, *Allott*; soft twin eggs and coo *W2-3*, *1848*. The autograph MS has only a cancelled (hypermetrical) reading, 'soft brace and above our heads coo'.

THE EVE OF ST AGNES

Written between 18 January and 2 February 1819; revised September 1819. Published *1820*. According to *W*2, Mrs Isabella Jones proposed the subject to Keats, but the poem's emotional atmosphere should be connected with his relationship with Fanny Brawne, whom Keats had met in autumn 1818, coming to some kind of 'understanding' with her on 25 December 1818.

Text based on *1820*. Keats's revisions in September, which added an extra stanza after l. 54, and altered ll. 314–22 and 375–7 in addition to other smaller changes, provoked violent reactions. Woodhouse reported to Keats's publisher, John Taylor, on 19 September: '[Keats] had the Eve of St A[gnes] copied fair: He has made trifling alterations, inserted an additional stanza early in the poem [see l. 54*n*] to make the *legend* more clearly intelligible, and correspondent with what afterwards takes place, particularly with respect to the supper & the playing on the Lute. – he retains the name of Porphyro – has altered the last 3 lines [see ll. 375–7*n*] to leave on the reader a sense of pettish disgust, by bringing Old Angela in (only) dead stiff & ugly. . . . There was another alteration, which I abused for "a full hour by the *Temple* clock." You know if a thing has a decent side, I generally look no further – As the poem was orig[inall]y written, *we* innocent ones (ladies & myself) might very well have supposed that Porphyro, when acquainted with Madeline's love for him, & when "he arose, Etherial flushd &c. &c." (turn to it [ll. 314–22]) set himself at once to persuade her to go off with him, & succeeded & went over the "Dartmoor black" (now changed for some other place [l. 351*n*]) to be married in right honest chaste & sober wise. But, as it is now altered, as soon as M[adeline] has confessed her love, P[orphyro] winds by degrees his arm round her, presses breast to breast, and acts all the acts of a bonâ fide husband, while she fancies she is only playing the part of a Wife in a dream [ll. 314–15]. This alteration is of about 3 stanzas [in fact, it affects only two stanzas]; and tho' there are not improper expressions but all is left to inference, and tho' profanely speaking, the Interest on the reader's imagination is greatly heightened, yet I do apprehend it will render the poem unfit for ladies, & indeed scarcely to be mentioned among the "things that are"' (*L* II, pp. 162–3). Taylor's response was unequivocal: if Keats 'will not so far concede to my Wishes as to leave the passage [ll. 314–22] as it originally stood, I must be content to admire his Poems with some other Imprint' (*L* II, p. 183). Keats's initial reaction to this threat of censorship was angry. Woodhouse reports, 'He says he does not want ladies to read his poetry: that he writes for men – & that if in the former poem [i.e., the original version of the consummation] there was an opening for doubt what took place, it was his fault for not writing clearly & comprehensibly – that he should despise a man who would be such an eunuch in sentiment as to leave a maid, with that Character about her, in such a situation: & sho[ul]d despise himself to write about it &c &c &c – and all this sort of Keats-like rhodomontade' (*L* II, p. 163). Keats finally gave way, and there is a cryptic note in *W*2, 'Keats left it to his publishers to adopt which [alterations] they pleased, and to revise the whole'. However, he went through the proofs of the poem in *1820*, and insisted that some of the revisions be included, so that the received text bears a somewhat ambiguous authorial approval.

Stillinger, pp. 158–66, gives an involved but persuasive case for adopting some of the revisions, arguing that the text should follow Keats's final intentions. He assumes that the *1820* text received Keats's approval, except in those places where the sexual or religious sensibilities of his publishers censored his wishes. Thus, the readings of the revised draft at ll. 98, 143, and 145–7, might be regarded as blasphemous, and ll. 314–22 and the stanza added after l. 54 make the poem's handling of sexuality more explicit, and would have been cut by Woodhouse and Taylor. These alterations, he argues, should be incorporated into the text of the poem.

While Stillinger's hypothesis is a convincing account of what Keats's wishes may have been in September 1819, there are other factors to be considered. Keats's alteration of ll. 375–7, so as 'to leave on the reader a sense of pettish disgust, by bringing Old Angela in (only) dead stiff & ugly' is as important a part of Keats's September 1819 revision as making the consummation of Madeline and Porphyro more explicit – all these changes being aimed at making the poem less 'smokeable', that is, less self-indulgent or sentimental. Keats wanted to make sure the poem could not be mocked for any suspicion of naivety. Stillinger's account assumes that Keats's publisher was right to persuade him out of this alteration, but wrong to make him change ll. 314–22, or that Keats himself changed his mind (on which there is no evidence). In this situation, it may be more reasonable to regard the revisions as alterations made by a writer who no longer trusted his original inspiration – the text of *La Belle Dame sans Merci* exhibits the same difficulty, and editors have agreed in following the original version of the poem, rather than the more conventional later text (see p. 637). In that case, the decision finally rests on the reader's critical judgement – which makes the better poem? The crux is ll. 314–22. Woodhouse's objection is not, it should be noted, to the sexuality in itself (indeed, he admits that 'profanely speaking, the Interest on the reader's imagination is greatly heightened'), but to the fact that Keats's alteration makes the fact of consummation *overt*. In fact, the earlier version, though not explicit, can certainly be read as implying consummation, while leaving the ladies and the 'innocents' free to accept a more sublimated interpretation. There is also the problem of diction. Is the phrase, 'Solution sweet', which describes the mingling of the scents of the rose and violet, an appallingly coy periphrasis for the sexual act, or is it a characteristically Keatsian triumph of sensual suggestivity, whose success depends upon the narrowness with which the diction skirts tastelessness? In all, it seems to me that the revised version coarsens this stanza and the balance of the poem, and that Stillinger's reconstructed text depends too heavily upon hypothesis.

The original draft of the poem is now in Harvard Library (referred to as *H* below). *W*1 contains stanzas 1–7, which are missing from the autograph, and *W*2 is a transcript of Keats's original draft. In the margin of *W*2 Woodhouse transcribed the revisions which Keats made to the poem in September 1819 (referred to as *Revised Draft* below). The notes record some of the more interesting early readings from *H* and *W*1–2, and some of the readings in the *Revised Draft*, which were finally rejected in *1820*. For a full record of the draft readings, see *G*; for details of George Keats's transcript, which differs from *W*2, see *Ridley*, pp. 180–90.

Keats's source for the poem is to be found in Burton and in John Brand's *Popular Antiquities* (1813 edn), I, pp. 32–4: 'On the eve of [St Agnes] ... many kinds of divination are practised by virgins to discover their future husbands. ... This is called fasting St Agnes's Fast. The following lines of Ben Jonson allude to this: "And on sweet St Agnes's night / Please you with the promis'd sight, / Some of husbands, some of lovers, / Which an empty dream discovers". ...' In the *Anatomy of Melancholy* (1813 edn, III 2 iv i) Robert Burton says: ''Tis their only desire, if it may be done by art, to see their husband's picture in a glass: they'll give any thing to know when they shall be married; how many husbands they shall have, by Cromnyomantia, a kind of divination, with onions laid on the altar on Christmas / eve; or by fasting on St Agne's [*sic*] eve or night, to know who shall be their first husband. ...' Keats's handling of the story is deeply influenced by *Romeo and Juliet* – the lovers are opposed by their families and helped by an old servant (Angela or the Nurse). The medieval atmosphere of the poem was affected by Keats's impressions of gothic architecture (see *Jack*, pp. 191–5, and *Gittings* [1954], pp. 64–82), and by Mrs Radcliffe's novels, Scott's *Lay of the Last Minstrel* (1805), and Coleridge's *Christabel* (1816). The influence of Boccaccio has also been seen in the poem – see *Finney*, pp. 541–3, and *Ridley*, pp. 139–42. *Gittings* (1968), pp. 279–81, suggests that Lasinio's engraving of Orcagna's *The Triumph of Death* may have affected the poem.

Keats was somewhat dismissive about his 'little poem', and thought it too 'smokeable', that is, like *Isabella*, open to mockery because too luxurious and sentimental (*L* II, pp. 58, 174). When he came to write *King Stephen*, Keats remarked that he wished 'to diffuse the colouring of St Agnes's eve throughout a Poem in which Character and Sentiment would be the figures to such drapery' (*L* II, p. 234). Hunt thought the poem 'the most delightful and complete specimen' of Keats's genius, and analysed the poem at length in his *Imagination and Fancy* (1844), which is reprinted in *Critical Heritage*, pp. 275–84. *Ridley*, pp. 96–180, gives a close study of the texture of the poem, based on Keats's drafts, and *Bate* (1945), pp. 91–117, analyses its technique. The main critical issue is the exact relationship between the high romance of the main action and the realistic elements in the framework. For Douglas Bush the poem is 'no more than a romantic tapestry of unique richness of colour', *Selected Poems and Letters* (1959), p. xvi. Other readers have seen the poem as an attempt to dramatize Keats's ideas about the nature of the imagination, and give the poem a metaphysical reading – see E. Wasserman, *The Finer Tone* (1953), pp. 97–137, and R. A. Foakes, *The Romantic Assertion* (1958), pp. 85–94. *Stillinger*, pp. 67–93, takes a more down-to-earth approach, seeing Madeline as a dreamer turning away from reality. See also Miriam Allott's essay in *John Keats: A Reassessment*, ed. K. Muir (1958), pp. 39–62, Harold Bloom's *The Visionary Company* (1961), pp. 369–75, John Bayley, 'Keats and Reality',

Proceedings of the British Academy, XLVIII (1962), pp. 91–125, *Bate* (1963), pp. 438–51, and *Jones*, pp. 232–48.

Title] Keats always referred to the poem as 'St Agnes' Eve' as do the *MSS*. The title in *1820* may have been suggested by Woodhouse or Taylor.

5 *Beadsman* 'one paid or endowed to pray for others; a pensioner or almsman charged with the duty of praying for the souls of his benefactors' (*OED*).

8 *without a death* at death the soul goes up to heaven as the breath of the Beadsman, condensing in the cold air, appears to do. The Beadsman's breath also resembles clouds of incense.

12 *meagre* emaciated, thin.

14–15 Keats visited Chichester Cathedral in January 1819, and he may be remembering the effigies there. The rails of the tombs confine the dead as the souls of the dead are confined in purgatory.

21 *Flattered to tears* 'in this word "flattered" is the whole theory of the secret of tears; which are the tributes ... of self-pity to self-love.... Yes, the poor old man was moved, by the sweet music, to think that so sweet a thing was intended for his comfort as well as others.' He felt that the mysterious kindness of heaven did not omit even his poor, old, sorry case ... and as he wished to live longer, he began to think that his wish was to be attended to' (Leigh Hunt in *Imagination and Fancy*, reprinted in *Critical Heritage*, pp. 276–7).

26 *reprieve* here, redemption.

27 *sake*] *1820, Revised Draft*; souls *W1–2. Between Stanzas 3 and 4 W1–2 give an additional stanza*: But there are ears may hear sweet melodies, / And there are eyes to brighten festivals, / And there are feet for nimble minstrelsies, / And many a lip that for the red wine calls. – / Follow, then, follow to the illumined halls, / Follow me youth – and leave the eremite – / Give him a tear – then trophied banneral / And many a brilliant tasseling of light / Shall droop from arched ways this high baronial night.

28 *prelude* introductory piece of music.

31 *snarling* descriptive both of the noise of the trumpets and of the rough temper of the host and his company.

32 *pride* splendour.

37 *argent* silver (heraldic).

39 *faerily*] *Garrod* (*OSA*); fairily *1820, G, Allott*. Keats uses the spelling 'Faery' at ll. 70 and 343 in *1820*, and it appears to be his preferred spelling. 'Faerily' means 'enchantedly'.

52–4 compare with the undated chap-book, *Mother Bunches Closet newly broke open*, cited by *Ridley*, p. 110: 'When thou liest down lie *as straight as thou canst*, lay thy hands under thy head and say "Now St Agnes play thy part, / And send to me my own sweetheart; / And show me such a *happy bliss*, / This night of him to have a kiss."'

54] *Revised Draft adds a stanza*: '"Twas said her future lord would there appear / Offering as sacrifice – all in the dream – / Delicious food even to her lips brought near: / Viands and wine and fruit and sugar'd cream, / To touch her palate with the fine extreme / Of relish: then soft music heard; and then / More pleasures / followed in a dizzy stream / Palpable almost; then to wake

623   NOTES FOR PP. 313-15

again / Warm in the virgin morn, no weeping Magdalen.' On the reasons for Keats's addition of this stanza, which seeks to make the story clearer, particularly 'with respect to the supper and the playing on the lute', see headnote. On the additional stanza, J. Stillinger remarks: 'Once the possibility of sexual references had been opened, the lines describing "More pleasures ... in a dizzy stream", "virgin morn", and "weeping Magdalen" (very likely an allusion to the deserted unwed mother of Book VI of *The Excursion*, who is called a "weeping Magdalene" and a "rueful Magdalene" in ll. 814, 987) would similarly have rendered the poem, by the publishers' standard, "unfit for ladies"' (*Stillinger*, p. 163). On the heroine's name, see the following note.

55   *Madeline*   see Keats's letter to Reynolds of 14 March 1818, '... by the holy Beaucoeur, – which I suppose is the virgin Mary, or the repented Magdalen, (beautiful name that, Magdalen) ...' (*L* I, p. 246). Compare with the 'weeping Magdalen' of *Revised Draft* (l. 54*n*).

58   *sweeping train*   'I do not use *train* for *concourse of passers by* but for *Skirts sweeping along the floor*' (*L* II, p. 295).

62   *But she saw not*   but because she saw not.

67   *timbrels*   tambourines.

70   *amort*   'in the state or act of death; inanimate; *fig.* spiritless' (*OED*).

71   *lambs unshorn*   after St Agnes's death, her parents saw her in a vision, with a white lamb standing by her side. See further, ll. 115–17*n*.

75   *Porphyro*   Keats called his hero 'Lionel' in earlier drafts. The connotations of the name finally chosen are various:

 1. *porphyro* is from the Greek for purple
 2. 'porphyry' is a beautiful and hard rock, often used by poets to mean a beautiful red stone taking a high polish
 3. 'Porphyrius' or 'Porphyry' was a neo-Platonic philosopher and enemy of Christianity (A.D. 233–*c*. 306).

A 'metaphysical' reading of the poem would emphasize 3, but the context of 'Porphyro, with heart on fire' suggests rather 1 and 2, and connects with the 'purple riot' (l. 138) of the young man's beating heart.

77   *Buttressed from moonlight*   Porphyro stands in the shadow cast by a buttress.

85   *barbarian hordes*   the hordes that attacked Rome (see the 'citadel' of the preceding line).

88   *Against his lineage*   Porphyro's family is involved in a feud with Madeline's (compare with the feud between the Capulets and the Montagus in *Romeo and Juliet*).

90   *beldame*   an aged woman, used in the sixteenth century as a form of address for nurses.

91 ff.   the portrait of Angela is inspired by the nurse in *Romeo and Juliet*, but also owes something to the ageing female attendants who appear in Gothic romances of the period.

98   *Porphyro*] Jesu *all MSS*. Probably changed for *1820* at the insistence of Keats's publishers.

105 *gossip* Elizabethan word for a talkative woman or female friend (derived from 'god-sip', god-relation).

112–13 Gittings (1954), p. 71, suggests the 'moonlight room' was based on Keats's memory of the Pulpitum in the Vicar's Hall, Chichester.

115–17 the feast of St Agnes is celebrated on 21 January in the basilica of St Agnes fuori le mura at Rome. Two unshorn lambs are presented and blessed at the altar, and their wool woven into the pallium by the nuns.

124 *conjuror plays* Madeline plans to play the part of a wizard, conjuring up spirits or visions.

126 *mickle* much (Spenser).

133 *brook* restrain.

134 *enchantments cold* whatever Madeline manages to conjure up will not be warm or living.

138 *purple riot* see l. 75*n*.

143 *Go, go*] O Christ *all MSS*.

145 *by all saints I swear*] by the great St Paul *all MSS*. The introduction of St Paul in *all MSS* gives an ironic note, in view of his emphasis upon chastity and purity.

146 *Quoth*] Sweareth *all MSS*.

147 *whisper its last prayer*] unto heaven call *all MSS*.

153 *beard* affront, defy.

162 *betide her weal or woe* whether good or ill befalls her.

163–252 the secret admission of the hero into the heroine's room is, of course, a stock device, which Keats could have taken from the Gothic novel. He was also perhaps influenced by *Cymbeline* II. 2., where the voyeur is the villain.

168 *faeries*] Garrod (*OSA*); fairies *1820, G, Allott*. See l. 39*n*.

169 *pale enchantment* Madeline's dream is pale and faint when compared to Porphyro's physical presence.

171 *Since Merlin paid his Demon all the monstrous debt* the reference has puzzled commentators. Merlin, whose demon-father gave him his magical powers, was infatuated with Nimue, and disclosed his secrets to her, which she then used to destroy him. The night of Merlin's death was one dominated by magic spells and supernatural presences, which provides an ominous parallel with the magic and fairies surrounding Keats's two lovers.

173 *cates* delicacies.

174 *tambour frame* embroidery frame.

182 *slowly*] quickly *H, Revised Draft, W1–2*.

188–9] There he in panting covert will remain / From Purgatory sweet to view what he may attain *W1 (pencilled in)*.

188 *covert* hiding-place.

198 *frayed* frightened (Spenser). Compare *Endymion* II, 245 and *n*.

204–5 Madeline's heart is beating with expectant excitement.

206 *tongueless nightingale* Stillinger suggests that this 'image embraces the entire story of the rape of Philomel, and with it [Keats] introduces a further note of evil that prevents us from losing ourselves in the special morality of fairy romance', *Stillinger*, pp. 76–7.

208–16 Keats may have taken details for this description from the neo-Gothic chapel at Stansted; see *Gittings* (1954), pp. 79–80. But contemporary literary sources, such as Scott's *Lay of the Last Minstrel* (1805) II. xi played their part.

209 *imag'ries* patterns, designs.

210 *knot-grass* 'a common weed in waste ground, with numerous intricately-branched creeping stems, and small pale pink flowers' (*OED*).

211 *diamonded with panes* compare with the same image in *Fragment of 'The Castle Builder'* 28–30.

213 *damasked* damask is a rich fabric (originally from Damascus), woven with elaborate designs.

215 *emblazonings* heraldic devices.

216 *shielded scutcheon* coat-of-arms with royal quarterings on a field gules (i.e., 'blushed with blood').

222 *glory* halo, nimbus.

226–43 see *Ridley*, pp. 153–6, for a discussion, based on the earlier drafts, of Keats's difficulties with this passage. For Keats's previous handling of a similar scene, see *Fancy* 84–7.

229 *Loosens her fragrant bodice*] *1820*; Keats had several attempts at this phrase in his autograph MS (*H*) – 'Loosens her bursting bodice from her', 'Loosens her bodice lace', 'Loosens her bodice string', 'Loosens her bodice and her bosom bare', 'Loosens her fragrant bodice and doth bare'.

241 *Clasped like a missal where swart Paynims pray* either, shut up with clasps because Mohammedans and pagans do not use Christian prayer-books, or, a missal clasped in the hand of a believer surrounded by unbelievers.

244 *paradise* often used to describe the transports of passionate love. *Ridley* 143 cites Mrs Radcliffe's *The Italian* (1797) I, chapter i: 'From this moment Vivaldi seemed to have arisen into a new existence; the whole world to him was Paradise'.

247 *slumbrous tenderness* a periphrasis for audible breathing in sleep, rather than snoring. In Porphyro's imagination, Madeline's gentle breathing is hopefully metamorphosed into the excited breathing of a passionate (waking) lover.

257 *drowsy Morphean amulet* 'amulet' means both a charm against evil, disease, or witchcraft, and 'all medicines . . . whose virtue or mode of operation is occult' (*OED*). Morpheus is the god of sleep, hence Porphyro wants a sleeping charm or potion. *Stillinger*, pp. 78–9, gives a reminder that Lovelace used drugs in order to rape Clarissa in Richardson's novel.

258 *clarion* either, a shrill-sounding trumpet with a narrow tube, or, the sound of a trumpet or any similar rousing sound.

259 *clarinet*] *all M S S, Garrod* (*O S A*); clarionet *1820, G, Allott*. 'Clarionet', though a variant spelling of clarinet, is probably a misprint in *1820*. Not only does it repeat 'clarion' in the preceding line, but it makes the line hypermetrical.

260 According to *Cowden Clarke*, p. 143, when 'repeating the passage when Porphyro is listening to the midnight music in the hall below' Keats said, 'that line . . . came into my head when I remembered how I used to listen in bed to your music at school.'

262–75 compare with *Endymion* II, 440–53.

265 *gourd* melon.

266 *soother* more soothing. For Keats the word also suggests 'smoother'. See *Sleep and Poetry* 180n (p. 552).

267 *tinct* coloured, tinged (Elizabethan). In his *Imagination and Fancy* (1844), Hunt commented on the line, 'Here is delicate modulation, and super-refined epicurean nicety . . . [which makes] us read the line delicately, and at the tip-end, as it were, of one's tongue' (*Critical Heritage*, p. 280).

268 *Manna* apparently used to mean a fruit; see *Endymion* I, 766n (p. 567).

268 *argosy* 'a merchant-vessel of the largest size and burden' (*OED*).

269 *Fez* Moroccan town.

270 *Samarkand* an ancient Persian city and market, legendary for its wealth. Silk was one of its staples.

277 *eremite* a recluse or anchorite, a hermit (poeticism). Used again in *The Eve of St Mark* 95 and '*Bright star! . . .*' 4.

280 *unnervèd* weakened, unsinewed.

285 *Broad golden fringe* the fringe of Porphyro's table-cloth.

288 *woofèd* woven.

290 *Tumultuous* presumably refers to the tumult of notes caused by Porphyro playing.

292 '*La belle dame sans mercy*' title of a poem by Alain Chartier written in 1424. See *La Belle Dame sans Merci* headnote (p. 638).

294–7 follows the pattern for such scenes in the Gothic romances. *Ridley* (p. 143) cites Mrs Radcliffe's *The Mysteries of Udolpho* (1794), 'She gazed at him for a moment in speechless affright, while he, throwing himself on his knee at the bedside, besought her to fear nothing.'

296 *affrayèd* startled, frightened (archaic).

297 *pale as smooth-sculptured stone* possibly recalling Mrs Radcliffe's *The Mysteries of Udolpho* (1794), 'his countenance became fixed, and touched as it now was by the silver whiteness of the moonlight, he resembled one of those marble statues of a monument which seem to bend, in hopeless sorrow, over the ashes of the dead. . .' (cited by *Ridley*, p. 166).

310 *spiritual and clear* Porphyro's eyes were 'spiritual' in her dream because lacking bodily substance, and they were 'clear' because not 'piteous' (l. 305).

313 *complainings* the song he sang.

314–22] *Revised Draft has:* 'See while she speaks his arms encroaching slow / Have zon'd her, heart to heart – loud, loud the dark winds blow. / For on the midnight came a tempest fell. / More sooth for that his close rejoinder flows / Into her burning ear; – and still the spell / Unbroken guards her in serene repose. / With her wild dream he mingled as a rose / Marryeth its odour to a violet. / Still, still she dreams – louder the frost wind blows'. On the reactions of Woodhouse and Taylor to this passage, see headnote.

323 *alarum* call to arms, a warning of danger, especially a sudden peal rung out on a tocsin (*OED*).

NOTES FOR PP. 322-3

325 *flaw-blown sleet* as a noun 'flaw' meant 'a sudden burst or squall of wind ... usually of short duration' (*OED*). In Elizabethan usage the noun could mean a flake of snow or a spark of fire, as well as a fragment. Harold Bloom in *The Visionary Company* (1961), p. 373, comments, 'the flaw is in nature and in the spirituality that merely repudiates that law'. Compare with *A Dream* ('As Hermes once ...') 10-11, 'the flaw / Of rain and hail-stones'.

333 *A dove forlorn and lost with sick unprunèd wing* compare with 'like ring-dove frayed' (l. 198). 'Unprunèd' is an archaic variant of 'unpreenèd'.

336 *vermeil* bright scarlet, vermilion (Spenser).

340-42] I have found, but cannot rob thy downy nest; / Soft Nightingale, I'll keep thee in a cage / To sing to me. But hark! the blended tempest's rage *W1-2 and H (with minor differences)*.

342 *rude infidel* compare with the 'swart Paynims' of l. 241.

343 *elfin-storm from faery land* 'elfin' here suggests the magical and mysterious origin of the storm. Although the storm and 'faery land' are regarded as beneficent by Porphyro, compare with the dangerous attractions of the 'elfin grot' in *La Belle Dame sans Merci* 29 and the 'deceiving elf' of fancy in *Ode to a Nightingale* 74 and *n* (p. 657). So too, 'faery land' is echoed in the 'faery lands forlorn' of *Ode to a Nightingale* 70.

344 *haggard seeming* as a noun 'haggard' means 'a wild (female) hawk caught when in her adult plumage' or, until *c*. 1680, 'a wild and intractable person (at first, a female); one not to be captured' (*OED*). More probably, the adjective is intended, with 'seeming' (appearance) as the noun. From 1807 'haggard' could mean 'Gaunt or scraggy-looking, from the loss of flesh with age' (*OED*), but other senses are relevant. It was originally used to describe a wild or forward falcon 'that preyed for her selfe long before she was taken' (Cotgrave), and hence meant 'wild, untamed' (sixteenth and seventeenth centuries).

344 *boon* favour, gift (poeticism).

349 *Rhenish* wine from the Rhine valley; the usage is Elizabethan.

350-51] Put on warm clothing sweet, and fearless be / Over the Dartmoor black I have a home for thee *H, W1-2*.

353 *dragons* 'dragon' was a variant spelling of 'dragoon' until 1849 (*OED*). The details in the following line describing the 'dragons' at 'glaring watch ... with ready spears' certainly suggest that they are soldiers on guard (though dragoons were actually cavalrymen armed with carbines). The choice of spelling suggests that 'dragon' (a mythical monster) was also present in Keats's mind.

355 *darkling* darksome, obscure. For Keats's later adverbial usage, compare with 'Darkling I listen', *Ode to a Nightingale* 51.

357-60 As *Allott* notes, perhaps suggested by Byron's *Siege of Corinth* (1816) 620-7, 'Like figures on arras, that gloomily glare, / Stirred by the breath of the wintry air / So seen by the dying lamp's fitful light, / Lifeless, but life-like, and awful to sight.... Fearfully flitting to and fro, / As the gusts on the tapestry come and go ...'.

357 Keats had difficulties with this line. *H* includes the following attempts –
'The Lamps were flickering death shad[e]s on the wall', 'Without, the Tempest kept a hollow roar', 'The Lamps were dying in ...', 'But here and there a Lamp was flickering out'.

361–2] *H has the following attempt* – Like spirits into the wide-paven hall / They glide, – and to the iron porch in haste they glide....

366] But with his calmed eye his Mistress owns. *H (cancelled)*.

371 *fled away into the storm*] fled into a night of storms *H (cancelled)*.

375–8] *Angela ... cold*] Angela went off / Twitch'd with the Palsy; and with face deform / The beadsman stiffen'd, 'twixt a sigh and laugh / Ta'en sudden from his beads by one weak little cough *Revised Draft*. Woodhouse recorded that Keats meant the lines 'to leave on the reader a sense of pettish disgust, by bringing Old Angela in (only) dead stiff & ugly. – He says he likes that the poem should leave off with this Change of Sentiment. . . .' (*L* II, pp. 162–3). On the reasons for rejecting this reading and other of Keats's revisions, see headnote. The harsh tone and satirical note is in keeping with Keats's wish to make the poem less 'smokeable' (see headnote).

376 *meagre face deform* a Miltonic construction. *Allott* makes the interesting suggestion that Keats is half-consciously recollecting the vision of disease and death which are to become the lot of mankind when Adam and Eve are expelled from Eden, *Paradise Lost* XI, 480–92. 'Meagre' is used to describe the Beadsman in l. 12.

THE EVE OF ST MARK

This unfinished poem was written 13–17 February 1819. Published *1848*, copied with changes (without ll. 115–19) on 20 September (*L* II, pp. 201–4). Text from British Museum holograph (Egerton 2780), which Stillinger argues for as the authoritative MS. (*Texts*, pp. 220–2). *G* and *Allott* add the fragment, 'Gif ye wol stonden hardie wight', after l. 99. *Allott* follows *W2*, which derives from the British Museum MS. She also includes Keats's first (cancelled) attempt at ll. 69–70 as a separate couplet.

Keats wrote the fragment shortly after returning from his visit to Chichester and Bedhampton, which is recollected in the atmosphere of the poem – 'Some time since I began a Poem call'd "the Eve of St Mark" quite in the spirit of Town quietude. I th[i]nk it will give you the sensation of walking about an old county Town in a coolish evening. I know not yet whether I shall ever finish it. . . .' (*L* II, p. 201). At the time of its composition, Keats was confined to his rooms with a sore throat, and the subject, like that of its companion-piece *The Eve of St Agnes*, was probably suggested by Mrs Isabella Jones. The superstition is recounted in John Brand's *Popular Antiquities* (1813 edn) II, p. 166: 'It is customary in Yorkshire, as a clergyman of that county informed me, for the common people to sit and watch in the church porch on St Mark's Eve [24 April], from eleven o'clock at night till one in the morning. The third year (for this must be done thrice), they are supposed to see the ghosts of all those who are to die next year, pass by into the church. When any one sickens that is thought to have been seen in this manner, it is presently whispered about that he will not recover, for that such, or such an one, who has watched St Mark's Eve, says so. This superstition is in such force, that, if the patients themselves hear of it, they almost despair of recovery. Many are said to have actually died by their imaginary fears on the occasion; a truly lamentable, but by no means incredible, instance of human folly.'

In *The Eve of St Mark* Keats's medievalism drew on his liking for Chatterton. The name of his heroine, Bertha, is the same as that of Chatterton's in *Aella, a Tragic Interlude* (1777), and the imitation of Middle English (ll. 99–114) is more closely related to Chatterton's attempts in this direction than to Chaucer or Gower. Although Keats had used octosyllabic lines earlier (see headnote to *Fancy*, p. 617), he was also indebted to Coleridge's *Christabel* (1816). *Gittings* (1954), pp. 86–92, has demonstrated that details in the poem are taken from Keats's stay at Chichester, his memories of Stansted Chapel, and the furniture in Mrs Isabella Jones's lodgings. D. G. Rossetti speculated on Keats's intended conclusion: 'I judge that the heroine – remorseful after trifling with a sick and now absent lover – might make her way to the minster-porch to learn his fate by the spell, and perhaps see his figure enter but not return' (*John Keats: Criticism and Comment* [1919], pp. 13–14).

The fragment anticipates the Pre-Raphaelites, and Rossetti thought that, with *La Belle Dame sans Merci*, it gives '... the chastest and choicest example of his maturing manner, and shows astonishingly real medievalism for one not bred as an artist' (ibid., p. 9). For a recent discussion, see D. Luke, '*The Eve of St Mark*: Keats's "Ghostly Queen of Spades" and the Textual Superstition', *Studies in Romanticism*, IX (1970), pp. 161–75. S. M. Sperry takes the discussion further in *Keats the Poet* (1974), pp. 221–8.

2 *Twice*] Thrice *L*. 'Twice holy' since it is both the Eve of St Mark and a Sunday (see l. 1).

5 *April rains* the Eve of St Mark was on 24 April.

8 *unmatured*] immatured *L*.

13 *Twice*] Thrice *L*.

14–22 compare with the description of Corinth in *Lamia* I, 352–61.

16 *fireside orat'ries* the citizens' (large) fireplaces are imagined as being 'oratories' (small rooms, or chapels, for prayer).

20 *folk*] crowd *L*.

22 *organs*] MSS; organ *1848*, *G*, *Allott*. The emendation is not needed. 'Organs' can be regarded as an archaic use of the plural (a 'set of organs'), or there may be more than one church in the town (and hence a possible distinction between 'even-song' and 'vesper prayer' in l. 18 above).

27 *two*] fair *L*.

28 *golden broideries* the gold-leaf used in illuminating the 'curious volume'.

30–38 these details are based on Lewis Way's stained glass windows in Stansted Chapel, near Bedhampton. See *Gittings* (1954), pp. 87–9, who also gives a photograph of the windows. The chapel may also have provided details for *The Eve of St Agnes* 208–16 and *n* (p. 625).

32 *'mid*] and *1848*; in *G*.

33 *Aaron's breastplate*] Moses's breastplate *W2* (marginally), *1848*, *Garrod*

(*OSA*). The 'breastplate', a richly embroidered cloth, set with precious stones engraved with the names of the twelve tribes of Israel, was part of Aaron's insignia as high-priest. It is described in Exodus xxviii 15–30, and Moses's consecration of Aaron and his sons is recorded in Leviticus viii 1–14.

33–4 *the seven / Candlesticks John saw in Heaven* for St John's vision of the seven-branched golden candlestick, symbolizing the seven churches of Asia, see Revelation i 13–20. The symbol has a prominent place on the left of Lewis Way's window at Stansted Chapel (see ll. 30–38*n*).

35 *The wingèd Lion of Saint Mark* St Mark's emblem, a winged lion, is derived from one of the four apocalyptic beasts who appear before God's throne in Revelation iv 6–9.

36–8 For a description of the ark of the covenant, surmounted by 'the cherubims of glory', see Hebrews ix 4–5. It figures prominently in Lewis Way's window at Stansted Chapel (see ll. 30–38*n*).

38 *golden mice* the Philistines captured the ark from the Israelites at Ebenezer. When they returned it they sent five golden mice, along with other propitiatory and symbolic gifts. See 1 Samuel vi 4.

53 *pleated*] plaited *W*2 (*marginally*), *1848*, *G*. Bertha's 'pleated lawn-frill' is a collar made of fine linen, sewn and ironed into pleats.

56 *imageries* pictures. Compare with the 'carven imag'ries' of *The Eve of St Agnes* 209.

59 *townwards*] homewards *L*, *1848*, *G*, *Allott*.

69–70] The Maiden lost in dizzy maze / Turn'd to the fire and made a blaze *Draft* (*deleted*); *W*2, *Allott adopts as extra couplet*.

70] And struck a swart lamp from the coal *L*.

75 *ceiling beam*] *Allott*; ceiling, beam, *L*; ceiling-beam *1848*, *G*.

76–82 Keats's description of Mrs Isabella Jones's rooms in Gloucester Street mentions a parrot (*L* I, pp. 402–3). Gittings (1954), pp. 90–91, thinks that the other details in this passage are drawn from the same source, the 'winter screen' being of East-Indian lacquer work, and the 'Lima mice' Keats's mishearing of 'lemur mice', a small nocturnal mammal found mainly in Madagascar. Mrs Jones's furnishings are also probably referred to in *Fragment of 'The Castle-builder'* 25–69 (see headnote, p. 608).

80 *legless birds of Paradise* the Bird of Paradise, notable for its brilliantly coloured plumage. Keats alludes to the legend that the birds never alight – *OED* 'Bird' 7 cites, 'The Birds of Paradise ... reside Constantly in the Air' (1638). Tennyson has, 'Like long-tailed birds of Paradise / That float through Heaven, and cannot light' (*The Day-Dream*, L'Envoi 7–8).

81 *Macaw ... Av'davat* a macaw is a parrot with gaudy plumage, found in the tropical and sub-tropical regions of America. The avadavat (properly, 'amadavat') is an Indian song-bird, brown in colour with white spots.

85 *wildest*] gastly *L*.

86 *ghostly Queen of Spades* the Queen of Spades is the death card.

89–92 St Mark's life, of which little is known, was the subject of many legends.

93 *eremite* a recluse or anchorite, a hermit.

94 *star ... dagger* symbols used to mark footnotes in the manuscript.

96 *crow-quill* 'a quill from a crow's wing, used as a pen for fine writing' (*OED*).

99-114 Preceded in *G* and *Allott* by 'Gif ye wol stonden hardie wight' (see headnote). Keats commented, 'What follows is an imitation of the Authors in Chaucer's time – 'tis more ancient than Chaucer himself and perhaps betwe[e]n him and Gower' (*L* II, p. 204). The imitation of Middle English is inaccurate, and indebted to Chatterton.

99 *swevenis* dreams.

102 *crimpede* 'to crimp' means 'to compress or pinch into minute parallel plaits or folds; to frill' (*OED*).

105 *Gif that the modre* if that the mother.

106 *solitarinesse* as *Allott* points out, Burton's *Anatomy of Melancholy* has a section on 'Solitariness' (I 3 i 2). Keats was fond of this line, and quoted it in his letter to Reynolds of 21 September 1819 and to George and Georgiana Keats (*L* II, p. 166, p. 209).

112 *Somdel* somewhat, something.

113 *auctorith* a verb formed from 'auctor', a Middle English form of 'author'.

115 *eyelids*] eye had *W*2, *Allott*.

119 *Venice* St Mark is the patron saint of Venice, and Keats refers to his shrine in St Mark's Cathedral.

'GIF YE WOL STONDEN HARDIE WIGHT'

Date uncertain. First printed H. B. Forman. *G* and *Allott* include as part of *The Eve of St. Mark* (after l. 98). However, the fragment is on the back of the Morgan Library draft of ll. 99–114, and copied separately at the end of *W*2. See *Texts*, pp. 220–2.

1 *wight* man.

3 *pardie* by God (par Dieu).

5 *Approchen*] Appouchen *G* (*following Morgan Library MS*). 'Appouchen' is a slip, and does not make sense.

9 *ilka ... carle* 'ilka' based on 'ilch', 'iche', meaning each or every; 'carle' means a man of the common people, especially a villein.

10 *in parle* literally, in speech, conversation, or argument.

'WHY DID I LAUGH TONIGHT?'

Written before 19 March 1819, when Keats copied it out for George and Georgiana Keats (*L* II, p. 81). Published *1848*. The sonnet may have been written *c*. 8 March since l. 7 echoes the idea expressed in Keats's letter to Haydon of that date – 'I will not spoil my love of gloom by writing an ode to darkness ...' (*L* II, p. 43). Keats introduced the poem to his brother and his sister-in-law with the following comments, 'I am ever affraid that your anxiety for me will lead you to fear for the violence of my temperament continually smothered down: for that reason I did not intend to have sent you the following sonnet – but look over the last two pages and ask yourselves whether I have not that in me which will well bear the buffets of the world. It will be the best

632 NOTES FOR PP. 328–9

comment on my sonnet; it will show you that it was written with no Agony but that of ignorance; with no thirst of any thing but knowledge when pushed to the point though the first steps to it were t[h]rough my human passions – they went away, and I wrote with my Mind – and perhaps I must confess a little bit of my heart –' (*L* II, p. 81). Text based on *L*.

4 *once –*] *L, Allott*; once. *1848, G*.

6 *Say, wherefore*] *L, Allott*; I say, why *1848, G*.

9 *this being's lease* the conditions on which my being is given. Compare with *Macbeth* IV. 1. 98–100, 'Macbeth / Shall live the lease of nature, pay his breath / To time and mortal custom. . . .'

10 the line means, 'allows my fancy (imagination) to extend itself and realize its fullest pleasures'.

11 *on this very midnight cease* anticipates *Ode to a Nightingale* 56, 'To cease upon the midnight . . .'.

11 *could*] *L, Allott*; would *1848, G*.

12 *ensigns* flags, banners.

12 *shreds.*] *L, Allott*; shreds; *1848, G*.

14 *Death intenser*] Death's intenser *Allott*. *Allott*'s reading is in error. In *L* Keats wrote 'Deaths is' for 'Death is' on the *second* occurrence of the word in this line.

FAERY BIRD'S SONG

Probably written before 15 April 1819, when Keats wrote '*When they were come unto the Faery's Court*' (see headnote, p. 633). Published *Plymouth and Devonport Weekly Journal*, 18 October 1838, and *1848*. Charles Brown attached a note to Keats's autograph MS, 'A faery Song – written for a particular purpose at the request of C.B.', and included the poem at the end of Chapter IV in his 'The Fairies' Triumph' in his MS Notebook, now at Hampstead. The Princes Elmy and Azameth, whose family is being persecuted by King Boulimar, are grieving over the flower, Love's Hope (really their brother, Selrik, who has been metamorphosed), which turns to dust when they pluck it: at this point, 'a bird of lovely form and brilliant plumage . . . gazed down on them with its mild dove-like eyes, and warbled its song to them.' For further details, and an account of Brown's story, see J. Stillinger, 'The Context of Keats's "Fairy Song"', *KSJ*, X (1961), pp. 6–8.

Title] untitled in Keats's MS, *Allott*; Fairy's Song *G* (*from R. M. Milnes's transcript*); Faery Bird's Song *Plymouth and Devonport Weekly Journal*; Faery Song *1848*. The title is adopted as the most accurate description of the poem.

FAERY SONG

Probably written before 15 April 1819 with preceding poem (see headnote). Published *Plymouth and Devonport Weekly Journal*, 25 October 1838, *1848*. The singer is probably one of the good fairies in Brown's story.

Title] *1848*; Faery Dirge *Plymouth and Devonport Weekly Journal*.

11 *Favonian* of or pertaining to the west wind, hence, gentle, propitious.

12   *soothly*   truthfully (but see *Sleep and Poetry* 180n, p. 552).

'WHEN THEY WERE COME UNTO THE FAERY'S COURT'

Written as a 'little extempore' on 15 April 1819 in Keats's journal letter of 14 February–3 May to George and Georgiana Keats (*L* II, pp. 85–8). Published *Macmillan's Magazine*, August 1888 (in part), and *Forman* (1890) (in full). Text based on *L*, the single source. F. Page considered that the poem shows Keats, depicted by the Dwarf, examining 'his conscience as a poet', and that the Princess represents poetry, the Ape Wordsworth, and the Fool Coleridge, *Dublin Review*, CCI (1937), pp. 87–97. *Gittings* (1954), pp. 107–9, followed by *Bate* (1963), pp. 470–71, explains it as a family joke, 'quizzing' Georgiana as the vain Princess, and giving George the part of the Ape, Keats that of the Dwarf, and Tom Keats the part of the Fool. It is more probable, as *Allott* suggests, that the fragment developed from the Dwarf and Ape who aided King Boulimar in his pursuit of the Princess Floramente in Brown's 'The Fairies' Triumph' (see headnote to *Faery Bird's Song*, p. 632). Keats may also have remembered Le Grand's 'The Mule without a Bridle' in G. L. Way's translation (1796) of his *Fabliaux*: see P. Mann, 'Keats's Reading', *Keats-Shelley Memorial Bulletin*, XIII (1962), pp. 41–3. The use of heroic couplets echoes Keats's recent reading of Dryden.

1   *unto*] into *Forman* (1890), *G*.
12   *Persian feathers*   oriental-style head-dresses, decorated with feathers, were fashionable women's wear at the time.
14   *Otahaeitan mule*   A. D. Atkinson traces the allusion to Cook's *Voyages*, in *N&Q*, 4 August 1951, p. 343. Tahiti had recently been the object of Christian missionaries.
33–5   *Gittings* (1954), p. 108, and *Bate* (1963), p. 471, think these lines refer to Tom Keats's death.
46   *A-quavering*] Quavering *G*. *G* adopts a rejected reading. Another attempt was 'They quaver'd'. *Forman* (1890) has 'And quavered'.
46   *three*] *Allott*; thee *L*; the *Forman* (1890), *G*.
53   *and then at him*] *Forman* (1890), *G*, *Allott*; and at him *L*.
66   *C'up, biddy*] *G*, *Allott*; cup biddy *L*. *G*'s emendation makes clear that Keats meant an abbreviation of 'Come up, biddy'.
67–8   as *Allott* notes, Keats may be recollecting *Hamlet* IV. 2. 17–19, 'such officers do the king best service in the end: he keeps them, like an ape, in the corner of his jaw....'.
76   *pricked*] *Forman* (1890), *G*, *Allott*; prick *L*.
80   the Mule quotes *King Lear* IV. 6. 107 and *Romeo and Juliet* III. 1. 133.
85   *rubbed*] *Forman* (1890), *G*, *Allott*; rub *L*.
90, 93   possibly suggested by Captain Cook's account of the Tahitans' thievery (see l. 14*n*). *Gittings* refers to Keats's letter to George and Georgiana Keats in which he suggests Georgiana might set up a 'whiskey shop for the Monkeys [Red Indians]' (*L* II, p. 92), and argues that the reference is to America.
93   *Shammed*] *G*, *Allott*; Sham'd *L*, *Forman* (1890).

'THE HOUSE OF MOURNING WRITTEN BY MR SCOTT'

Date conjectural, but *Allott* points to the personal allusion in ll. 8–14 which indicates that it was probably written in mid-April 1819, and its light-heartedness is in keeping with the preceding and following poems. Published *Finney*, who proposes a date in June 1819, and reproduces the single transcript in *W*3. *Gittings* (1954), p. 112, thinks that ll. 1–7 may have been written by Woodhouse, who was, among other things, a publisher's reader. Stillinger (*Texts*, p. 274) thinks the attribution doubtful, and suggests Woodhouse as possible author. More likely, the whole is Keats's, reflecting his recent experiences and parodying Wordsworth's list of delights in *Composed in the Valley near Dover, on the Day of Landing* (1807), the poem referred to in the last line of Keats's sonnet.

1 Keats's publishers, Taylor and Hessey, had published John Scott's volume of poems in 1817.

2 *the Magdalen* Magdalen Hospital in St George's Fields, a home for reformed prostitutes founded in the eighteenth century.

4 *uphill to a friend's cot* possibly a reference to Hampstead.

7 *drunkenness from beer* an unpleasant kind of inebriation as opposed to that caused by wine, of which Keats was fond.

8 *Haydon's great picture* Keats refers to Haydon's *Christ's Triumphal Entry into Jerusalem* which was progressing slowly in April (see *L* II, p. 83). Haydon's ill-timed request for financial help had already begun to turn Keats against him (*L* II, pp. 53–5).

10 *the voice of Mr Coleridge* Keats met Coleridge on 11 April 1819, and commented, 'I heard his voice as he came towards me – I heard it as he moved away – I heard it all the interval – if it may be called so' (*L* II, p. 89).

11–12 *a pipe...neighbour* on 15 April 1819 Keats complained gently of the racket made by Brown's nephews (*L* II, p. 83).

CHARACTER OF CHARLES BROWN

Written 16 April 1819 (*L* II, p. 89). Published *1848*. This extempore *jeu d'esprit* was a hit at Brown who, Keats reported, '... this morning is writing some spenserian stanzas against Mrs Miss Brawne and me; so I shall amuse myself with him a little: in the manner of Spenser –' (*L* II, p. 89). Keats was staying with Brown at Wentworth Place, Hampstead, and the Brawnes had moved in next door on 3 April. Charles Brown (1787–1842) met the poet in summer 1817, and their friendship was cemented by their Scottish walking tour in June–August 1818. Keats went to live in his house on 1 December, after the death of Tom. The ironic *Character* is a prolonged private joke. Brown was anything but 'melancholy' (l. 1), was heavily-built and bald (ll. 2–5), and was far from being a beardless youth – ll. 6–8 refer to Brown's buffoonery when staying with Keats at Chichester in January 1819, when Sarah Mullins persuaded him to shave off his whiskers and Brown, the following morning, dressed up as a woman (*L* II, p. 36). The remainder of the poem is equally pointed. Brown, an experienced and travelled man who had retired early from business, enjoyed both liquor and flirting. Keats's letters contain several references to Brown's liking for women, and his house-keeper,

635 NOTES FOR PP. 333-4

Abigail O'Donaghue (whom he may have married illegally in the summer of 1819), bore him a son. Keats, who enjoyed his extrovert energy, once remarked that the Devil was 'Brown's Muse' (*L* II, p. 65). The *Character* was written only two days after Brown had composed a valentine to Fanny Brawne, playing upon his baldness and personal untidiness (the four extant stanzas are given by *Bate* [1963], p. 453*n*). In July Keats confessed to Fanny Brawne that he had felt he was being done to 'death by inches' when she had been 'in the habit of flirting with Brown' (*L* II, p. 303). The two men later collaborated in writing *Otho the Great* (see headnote p. 662). A dependable, generous, and methodical man, Brown was of great assistance to Keats in the coming months, though he did not, as Keats wanted, accompany the poet to Italy during his last illness. Brown's transcripts and his concern for Keats's poetry were to make a lasting contribution to Keats studies.

1 *to weet*   'to wit', 'to be sure'.
1 *carle*   here, churl (but see *The Eve of St Mark* 109*n*, p. 631).
3 *parle*   discourse.
9 *Persian*   see '*When they were come unto the Faery's Court*' 12*n* (p. 633).
10 *half-and-half*   'a drink of ale and beer, or beer and porter, in equal quantities' (Partridge).
13 *swine-herd*] *L*; swine-head *1848*, *G*, *Allott*. The meaning is, 'Brown disdained to drink from the wassail bowl with the common run of mankind'. *1848*'s emendation gives the sense, 'Brown ignored the image of the swine's head carved on a drinking-cup'.
15 *Lemans*   mistresses, lovers.
16-17 *after water-brooks ... Panted*   see Psalms xlii 1, 'As the hart panteth after the water brooks, so panteth my soul after thee, O God.'
18 *gillyflowers*   fragrant flowers, esp. the clove-scented pink, white stocks, or wall-flowers.
20 *Tipping the wink*   to warn or signal with a wink (slang).
21 *olden Tom or ruin blue*   both names for gin. 'Blue ruin' was a gin of poor quality (*OED*).
22 *cheery*] *L*, *Allott*; cherry *1848*, *G*. As *Allott* points out, Keats probably intended the pun. 'Nantz' means brandy (originally from Nantes).
24 *beating up the watch*   was a traditional sport of the London rake.
26-7 see Isaiah iii 16, 'the daughters of Zion are haughty ... walking and mincing as they go, and making a tinkling with their feet'.

A DREAM, AFTER READING DANTE'S EPISODE OF
PAOLA AND FRANCESCA

Written *c.* 16 April 1819, when Keats copied it out for George and Georgiana Keats (*L* II, p. 91). Published *Indicator*, 28 June 1820 (signed 'Caviare'), *London Magazine*, November 1821, *1848*. Text based on *1848* emended against *L*, with some first gropings noted from Keats's draft in the copy of Cary's *Dante* (Ashley Library, referred to below as *Draft*) which he gave to Fanny Brawne.

636 NOTES FOR P. 334

Keats had been reading Cary's translation of Dante, *Inferno* V, and gives the following account of the sonnet's genesis: 'The fifth canto of Dante pleases me more and more – it is that one in which he meets with Paulo [*sic*] and Francesca – I had passed many days in rather a low state of mind and in the midst of them I dreamt of being in that region of Hell. The dream was one of the most delightful enjoyments I ever had in my life – I floated about the whirling atmosphere as it is described with a beautiful figure to whose lips mine were joined as it seem'd for an age – and in the midst of all this cold and darkness I was warm – even flowery tree tops sprung up and we rested on them sometimes with the lightness of a cloud till the wind blew us away again – I tried a Sonnet upon it – there are fourteen lines but nothing of what I felt in it – o that I could dream it every night – ' (*L* II, p. 91). Keats's feelings were obviously related to his emotions towards Fanny Brawne, and the fact that his 'lovers need not tell / Their sorrows' (ll. 11–12) is probably related to a dislike of his friends' curiosity about his relationship – in June he wrote to Fanny, 'My friends have behaved very well to me in every instance but one, and there they have b[e]come tattlers, and inquisitors into my conduct: spying upon a secret I would rather die than share it with any bodies confidence. . . . If I am the Theme, I will not be the Friend of idle Gossips. Good gods what a shame it is our Loves should be so put into the microscope of a Coterie' (*L* II, pp. 292–3). E. Schneider remarks that the dream 'exhibits several of the features that in [opium] addicts are commonly attributed to the drug. . . . Keats made of this [dream] a sonnet, the close of which might have been thought inspired by the opium eater's confessions except that De Quincy had not yet celebrated his pleasures and pains in print', *Coleridge, Opium, and 'Kubla Khan'* (1953), p. 50.

Title] *Indicator, Garrod* (*O S A*); *no title in L, Draft, Allott*; A Dream *London Magazine*; On a Dream *1848, G*. The most fully descriptive title is the one adopted. Keats does not seem to have given the poem a title.

1–8 for the myth of Hermes's rescue of Io, see *Dictionary of Classical Names* under 'Io' (p. 708).

3–5 recollects *Paradise Lost* XI, 129–33.

3 *spright* disembodied spirit (a variant spelling of 'sprite').

4 *bereft* Rossetti noted the 'singular defect' of the false rhyme 'slept / bereft' (*John Keats: Criticism and Comment*, 1919, pp. 6–7).

5 *dragon-world*] *G, Allott*; dragon world *L, Indicator*; Dragon-world *Draft, London Magazine, 1848*.

7 *to*] all texts but for *Indicator* which has *unto*.

7 *snow-cold*] snow-clad (*cancelled reading in L*). Keats's first attempt read 'But not olympus-ward to serene skies' (*Draft*).

8 *that*] *Draft, L, London Magazine, G, Allott*; a *Indicator, 1848, Garrod* (*OSA*).

9–11 based on Cary's translation of the *Inferno* V, 32–4, '. . . The stormy blast of hell / With restless fury drives the spirits on / Whirled round and dash'd amain with sore annoy . . .' and VI, 9, 'Large hail, discolour'd water, sleety flaw . . .'.

10   *in ... whirlwind*] 'mid ... world-wind *Indicator*.
10   *flaw*   see *The Eve of St Agnes* 325n (p. 627).
11–12   either, the lovers have no need to speak since their sorrow is apparent, or because they are safe from prying questions (see headnote for the possible biographical background).
12, 13   *Pale*   foreshadows the use of the word in *La Belle Dame sans Merci* 2, 37–8, 46.

LA BELLE DAME SANS MERCI. A BALLAD

Written 21 April 1819 (*L* II, pp. 95–6). Published *Indicator*, 10 May 1820 (signed 'Caviare') and *1848*. The *Indicator* version is a revision of the first draft which Keats wrote in his journal-letter to George and Georgiana Keats, and introduces several changes (see notes), which most editors have agreed are for the worse. Bate (1963), p. 479n, says, 'The revisions were made when Keats was far too ill to have any confidence at all in his own judgement (early May, 1820); and then the revised poem was printed by Hunt in the *Indicator*. ... One can only suppose that Hunt – possibly Woodhouse – thought, with myopic good-will, that the magic, dreamlike quality of the poem would be considered "sentimental"....' Text based on *L*, from which *1848* is derived.

The poem is an oblique expression of some aspects of Keats's feelings for Fanny Brawne, and its dreamlike atmosphere should be compared with that of the preceding poem. Literary echoes abound, reaching from Alain Chartier's medieval French poem, which supplies the title, to Elizabethans like Spenser, William Browne and Robert Burton, and up to Keats's contemporaries, Wordsworth and Coleridge. Cary's translation of *Dante* also affected the poem. The main source for the heroine is in Spenser's enchantresses, especially Duessa's seduction of the Red Cross Knight, the story of Cymochles and Phaedria and that of the false Florimel (*Faerie Queene* I. ii, ix, II. vi, and III–IV). As Janice N. Sinson points out (*John Keats and the Anatomy of Melancholy* [1971], pp. 17–19), the figure of the knight-at-arms was probably suggested by Burton's description of those suffering from the cold humour of melancholy – 'As Bellerophon in Homer ... That wandered in the woods, sad all alone Forsaking men's society, making great moan; they delight in floods and waters, desert places, to walk alone in orchards, gardens, private walks, back lanes; averse from company ... He forsook the city and lived in hollow trees, upon a green bank by a brookside, or confluence of waters, all day long and all night.... They are much given to weeping and delight in waters, ponds, pools ... they are pale of colour, slothful, apt to sleep, much troubled with the headache' (*Anatomy of Melancholy* [1813 edn] I 3 i 2, I, pp. 280–85). Keats could also have drawn on the ballad tradition which supplied his form – *Thomas the Rymer*, for instance, gives the story of a thirteenth-century poet chosen for her lover by the Queen of Elfland, and had been recently reprinted in Scott's *Border Minstrelsy* (1802–3), and elsewhere. He would also have found traditional ballads treating similar material in Percy's *Reliques of Ancient Poetry* (1765), but Wordsworth's and Coleridge's use of the ballad form was also important (see l. 15n). Further on the sources, see Finney, pp. 593–9, Robert

Graves's *The White Goddess* (1948), pp. 374–80, and Gittings (1954), pp.113–23 (but see the comments of F. W. Bateson and K. Muir in *Essays in Criticism*, IV (1954), pp. 432–40).

Like *The Eve of St Mark*, this poem held a particular attraction for the Pre-Raphaelites: see Rossetti's remark cited in the headnote to the earlier poem, p. 629, and G. H. Ford's *Keats and the Victorians* (1944), pp. 121–2. Recent critics differ widely over the meaning of the poem, and whether La Belle Dame is wilfully cruel to the knight, or whether it is the knight's inability to maintain the vision that causes his return to the 'cold hill side'. Earlier critics saw the lady as a Circe, deliberately leading men to their destruction, while Graves sees the poem as a celebration of the poet's destruction by his muse: 'That the Belle Dame represented Love, Death by Consumption ... and Poetry all at once can be confirmed by a study of the romances from which Keats developed the poem' (op. cit. p. 378). K. M. Wilson identifies her as the 'demon Poesy' in *The Nightingale and the Hawk* (1964), pp. 141–2, 144. David Perkins sees the poem as 'not only uncertain but a poem about uncertainty' in *The Quest for Permanence* (1959), pp. 259–62. Harold Bloom relates it to Blake's vision of Ulro with the knight being allowed to dream the truth only to awake in the withered natural world (*The Visionary Company* [1961], pp. 375–8), while *Bate* (1963), pp. 478–81, stresses that 'in this ballad all clues to ready judgement are withheld'.

Title] A Ballad *not in* L. According to Leigh Hunt in the *Indicator* Keats took his title from Alain Chartier's poem *La Belle Dame sans Mercy* (1424), which was included and translated in *The Poetical Works of Geoffrey Chaucer* (1782 edn). The title is quoted in *The Eve of St Agnes* 292.

1, 5] Ah! what can ail thee, wretched wight, *Indicator*.

3 *has*] is *Indicator*. See l. 47n. Compare the line with *The Eve of St Mark* 10, 'rivers new with spring-tide sedge'.

6 *haggard* 'gaunt or scraggy-looking from the loss of flesh' (*OED*). See also the note on 'haggard seeming', *The Eve of St Agnes* 344n (p. 627).

9, 11 *lily ... rose* poetic commonplace for the white and red of the face, but usually applied to beautiful women rather than, as here, to a man.

9 *a lily*] death's lilly L (*cancelled*).

11 *a fading rose*] death's fading rose L (*cancelled*).

13 *meads*] Wilds L (*cancelled*).

15–16 the simplicity of the whole stanza owes a debt to Wordsworth's handling of the ballad, though, as Harold Bloom points out in *The Visionary Company* (1961), p. 377, ll. 15–16 are paralleled by Coleridge's 'Night-Mare LIFE-IN-DEATH'—'*Her* lips were red, *her* looks were free, / Her locks were yellow as gold: / Her skin was white as leprosy...' (*The Rime of the Ancient Mariner* [1797], 190–94).

17–24 stanzas v and vi are transposed in *Indicator*.

17 recollects the garlands made for the false Fidessa and false Florimel in the *Faerie Queene* I. ii. 30, III. vii. 17, the latter being mentioned in Keats's journal-letter shortly before writing the poem (*L* II, p. 93).

639 NOTES FOR PP. 335-6

18 *fragrant zone* a girdle or belt made of flowers (poeticism).
20 *made sweet moan* compare *Ode to Psyche* 30, 'virgin-choir to make delicious moan'. A poetic archaism which occurs in both Spenser and Chaucer.
23 *sidelong would she bend*] sideways would she lean *Indicator*.
26 *manna-dew* see *Endymion* I, 766n (p. 567). Compare Coleridge, *Kubla Khan* (1816) 53-4, 'For he on honey-dew hath fed, / And drunk the milk of Paradise'.
29 *elfin* for Keats's use of this word, see *The Eve of St Agnes* 343n (p. 627).
30 *and sighed full sore*] and there she sighed full sore *L* (*cancelled*); gazed and sighed deep *Indicator*.
31 *wild wild*] wild sad *Indicator*.
32 *With kisses four*] So kissed to sleep *Indicator*. Keats commented to George and Georgiana Keats, 'Why four kisses – you will say – why four because I wish to restrain the headlong impetuosity of my Muse – she would have fain said "score" without hurting the rhyme – but we must temper the Imagination as the Critics say with Judgment. I was obliged to choose an even number that both eyes might have fair play: and to speak truly I think two a piece quite sufficient – Suppose I had said seven; there would have been three and a half a piece – a very awkward affair – and well got out of on my side – ' (*L* II, p. 97). Graves relates the kisses to Tom's death, suggesting that two of the kisses are the 'pennies laid on the eyes of death', and that the *Indicator* revisions were unconscious attempts to circumscribe the 'painful doubleness' of the tragic vision and that the alteration of 'wild wild' (l. 31), 'meaning ... elf-wild and horror-wild ... would have the same effect', *English Poetry* (1922), p. 54.
33 *she lullèd me asleep*] we slumbered on the moss *Indicator*.
35 *dreamt*] *L*; dreamed *all other texts*.
36 *hill*] *L*, *Indicator*, *G*, *Allott*; hill's *1848*. *1848*'s reading regularizes 'hill's' to match l. 44. The *Indicator* version regularizes the other way round. Certainly it is neater to have either 'hill' / 'hill' or 'hill's' / 'hill's' at ll. 36 and 44, but the delicate modulations and echoes in the poem depend upon small variations, and I have followed *G* in keeping to the irregularity in *L*. For a similar problem over tense, see l. 47n. *Texts* (pp. 232-4) prefers 'hill's'.
37-8 compare with the 'pale' figure in *A Dream* ('As Hermes once ...') 12-13, which, like this poem, was influenced by Keats's reading of Cary's translation of the *Inferno* V. The warnings given by the 'kings and princes' (ll. 37-42) are probably indebted to *Pericles* I. 1. 34-40.
39 *They*] Who *Indicator*.
40 *Thee hath*] *L*; Hath thee *all other texts*.
41 *gloam*] gloom *Indicator*. 'Gloam' (twilight) is Keats's invention based on 'gloaming'.
42 *gapèd wide*] wide agape *L* (*cancelled*). *L* shows that Keats attempted to start the line with 'All tremble ...'
44 *hill's*] hill *Indicator*, *Allott*. See l. 36n.
45 *sojourn*] wither *L* (*cancelled*).
47 *is*] *L*, *Indicator*, *1848*, *Allott*; has *G*. Where *G* regularizes to 'has' to avoid the change of tense from 'has' at l. 3, the *Indicator* version puts both into

640 NOTES FOR PP. 336-8

the present tense. The tense-change, however, is part of the poem's characteristic eeriness, and Keats's original reading in *L* is adopted. See l. 36n for a similar problem with 'hill' / 'hill's'.

SONG OF FOUR FAERIES

Written 21 April 1819. Published *1848*. Keats wrote the first draft in his journal-letter to George and Georgiana Keats of 14 February–3 May, immediately after composing *La Belle Dame sans Merci* and just before he wrote the important passage on the 'Vale of Soul-making' (*L* II, pp. 97–100). Text based on Keats's autograph MS at Harvard (referred to as *H*). See *Texts*, pp. 234–5. The spelling 'Faery' is preferred in *L*, and has been adopted throughout. For Keats's earlier handling of fairies, see *Faery Bird's Song* and *Faery Song* (p. 632) and (possibly) 'Had I a man's fair form ...' (p. 540). Here the fairies are fused with the spirits of the four elements, and Keats's handling of them was probably affected by his recent reading of Burton's discussion of Melancholy in terms of the medieval 'humours', hot, cold, moist, and dry (see *Gittings* [1954], p. 117).

Title **Salamander ... Dusketha, Breama** a salamander is a 'lizard-like animal supposed to live in, or to be able to endure, fire', hence a mythical 'spirit supposed to live in fire' (*OED*). 'Dusketha' is invented from 'dusk', and 'Breama' from the fish, 'bream'.

9 *Nimbly*] *H* (*marginally*), *W*2, Allott; Faintless *L*; Faintly *1848*, *G*.

16 *bitumen*] *H*, *L*, Allott; bitumen. *1848*, *G*. Bitumen means pitch, though as the term was generic, and could include naphtha, 'spumy bitumen' may be a periphrasis for an inflammable spirit such as naphtha. For Keats's use of 'spumy' see *To Homer* 7. The phrase has its origin in Thomson's *The Seasons* (1730), *Summer* 1108–9, 'Thence nitre, sulphur and the fiery spume / Of fat bitumen, steaming on the day ...'.

18 *aloof.*] Allott; aloof *L*; aloof; *H*; aloof, *1848*, *G*.

19 *their*] my *L*.

20 *live tapestries* the forms made by the flames.

23 *Spirit*] Spright *L* (*and throughout*).

28 *asphodel* an immortal flower, supposed to cover the Elysian Fields. See *Endymion* II, 663n (p. 574).

32 *sedge-buried*] sedge shaded *L*.

37–8 *Queen ... Oberon* Titania and Oberon are the fairy king and queen in *A Midsummer Night's Dream*.

39 *Faery*] *L*, *H*, *G*, Allott, *with varied spelling*; Fairy! *1848*.

40 *Soothly* truly, but see *Sleep and Poetry* 180n (p. 552).

46] Far beyond the search and quest *L*.

47 *presenced*] *H*, *W*2, *G*, Allott; browed *L*, *1848*. *W*2 completes the couplet with, 'When his arched course is done'.

52 *Vesper* the evening star, Hesperus.

57 *drouthy* dry (variant of 'droughty').

61 *unlucent* dull (coinage).

641 NOTES FOR PP. 338–40

64 *aguish* tending to give ague (an acute fever), but also here, damp and chilly.
74 *lizard-sided* Dusketha in some ways resembles a salamander.
78 *essence* see *Endymion* I, 777–81*n* (p. 567).
98 *whist*] *Allott*; wist *all other texts*. The word means silent, hushed, quiet. Allott cites Milton's *Nativity Ode* 64, 'The Windes with wonder whist . . .'.
100 *twilight* here used as a verb (*OED*'s first example dates from 1866).

TO SLEEP

Probably written late April 1819. Published *Plymouth and Devonport Weekly Journal*, 11 October 1838, *1848*. This experimental sonnet and the four following poems (which include the *Ode to Psyche*) were written out between 30 April and 3 May in Keats's journal-letter of 14 February–3 May 1819 (*L* II, pp. 104–9). Their order of composition is not clear from Keats's comments, and my interpretation of the evidence differs somewhat from Mrs Allott's, who arranges them as follows: 1. *To Sleep* 2. *On Fame (I)* ('Fame, like a wayward girl . . .') 3. *On Fame (II)* ('How fevered is the man . . .') 4. *Ode to Psyche* and 5. '*If by dull rhymes . . .*' Bate (1963), p. 497, assumes that the four sonnets precede the *Ode to Psyche*. For a brief justification of the order adopted here, see headnotes to the four following poems. *To Sleep* is clearly one of the 'two or three lately written' sonnets Keats referred to (*L* II, p. 104).

The importance of the exact order lies in the relationship between these experiments with the sonnet structure and Keats's evolution of the stanzaic structure of the *Ode to Psyche* and the subsequent odes. In this sonnet Keats breaks away from the Shakespearean form in the sestet, which he rhymes *bc e f e f*, both avoiding the final couplet, and tying the sestet's rhymes into that of the octet, thus achieving a more fluid movement. For Keats's dissatisfaction with the Shakespearean and Petrarchan forms, see his introductory remarks on '*If by dull rhymes . . .*' (quoted in headnote, p. 642). Keats's first draft is in his copy of Milton in the Hampstead Museum, and is printed in *Garrod* (*OSA*), p. 466. Text from Keats's later album transcript (see *Texts*, pp. 235–7).

5 *soothest* most soothing, a superlative invented by Keats. Probably also contains the idea of smoothness (see *Sleep and Poetry* 180*n*, p. 552).
8 *lulling*] dewy *L*, *W*2 (*with* 'lulling' *in the margin and a note recording that the correction is in Keats's handwriting*).
11–12 *hoards* / *Its strength for darkness*] *W*2 (*pencilled over* 'lords'), *Album*, *Allott* lords / Its strength, for darkness *1848*; lords / Its strength for darkness *L*, *G*. 'Hoards' appears to be Woodhouse's alteration, but was adopted by Keats in his album transcript (*Texts*, p. 237). None of these readings is entirely satisfactory. Garrod (*OSA*) thinks 'hoards' is Woodhouse's emendation. He defends 'lords' by citing its use in *Endymion* II, 891, 'And all the revels he had lorded there', and comments, 'There "lorded" means "captained", "marshalled", with some added suggestion of ostentation . . . [hence] Conscience marshals, arrays, disposes proudly and boastfully, its power for darkness.' The real difficulty lies in the mixture of images. It is the duty of conscience to

probe our darkest secrets, which may well be likened to a mole's burrowing, but a mole is hard to see either as a hoarder or as a military leader. (The punctuation of *1848* is an interesting emendation, but must be rejected because *L* gives one of its rare commas after 'darkness'.)

'IF BY DULL RHYMES OUR ENGLISH MUST BE CHAINED'

Probably written before 30 April 1819 (though *Allott* places between 30 April and 3 May). Published *1848*. Keats copied out the sonnet for George and Georgiana Keats on 3 May with the heading 'Incipit altera Sonneta' and writing immediately after the last line, 'Here endeth the other Sonnet' (*L* II, pp. 108–9), so fulfilling his promise (*L* II, p. 104) to copy out 'two or three lately written' sonnets. He commented, 'I have been endeavouring to discover a better sonnet stanza than we have. The legitimate [Petrarchan sonnet] does not suit the language over-well from the pouncing rhymes – the other kind [the Shakespearean] appears too elegaic – and the couplet at the end of it seldom has a pleasing effect – I do not pretend to have succeeded – it will explain itself. . . .' (*L* II, p. 108). See *To Sleep* and the two sonnets *On Fame* for these experiments, and the headnote of the *Ode to Psyche* (immediately following) for their relationship with the stanzaic structure of Keats's odes. (For an earlier experiment, see '*Woman! when I behold thee flippant, vain*'.) After these four sonnets, Keats did not use the form again until October 1819, and his three last sonnets are all Shakespearean (see headnote to '*The day is gone, and all its sweets are gone*', p. 682).

ODE TO PSYCHE

Written between 21 April and 30 April 1819. On 30 April Keats called this 'Poem' (as opposed to sonnet) 'the last I have written' (*L* II, p. 105): he had written *La Belle Dame sans Merci* and *Song of Four Faeries* on 21 April. Published *1820*. Important variants are given from the text Keats copied out in *L*, and from his autograph draft (now in the Morgan Library, referred to as *M* – reproduced in *Gittings* [1970], p. 51).

Keats commented on the *Ode*, it '. . . is the first and the only one with which I have taken even moderate pains – I have for the most part dash'd of[f] my lines in a hurry – This I have done leisurely – I think it reads the more richly for it and will I hope encourage me to write other thing[s] in even a more peacable and healthy spirit. You must recollect that Psyche was not embodied as a Goddess before the time of Apuleius the Platonist who lived after the Augustan age, and consequently the Goddess was never worshipped or sacrificed to with any of the ancient fervour – and perhaps never thought of in the old religion – I am more orthodox tha[n] to let a he[a]then Goddess be so neglected –' (*L* II, pp. 105–6).

Although the legend of Psyche and Cupid had attracted a good deal of commentary, Keats's letter indicates his dependence upon *Lemprière*: 'PSYCHE, a nymph whom Cupid married and carried into a place of bliss, where he long enjoyed her company. Venus put her to death because she had robbed the world of her son; but Jupiter, at the request of Cupid, granted immortality to Psyche. The word signifies *the soul*, and this personification of Psyche is posterior to the Augustan age, though still it is connected with ancient mythology. Psyche is generally represented with the wings of a butterfly, to intimate the lightness of the soul, of which the butterfly is the symbol, and on that account, among the ancients, when a man had just expired, a butterfly appeared fluttering above, as if rising from the mouth of the deceased.' (In Greek, 'Psyche' means both the soul, and a butterfly.)

Keats's Cupid (named only as 'the wingèd boy' and 'the warm Love') should be identified with Eros. Spence's account is helpful: 'As to the Cupids; they were supposed of old to be very numerous: but there were two, which were the chiefs of all that number. ... One of these chief Cupids was looked on as the cause of love; and the other, as the cause of its ceasing. Accordingly, the antiquarians now at Florence usually call the two little Cupids at the foot of the Venus of Medici, by the names of Eros and Anteros ... the antient artists ... always represent [Cupid] as young, pleasing, and handsome. I remember a pretty statue ... in which he appears like a youth of about seventeen, or eighteen years old; and Raphael, (who may almost pass for an authority, when we are speaking of Roman antiquities) represents him as about the same age, in his marriage of Cupid and Psyche. But the most common way of representing Cupid, in the works of the antients themselves, is quite as a child; of not above seven or eight years old; and sometimes, even younger than that. ... His wings are ornamental as well as useful; and were probably sometimes represented in the paintings of the antients, as of various and pleasing colours ... the butterfly is generally used by the Greek artists as an emblem for the human soul; and a Cupid fondling or burning a butterfly, is just the same with them as a Cupid caressing or tormenting the goddess Psyche, or the soul' (*Polymetis*, pp. 69–71).

Keats had previously described the apotheosis of Psyche in '*I stood tiptoe . . .*' 141–50. The *Ode to Psyche* assumes that Psyche is already a goddess, but the experiences described in the poem are drawn from her earlier meetings with Cupid, as they had been described in William Adlington's translation of Apuleius's *The Golden Ass* (1566). Adlington interprets the story as showing how Love (Cupid as Eros), hitherto mischievous, has been won over to the mind or soul, and Keats's *Ode* echoes verbal details of his description of Psyche's wanderings – 'Thus poore Psyches being left alone, weeping and trembling on the toppe of the rocke, was blowne by the gentle aire and of shrilling Zephyrus, and caried from the hill with a meek winde, which retained her garments up, and little by little brought her downe into a deepe valley, where she was laid in *a bed of most sweet and fragrant flowers. Thus faire Psyches being sweetly couched among the soft and tender hearbs, as in a bed of sweet and fragrant floures* [compare ll. 7–15], and having qualified the thoughts and troubles of her restlesse mind, was now well reposed. And when she had refreshed her selfe sufficiently with sleepe, she rose with a more quiet and pacified minde, and fortuned to *espy a pleasant wood invironed with great and mighty trees. Shee espied likewise a running river as cleare as crystall: in the midst of the wood well nigh at the fall of the river was a princely Edifice, wrought and builded not by the art or hand of man* [compare ll. 50–62]' (C. Whibley's reprint [1893], p. 102, of 1639 edn of *Apuleius*). In Apuleius, however, the 'princely Edifice' is Cupid's palace, where Psyche is visited by her lover only at night. Psyche, who fears her lover may be a serpent, hides a burning lamp, intending to cut off his head, but when she sees Cupid she falls to her knees and he is woken by a drop of burning oil, and flees. Psyche then has to suffer a period of expiatory wandering, which includes a journey over the 'ridge' of a 'mountain' (see l. 55), and a trip to the underworld, before Cupid escapes through a 'window of the chamber where hee was inclosed', and successfully petitions Jupiter for Psyche's immortality.

Keats's interest in the story, particularly in Psyche's period of suffering, should be connected with his account of the 'vale of soul-making', written a few days before that he copied out the *Ode to Psyche* in his journal-letter: 'I say *'Soul making'* Soul as distinguished from an Intelligence – There may be intelligences or sparks of the divinity in millions – but they are not Souls till they acquire identities, till each one is personally itself. I[n]telligences are atoms of perception – they know and they see and they are pure, in short they are God – how then are Souls to be made? ... How, but by the medium of a world like this? This point I sincerely wish to consider because I think it a grander system of salvation than the chrystain [*sic*] religion – or rather it is a system of Spirit-creation – This is effected by three grand materials acting the one upon the other for a series of years – These three grand Materials are the *Intelligence* – the *human heart* (as distinguished from intelligence or Mind) and the *World* or *Elemental space* suited for the proper action of *Mind and Heart* on each other for the purpose of forming the *Soul or Intelligence destined to possess the sense of Identity*.... Do you not see how necessary a World of Pains and troubles is to school an Intelligence and make it a soul? A Place where the heart must feel and suffer in a thousand diverse ways! Not merely is the Heart a Hornbook, It is the Minds Bible, it is the Minds experience, it is the teat from which the Mind or intelligence sucks its identity – As various as the Lives of Men are – so various become their souls, and thus does God make individual beings, Souls, Identical Souls of the sparks of his own essence – This appears to me a faint sketch of a system of Salvation which does not affront our reason and humanity – I am convinced that many difficulties which christians labour under would vanish before it ... It is pretty generally suspected that the chr[i]stian scheme has been coppied from the ancient persian and greek Philosophers. Why may they not have made this simple thing even more simple for common apprehension by introducing Mediators and Personages in the same manner as in the he[a]then mythology abstractions are personified – Seriously I think it probable that this System of Soul-making – may have been the Parent of all the more palpable and personal Schemes of Redemption, among the Zoroastrians the Christians and the Hindoos. For as one part of the human species must have their carved Jupiter; so another part must have the palpable and named Mediatior and saviour, their Christ their Oromanes and their Vishnu. ...' (*L* II, pp. 102–3). For Keats's earlier ideas of 'fellowship with essence', see *Endymion* I, 777–81 and n (p. 567); for his ideas on the origins of myth, which were strongly influenced by Wordsworth, see '*I stood on tip-toe* . . .' 125–204 and n (p. 550) together with Appendix 1 (p. 499).

As might be expected, Keats's handling of the legend was affected by his reading of Spenser's 'Garden of Adonis' in the *Faerie Queene* (see particularly III. vi. 49–50), and by Mrs Tighe's *Psyche* (1811). Milton provides further parallels, as does (more surprisingly) Erasmus Darwin's *The Botanic Garden*. On these echoes and on the iconographic tradition, see *Jack*, pp. 201–13.

In the *Ode to Psyche* Keats evolved the stanza structure for the remaining odes. It developed from his experiments with the sonnet (see headnotes to '*Woman! when I behold you flippant, vain*', *To Sleep* and '*If by dull rhymes* . . .', pp. 538, 641, 642), and offered a form which could be sustained over the several stanzas of an ode, without losing what Keats called the 'interwoven and complete' character of the sonnet. Further, see the discussions of H. W. Garrod, *Keats* (1926), pp. 83–90, *Ridley*, pp. 195–210, *Bate* (1945), pp. 125–33, and *Bate* (1963), pp. 494–8. *Ridley*, pp. 197–210, explores the *Ode*'s structure as an anticipation of the later odes, following Garrod who, unlike most critics, also thought that Keats meant to portray *Cupid* waiting for Psyche in the last stanza – 'The open window and the lighted torch – they are to admit and attract the timorous *moth-goddess*, who symbolizes melancholic love . . . Keats has . . . identified the Psyche who is the soul (love's soul) with the Psyche which means moth . . . we encounter her again, brought into darker shadow, in the *Ode on Melancholy*' (*Keats* [1926], p. 99). Kenneth Allott gives a more positive interpretation of 'the Cinderella of Keats's great Odes', and suggests that it argues 'that love, poetry and indolence are the natural medicines of the soul against the living death it must expect from "cold philosophy"' (*John Keats: A Reassessment*, ed. K. Muir [1959], pp. 74–94). For other readings exploring the symbolic meanings of the poem, see David Perkins's *The Quest for Permanence* (1959), pp. 221–8, Harold Bloom's *The Visionary Company* (1961), pp. 389–97, which presents Keats's Psyche as 'a sexual Goddess who renews consciousness and thus renews the earth', *Bate* (1963), pp. 487–98, and *Jack*, pp. 201–13, who sees the *Ode* as an 'Act of Pagan Worship'.

1 *numbers* verses.
2 *By sweet enforcement and remembrance dear* compare Milton's *Lycidas* 4, 6, '. . . with forc'd fingers rude. . . . Bitter constraint, and sad occasion dear . . .'.
4 *soft-conchèd* like a soft shell.
5 compare Spenser, *Amoretti* lxxvii, 'Was it a dreame, or did I see it playne . . .?'
6 *awakened eyes* eyes which were not dreaming, obviously, but also suggests that imaginative perception is a heightened form of everyday seeing. Compare *Ode to a Nightingale* 79n. *L* has 'awaked' for 'awakened'.
7–15 for the debt to Adlington's translation of Apuleius, see headnote.
10 *roof*] fan *M*, *L*. The alteration creates an unrhymed line.
14 *silver-white*] freckle pink *M* (*marginally*), *L*.
14 *Tyrian*] syrian *M*, *L*. Probably an emendation in *1820*, since all MSS

read 'syrian', which makes no sense in the context. 'Tyrian' means 'purple', after a dye once made at Tyre.

16 *pinions* wings.

17 *bade*] bid *M, L, G*.

20 *eye-dawn*] dawning *M* (*cancelled*). As the sleeping pair awaken, so does the love in their eyes. 'Aurorean' means belonging to Aurora, goddess of dawn.

21 *the wingèd boy* Cupid, on whom see headnote.

22 *dove* Psyche is not traditionally depicted as a dove, but see Mrs Tighe's *Psyche* (1811) II, 3, 'Oh, Psyche, happy in thine ignorance . . . Pure spotless dove!'

23/24] *no stanza division here in Allott*. In *L*, ll. 24-35 are given, but there is no paragraph given at l. 50.

25 *Olympus' faded hierarchy* the Olympians are faded because they have been surpassed by Psyche's beauty. Compare with Keats's notions of progress in *Hyperion* II, 228-9, '. . . 'tis the eternal law / That first in beauty should be first in might. . . .'

26 *Phoebe's*] *Keats made two attempts in M* (Night's wide full *and* Night's orb'd) *before settling on* Phoebe's.

26 *sapphire-regioned star* with the phrase, 'Sapphire-regioned', compare *On Visiting the Tomb of Burns* 7 and *The Eve of St Agnes* 319, '. . . the sapphire heaven's deep repose . . .'. Probably all drawn from *Paradise Lost* IV, 604-5, '. . . now glowd the Firmament / With living Saphirs. . .'. See David Perkins, *KSJ* II, (1953), pp. 54-5. Phoebe's 'star' is the moon, whose chastity is contrasted with the evening star, Venus, who appears as Vesper in the following line.

30-35 recollects Milton's account of the death of the classical divinities in *On the Morning of Christ's Nativity* 173-80. In *M* Keats first wrote 'nor' for 'no' throughout this passage.

30 *make delicious moan* compare *La Belle Dame sans Merci* 20 and *n* (p. 639). For 'delicious' *M* has 'melodious'. The 'virgin-choir' is made up of the virgins attendant upon pagan shrines.

34-5 *no heat / Of pale-mouthed prophet dreaming* pagan priests or priestesses might be inspired to speak as the mouthpiece ('oracle') of the deity. As 'prophet' he would speak through the power of the god, and his message would be sublime ('heated'), though the speaker himself would be rapt and pale in his trance, 'dreaming' truth.

36 *brightest*] Bloomiest *M, L*.

37 *fond believing lyre* hymns sung by unquestioningly faithful worshippers. The prime sense of 'fond' is 'affectionate' or 'devoted', but the earlier meaning of 'foolish' or 'doting' is also present.

38-45 again, this recalls Milton's *On the Morning of Christ's Nativity* 184-91. See also Appendix 1 for Wordsworth's views on the creation of the pagan deities, which influenced Keats.

41 *lucent fans* bright, shining, wings.

42 *faint* compare with 'faded', l. 25.

647   NOTES FOR PP. 341-2

43 *by mine own eyes inspired*   as opposed to the 'pale-mouthed prophet' of l. 35, who was directly inspired by the deity. Keats goes on in ll. 44–9 to repeat ll. 30–35 with variations.

45] *M has a cancelled line in the margin* Thy altar heap'd with flowers.

50 *fane*   temple (poeticism).

50–62   compare the mental landscape which Keats creates for Psyche's temple with the setting for the sacrifice to Pan in *Endymion* I, 63–106. See also the passage from Adlington's *Apuleius* cited in the headnote above. Keats may have been influenced by hearing lectures on the brain's structure as a student; see C. W. Hagelman, 'Keats's Medical Training and the Last Stanza of the *Ode to Psyche*' *KSJ*, XI (1962), pp. 73–82.

54–5   compare with *Endymion* I, 85–6, '... the space of heaven above, / Edged round with dark tree tops...'. See also Keats's description of the landscape round Derwentwater, '... perpendicular Rocks, all fledged with Ash...' (*L* I, p. 306).

56–7   compare with the passage from Adlington's *Apuleius* cited in headnote above.

62–3 *With all the gardener Fancy e'er could feign, / Who breeding flowers, will never breed the same*   Fancy does not have for Keats the downgraded meaning given it by Coleridge in his distinction between Imagination and Fancy. Rather it points 'in the direction of Invention and the "marvellous" – of making and feigning' (*Jones*, pp. 165–7). The notion of Fancy as a gardener who aids and improves nature is common in Renaissance discussions of the imagination, and something of that meaning is present here. As David Perkins points out 'the word "feign" recalls the partial disillusion at the close of the *Ode to a Nightingale*: "Adieu! the fancy cannot cheat so well / As she is famed to do, deceiving elf"' (*The Quest for Permanence* [1959], p. 227). The 'flowers' will always be different because the Fancy (Imagination) always creates anew.

65 *shadowy thought*   'either musing thought that evolves obscurely or, perhaps, thought that is shadowy as the mere ghost of sensations' (*Allott*).

66–7   usually interpreted to mean that Psyche waits in the fane to welcome Cupid. For Garrod's belief that Cupid is waiting for Psyche, see headnote. *Jones*, pp. 204–7, thinks that neither reading should be wholly excluded.

ON FAME (1) ('Fame, like a wayward girl, will still be coy')

Written 30 April 1819. Published *Ladies' Companion* (New York), August 1837, *Odd Fellow*, 8 January 1842, *1848*. On 30 April in his journal-letter of 14 February–3 May 1819, Keats reports, 'Brown has been rummaging up some of my old sins – that is to say sonnets ... I have just written one on Fame' (*L* II, p. 104). The sonnet's structure is Shakespearean, unlike the other experimental sonnets written at this time (see headnotes to *To Sleep* and '*If by dull rhymes ...*', pp. 641–2). Keats's reading of Dryden influenced the subject and its treatment.

Title] *1848, G*; Another on Fame *L*; untitled, *Allott*.

648 NOTES FOR PP. 342-4

8 *scandal* defame. Used as a verb up to the seventeenth century. See Dryden, *The Flower and Leaf* (1700), 606-7, '... for Defence / Against ill Tongues that scandal Innocence'.

9 *Nilus-born* gipsies ('Egyptians') were thought to originate from that country.

10 *jealous Potiphar* Potiphar was jealous of Joseph, who had attracted the desire of his master's wife.

12 *artists lovelorn*] lovelorn artists *L, Ladies' Companion, Allott*; lovesick artists *Odd Fellow*.

ON FAME (II) ('How fevered is the man who cannot look')

Written 30 April 1819. Published *1848*. An extempore sonnet, written while Brown was transcribing the preceding poem (*L* II, p. 104). The rhyme scheme is another experiment with the sonnet structure (see headnotes to *To Sleep* and '*If by dull rhymes* ...', pp. 641, 642).
Title] *1848, G*; untitled *Allott*.

1 *How fevered is the man*] How is that Man misled *altered to* How fever'd is that Man *L*.

7-8] As if a clear Lake meddling with itself / Should cloud its pureness with a muddy gloo[m] *L. Allott* reports that in *W*2 Woodhouse commented, 'The objection to these lines was probably that "itself" was thus made to rhyme to itself [see l. 5]. But the author ... forgot that he left an allusion in the 12th line to those thus erased'.

7 *elf* see *Ode to a Nightingale* 73-4n (p. 657).

13 *teasing the world for grace*] leasing the world for grace *over* his own bright name deface *L*.

14] *L gives the cancelled line* 'And spoil burn our pleasures in his selfish fire' – The 'fierce miscreed' is the pursuit of fame.

'TWO OR THREE POSIES'

Written *c*. 1 May 1819. Published *Forman* (1883). Keats wrote the lines in his letter to Fanny, which is conjecturally assigned to this date by H. E. Rollins (*L* II, p. 56). On 'Two or three' rhymes, see *Forman* (1938-9) IV, pp. 204-5, and *KSJ*, IX (1960), p. 85.

2 *simples* plants or herbs used for medicinal purposes.

20 *Mrs —* Mrs Abbey, wife of Richard Abbey who acted as the Keats children's guardian from 1810. Relations between the guardian and his wards were uneasy.

ODE ON A GRECIAN URN

Date conjectural. Published *Annals of the Fine Arts*, XV (January 1820), *1820*. Text follows *1820*, except for one or two minor alterations in punctuation, and a substantive change of punctuation in ll. 49-50 (see note). Variants recorded from *Annals*, George Keats's transcript now in the British Museum (referred to as *BM* – it is reproduced by *Gittings*, 1970, pp. 44-9), and the transcript in *W*2. Dated '1819' (*G* in error) in Dilke's transcript (Hampstead). As *Gittings* (1970), ppl 69-70, argues, the *Ode on a Grecian Urn* was probably written after reading two articles by B. R. Haydon, which were published in the *Examiner* on 2 and 9 May, and which are echoed by Keats's poem (see l. 28*n*). This *Ode* is usually placed after the *Ode to a Nightingale*, but see headnote (p. 653) for the order adopted here.

Keats's urn is not based on any single Greek vase or urn, but is a composite drawn from several sources. A drawing of the Sosibios Vase was made by Keats from Henry Moses's *A Collection of Antique Vases, Altars, Paterae ...* (1814), but the Townley and Borghese vases may also have influenced him. Further, see *Jack*, pp. 214-24, 281-9 (Plates XXIX-XXXVII reproduce the main influences, and Plate XXX reproduces Keats's drawing), and N. Machin, 'The Case of the Empty-handed Maenad', *Observer Magazine* (Colour Supplement), 28 February 1965. However, the heifer being led to sacrifice on the South Frieze of the Elgin Marbles probably supplied details for the fourth stanza (*Jack*, p. 219), and Wedgwood's reproductions of classical motifs and forms also played a part. For the latter, see D. E. Robinson's 'Ode on a "New Etrurian Urn" (A Reflection of Wedgwood Ware in the Poetic Imagery of John Keats)', *KSJ*, XII (1963), pp. 11-35. Keats himself had earlier described a pagan sacrifice in *To J. H. Reynolds, Esq.* 20-22 (see ll. 31-40*n*) and *Endymion* I, 106-231. *De Selincourt* points out the thematic similarity between Wordsworth's sonnet *Upon the Sight of a Beautiful Picture* (1815) and Keats's *Ode*, and *Gittings* (1954), pp. 136-7, believes that Keats's reading of Burton's *Anatomy of Melancholy* gave 'hints for the main theme and much of the general philosophy'.

The *Ode*'s success or failure as a poem, and its meaning, have been much debated. Discussion has centred on the interpretation of the poem's last two lines (see ll. 49-50*n*). E. Wasserman in his *The Finer Tone* (1953) decides, 'The intention of the poem must be to hold up art as the source of the highest form of wisdom', and uses Keats's letter of 22 November 1817 (*L* I, pp. 184-6) and the passage on the 'Pleasure Thermometer' (*Endymion* I, 777 ff.) to support his view. However, *Murry* (1930), pp. 71-92, related its meaning to Keats's ideas on the 'Vale of Soul-making', written shortly before the *Ode* (*L* II, pp. 101-4, quoted in part in headnote to *Ode to Psyche*, p. 644). F. W. Bateson in *English Poetry : A Critical Introduction* (1950), pp. 217-22, discerns '... a necessity for uniting Romanticism ("beauty") and realism ("truth"), the subconscious with the conscious mind, the feeling with the concept, poetry and philosophy', while Douglas Bush argues that Keats 'cannot convince himself that love and beauty on marble are better than flesh-and-blood experience' in his 'Keats and his Ideas' in *The Major English Romantic Poets*, ed. C. D. Thorpe *et al.* (1957), p. 241. Cleanth Brooks's important essay, 'Keats's Sylvan Historian: History without Footnotes', in *The Well Wrought Urn* (1947), pp. 139-52, should be compared with the reply by William Empson in *The Structure of Complex Words* (1951), pp. 368-74. See also *Bate* (1963), pp. 510-20. An account of the major interpretations is given by *Pettet*, pp. 375-81; see also P. Hobsbaum, 'The "Philosophy" of the Grecian Urn; A Consensus of Readings', *Keats-Shelley Memorial Bulletin*, XV (1965). Several important readings are brought together in *Twentieth Century Interpretations of Keats's Odes*, ed. J. C. Stillinger (1968), and most general works on Keats contain further discussions.

Title] On a Grecian Urn *Annals*. Keats realized that the function of Grecian urns was to preserve the ashes of the dead – 'Why, I have shed / An urn of tears, as though thou wert cold-dead' (*Endymion* III, 431–2). See also *Lamia* II, 94.

1 *still unravished bride of quietness* in the *Annals* version, a comma is added after 'still', so making the word into an adjective ('motionless'). The punctuation in *1820*, etc., makes 'still' an adverb, suggesting that the bride may yet be ravished, without denying the possibility of a play on the adjectival sense. The urn is intact – unravished as a bride, or unbroken as an art object. Its virginal chastity is 'unravished' either by the infidelity of speaking, or by a marital consummation with 'quietness'.

2 *foster-child of silence and slow time* since the death of its maker (its father), the urn has been fostered by time and silence.

3 *Sylvan historian* the pictures on the urn's sides depicting a 'flowery tale' from the past make it an 'historian', both in the sense of tale-teller and recorder of the past. 'Sylvan' means 'belonging to the woods' (compare 'Pastoral', l. 45 and *n*).

8 *men or gods*] Gods or Men *Annals*. Compare 'deities or mortals' (l. 6). Keats and his contemporaries were uncertain of the meaning of the figures on Greek vases and urns.

9 *What mad pursuit?*] What love? what dance? *BM, W2, Annals*.

10 *timbrels* tambourines.

11–14 compare Wordsworth, *The Excursion* (1814) II, 710–12, 'Music of finer tone; a harmony / So do I call it, though it be the hand / Of silence, though there be no voice...'.

13 *sensual* belonging to the world of the senses.

15–30 these lines are often interpreted as showing Keats's ambivalent feelings towards the urn, since the lovers remain perpetually unsatisfied.

16 *can those trees be bare*] bid the spring adieu *Annals*.

18 *yet*] O *BM, W2, Annals*.

19–20 compare *Ode to a Nightingale* 29–30.

21, 23, 25 for the repetition of 'happy' here, compare *Ode to Psyche* 22, 'O happy, happy dove', and *Ode to a Nightingale* 5–6.

28 *All breathing human passion far above* in 1818 Hazlitt said in a lecture, 'Greek statues are marble to the touch and to the heart.... In their faultless excellence they appear sufficient to themselves. By their beauty they are raised above the frailties of passion or suffering' (*Works*, ed. P. P. Howe [1930–4] V, p. 11). B. R. Haydon, in the second of his articles on Raphael's cartoon, *The Sacrifice at Lystra*, claimed that he 'seemed to disdain to imitate creatures who are weak enough to yield to passion and took refuge from the poverty of this world's materials in ... imagining a higher order of beings and a world of his

own' (*Examiner*, 9 May 1819). For the possible influence of Haydon's articles on the poem, see J. R. MacGillivray, *TLS*, 9 July 1938, pp. 465–6.

28–30 Bate (1963), p. 514 comments '... more is being deprived the figures on the urn than is bestowed. They are now conceived negatively, through what they lack; and in only the weak final line does their lack suggest much advantage. "All breathing human passion" is a weighted phrase: "above", half ironic, loses its evaluative force and begins to connote unawareness. "Cloy'd" at least implies fulfillment. Finally a "heart high-sorrowful" is able to experience the mystery of sorrow....'

30/31 *Jack*, p. 286, thinks that the poem initially ended here.

31–40 compare with the description of a Greek sacrifice in *To J. H. Reynolds, Esq.* 20–22, 'The sacrifice goes on; the pontiff knife / Gloams in the sun, the milk-white heifer lows, / The pipes go shrilly, the libation flows...'. The 'heifer lowing at the skies' (l. 33) is probably based on a detail in the Elgin Marbles, while the passage as a whole owes a debt to Claude Lorraine's paintings, particularly perhaps his *View of Delphi with a Procession* and his *Landscape with the Father of Psyche sacrificing at the Milesian Temple of Apollo* (see *Jack*, pp. 219–22).

34 *flanks*] sides *BM*, *W*2.

37–40 *emptied ... desolate* the description of the festival of Hyacinthia in Lemprière concludes, '... all were eager to be present at the games, and the city was almost desolate, and without inhabitants'. The effect of the two words here, which can be read as suggestive of the implicit emptiness of the urn's world, may be compared with the use of 'forlorn' in *Ode to a Nightingale* 71–2, and prepares for 'Cold Pastoral' in l. 45.

41 *O Attic shape! Fair attitude!* 'Attic' means Grecian. 'Attitude' is used both with the technical sense of 'The disposition of a figure in statuary or painting; hence, the posture given to it', and 'A posture of the body proper to or implying some mental action or state' (*OED*). Compare *Specimen of an Induction to a Poem* 7. The modern meaning, 'habitual mode of regarding anything', developed only in the mid-nineteenth century.

41–2 *with brede* / *Of marble men and maidens overwrought* on the force of 'marble', see l. 28n. 'Brede' puns on 'breed' and 'brede', a variant spelling of braid, used as a poeticism for anything interwoven or plaited. Collins's *Ode to Evening* (1747), 7, has, 'With brede etherial wove...'. The reference is to the figures depicted moving round the urn. 'Overwrought' means fashioned over the surface of the urn, but it could also mean at this period, 'Exhausted by overwork; worked up to too high a pitch; over-excited' (*OED*). According to the *OED*, the modern sense, 'Elaborated to excess; over-laboured', was not used until 1839.

42 *maidens overwrought*] maidens, overwrought *BM*, *W*2.

44 *tease us out of thought* two, not necessarily exclusive, readings are possible: either, defeats our attempts to reason, or, raises us beyond merely intellectual speculation to an intuitive level. Keats had earlier used the phrase in *To J. H. Reynolds, Esq.* 77. In the *Ode to a Nightingale* 34 it is the 'dull brain' that 'perplexes and retards', and in the *Ode to Psyche* the poet sees the vision as he wanders 'thoughtlessly' (l. 7).

45 *Cold Pastoral* the urn is immortal, but also cold and inhuman. Compare Keats's use of 'cold Beauty' in *On Visiting the Tomb of Burns* 8. As a noun, 'pastoral' refers to the genre portraying the life of shepherds.

47 *shalt*] wilt *BM, W2, Annals*.

48 *a*] as *BM, W2*.

49–50] Beauty is truth, – Truth Beauty, – that is all / Ye know on Earth, and all ye need to know. *BM, W2*; Beauty is Truth, Truth Beauty. – That is all / Ye know on Earth, and all ye need to know. *Annals*; 'Beauty is truth, truth beauty,' – that is all / Ye know on earth, and all ye need to know. *1820, Garrod (OSA), Allott; G follows 1820, but omits the inverted commas.* This is a much debated crux. The problem is who speaks the last lines. Unfortunately, no autograph MS exists for this poem, though Keats saw the *1820* volume through the press, which gives it some priority. The following interpretations are possible:

1 both lines are spoken by the urn, and addressed to man
2 the lines are spoken by the poet to the urn
3 the lines are spoken by the poet to the figures on the urn
4 'Beauty is truth, truth beauty' is spoken by the urn, and the remainder is the poet speaking to his readers
5 the motto, as in preceding reading, is spoken by the urn, but the poet then addresses the urn, not mankind.

Critics have argued for all these possibilities, and the lack of any definitive evidence means that the punctuation adopted must depend upon the reader's sense of the whole poem. However, it should be pointed out that in ll. 44–8 Keats identifies himself with mankind ('us', 'ours'), while the last two lines switch to 'Ye', and so address mankind, which makes 1 seem the more likely meaning, and I have punctuated the *1820* text accordingly. (The inverted commas round the motto in *1820* emphasize its aphoristic quality, suggesting that it is in an inscription on the urn itself – it is possible that *1820* avoided enclosing both lines in inverted commas because the resultant '"..."..."' would have been ungainly. For Keats's use of quotation, compare *To Charles Cowden Clarke* 100.) Further, see A. Whitley, 'The Message of the Grecian Urn', *Keats-Shelley Memorial Bulletin*, V (1953), pp. 1–3, and *Stillinger*, pp. 167–73. The reading adopted here means that Keats does not necessarily identify himself with the urn's message.

Many parallels for the Beauty–Truth formulation have been cited, ranging from Plato to Boileau's 'Rien n'est beau que le vrai' (*Épître* IX, 43), to Shaftesbury's '*all* Beauty is TRUTH' (*Sensus Communis* IV iii). The relationship between the two terms was, however, a widespread topic in the eighteenth century, and was a common Romantic concern. In November 1817 Keats had written, 'What the Imagination seizes as Beauty must be truth – whether it existed before or not' (*L* I, p. 184), and in October 1818 he spoke of '... the yearning Passion I have for the beautiful, connected and made one with the ambition of my intellect' (*L* I, p. 404). It is connected with his idea that 'the excellence of every Art is its intensity, capable of making all disagreeables evaporate, from their being in close relationship with Beauty & Truth...' (*L* I, p. 192). The final lines are seen by some critics as a blemish because grammatically meaningless (T. S. Eliot), as irrelevant (Murry), as a strained attempt to resolve the tensions in the poem; or as an appropriate dramatization of the urn's view of things (Cleanth Brooks).

ODE TO A NIGHTINGALE

Dated 'May 1819' in *W*1–2, but exact date conjectural. Normally placed before the *Ode on a Grecian Urn*. The main evidence for the conventional dating early in May is twofold. Metrically the *Ode to a Nightingale* (with the shorter eighth line) stands between the *Ode to Psyche* and the *Ode on a Grecian Urn* (which has a long eighth line, like the two later odes). Secondly, the parallels between the second stanza and Keats's letter to Fanny of 1(?) May 1819 (see ll. 11–13*n*) argue for a date *c*. 1 May. However, there are other parallels with much earlier letters in the poem (see l. 69*n*). The fifth stanza, with its reference to 'mid-May's eldest child' (l. 48) and to the hawthorn, etc. (see ll. 44–50*n*), suggests the poem was written in the middle of the month. Hence, it is given here after the *Ode on a Grecian Urn* (possibly written *c*. 9 May, see headnote p. 648). *Ward* (1963), pp. 283, 433, also argues for the later dating.

Published *Annals of the Fine Arts*, July 1819, *1820*. Some variants are noted from Keats's draft, now in the Fitzwilliam Museum, Cambridge (*C*), and *Annals*. The draft MS is reproduced in *Gittings* (1970), pp. 36–43.

Twenty years after the event, Charles Brown recalled the poem's composition: 'In the spring of 1819 a nightingale had built her nest in my house. Keats felt a tranquil and continual joy in her song; and one morning he took a chair from the breakfast-table to the grass-plot under a plum-tree, where he sat for two or three hours. When he came into the house, I perceived he had some scraps of paper in his hand, and these he was quietly thrusting behind the books. On inquiry, I found those scraps, four or five in number, containing his poetic feeling on the song of our nightingale. The writing was not well legible; and it was difficult to arrange the stanzas on so many scraps. With his assistance I succeeded, and this was his "Ode to a Nightingale", a poem which has been the delight of every one' (*KC* II, p. 65). Brown's story has been called into doubt because Keats's draft (*C*) is written on two sheets of paper only. *Gittings* (1970), p. 65, thinks that Brown conflated his memories of the poem's composition with Keats's later struggle with the MS of the *Ode on Indolence*. The spring of 1819 was unusually warm (see ll. 44–50*n*), and Keats's moods were always influenced by the weather – see, for instance, his reaction against the cold summer of Scotland in *On Visiting the Tomb of Burns*. On 1(?) May he wrote to Fanny, 'O there is nothing like fine weather...' (*L* II, p. 56).

Although the nightingale is a common subject for Romantic poetry, Keats probably recalled Coleridge's *To the Nightingale* (1796) and *The Nightingale: A Conversation Poem* (1798), and in his conversation with Coleridge on 11 April 1819 the older man had '... broached a thousand things ... Nightingales, – Poetry – on Poetical sensation – Metaphysics – Different genera and species of Dreams – Nightmares – a dream accompanied by a sense of touch – single and double touch...' (*L* II, pp. 88–9). Keats had also attended Hazlitt's lectures on English poetry, and may have remembered his remarks about the cuckoo – 'The cuckoo, "that wandering voice", that comes and goes with the spring, mocks our ears with one note from youth to age; and the lap-wing, screaming round the traveller's path, repeats for ever the same sad story of Tereu and Philomel!' (*Works*, ed. P. P. Howe [1930–34] V, pp. 103–4). The poem also has signs of a recent re-reading of Wordsworth. For Keats's earlier imaginative response to the nightingale's song, see the cancelled readings in *Endymion* I, 494–5*n* and 665–6*n* (pp. 565, 567).

Like many of the greatest Romantic odes, Keats's poem explores the nature and limits of artistic creation, setting the suffering of mankind against the immortality of the bird's song. It also takes up the Keatsian concern with the paradoxical association of pleasure and pain. Earlier critics saw the poem as an endorsement of the beauty of art as contrasted with the transience of mortal experience, but later writers have been sharply aware of the tensions within the poem. H. W. Garrod has remarked that the nightingale begins as a particular bird, but is imaginatively transformed into a myth in the course of the poem (*Keats* [1926], pp. 113–14). J. Spens examines the influence of Hazlitt and Wordsworth, in *RES*, III (1952), pp. 234–43, and *Ridley*, pp. 218–31, analyses its relationship with Keats's earlier work. F. R. Leavis gives a valuable discussion of the poem in *Revaluation* (1936), pp. 244–52, and Cleanth Brooks has defined the theme of the poem as the 'following paradox: the world of the imagination offers a release from the painful world of actuality, yet at the same time it renders the world of actuality more painful by contrast' (*Modern Poetry and the Tradition* [1939], p. 31): see also the discussion of the poem in his joint volume with R. P. Warren, *Understanding Poetry* (1960) pp. 426–30. Marshall McLuhan discusses the poem's musical organization in 'Aesthetic Pattern in Keats's Odes', *University of Toronto Quarterly*, XII (1943), pp. 167–79, and G. Wilson Knight has a discerning study in *The Starlit Dome* (1941), pp. 258–307. See further, Allen Tate, 'A Reading of Keats' in *The Man of Letters in the Modern World* (1955), pp. 193–210, R. H. Fogle, 'Keats's *Ode to a Nightingale*', *PMLA*, LXVII (1953,) pp. 211–22, Pettet, pp. 251–81, David Perkins, *The Quest for Permanence* (1959), pp. 244–57, and *Bate* (1963), pp. 500–509. Most general works on Keats contain a discussion of the poem, and K. M. Wilson's *The Nightingale and the Hawk* (1964) gives a basically Jungian interpretation of Keats's work, focusing on the *Ode*.

Title] Ode to the Nightingale *C*, *Annals*. The nightingale starts singing in England in mid-April.

1–4 probably echoes Horace's *Epode* XIV, 1–4, *Mollis inertia cur tantam diffuderit imis | oblivionem sensibus, | pocula Lethaeos ut si ducentia somnos | arente fauce traxerim* ... ('... why soft indolence has diffused as great forgetfulness over my inmost senses as if with parched throat I had drained the bowl that brings Lethean sleep ...').

NOTES FOR P. 346

1 *drowsy numbness pains*] painful numbness falls *C* (*cancelled*). The words 'Small winged Dryad' which occur upside-down at the bottom of the second page of *C* probably represent a false start. The relationship between 'drowsy numbness' and creative insight is common in Keats (see J. Holloway, *The Charted Mirror* [1960], pp. 40–52).

2 *hemlock* a plant which produces a powerful sedative, and from which it is also possible to produce a poison.

4 *past*] hence *C* (*cancelled*). 'Lethe-wards' recalls that souls waiting in Hades to be reborn drink the waters of Lethe in order to forget their past existence.

7 *light-wingèd Dryad* see l. 1*n* for a variant of this phrase which seems to be Keats's first attempt to begin the poem.

11–13 compare with Keats's remarks in his letter to Fanny on 1(?) May 1819, '... and, please heaven, a little claret-wine out of a cellar a mile deep ... a rocky basin to bathe in, a strawberry bed to say your prayers to Flora in ...' (*L* II, p. 56). See also '*Hence Burgundy, Claret and Port*' 1–2*n* (p. 590).

11 *vintage* wine.

12 *Cooled a long age*] Cooling an age *C* (*cancelled*).

14 *Provençal song, and sunburnt mirth* the festivities at the grape-harvest. Provence was also the home of the medieval troubadours.

15 *warm South* wine from the Mediterranean.

16 *the true, the blushful Hippocrene* a periphrasis for wine. 'Hippocrene' is 'a fountain of Boeotia, near mount Helicon, sacred to the muses' (*Lemprière*), and hence the fountain of inspiration. Keats may be playing on the difference between 'blushful' (red) wine and the colourlessness of water, but *Baldwin*, p. 49, says, '... the waters of [Hippocrene] were violet-coloured, and are represented as endowed with voice and articulate sound'.

17 *beaded*] clustered *C*. Altered when Keats decided to use the word at l. 37.

17–18 compare *Endymion* II, 441–4.

19 *leave the world unseen* unseen by mankind, and (as a secondary meaning) not seeing the world.

20 *away*] *not in Annals* (presumably omitted to avoid a twelve syllable line).

21 *dissolve* 'to release from life ... to die, depart' (*OED*, which gives the last instance of the usage as 1736), but also with the idea of melting, which was a current meaning (compare *Endymion* I, 98–100). See also *Paradise Lost* VIII, 291.

25–6 *palsy ... youth* although not capitalized, *Allott* regards these as personifications.

26 *pale, and spectre-thin, and dies* pale and thin, and old and dies *C* (*cancelled*). Usually seen as a reference to Tom Keats, who died of tuberculosis 1 December 1818. Compare Keats's remark to Fanny on 12 April 1819, '... any place very confined would soon turn me pale and thin ...' (*L* II, p. 52), and Wordsworth's *The Excursion* IV, 760, 'While man grows old, and dwindles, and decays. ...'.

27 *sorrow*] grief *C* (*cancelled*).

656 NOTES FOR PP. 346-7

27-9 compare Keats to Bailey on 21 May 1818, 'I have this morning such a Lethargy that I cannot write ... my hand feels like lead – and yet it is an unpleasant numbness it does not take away the pain of existence. ...' (*L* I, p. 287).

29-30 compare *Ode on Melancholy* 21-3.

31 *to thee*] with thee *C* (*cancelled*).

32 *Bacchus and his pards* 'pards' are leopards. For Bacchus' rout, see entry under 'Bacchus' in *Dictionary of Classical Names* (p. 701).

33 *viewless* invisible (and may also suggest that the flight of 'Poesy' is so high as to make the world invisible).

36 *haply* by chance, perhaps. With 'Queen-Moon', compare Coleridge's *To the Nightingale* (1796) 7-8, 'How many wretched Bards address *thy* name, / And hers, the full orb'd Queen that shines above.' In l. 16 Coleridge refers to the nightingale as 'Minstrel of the Moon'.

37 *Clustered* see l. 17*n*. 'Fays' are fairies.

38-50 compare with Coleridge's *The Nightingale: A Conversation Poem* (1798) 4-11, 26, 52-7.

40 *Through verdurous*] Sidelong *C* (*cancelled*).

42 *soft incense*] blooms *C* (*cancelled*). For an early use of 'incense' to mean scent, see *Calidore* 155 and *n* (p. 542).

43 *embalmèd darkness* the night is full of the scent of flowers. 'Embalmed' also anticipates the concern with death in ll. 51-60.

44-50 the 'seasonable month' is May. On 3 May Keats wrote, '... every thing is in delightful forwardness; the violets are not withered, before the peeping of the first rose ...' (*L* II, p. 109). Since the violets are 'Fast-fading' in l. 47, I take it that the description refers to mid-May 1819. Hawthorn's white flowers come out in May, and the musk-rose (*rosa moschata*) does not flower until June (and is, therefore, 'mid-May's eldest [most forward] child'). For Keats's liking for the musk-rose, see *To a Friend who Sent me some Roses* 5-6 and 6*n* (p. 543). The 'eglantine' is the sweet-briar (see *Endymion* IV, 697*n*).

49 *dewy*] sweetest *C*, *Annals*.

51 *Darkling* in the dark (compare 'darkling way' in *The Eve of St Agnes* 355). Compare *Paradise Lost* III, 37-40, 'Then feed on thoughts, that voluntarie move / Harmonious numbers; as the wakeful Bird / Sings darkling, and in shadiest Covert hid / Tunes her nocturnal Note. . .'.

52 *half in love* only one aspect of Keats's feelings are involved. In the next stanza he revolts against the idea of death.

54 *quiet*] painless *C*.

55 *rich to die* compare 'some rich anger', *Ode on Melancholy* 18.

56 *To cease upon the midnight* compare '*Why did I laugh tonight?* ...' 11.

57 *forth*] thus *C*, *Annals*.

59 *wouldst*] would *C*.

60 *To thy high requiem become a sod* Keats first wrote 'For' instead of 'To', and his first attempt at the line was 'But requiem'd ' . .' (*C*). The poem will become part of the earth through his death, while the nightingale's continuing song is transformed into a mass for the dead.

61 *immortal Bird* immortal because its song is unaltered from age to age. The line has been attacked as nonsense, most notably by Robert Bridges (*The Poems of John Keats*, ed G. Thorn-Drury [1896], p. lxiv).

62 compare Wordsworth, *The Excursion* IV, 761-2, 'And countless generations of mankind / Depart; and leave no vestige where they trod ...' See l. 26n for an echo of Wordsworth's preceding line.

64 *clown* countryman, peasant.

66-7 *sad heart of Ruth ... alien corn* Ruth, a Moabitess, accompanied her mother-in-law, Naomi, to Bethlehem. There, in an alien country, she became a gleaner in the fields of Boaz (Ruth ii 1-3).

69 *magic casements*] wide casements *C* (*cancelled*). Compare with 'The windows as if latched by fays and elves', *To J. H. Reynolds, Esq.* 50, and the references to windows in Keats's letters – 'I should like the window to open onto the Lake of Geneva ...' (*L* II, p. 46; see also *L* I, p. 403).

70 *perilous*] keelless [?] *or* ruthless [?] *C* (*cancelled*). The cancelled word is illegible. See further, Ridley, pp. 229-30, N. Ford, *KSJ*, I (1952), pp. 11-12, and Gittings (1970), pp. 40-41, 67.

70, 71 *forlorn* 'in the first instance, "forlorn" is being used primarily in its archaic sense of "utterly lost". The faery lands are those of a past which is remote and far away. But the meaning of "forlorn" is definitely shifted as the poet repeats the word ... its meaning "pitiable; left desolate" ... describes the poet's own state' (Cleanth Brooks, *Modern Poetry and the Tradition* [1939], p. 31).

71-2 *bell ... toll* the image of a church-bell tolling for a funeral continues the religious imagery of 'high requiem' (l. 60) and is continued by 'plaintive anthem' in l. 75.

72 *to my sole self*] unto myself *C*. 'Sole' means solitary, lonely, with probably some suggestion of the meaning, exclusive of all others.

73-4 *the fancy ... deceiving elf* interpreted by *Allott* as meaning 'Fancy is like a will-o'-the-wisp', as in *Endymion* II, 277-9. But 'elf' has several meanings in Keats (see *Endymion* II, 277n, 461n, pp. 572, 573), and here is feminine in gender and means 'faery'. In 1819 the word is usually connected in Keats's mind with the ambiguously attractive or frightening, as in the 'elfin-storm from faery land, / Of haggard seeming, but a boon indeed' (*The Eve of St Agnes* 343-4), or the 'elfin grot' of *La Belle Dame sans Merci* 29. Lamia is described as being like 'some penanced lady elf' (see *Lamia* I, 55 and *n*, p. 668), and as having 'elfin blood' (I, 147). The 'meddling elf' of *On Fame II* ('How fevered is the man ...') 7 is, however, an instance of Keats using the traditional meaning, a mischievous and diminutive spirit. Keats's phrasing has been sharply attacked by Robert Bridges in *The Poems of John Keats*, ed. G. Thorn-Drury (1896), p. lxiv, and by Kingsley Amis in 'The Curious Elf, A Note on Rhyme in Keats', *Essays in Criticism*, I (1951), p. 191, who comments, in a discussion of Keats's 'weakness in handling rhyme', 'After the climax of the preceding stanza, and the vigour of the first two lines of this one,

658 NOTES FOR P. 348

the elf's appearance here is doubly unwelcome ... it [has] nothing to add in precision, it even hinders the reader from grasping how "the fancy" appears in the poet's imagination.'

74 *famed*] *above* fam'd *W*2 *has* feigned J.H.R. *C could be read either as* fam'd *or* fain'd. (See *Jones*, pp. 165-8, for an interesting discussion of Reynolds's 'feigned'.)

75 *plaintive anthem* see l. 71-2n.

77-8 *buried deep | In the next valley-glades* compare with Keats's description of Ambleside water-fall, '... it is buried in trees, in the bottom of the valley ...' (*L* I, p. 300).

79 *vision, or a*] vision real or *C*; vision? or a *Annals*. Compare *Ode to Psyche* 5-6. With the phrase 'waking dream' compare Wordsworth, *Yarrow Visited* (1814), 3, 'a waking dream', *Immortality Ode* (1807) 56-7, 'Whither is fled the visionary gleam? / Where is it now, the glory and the dream?', *The Excursion* (1814) II, 833, 'By waking sense or by the dreaming soul'; *The Merry Wives of Windsor* III. 5. 123-4, 'Hum! ha! Is this a vision? Is this a dream? Do I sleep?'; Hazlitt, 'On Chaucer and Spenser' (1818), 'Spenser was the poet of our waking dreams ... lulling the senses into a deep oblivion of the jarring noises of the world, from which we have no wish to be ever recalled' (*Works*, ed. P. P. Howe [1930-4] V, p. 44).

80 *Do I wake or sleep?* is reality the ecstatic world of the nightingale's song, or the everyday world he has 'awakened' to?

ODE ON MELANCHOLY

Date of composition conjectural, but probably May 1819. The theme is related to that of the *Ode to a Nightingale* and the *Ode on a Grecian Urn*, and the echoes of Burton's *Anatomy* also connect it with this period. Published *1820*. Keats's draft (referred to as *K*) is reproduced by *Gittings* (1970), pp. 60-63, and the two leaves are now divided between R. H. Taylor of Princeton and the Berg Collection in the New York Public Library. The poem explores the relationship between melancholy and delight, beauty and transience. It has often been regarded as inferior to the preceding odes, and the first stanza thought to suffer from macabre extravagance (see Douglas Bush, *John Keats* [1966], pp. 144-8). For Keats's cancelled first stanza, which dwelt more emphatically on the macabre, see l. 1n. Discussions of the poem's richness and complexity can be found in William Empson's *Seven Types of Ambiguity* (1947 edn), pp. 214-17, *Bate* (1963), pp. 520-24, Harold Bloom's *The Visionary Company* (1961), pp. 403-6, and in Robin Mayhead's commentary in *John Keats* (1967), pp. 58-65.

1 *No, no, go not to Lethe*] a modulation from the cancelled first stanza preserved in *W*2 (printed in *1848* with 'shrouds' for 'creeds' in l. 3): 'Though you should build a bark of dead men's bones, / And rear a phantom gibbet for a mast, / Stitch creeds together for a sail, with groans / To fill it out, bloodstained and aghast; / Although your rudder be a dragon's tail / Long sever'd, yet still hard with agony, / Your cordage large uprootings from the skull / Of bald Medusa, certes you would fail / To find the Melancholy – whether she / Dreameth in any isle of Lethe dull.' Unlike most critics, who find the stanza strained, Harold Bloom comments, 'The "whether" in the ninth line may be read as "even if ".This remarkable and grisly stanza is more than the reverse of an invitation to the voyage. Its irony is palpable; its humour is in the enormous labor of Gothicizing despair which is necessarily in vain, for the mythic beast, Melancholy, cannot thus be confronted. The tone of the stanza changes with the dash in line 9; with it the voice speaking the poem ceases to be ironical ... By excluding the original first stanza, Keats lost a grim humour that finds only a thin echo at the poem's close. That humour, in juxtaposition to the poem's intensities, would have been parallel to successful clowning in a tragedy' (*The Visionary Company* [1961], pp. 403-4).

2 *Wolf's-bane*] Hensb[ane] *K* (*cancelled*). 'Hensbane', like wolf-bane (aconite), is a poisonous plant.

4-5 *nightshade, ruby grape of Proserpine ... rosary of yew-berries* Deadly Nightshade is a poisonous plant with bright red berries, and hence is the 'ruby grape' of Proserpine, Queen of the Underworld. The yew-tree also has small red berries which are poisonous.

6 *beetle* death-watch beetle.

6-7 *nor the death-moth be / Your mournful Psyche* the Death's Head moth is a large species of hawk-moth, having marks on the back of the thorax resembling a human skull. As Psyche (the soul) was represented as a moth or butterfly (see *Ode to Psyche* headnotes, p. 643), the sense is ironical – 'do not let the Death's Head moth become the antitype of Psyche ("Your mournful [as opposed to joyous] Psyche")'.

8 *sorrow's mysteries* Melancholy is regarded, throughout the poem, as a Goddess to whom proper observances are due. In the final stanza, Melancholy has a 'shrine' in the 'temple of Delight' with its 'trophies' (see l. 30*n*). The 'wine' of ll. 1-2, the wreath of ll. 3-4, the 'rosary' of l. 5, and 'sorrow's mysteries' are all associated with the rites of worship, though mixing Christian and pagan aids to devotion.

9 *shade to shade* plays on 'shade' (shadow) and 'shade' (spirit, ghost).

9 *drowsily*] heavily *and* sleepily *K* (*cancelled*).

11-14 these lines develop the paradox that though Melancholy produces showers of tears, the tears are, like April showers, the bringer of new and fresh life.

11 *fall*] come *K* (*cancelled*).

14 *hill*] hills *K* (*and all transcripts*). The singular in *1820* is possibly a misprint which slipped Keats's attention, but in context its particularity is effective.

15 *glut ... on* 'take one's fill of thinking, gazing, etc., on something' (*OED*). Compare Thomas Carew's *Separation of Lovers* (1639), 13-14. 'Love doth with an hungry eye / Glut on beauty...'. Probably also with some suggestion of the sense, 'To gratify to the full (... esp. a ferocious or lustful desire)' (*OED*). See further, *On the Sea* 3*n* (p. 558).

18-20 *Gittings* (1970), p. 79, comments that these lines '... have been accused of masochism, sadism ... and, what is perhaps worse, of painting a rather silly and "Cockney" picture of the young poet flirtatiously holding on to his girl-friend's wrists while she struggles to get away'. The lines can be compared to *Lamia* II, 73–6. However, *K* has 'Mistress' and the 'She' of l. 21 must refer to Melancholy: as Robin Mayhead observes, 'The "mistress" may thus be regarded as either a "real" woman, a personification of melancholy, or both' (*John Keats* [1967], p. 64).

21   *She dwells with Beauty*] She lives in Beauty *K*.

23–6   compare Burton's *Anatomy of Melancholy* I 2 iii 5, '... in the Calends of January Angerona [identified with Melancholy, II 1 iii] had her holy day, to whom in the Temple of Volupia, or Goddess of Pleasure, their Augurs and Bishops did yearly sacrifice' (1813 edn I, p. 141). Compare also Hazlitt's 'On Poetry in General', where he remarks, 'The poetical impression of any subject is that uneasy, exquisite sense of beauty or power that ... strives ... to enshrine itself ... in the highest forms of fancy, and to relieve the aching sense of pleasure by expressing it in the boldest manner' (*Works*, ed. P. P. Howe [1930–34] V, p. 3).

24   compare *Isabella* 103–4, 'Even bees, the little almsmen of spring-bowers, / Know there is richest juice in poison-flowers.'

27   *him*] those *K* (*cancelled*).

29   *sadness*] anguish *K*.

30   *cloudy trophies*   trophies of victory were displayed in classical temples. Keats could also be thinking of the battle honours displayed in many English churches and cathedrals. Compare also Shakespeare, *Sonnet* xxxi 9–10, 'Thou art the grave where buried love doth live, / Hung with the trophies of my lovers gone...'.

ODE ON INDOLENCE

Probably written late May or early June 1819. Published *1848*, which forms the basis of the text with some variants adopted from *W2*. Charles Brown's transcript has the stanzas in a different order (1, 2, 4, 6, 3, 5) but with the stanza numbers altered to correspond with *W2*'s order. *W2*'s order (1, 2, 3, 4, 5, 6) was adopted in *1848*, though R. M. Milnes based his text on Brown's transcript. Like *Allott*, the order followed here is that of *W2* and *1848*. *G* constructed a fresh order (1, 2, 5, 3, 4, 6), which has no obvious advantages. (*Allott* gives the order in Brown's transcript as 1, 2, 5, 6, 4, 3, but this seems to be a misunderstanding of Garrod's notes in *G* and *OSA*.)

The date of the poem's composition is suggested by Keats's letter of 9 June to Sarah Jeffrey: 'I have been very idle lately, very averse to writing; both from the overpowering idea of our dead poets and from abatement of my own love of fame. I hope I am a little more of a Philosopher than I was, consequently a little less of a versifying Pet-lamb [compare ll. 53–4].... You will judge of my 1819 temper when I tell you that the thing I have most enjoyed this year has been writing an ode to Indolence' (*L* II, p. 116). A letter from George on 12 May had forced Keats to take stock of his situation, and he thought for a while of looking for a post as surgeon on a ship. Poetry was bringing neither money nor fame, and financial security was essential before he could marry Fanny

661 NOTES FOR PP. 349-51

Brawne. On 31 May he wrote, 'Yes, I would rather conquer my indolence and strain my ne[r]ves at some grand Poem – than be in a dunderheaded indiaman [a ship of the East Indian Company]' (*L* II, p. 113). The *Ode on Indolence* is the only ode concerned with the poet himself, rather than something exterior, and the figures on the urn, Fame, Love and Poesy, which are rejected in favour of Indolence, are a direct reflection of his personal crisis. Keats had been sorting out his affairs, and apparently going over his papers. He came across a passage written on 19 March, which provided the basis of the *Ode* – 'In this state of effeminacy the fibres of the brain are relaxed in common with the rest of the body, and to such a happy degree that pleasure has no show of enticement and pain no unbearable frown. Neither Poetry, nor Ambition, nor Love have any alertness of countenance as they pass by me: they seem rather like three figures on a greek vase – a Man and two women – whom no one but myself could distinguish in their disguisement. This is the only happiness; and is a rare instance of advantage in the body overpowering the Mind' (*L* II, pp. 78-9). The *Ode* rehandles and echoes ideas and lines used earlier in the *Ode to Psyche*, the *Ode on a Grecian Urn*, the *Ode to a Nightingale*, and the two sonnets *On Fame* (see notes below). For discussions of the *Ode*, generally considered markedly inferior to the major odes, see *Gittings* (1954), pp. 143-6, Harold Bloom's *The Visionary Company* (1961), pp. 410-11, and *Bate* (1963), pp. 527-30.

Motto 'Consider the lilies of the field, how they grow; they toil not, neither do they spin', Matthew vi 28.

9 *betide* happen to, befall (poeticism).
10 *Phidian* Phidias (c. 490–c. 448 B.C.), sculptor of the Periclean age, responsible, among many other works, for the Elgin Marbles.
12 *masque*] mask *1848*, Garrod (*OSA*).
20 compare Keats's comment on 17 March, 'I do not know what I did on monday – nothing – nothing – nothing – I wish this was any thing extraordinary' (*L* II, p. 77).
21-2 possibly echoes the witches' prophecy in *Macbeth* IV. 1. Further, see l. 34*n*.
33 *Ambition –*] *W*2, *G*, *Allott*; Ambition! *1848*.
33-4 compare with *On Fame* (I) and (II).
34 *man's little heart's short fever-fit* echoes *Macbeth* III. 2. 23, 'After life's fitful fever he sleeps well...'. This, together with the possible echo in ll. 21-2 above, may indicate that Keats was thinking of Ambition, Love and Poesy as his equivalent of the three witches who tempt Macbeth to damnation. The line also recalls *Ode to a Nightingale* 23-4.
38 *annoy* pain, harm (Spenser).
41 *A third time*] *W*2, *G*, *Allott*; And once more *1848*. The alteration avoids the repetition of the opening words of l. 21 above. But this line, with its 'alas! wherefore?', refers to something that has already happened.
43-6 compare *Ode on Melancholy* 12-14.
47-8 compare *Ode to Psyche* 66-7.
52 compare *Ode to Psyche* 15.

53-4 *dieted with praise | A pet-lamb in a sentimental farce* the idea is repeated in Keats's letter to Sarah Jeffrey cited in the headnote. It reflects Keats's attempted unconcern with what reviewers wrote. His meaning is, 'The praise reviewers give is worthless, it is like the sentimentality of caressing a lamb (which is in any case harmless)'. Compare with Keats's views of 8 October 1818, 'Praise or blame has but a momentary effect on the man whose love of beauty in the abstract makes him a severe critic of his own Works. My own domestic criticism has given me pain without comparison beyond what Blackwood or the Quarterly could possibly inflict' (*L* I, pp. 373-4).

59 *my idle sprite* Keats has used the phrase earlier in *A Dream* ... 3.

OTHO THE GREAT. A TRAGEDY IN FIVE ACTS

Written between July and 23 August 1819, in collaboration with Charles Brown. Published *1848*. Text (unlike *G*) from Brown's revised fair copy (now in Harvard College Library); see *Texts*, pp. 250-4. Keats's autograph is now divided between several American libraries; see *G*, pp. xliii-vi, and *Allott*, Appendix C. Keats had started the play before Brown's arrival in Shanklin, Isle of Wight, and the two men left for Winchester on 12 August. Brown later recorded, 'I engaged to furnish him with the fable, characters, and dramatic conduct of a tragedy, and he was to embody it into poetry. The progress of this work was curious; for, while I sat opposite to him, he caught my description of each scene, entered into the characters to be brought forward, the events, and every thing connected with it. Thus he went on, scene after scene, never knowing nor inquiring into the scene which was to follow, until four acts were completed. It was then he required to know, at once, all the events which were to occupy the fifth act. I explained them to him; but, after a patient hearing, and some thought, he insisted on it that my incidents were too numerous, and, as he termed them, too melodramatic. He wrote the fifth act in accordance with his own view' (*KC* II, p. 66). Brown sent the completed tragedy to Drury Lane, where Charles Kean expressed an interest in the lead, though the play was turned down both there and at Covent Garden. Its first performance was given on 26 November 1950 at St Martin's Theatre, London.

Keats regarded *Otho the Great* as Brown's 'child', his role being that of 'Midwife' (*L* II, p. 157). His references to the play display a degree of flippancy. He wrote to Dilke on 31 July, 'Brown and I are pretty well harnessed again to our dog-cart. I mean the Tragedy which goes on sinkingly ...' (*L* II, p. 135), and on 5 August he said to Fanny Brawne, '... I leave this minute a scene in our Tragedy and see you ... through the mist of Plots speeches counterplots and counterspeeches – The Lover [Ludolph] is madder than I am – I am nothing to him ...' (*L* II, p. 137). Keats's reasons for writing the tragedy, which interrupted the composition of *Lamia* and *The Fall of Hyperion*, were mixed. It was a first step towards attempting a play of his own; on 14 August he wrote to Bailey, 'It was the opinion of most of my friends that I should never be able to write a scene – I will endeavour to wipe away the prejudice.... One of my Ambitions is to make as great a revolution in modern dramatic writing as Kean has done in acting' (*L* II, p. 139). He also needed a financial success – 'My name with the literary fashionables is vulgar ... a Tragedy would lift me out of this mess. And mess it is as far as regards our Pockets ...' (*L* II, p. 186). The money which Brown had lent Keats was apparently meant to be repaid from any profits the play might bring in, and, as a friend, Keats felt obliged to help with a scheme which Brown believed would be successful. Their hopes were not unreasonable. Brown had contacts in the theatres, the tragedy was intended as a vehicle for Kean, and Brown's comic opera, *Narensky*, had been put on at Drury Lane in 1814, and earned £300. Unfortunately, the two theatres were losing money, taste was changing, and unknown to Keats or Brown until after the play was written, Kean was planning a tour of America.

Otho the Great deals with the Hungarian uprisings of AD 953–4, in which Ludolf and his brother-in-law, Conrad, Duke of Franconia, unsuccessfully tried to overthrow Otto I (AD 936–73). It is conventional Romantic historical melodrama, strongly influenced by Keats's reading of Elizabethan drama. For discussions of the tragedy, see G. Wilson Knight's *The Starlit Dome* (1943), pp. 306–7, Bernice Slote's *Keats and the Dramatic Principle* (1958), pp. 104–20, and *Bate* (1963), pp. 562–8.

I. 1. 5   *furled*] struck *autograph MS*, Allott.

I. 1. 6   *glide ... saved*] sail ... safe *autograph MS*, Allott.

I. 1. 9   *petards*   small engines of war used to blow in a door or a gate, or to make a breach in a fortification (*OED*).

I. 1. 13   *rich*] sweet *autograph MS*, Allott.

I. 1. 16   *Auranthe*   an invented character.

I. 1. 41   *Now*] How *autograph MS, G,* Allott.

I. 1. 81   *ratio*] ration *1848*, Garrod (*OSA*), Allott.

I. 2. 6   *illustrious*] imperial *autograph MS, G*.

I. 2. 51   *Monarch*] Caesar *autograph MS, G.* Otto I was a Roman Emperor.

I. 2. 55   *rhomb*   a formation of troops disposed in a lozenge shape.

I. 2. 59   *Saladin*   an anachronism. Saladin (1137–93), the Saracen ruler of Syria and Egypt, recently presented by Scott as a chivalric and noble figure.

I. 2. 81   *no*] *MSS, G,* Allott *give four exclamations of* no; *1848 three.*

I. 2. 85   *Gersa*   Géza, first King of Hungary (AD 971–97), who did not actually meet Otto, but made peace in 972.

I. 2. 88   ] Slow in the demure proudness of despair *autograph MS, G,* Allott.

I. 2. 137   *Otho*] Caesar *autograph MS, G*.

I. 2. 172   *cates*] cakes *1848*. 'Cates' is an Elizabethan word meaning 'dainties'.

I. 2. 175   *basement*   base, foundation.

I. 3. 66   *housings*   a cloth covering put on a horse for defence or ornament.

II. 1. 56   *a tight leech*] Sigifred *autograph MS, G*.

II. 1. 91   *swart*   black.

II. 1. 128   *fatted calf*   the fatted calf was killed to celebrate the return of the Prodigal Son; see Luke XV 23–4.

II. 1. 129   *hecatombs*   see *Endymion* IV, 39*n* (p. 581).

II. 1. 132–3   a reference to the building of the Tower of Babel (Genesis xi 1–9).

II. 2. 16   *it is*] 'tis one *autograph MS, G, Allott*.

II. 2. 62   *wen*   a wart, or tumour (esp. on the face).

II. 2. 63   *imp*   a little demon or devil.

II. 2. 101   *fledgy*   feathery.

III. 1. 8   *limbo*] white limbs *1848*. Milnes's alteration has no authority.

III. 1. 16   *Henry the Fowler*   Henry I, father of Otto I, was given this nickname.

III. 1. 17   *louted*   bowed (Spenser).

III. 1. 21   *Europe's thronèd*] a well-judging *autograph MS, G, Allott*. See *Texts*, p. 254. *G* records inaccurately.

III. 2. 17   followed in *autograph MS*, Fair copy *(cancelled)*, *G* by the line, 'Devoted, made a slave to this day's joy'. Not in *Garrod (OSA)*.

III. 2. 48   followed in *autograph MS, G* by the line, 'Otho. Come, come, a little sober reason.' *Garrod (OSA)* has 'sense' for 'reason'.

III. 2. 51   *stun*   see *Endymion* II, 247 *n* (p. 571).

III. 2. 59   followed in *autograph MS, G* by the line, 'Mad Churchman, would'st thou be impal'd alive?'

III. 2. 67   *toils*   nets.

III. 2. 74   *yerk*   to lash, beat (as with sharp words or treatment) (*OED*).

III. 2. 83   *yawn*] roar *autograph MS, G, Allott*.

III. 2. 125   *newly-shent*   newly disgraced.

III. 2. 160   *tedious*] hideous *1848* (a misreading).

III. 2. 204   *Bald*] Bold *1848* (misreading). Compare *Lamia* II, 245, 'bald-head philosopher'.

III. 2. 260   *minion*   darling, favourite, especially of a monarch.

III. 2. 272   two extra lines in *autograph MS* are included in *G*, 'Erminia! dream tonight of better days / Tomorrow makes them real – once more good morrow.'

III. 2. 279   *mere*] more *1848* (misreading).

IV. 1. 69   *lords*] nobles *autograph MS, G*.

IV. 1. 99   *Abbot*] father *autograph MS*, Fair copy (originally), *G*.

IV. 1. 103   *stickle*   scruple, hesitate.

IV. 1. 184   *Oh! Oh! Oh!*] not in *1848, Allott*.

IV. 2. 2   ] *autograph MS, G, Allott*; crossed out in Fair copy, not in *1848*.

IV. 2. 6   *bade*] bid *autograph MS, Garrod (OSA), Allott*.

IV. 2. 38   *rubious*   rosy, red. Compare *Lamia* I, 163, 'rubious-argent'.

IV. 2. 91   *battailous*   prepared for battle (Spenserian).

IV. 2. 103   *fresh*] last new, *1848, Allott*.

IV. 2. 106   *wittol*   a contented cuckold.

IV. 2. 138   followed in *autograph MS, G* by the line, 'Jackall, lead on: the lion preys tonight'.

V. 1. 11   ] If he escape me, may I die a death *autograph MS, G*.

V. 2. 8   *AURANTHE rushes in*] *autograph MS, G, Allott*; Enter Auranthe *Fair copy, 1848*.

V. 4. 38   Fill full] *autograph MS, G, Allott*; Fill, fill, *Fair copy, 1848*.

V. 4. 44   *A whisper in this silence that he's*] *Fair copy, 1848* (see *Texts*, p. 253); This silence whisper that he's *autograph MS, G, Allott*.

V. 5. 3, 4   *sleep ... dreaming*] dream ... sleeping *autograph MS, G, Allott*.

V. 5. 116   *Certes* assuredly.

V. 5. 164   *pight* mentally determined. Compare *King Lear* II. 1. 64–5, 'When I dissuaded him from his intent / And found him pight to do it...'. See also *Endymion* II, 60n (p. 570).

V. 5. 191   ] added in Keats's hand in *Fair copy*; not in *autograph MS, 1848*; *G* prints as last line of the play; *Allott* prints as l. 191 but places the question mark after 'father' (the *MS* punctuates 'hand – father').

LAMIA

Part I written between *c*. 28 June and 11 July 1819 during Keats's trip to the Isle of Wight with James Rice, completed at Winchester between 12 August and *c*. 5 September, and revised in March 1820 (see *L* II, pp. 128, 139, 157, 276). Published *1820*. Some variants are given from the fragments of Keats's draft now preserved in the University of Texas, Harvard, and elsewhere (further, see *G*), from Keats's fair copy (Harvard), and from the 'sample of the Story' which Keats sent to Taylor (see II, 199–220n). For the alterations made in the proofs, and Woodhouse's part in these, see W. A. Coles's 'The Proof Sheets of Keats's "Lamia"', *Harvard Library Bulletin*, VIII (1954), pp. 114–19. The gap between the composition of Part I in June and July, and the writing of Part II in August and September, was caused by Keats's diversion of his energies into the writing of *Otho the Great* (see headnote, p. 662), and his rewriting of *Hyperion*.

Lemprière gives the following account of a 'Lamia' – 'Certain monsters of Africa, who had the face and breast of a woman, and the rest of the body like that of a serpent. They allured strangers to come to them, that they might devour them, and though they were not endowed with the faculty of speech, yet their hissings were pleasing and agreeable. Some believed them to be witches, or rather evil spirits, who, under the form of a beautiful woman, enticed young children and devoured them....' Keats omitted the child-devouring aspect, and his sympathetic treatment of Lamia resembles Coleridge's handling of the ambiguously attractive Geraldine in *Christabel* (1816); compare also with the enchantress in T. L. Peacock's *Rhododaphne* (1818).

Keats printed his prime source, Burton's *Anatomy of Melancholy* III 2 i 1, at the end of the poem in *1820*: 'Philostratus, in his fourth book *de Vita Apollonii*, hath a memorable instance in this kind, which I may not omit, of one Menippus Lycius, a young man twenty-five years of age, that going betwixt Cenchreas and Corinth, met such a phantasm in the habit of a fair gentlewoman, which taking him by the hand, carried him home to her house, in the suburbs of Corinth, and told him she was a Phoenician by birth, and if he would tarry with her he should hear her sing and play, and drink such wine as never any drank, and no man should molest him; but she, being fair and lovely, would live and die with him, that was fair and lovely to behold. The young man, a philosopher, otherwise staid and discreet, able to moderate his passions, though not this of love, tarried with her a while to his great content, and at last married her, to whose wedding amongst other guests, came Apollonius; who, by some probable conjectures, found her out to be a serpent, a lamia; and that all her furniture was, like Tantalus' gold, described by Homer, no substance but mere illusions. When she saw herself descried, she wept, and desired Apollonius to be silent, but he would not be moved, and thereupon she, plate, house, and all that was in it, vanished in an instant: many thousands took notice of this fact, for it was done in the midst of Greece.' Keats added Lycius's death, and made Apollonius's role much more equivocal than it is in Burton's straightforward account of witchcraft uncovered by the wisdom of philosophy. The episode of Hermes and the nymph (I, 1–145) is indebted to Keats's reading of Ovid's *Metamorphoses* II, 722–832, and also influenced by Marlowe's *Hero and Leander* (1598) I, 386–464. Woodhouse (*L* II, p. 164) noted the parallel between Lamia's magical house (I, 388–93) and the secret palace which occurs in 'The Story of Prince Ahmed, and the Fairy Pari Banou', which was reprinted along with oriental tales in Henry Weber's *Tales of the East* (1812), where Keats probably read it. The versification is based on Dryden's heroic couplets (see *L* II, p. 165), and is discussed by *Ridley*, pp. 241–50, and *Bate* (1945), pp. 146–71.

In writing *Lamia* Keats sought for a clarity and objectivity which he felt had been lacking in *Isabella* and *The Eve of St Agnes*. On 11 July 1819 he wrote to Reynolds, 'I have great hopes of success, because I make use of my Judgment more deliberately than I yet have done....' (*L* II, p. 128). He particularly wished to avoid the charge of mawkishness, and said to Woodhouse on 22 September 1819, '... The Pot of Basil [Isabella] ... is too smokeable ... There is too much inexperience of li[f]e, and simplicity of knowledge in it. ... I intend to use more finesse with the Public. It is possible to write fine things which cannot be laugh'd at in any way. Isabella is what I should call were I a reviewer "A weak-sided Poem" with an amusing sober-sadness about it ... in my dramatic capacity I enter fully into the feeling: but in Propria Persona I should be apt to quiz it myself – There is no objection of this kind to Lamia – A good deal to St Agnes Eve – only not so glaring ...' (*L* II, p. 174). Keats's attempt to stop himself from identifying with the feelings of his characters appears most obviously in the authorial asides, which owe something to Byron's manner (see, for instance, I, 328–39). In *1820* Keats placed the poem first – '... I am certain there is that sort of fire in it which must take hold of people in some way – give them either pleasant or unpleasant sensation. What they want is a sensation of some sort' (*L* II, p. 189).

Reactions to *Lamia* have been mixed. Leigh Hunt's enthusiastic reception was offset by the mockery of an anonymous reviewer in the *London Magazine* in August 1820 (see *Critical Heritage*, pp. 184–92, 165–70; for Lamb's attitude see pp. 158-9). Robert Bridges thought it 'the most perfect of his free narratives' (introduction to *The Poems of John Keats*, ed. G. Thorn Drury [1896], p. lxi). Various attempts have been made to give the poem a biographical interpretation. Middleton Murry writes, 'Keats is Lycius, Fanny Brawne is the Lamia, and Apollonius is Charles Brown the realist trying to break Fanny's spell over Keats by insisting upon her as the female animal.... The truth about the Lamia is that Keats himself did not know whether she was a thing of beauty or a thing of bale' (*Murry* [1925], pp. 157-9). For a summary of such readings, see *Bate* (1963), p. 548. The narrative may be more truly seen as a dramatization of the rival claims of emotions and thought, and of the dangers and attractions of love. N. F. Ford believes that it is Keats's attempt to discredit finally the power of the 'dream world' (*The Prefigurative Imagination of Keats* [1951], p. 144), while Miriam Allott sees it as an anguished protest against Apollonius's 'Philosophy', whose kind of 'truth' Keats is too honest to deny, despite its destruction of Lamia and Lycius ('"Isabella", "The Eve of St Agnes" and "Lamia"' in *John Keats: A Reassessment*, ed. K. Muir [1958], pp. 52-62). Other readings are given by *Pettet*, pp. 227-40, Bernice Slote, *Keats and the Dramatic Principle* (1958), pp. 138-92, David Perkins, *The Quest for Permanence* (1959), pp. 263-76, *Bate* (1963), pp. 547-61, and *Jones*, pp. 242-60.

PART I

I, 1-6 Keats begins by taking the reader back to a Grecian world in which the Olympian gods still ruled. The idea that the classical nymphs, satyrs and gods were displaced by the fairies of English folk-lore is common in Elizabethan and seventeenth-century literature. Burton's *Anatomy of Melancholy* I 2 i 2 has, 'Terrestrial devils are those *lares, genii, faunes, satyrs*, wood-nymphs, foliots, fairies, *Robin Goodfellows, Trulli*, etc. ... Some think it was they alone that kept the heathen people in awe of old.... Of this range was Dagon among the Philistines [etc.] ... some put our fairies into this rank, which have been in former times adored with much superstition....' (1813 edn I, pp. 67-8). Gittings (1954), p. 224, cites Dryden's *The Wife of Bath Her Tale* 1-4, 'In Days of Old, when *Arthur* fill'd the Throne, / Whose Acts and Fame to Foreign Lands were blown, / The King of Elfs and little fairy Queen / Gamboll'd on Heaths, and danc'd on ev'ry Green'. See too *The Faerie Queene* II. x. 70-71.

I, 6 (and 46) *brakes* clump of bushes, thicket.

I, 7-145 this introductory episode demonstrates the reciprocal help which Hermes and Lamia are able to give one another in the non-human world, and is contrasted with Lamia's failure to achieve a lasting union in the human world. See the comments of E. Wasserman, *The Finer Tone* (1953), pp. 158-64.

I, 7 *ever-smitten* Hermes was known for the frequency of his amours.

I, 13 *sacred island* Crete was sacred because 'Jupiter was secretly educated in a cave on Mount Ida, in Crete' (*Lemprière*).

I, 16 *on land they withered* because Tritons live in the sea.

I, 26] *Garrod* (*O S A*), *Allott* (*following the Fair copy*) *begin a new paragraph here.*

I, 36 *gentle* noble, generous, courteous (Chaucer, Spenser).

I, 46 *cirque-couchant* a Keatsian coinage meaning 'lying coiled in circles'. It is intended to have heraldic overtones.

I, 47–52 The description was probably suggested by *Paradise Lost* IX, 498–503, and by Burton (see *Gittings* [1954], p. 149).

I, 47 *gordian* intricate, like the Gordian knot.

I, 50 *Eyed like a peacock* the brightly coloured circles on a peacock's tail are called 'eyes'.

I, 55 *some penanced lady elf* in fairy tales it is a common punishment to transform a character into an animal. On 'elf', see *Ode to a Nightingale* 73–4n (p. 657). *Allott* points out that lamiae were sometimes called elves or fairies.

I, 57–8 *Upon her crest... Ariadne's tiar* 'according to some writers, Bacchus loved [Ariadne] after Theseus had forsaken her, and he gave her a crown of seven stars, which, after her death, were made a constellation' (*Lemprière*).

I, 64–5 on Lamia's 'serpent speech' see the passage from *Lemprière* quoted in headnote.

I, 66–7 *on his pinions lay, / Like a stooped falcon* Hermes is hovering, prior to dropping on his prey. Strictly speaking, 'stoop', used of a falcon, does not mean hovering, but descending, swooping down.

I, 75 compare with the description of Apollo in *Hyperion* III, 81–2.

I, 76 *purple flakes* fleecy clouds, reddened by the sun. 'Purple' is the colour of passion in Keats.

I, 78 *Phoebean dart* a ray of sunlight.

I, 80 *gentle* see l. 36n.

I, 81–90 for the details about Hermes referred to here, see *Dictionary of Classical Names* under Mercury (p. 709).

I, 84 *wreath* the coiled lamia.

I, 107 *weird syrops* mysterious or supernatural syrups ('syrop' is a poetic spelling, archaic in flavour).

I, 116 *swift-lisping* describes the serpent's voice.

I, 130 *Dashed* confounded, abashed.

I, 133 *lithe* as *Allott* points out, the word is suggested by the snakes traditionally depicted as entwined round Hermes's caduceus (wand).

I, 141 *bland* gentle, soft.

I, 143 *lees* dregs, esp. of wine. Compare the phrase, 'Drain to the lees'.

I, 145 compare *Ode on a Grecian Urn* 25–30.

I, 146–70 Woodhouse thought this metamorphosis of Lamia from serpent into woman 'quite Ovidian, but better' (*L* II, p. 164).

I, 147 *elfin* see *Ode to a Nightingale* 73–4n (p. 657).

I, 148 *besprent* sprinkled (Spenser).

I, 152–64 *Flashed phosphor and sharp sparks... colours all inflamed... deep volcanian yellow... lava... left* the description of Lamia's transformation from serpent into woman '... resembles nothing so much as the effects of a violent chemical reaction. Both in what it depicts and what it implies, the passage is marked by a brilliant mocking irony. A sort of chemical analysis or separation of elements takes place. Lamia's bright emblems and colours are overrun and dwindle to a little pile of charred remains....', S. M. Sperry,

'Keats and the Poetic Chemistry of Creation', *PMLA*, LXXXV (1970), pp. 275–6.

I, 155 *volcanian* sulphur.

I, 158 *brede* plaited or interwoven material. See *Ode on a Grecian Urn* 41–2n (p. 651).

I, 163 *rubious-argent* another Keatsian coinage, by analogy with heraldic colouring. The meaning is 'ruby-silver'. 'Rubious' is used in *Otho the Great* IV. 2. 38. 'Rubious' occurs in Shakespeare, *Twelfth Night* I. 4. 30–31, but the *OED* records no other examples until Keats.

I, 167 *luting soft* Woodhouse objected to the words, but they were retained by Keats. See *KC* I, p. 112.

I, 174 *Cenchreas' shore* Cenchreas (or Cenchrea) was the port for Corinth.

I, 176] The rugged paps of little Perea's rills *Fair copy*. The alteration of 'paps' and 'little' was due to Woodhouse's suggestions in the proofs.

I, 179 *Cleone* a village to the south of Corinth.

I, 182 *passionèd* probably drawn from Keats's reading of Shakespeare. *OED* defines the intransitive verb as 'To show, express, or be affected by passion or deep feeling; formerly esp. to sorrow', and cites *Two Gentlemen of Verona* IV. 4. 163–4, ''twas Ariadne passioning / For Theseus' perjury ...', and *The Tempest* V. 1. 22–4, 'shall not myself, ... / Passion as they?' See also *Endymion* I, 248n (p. 563).

I, 188 *Spread a green kirtle to the minstrelsy* spread her skirts round her on the ground while sitting to hear singers.

I, 191 *sciential* endowed with knowledge. Compare *Paradise Lost* IX, 837–8, 'sciential sap, deriv'd / From Nectar, drink of Gods ...'.

I, 195 *dispart* distinguish.

I, 198 *unshent* unsullied. Compare *Sleep and Poetry* 379, 'unshent by foam'.

I, 206 *faint Elysium* Elysium (the western isle where the souls of the virtuous go) is 'faint' either because dimly discerned, or because it is inhabited by insubstantial spirits.

I, 210 *glutinous* sticky, gluey, here referring to the resin oozing from the pine tree.

I, 211 *Pluto's gardens palatine* the palatial gardens of Pluto, god of the underworld.

I, 212 *Mulciber's ... piazzian* for Mulciber, see 'Vulcan' in *Dictionary of Classical Names* (p. 718). 'Piazzian' is used to suggest a piazza surrounded by colonnades. Compare with Mulciber's construction of Pandemonium in *Paradise Lost* I, 713–15, 'Built like a Temple, where *Pilasters* round / Were set, and Doric pillars overlaid / With Golden Architrave ...'.

I, 229 *Jove heard his vows* Jupiter was one of the gods who had care over marriage.

I, 230 *freakful* see *To B. R. Haydon* 8n (p. 557).

I, 236 *Platonic*] platonian *Fair copy*. The alteration was suggested by Woodhouse in the proofs.

NOTES FOR PP. 420-24

I, 238 *drear* drear to Lamia.

I, 244 *syllabling* compare Milton's *Comus* 208, '... airy tongues, that syllable mens names...'.

I, 256 *his chain* Lamia has enchained Lycius.

I, 260] Thou to Elysium gone, here for the vultures I *Fair copy*.

I, 265-7 Lycius speculates that Lamia is one of the stars of the constellation of Pleiades, descended to earth, who would therefore need a proxy to take her place in the heavens. Further, see *Dictionary of Classical Names*. Lycius's speculations about the nature of his love in this passage (ll. 261-70) should be compared with *Endymion* II, 687-94.

I, 275 *nice* discriminating.

I, 283 *essence* the insubstantial element of which gods are made. See *Endymion* I, 777-81n (p. 567).

I, 288 *complain* complaint (poeticism).

I, 293 *amenity* the quality of being pleasurable or agreeable.

I, 300 the stars are so entranced by Lamia's song that they cease twinkling, just as a human might hold his breath.

I, 307 *subtle fluid* immaterial, ethereal liquid (a semi-technical phrase perhaps, echoing Renaissance chemical ideas).

I, 317-20 Adonis's yearly festival, a fertility rite, was held in Venus's temple. Hence, the freshly gathered herbs and flowers are 'amorous'. Gittings (1954), p. 224, cites Dryden's *The First Book of Ovid's Art of Love* 80-81, 'Or *Venus*' Temple; where, on Annual Nights,/They mourn *Adonis* with *Assyrian* rites...'. The passage recollects Marlowe's *Hero and Leander* I, 91-3, 131-4.

I, 323 *lays* songs. Her words are music to his ears.

I, 328-33 Keats is imitating Byron's man-of-the-world style in *Don Juan*.

I, 329 *Peris* a race of superhuman beings or good genii, endowed with grace and beauty, in Persian mythology.

I, 330 *treat* a colloquial usage which *OED* dates from 1805, meaning 'a great pleasure, delight, or gratification'.

I, 333 *Pyrrha's pebbles* see under 'Deucalion' in *Dictionary of Classical Names* (p. 703).

I, 347 *comprised* wrapped up in, absorbed.

I, 352 *temples lewd* 'lewd' may have its older meaning, 'ignorant'. But *Lemprière* notes that 'only women were admitted [to the Adonia, the festivals of Adonis], and such as did not appear were compelled to prostitute themselves for one day'. Burton's *Anatomy of Melancholy* III 2 ii 1 says of Corinth, '... every day strangers came in, at each gate, from all quarters. In that one temple of Venus a thousand whores did prostitute themselves ... all nations resorted thither as to a school of Venus' (1813 edn II, 212). Compare with Lamia's attendance at 'Cupid's college' (I, 197-9).

I, 375 *Apollonius* Apollonius of Tyana, a Pythagorean philosopher who lived in the first century A.D. According to *Lemprière* he was 'well skilled in the secret arts of magic'. He was also an advocate of moral and religious reform.

I, 380 *phosphor* Phosphor was another name for Venus, the morning star,

671 NOTES FOR PP. 424-7

and hence, before 1820, meant 'light-giving, phosphorescent' as an adjective (*OED*).

I, 386 *Aeolian* like the sound of a wind-harp (see *Ode to Apollo* 34n, p. 536).

I, 394-6] Keats's draft shows he had difficulty in controlling the tone of the poem at this point. A first attempt reads, '... but what can foil / The winged verse? What Poesy not win / The humblest Muse unwe[a]ried of her toil...'. Keats then tried, 'This flitter-winged verse perhaps might tell / If it durst speak, what it should dare to speak / But this is Poesy's long ember week / And ... against fashion folly 'tis to sin...'.

I, 397 *world,*] *Draft, Allott*; world *1820, G*. The meaning of ll. 396-7 is, 'Many readers with tender sensibilities would be happy to leave the lovers at this point, safe from the world: they would not believe that the story could have the unhappy ending which is portrayed in Part II.'

PART II

II, 6 *non-elect* the 'elect' are those people chosen by God for eternal life.

II, 9 *clenched it quite* proved it conclusively.

II, 12-15 *Love, jealous grown ... floor* Cupid jealously guards such perfect love against the possibility of intruders. There may also be some suggestion that Cupid is himself jealous of such complete love.

II, 16 *For all this* despite all this.

II, 22 *two marble shafts* two small columns supporting the lintel of the window.

II, 24 *tithe* a very small part.

II, 26 *suburb hill* a hill outside the city walls.

II, 29 *a thought a-buzzing*] *Draft, Fair copy, G, Allott*; a thought, a buzzing *1820*.

II, 31 *purple-linèd* Lamia's palace is purple to suggest both opulence and passion.

II, 32 *bourne* limit, boundary.

II, 34 *penetrant* piercing, acute (archaic).

II, 36 *empery* empire, the territory of an absolute or powerful ruler.

II, 45] *followed in Fair copy by* Too fond was I believing, fancy fed / In high deliriums, and blossoms never shed!

II, 48 *silver planet, both of eve and morn* Venus, the morning and evening star.

II, 52 *trammel* enmesh.

II, 73-7 compare *Ode on Melancholy* 18-20.

II, 76 *sanguineous* flushed with anger.

II, 78 *mitigated* moderated.

II, 80 *The serpent* see 'Python' in *Dictionary of Classical Names* (p. 715). 'Certes' is a Spenserian word meaning 'assuredly'.

II, 81-3 *She burnt, she loved the tyranny ... paramour* Keats commented on this passage, 'Women love to be forced to do a thing, by a fine fellow – *such as this*....' (*L* II, p. 164).

II, 81 after this line the *Fair copy* has, 'Became herself a flame – 'twas worth an age / Of minor joys to revel in such rage.' For Keats's initial, and longer, attempt at ll. 81–102, see G.

II, 105 Lamia 'betrays' Lycius into a 'deep sleep' by a magic spell.

II, 114 *pompousness* desire for display, ostentation.

II, 118 *subtle servitors* Lamia's servants are immaterial spirits. They are called 'viewless servants' at l. 136.

II, 122–62, 199–220 Keats copied out an early version of these passages in a letter to Taylor on 5 September 1819 (*L* II, pp. 157–9) which differs importantly from *1820*, especially ll. 199–220 (see note). One or two other variants are also recorded in the notes.

II, 123 *made moan* see *La Belle Dame sans Merci* 20n (p. 639).

II, 128–30 *Two palms and then two plantains ... aislèd place* may remember a passage from Burton, cited by *Allott* – '... palm-trees ... are both he and she, and express not a sympathy but a love passion ... the two trees bend, and of their own accords stretch out their boughs to embrace and kiss each other' (*Anatomy of Melancholy* III 2 i 1, 1813 edn II, p. 193).

II, 133 *with odours*] a perfume *L*.

II, 134 *Silently*] Silverly *L, Fair copy*.

II, 136 *viewless* invisible. See l. 118n, and *Ode to a Nightingale* 33n (p. 656).

II, 137 *fretted*] splendid cornicing *L*. 'Fretted' means adorned with fretwork, that is carved or embossed work in patterns.

II, 138 *marbled plain*] wainscoted *L, Fair copy*.

II, 142 *faded at self-will* made herself disappear.

II, 147–8] O senseless Lycius! Dolt! Fool! Madman! Lout! / Why would you murder happiness like yours? *L*.

II, 155 *demesne* strictly, a territory held in possession, but refers here to Lamia's palace.

II, 160 *daffed* played the fool with, or, daunted (Northern dialect). Compare '*Ah, ken ye what I met the day*' 35, 'Tam was daffèd like a chick...'.

II, 175 *lucid* bright, shining.

II, 183–5 *spherèd tables ... paws* compare J. Potter's *Antiquities of Greece* (1697), '... the Greeks made their tables ... spherical, in imitation of the world. ... The most common support of these tables was an ivory foot, cast in the form of a lion, a leopard or some other animal' (II, pp. 376–7, cited by *Allott*). Keats could also have been influenced by contemporary furniture, which was often neoclassical in inspiration.

II, 185 *libbard's* leopard's (archaic).

II, 199–220 the version in *L* makes a sharp contrast between the splendour of Lamia's palace, and the satiric presentation of the drunken guests. 'Soft went the music, and the tables all / Sparkled beneath the viewless banneral / Of Magic; and dispos'd in double row / Seem'd edged Parterres of white bedded snow, / Adorne'd along the sides with living flowers / Conversing, laughing after sunny showers: / And, as the pleasant appetite entic'd, / Gush came the wine, and sheer the meats were slic'd. / Soft went the Music; the flat salver sang / Kiss'd by the emptied goblet, – and again it rang: / Swift bustled by the servants: – here's a health / Cries one – another – then, as if by stealth, / A Glutton drains a cup of Helicon, / Too fast down, down his throat the brief delight is gone. / 'Where is that Music?' cries a Lady fair. / 'Aye, where is it my dear? Up in the air?' / Another whispers 'Poo!' saith Glutton 'Mum!' / Then makes his shiny mouth a napkin for his thumb. &&&–'. This passage occurs after l. 162 in *L*. Woodhouse copied it out in the proofs out of interest (*Texts*, p. 256), *not* because it was being considered for inclusion (W. A. Coles, 'The Proof Sheets of Keats's "Lamia"', *Harvard Library Bulletin*, VIII (1954), p. 115).

II, 213 *at meridian height* at its height, as the sun at midday.

II, 217 *osiered* woven. The osier is a kind of willow whose branches are made into baskets.

II, 224 *willow ... adder's tongue* emblems of grief, but Adder's Tongue (a fern) was formerly used as a soothing and healing herb.

II, 225–6 *let us strip for him | The thyrsus* Lycius's wreath is to be made from the ivy and vine-leaves twisted round Bacchus's thyrsus (wand).

II, 229–37 *Do not all charms fly | At the mere touch of cold philosophy? ... Unweave a rainbow* Keats knew Hazlitt's lecture *On Poetry in General* in 1818, in which he remarked, 'It cannot be concealed ... that the progress of knowledge and refinement has a tendency to circumscribe the limits of the imagination, and to clip the wings of poetry' (*Works*, ed. P. P. Howe [1930–34] V, p. 9). At a dinner-party at Haydon's on 28 December 1817, Keats agreed with Lamb that Newton had 'destroyed all the Poetry of the rainbow, by reducing it to a prism', and had drunk 'Newton's health, and confusion to mathematics' (*The Diary of B. R. Haydon*, ed. W. B. Pope [1960], II, p. 72). Compare with Keats's remark on the rainbow in his review of Kean's acting (Appendix 5, p. 529). Further, see S. M. Sperry, 'Keats and the Chemistry of Poetic Creation', *PMLA*, LXXXV (1970), pp. 276–7.

II, 237 *Unweave a rainbow* compare *Endymion* II, 230–31, where Keats speaks of the 'interwoven' colours in a rainbow.

II, 246 *fixed his eye* Apollonius is now like a snake.

II, 275 *deep-recessèd vision* probably describes the blankness of Lamia's dying eyes. *Allott* glosses as 'sunken eyes'.

II, 277 *juggling* conjuring.

II, 289 *his demon eyes* Apollonius has now taken over Lamia's role as a 'demon' – compare I, 56.

II, 297–8] That youth might suffer have I shielded thee / Up to this very hour, and shall I see / Thee married to a Serpent? Pray you Mark, / Corinthians! A Serpent, plain and stark! *Fair copy*. Taylor, Keats's publisher, apparently objected to the word 'stark', which does not occur in *1820*. See W. A. Coles, 'The Proof Sheets of Keats's "Lamia"', *Harvard Library Bulletin*, VIII (1954), pp. 118–19.

II, 301 *perceant* piercing (Spenser).

'PENSIVE THEY SIT, AND ROLL THEIR LANGUID EYES'

Written 17 September 1819 in Keats's journal-letter to George and Georgiana Keats (*L* II, p. 188). Published *World* (New York), 25 June 1877, Forman (1883). Text based on *L*. Keats prefaced the poem with the following remarks, 'Nothing strikes me so forcibly with a sense of the rediculous as love – A Man in love I do think cuts the sorryest figure in the world – Even when I know a poor fool to be really in pain about it, I could burst out laughing in his face – His pathetic visage becomes irrisistible ... Somewhere in the Spectator [No. 371] is related an account of a Man inviting a party of stutter[e]rs and squinters to his table. 't would please me more to scrape together a party of Lovers, not to dinner – no to tea. The[re] would be no fighting as among Knights of old –' (*L* II, pp. 187–8). For similar fragments, see '*And what is love* ...' and *Fragment of the 'Castle Builder'*.

9 *Humane Society* refers to the Royal Humane Society, founded in 1774.
10–13 *Mr Werter* Keats had probably read Daniel Malthus's translation of Goethe's *The Sorrows of Werther* (1783) – 'Every moment I am myself a destroyer. The most innocent walk deprives of life thousands of poor insects ...' (I, p. 144). See D. B. Green, *N & Q*, 16 September 1950, pp. 410 ff.
15 *cauliflower* an untrimmed wick.
16 *winding sheet* 'a mass of solidified drippings of grease clinging to the side of a candle, resembling a sheet folded in creases, and regarded as an omen of death or calamity' (*OED*).
17 *Circus gay* Piccadilly Circus.
23 *Wapping* an unfashionable area near the docks in East London.

TO AUTUMN

Written *c*. 19 September 1819 at Winchester. Published *1820*. Some variants noted from Keats's draft, now in Harvard (referred to as *K* – it is reproduced in *Gittings* [1970], pp. 56–9) and the version copied out in Keats's letter to Woodhouse of 21–2 September (*L* II, pp. 170–71). The number of alterations in the second stanza of Keats's MS led *Ridley*, p. 282, to guess that it is a late addition.

Keats described the poem's occasion in his letter to Reynolds of 21 September. 'How beautiful the season is now – How fine the air. A temperate sharpness about it. Really, without joking, chaste weather – Dian skies – I never lik'd stubble fields so much as now – Aye better than the chilly green of the spring. Somehow a stubble plain looks warm – in the same way that some pictures look warm – this struck me so much in my sunday's walk that I composed upon it. . . . I somehow always associate Chatterton with autumn. He is the purest writer in the English Language' (*L* II, p. 167). *Gittings* (1954), p. 187, has pointed out the echoes of Chatterton's *Aella*, though there are also echoes of Wordsworth, and Coleridge's *Frost at Midnight* (1798), 65–75. Keats's probable debt to paintings is discussed by *Jack*, pp. 232–43. The stanza structure is closely related to that of the odes of April and May, but extended to eleven lines and including a couplet (first stanza: *a b a b c d e d c c e*; the

675   NOTES FOR P. 434

other two: *a b a b c d e c d d e*). 'The effect of the couplet, placed thus, is to sustain the approaching close at a momentary crest before the stanza subsides in the final line' (*Bate* [1963], p. 581*n*).

To Autumn is often regarded as the most achieved of Keats's odes. 'The *Ode to a Nightingale*, for example, is a less "perfect" though a greater poem. The distinctive appeal of *To Autumn* lies not merely in the degree of resolution but in the fact that, in this short space, so many different kinds of resolution are attained' (*Bate* [1963], p. 581). The ode's meaning is implicit rather than explicit. Autumn's particular beauty is dependent upon its transience, and the stanzas can be seen as moving through the season, beginning with pre-harvest ripeness, moving to the repletion of harvest itself, and concluding with the emptiness following the harvest, but preceding winter. It also progresses from the tactile senses, to the visual, culminating in the auditory senses, and focuses first on the vegetable world, then on the human activity in gathering the harvest, and concludes in the world of animals, birds, and insects. It has also been read as a movement from morning to evening. The interconnectedness of maturity, death, and regeneration is implicit throughout. Readings of the poem include *Ridley*, pp. 281–90, F. R. Leavis's account in *Revaluation* (1936), pp. 262–6, A. Davenport's 'A Note on *To Autumn*' in *John Keats: A Reassessment*, ed. K. Muir (1958), pp. 95–101, B. C. Southam's 'The Ode *To Autumn*' in *KSJ*, IX (1960), pp. 91–8, Harold Bloom in *The Visionary Company* (1962), pp. 421–5, *Bate* (1963), pp. 580–85, and *Jack*, pp. 232–43.

1–2 compare Wordsworth's *The Excursion* (1814), V, 400, '... mellow Autumn, charged with bounteous fruit...', but also Keats's own treatment of autumn, especially '*After dark vapours have oppressed our plains*' 9–11, *Endymion* I, 439–41, 991, II, 416, IV, 422–3, 814, and *Otho the Great* IV. 1. 166–7.

2 *maturing sun* the sun matures the fruit, but may also be seen as itself maturing in the course of autumn.

4 *With fruit the vines*] The Vines with fruit *K, L*.

6 *fruit with ripeness*] fruits with sweetness *K*.

7 *plump* compare *Endymion* IV, 377, 'Ere a lean bat could plump its wintry skin...'.

8 *sweet*] white *K, L*.

12 *oft amid thy store*] for thy haunts are many *K* (*cancelled*).

12–22 the personifications in this stanza draw directly from English country life, but may owe a debt to pictorial traditions. Autumn sitting in the granary, her hair 'soft-lifted by the winnowing wind' (ll. 12–15), resembles Giulio Romano's *Psyche Asleep among the Grain*; Autumn as a sleeping reaper (ll. 16–18) recalls the engravings done for Thomson's *Seasons* (1807) after paintings by William Hamilton; Autumn carrying a basket on her head (ll. 19–20) has a general likeness to a figure in Poussin's *Autumn, or the Grapes of the Promised Land* (see *Jack*, pp. 236–40 and Plates XXXVIII–XLI). As *Jack* points out, 'about each of [these figures] there is even a slight suggestion of the classical figure of Ceres'. Keats has departed from tradition in making Autumn female.

13 *abroad*] for thee *K* (*cancelled*).

676 NOTES FOR PP. 434–5

14 *sitting careless on a granary floor* both sitting casually, and, sitting without cares since the harvest is safely gathered.

15] *followed in K by a cancelled line* While bright the Sun slants through the husky barn; –

16] Or sound asleep in a half reaped field *K* (*cancelled*).

17–18] Dosed with red poppies; while thy reeping hook / Spares for some slumbrous minutes while warm slumbers creep *K* (*cancelled*). For 'Drowsed' *K* has 'Dosed' and *L* 'Dased'. Poppies are associated with sleep, and before modern agricultural weed control they were common in fields of grain.

18 *swath* the width of corn cut by a scythe.

19–20 F. R. Leavis says, 'In the step from the rime-word "keep", across (so to speak) the pause enforced by the line-division, to "Steady" the balancing movement of the gleaner is enacted' (*Revaluation* [1936], pp. 263–4).

20 *a*] the *K*.

22 *oozings*] oozing *K*.

25 *barrèd ... bloom*] a gold ... gilds *K* (*cancelled*). The use of 'bloom' suggests that paradoxically the dying day is a reminder of the 'bloom' of regeneration.

26 *And touch*] Touching the *K* (*cancelled*). In his letter to Reynolds (see headnote), Keats remarked, 'Somehow a stubble plain looks warm. . .'.

26 *hue:*] *L*; hue —*K*; hue; *1820*, *G*; hue. *Allott*.

27 '"wailful choir" and "mourn", while deftly characterizing the thin noise made by a cloud of gnats, cannot help also linking with the idea of a funeral dirge for the dying year' (Robin Mayhead, *John Keats* [1967], p. 100).

28 *sallows* willows. *G* has 'shallows' (probably a misprint, since Garrod [*OSA*] has 'sallows'). For Keats's earlier use of the word, see '*I stood tiptoe . . .*' 67.

29 *or*] and *K*, *L*.

30 *bourn* almost certainly Keats meant 'boundary', but 'bourn', meaning a stream, would make sense.

31 *Hedge-crickets sing* in *On the Grasshopper and Cricket* 3–5 the grasshopper is associated with early summer, and in ll. 10–12 the cricket associated with winter. Keats's made-up word, 'hedge-cricket', indicates that both associations are present.

31 *with treble soft*] again full soft *K*.

33 *And gathering*] Then Gathering *K* (*which at first had* And now flock still); And gather'd *L*.

THE FALL OF HYPERION. A DREAM

Begun mid-July 1819 at Shanklin in the Isle of Wight; 'given up' *c.* 21 September (*L* II, p. 167), though Keats probably continued to tinker with the text after that date. Published by R. M. Milnes as 'Another Version of Keats's *Hyperion*' in *Biographical and Historical Miscellanies of the Philobiblon Society, 1856–7* (1856). Milnes was much freer with Keats's text in *1856* than he had been in *1848* (see *G*, pp. xlv–xlvi), and the text given here is based on the transcript in *W*2, with some variants noted from *1856* and from the extracts copied out by Keats in his letter to Woodhouse of 21 September 1819 (*L* II, pp. 171–2).

Keats's attempted reconstruction of the earlier *Hyperion* (put aside in April 1819), is influenced by his reading of Milton and Dante, whose *Divina Commedia* he had been studying both in Cary's translation and the original. Further, see J. L. Lowes, '*Hyperion* and the *Purgatorio*', *TLS*, 11 January 1936, and 'Moneta's Temple' *PMLA*, LI (1936), pp. 1098–1113, F. R. Leavis in *Revaluation* (1936), pp. 269–70, and J. Saly, 'Keats's Answer to Dante: *The Fall of Hyperion*' *KSJ*, XIV (1965), pp. 65–78. Keats testified to his admiration for Milton when writing to Reynolds on 24 August 1819 – 'I am convinced more and more day by day that fine writing is next to fine doing the top thing in the world; the Paradise Lost becomes a great wonder – The more I know what my diligence may in time probably effect; the more does my heart distend with Pride and Obstinacy . . .' (*L* II, p. 146). Keats's ostensible reason for abandoning *The Fall of Hyperion* was his reaction against its Miltonism: 'I have given up Hyperion – there were too many Miltonic inversions in it – Miltonic verse cannot be written but in an artful or rather artist's humour. I wish to give myself to other sensations. English ought to be kept up' (to Reynolds, 21 September 1819, *L* II, p. 167). He also told George and Georgiana Keats, '. . . I have but lately stood on my guard against Milton. Life to him would be death to me' (*L* II, p. 212). But other factors were at work. Moneta's admonitions in Canto I had already dealt with his main theme, and the strain of sustaining a vision dealing exclusively with supernatural beings was considerable (even *Paradise Lost* had not attempted this). Failing health further discouraged Keats – his tuberculosis probably moved into its active stage in September (*Bate* [1963], pp. 614–16).

In his rehandling of the earlier *Hyperion*, Keats adopted the dream vision structure, in which Moneta was to relate the fall of the Titans. After an induction (I, 1–18), *The Fall of Hyperion* deals with the nature of poetry and the poet, the distinction between the poet and the dreamer, and the problem of human suffering. At I, 294, Keats picks up the original narrative with the entry of Saturn and Thea, concluding with the appearance of Hyperion in Canto II. The movement from the pleasant garden (I, 19–46) to the 'antichamber of this dream' (I, 47–end) recalls the 'Chamber of Maiden-Thought' which Keats had described a year earlier, in his letter to Reynolds of 3 May 1818: '. . . I compare human life to a large Mansion of Many Apartments, two of which I can only describe, the doors of the rest being as yet shut upon me – The first we step into we call the infant or thoughtless Chamber, in which we remain as long as we do not think – We remain there a long while . . . but are at length imperceptibly impelled by the awakening of the thinking principle – within us – we no sooner get into the second Chamber, which I shall call the Chamber of Maiden-Thought, than we become intoxicated with the light and atmosphere, we see nothing but pleasant wonders, and think of delaying there for ever in delight: However among the effects this breathing is father of is that tremendous one of sharpening one's vision into the heart and nature of Man – of convincing ones nerves that the World is full of Misery and Heartbreak, Pain, Sickness and oppression – whereby This Chamber of Maiden Thought becomes gradually darken'd and at the same time on all sides of it many doors are set open – but all dark – all leading to dark passages – We see not the ballance of good and evil. We are in a Mist – *We* are now in that state – We feel the "burden of the Mystery", To this point was Wordsworth come, as far as I can conceive when he wrote "Tintern Abbey" . . .' (*L* I, pp. 280–81).

Nineteenth-century critics preferred *Hyperion* to the later version, though this emphasis has been largely reversed. J. M. Murry called it 'the profoundest and most sublime of his poems' (*Murry* [1925], p. 169). See also *Ridley*, pp. 266–80, K. Muir's 'The Meaning of *Hyperion*', in *John Keats: A Reassessment*, ed. K. Muir (1958), pp. 111–22, Robin Mayhead, *John Keats* (1967), pp. 107–11, *Bate* (1963), pp. 585–605, *Jones*, pp. 91–104, and the discussions, cited above, of Keats's debt to Dante.

I, 1–11   Keats copied these lines out for Woodhouse, calling them 'a sort of induction' (*L* II, p. 172).

I, 1   *Fanatics*   religious enthusiasts.

I, 3   *fashion*   carries the sense of 'fashionings', hence suggests invention, imagination.

I, 10   *charm*] chain *1856*.

I, 15   *tongue.*] *1856*, *Allott*, *Garrod* (*OSA*); tongue, *G*.

I, 24   *Turning*] Twining *1856*.

I, 25–7   compare *Ode to Psyche* 59–61, The 'bells' of l. 26 refer to the bell-like flowers which hang from the trellis.

I, 31–4   compare *Paradise Lost* V, 303–7, 326–8, 341–4.

I, 35   *fabled horn*   the cornucopia, Ceres's emblem of fruitfulness (referred to in *Lamia* II, 186–7). Ceres was Proserpine's mother.

I, 48–51   the Caliphs ruled the Mohammedan world after Mohammed's death. Like the cardinals of the Catholic Church in Renaissance Italy ('the scarlet conclave of old men'), they were commonly thought to have used poisonings to further their intrigues.

I, 48   *soon-fading*] *W2* records 'originally death-doing'.

I, 56   *Silenus*   possibly a recollection of a detail of the Borghese Vase (*Jack*, Plate XXXVII).

I, 64   *spread*] sail *L*.

I, 68   *superannuations*   glossed by *Allott* as 'Obsolete remains. The effectiveness of the line depends on Keats's use of the abstract noun "superannuation" (an archaism for infirmity or decay) as a concrete noun in the plural.'

I, 70   *faulture*   a Keatsian invention. The text in *L* II, p. 171, gives 'failing'. *OED* suggests 'Decayed remnants'.

I, 74   *asbestos*   'a mineral of fibrous texture, capable of being woven into an incombustible fabric' (*OED*).

I, 75   *Or in that place the moth could not corrupt*   compare Matthew vi 20, '. . . lay up for yourselves treasures in heaven, where neither moth nor rust doth corrupt.'

I, 77 *imageries* patterns woven into the cloth (*OED*).

I, 96 *One ministering* Moneta, the temple's priestess.

I, 97 *mid-May*] G, Allott; midway *W2*; midday *1856*. The emendation was suggested by A. E. Housman, *TLS*, 8 May 1924.

I, 103 *Maian incense* a scent like that of the flowers of May. The goddess Maia is celebrated in Keats's *Ode to May*.

I, 116 *gummèd leaves* the leaves of some kind of tree with sweet-smelling gum.

I, 122–31 *a palsied chill . . . not* Keats had seen his mother and his brother die, and had been a medical student. The description of the onset of death is accurate.

I, 135–6 *As once . . . Heaven* a reference to Jacob's Ladder, Genesis xxviii 12. See also *Paradise Lost* III, 510–22.

I, 137 *hornèd shrine* ancient altars were adorned with horns – see I, 237.

I, 141 *veilèd shadow* Keats's description of Moneta as a 'shade' or 'shadow' probably echoes Dante's use of *ombra* in the *Purgatorio*. But, as Allott points out, Keats's mysterious figure is affected by ideas of the Egyptian goddess, Isis. According to *Lemprière* Isis was goddess of the moon, and together with Osiris, 'comprehended all nature and all the gods of the heathens. . . . The word *Isis*, according to some, signifies *ancient*, and, on that account, the inscriptions on the statue of the goddess were often in these words: *I am all that has been, that shall be, and none among mortals has hitherto taken off my veil.*'

I, 144–5 *dated on / Thy doom* delayed the moment of your death.

I, 147–59 A. C. Bradley points out the parallel with Shelley's preface to *Alastor* (1816), which distinguishes between everyday egotism, which is 'morally dead', and the necessary 'self-centred seclusion' of the poet (*Oxford Lectures on Poetry* [1909], pp. 242–3). For Keats's view that poetic power depends on a knowledge of human suffering, see *Hyperion* III, 113–20. See also his ideas on the 'Chamber of Maiden-Thought' quoted in the headnote.

I, 152 *fane* temple (poeticism).

I, 155 *sooth* means both 'true' and 'smooth' (see *Sleep and Poetry* 180*n*, p. 552).

I, 157 compare *Sleep and Poetry* 122–5.

I, 161–2 *visionaries . . . dreamers* the words are used here as synonyms (compare I, 12–14).

I, 166] *in W2 followed by a cancelled couplet*: Mankind thou lovest; many of thine hours / Have been distempered with their miseries. . . .

I, 169 *fever* Keats associates 'fever' with poetic inspiration. On 21 September 1819 he described his attempt to gain a 'more thoughtful and quiet power'. He was, he said, '. . . exerting myself against vexing speculations, scarcely content to write the best verses for the fever they leave behind. I want to compose without this fever' (*L* II, p. 209). Paradoxically, the poet's function is that of the physician, who 'pours out balm upon the world' (I, 184, 201).

I, 171–6 ordinary men are able to compartmentalize their experiences of joy and sorrow, but the dreamer/poet cannot achieve this degree of unawareness.

I, 172   *sole*   single, solitary.

I, 183-4   *By such propitious parley medicined | In sickness not ignoble* the poet is grateful to Moneta for her timely, even hopeful ('propitious') words, which act like a medicine for a sickness (poetry/dreaming), which he can now see is not ignoble. It is not ignoble because the suffering is a source of imaginative insight.

I, 187-210   ] *not in 1856*. Woodhouse records, 'Keats seems to have intended to erase this [I, 187-9] & the 21 follow[in]g verses'. This powerful personal passage is a digression – see the repetitions at ll. 187 and 211, and ll. 194-8 and 216-20. *Allott* includes the lines for the light they throw on Keats's thinking but *Texts* (p. 262) argues for their inclusion on textual grounds.

I, 199-202   *The poet and the dreamer are distinct ... vexes it*   the poet offers solace through his imaginative insight into the dark truths of reality, whereas the 'dreamer' vexes the world because his dream is merely self-indulgent.

I, 205   *misty pestilence*   for Apollo's power over illness and disease, see *Dictionary of Classical Names*.

I, 207-8   Byron is probably Keats's chief target. A 'hectorer' is a blusterer. For Keats's earlier attack on contemporary poetry, see *Sleep and Poetry* 231-5 and *nn* (p. 553).

I, 222   *Is all spared*   is all that is spared. The 'war' referred to is that between the Titans and the Olympians.

I, 226   *Moneta*   another name for Mnemosyne, who appears in *Hyperion*. For the meaning of the change, see *Dictionary of Classical Names* under Moneta.

I, 245   *swooning vivid through my globèd brain*   'swooning vivid' has the force of a compound and means that the scenes are so vivid as to cause swooning. 'Globèd brain' should be compared to *Ode to Psyche* 50-62 and *n* (p. 647).

I, 246   *electral*   charged, as if by electricity.

I, 256-62   with this description of Moneta's face compare the unveiling of Beatrice in Dante's *Purgatorio* XXXI, 136-44. Keats is reworking his own earlier portraits of Thea and Mnemosyne in *Hyperion*, I, 34-6 and III, 59-60.

I, 257   see Robin Mayhead's discussion of ll. 256-62 in *John Keats* (1967), p. 4, '... there is a certain oddity in the word "bright". Its obvious function is to define the extreme and frightening whiteness of Moneta's face; it is bright in the same way that the lily and the snow [l. 262] are "bright". But ... "bright", after all, cannot help suggesting radiance and life, both of which are opposed to "wan" and "deathwards progressing" [ll. 256, 260]'.

I, 264-71   *But for her eyes ... upward cast*   the dramatic shift from Moneta's 'wan' face to her eyes, which are 'benignant' and 'visionless entire' though half-closed, provides an analogy with the disinterested objectivity yoked with suffering, characteristic of the true poet in Keatsian terms. Moneta can thus offer solace to the speaker, as the poet can to mankind.

I, 266   *Soft-mitigated*] *G, Allott*; Soft mitigated *W2, Garrod* (*OSA*); Soft, mitigated *1856*.

I, 267   *visionless*   because not seeing 'external things' (l. 268), but turned inward on her own visions.

681 NOTES FOR PP. 442-5

I, 276-8 *hollow brain ... the dark secret chambers of her skull* compare with 'globèd brain' (I, 245), and the temple built in the poet's brain in *Ode to Psyche* 51-2, 60.

I, 277 *enwombèd*] environ'd *1856*; envisioned *Forman* (1883).

I, 282 *Shade of Memory* Moneta, whose other name, Mnemosyne, means 'memory'. See Moneta in *Dictionary of Classical Names*.

I, 283 *adorant* a neologism for 'adoring'.

I, 285 *golden age* the Golden Age of Saturn's rule.

I, 288 *Omega* the last letter of the Greek alphabet; hence, Moneta is the only Titan left after the war with the Olympians.

I, 294 the first version of *Hyperion* begins with this line.

I, 303 *ken* range of perception.

I, 308 *half-unravelled web* either, a use of the archaic sense of 'unravel', to reveal or disclose (so that the phrase means 'half-disclosed pattern'), or a piece of cloth whose threads are working loose. The sense is that Keats only half-perceives Moneta's 'lofty theme'.

I, 312 *zoning of a summer's day* duration of a summer's day (based on the idea of the sun 'zoning', that is, following its course across the sky).

I, 326 *ancient mother* Tellus (Earth).

I, 331 *Mnemosyne* the Greek name for Moneta, the poet's guide.

I, 336-46 compare with the description of Thea in *Hyperion* I, 26-44. Keats omits the stress on Thea's superhuman size which marks the earlier version (I, 26-36) since he wishes to suggest that she is closer to human sorrow than Moneta. The passage may owe something to Keats's recollection of a Wedgwood design, 'Maternal Affection': see D. Robinson, *KSJ*, XVI (1967), p. 24. 'Statuary' here means both 'stature' and 'statuesqueness'.

I, 341 *vanward*] venom'd *1856*.

I, 348 *hollow*] *not in 1856*. 'Hollow' makes the line hypermetrical, and did not occur in the first version, *Hyperion* I, 46.

I, 350 *tune*] tone *1856*. *Hyperion* I, 48 has 'tone'.

I, 352 *this-like Hyperion* I, 50 has 'these like'.

I, 354 for the influence of *King Lear* on Keats's conception of Saturn, see *Hyperion* I, 98-103*n* (p. 611).

I, 356 *cry*] say *1856*. *Hyperion* I, 54 has 'say'.

I, 362 *captious* replaces 'conscious' in *Hyperion* I, 60.

I, 373-4 takes the place of *Hyperion* I, 73-5, 'Those green-robed senators of mighty woods, / Tall oaks, branch-charmèd by the earnest stars, / Dream, and so dream all night without a stir...'.

I, 379 *pressed* in *Hyperion* I, 80, 'touched'.

I, 384-99 expands *Hyperion* I, 83-5, 'One moon, with alteration slow, had shed / Her silver seasons four upon the night, / And still these two were postured motionless...'.

I, 395 *every*] ever *G, Allott*. The emendation of *G* and *Allott* follows the suggestion of J. C. Maxwell. However, as Mr Maxwell has subsequently informed me, the phrase 'each day by day' occurs in Thomas Hardy's *The*

682 NOTES FOR PP. 446-9

Dynasts Part 2 II 6 (Wessex edn, *Verse* II [1920], p. 250), which supports the reading of both *W*2 and *1856*, 'every day by day'.

I, 411 *solitary Pan* presumably Pan is solitary because the Golden Age, which had flourished under Saturn, is no more. Further, see *Dictionary of Classical Names* (p. 713).

I, 412-38 Saturn's speech in *Hyperion* I, 95-134 is longer. Keats's revision alters the tone, making Saturn more querulous, and giving him less hope.

I, 426 *shaking palsy*] aching palsy *1856*, Allott.

I, 431 *those imps* his children, the Olympians, who led by Jupiter had revolted against the Titans.

I, 441-5 the poet is distressed by the dichotomy between Saturn's god-like appearance (he is a 'large-limbed vision'), which would be suited by tragic tones, and the pathos of his words, which sound like those of an old man rather than a god.

I, 442 *pleasant*] *not in 1856*. The line is hypermetrical.

II, 1-49 a reworking of *Hyperion* I, 158-204.
II, 1-3 compare *Paradise Lost* V, 571-4.
II, 12 *in their doom* in *Hyperion* I, 163, 'in sharp pain'.
II, 15 *orbèd fire* the sun. Hyperion was god of the sun.
II, 18 *prodigies* unnatural events.
II, 20 *gloom-bird's even screech* the owl's hooting in the evening. The owl is a bird of ill-omen. *Hyperion* I, 171 has 'hated' for 'even'.
II, 22 followed in *Hyperion* I, 173-4 by the line, 'Or prophesyings of the midnight lamp ...', which is included in *1856*.
II, 24-30 *His palace ... angerly* see *Hyperion* I, 176-82n.
II, 25 *glowing*] shining *1856*.
II, 48 *Is sloping* altered from 'Came slope' of *Hyperion* I, 204 in order to avoid the Miltonic effect. So, too, the following lines in *Hyperion* (I, 205-8), which are heavily Miltonic, are omitted.
II, 50 *Mnemosyne* Moneta.
II, 53-6 reworks *Hyperion* I, 213-20.
II, 56 *diamond-pavèd*] diamond-paned *1856*.
II, 60 *Hours* the attendant nymphs of the sun ('Horae').

'THE DAY IS GONE, AND ALL ITS SWEETS ARE GONE!'
Probably written on 10 October 1819, the evening after visiting Fanny Brawne for a few hours in Hampstead. The following day he wrote, 'My sweet Girl, I am living to day in yesterday: I was in a complete fascination all day. I feel myself at your mercy.... You dazzled me – There is nothing in the world so bright and delicate' (*L* II, p. 222). Here, as in his two remaining sonnets ('*I cry your mercy ...*' and '*Bright star! ...*'), Keats returns to the Shakespearean form. For his experiments in April 1819, see headnotes to *To Sleep* and '*If by dull rhymes ...*' (pp. 641-2). Published *Plymouth and Devonport Weekly Journal*, 4 October 1838, *1848*. Keats's draft, now in the Morgan Library, has 'tranc'd' for 'light' (l. 3) and transposes ll. 5-8 and 9-12.

683 NOTES FOR PP. 449–51

4 *accomplished* perfect.
8 *warmth, whiteness* compare '*I cry your mercy . . .*' 8, 'That warm, white, lucent, million-pleasured breast. . .'.
9 *shut of eve* compare *Lamia* II, 107, 'at blushing shut of day'.
13 *love's missal* love's prayer-book. With the religious images, compare *To [Fanny]* 25–6, '*Bright star! . . .*' 4, *Ode to Fanny* 50–53.

'WHAT CAN I DO TO DRIVE AWAY'

Dated c. Oct. 1819 in *1848*, where it was first published. Possibly written c. 13 October 1819, when Keats wrote to Fanny Brawne, 'This moment I have set myself to copy some verses out fair ['*The day is gone . . .*'?]. I cannot proceed with any degree of content. I must write you a line or two and see if that will assist in dismissing you from my Mind for ever so short a time [this poem]. Upon my soul I can think of nothing else. . . . I cannot exist without you – I am forgetful of every thing but seeing you again – my Life seems to stop there – I see no further. . . . I could be martyr'd for my Religion – Love is my religion – I could die for that. . . . You have ravish'd me away by a Power I cannot resist; and yet I could resist till I saw you; and even since I have seen you I have endeavoured often "to reason against the reasons of my Love"' (*L* II, pp. 223–4). Like '*I cry your mercy . . .*', this poem is an expression of Keats's confused feelings on fully admitting to his love for Fanny Brawne. He half-feared that his passion might displace his ambitions as a poet. Stillinger (*Texts*, pp. 264–5) points out that the date and *Allott*'s title, *To [Fanny]*, are based on Milnes's conjecture.

7–9 compare Keats's remarks on 25 July 1819, '. . . I am indeed astonish'd to find myself so careless of all charms but yours – remembring as I do the time when even a bit of ribband was a matter of interest with me' (*L* II, p. 133).
10 *parti-coloured* Keats was aware of the uneven quality of his poetry.
17 *throes* is convulsed in throes. A rare verb according to *OED*, which cites *The Tempest* II, 1. 225, 'A birth . . . which throes thee much to yield'.
18 compare Chaucer, *Troilus and Criseyde* V, 225, 'How shal I do? When shal she com ageyn . . .?'
25–6 for the religious imagery, see '*The day is gone . . .*' headnote and l. 13 and *n* (above).
31–43 Keats refers to his brother George's difficulties in America, and the country is depicted as antipathetic to the pastoral world.
33 *wrecked*] *wretched Allott (following H. B. Forman's emendation)*.
35 *urns* depicted in neoclassical literature and art as the source of rivers or streams.
42 *flowers*] *Garrod (OSA)*; *bad flowers 1848, G*; *bud flowers Allott*. H. B. Forman guessed that Keats first wrote 'buds', and then replaced it with 'flowers', but forgot to cancel 'bud'.
43 alludes to Pope's *An Essay on Man* (1733) I, 294, 'One truth is clear, "Whatever is, is right". . .'.

48-9 compare *'Bright star! . . .'* 10, 'Pillowed upon my fair love's ripening breast. . .'.

54 *O, the sweetness of the pain* a line used earlier in *'Welcome joy, and welcome sorrow'* 23.

'I CRY YOUR MERCY, PITY, LOVE – AY, LOVE!'

Probably written in October 1819. Published *1848*. On 19 October Keats wrote to Fanny Brawne, 'I shold like to cast the die for Love or death – I have no Patience with any thing else. . .' (*L* II, p. 224).

8 compare with *To [Fanny]* 48-9.

10 *Withhold*] Without *G* (*with no authority*; Garrod [*OSA*] has Withold).

11 *thrall* servant, subject; also suggests an enthralled subject. Compare *La Belle Dame sans Merci* 39-40, 'La Belle Dame . . . / Hath thee in thrall. . . .' See also *Calidore* 103, *Endymion* III, 333 for Keats's use of the word.

'BRIGHT STAR! WOULD I WERE STEADFAST AS THOU ART'

Date conjectural. Published *Plymouth and Devonport Weekly Journal*, 27 September 1838, *1848*. Text based on Keats's autograph in Severn's copy of Shakespeare (now in the Keats Museum at Hampstead). Brown's transcript of an earlier version is now in Harvard College Library.

There has been a good deal of disagreement over the date of this sonnet's composition. It was long regarded as Keats's last poem, written *c.* 29 September 1820, when he copied it out in Severn's copy of Shakespeare during his voyage to Italy. The discovery of Brown's transcript of an earlier version (*Colvin* [1917], pp. 493-4), which is dated '1819', made the date in 1820 impossible. Three main dates have been suggested:

1 *October 1818*: Keats's description of Windermere in his letter to Tom of 25-7 June 1818 provides a parallel with ll. 1-4 (see *n*). Gittings (1954), pp. 25-36, and *Gittings* (1956), pp. 54-68, argue that Keats re-read this passage in October, and that the poem is addressed, not to Fanny Brawne, but to Mrs Isabella Jones, with whom Gittings believes Keats had an affair. This dating ignores Brown's date, '1819', the single piece of MS evidence, and is considered unlikely by most scholars (see J. M. Murry, *Keats* [1955], pp. 113-23, for a reply).

2 *July 1819*: This date depends upon the parallel between the sonnet and the conclusion of Keats's letter to Fanny Brawne, written 25 July 1819, 'I will imagine you Venus tonight and pray, pray, pray to your star like a Hethen. Your's ever, fair Star' (*L* II, p. 133). However, Fanny is here imagined as the evening star, Venus, and in the sonnet Keats is thinking of the North Star (see too, *Bate* [1963], p. 539*n*).

3 *October–November 1819*: the fact that Fanny Brawne transcribed the poem in the copy of Cary's *Dante*, which Keats had given her, associates it with her. The return to the sonnet form connects it with '*The day is gone . . .*', which can be dated 10 November 1819 (see headnote, p. 682), and with '*I cry your*

685 NOTES FOR P. 452

mercy ...'. There are sufficient similarities between the themes and wording of these two sonnets, *To [Fanny]*, and '*Bright star!* ...', to regard them as a group. *Bate* [1963], p. 618, settles for a date in October–December 1819, and *Allott*, though she argues for October–November, places the sonnet after *The Cap and Bells*, written November–December 1819. See also A. Ward, 'The Date of Keats's *Bright Star* Sonnet', *Studies in Philology*, LII (1955), pp. 75–85.

H. W. Garrod's view of the conclusion of the poem is disapproving – '... the octave ... is good and noble, the sestet (which is full of textual variants) is vicious and ineffective. ... The poet asks of the Star only steadfastness and unchangeability. But do they really matter to him? Does the Bright Star really stand for anything in which the sonnet culminates?' (*Garrod [OSA]*, pp. 468–9). Other readings include F. W. Bateson, *English Poetry* (1950), pp. 11–12, *Ward* (1963), pp. 297–8, Harold Bloom, *The Visionary Company* (1961), pp. 456–8, *Bate* (1963), pp. 359*n*, 539, 618–20, and B. Ormerod 'Nature's Eremite: Keats and the Liturgy of Passion', *KSJ*, XVI (1967),' pp. 73–7.

Title] Keats's Last Sonnet *1848 (the MSS are untitled)*.

1–4 compare Keats's description of Windermere in his letter to Tom on 25–7 June 1818, '... the two views we have had of it are of the most noble tenderness – they can never fade away – they make one forget the divisions of life; age, youth, poverty and riches; and refine one's sensual vision into a sort of north star which can never cease to be open lidded and stedfast over the wonders of the great Power' (*L* I, p. 299). Both this description and the sonnet recall Wordsworth's *The Excursion* (1814) IV, 691–3, 'Looked on the Polar Star, as on a Guide / And Guardian of their course, that never closed / His steadfast eye. ...' But star imagery is widespread in Keats's poetry: compare 'the lidless-eyèd train / Of planets' (*Endymion* I, 598–9), 'the same bright, patient stars' (*Hyperion* I, 353), and the description of Porphyro, 'Ethereal, flushed, and like a throbbing star / Seen mid the sapphire heaven's deep repose', *The Eve of St Agnes* 318–19.

2 *aloft*] amid *Brown's transcript*. 'Aloft' means both 'aloft in the night sky' and 'above the night sky'.

3 *And*] Not *Brown's transcript*.

4 *patient*] devout *Brown's transcript*. 'Eremite' means recluse or anchorite. See *The Eve of St Agnes* 277 and *n* (p. 626).

5 *moving*] morning *Brown's transcript*.

6 *pure ablution* 'ablution' refers to the religious rites of purification (see 'priestlike' in the preceding line). Literally, it means washing clean, which is what the tides ('moving waters') do to the seashore twice a day.

7–8 possibly a clue to the poem's composition in late October. *Allott* cites the *Annual Register*, 23 October 1819, which reported a heavy snowfall the previous day.

7 *mask*] masque *Draft*.

686 NOTES FOR P. 452

10–14] Brown's transcript reads: 'Cheek-pillow'd on my Love's white ripening breast / To touch, for ever, its warm sink and swell, / Awake, for ever, in a sweet unrest, / To hear, to feel her tender-taken breath, / Half passionless, and so swoon on to death.' With l. 10, compare *To [Fanny]* 48–9 and '*I cry your mercy . . .*' 8.

11 *swell and fall*] sink and swell *Brown's transcript*; fall and swell *1848*. *G* and *Allott* follow *1848*'s emendation, which avoids the more obvious order, and like *Brown's transcript*, makes 'swell' the rhyme-word.

14 compare Keats's letter to Fanny Brawne on 25 July 1819, 'I have two luxuries to brood over in my walks, your Loveliness and the hour of my death' (*L* II, p. 133). For the use of 'swoon' in an erotic context, see *Endymion* I, 398, 'His senses had swooned off. . .'.

KING STEPHEN. A FRAGMENT OF A TRAGEDY

Possibly begun late August 1819 and put aside in November 1819 (the date given on Brown's transcript). Published *1848*. Text based on *1848* with some corrections from Keats draft (now in Harvard Library – referred to as *K*). Brown recorded some twenty years later: 'As soon as Keats had finished *Otho the great* I pointed out to him a subject for an english historical tragedy in the reign of Stephen, beginning with his defeat by the Empress Maud, and ending with the death of his son Eustace, when Stephen yielded the succession to the crown to the young Henry. He was struck with the variety of events and characters which must necessarily be introduced; and I offered to give, as before [in *Otho the Great*] their dramatic conduct. "The play must open", I began, "with the field of battle, when Stephen's forces are retreating" – "Stop!" he said, "stop! I have been already too long in leading-strings. I will do all this myself." He immediately set about it, and wrote two or three scenes, about 130 lines' (*KC* II, p. 67). *Bate* (1963), pp. 568, 621, believes the fragment was written in the first two weeks of November.

In 1135 Stephen seized the English crown on the death of his uncle, Henry I, even though Henry had previously persuaded his barons to recognize his daughter as heir to England and Normandy. Stephen was defeated at Lincoln in 1141 by the Empress Maud, and in 1154 Henry II became king. For Keats's sources, see *Lowell* II, pp. 361–2, *Finney*, pp. 728–31, and *Allott*. The part of Stephen was written with Edmund Kean in mind, but Kean left for an American tour in autumn 1819. This, together with lack of confidence in his dramatic powers, probably caused Keats to give up the play. On 17 November he wrote to Taylor, 'The little dramatic skill I may as yet have however badly it might show in a Drama would I think be sufficient for a Poem – I wish to diffuse the colouring of St Agnes eve throughout a Poem in which Character and Sentiment would be the figures to such drapery – Two or three such Poems, if God should spare me, would be a famous gradus ad Parnassum altissimum – I mean they would nerve me up to the writing of a few fine Plays – my greatest ambition – when I do feel ambitious' (*L* II, p. 234). See Bernice Slote, *Keats and the Dramatic Principle* (1958), pp. 114–15.

Sub-title] *Brown's transcript*; A Dramatic Fragment *1848*.

I. 1. 1   *vein-swollen front*   compare *Lamia* II, 77, 'whose brow had no dark veins to swell'. The parallel argues for the hypothesis that *King Stephen* was begun in August.

I. 1. 9   Robert, Earl of Gloucester, half-brother of the Empress, raised the siege of Lincoln with the help of Ranulf, Earl of Chester, his son-in-law.

I. 1. 19–21   *De Redvers ... Baldwin*   as *Allott* points out Keats has confused Baldwin de Redvers, who was opposed to Stephen, and Baldwin Fitz-Gilbert, a courageous warrior, who addressed the army on Stephen's behalf.

I. 2. 18   *Duke of Bretagne*   Alan, Earl of Brittany, was the leader of the Breton supporters of Stephen.

I. 2. 35–50   compare *Macbeth* I. 2.

I. 2. 40   *morion*   an anachronism – 'A kind of helmet, without beaver or visor, worn in the sixteenth and seventeenth centuries' (*OED*). The word occurs in Spenser. It is used accurately in Scott's *Marmion* (1808) I, ix, '... with musquet, pike, and morion'.

I. 2. 51   *hilts*] *K, G, Allott*; hilt *1848*.

I. 2. 52   *Mars*] *K, G, Allott*; man *1848*.

I. 3. 5   *comes*] *K, G*; come *1848, Allott*.

I. 3. 5–6   *O, for a sword ... A noble sword!*   compare *Richard III* V. 4. 7, 'A horse! A horse! My kingdom for a horse!' Richard was one of Kean's parts. See I. 4. 57–8n.

I. 3. 11   *truck*   barter.

I. 3. 16   *dips*] dip *K, G, Allott*.

I. 3. 25   *vail*   submit.

I. 3. 45   *hilts*] *K, G, Allott*; hilt *1848*.

I. 4. 1   *Boulogne*   King Stephen, who married the daughter of Count Eustace of Boulogne.

I. 4. 9   *I will*] will I *K, G.* Garrod (*OSA*) follows *1848*.

I. 4. 13   *trenching*   encroaching, that is, advancing trenches towards a besieged enemy.

I. 4. 20   *dooming*] a dooming *K, G*.

I. 4. 55   *rubiest*   compare 'rubious health' (*Otho the Great* IV. 2. 38) and 'rubious-argent' (*Lamia* I, 163).

I. 4. 57–8   compare *Richard III* I. 1. 1–2., 'Now is the winter of our discontent / Made glorious summer by this sun of York ...' (for another echo, see I. 3. 5–6n). Matthew Prior's *English Ballad on the Taking of Namur* (1707), 83–4 reads, '... that mighty year / When you turn'd June into September ...'.

'THIS LIVING HAND, NOW WARM AND CAPABLE'

Probably written November–December 1819. The lines were written on a page of the manuscript of *The Cap and Bells*, probably during the composition of that poem. (See *Finney*, p. 740, for a reproduction of the MS, now in Harvard Library.) Formerly thought to be addressed to Fanny Brawne; now generally regarded as a fragment meant for later use in a play or poem.

1–3   *This living hand ... tomb*   compare *The Fall of Hyperion* I, 18, 'When this warm scribe my hand is in the grave ...'

THE CAP AND BELLS: OR, THE JEALOUSIES.
A FAERY TALE – UNFINISHED

Written November–December 1819. Published *1848* (ll. 217–56 appeared in the *Indicator*, 23 August 1820). The larger part of Keats's draft (referred to as *K* below) is now divided between the Morgan, Huntington, and Harvard libraries, and together with Woodhouse's transcript (*W*2), corrects some misreadings in *1848*. *K* includes a few revisions made after Brown's lost transcript.

Charles Brown later described the circumstances in which the poem was written: 'By chance our conversation turned on the idea of a comic faery poem in the Spenser stanza, and I was glad to encourage it. He had not composed many stanzas before he proceeded in it with spirit. It was to be published under the feigned authorship of Lucy Vaughan Lloyd, and to bear the title of *The Cap and Bells*, or, which he preferred, *The Jealousies*. This occupied his mornings pleasantly. He wrote it with the greatest facility; in one instance I remember having copied (for I copied as he wrote) as many as twelve stanzas before dinner. In the evenings, at his own desire, he was alone in a separate sitting-room, deeply engaged in remodelling his poem of "Hyperion" into a "Vision"' (*KC* II, pp. 71–2). (Keats was probably tinkering with *The Fall of Hyperion* rather than remodelling it; see headnote, p. 676). Keats gave up the poem under the pressures of personal trouble (*KC* II, p. 72), probably connected with George Keats's trip to England 9–28 January 1820. On 3 February Keats's first haemorrhage occurred, but he still hoped to return to the poem when his health improved (*L* II, pp. 268, 299).

Brown stresses the unfinished nature of the poem. *1848* printed the following note: 'This Poem was written subject to future amendments and omissions: it was begun without a plan, and without any prescribed laws for the supernatural machinery. – CHARLES BROWN.' Brown also recorded that it '... was written chiefly for amusement; it appeared to be a relaxation. ... When I noticed certain startling contradictions, his answer used to be – "Never mind Brown; all these matters will be properly harmonized when we divide it into Cantoes"' (*KC* II, p. 99). The idea for the poem may have come from Keats's earlier involvement in Charles Brown's prose story, *The Fairies' Triumph*, a humorous fantasy, with satirical touches (see the headnote to *Faery Bird's Song*, p. 632, and compare the satirical vein of *The Cap and Bells* with that in '*When they were come unto the faery's court*'. The pattern of crossed love, with immortals pursuing mortal lovers, is probably indebted to *A Midsummer Night's Dream*. As Brown noted, *The Cap and Bells* were written without a plan, and several more or less unrelated themes can be discerned. There is a certain amount of topical satire (see the passages on gaslight and on hackney coaches, ll. 210–16 and 225–61); political satire directed against the Prince Regent, who, like Elfinan, disliked the bride (Princess Caroline) chosen for him (see ll. 145–62); literary satire, in which Elfinan portrays Byron (see ll. 610–13*n*); and self-parody of Keats's own work (see, for instance, ll. 169*n*, 418–19*n* and 737–8*n*). It is also possible that Keats drew an oblique parallel between his story and his relationship with Fanny Brawne. *Gittings* (1956), pp. 115–43, and *Gittings* (1968), pp. 368–73, argue both for the biographical

interpretation and for the notion that the poem was meant as a satire on the
rivalry between the Lake Poets and the 'Cockney' writers (identifying Elfinan
with Byron, Eban with Hazlitt, Hum with Leigh Hunt and Charles Lamb, and
Crafticanto as 'Southey with a dash of Wordsworth'). This plays down the
political satire, and seems too precise a schematization for such an undeveloped
fragment. Further on the allusions, see *Finney*, pp. 732–7, and P. Mann,
'Keats's Indian Allegory', *KSJ*, VI (1957), pp. 4–9. Keats had some hopes
of making a popular success with the poem, but 'Everything was against it:
his health, anxieties about money, dejection because marriage was impossible
for years to come, wavering confidence in the quality of his previous work, and,
finally, lack of any real interest in the poem itself' (*Bate* [1963], p. 623).
Title] The jealousies A faery Tale by Lucy Vaughan Lloyd of China Walk,
Lambeth *W*2.

1 *Hydaspes* Keats was probably thinking of the Ganges: compare *Paradise
Lost* III, 436, '*Ganges* or *Hydaspes Indian* streams...'.

4 *Elfinan* borrowed from Spenser, *The Faerie Queene* II. x. 72.

4–5 *famed ... fair* satirizes the habits of the Prince Regent. As a fairy
prince, Elfinan ought not to love mortals.

9 *Jones* (p. 260n) comments, '... the abandoned satire *Cap and Bells* recalls
Lamia in its illicit mixing of human and non-human loves and its fairy Emperor who "lov'd girls smooth as shades, but hated a mere shade".'

14 *Zendervester* the Zend-Avesta is the sacred book of the Zoroastrian religion.

18 *Caricature ... tart lampoon* satiric attacks on the Prince Regent reached
new heights when he sought for a divorce in 1819–20.

19–31 George III and his ministers had arranged for the Prince Regent's
marriage to Princess Caroline of Brunswick in 1795.

31 *Bellanaine* 'beautiful dwarf', from *bella* (Italian) and *naine* (French).
Queen Caroline was short in stature. It may also be, as Finney thought, a near-anagram of the name of Byron's wife, Anne Isabella Milbank (see ll. 610–13
and *n*).

44 *promener à l'aile* take a walk, as suits a fairy, by flying.

45 *somerset* a corruption of 'somersault', current from the sixteenth to
nineteenth centuries.

49–53 *Crafticant ... flying footman* probably meant as a satire against the
Tory ministers who supported the Prince Regent.

59 *chouse* dupe, trick, deceive (used earlier in '*All gentle folks who owe a
grudge*' 47).

64 *beauteous mortal* like Elfinan, Bellanaine loves a mortal.

86–95 probably aimed in part at Byron, who had published Cantos I and
II of *Don Juan* in July 1819. But also, as *Allott* points out, attacking the
'Delicate Investigation' of 1806 into Princess Caroline's morals.

88 *Parpaglion* an invented name. *Allott* notes that *paglia* (Italian) means
straw or chaff.

90 *Panthea* from *The Faerie Queene* II. x. 73.

91 *hypercritic*] hypocritic *W*2, *Allott*.

NOTES FOR PP. 463–7

107 *seems*] seem *K*; seemed *W2, Allott*.

114 *Angle-land* England

129 *suburb* neighbouring.

135–62 the Prince Regent's efforts to divorce Caroline had made his relations with the Whig ministers worse.

145–62 the alterations of the numbering in *K* indicate that these two stanzas are 'an afterthought or subsequent insertion' (*G*, pp. xlvi–vii).

145 *chancellor* perhaps Nicholas Vansittart, Baron Bexley, who was Chancellor of the Exchequer from 1812 to 1822.

147, 149 *Palfior, Phalaric* invented names.

150 *tip-toe marquis* perhaps the Marquis of Lansdowne, '... whose refusal to sit upon the Green Bag Committee in the House of Lords was both "moral" and "gallant"' (*Forman* [1883] II, p. 495).

151 *upon tick* on credit (colloquial).

161 *zany* mountebank (a word originating in the *Commedia dell'arte*), or, more loosely, buffoon, simpleton.

162 *Biancopany* H. B. Forman pointed out that the reference is to Samuel Whitbread (*bianco* plus *pane* in Italian). He was a staunch supporter of the Princess, and came from the famous brewing family.

169 *Bertha* the name of the heroine of Keats's *The Eve of St Mark*. The element of self-parody in the following passage is marked, and appears elsewhere in the poem.

170 *pleatings*] *K, Garrod* (*OSA*), *Allott*; plaitings *W2, 1848, G*.

178–80 an echo of Thomas Moore's satire on the Prince Regent in *The Insurrection of the Papers* (1812), 17–18.

180 *felon*] *K, W2, G, Allott*; fellow *1848*.

181 *Eban* the name suggests 'ebony'. Black house-servants and pages were not unusual in the period.

188 *Hum* a colloquial abbreviation of 'humbug'. *Allott* points out that Moore used the name to satirize the Prince Regent in his 'Fum and Hum, the Two Birds of Royalty', *Poetical Works of Thomas Moore*, ed. A. D. Godley (1910), pp. 452–3.

190–98 Elfinan's actions were possibly suggested by Tipu Sultan, who sent a diamond ring to France with his envoys, and was notorious for his callous cruelty. Further, see l. 333*n*.

193 *bowstrung* a Turkish method of execution (by strangling) in the seventeenth century.

207 *For shortest*] *K* (later revision); And for short *W2, 1848, G, Allott*. See *Texts*, p. 269.

208 *houses*] *K, G, Allott*; dealers *W2, 1848*.

210–16 retail traders stayed open as long as possible. London's first gas lighting was installed *c*. 1807.

215 *scathe* harm, damage (Spenser).

222 *hurdy-gurdies* an early form of barrel-organ, used by street musicians.

226–61 Brown commented, 'What can be better than [Keats's] description of a London hackney-coach? – yet how much misplaced!' (*KC* II, p. 99).

691 NOTES FOR PP. 467–70

226 *string* the check-string, used by the passenger to tell the driver to stop.
227 etc. *Jarvey* a hackney-coachman, or the vehicle itself. Used here to refer to the driver, horse, and coach as if they were one.
229 *linsey-woolsey* an inferior cloth, made from a mixture of wool and flax.
234 *in a litter* puns on the two meanings.
235 *crop* craw, stomach.
238 *fiddle-faddle* trifling, fussy.
240 *lazar-house* see *Isabella* 124n (p. 598).
251–2 *tilburies . . . phaetons . . . Curricles . . . mail-coaches* mail-coaches were introduced at the end of the eighteenth century; the other vehicles are varieties of light carriages.
256 *Louted* bowed (Spenserian).
257 *Certes* assuredly (Spenserian).
261 in *K*, stanza xxix is followed by a cancelled stanza; "Ho! Ho thought Eban so this Signor Hum / A Conversazione holds tonight / Wheneer he beats his literary drum / The learned muster round all light and tight / Drest in best black to talk by candle light.' / E'en while he thought, for eighteen penny fare / He paid a half penny by cuning sleight / Made argent; then with self-contented Air / Broke through the crowd to Hums, and all the world was there.' Gittings (1956), pp. 125–9, claims that this is a satire on Leigh Hunt.
288 *figure* horoscope.
290 *chalk* for making magic circles.
291 *aqua-vitae* 'a term of the alchemists applied to . . . unrectified alcohol' (*OED*). Also, spirits, especially brandy.
292 *dentes sapientiae* wisdom teeth, to be used for magical purposes.
293 *Our barber tells me* barbers at this time pulled teeth and let blood as well as tending hair.
295 *grains of Paradise* the seed-pods of the plant *Amomum Meleguetta* used as a medicine and spice from the Middle Ages.
297 *sly*] *1848* has 'slight' in error. A 'sly douceur' is a bribe (*OED* gives examples from 1763 to 1818).
304–6 *with one shoe . . . John* Keats is playing on the nursery rhyme, 'Diddle, diddle dumpling, my son John, / Went to bed with his trousers on. / One shoe off, and one shoe on, / Diddle, diddle dumpling, my son John.' Gittings (1956), p. 130, points out that Charles Lamb had tipsily insulted an acquaintance of Wordsworth's by singing this rhyme at him during the 'immortal dinner' at Haydon's, which Keats attended, on 28 December 1817.
310 *two pair* a 'pair' is a 'pair of stairs', often used to mean flight or storey. Hence, 'Two pair' meant the second floor or storey (*OED*).
311 *Salpietro* saltpetre, used here either as an exclamation, or as a name.
314 *yelping*] *G, Allott*; whelping *K, W2, 1848*. H. B. Forman is responsible for the emendation. In ll. 312–13 the dog is referred to as a male.
319 *rattan* a cane used for giving beatings.
333 *Man-Tiger-Organ* P. Mann, *KSJ*, VI (1957), pp. 4–9, has identified this as the famous mechanical tiger made for Tipu Sultan. It is almost life-size, and when set in motion attacks the model of an English officer, making

appropriate noises. The tiger represents Tipu himself, a fanatical Moslem who attacked the Christians. After Tipu Sultan's defeat at Seringapatam in 1799, the tiger was captured, and eventually put on display in East India House in 1818, where Keats probably saw it. (It is now in the Victoria and Albert Museum.) *Gittings* (1956), pp. 126–7, notes a striking resemblance between this passage and a childhood dream of Leigh Hunt's.

341 *senna-tea* administered as a purgative.

347 *treen* trees (dialectal). *1848* has 'green', *K* has 'treen'.

357 *Chaldean* the Chaldeans were famous for their occult knowledge, hence extended to mean soothsayer, astrologer.

365 *1848* and *W2* give a footnote: 'Mr Nisby is of opinion that laced coffee is bad for the head. Spectator.' 'Nantz' is brandy from Nantes.

389–96 probably suggested by *A Midsummer Night's Dream* II. 1. 120–35.

396 *ope*] oped *G, Allott*. *K* has either 'open' or 'ope' (*Texts*, p. 270).

398 *bam* a hoax or imposition (slang).

403 *Cham* *1848* and *W2* give a footnote: 'Cham is said to have been the inventor of Magic. Lucy learn'd this from Bayle's Dictionary, and had copied a long Latin note from that work.' P. Bayle's *Dictionnaire Historique* was first published in 1695–7.

411 *palatine* possibly meant as an adverb meaning 'royally'. But see the individual use of the word in *Lamia* I, 211.

416 *Admiral de Witt* John de Witt (1625–72) led the Dutch against the British fleet in 1667.

418–19 compare with *Ode to a Nightingale* 11–17.

419 *one*] *K, G, Allott*; the *W2, 1848*.

422 *save 'the creature'*] *K, W2, G*; catch the treasure *1848*, *Garrod* (*OSA*); catch 'the creature' *Allott*. *1848*'s alteration was probably to avoid the colloquialism 'creature', meaning strong drink.

427 *Ottoman* 'a cushioned seat like a sofa, but without back or arms ... or a small article of the same kind used as a low seat or footstool' (*OED*).

429 *lady's-fingers* small biscuit or cake. 'Candy wine', as *Allott* notes, probably means sweet wine, or wine from Kandy (Ceylon).

434 *Mago* Keats's abbreviation of 'magician'.

443 *Midsummer*] May 1392 *K* (*cancelled*).

468 *or head*] head *W2, Allott*.

468 *fay* an archaic form of 'faith', but also means 'fairy'.

478 *repeater* a repeating watch or clock.

500 *Moore* a reference to *Old Moore's Almanac*, first published in 1699.

503–4 parodies *The Eve of St Mark*.

505 *'gan*] *K, W2, G, Allott*; 'gan to *1848*.

512–13 *old* | *And legend-leavèd book* compare with Bertha's 'curious volume' in *The Eve of St Mark* 25–38.

521 *Uplift*] *G, Allott*; Up lift *K*; But lift *W2, 1848*.

522 *where I wait for guerdon fit*] *K, G, Allott*; not in *W2, 1848*.

523 *that*] this *G, Allott*.

527 *I*] I'll *W2, Allott*.

NOTES FOR PP. 476–83

539 *cold pig* to 'give cold pig' is 'To awaken by sluicing with cold water or by pulling off the bed-clothes' (E. Partridge, *A Dictionary of Slang* [1949], p. 169). A mocking reference to the 'extreme unction' in preceding line.

544 *Whew*] the word is not clearly written in *K* or *W2*. *1848* has 'Where'.

547 *pigsney* darling, pet (addressed to women, and derived from 'pig's eye').

563 *Hark! Hark!*] Hark! Hah! *K*, *G*.

565 *view*] see *W2*, Allott.

586 *Gentlemen pensioners* gentlemen-at-arms.

587 *Janizaries* formerly a body of Turkish infantry who made up the Sultan's guard and the main part of his standing army.

600 *Hocus* a conjuror or trickster (an abbreviation of 'hocus-pocus').

610–13 *Farewell ... fare thee well! ... By'r Lady* Keats quotes from Byron's poem *Fare thee well* (1816), 1–2, written after separating from his wife Annabelle Milbank. The poem caused a controversy on its appearance, and was reprinted in 1819. 'Bellanaine' is a partial anagram of Annabelle (see l. 31*n*), while 'By'r Lady' plays upon her married name, Lady Byron.

615 *smoke* uncover, perceive. The word could also mean ridicule, mock, a possible sense here.

664 *reek* emit smoke, vapour, steam, etc.

666 *respire* breathe, take breath (poeticism).

671 *her hoop* her hoop-skirt.

679 *Balk* Balkh was an ancient city in Persia.

680 *griffin* perhaps a reference to the griffin on St Mary's Church, Cheapside, which Keats would have known as a boy.

684 *marrowbones* used as a jocular term for the knees.

690 *Cinque-parted* grouped in fives.

691 *green-faned cedars*] green-fanned cedars Allott. The emendation is unnecessary. The upright trunk and green canopy of the cedar can be regarded as a 'fane' (temple). Compare *Ode to Psyche* 48, 50–54.

692 *dozed*] *G*, Allott; dos'd *K*, *W2*, *1848*.

694 *kettledrum* that is, a kettle-drummer.

695 *It went for apoplexy* his death was thought by most people to have been caused by apoplexy.

696 *Left it to pay the piper* Crafticanto left his gold watch in compensation for the death of the kettle-drummer (whose burial might call for a piper?).

697 *maugre* in spite of (archaic).

700 *revokes* in whist, the failure to follow suit when a card of the required suit is held.

707 *hoity-toity* huffy, petulant, or haughty, rather than flighty or frolicsome.

737–8 another example of self-parody. Compare *Hyperion* II, 305–6, '. . . like sullen waves / In the half-glutted hollows of reef-rocks. . .'. On the use of 'glut', see *On the Sea* 3*n* (p. 558).

744 *plenty horn* cornucopia.

751 *Basilic* an archaic form of 'Basilica', originally a royal palace, 'thence,

a large oblong building or hall, with double colonnades and a semicircular apse at the end, used for a court of justice and place of public assembly', and then applied to a building of this kind, used for Christian worship (*OED*). Keats may have St Paul's Cathedral in mind.

759 *Congées* bows.

770 *bag-wigs* eighteenth-century wigs, with the back hair enclosed in a bag, worn by the well-to-do.

793–4] *W2*; not in *K*, *1848*. First printed by *G*.

TO FANNY

Allott is probably correct in dating this February 1820. Published *1848*. Some corrections from Keats's fragmentary early draft, now in Harvard Library (referred to as *K*). After his first haemorrhage on 3 February 1820, Keats was confined indoors, and sometime in February he offered Fanny Brawne the opportunity to free herself from their engagement. Her refusal to do so did not quieten his jealousy for long, and it was exacerbated by his own helplessness, and the fact that she was living next door in Wentworth Place. See *Allott* for a convincing array of parallels between the poem and Keats's letters written to Fanny Brawne in this period.

Title] Ode to Fanny *K, G, Allott*.

3 *tripod* the oracles in Apollo's temple at Delphi 'were always delivered by a priestess, called the Pythia ... [who] placed herself on a tripod, or three-legged stool, made full of holes, directly upon the chasm'; there she was possessed, and her 'wild and incoherent speeches were written down by the priest, digested into order, arranged in hexameter verse, and delivered to the suppliant' (*Baldwin*, pp. 48–50). Apollo was both 'the author of plagues and contagious diseases' (as sun-god), and the 'God of medicine' (pp. 66–7).

8 *out*] *1848*'s 'not' is a misprint, followed by *Garrod* (*OSA*).

40 *blow-ball* 'the globular seeding head of the dandelion' (*OED*).

46 *has*] *K, G, Allott*; his *1848*.

51–3] for the religious imagery, see 'The day is gone ...' 13 and *n* (p. 683).

54 *the just new-budded flower* compare 'The day is gone ...' 5, '... the flower and all its budded charms...'.

56 *last*] *K, G, Allott*; lost *1848, Garrod (OSA)*.

'IN AFTER-TIME, A SAGE OF MICKLE LORE'

Probably written *c*. July 1820. Published *Plymouth and Devonport Weekly Journal*, 4 July 1839, *1848*. *Allott* points out that it was in July that Keats was 'marking the most beautiful passages' for Fanny Brawne in his copy of Spenser (*L* II, p. 302), and that the lines were written out in this copy (now lost). When publishing it in the *Plymouth and Devonport Weekly Journal*, Brown called the verses 'the last stanza of any kind that [Keats] wrote before his lamented death'. R. M. Milnes wrote, '[Keats] expressed this *ex post facto* prophecy, his conviction of the ultimate triumph of freedom and equality by the power of transmitted knowledge' (*1848* I, p. 281). Keats's stanza describes the re-education of Spenser's Giant, who wanted to level the world to equality (*The Faerie Queene* V. ii. 30–54). In Spenser, Artegall (Justice) and his squire Talus defeat the Giant and prove his simple-mindedness. In Keats's version the Giant, with the help of the knowledge spread by Typographus (the printed word), destroys Spenser's heroes.

1 *mickle lore* much learning.

THREE UNDATED FRAGMENTS

I. Probably written February 1816, as it appears in Keats's MS containing *To [Mary Frogley]*. Published *G*.
II. Undated. Published J. M. Murry, *The Poems and Verses of John Keats* (1930) from Keats's MS in Harvard Library, which has both verses on a single piece of paper. Murry and *G* print both verses; *Allott* only the second, giving l. 4 as a variant of l. 8.
III. Undated. Published *G*, from Keats's MS then owned by M. B. Forman.

Doubtful Attributions

'SEE, THE SHIP IN THE BAY IS RIDING'

Published *G* from the transcript in *W*3. Woodhouse noted, 'This poem K. said had not been written by him. He did not see it; but I repeated the first four lines to him'. Unfortunately, it is not entirely clear that Woodhouse is referring to this particular poem. Garrod included it with Keats's poems, 'but with no belief in its authenticity' (*G*, p. lxxii).

THE POET

Probably written by Keats's publisher, John Taylor. See M. A. E. Steele, 'The Authorship of *The Poet* . . .' *KSJ*, V (1956), pp. 69–79. Lowell, Finney, and Garrod include it among Keats's poems, the text of *G* being based on the transcript in *W*3. *Allott* follows what is probably Taylor's revised version, published in the *London Magazine*, October 1821, *Lowell*. The text here follows *W*3, as being the version usually attributed to Keats.

GRIPUS. A FRAGMENT

Undated. Published *Lowell*. The fragment occurs in *W*3, with no indication of its authorship or date. *Allott* considers it 'unKeatsian'. *Gittings* (1968), pp. 285–6, believes it has some reference to Charles Brown, Fanny Brawne and Keats, and was written early in 1819. Certainly, the fact that Woodhouse transcribed it suggests some connection with the Keats circle, and the liaison between Charles Brown and Abigail O'Donaghue, whom he may have married secretly and by whom he had a son, provides an obvious parallel with the relationship between Gripus and Bridget. Keats knew about Brown's liaison, which began before October 1819, and Abigail O'Donaghue became a part-time servant at Wentworth Place, though she did not move into the house until after Keats left for Italy. If *Gripus* does allude to Brown, the only person in the Keats circle likely to write a good-humoured piece mocking his vagaries would be Keats himself, and this fragment should perhaps be connected with the *Character of Charles Brown* (see headnote and *nn*, pp. 634–5). The undistinguished quality of *Gripus* does not exclude the possibility of Keats's authorship if the piece is assumed to be a casual and light-hearted private joke, and the word-play is typically Keatsian.

95 *redicule* a malapropism for 'reticule'. Compare 'excard' for 'discard', 'allegolly' for 'allegory' and 'nonplush' for 'nonplus' (ll. 111, 132, 173).

Dictionary of Classical Names

This guide is based on the works of reference which Keats is known to have used. Cowden Clarke, a schoolboy friend, attributed Keats's 'uncommon familiarity – almost consanguinity with the Greek mythology' to his early reading of Lemprière's *Bibliotheca Classica* (1788, 1st edn), Andrew Tooke's *Pantheon* (1722, 1st edn), and Joseph Spence's *Polymetis* (1747, 1st edn) (*KC* II, pp. 147–8). He also owned copies of the *Pantheon* (1806, 1st edn) compiled for the use of children by 'Edward Baldwin' [William Godwin], and John Potter's *Antiquities of Greece* (1697, 1st edn) (*KC* I, pp. 254, 258). Keats's notions of Greek mythology were importantly formed by his reading of the Elizabethan poets, particularly George Sandys's translation of Ovid, and the iconographic traditions in the visual arts were a further influence (see *Jack*).

Cross-references are indicated by ▷.

Acteon 'A famous huntsman. . . . He saw Diana and her attendants bathing near Gargaphia, for which he was changed into a stag, and devoured by his own dogs' (*Lemprière*). See *Endymion* I, 512–14.

Adonis 'Son of Cinyras, by his daughter Myrrha, was the favorite of Venus. He was fond of hunting, and was often cautioned by his mistress not to hunt wild beasts, for fear of being killed in the attempt. This advice he slighted, and at last received a mortal bite from a wild boar which he had wounded, and Venus, after shedding many tears at his death, changed him into a flower called anemony. Proserpine is said to have restored him to life, on condition that he should spend six months with her, and the rest of the year with Venus. This implies the alternate return of summer and winter. Adonis is often taken for Osiris, because the festivals of both were often begun with mournful lamentations, and finished with a revival of joy, as if they were returning to life again' (*Lemprière*). On the 'Adonian feast', see *Lamia* I, 317–20n (p. 670).

Aeaea An island off Italy, the birthplace of Circe. When she was expelled from Colchis by her subjects, her father carried her back to the island for safety. It was there that Ulysses encountered her.

Aeneas A Trojan prince, son of Anchises and Venus, who founded Rome, and the hero of Virgil's *Aeneid*.

Aeolus 'The king of storms and winds'. His kingdom, the Aeoliae, the seven islands between Italy and Sicily, now known as the Lipari Islands,

698 DICTIONARY OF CLASSICAL NAMES

were 'the retreat of the winds' (*Lemprière*).

Aethon One of the horses which drew the chariot of the sun.

Aetna Mount Etna, Sicily. 'The poets supposed that Jupiter had confined the giants [Titans] under this mountain. It was the forge of Vulcan, where his servants the Cyclops fabricated thunderbolts.'

Alecto 'One of the furies ... represented with her head covered with serpents, and breathing vengeance, war, and pestilence' (*Lemprière*).

Alexander King of Macedonia (356–23 B.C.), conqueror of the East. *King Stephen* I. 4. 34 refers to his generous treatment of the captured princesses, after defeating Darius in 333 B.C.

Alpheus ⟡ Arethusa.

Amalthea 'Daughter of Melissus king of Crete, fed Jupiter with goat's milk. Hence some authors have called her a goat, and have maintained that Jupiter, to reward her kindnesses, placed her in heaven as a constellation, and gave one of her horns to the nymphs who had taken care of his infant years. This horn was called the horn of plenty, and had the power to give the nymphs whatever they desired' (*Lemprière*).

Amphion The son of Jupiter by Antiope: '... he cultivated poetry, and made such an uncommon progress in music, that he is said to have been the inventor of it, and to have built the walls of Thebes at the sound of his lyre' (*Lemprière*). In *Endymion* III, 461 Keats fuses Amphion with Arion (*q.v.*), who had power over the sea.

Amphitrite 'Daughter of Oceanus and Tethys, married Neptune ... She had by him Triton, one of the sea deities.... She ... is often taken for the sea itself' (*Lemprière*).

Andromeda In order to placate the wrath of Neptune she was left to be devoured by a sea-monster. She was 'tied naked on a rock', but Perseus, returning from the conquest of the Gorgons, saw her from the air, was captivated, and turned the monster into a rock. He married Andromeda. *Lemprière* notes, 'Some say that Minerva made Andromeda a constellation in heaven after her death'.

Apollo Above all for Keats, god of the sun and poetry. According to *Baldwin*, 'Apollo was the son of Jupiter by Latona, the daughter of Coeus and Phoebe, two of the Titans'. Juno, Jupiter's wife, was jealous of the amour, and 'sent the serpent, Python, a monster bred from the slime occasioned by a deluge, to persecute' Latona. Apollo and Diana were born together there, and 'one of the first actions of Apollo, when he grew to man's estate, was to kill with his arrow the serpent Python, that had been the tormentor of his mother. Apollo was represented by the Greeks under the most beautiful figure they were able to conceive, young, unbearded with graceful hair, and a countenance, fair, animated and expressive. Beside the name of Apollo ... this God is often called by the poets Hyperion, and Titan; Hyperion one of the Titans having been ... the God of the sun, before that province was conferred upon Apollo. Apollo has various offices. He is the charioteer of the sun, or rather the sun itself; he drives his chariot every day through the circuit of heavens, and at night sinks below the waves to rest: he is drawn by four horses of the most extraordinary beauty and spirit, harnessed abreast: and, when represented in this office, his head is surrounded with a brilliant circle of rays. . . . Apollo is also the God of music and poetry: in this character he is represented with a lyre in his hand, and surrounded by the Nine Muses, the daughters of Jupiter by Mnemosyne, or Memory, one of the Titans. Apollo is the author of plagues and contagious diseases: this is an allegorical conception, as contagious diseases are most frequent and fatal when the heat of the sun is at the greatest. . . . Apollo is also the God of medicine. Lastly, Apollo is supposed to have instructed mankind in the art of foretelling future events: in all this there is a close connection: it is the sun, as he breaks forth in the spring, and pours upon us the genial warmth of summer, that inspires the mind with glowing conceptions and poetry, and the same turn of mind which makes men poetical, imbues them with sagacity beyond their fellows, and leads them with daring penetration to anticipate events to come; insomuch that in Latin the same word, *vates*, signifies a poet and a prophet' (pp. 45–7). *Lemprière* did not accept the identification of Apollo and Hyperion: 'Apollo has been taken for the Sun; but it may be proved by different passages in the ancient writers, that Apollo, the Sun, Phoebus, and Hyperion were all different characters and deities. . . .' For Apollo's metamorphosis into a god, see *Hyperion* III. Further on Keats's conception of the god, see *Jack*, pp. 176–90 and W. Evert, *Aesthetic and Myth in the Poetry of Keats* (1965), pp. 23–87.

Apollonius (of Tyana) 'A Pythagorean philosopher, well skilled in the secret arts of magic' (*Lemprière*). He was also noted as a moral reformist.

Arcadia, Arcady 'An inland country of Peloponnesus. . . . The country has been much celebrated by the poets, and was famous for its mountains. The inhabitants were for the most part all shepherds who lived upon acorns, were skilful warriors, and able musicians. They thought themselves more ancient than the moon. Pan the god of shepherds chiefly lived among them' (*Lemprière*).

Arethusa 'Alpheus is a beautiful river of Arcadia in Greece: Arethusa was one of the nymphs attendant upon Diana: coming one day, much fatigued with hunting, to the banks of the Alpheus, and smit with the limpidness of the stream, she threw off her clothes, and determined to bathe there. . . .' The river-god was struck by her charms, and Diana turned Arethusa into a fountain to escape his pursuit. 'Alpheus immediately put off the human figure . . . returned to his characteristic form of a river, and sought to mix his waters with those of the fountain Arethusa, the natural marriage of a river God: the nymph still in her new form shrunk away from this familiarity, and, aided by Diana, escaped under the bed of the sea, and rose again a fountain in the island of Ortygia: Alpheus however was too passionate a lover to be repulsed by any obstacles: he took the same course as Arethusa, and pursued her beneath the caverns of the sea . . . whatever fragment of wood . . . was cast into the river Alpheus in Arcadia, was observed ... to rise again in the fountain Arethusa ... ' (*Baldwin*, pp. 92–3).

Argonauts The ancient heroes who sailed with Jason in search of the Golden Fleece. The incident recounted in *Endymion* I, 347–54, in which Apollo's bow appears to the Argonauts, does not occur in Keats's usual sources, like *Lemprière*. *De Selincourt* (pp. 423–4) suggests that Shelley, who was moved by 'the Apollo so finely described by Apollonius Rhodius when the dazzling of his beautiful limbs suddenly shone over the dark Euxine' (*Prose Works*, ed. H. B. Forman [1880] III, p. 56), may have brought the incident to Keats's attention. The *Argonautica* had been translated by Francis Fawkes (1780), and was reprinted in *Chalmer's English Poets* (1810), XX, p. 271.

Argus Son of Arestor. 'As he had an hundred eyes, of which only two were asleep at one time, Juno set him to watch Io, whom Jupiter had changed into a heifer; but Mercury [Hermes] by order of Jupiter slew him, by lulling all his eyes asleep with the sound of his lyre' (*Lemprière*).

Ariadne Ariadne was deserted by her lover Theseus on the island of Naxos. 'According to some writers, Bacchus loved her after Theseus had forsaken her, and he gave her a crown of seven stars, which, after her death, were made a constellation' (*Lemprière*). Keats's description of Bacchus's 'swift bound' from his chariot, 'when his eye / Made Ariadne's cheek look blushingly' (*Sleep and Poetry* 334–6), was suggested by Titian's *Bacchus and Ariadne*, shown at the British Institution in 1816 (*Jack*, pp. 130–31).

Arion 'A famous Lyric poet and musician, son of Cyclos ... in the island of Lesbos'. He went to Corinth, obtained 'immense riches by his profession', and during his return voyage to Lesbos, the sailors attempted to rob and murder him. Arion '... begged that he might be permitted to play some melodious tune; and as soon as he had finished it, he threw himself into the sea. A number of dolphins had been attracted round the ship by the sweetness of his music; and it is said that one of them carried him safe on his back to Taenarus' (*Lemprière*).

Asia Daughter of Oceanus and Tethys in Hesiod, a Nereid according to Hyginus. In *Hyperion* II, 53–5 Keats invents a suitable parentage for her: there she is the daughter of Tellus (Earth) and Caf, an enormous mountain figuring in eastern tales. There is a 'horrible Kaf' in Beckford's *Vathek*, 'which in reality is no other than Caucasus' (1816 edn, p. 248).

Atlas 'One of the Titans, son of Japetus and Clymene'. Atlas was later changed into a mountain by Perseus. 'This mountain, which runs across the desarts of Africa east to west, is so high that the ancients have imagined that the heavens rested on its top, and that Atlas supported the world on his shoulders. Hyginus says, that Atlas assisted the giants in their wars against the gods, for which Jupiter compelled him to bear the heavens on his shoulders' (*Lemprière*).

701 DICTIONARY OF CLASSICAL NAMES

Aurora Goddess of dawn, '... generally represented by the poets drawn in a rose colored chariot, and opening with her rosy fingers the gates of the east...' (*Lemprière*).
Ausonia The ancient name for Italy.

Bacchus God of the vine, son of Jupiter and Semele, daughter of Cadmus. 'Bacchus is the Osiris of the Egyptians, and his history is drawn from the Egyptian traditions concerning that ancient king [on Osiris, see *Endymion* IV, 257n, p. 583].... His expedition into the east is celebrated. He marched, at the head of an army composed of men, as well as of women, all inspired with divine fury, and armed with thyrsuses, cymbals, and other musical instruments. The leader was drawn in a chariot by a lion and a tyger, and was accompanied by Pan and Silenus and all the Satyrs. His conquests were easy, and without bloodshed; the people easily submitted, and gratefully elevated to the rank of a god the hero who taught them the use of the vine, the cultivation of the earth, and the manner of making honey. Amidst his benevolence to mankind, he was relentless in punishing all ... disrespect to his divinity.... His figure is that of an effeminate young man, to denote the joys which commonly prevail at feasts.... The panther is sacred to him, because he went in his expedition covered with the skin of that beast.... He often appears naked, and riding upon the shoulders of Pan, or in the arms of Silenus, who was his foster-father.... According to Pliny, he was the first who ever wore a crown. His beauty is compared to that of Apollo, and, like him, he is represented with fine hair loosely flowing down his shoulders, and is said to possess eternal youth' (*Lemprière*). For Keats's treatment of Bacchus's rout, see *Endymion* IV, 193-277 and n (p. 583). *Baldwin* gives a fuller account of the traditionally youthful and effeminate image of Bacchus: 'Bacchus was ordinarily represented under the naked figure of a beautiful young man, but considerably plumper in his face and limbs, as might seem best to befit the generous living of the patron of the vine, and his countenance expressed the merry and jovial cast of thought which wine inspires: he was crowned with ivy and vine leaves, and bore in his hand the thyrsus, a dart twined about with the leaves of ivy and the vine' (p. 178). For Bacchus and Ariadne ▷ Ariadne.
Baiae 'A city of Campania near the sea ... famous for its delightful situation and baths, where many of the Roman senators had country-houses' (*Lemprière*). That is, the Bay of Naples, which was also Tasso's birthplace.
Bellona The Roman goddess of war.
Boreas God of the north wind.
Briareus One of the Titans. 'A famous giant, son of Coelus and Terra, who had 100 hands and 50 heads.... He assisted the giants in their war against the gods, and was thrown under mount Aetna, according to some accounts' (*Lemprière*).

Caria(n) ▷ Latmos.

Castor (and Pollux) Twin brothers, sons of Jupiter by Leda. After their death they became the constellation Gemini.

Centaurs 'A people of Thessaly, half men and half horses' (*Lemprière*).

Ceres 'The goddess of corn and of harvests, was daughter of Saturn and Vesta. She had a daughter by Jupiter, whom she called Pherephata, *fruit bearing*, and afterwards Proserpine.... Ceres was represented with a garland of ears of corn on her head, holding in one hand a lighted torch, and in the other a poppy, which was sacred to her' (*Lemprière*). For *Baldwin*'s interpretation of Ceres's festival, see *Hyperion* I, 316–18n (p. 613). 'Ceres's horn' was the cornucopia, or horn of plenty.

Cimmerian 'The country which [the Cimmerian people] inhabited, was supposed to be so gloomy, that, to mention a great obscurity, the expression *Cimmerian darkness* has proverbially been used; and Homer ... drew his images of hell and Pluto from the gloomy and dismal country where they dwelt' (*Lemprière*).

Circe 'A daughter of Sol and Perseis, celebrated for her knowledge of magic and venomous herbs'. She was expelled by the inhabitants of Colchis, and taken to the island Aeaea. Ulysses and his men visited the isle, and she changed all but Ulysses into swine: Ulysses himself was proof against her magic but not against her charms. Circe also 'showed herself cruel to her rival Scylla' (▷ Glaucus).

Clio 'The first of the Muses, daughter of Jupiter and Mnemosyne. She presided over history' (*Lemprière*).

Clymene Keats follows Hesiod in making her a Titan. She was 'a daughter of Oceanus and Tethys, who married Japetus, by whom she had Atlas, Prometheus, Menoetius, and Epimetheus' (*Lemprière*).

Coelus Otherwise known as 'Uranus', 'an ancient deity' of the heavens. 'He was son of Terra, whom he afterwards married'. His sons were the Titans, who led by Saturn overthrew him. In *Hyperion* I, 305–8 Keats ignores the hostility between Coelus and his sons.

Coeus One of the Titans.

Cupid See headnote to *Ode to Psyche* (p. 643).

Cybele Cybele's place in classical mythology was confused, and she was sometimes taken to be her mother, Tellus. 'The wife of Saturn is variously called Ops and Rhea, and Cybele ... she also sometimes bears the name of her mother (for she was the sister, as well as the wife, of Saturn): like [Tellus], she seems likewise to be the Earth, and in this character was invoked by the appellations of ... *Magna Mater* (the Great Mother) and the Mother of the Gods' (*Baldwin*, p. 33). 'Cybele was ... represented as a robust woman, far advanced in her pregnancy, to intimate the fecundity of the earth. She held keys in her hand, and her head was crowned with rising turrets, and sometimes with the leaves of an oak. She sometimes appears riding in a chariot drawn by two tame lions ...' (*Lemprière*).

Cyclades A cluster of island in the Aegean sea, near Delos.

Cyclops 'A certain race of men of gigantic stature, supposed to be the sons

703 DICTIONARY OF CLASSICAL NAMES

of Coelus and Terra. They had but one eye in the middle of the forehead; whence their name...' (*Lemprière*). Ulysses blinded the sleeping Cyclops so that he and his men could escape (*Odyssey* IX).
Cyther(e)a Cyprus, the birthplace of Venus.
Cynthia ▷ Diana.

Danae's son ▷ Perseus.
Daphne 'A daughter of the river Peneus ... of whom Apollo became enamoured.... Apollo pursued her; and Daphne, fearful of being caught, intreated the assistance of the gods, who changed her into a laurel' (*Lemprière*).
Darius ▷ Alexander.
Dedalus 'He was the most ingenious artist of his age'. He escaped from Minos's anger by making himself 'wings with feathers and wax, and carefully fitted them to his body, and that of his son.... They took their flight in the air from Crete; but the heat of the sun melted the wax on the wings of Icarus, whose flight was too high, and he fell into that part of the ocean, which from him has been called the Icarian sea' (*Lemprière*). Hence the adjectives, 'daedal' and 'dedalian'.
Delos 'One of the Cyclades.... It was called Delos from δηλος, because it suddenly made its *appearance* on the surface of the sea, by the power of Neptune ... who permitted Latona to bring forth [Apollo and Diana] there, when she was persecuted all over the earth, and could find no safe asylum'. Festivals were held on the island for the two gods, and Apollo had a famous temple there. 'The whole island of Delos was held in such veneration, that the Persians, who had pillaged and profaned all the temples of Greece, never offered violence to the temple of Apollo, but looked upon it with the most awful reverence' (*Lemprière*).
Delphian, Delphic 'Delphi was the place where Apollo is said to have killed the serpent Python: this place therefore, beyond all others in the world, was sacred to the god Apollo' (*Baldwin*, p. 66). Further on the oracles there, see *Ode to Fanny* 3n (p. 694).
Deucalion 'Deucalion was a prince who reigned in Thessaly, about fifty years later than the reign of Cecrops in Athens; both he and his wife Pyrrha owed their birth immediately to the Gods, he being the son of Prometheus, and she the daughter of Epimetheus, first cousins to Jupiter; the mother of Pyrrha was Pandora: in the time of Deucalion, Jupiter, exasperated with the crime and enormities of mankind, sent a flood which destroyed the whole world.' As the 'only pious and innocent persons then living', Deucalion and Pyrrha were saved by the use of a boat. The oracle they consulted after the flood subsided 'commanded them to cast the bone of their "Great Mother" over their shoulders ... at length they discovered that by their mother the oracle designed the earth, and that the bones of their mother were the pebbles scattered upon the surface: they obeyed the will of the Goddess; and the stones cast by Deucalion were turned into men; and those thrown by Pyrrha into women' (*Baldwin*, pp. 171-2). The

depiction of Deucalion 'mountained o'er the flood' (*Endymion* II, 195-7) is indebted to Ovid, *Metamorphoses* I, 316-29, where Deucalion waits on the top of Mount Parnassus while the flood rages below.

Diana Also called *Cynthia*, *Phoebe*, or *Hecate*. On the variety of names, Drayton's comment is helpful – 'PHOEBE, DIANA, HECATE, doe tell / Her Soueraintie in Heauen, in Earth and Hell', *The Man in the Moone*, *Poems* (1619) 486. She was the daughter of Jupiter and Latona, and so '... the twin-sister of Apollo, and like him has various offices: in heaven she is the moon, as Apollo is the sun; on earth she is the Goddess of hunters; and in Tartarus she is Hecate: it was also her office to watch over women on occasions of child-birth; and she was worshipped in all cross-ways, from which circumstance she obtained the name of Trivia (*three ways*). By the painters and sculptors she was most frequently represented in her character of a hunter: in this character she was attended by a bevy of nymphs, beautiful and exquisitely formed, herself more majestic, and taller by the head, than any of her followers; her legs were bare, well shaped and strong: her feet were covered with buskins; she had a bow in her hand, and a quiver full of arrows at her back. Diana is the Goddess of chastity, more prone to the pursuit of wild beasts than the indulgences of love: this is metaphorical: the silent moon with its mild and silver light, and that refreshing coolness which always accompanies a moon-light scene, was regarded as the very emblem of chastity. In her character of Hecate she is sometimes confounded with Proserpine, the queen of Tartarus: as Hecate however she is principally distinguished as the Goddess of magic and enchantments...' (*Baldwin*, pp. 51-2). For Diana and Endymion ▷ Endymion.

Dido Founder and queen of Carthage. She fell in love with Aeneas, who had been driven ashore on her shores. Aeneas was forced to leave Carthage in order to fulfill his destiny, the founding of Rome, and Dido's grief was such that she had herself burned to death on a funeral pyre. See also *Isabella* 99n (p. 598).

Dis ▷ Pluto.

Dolor Not a Titan, but so regarded by Keats. The name was suggested by Hyginus's *Auctores Mythographi Latini* (1742), which has '*ex Aethere et Terra, Dolor*' ('Grief, born from Air and Earth'), and shortly after mentions the Titans (3).

Doris 'A goddess of the sea, daughter of Oceanus and Tethys. She married her brother Nereus, by whom she had 50 daughters called Nereides. Her name is often used to express the sea itself' (*Lemprière*).

Dryads 'Nymphs that presided over the woods' (*Lemprière*). Unlike hamadryads, they were not tied to a particular tree, and could marry.

Dryope The reference in *Endymion* I, 495, is to the nymph who was ravished by Apollo. While on the bank of a lake sacred to the nymphs, she broke off a branch from a lotus-tree for her son to play with, and was in punishment transformed into a lotus herself (Ovid, *Metamorphoses*, IX, 371-9). The allusion is not likely to be to the other Dryope, mother of Pan, who was frightened of her child's appearance according to Chapman's *Homeric Hymn to Pan* 70-71, which was known to Keats.

Echo A nymph punished by Juno for her loquacity, 'and only permitted to answer to the questions which were put to her' (*Lemprière*). She fell in love with Narcissus, who spurned her. She pined away with grief until only her voice remained.

Elysium 'A place or island in the infernal regions, where ... the souls of the virtuous were placed after death. Their happiness is complete, the pleasures are innocent and refined. Bowers are forever green, delightful meadows with pleasant streams are the most striking objects. The air is wholesome, serene and temperate; the birds continually warble in the groves, and the inhabitants are blessed with another sun and other stars. ... To these innocent amusements some poets have added continual feasting and revelry, and they suppose that the Elysian fields were filled with all the incontinence and voluptuousness which could gratify the low desires of the debauchee' (*Lemprière*).

Enceladus 'A son of Titan and Terra, the most powerful of all the giants who conspired against Jupiter. He was struck with Jupiter's thunders, and overwhelmed under mount Aetna. Some suppose he is the same as Typhon. According to the poets, the flames of Aetna proceeded from the breath of Enceladus; and as often as he turned his weary side, the whole island of Sicily felt the motion, and shook from its very foundations' (*Lemprière*). Keats's Enceladus (*Hyperion* II, 308-45) is indebted to Milton's Moloch in *Paradise Lost* II, 43-105, and *Allott* cites Sandys's account of Typhon, 'the type of Ambition ... said to have reached Heaven with his hands, in regard of his aspiring thoughts ... This horrid figure ... agrees with rebellion' (*Ovid's Metamorphosis*, trans. G. Sandys [1640 edn], p. 96, commentary on Book V).

Endymion 'Diana is said to have fallen in love ... though she were the Goddess of Chastity: the object of her flame was Endymion, a shepherd of Caria: she saw him naked on the top of mount Latmos, and thought she had never beheld so beautiful a creature: as she was the most bashful and modest of existing beings, she cast him into a deep sleep, that she might kiss him unseen and undiscovered even by him she loved: every night she visited the beautiful shepherd, whom Jupiter endowed with perpetual youth, and every night she loved him better than the night before: the meaning of the fable is that Endymion was a great astronomer; that he passed whole nights upon mount Latmos contemplating the heavenly bodies ... and that he is said first to have explained the phenomenon of Diana, that is, the moon, and to have given a just account of their causes' (*Baldwin*, p. 206). *Bell's New Pantheon* (1790), drawing on Spence's *Polymetis*, gives the following explanation: 'It was this Diana, (the intelligence that was supposed to preside over the Moon) who was fabled to fall in love with Endymion ... it may appear, perhaps, to have been only a

706 DICTIONARY OF CLASSICAL NAMES

philosophical amour, or, what we call, platonic affection, and so may not interfere with her general character of chastity.'

Erebus 'A deity of hell, son of Chaos and Darkness ... The poets often used the word Erebus to signify hell, itself, and particularly that part where dwelt the souls of those who had lived a virtuous life, from whence they passed into the Elysian fields' (*Lemprière*).

Eurydice ▷ Orpheus.

Fauns ▷ Satyrs.

Favonius The west wind. Hence the adjective 'Favonian', meaning mild, gentle.

Flora 'The Goddess of flowers and gardens among the Romans. ... She was represented as crowned with flowers, and holding in her hand the horn of plenty' (*Lemprière*). Further, see *Sleep and Poetry* 101-21 and *n* (p. 551).

Ganymede 'A beautiful youth of Phrygia ... taken up to heaven by Jupiter ... and he became the cup-bearer of the gods in the place of Hebe' (*Lemprière*).

Glaucus 'A fisherman of Anthedon in Boeotia, son of Neptune and Nais. ... As he was fishing, he observed that all the fishes which he laid on the grass received fresh vigor as they touched the ground, and immediately escaped from him by leaping into the sea. He attributed the cause of it to the grass, and by tasting it, he found himself suddenly moved with a desire of living in the sea. Upon this he leaped into the water, and was made a sea deity by Oceanus and Tethys. ... After this transformation, he became enamoured of the Nereid Scylla. ... He is represented like the other sea deities with a long beard, dishevelled hair, and shaggy eyebrows, with the tail of a fish. He received the gift of prophecy from Apollo ...' (*Lemprière*). Of his relationship with Scylla, daughter of Typhon (or Phorcys), *Lemprière* says, 'Scylla scorned the addresses of Glaucus, and the god, to render her more propitious, applied to Circe, whose knowledge of herbs and incantations was universally admired. Circe no sooner saw him than she became enamoured of him, and instead of giving him the required assistance, she attempted to make him forget Scylla, but in vain. To punish her rival, Circe poured the juice of some poisonous herbs into the waters of the fountain where Scylla bathed. ...' Scylla was immediately transformed into a monster. 'This sudden metamorphosis so terrified her, that she threw herself into that part of the sea which separates the coast of Italy and Sicily, where she was changed into rocks ... which were universally deemed very dangerous to navigators. ...' The traditional story provided Keats with a starting-point for *Endymion* III, 318-638, which is freely adapted from Ovid, *Metamorphoses* XIII, 898-968, XIV, 1-74.

Graces, Three The goddesses who bestowed beauty and charm and were themselves the embodiment of both. They were the sisters Aglaia, Thalia, and Euphrosyne.

Gorgon There were three gorgons, Medusa being the chief. They had

707 DICTIONARY OF CLASSICAL NAMES

serpents in place of hair, and Medusa's face was so hideous that anyone who saw it was turned to stone. She was slain by Perseus.

Gyges A Titan, 'son of Coelus and Terra, represented as having a hundred hands. He, with his brothers, made war against the gods, and was afterwards punished in Tartarus' (*Lemprière*).

Hamadryads Female rural deities, who were mortal, unlike the Dryads. Their 'existence was indissolubly bound to that of the tree to which they belonged: they lived as long as the tree, and when the life of the tree was gone, the nymph also expired in the same moment: the deification of these beings was plainly nothing more than personifying the principle of vegetable life which appears and flourishes so wonderfully in trees...' (*Baldwin*, p. 95).

Hebe 'A daughter of Jupiter and Juno.... As she was fair, and always in the bloom of youth, she was called the goddess of youth, and made by her mother cup-bearer to all the gods. She was dismissed from her office by Jupiter, because she fell down in an indecent posture as she was pouring nectar to the gods at a grand festival, and Ganymedes, the favourite of Jupiter, succeeded her as cup-bearer.... She is represented as a young virgin crowned with flowers, and arrayed in a variegated garment' (*Lemprière*). For the Keatsian version of her slip before Jupiter, see *Fancy* 85.

Hecate ⇨ Diana. As the moon, Diana controlled the tides.

Helicon 'A mountain of Boeotia, on the borders of Phocis. It was sacred to the Muses, who had there a temple. The fountain Hippocrene flowed from this mountain' (*Lemprière*).

Hercules A hero famous for his Seven Labours. He built his own funeral pyre on Mount Oeta.

Hermes ⇨ Mercury.

Hesperides The three daughters of Hesperus, appointed to guard the golden apples which Juno had given Jupiter as a wedding gift. The garden of the Hesperides was sited beyond the ocean, and 'abounded with fruits of the most delicious kind' (*Lemprière*).

Hesperus (a) son of Iapetus, and father of the preceding. (b) 'The name of Hesperus was also applied to the planet Venus, when it appeared after the setting of the sun. It was called Phosphorus or Lucifer when it preceded the sun' (*Lemprière*).

Hippocrene See *Ode to a Nightingale* 16n (p. 655).

Horae Nymphs attendant on the sun. Also referred to as 'Hours'.

Hyacinth(us) A youth beloved by Apollo and Zephyrus. The latter was jealous of Hyacinth's love for Apollo, and while the two were playing at quoits, he blew the quoit so that it struck Hyacinth a fatal blow. 'Apollo was so disconsolate at the death of Hyacinthus, that he changed his blood into a flower, which bore his name, and placed his body among the constellations' (*Lemprière*).

708 DICTIONARY OF CLASSICAL NAMES

Hybla 'A mountain in Sicily, where thyme and odoriferous flowers of all sorts grew in abundance' (*Lemprière*).

Hymen The god of marriage, and son of Bacchus and Venus, or, alternatively, Apollo and one of the Muses.

Hyperion A Titan, son of Coelus and Terra. 'Hyperion is often taken by the poets for the sun itself' (*Lemprière*). *Baldwin* is of more help: 'Beside the name of Apollo, by which he is most commonly known, this God is often called by the poets Hyperion, and Titan; Hyperion one of the Titans having been according to some accounts the God of the sun, before that province was conferred upon Apollo' (p. 56). For Keats's handling of this figure, see *Hyperion* and *The Fall of Hyperion*, where he enlarges on these hints.

Iäpetus A Titan, son of Coelus and Terra.

Icarus ⟡ Dedalus.

Ida A mountain near Troy. It was here 'that the shepherd Paris adjudged the prize of beauty to the goddess Venus' (*Lemprière*). In *Endymion* II, 761 it may be used as a synonym for Venus herself.

Imaus 'A large mountain of Scythia' (*Lemprière*).

Io '... priestess of Juno at Argos, Jupiter became enamoured of her; but Juno, jealous of his intrigues, discovered the object of his affections, and surprised him in the company of Io. Jupiter changed his mistress into a beautiful heifer; and the goddess, who well knew the fraud, obtained from her husband the animal, whose beauty she had condescended to commend. Juno commanded the hundred-eyed Argus to watch the heifer; but Jupiter ... sent Mercury [Hermes] to destroy Argus, and restore her to liberty' (*Lemprière*).

Iris Goddess of the rainbow, and also one of the Oceanides (sea-nymphs).

Ixion 'Jupiter, displeased with the insolence of Ixion, banished him from heaven ... struck him with his thunder, and ordered Mercury to tie him to a wheel in hell, which continually whirls round. The wheel was perpetually in motion, therefore the punishment of Ixion was eternal' (*Lemprière*).

Jove ⟡ Jupiter.

Jupiter 'The most powerful of all the gods of the ancients ... son of Saturn and Ops. ... Saturn ... devoured all his sons as soon as born; but Ops ... secreted Jupiter ... [who] was educated in a cave on mount Ida [*Lamia* I, 13]. ... [Jupiter rebelled against Saturn, and defeated him]. Jupiter, now become the sole master of the empire of the world, divided it with his brothers. He reserved for himself the kingdom of heaven, and gave the empire of the sea to Neptune, and that of the internal regions to Pluto. ... He is generally represented as sitting upon a golden or ivory throne, holding in one hand, thunderbolts just ready to be hurled, and, in the other, a sceptre of cypr[ess]. His looks express majesty, his beard flows long and neglected, and the eagle stands with expanded wings at his feet'

(*Lemprière*). Jupiter was also one of the gods who had a care over marriage (*Lamia* I, 229).

Lamia See headnote to *Lamia* (p. 665).
Latmos 'A mountain of Caria near Miletus. It is famous for the residence of Endymion whom the moon regularly visited in the night . . .' (*Lemprière*). Hence 'Latmian', like 'Carian', is another name for Endymion.
Latona Mother of Apollo and Diana.
Leander A youth in love with Hero who swam the Hellespont to pass the night with her. One night he was drowned, and Hero drowned herself in her grief.
Leda Wife of Tyndarus, king of Sparta, who was visited by Jupiter in the form of a swan. She gave birth to two eggs, from which came Pollux and Helena, and Castor and Clytemnestra.
Lethe 'One of the rivers of hell, whose waters the souls of the dead drank after they had been confined for a certain space of time in Tartarus. It had the power of making them forget whatever they had done, seen, or heard before, as the name implies, $\lambda\eta\theta\eta$, *oblivion*' (*Lemprière*).
Lucifer ▷ Hesperus.
Lycaeus 'A mountain of Arcadia, sacred to Jupiter, where a temple was built in honour of the god Lycaeus. . . . It was also sacred to Pan, whose festivals, called Lycaea, were celebrated there' (*Lemprière*).

Maia The goddess of the month of May. 'She was the mother of Mercury by Jupiter. She was one of the Pleiades, the most luminous of the seven sisters' (*Lemprière*).
Mars The god of war, son of Jupiter and Juno, or Juno alone. 'The amours of Mars and Venus are greatly celebrated. The god of war gained the affections of Venus, and obtained the gratification of his desires, but Apollo, who was conscious of their familiarities, informed Vulcan of his wife's debaucheries. . . . Vulcan secretly laid a net around the bed, and the two lovers were exposed, in each others arms, to the ridicule and satire of all the gods, till Neptune prevailed upon the husband to set them at liberty' (*Lemprière*).
Medusa ▷ Gorgon.
Melpomene One of the Nine Muses. She presided over tragedy.
Memnon See *Hyperion* II, 374–6n (p. 615).
Mercury The Roman name given to Hermes. 'Mercury is the son of Jupiter, by Maia the daughter of Atlas, and grand-daughter of Iapetus one of the Titans: his peculiar office in the council of Olympus, is that he is the messenger of the Gods, and particularly of Jupiter: for this purpose he is furnished with a winged hat, called *petasus*, and with wings to be worn on his feet, called *talaria*: the figure given to him by the statuaries is that which is best adapted for nimbleness and celerity; and nothing is more obvious than that those properties of the human figure which are best fitted for these purposes, are closely allied to the perfection of symmetry and

710 DICTIONARY OF CLASSICAL NAMES

beauty. Mercury also possessed certain attributes intimately connected with magic and enchantment; and in this character he bore a wand, called *caduceus*: this wand had wings at the top, and two serpents wreathed themselves about the stalk: it was endowed with such virtues, that whoever it touched, if awake, would immediately sink into a profound sleep, and, if asleep, would start up full of life and alacrity: when it touched the dying, their souls gently parted from the mortal frame: and, when it was applied to the dead, the dead returned to life: it also had sovereign power in appeasing quarrels. ... It is in virtue of the caduceus that Mercury is represented not only as one of the celestial, but also one of the infernal deities; it was his office to conduct the spirits of the departed to the boat of Charon ... and again ... it was Mercury who led the spirits back, after having resided for some time in the nether or lower world, to revisit the cheerful beams of the sun. There are many things related of this God, which forcibly suggest to us the idea of a man, who for his great and essential services to his fellow beings was worshipped as a divinity after his death. He is said to be the inventor of letters; and his Greek name, Hermes, is derived from a word in that language which signifies "to interpret" or "explain": in this quality Mercury is the God of eloquence, as Apollo is the God of poetry. ... Mercury is further presented as the inventor of traffic [trade], and is said to have introduced the use of weights, measures and contracts: this is one of the fruits of civilization. ... Traffic however is too apt to degenerate into a system of fraud. .. the licentiousness of Greek imagination has taken hold of this, and has indecorously represented Mercury as the God of thieves ...' (*Baldwin*, pp. 56–8). Mercury is presented as the conductor of the dead, the 'star of Lethe', in *Lamia* I, 81, and as a thief in *The Cap and Bells* 619.

Midas A king of Phrygia, whose avarice led him to ask Bacchus for the ability to turn everything he touched to gold. The wish was granted with disastrous results.

Minerva Also known as Pallas Athene. 'The goddess of wisdom, war, and all the liberal arts, was produced from Jupiter's brains without a mother. ... She generally appeared with a countenance full more of masculine firmness and composure, than of softness and grace. Most usually she was represented with a helmet on her head, with a large plume nodding in the air. In one hand she held a spear, and in the other a shield, with the dying head of Medusa upon it' (*Lemprière*).

Minos 'Within the palace of Pluto were to be found the three judges of Hell, Minos, Rhadamanthus, and Aeacus: the two first of these had once been men, and were the authors of the famous laws of Crete: Minos and Rhadamanthus were placed by the Greeks as the final judges of the spirits of men departed, in consequence of the consummate excellence they had displayed as lawgivers and judges while they lived upon earth' (*Baldwin*, p. 128).

Mnemosyne 'A daughter of Coelus and Terra, mother of the nine Muses, by Jupiter. ... The word *Mnemosyne* signifies *memory*, and therefore the poets have rightly called memory the mother of the muses, because it is to that mental endowment that mankind are indebted for their progress in science' (Lemprière). In Hesiod she is a Titan, and is presented as such in *Hyperion*, where she deserts the Titans in order to join Apollo (III, 76–9). See also 'Moneta' below.

Momus 'The god of pleasantry among the ancients' (Lemprière).

Moneta In *The Fall of Hyperion* the priestess, Moneta, takes the role played by Mnemosyne, the Titan, in the earlier *Hyperion*. 'Moneta' was one of the surnames given to the Roman goddess Juno, but the identification of the two figures is based on Hyginus's *Auctorii Mythographi Latini* (1741), 3–4, where she is described as Jupiter's child by Memory (Mnemosyne also meant 'memory'). See 'Mnemosyne' above.

Morpheus 'A minister of the god Somnus.... He is sometimes called the god of sleep' (Lemprière).

Mulciber ⇨ Vulcan.

Naiad 'Certain inferior deities who presided over rivers, springs, wells, and fountains. The Naiades generally inhabited the country and resorted to the woods or meadows near the stream over which they presided.... They are represented as young and beautiful virgins often leaning upon an urn, from which flows a stream of water' (Lemprière).

Naiad Zephyr For this Keatsian composite deity, see *To Charles Cowden Clarke* 6 and *n* (p. 544).

Nais Mother of Glaucus and one of the Oceanides (sea-nymphs).

Narcissus 'A beautiful youth ... born at Thespis in Boeotia. He saw his image reflected in a fountain, and became enamoured of it, thinking it to be the nymph of the place. His fruitless attempts to approach this beautiful object so provoked him that he grew desperate and killed himself. His blood was changed into a flower, which still bears his name' (Lemprière). For Narcissus and Echo ⇨ Echo. See also '*I stood tip-toe* ...' 163–80 and *n* (p. 550).

Nemesis 'One of the infernal deities, daughter of Nox. She was the goddess of vengeance always prepared to punish impiety, and at the same time liberally to reward the good and virtuous.... Her power did not only exist in this life, but she was also employed after death to find out the most effectual and rigorous means of correction' (Lemprière).

Neptune One of the Olympians, and son of Saturn. 'Neptune shared with his brothers the empire of Saturn, and received as his portion the kingdom of the sea.... He was generally represented sitting in a chariot made of a shell, and drawn by sea horses or dolphins. Sometimes he is drawn by winged horses, and holds his trident in his hand, and stands up as his chariot flies over the surface of the sea' (Lemprière).

Nereids 'Nymphs of the sea, daughters of Nereus and Doris. They were fifty, according to the greater number of mythologists' (Lemprière).

Nereus 'A deity of the sea, son of Oceanus and Terra'. Father of the Nereids. 'Nereus was generally represented as an old man with a long

712 DICTIONARY OF CLASSICAL NAMES

flowing beard, and hair of an azure color. The chief place of his residence was in the Aegean sea, where he was surrounded by his daughters, who often danced in chorusses round him. He had the gift of prophecy, and informed those that consulted him of the different fates that attended them. . . . The word *Nereus* is often taken for the sea itself. Nereus is sometimes called the most antient of all the gods' (*Lemprière*).

Nestor King of Pylos, one of the oldest of the Greek leaders in the Trojan War, which he survived.

Niobe 'She married Amphion . . . by whom she had ten sons and ten daughters [other writers give other figures]. . . . The number of her children encreased her pride, and she had the imprudence not only to prefer herself to Latona who had only two children, but she even insulted her. . . . This insolence provoked Latona. She entreated her children to punish the arrogant Niobe. Her prayers were heard, and immediately all the sons of Niobe expired by the darts of Apollo, and all the daughters except Chloris were equally destroyed by Diana; and Niobe, struck at the suddenness of her misfortunes, was changed into a stone' (*Lemprière*). Keats also knew the account in Ovid, *Metamorphoses* VI, 165–312. For the pictorial traditions, see *Jack*, pp. 152–3.

Nox 'One of the most antient deities among the heathens, daughter of Chaos. From her union with her brother Erebus, she gave birth to the Day and the Night. . . . She is called by some of the poets the mother of all things, of gods as well as of men, and therefore she was worshipped with great solemnity by the antients' (*Lemprière*). Compare *Paradise Lost* II, 970, '*Chaos* and *ancient Night*'.

Oceanus 'A powerful deity of the sea, son of Coelus and Terra. . . . According to Homer, Oceanus was the father of all gods. . . . He is generally represented as an old man with a long flowing beard, and sitting upon the waves of the sea. He often holds a pike in his hand, while ships under sail appear at a distance, or a sea monster stands near him. Oceanus presided over every part of the sea, and even the rivers were subjected to his power. The ancients were superstitious in their worship to Oceanus, and revered with great solemnity a deity to whose care they entrusted themselves when going on any journey' (*Lemprière*).

Ops A daughter of Coelus and Terra. Often identified with Cybele, as the wife of Saturn and mother of Jupiter, hence known as mother of the gods.

Oread 'Nymphs of the mountains. . . . They generally attended upon Diana, and accompanied her in hunting' (*Lemprière*).

Orion A celebrated giant. His eyes were treacherously put out by Oenopion, king of Chios. 'Orion, finding himself blind when he awoke, was conducted by the sound to a neighbouring forge, where he placed one of the workmen on his back, and, by his directions, went to a place where the rising sun was seen with the greatest advantage. Here he turned his face towards the luminary, and . . . he immediately recovered his eye sight, and

713 DICTIONARY OF CLASSICAL NAMES

hastened to punish the perfidious cruelty of Oenopion' (*Lemprière*). Keats probably knew Poussin's *Landscape with Orion*; see *Jack*, p. 156.

Orpheus A Thracian shepherd, son of Calliope and Apollo, who was given a lyre by the latter. The power of Orpheus's music was such that it could move even inanimate things. When his wife Eurydice died, he went down to the infernal regions, and so charmed Pluto that she was released, on condition that Orpheus would not look back until they reached the earth. He was just about to put his foot on the earth when he looked back. Eurydice vanished.

Pallas ⇨ Minerva.

Pan The account given by *Lemprière* reflects Pan's uncertain position in classical mythology. 'PAN was the god of shepherds, and of all the inhabitants of the country. He was the son of Mercury by Dryope, according to Homer ... the name of *Pan* ... signifies *all* or *every thing*. Pan was monster in appearance, he had two small horns on his head, his complexion was ruddy, his nose flat, and his legs, thighs, tail, and feet, were those of a goat. ... Bacchus was greatly pleased with him, and gave him the name of Pan. The god of shepherds resided chiefly in Arcadia, where the woods and the most rugged mountains were his habitation. He invented the flute with seven reeds, which he called *Syrinx*, in honor of a beautiful nymph of the same name, to whom he attempted to offer violence, and who was changed into a reed. He was continually employed in deceiving the neighbouring nymphs, and often with success. ... The worship of Pan was well established particularly in Arcadia, where he gave oracles on mount Lycaeus. ... The worship, and the different functions of Pan, are derived from the mythology of the antient Egyptians. This god was one of the eight great gods of the Egyptians. ... He was worshipped with the greatest solemnity all over Egypt. His statues represented him as a goat, not because he was really such, but this was done for mysterious reasons. He was the emblem of fecundity, and they looked upon him as the principle of all things. ... Some suppose that he appeared as a goat because when the gods fled into Egypt, in their war against the giants, Pan transformed himself into a goat, an example which was immediately followed by all the deities. Pan, according to some, is the same as Faunus, and he is the chief of all the Satyrs. Plutarch mentions, that in the reign of Tiberius, an extraordinary voice was heard near the Echinades in the Ionian sea, which exclaimed, that the great Pan was dead'. See also *Endymion* I, 232-306n (p. 563).

Paphos A city in Cyprus, the birthplace of Venus, with a famous temple to the goddess.

Pegasus 'A winged horse sprung from the blood of Medusa. ... As soon as he was born he left the earth, and flew up into heaven, or rather, according to Ovid, he fixed his residence on mount Helicon, where by striking the earth with his foot, he instantly raised a fountain, which has been called Hippocrene. He became the favourite of the Muses. ...

DICTIONARY OF CLASSICAL NAMES

Pegasus ... was placed among the constellations by Jupiter' (*Lemprière*). Further, see *Sleep and Poetry* 101–21n (p. 551).

Peona See *Endymion* I, 408n (p. 564).

Perseus Son of Danae, who saved Andromeda. ▷ Andromeda.

Philomel Sometimes used simply as a synonym for 'nightingale'. The name means 'lover of song'. In *Lemprière* Philomela is ravished by her brother-in-law, Tereus, and her tongue cut out to prevent her telling what had happened. Though locked up in a 'castle', she described her misfortunes on a piece of tapestry, which she sent to Procne, her sister and Tereus's wife. Procne killed her son Itylus, and served him up as a dish to Tereus. Just as Tereus was going to stab Procne and Philomela, 'he was changed into a hoopoe, Philomela into a nightingale, Procne into a swallow, and Itylus into a pheasant. ... Procne and Philomela died through excess of grief and melancholy, and as the nightingale's and swallow's voice is peculiarly plaintive and mournful, the poets have embellished the fable by supposing, that the two unfortunate sisters were changed into birds'.

Phoebe A Titan and the mother of Diana. But also another name for Diana herself. ▷ Diana.

Phoebus 'A name given to Apollo or the sun. This word expresses the brightness and splendor of that luminary' (*Lemprière*).

Phorcus Regarded by Keats as a Titan. 'A sea deity, son of Pontus and Terra, who married his sister Ceto, by whom he had the Gorgons, the dragon that kept the apples of the Hesperides, and other monsters' (*Lemprière*).

Phosphorus ▷ Hesperus.

Pleiades 'A name given to seven of the daughters of Atlas. ... They were placed in the heavens after death, where they formed a constellation called Pleiades, near the back of the bull in the Zodiac' (*Lemprière*).

Pluto Also known as 'Dis'. 'Son of Saturn and Ops, inherited his father's kingdom with Jupiter and Neptune. He received as his lot the kingdom of hell, and whatever lies under the earth, and as such he became the god of the infernal regions, of death and funerals. ... He is looked upon as a hard-hearted and inexorable god, with a grim and dismal countenance ...' (*Lemprière*). Pluto took Proserpine as his wife. ▷ Proserpine.

Pollux ▷ Castor.

Pomona 'A nymph at Rome who was supposed to preside over gardens, and to be the goddess of all sorts of fruit-trees' (*Lemprière*). ▷ Vertumnus.

Porphyrion A Titan in Keats. 'A son of Coelus and Terra, one of the giants who made war against Jupiter. He was so formidable, that Jupiter, to conquer him, inspired him with love for Juno, and while the giant endeavoured to obtain his wishes, he, with the assistance of Hercules, overpowered him' (*Lemprière*).

Prometheus 'A son of Iapetus by Clymene, one of the Oceanides. ... According to Apollodorus, Prometheus made the first man and woman that ever were upon the earth, with clay, which he animated by means of the fire which he had stolen from heaven' (*Lemprière*).

715 DICTIONARY OF CLASSICAL NAMES

Proserpine 'A daughter of Ceres by Jupiter.... Proserpine made Sicily the place of her residence, and delighted herself with the beautiful views, the flowery meadows, and limpid streams.... In this solitary retreat, as she amused herself with her female attendants in gathering flowers, Pluto carried her away into the infernal regions, of which she became queen. Ceres was so disconsolate at the loss of her daughter, that she travelled all over the world, but her inquiries were in vain.... Jupiter, to appease the resentment of Ceres, and sooth her grief, permitted that Proserpine should remain six months with Pluto in the infernal regions, and that she should spend the rest of the year with her mother on earth. As queen of hell, and wife of Pluto, Proserpine presided over the death of mankind...'. In some traditions she is identified with Hecate (one of Diana's names), and this may be relevant to her introduction in *Endymion* I, 944-6.

Psyche See headnote to *Ode to Psyche* (p. 643).

Pylos ⟡ Nestor.

Pyrrha ⟡ Deucalion.

Pythia The priestess of Apollo's shrine at Delphi. Further, see *Ode to Fanny* 3n (p. 694).

Python 'A celebrated serpent sprung from the mud and stagnated waters which remained on the surface of the earth after the deluge of Deucalion. Some, however, suppose that it was produced from the earth by Juno, and sent to persecute Latona, who was then pregnant by Jupiter ... she gave birth to Apollo and Diana [on Delphos]. Apollo, as soon as he was born, attacked the monster, and killed him with his arrows ...' (*Lemprière*).

Rhadamanthus 'A son of Jupiter and Europa. He was born in Crete.... He passed into some of the Cyclades, where he reigned with so much justice and impartiality, that the antients have said he became one of the judges of hell, and that he was employed in the infernal regions in obliging the dead to confess their crimes, and in punishing them for their offences' (*Lemprière*).

Sappho Famous Greek poetess of Lesbos (*fl. c.* 600 B.C.). 'She conceived such a passion for Phaon, a youth of Mitylene, that upon his refusal to gratify her desires, she threw herself into the sea from mount Leucas' (*Lemprière*).

Saturn Son of Coelus or Uranus by Terra. Leader of the Titans, who were overthrown by his sons, led by Jupiter, who established the Olympian rule. In the two *Hyperions*, Keats passes over the traditional story that Saturn attempted to devour his children as soon as they were born, for fear that he would be displaced by them. Keats also transposes the Saturnian Golden Age, normally supposed to have happened after Saturn was defeated by Jupiter, to a period before the Olympian wars had taken place. *Lemprière* gives the traditional account: 'Jupiter banished [Saturn] from his throne, and the father fled for safety into Italy, where the country retained the name

716 DICTIONARY OF CLASSICAL NAMES

of *Latium*, as being the place of *concealment* (*lateo*). Janus, who was then king of Italy, received Saturn with marks of attention, he made him his partner on the throne; and the king of heaven employed himself in civilizing the barbarous manners of the people of Italy, and in teaching them agriculture and the useful and liberal arts. His reign there was so mild and popular, so beneficent and virtuous, that mankind have called it the *golden age*, to intimate the happiness and tranquillity which the earth then enjoyed.' Keats not only makes Saturn more beneficent, but he does not present Saturn with his usual symbol, a scythe, which allowed *Baldwin* (and others) to identify him with Time. The freedom in handling Saturn received some support from the multiplicity of interpretations of his significance. Earlier writers had identified him with Moloch, with Nimrod the founder of Babylon, with Noah (who Bochart regarded as the father of mankind after the deluge, another 'golden age'), or (following the Abbé Pluché) with the Egyptian god, Osiris.

Satyrs 'Demigods of the country, whose origin is unknown. They are represented like men, but with the feet and the legs of goats, short horns on the head, and the whole body covered with thick hair. They chiefly attended upon Bacchus, and rendered themselves known in his orgies by their riot and lasciviousness. The first fruits of every thing were generally offered to them. The Romans promiscuously called them Fauni, Panes and Sylvani' (*Lemprière*).

Scylla ▷ Glaucus.

Semele The mother of Bacchus by Jupiter.

Silenus 'A demi-god, who became the nurse, the preceptor, and attendant of the god Bacchus. He was, as some suppose, son of Pan, or according to others, of Mercury, or of Terra. . . . Silenus is generally represented as a fat and jolly old man, riding on an ass, crowned with flowers, and always intoxicated. . . . Some authors assert, that Silenus was a philosopher, who accompanied Bacchus in his Indian expedition, and assisted him by the soundness of his counsels' (*Lemprière*).

Sirens 'Sea nymphs who charmed so much with their melodious voice, that all forgot their employments to listen with more attention, and at last died for want of food' (*Lemprière*).

Syrinx An Arcadian nymph fled to the River Lodon to escape the attentions of Pan, and was metamorphosed into a reed from which Pan made his flute.

Tartarus 'The Greeks . . . separated the infernal region into two principal divisions, Tartarus, or the abode of woe, and Elysium, or the mansions of the blessed; Erebus was a general name for both . . .' (*Baldwin* 119).

Tellus 'A divinity, the same as the earth, the most antient of all the gods after Chaos'. Mother of the Titans, and also known as Cybele (*Lemprière*).

717 DICTIONARY OF CLASSICAL NAMES

Tempe 'A valley in Thessaly, between mount Olympus at the north, and Ossa at the south, through which the river Peneus flows into the Aegean. The poets have described it as the most delightful spot on the earth, with continually cool shades, and verdant walks, which warbling birds rendered more pleasant and romantic. Tempe extended about five miles in length, but was scarce one acre and a half wide' (*Lemprière*).

Tethys 'The greatest of the sea deities, was wife of Oceanus, and daughter of Uranus and Terra. She was mother of the chiefest rivers of the universe, such as the Nile, the Alpheus ... and about 3000 daughters called Oceanides' (*Lemprière*).

Thalia One of the Nine Muses 'who presided over festivals, pastoral and comic poetry' (*Lemprière*). Her symbols are a comic mask, a shepherd's staff, or a wreath of ivy. She was also one of the Three Graces.

Thea 'A daughter of Uranus and Terra' (*Lemprière*).

Themis In Keats, who follows Hesiod, one of the Titans. 'A daughter of Coelus and Terra' according to *Lemprière*.

Thessaly A region in Greece, to which Apollo was exiled.

Thetis 'One of the sea deities, daughter of Nereus and Doris, often confounded with Tethys, her grand mother' (*Lemprière*).

Titans 'A name given to the sons of Coelus and Terra. They were forty-five in number, according to the Egyptians. Apollodorus mentions thirteen, Hyginus six, and Hesiod twenty, among whom are the Titanides. The most known of the Titans are Saturn, Hyperion, Oceanus, Iapetus, Cottus, and Briareus, to whom Horace adds, Typhoeus [Typhon], Mimus, Porphyrion, Rhoetus, and Enceladus, who are by other mythologists reckoned among the giants. They were all of a gigantic stature, and with proportionable strength' (*Lemprière*). *Baldwin* adds further names: '... the Titans were Oceanus, Coeus, Creus, Hyperion, Iapetus, Cottus, Gyges and Briareus: they had an equal number of sisters with whom they married, Oceanus to Tethys, Coeus to Phoebe, Hyperion to Theia, and Iapetus to Clymene' (p. 37). In making up the Miltonic roll-call in *Hyperion* II, 19–81, Keats chose from among these names, and added the name of 'Dolor'. *Lemprière* warned his reader, 'The wars of the Titans are very celebrated in mythology. They are often confounded with that of the giants; but it is to be observed, that the war of the Titans was against Saturn, and that of the giants against Jupiter'. Keats chose to ignore the distinction, and the two *Hyperions* present a conflict between the Titans and the Olympians.

Triton 'A sea deity, son of Neptune, by Amphitrite. ... He was very powerful among the sea deities, and could calm the sea and abate storms at pleasure. He is generally represented as blowing a shell, his body above the waist is like that of a man, and below, a dolphin. Some represent him with the fore feet of a horse. Many of the sea deities are called Tritons, but the name is generally applied to those only who are half men and half fishes' (*Lemprière*).

Typhon A Titan in Keats. 'A giant whom Juno produced by striking the earth' (*Lemprière*). Sometimes identified with Typhoeus, another giant, and

son of Tartarus and Terra: Jupiter put Typhoeus to flight with his
thunderbolts, and 'crushed him under mount Aetna' (*Lemprière*).
◊ Enceladus.

Urania (a) 'One of the Muses, daughter of Jupiter and Mnemosyne, who
presided over astronomy. ... She was represented as a young virgin
dressed in an azure colored robe, crowned with stars and holding a globe in
her hands, and having many mathematical instruments placed round'.
(b) 'A sirname of Venus, the same as *Celestial*. She was supposed, in that
character, to preside over beauty and generation, and was called daughter of
Uranus or Coelus by the Light' (*Lemprière*).
Uranus Another name for Coelus, god of the heavens.

Venus (a) The name given to the evening star (i.e. Venus Urania).
(b) '... the goddess of beauty, the mother of love, the queen of laughter,
the mistress of graces and pleasures, and the patroness of courtezans. ...
She arose from the sea near the island of Cyprus ... whither she was
wafted by the zephyrs, and received on the sea shore by the seasons,
daughters of Jupiter and Themis. ... Venus became mother of ... Cupid
and Anteros by Mars [◊ Mars]. ... The power of Venus over the heart,
was supported and assisted by a celebrated girdle, called a *zone*, by the
Greeks, and *cestus*, by the Latins. This mysterious girdle gave beauty,
grace and elegance, when worn even by the most deformed; it excited love,
and kindled extinguished flames ...' (*Lemprière*). The dove was one of her
emblems. For her love for Adonis ◊ Adonis.
Vertumnus 'A deity among the Romans, who presided over the spring and
orchards. He endeavoured to gain the affections of Pomona; and to effect
this, he assumed the shape and dress of a fisherman, of a soldier, a peasant,
a reaper, etc. but all to no purpose, till under the form of an old woman, he
prevailed upon his mistress and married her. He is generally represented as
a young man crowned with flowers, covered up to the waist, and holding
in his right hand fruit, and a crown of plenty in his left' (*Lemprière*).
Vesper Another name for Venus, as evening star. ◊ Hesperus.
Vesta The Roman goddess of the hearth.
Vulcan 'A god of the antients who presided over fire, and was the patron
of all artists who worked iron and metals. ... The Cyclops ... were his
ministers and attendants, and with him they fabricated, not only the
thunderbolts of Jupiter, but also arms for the gods and the most celebrated
heroes. His forges were supposed to be under mount Aetna ... as well as in
every part of the earth where there were volcanoes' (*Lemprière*). Vulcan was
identified by later writers with Mulciber.

DICTIONARY OF CLASSICAL NAMES

Zephyr(us) 'One of the winds, son of Atreus and Aurora, the same as the Favonius of the Latins. ... Zephyr was said to produce flowers and fruits by the sweetness of his breath ... he was represented as a young man of delicate form, with two wings on his shoulders, and with his head covered with all sorts of flowers. He was supposed to be the same as the west wind' (*Lemprière*). On occasion Keats seems to regard 'zephyrs' (winds) as feminine. See *To Charles Cowden Clarke* 6n (p. 544).

Index of Titles

Acrostic 256
Addressed to [Haydon] ('Great spirits now on earth are sojourning') 75
Addressed to Haydon ('Highmindedness, a jealousy for good') 74
A Dream, after reading Dante's Episode of Paolo and Francesca 334
'After dark vapours have oppressed our plains' 96
'Ah! ken ye what I met the day' 262
'Ah, who can e'er forget so fair a being' *see under* 'Woman! when I behold thee flippant, vain'
'All gentle folks who owe a grudge' 264
'And what is love? It is a doll dressed up' 282
Apollo to the Graces 218
'As from the darkening gloom a silver dove' 40
'Asleep! O sleep a little while, white pearl!' 232

'Blue! 'Tis the life of heaven, the domain' 227
'Bright star! would I were steadfast as thou art' 452

Calidore. A Fragment 58
'Can death be sleep, when life is but a dream' 40
Character of Charles Brown 333

Daisy's Song 230

Endymion: A Poetic Romance 106
Extracts from an Opera 229

Faery Bird's Song 328
Faery Song 329
Fancy 307
'Fill for me a brimming bowl' 38
Folly's Song 230
'For there's Bishop's Teign' 232
'Four seasons fill the measure of the year' 232
Fragment of the 'Castle Builder' 280

'Gif ye wol stonden hardie wight' 327
'Give me Women, Wine, and Snuff' 55

INDEX OF TITLES

'God of the meridian' 222
Gripus 489

'Happy is England! I could be content' 95
'Hence Burgundy, Claret, and Port' 222
'Hither, hither, love' 103
'How many bards gild the lapses of time!' 72
'Hush, hush! tread softly! hush, hush my dear!' 311
Hyperion. A Fragment 283

'I am as brisk' 487
'I cry your mercy, pity, love – ay, love!' 451
'If by dull rhymes our English must be chained 340
Imitation of Spenser 37
'In after-time, a sage of mickle lore' 487
'In drear-nighted December' 217
Isabella; or, The Pot of Basil 239
'I stood tip-toe upon a little hill' 76

'Keen, fitful gusts are whispering here and there' 74
King Stephen. A Fragment of a Tragedy 452

La Belle Dame sans Merci. A Ballad 334
Lamia 414
'Light feet, dark violet eyes, and parted hair' *see under* 'Woman! when I behold thee flippant, vain'
Lines on the Mermaid Tavern 225
Lines Rhymed in a Letter Received (by J. H. Reynolds) from Oxford 104
Lines Written in the Highlands after a Visit to Burns's Country 266
Lines Written on 29 May The Anniversary of the Restoration of Charles the 2nd 44

Nebuchadnezzar's Dream 217

'O blush not so! O blush not so!' 221
Ode ('Bards of Passion and of Mirth') 309
Ode on a Grecian Urn 344
Ode on Indolence 349
Ode on Melancholy 348
Ode to a Nightingale 346
Ode to Apollo ('God of the golden bow') 98
Ode to Apollo ('In thy western halls of gold') 43
Ode to May. Fragment 255
Ode to Psyche 340
'Of late two dainties were before me placed' 266
'O grant that like to Peter I' 487
'O! how I love, on a fair summer's eve' 63

INDEX OF TITLES

'O, I am frightened with most hateful thoughts'   231
'Old Meg she was a gipsy'   257
On a Leander Gem which Miss Reynolds, my Kind Friend, Gave Me   101
On Fame (I) ('Fame, like a wayward girl, will still be coy')   342
On Fame (II) ('How fevered is the man, who cannot look')   343
On First Looking into Chapman's Homer   72
On Leaving some Friends at an Early Hour   73
On Peace   38
On Receiving a Curious Shell, and a Copy of Verses, from the Same Ladies   46
On Receiving a Laurel Crown from Leigh Hunt   97
On Seeing a Lock of Milton's Hair. Ode   219
On Seeing the Elgin Marbles   99
On Sitting Down to Read *King Lear* Once Again   220
On the Grasshopper and Cricket   94
On the Sea   101
On *The Story of Rimini*   100
On Visiting Staffa   268
On Visiting the Tomb of Burns   257
'O Solitude! if I must with thee dwell'   50
Otho the Great. A Tragedy in Five Acts   353
'O thou whose face hath felt the Winter's wind'   228
'Over the hill and over the dale'   235
'O! were I one of the Olympian twelve'   229

'Pensive they sit, and roll their languid eyes'   433

'Read me a lesson, Muse, and speak it loud'   270
Robin Hood   223

'See, the ship in the bay is riding'   488
Sleep and Poetry   82
Song ('Hush, hush! tread softly! hush, hush my dear!')   311
Song ('I had a dove and the sweet dove died')   310
Song ('Spirit here that reignest!')   279
Song ('Stay, ruby-breasted warbler, stay')   48
Song of Four Faeries   336
Sonnet to A[ubrey] G[eorge] S[pencer]   229
Specimen of an Induction to a Poem   56
'Spenser! a jealous honourer of thine'   227
Stanzas   102
Stanzas on some Skulls in Beauly Abbey, near Inverness   272
'Sweet, sweet is the greeting of eyes'   256

The Cap and Bells; or, The Jealousies   459
'The day is gone, and all its sweets are gone!'   449

INDEX OF TITLES

The Eve of St Agnes 312
The Eve of St Mark 324
The Fall of Hyperion. A Dream 435
'The House of Mourning written by Mr Scott' 332
The Human Seasons 232
'The Stranger lighted from his steed' 231
'They weren fully glad of their gude hap' 487
'Think not of it, sweet one, so' 105
'This living hand, now warm and capable' 459
'This mortal body of a thousand days' 263
Three Undated Fragments 487
''Tis "the witching time of night"' 276
To — ('Had I a man's fair form, then might my sighs') 55
To — ('Time's sea hath been five winters at its slow ebb') 226
To a Friend who Sent me some Roses 63
To Ailsa Rock 263
To Autumn 434
To a Young Lady who sent me a Laurel Crown 73
To B. R. Haydon, with a Sonnet Written on Seeing the Elgin Marbles 100
To Charles Cowden Clarke 68
To Chatterton 40
To Emma 47
To Fanny 485
To George Felton Mathew 50
To G[eorgiana] A[ugusta] W[ylie] 95
To Homer 255
To Hope 41
To J[ames] R[ice] 238
To J. H. Reynolds, Esq. 235
To Kosciusko 94
To Leigh Hunt, Esq. 96
To Lord Byron 39
To [Mary Frogley] 53
To Mrs Reynolds's Cat 218
To my Brother George ('Full many a dreary hour have I passed') 64
To my Brother George ('Many the wonders I this day have seen') 64
To my Brothers 75
'To one who has been long in city pent' 62
To Sleep 339
To Some Ladies 45
To the Ladies who Saw Me Crowned 98
To the Nile 226
Translated from Ronsard 276
'Two or three posies' 343

'Upon my life, Sir Nevis, I am piqued' 270

INDEX OF TITLES

'Welcome joy, and welcome sorrow' 278
'What can I do to drive away' 450
'When I have fears that I may cease to be' 221
'When they were come unto the Faery's Court' 329
'Where be ye going, you Devon maid?' 234
'Where's the Poet? Show him! show him' 280
'Why did I laugh tonight? No voice will tell' 328
'Woman! when I behold thee flippant, vain' 49
Written in Disgust of Vulgar Superstition 93
Written on a Blank Space at the End of Chaucer's Tale of *The Floure and the Leafe* 97
Written on the Day that Mr Leigh Hunt left Prison 41

Index of First Lines

After dark vapours have oppressed our plains 96
Ah! ken ye what I met the day 262
Ah, who can e'er forget so fair a being *see under* Woman! when I behold thee flippant, vain
Ah! woe is me! poor silver-wing! 329
All gentle folks who owe a grudge 264
And gold and silver are but filthy dross 489
And what is love? It is a doll dressed up 282
As from the darkening gloom a silver dove 40
As Hermes once took to him feathers light 334
As late I rambled in the happy fields 63
Asleep! O sleep a little while, white pearl! 232
A thing of beauty is a joy for ever 107
At morn, at noon, at eve, and middle night 488

Bards of Passion and of Mirth 309
Before he went to live with owls and bats 217
Blue! 'Tis the life of heaven, the domain 227
Bright star! would I were steadfast as thou art 452
Byron! how sweetly sad thy melody! 39

Can death be sleep, when life is but a dream 40
Cat! who hast passed thy grand climacteric 218
Chief of organic numbers! 219
Come hither all sweet maidens soberly 101

Dear Reynolds! as last night I lay in bed 235
Deep in the shady sadness of a vale 283

Ever let the Fancy roam 307

Fair Isabel, poor simple Isabel! 239
Fame, like a wayward girl, will still be coy 342
Fanatics have their dreams, wherewith they weave 435
Fill for me a brimming bowl 38
For there's Bishop's Teign 232
Four seasons fill the measure of the year 232

728 INDEX OF FIRST LINES

Fresh morning gusts have blown away all fear 73
Full many a dreary hour have I passed 64

Gif ye wol stonden hardie wight 327
Give me a golden pen, and let me lean 73
Give me Women, Wine, and Snuff 55
Give me your patience, sister, while I frame 256
Glory and loveliness have passed away 96
God of the golden bow 98
God of the meridian 222
Good Kosciusko, thy great name alone 94
Great spirits now on earth are sojourning 75

Had I a man's fair form, then might my sighs 55
Hadst thou lived in days of old 53
Happy, happy glowing fire! 336
Happy is England! I could be content 95
Hast thou from the caves of Golconda a gem 46
Haydon! forgive me that I cannot speak 100
Hearken, thou craggy ocean pyramid! 263
He is to weet a melancholy carle 333
Hence Burgundy, Claret, and Port 222
Highmindedness, a jealousy for good 74
Hither, hither, love 103
How fevered is the man who cannot look 343
How many bards gild the lapses of time! 72
Hush, hush! tread softly! hush, hush my dear! 311

I am as brisk 487
I cry your mercy, pity, love – ay, love! 451
If by dull rhymes our English must be chained 340
If shame can on a soldier's vein-swollen front 452
I had a dove and the sweet dove died 310
In after-time, a sage of mickle lore 487
In drear-nighted December 217
Infatuate Britons, will you still proclaim 44
In midmost Ind, beside Hydaspes cool 459
In short, convince you that however wise 280
In silent barren Synod met 273
In thy western halls of gold 43
I stood tip-toe upon a little hill 76
It keeps eternal whisperings around 101

Keen, fitful gusts are whispering here and there 74

Light feet, dark violet eyes, and parted hair *see under* Woman! when I behold thee flippant, vain
Lo! I must tell a tale of chivalry 56

INDEX OF FIRST LINES

Many the wonders I this day have seen 64
Minutes are flying swiftly, and as yet 97
Mother of Hermes! and still youthful Maia! 255
Much have I travelled in the realms of gold 72
My heart aches, and a drowsy numbness pains 346
My spirit is too weak – mortality 99

Nature withheld Cassandra in the skies 276
No, no, go not to Lethe, neither twist 348
Not Aladdin magian 268
No! those days are gone away 223
Now Morning from her orient chamber came 37
Nymph of the downward smile, and sidelong glance 95

O blush not so! O blush not so! 221
O Chatterton! how very sad thy fate! 40
O come, dearest Emma! the rose is full blown 47
Of late two dainties were before me placed 266
Oft have you seen a swan superbly frowning 68
O Goddess! hear these tuneless numbers, wrung 340
O golden-tongued Romance, with serene lute! 220
O grant that like to Peter I 487
O! how I love, on a fair summer's eve 63
O, I am frightened with most hateful thoughts! 231
Old Meg she was a gipsy 257
One morn before me were three figures seen 349
O Peace! and dost thou with thy presence bless 38
O soft embalmer of the still midnight 339
O Solitude! if I must with thee dwell 50
O that a week could be an age, and we 238
O thou whose face hath felt the Winter's wind 228
Over the hill and over the dale 235
O! were I one of the Olympian twelve 229
O what can ail thee, knight-at-arms 334

Pensive they sit, and roll their languid eyes 443
Physician Nature! let my spirit blood! 485

Read me a lesson, Muse, and speak it loud 270

St Agnes' Eve – Ah, bitter chill it was! 312
Season of mists and mellow fruitfulness 434
See, the ship in the bay is riding 488
Shed no tear – O, shed no tear! 328
Small, busy flames play through the fresh-laid coals 75
So, I am safe emergèd from these broils! 353

INDEX OF FIRST LINES

Son of the old moon-mountains African! 226
Souls of Poets dead and gone 225
Spenser! a jealous honourer of thine 227
Spirit here that reignest! 279
Standing aloof in giant ignorance 255
Stay, ruby-breasted warbler, stay 48
Sweet are the pleasures that to verse belong 50
Sweet, sweet is the greeting of eyes 256

The church bells toll a melancholy round 93
The day is gone, and all its sweets are gone! 449
The Gothic looks solemn 104
The House of Mourning written by Mr Scott 332
The poetry of earth is never dead 94
There is a joy in footing slow across a silent plain 266
There was a naughty boy 258
The stranger lighted from his steed 231
The sun, with his great eye 230
The town, the churchyard, and the setting sun 257
They weren fully glad of their gude hap 487
Think not of it, sweet one, so 105
This living hand, now warm and capable 459
This mortal body of a thousand days 263
This pleasant tale is like a little copse 97
Thou still unravished bride of quietness 344
Time's sea hath been five years at its slow ebb 226
'Tis 'the witching time of night' 276
To one who has been long in city pent 62
Two or three posies 343

Unfelt, unheard, unseen 102
Upon a Sabbath-day it fell 324
Upon a time, before the faery broods 414
Upon my life, Sir Nevis, I am piqued 270

Welcome joy, and welcome sorrow 278
What can I do to drive away 450
What is more gentle than a wind in summer? 82
What is there in the universal Earth 98
What though, for showing truth to flattered state 41
What though, while the wonders of Nature exploring 45
When by my solitary hearth I sit 41
When I have fears that I may cease to be 221
When they were come unto the Faery's Court 329
When wedding fiddles are a-playing 230
Where be ye going, you Devon maid 234
Where didst thou find, young Bard, thy sounding lyre? 229

Where's the Poet? Show him! show him   280
Which of the fairest three   218
Who loves to peer up at the morning sun   100
Why did I laugh tonight? No voice will tell   328
Woman! when I behold thee flippant, vain   49

Young Calidore is paddling o'er the lake   58
You say you love; but with a voice   102

*More about Penguins
and Pelicans*

Penguinews, which appears every month, contains details of all the new books issued by Penguins as they are published. From time to time it is supplemented by *Penguins in Print*, which is our complete list of almost 5,000 titles.

A specimen copy of *Penguinews* will be sent to you free on request. Please write to Dept EP, Penguin Books Ltd, Harmondsworth, Middlesex, for your copy.

In the U.S.A.: For a complete list of books available from Penguins in the United States write to Dept CS, Penguin Books, 625 Madison Avenue, New York, New York 10022.

In Canada: For a complete list of books available from Penguins in Canada write to Penguin Books Canada Ltd, 41 Steelcase Road West, Markham, Ontario.

Penguin English Poets

General Editor: Christopher Ricks
Professor of English, University of Cambridge

ROBERT BROWNING: THE RING AND THE BOOK
Edited by Richard D. Altick

WILLIAM BLAKE: THE COMPLETE POEMS
Edited by Alicia Ostriker

LORD BYRON: DON JUAN
Edited by T. G. Steffan, W. W. Pratt and E. Steffan

JOHN DONNE: THE COMPLETE ENGLISH POEMS
Edited by A. J. Smith

SIR GAWAIN AND THE GREEN KNIGHT
Edited by J. A. Burrow

SAMUEL JOHNSON: THE COMPLETE ENGLISH POEMS
Edited by J. D. Fleeman

BEN JONSON: THE COMPLETE ENGLISH POEMS
Edited by George Parfitt

JOHN KEATS: THE COMPLETE POEMS
Edited by John Barnard

CHRISTOPHER MARLOWE: THE COMPLETE POEMS
AND TRANSLATIONS
Edited by Stephen Orgel

ANDREW MARVELL: THE COMPLETE POEMS
Edited by Elizabeth Story Donno

EDMUND SPENSER: THE FAERIE QUEENE
Edited by Thomas P. Roche Jnr and C. Patrick O'Donnell Jnr

HENRY VAUGHAN: THE COMPLETE POEMS
Edited by Alan Rudrum

WALT WHITMAN: THE COMPLETE POEMS
Edited by Francis Murphy

WILLIAM WORDSWORTH: THE PRELUDE (A PARALLEL TEXT)
Edited by J. C. Maxwell

WILLIAM WORDSWORTH: THE POEMS (in two volumes)
Edited by John O. Hayden

Some Penguin Anthologies

POETRY OF THE THIRTIES
Edited by Robin Skelton

POETRY OF THE FORTIES
Edited by Robin Skelton

SCOTTISH LOVE POEMS: A PERSONAL ANTHOLOGY
Edited by Antonia Fraser

THE PENGUIN BOOK OF RESTORATION VERSE
Edited by Harold Love

THE PENGUIN BOOK OF ENGLISH ROMANTIC VERSE
Edited by David Wright

THE PENGUIN BOOK OF ELIZABETHAN VERSE
Edited by Edward Lucie-Smith

THE PENGUIN BOOK OF JAPANESE VERSE
Edited by Geoffrey Bownas and Anthony Thwaite

THE PENGUIN BOOK OF ENGLISH VERSE
Edited by John Hayward

THE PENGUIN BOOK OF LATIN AMERICAN VERSE
Edited by E. Caracciolo-Trejo

THE PENGUIN BOOK OF AUSTRALIAN VERSE
Edited with an Introduction by Harry Heseltine

THE METAPHYSICAL POETS
Introduced and edited by Helen Gardner